Parish Law

Being a Digest of the Law Relating to Parishes

JOHN STEER

CAMBRIDGE
UNIVERSITY PRESS

CAMBRIDGE UNIVERSITY PRESS

Cambridge, New York, Melbourne, Madrid, Cape Town, Singapore,
São Paolo, Delhi, Dubai, Tokyo, Mexico City

Published in the United States of America by Cambridge University Press, New York

www.cambridge.org
Information on this title: www.cambridge.org/9781108024938

This edition first published 1830
This digitally printed version 2010

ISBN 978-1-108-02493-8 Paperback

CAMBRIDGE LIBRARY COLLECTION

Books of enduring scholarly value

History

The books reissued in this series include accounts of historical events and movements by eye-witnesses and contemporaries, as well as landmark studies that assembled significant source materials or developed new historiographical methods. The series includes work in social, political and military history on a wide range of periods and regions, giving modern scholars ready access to influential publications of the past.

Parish Law

John Steer (*fl.* 1830) was a barrister and writer on legal issues best remembered for this detailed survey of the state of parish laws in the early nineteenth century. In this period the parish was the main institution of rural administration, and parishes were responsible for both ecclesiastical and civil matters, these being administered by the parish vestry. This volume, first published in 1830, contains a clear and comprehensive review of the many laws relating to the responsibilities of the parish. Organising the text according to parish institution, Steer provides a thorough description of legislation which governs all aspects of parish activities, including the parish vestry, Poor Law and church administration, and the duties of Justices of the Peace, with the legal statutes and pertinent legal cases included. This volume was published in multiple editions during the nineteenth century, and provides a rich resource for the study of contemporary life.

PARISH LAW:

BEING

A DIGEST OF THE LAW

RELATING TO

PARISHES.
CHURCHES AND CHAPELS.
PARISH REGISTERS.
MINISTERS OF CHURCHES AND CHAPELS.
VESTRIES AND PARISH MEETINGS.
CHURCHWARDENS.
PARISH CLERKS.
SEXTONS AND BEADLES.
DISSENTERS.
HIGHWAYS.
PARISH AND COUNTY RATES.
WATCHING AND LIGHTING PARISHES.
WEIGHTS AND MEASURES.
DISORDERLY HOUSES.
MILITIA AND JURY LISTS.
JUSTICES OF THE PEACE.
CONSTABLES, WATCHMEN, &c.
VAGRANTS.
LUNATICS.
OVERSEERS, GUARDIANS, &c. &c.

AND THE

RELIEF, SETTLEMENT, AND REMOVAL

OF

THE POOR.

BY JOHN STEER, ESQ.

BARRISTER AT LAW.

LONDON:
SAUNDERS AND BENNING, LAW BOOKSELLERS,
(SUCCESSORS TO J. BUTTERWORTH AND SON,)
43, FLEET STREET.

1830.

PREFACE.

There are several hundred volumes already in the hands of the public, upon the various subjects comprehended in that extensive department of our Jurisprudence, which is designated by the title to this work. The fact of so many members of the learned profession having, from time to time, devoted their attention to the subject, and the enormous amount of labour which has been devoted to it, sufficiently demonstrate its importance.

In the midst of this abundance and variety, it is a little singular, that a compendium of the whole has not been offered to the patronage of the profession. Burn's Justice, however excellent in itself, is at once too comprehensive and too exclusive for the purpose. It contains much which does not belong, and omits a great deal which is essential, to a complete treatise upon the subject; being, as its name imports, more adapted for the county magistrate, than for the parish officer.

The complex and multifarious duties and interests, civil and ecclesiastical, of this (not inaptly called) little republic—the rights and responsibilities of its officers—the mode of their election– the extent, and duration, with the means of redress for the abuse, of their authority—the sources of Parish revenue, and the restraints upon its misapplication—the general maxims of its internal government, and the nature of its tributory obligations to the county in which it is included,—these are the great outlines of Parish Law:

and to collect and arrange the details in one entire system, is the task which I have attempted to perform.

Independently of the general recommendation of such a work, arising from these considerations, the disposition which is spreading among Parishes, to investigate and enforce the authority of the great body of the inhabitants, over all matters of revenue and expenditure, suggested an additional motive to the undertaking. Especial care, therefore, has been taken, to explain the authority, rights, and powers of Select Vestries, whether established by prescription, or under the statutes passed for the purpose; and, in short, of parish meetings of every description.

It may be expedient here to state with somewhat more particularity, the general contents of the volume. In the first place, the institution of Parishes, with the mode of preserving the evidence of their boundaries, is considered. The Law respecting the Church, and the rights and duties of its members, from the highest to the lowest, among those who officiate in its sanctuary, is also explained; and its civil constitution, with the authority of its officers of every denomination; the mode of their appointment, and their responsibilities, with the nature of the obligation imposed upon the people, whether in the shape of Tithes or Rates, for its becoming support, complete this part of the work.

The summary of the Poor Laws methodically arranged, and embracing the leading principles and decisions under the several heads of Settlements, Rates, Relief, Removal, Appeals, &c. &c., though concise, it is hoped will be found complete, and practically useful, considering how much may be compressed into a comparatively small space, if the Law *only*, in a brief and intelligible form, is included.

In addition to the several parish officers, as Churchwardens, Overseers, Guardians of the Poor, Clerks, Sextons, &c.

&c.; the authority and duties of Constables, Tithing Men, Beadles, and all others holding Parish appointments, whether arising out of its Ecclesiastical or Civil Institutions, are fully investigated; so that the work may afford a ready means of information to those whose avocations, employments, or pursuits, render it expedient that they should be well instructed in any, or in the several branches, of Parish Law.

Although the line of demarcation between the civil rights of Churchmen and Dissenters has been gradually fading away before the more enlightened policy of modern times, most of the regulations relating to dissenting places of worship, and many enactments passed in deference to individual religious scruples, still remain. They are modifications of the general rules of municipal government, and will therefore be found under their proper heads.

I owe some apology to my friends for the delay in the publication beyond the period at which it was promised. My excuse is, an anxiety to render the volume as complete as possible, by including the several acts which were in the contemplation of the legislature during the present session, relating to the Poor, and other Parish matters. Those which have actually passed, I have inserted, the others are relinquished, without any probability that they will be again brought forward at any definite period. In waiting for this result, I have been also enabled to include all the cases relating to settlements, highways, &c. decided in the Court of King's Bench to the end of Trinity term.

JOHN STEER.

15, Chancery Lane,
July 12, 1830.

TABLE OF CONTENTS.

CHAP. VII.—*Highways.*

CHAP. VIII.—*Highway Acts.*

CHAP. IX.—*Parish Vestries.*

CHAP. X.—*Select Vestries.*

CHAP. XI.—*Justices of the Peace.*

CHAP. XII.—*Constables.*

CHAP. XIII.

CHAP. XIV.—*Weights and Measures.*

CHAP. XV.—*Disorderly Houses.*

CHAP. XVI.—*Vagrants.*

CHAP. XVII.

CHAP. XVIII.

CHAP. XIX.

CHAP. XX.—*Poor Rates.*

CHAP. XXI.—*Overseers of the Poor.*

CHAP. XXII.—*Incorporated Districts.*

CHAP. XXIII.—*Relief of the Poor.*

CHAP. XXV.—*Parochial Settlements.*

CHAP. XXVI.—*Removal of Paupers.*

CHAP. XXVII.

A TABLE

OF

THE NAMES OF CASES.

CITED IN THE WORK.

C.

C.

D.

S.

PARISH LAW,

&c. &c.

CHAP. I.—PARISHES.

SECTION I. *Origin of Parishes.*
II. *Boundaries of Parishes.*
III. *Division of Parishes.*
IV. *Parishioners.*

SECTION I.—ORIGIN OF PARISHES.

Their History Uncertain.] As the ecclesiastical division of the kingdom was not commenced till a long time after the introduction of Christianity, and as those who were most active and most immediately interested in its establishment, were also the historians of the times, it seems a little singular that the information respecting the infancy and extension of religious institutions, in this country, should be so scanty and uncertain.

It is agreed among ecclesiastical writers, that dioceses (*dioichia*) existed anterior to parishes, and that it was only when the number of converts within the district over which the bishop exercised his functions, became too large for him, even with the aid of his presbyters, to minister to their spiritual wants, that parishes were instituted. Besides, the erection of churches in different parts of the country as the religion spread among the people, would afford an additional reason, as a matter of convenience, for the division into smaller portions, of the districts over which the bishop still maintained a general controul and superintendence.

Limits how Determined.] Thus in process of time the presbyters and priests, who were little more than the curates or messengers to the higher dignitaries, became settled in the towns and villages, distant from the cathedral churches, (in which the bishops themselves officiated,) and the limits of their spiritual superintendence being co-extensive with the habitations of the persons who resorted to their churches, those districts were eventually marked out and determined, which were afterwards called and known by the distinctive appellation of parishes; though in the more early times, it is probable that dioichia and paroichia were terms applied to either division indiscriminately. (Com. Dig. Parish, 3 Burn. Ec. L. 61.)

Protestant Hierarchy.] It will not be considered very much out of place to state, in general terms, the orders and degrees of the hierarchy of the Protestant church, as it exists at the present day. The ecclesiastical division of the kingdom is primarily into two provinces, those of Canterbury and York. A *province* is the circuit of an archbishop's jurisdiction. Each province contains divers dioceses, or sees of suffragan bishops; they are styled suffragans in respect of their relation to the archbishop of their province; but formerly each archbishop and bishop had also his suffragan to assist him in conferring orders, and in other spiritual parts of his office within his diocese. These, in our ecclesiastical law, are called suffragan bishops, and resemble the *chorepiscopi* or *bishops of the country,* in the early times of the Christian church. How this *inferior* order of bishops *may* be elected and consecrated, is regulated by the 26 Hen. VIII. c. 14.; but it is not usual to appoint them. They should not be confounded with the *coadjutors* of a bishop, who are appointed in case of the bishop's infirmity to superintend his *jurisdiction* and *temporalities,* neither of which was within the interference of the former. (1 Gibs. Cod. 1st ed. 155.) The province of Canterbury includes twenty-one dioceses, viz. of ancient foundations,—Rochester his principal chaplain, London his dean, Winchester his chancellor, Norwich, Lincoln, Ely, Chichester, Salisbury, Exeter, Bath and Wells, Worcester, Coventry and Litchfield, Hereford, Llandaff, St. David, Bangor and St. Asaph, with four founded by Hen. VIII. erected from the ruins of dissolved monasteries, viz. Gloucester, Bristol, Peterborough, and Oxford. The province of York has four only, though anciently more: they are Chester, Durham, Carlisle, and the Isle of Man, which was annexed to the province of York by king Henry VIII. Every diocese is divided into archdeaconries, whereof there are sixty in all; each archdeaconry into rural deaneries, which are the circuit of the archdeacon's and rural dean's jurisdiction; and every deanery is divided into two parishes.

Parish Defined.] A parish is that circuit of ground which is committed to the charge of one parson or vicar, or other minister having cure of souls therein. These districts are computed to be near ten thousand in number. (Camden's Brittannia.)

Date of Parishes.] Mr. Camden (in his Brittannia) says, England was divided into parishes by Archbishop Honorius about the year 630. Sir Henry Hobart, (Hob. 296,) lays it down, that parishes were first erected by the council of Lateran, which was held A. D. 1179. Each widely differing from the other, and both of them perhaps from the truth; which will probably be found in the medium between the two extremes. For Mr. Selden has clearly shewn, (Of Tithes. c. 9,) that the clergy lived in common without any division of parishes, long after the time mentioned by Camden. And it appears from the Saxon laws, that parishes were in being long before the date of that council of Lateran, to which they are ascribed by Hobart.

Extent of Parishes.] It seems to be tolerably certain, that the boundaries of parishes were originally ascertained by those of a manor or manors: since it very seldom happens that a manor extends itself over more parishes than one, though there are often many manors in one parish. The lords, as Christianity spread itself, began to build churches upon their own demesnes, or wastes, to accommodate their tenants in one or two adjoining lordships; and, in order to have divine service regularly performed therein, obliged all their tenants to appropriate their tithes to the maintenance of the one officiating minister, instead of leaving them at liberty to distribute them among the clergy of the diocese in general; and this tract of land, the tithes whereof were so appropriated, formed a distinct parish. Which will well enough account for the frequent intermixture of parishes one with another. For if a lord had a parcel of land detached from the main of his estate, but not sufficient to form a parish of itself, it was natural for him to endow his newly erected church with the tithes of those disjointed lands; especially if no church was then built in any lordship adjoining to those out-lying parcels. (1 Bla. Com. 113.)

How Number Increased.] Thus parishes were originally formed; and parish churches endowed with tithes that arose within the circuit assigned. Their number has been added to, by some of the most extensive ones, being divided into two or more, when a greatly increased population rendered such a measure highly expedient for the spiritual welfare of the people. As will readily be presumed, this has been the case in London and Westminster, and several other towns, which from their magnitude, and advancement in civilization, were the chief objects of ecclesiastical watchfulness and regard.

The churches in these new divisions were sometimes of considerable antiquity, and by this means acquired the distinctive appellation of the parish church, whilst others were erected, as the number of communicants increased, subordinate, and in some respects tributary to the former.

Bishop defined Limits.] This gradual reduction of the whole kingdom into definite portions, is corroborated by the testimony of Bishop Kennet, in his Parochial Antiquities (see p. 585 et seq.) upon whose authority it may be stated, that in the earlier periods of our ecclesiastical history, the limits of these new parishes were always appointed by the bishop, who was guided probably in settling the boundaries, by the extent of the founders lands, when the church was built by a layman, or by some cogent reasons arising from individual interests or public convenience.

Tithes Assigned.] If the bishop gave the new church a right of burial, the lord of the manor might (with his approbation and not otherwise) give some part of the tithes to that church, which before were due to the mother church; but if this right were not conceded, then the edifice remained a chapel; and if the lord of the manor would have a curate, he was to maintain him at his own charge. However, in some instances, one third of the tithes, were by authority of the bishop, allowed to the newly erected church, and the remainder was reserved to the old one, which was standing before this smaller parish was carved out of the larger district; and hence it was, that when a question arose whether a foundation of this kind were a parish church, or merely a chapel, it was to be decided by the bishop's certificate. But the dominion of the church was preserved in all cases, unless it was clearly made out that it had been duly surrendered, and upon an adequate consideration. Thus upon a question whether the inhabitants of a chapelry ought to contribute to the repairs of the mother church, it was held that a chapelry may be exempt by prescription, where it buries and christens within itself, and has never contributed to the mother church; for in that case, it shall be intended coeval, and not a later erection, but if it appears that the chapel could only be an erection in *ease* and favour of those of the chapelry, and that when they prevailed upon the bishop to consecrate them a burial-place, they in consideration thereof agreed to pay towards the reparation of the mother church, they remain liable. (Ball v. Cross, Holt, R. 138. 1 Salk. 164.)

Parish in separate Parts.] In some few instances, parishes seem to interfere with each other, that is, when a place or district in the middle of another parish, belongs to a parish that is distant; but that hath generally happened by an unity of possession, when the lord of a manor was at the charge to erect a new church, and make a distinct parish of his own demesnes, some of which lay in the compass of another parish. (1 Still. 244.)

SECTION II.—BOUNDARIES OF PARISHES.

Boundaries Traditionary.] The boundaries of parishes in most instances depend upon ancient and immemorial custom, having been originally established according to the particular circumstances of the times or districts. (Still. 243.) They were settled long after the foundation of churches, and were afterwards much varied, and in many cases abridged and narrowed, as new churches were built. (Lousley v. Hayward, 1 Younge & J. 586.)

Motives to define Bounds.] For a long period, a sufficient inducement to define the boundaries of parishes accurately, did not present itself; but when it became part of the law, to require the attendance of the people upon the services of religion at the *parish* church, and numerous civil duties were conferred upon them as *parishioners,* it then was felt to be of consequence to have the limits of each parish ascertained and settled. For this purpose, perambulations were made, and are, in many places, still continued.

Perambulations.] These perambulations, though of evident utility, were in the times of popery accompanied with great abuses. They were usually performed in rogation week, whence the rogation days were anciently called *gange days,* from the Saxon *gan* or *gangen,* to go.

The processions upon these occasions were accompanied with many ceremonials of popish superstition; with banners flying, which, according to a constitution of Archbishop Winchelsey, the parishioners were to find at their own charge, (Lind. 252,) and hand-bells, lights, and other pageantry. When they arrived at a spot upon which a cross was erected, the procession halted, and certain rites were performed, but their resting-places were chiefly selected for the purposes of feasting and revelry; and in process of time, they came to demand as a right, what was dispensed originally from the hospitality of some of the wealthier yeomen, or lords of the manors residing upon or near to the boundary. However, though repeated attempts were made to establish this right by legal proceedings, the custom was not sanctioned by any public tribunal, but on the contrary, was declared to be against law and reason. (Gibs, 213. 2 Roll's Rep. 259. Moor, 916. 2 Lev. 163.)

Ceremonies Abridged.] At length the irregularities and excesses committed on these occasions, attracted the reprehension of the sovereign, for we find that processions in the manner they had been performed, were forbidden by injunctions from Queen Elizabeth, though it was at the same time required, that for the retaining of the perambulations of the circuits of parishes, the people should, once in the year, at the time accustomed, with the curate and the substantial men of the parish, walk about the parishes as they were accustomed, and at their return to the church, make their common prayers. And the curate attending such perambulations, was at certain convenient places to admonish the people to give thanks to God, (in the beholding of his benefits,) and for the increase and abundance of his fruits upon the face of the earth; with the saying of the 103d Psalm. At which time he was also to inculcate these or such like sentences:—*Cursed be he which translateth the bounds and dolles of his neighbour,* or such other order of prayers as should be lawfully appointed. (Gibs. 213.)

Perambulate over Private Lands.] It is said in the case of Goodday v. Michell, reported in Cro. Eliz. 441. Owen. 72, that it is not to be doubted that parishioners may well justify the going over any man's lands in their perambulations, according to their *usage* or custom; and to abate all nuisances in their way. (See F. N. B. 185. B. Ent. 158. See also Vin. Ab. Perambulation.)

Bounds settled by Law.] When from the neglect to perambulate, or from other causes, the bounds of parishes have become confused and difficult to determine, the proper mode to have them ascertained is by an action at law. And the books of common law agree in the maxim, that the bounds of parishes, though coming in question in a spiritual matter, shall be tried in the temporal court, (Transam's case, Cro. Eliz. 178, 228.) though the provincial constitutions mention the bounds of parishes amongst the matters which belong to the ecclesiastical court, and say they cannot belong to any other. (Gibs. 212.) The superior authority of the common law cannot however be disputed, though the rule seems to be, that the spiritual courts having jurisdiction in other matters, wherein the question of boundary may arise collaterally, are still at liberty to proceed. Thus, if the question of boundary arises incidentally, and the ecclesiastical court has jurisdiction in the *principal* point, the Court of K. B. will not grant a prohibition to stay trial. (Full v. Hutchins, Cowp. 424.) But there are few instances in which the ecclesiastical courts are permitted to proceed, where a question of this nature is involved, if a prohibition is sued out in due time, that is before trial. (Banister v. Hopton, 10 Mod. 12. Paxton v. Knight, 1 Burr. 314.)

Between Spiritual Persons.] If the suit is between a rector and vicar, though the former is an impropriator, it shall be tried in the spiritual court, and no prohibition shall go. If it be a proceeding to determine a case of tithes, the right to which depends on the lands lying in a vill *within* the parish, or in the other part of the parish, in such case, the Court of King's Bench declared that the question was triable in the ecclesiastical court. (2 Rolls. Abr. 312.)

Thus in a suit between the parson impropriate and the vicar of the same parish, wherein the vicar claimed all the tithes of the village of D. within the parish, and the question between them was whether certain lands, whereof the vicar claimed the tithes, were within the village of D. or not; yet, inasmuch as the suit was between spiritual persons, viz. the parson and vicar, although the parson was a layman, and the parsonage appropriate a lay fee, it was held to be triable in the same court. (*Ibid.*)

Between Parson and Layman.] But in a case between a clergyman and a layman, where a vicar sued for tithes, arising *inter loca decimabilia* of such a parish and the defendant suggested that the lands were in another parish, and that he had paid tithes to the parson there, this shall be tried at law. (Stransham v. Cullington, Cro. Eliz. 228.) So, if it be disputed, between the parties whether certain lands for which tithes are demanded be in one parish or another, the question is triable at common law. (Transam's case, Cro. Eliz. 178. 1 Keb. 369.) Because, though the bounds of vills may be triable by the ecclesiastical courts, those of parishes are not. (Petler v. Yaleman, 1 Lev. 78. 1 Sid. 89.)

Commission to settle Bounds.] It is laid down in the books, that the boundaries of counties, of towns, and of manors may, by the *assent* of the parties, be ascertained and settled by a commission *de perambulatione faciendâ,* issued to the sheriff or to other persons. (Vin. Ab. tit. Perambulation.) And where the lands of private individuals have become confused from having been for a long period in the same occupation, the Court of Chancery, without such assent, will grant a *commission* for this purpose, if it is shown that the confusion has arisen from the misconduct of the defendant or of those under whom he claims. (Speer v. Crawter, 2 Meriv. 410.) Still upon these occasions the granting the commission is not of course as respects *legal* estates: there must be some *equitable* circumstances. (Wake v. Conyers, 1

Edin. Rep. 331. 2 Cox. 360. Willis v. Parkinson, 2 Meriv. 507.) There seems no reason why the boundaries of parishes should not be settled in the same way as those of counties and towns, where they are in dispute, but it is said that a bill will not lie for an issue or commission for this purpose; except, perhaps, all parties concerned, or who have a probable interest, are before the court. (St. Luke's v. St. Leonard's, 1 Bro. C. C. 40; Atkyns v. Hatton, 2 Anstr. 386.)

Bounds now known.] The necessity for a commission or any other legal proceeding for the purpose of ascertaining the boundaries of parishes must be daily diminishing; as in those places where perambulations are neglected, the limits of parishes are known either from the municipal records or by other means equally satisfactory. And in those cases where the lines of demarcation traverse extensive wastes or commons, the legislature has provided the means, when it becomes important, by such lands being brought into cultivation, of determining with exactness their parochial locality.

Wastes near Parish.] By the 17 Geo. 2. c. 37, it is enacted, that where there shall be any dispute, in what *parish* or place, improved wastes, and drained and improved marsh-lands lie, and ought to be rated, the occupiers of such lands, or houses built thereon, tithes arising therefrom, mines therein, and saleable underwoods, shall be rated to the relief of the poor, and to all other parish rates within such parish or place which lies nearest to such lands; and if, on application to the officers of such parish or place to have the same assessed, any dispute shall arise, the justices of the peace at the next sessions after such application made, and after notice given to the officers of the several parishes and places adjoining to such lands, and to all others interested therein, may hear and determine the same on the appeal of any person interested, and may cause the same to be equally assessed, whose determination therein shall be final. But this shall not determine the boundary of any parish or place, other than for the purpose of rating such lands to the relief of the poor, and other parochial rates. (s. 1, 2.) And by the 2. and 3. Ed. 6. c. 13. s. 3, every person who shall have any beasts or other cattle titheable, depasturing on any waste or common whereof the parish is not certainly known, shall pay the tithes thereof where the owner of the cattle dwells.

By Inclosure Acts.] And by the 41 Geo. 3. c. 109. s. 3, commissioners appointed in or by virtue of inclosure acts, are authorised and required by examination of witnesses upon oath or affirmation, which any one of such commissioners is empowered to administer, and by such other legal ways and means as he or they shall think proper, to inquire into the boundaries of such several parishes, manors, hamlets, or districts; and in case it shall appear to such commissioners, that the boundaries of the same respectively are not then sufficiently ascertained and distinguished, such commissioners shall ascertain, set out, determine, and fix the same respectively; and after the said boundaries shall be so ascertained, &c. the same shall be the boundaries of such parishes, manors, hamlets, or districts.

Notice of fixing Bounds.] Provided always, that such commissioners, before they proceed to ascertain and set out the boundaries of such parishes, manors, hamlets, or districts, shall give public notice, by writing, under their hands, to be affixed on the most public doors of the churches of such parishes, and also by advertisement, and also by writing to be delivered to, or left at the last or usual places of abode of the respective lords, or stewards of the lords of the manors, in which the lands to be inclosed shall be situate, and of such adjoining manors, ten days at least before the time of setting out such boundaries, of their intention to set out and determine the same respectively.

Publishing Bounds.] And such commissioners shall, within one month after their ascertaining, &c. the same boundaries, cause a description thereof, in writing, to be delivered to, or left at, the places of abode of one of the churchwardens or overseers of the poor of the respective parishes, and also of such respective lords or stewards.

Appeal against Bounds.] "Provided, that if any persons interested in the said determination of the said commissioners shall be dissatisfied therewith, such persons may appeal to the justices for the county, at any general quarter-sessions held within four calendar months after the aforesaid publication of the said boundaries; the appellants giving eight days' notice of such appeal, and of the matter thereof in writing to the commissioners; and the decision of the said justices therein, shall be final, and not removable by *certiorari*, or any other process whatsoever into any of his Majesty's Courts of Record, at Westminster or elsewhere."

Error of Commissioners.] But unless the commissioners appointed by any such act pursue the authority given them, strictly, their proceedings may be invalidated. Thus, where they duly fixed and settled the boundaries, and published them accordingly, but the boundaries mentioned in their *award* varied from those *advertised*, it was held, that their award was not binding as to the boundaries of the parish. (R. v. Washbrook, 4 Barn. and Cres. 732; 7 Dowl. and Ryl. 221.)

Incompetent Witnesses.] The parson cannot give evidence on a question relating to the bounds of his parish, for he is interested to enlarge them, and, consequently, his tithes. (Wharton v. Robinson, 7 Mod. 63.) Nor a parishioner *actually* rated, though, if he be merely liable to be rated, his evidence is admissible. (Deacon v. Cook, 2 East. 562.)

SECTION III.—DIVISION OF PARISHES.

Expediency thereof.] The increase of population, and a becoming zeal for the character and influence of the Protestant establishment, which were in some measure impaired by the unwearied and extended labours of sectarianism, induced the legislature, towards the close of the late reign, to appropriate large sums of money for the erection of new churches. It was an important part of the general scheme, to give to the churches so to be established a peculiar district, in the nature of a separate parish, wherever it might be found expedient.

Power to divide Parishes.] Accordingly the statutes passed on the subject provide, that if the commissioners, appointed to carry this object into effect, shall think it expedient to divide any parish into two or more *separate parishes, for all ecclesiastical purposes,* they may, with the consent of the bishop of the diocese, under his hand and seal, apply to the patron of the parish church for his consent, and upon his signifying it under his hand and seal, the commissioners shall represent the whole matter to the King in council, stating the proposed bounds of such division, with the relative proportions of glebe lands, tithes, moduses, and other endowments, and the estimated amount of fees, oblations, or other ecclesiastical dues or profits within each division; upon which his Majesty in Council may direct such division to be made. Provided that it shall not completely take effect till after the death, resignation, or avoidance of the existing incumbent. (58 Geo. 3. c. 45. s. 16.)

Tithes assigned.] Incumbents of the churches of each division of the parish are empowered to recover the tithes, &c. assigned to them, in like manner as the incumbent of the original parish. (s. 17.)

Existing Incumbencies.] New churches of such divided parishes shall, during the existing incumbency, remain chapels of ease, and be served by a curate nominated by the incumbent, and licensed by the bishop, and paid as after directed. (s. 18.)

New Parish a Rectory, &c.] Every separate parish, when the division shall become complete, shall be a rectory, vicarage, donative, or perpetual curacy, according to the nature of the original church of the parish so divided, and subject to the same jurisdiction and laws. (s. 19.)

Donatives and perpetual curacies shall lapse in six months like benefices, but no spiritual person appointed thereto shall be removable at the pleasure of the party appointing. (s. 20.)

Consolidated Chapelries.] The 59 Geo. 3. c. 134. s. 6. reciting that a considerable population is frequently collected at the extremities of parishes or in extra-parochial places contiguous to each other, at a distance from the churches or chapels thereof, enacts, that it shall be lawful for the commissioners, with such consent as is required by the 58 Geo. 3. c. 45. s. 16. (see *ante* 10.) to consolidate any such contiguous parts into a *separate* DISTRICT *for all ecclesiastical* purposes; and to cause such district to be named, and ascertained by prescribed bounds, and such name and bounds, when approved by his Majesty in council, to be enrolled in Chancery, and in the registry of the diocese; and to make grants or loans for building any chapel, with or without cemeteries, for the use of such district, under such regulations as may appear most expedient; and to constitute any such district a *consolidated chapelry*, with similar privileges as to marriages, burials, &c. and with like provisions as to its government, as if such chapelry were a distinct parish; and to be subject to all other laws relative to holding benefices and churches.

It is further provided, that it shall be lawful for the commissioners, with the consent of the bishop, in dividing any parish and apportioning the glebe or other endowments, to apportion also the permanent charges in respect thereof, or affecting the same, or the incumbent; and the charges so apportioned shall thereafter be borne by each division, or the spiritual person serving it. (59 G. 3. c. 134. s. 9.)

Districts, or Parishes.] If the commissioners shall think it not expedient to make such divisions into *separate parishes* as aforesaid, but into *ecclesiastical districts*, they may report accordingly to his Majesty in council, who may direct such division into ecclesiastical districts as aforesaid, to be made. (58 G. 3. c. 45. s. 21.)

Bounds enrolled.] Boundaries of new parishes created by any complete division, and of ecclesiastical districts, shall be ascertained, and the description of such bounds enrolled in Chancery and registered in the registry of the diocese, and notice thereof given as the commissioners shall direct, (s. 22,) and such boundaries shall continue the boundaries of such parishes or districts, (s. 24.)

District Parishes.] Such districts shall be separate and distinct *district parishes*, and the churches and chapels assigned to them when consecrated, shall be district parish churches, for all purposes of ecclesiastical worship and performance of ecclesiastical duties, and as to all marriages, christenings, churchings, and burials, and the registry thereof. And in relation to all fees, oblations, and offerings, and as to all other purposes. (s. 24.)

But such divisions are not to affect any lands, glebe, tithes, moduses or endowments of the original church, (s. 30,) nor any poor or other parochial rate, or the persons interested therein, except church rates, as regulated by the act, s. 31. See "CHURCHWARDENS," *post*.

Subject to same Laws.] All acts, laws, and customs, relating to publishing banns of marriage, marriages, christenings, churchings, and burials, and the registering thereof, and to all ecclesiastical fees, oblations or offerings, shall apply to all districts, and consolidated or district chapelries, and divisions of any parishes, or extra-parochial places, whereof the boundaries shall be enrolled in Chancery under the provisions of these acts, and in the churches and chapels whereof banns shall be allowed to be published, and marriages, christenings, churchings, or burials, shall be allowed to be solemnized, and to the churches and chapels thereof, and to the ecclesiastical persons having cure of souls therein, or serving the same in like manner, as if the same had been ancient, separate, and distinct parishes and parish churches by law. (59 Geo. 3. c. 134, s. 17.)

Chapelry converted to Parish.] It shall be lawful for the commissioners with the consent of the ordinary, patron, and incumbent, on the next avoidance, to convert any district chapelry, made under these acts, into a separate and *distinct parish* for ecclesiastical purposes, or into a *district* parish, where a suitable residence and competent maintenance can be procured and established for the minister and his successors; compensation being provided for all fees and ecclesiastical dues, which may be thus lost to the original parish. (3 Geo. 4. c. 72. s. 16.)

SECTION IV.—PARISHIONERS.

Definition.] Parishioner is a very large word, and takes in not only inhabitants of the parish, but persons who are *occupiers* of lands that pay the several rates and duties, though they are not resiant, nor do contribute to the ornaments of the church.

Of Inhabitants] Inhabitants is still a larger word: it takes in housekeepers, though not rated to the poor; and also persons who are not housekeepers; as for instance, such who have gained a settlement, and by that means become inhabitants. Such is the language of Lord Chancellor Hardwicke, in the Attorney-General v. Parker, (3 Atk. 577.) And upon the same principle it was held, that an allegation, of a custom in *parishioners* to elect a curate, is not supported by proof of such a custom in parishioners *paying church rates only.* (Arnold v. Bishop of Bath and Wells, 5 Bing. 316.)

Variable Import.] The word inhabitant varies in its import, according to the subject to which it is applied. It may be said generally, that such an *occupier* is an inhabitant for all purposes of pecuniary charge; for the church rate, to which by law all inhabitants are said to be contributory; to the repairs of the highways by the common law; to the repair of bridges, by the statute 22 H. 8. c. 5, if not by the common law. Lord Coke, in his commentary on this statute, 2 Inst. 702, after observing that the word *inhabitant* is the largest word of the kind, and describing all occupiers as inhabitants within the meaning of the statute, says "that servants are not within the statute." (Per Abbott, C. J. R. v. Adlard, 4 Barn. & Cres. 778.)

When Resiant.] "The word inhabitant may mean either occupier or resiant; the latter is the proper sense, when it is used to denote persons on whom a personal (and not a pecuniary) charge is to be imposed. Per Bayley, J. (Donne v. Martyr, 8 Barn. & Cres. 69; 2 Man. and Ryl. 98); and the same doctrine was stated by Abbot, C. J. in R. v. Adlard, *(supra.)*

Casual Sojourners.] Casual sojourners seem not to come within either of these descriptions; as if a man take up a lodging for a week in a town, he shall not be charged to the repair of the church, or such like. (See Holledges case, 2 Roll. Rep. 238. 1 Bot. 123.)

Power of Parishioners.] The general government of parishes, in matters of internal regulation, and the appointment of their public functionaries, is still vested, to some considerable extent, in the parishioners themselves, though their authority in this respect has in many instances been abridged by local customs and statutary provisions. The power of the general body is exercised in public assembly, usually in what are called vestry meetings; and if a vestry is called, every parishioner is bound to attend, or if he does not, he is bound by the acts of those who do. (Clutton v. Cherry, 2 Phil. Ec. Ca. 380.)

It would, however, be a needless repetition, to detail in this place their peculiar rights and privileges as against strangers, their reciprocal duties, and the obligations which are cast upon them as forming a portion of the larger municipal division,—the county in which they are situated. The law upon these subjects respectively, will be found in the other more appropriate parts of the work.

When Incompetent Witnesses.] In legal proceedings to which parishes become parties, though the interest of individual parishioners may be, in most cases, too minute to have any influence upon their evidence, yet they are generally held at common law, incompetent witnesses upon such occasions. Thus, in an action of trespass, the question being whether the locus in quo is a free wharf for the inhabitants of A., an inhabitant of A. is incompetent. (Prewit v. Tilley, 1 Car. and P. 140.) Nor can an owner of lands in the parish be received as a witness upon the trial of an issue upon a question of a modus in lieu of tithes. (Jones v. Carrington, *ib.* 328.)

Competent by Statutes.] To remedy the inconvenience which frequently arose from a too rigid observance of the above rule, it was found necessary to relax it by legislative enactment, and accordingly by the 54 Geo. 3. c. 170. s. 9. it is provided, that no inhabitant, or person rated, or liable to be rated, to any rates or cesses of any district, parish, township, or hamlet, or wholly or in part maintained by such rates, or executing or holding any office therein, shall be deemed on such account an incompetent witness for or against such district, parish, &c. in any matter relating to such rates or cesses, or relating to the boundary between such district, parish, &c. and any adjoining district, &c. or to any order of removal to or from such district, or to the settlement of any pauper in such district, or touching any bastards chargeable, or likely to become chargeable to such district, or touching the recovery of any sum for the charge or maintenance of such bastards, or the election or appointment of any officer or the allowance of the accounts of any officer of any such district.

The provision that no inhabitant *shall be deemed incompetent in any matter relating to the rates or cesses*, has received a liberal construction. In an action of trespass against the overseers of a township, where the principal point was, whether the lands in question were vested in the overseers under a local Act of Parliament, the court of Exchequer determined that a rated inhabitant of the township was not incompetent to be a witness for the defendants, although the lands in question if vested in them, would be vested in trust for the township, and in aid of the poor rates. (Meredith v. Gilpin and others, 6 Price, 146. See Rhodes v. Ainsworth, 1 Barn. & Ald. 87; Rex. v. Cottrell, 2 Chit. 487.)

Under Highway Acts.] So in proceedings for offences against the highway acts, the inhabitants of the parish or place in whose behalf such proceedings are taken, are competent witnesses. (13 G. 3. c. 78, s. 76; 3 G. 4. c. 126. s. 137.) But it has been said that the inhabitants of a parish indicted for not repairing a highway, are incompetent to give evidence *for the defendants.* (R. v. Wandsworth.)

It may however well be doubted, whether any inhabitant would be incompetent unless he were liable to some duty in respect of the highway in question. (See 54 G. 3. c. 170, *ante*, 14. 2 Stark, Ev. 673.)

CHAP. II.—CHURCHES.

SECTION I.—FOUNDING OF CHURCHES.

By whom founded.] It is a moot question among ecclesiastical writers, whether any person was at liberty upon the first planting of the Christian religion, to erect a church without the leave of the bishop. The general rule, however, seems to have been, that though the edifice might be raised, it could not be used for the purposes of devotion till it had been consecrated. It appears from Selden, vol. iii. pt. ii. 1121. ed. 1725, that in early times, by the pope's license, churches were founded or built by lords of manors, or other lay founders.

There are, it is true, upon record, instances of licenses being granted upon special occasions, for the performance of divine service before consecration, (Gibs. 190.); and another exception obtained in cases of extreme necessity; for if the church was destroyed by fire, the service might be performed in chapels, tents, or in the open air, before the consecrated altar-table; (De Cons. i. 30. Inst. J. C. ii. 18;) and in more recent times, a marriage had on the site or ruins of an old church, which was unroofed, and in part pulled down for the purposes of repair, was held valid, the publication of banns having been made in the church of an adjoining parish. (Stallwood v. Tredger. 2 Phil. Ec. Ca. 292.)

Manner of Founding.] The ancient manner of founding churches, after Christianity had become established in the kingdom, was for the founders to make application to the bishop of the diocese, and when his license had been obtained, the bishop or his commissioners fixed up a cross, and set forth the ground where the church was to be built; and then the founders proceeded with the building, and when the church was finished, and it was endowe l, and not till then, the bishop consecrated it. (Degge, part i. c. 12.)

Consecration.] In the church of England, every bishop is left to his own discretion as to the form of consecrating churches and chapels. But by the 21 Hen. 8. c. 13, for limiting the number of chaplains, one reason there assigned why a bishop may retain six chaplains, is because he must occupy that number in the consecration of churches.

Founding commemorated by Wakes, &c.] From the dedication of churches, fairs and wakes originated, to commemorate the munificence of those who had founded and endowed them. It was on this account that fairs were generally kept in churchyards, and even in the churches; till the indecency and scandal became so great as to require a reformation. But that wakes and fairs were originally exempt from this censure, if they were not, on the other hand, characterized by the manifestation of a due reverence for the occasion of their institution, and the interchange of the best feelings among the people, seems to be unquestionable.

Attempt to suppress Wakes, &c.] A celebrated writer on this subject says, this laudable custom of wakes prevailed for many ages, till the Puritans began to exclaim against it as a remnant of Popery: and by degrees, the humour grew so popular, that at the summer assizes held at Exeter in the year 1627, the Lord Chief Baron Walter and Baron Denham made an order for suppression of all wakes. And a like order was made by Judge Richardson, for the county of Somerset, for the year 1631. But on Bishop Laud's complaint of this innovating humour, the king commanded the last order to be reversed, which Judge Richardson refusing to do, an account was required from the Bishop of Bath and Wells, how the said feast days, church ales, wakes, and revels, were for the most part celebrated and observed in his diocese.

Wakes, Certificate in their favour.] The account goes on to state, that on receipt of the above instructions, the bishop sent for and advised with seventy-two of the most orthodox and able of his clergy, who certified under their hands, that on these feast days, (which generally fell on Sundays,) the service of God was more solemnly performed, and the church much better frequented, both in the forenoon and afternoon, than on any other Sunday in the year; that the people very much desired the continuance of them; that the ministers did in most places do the like, for these reasons, viz.—for preserving the memorial of the dedication of their several churches,—for civilizing the people,—for composing differences by the mediation and meeting of friends,—for increase of love and unity by these feasts of charity, and for relief and comfort of the poor.

On the return of this certificate, Judge Richardson was again cited to the council table, and peremptorily commanded to reverse his former order. After which it was thought fit to reinforce the declaration of King James, when perhaps this was the only good reason assigned for that unnecessary and unhappy license of sports: "We do ratify and publish this our blessed father's decree, the rather because of late in some counties of our kingdom, we find that under pretence of taking away abuses, there hath been a general forbidding, not only of ordinary meetings, but of the feasts of the dedication of churches, commonly called wakes."

Decline of Wakes, &c.] However, by such a popular prejudice against wakes, and by the intermission of them in the confusions that followed, they are now discontinued in many counties, especially in the east, and some western parts of England; but are commonly observed in the north, and in the midland counties. (Ken. Par. Ant. 609—614.) And in many instances, where churches or chapels have been erected within the last century, a similar commemoration has been annually celebrated, though discountenanced by the municipal authorities, on account of the disorders and profligacy which often attend them.

Increase of Churches.] The number of churches was augmented from time to time, chiefly by the piety of individuals, till the practice of bequeathing their property to pious uses was encouraged by the priests to such an alarming extent, that the statutes of mortmain were passed to prevent the continuance of the evil. In the late reign, however, several acts of Parliament were passed, authorising the gift, by deed or will, of land to the extent of five acres, or other property, not exceeding 500*l.* towards erecting, rebuilding, or providing any church or chapel, where the liturgy and rites of the united church of England and Ireland are observed, or any house of residence, &c. &c. (See 43 G. 3. c. 108; 51 G. 3. c. 115; 52 G. 3. c. 161.)

And a considerable addition has since been made under the powers of the 58 G. 3. c. 45; 59 G. 3. c. 134; and 3 G. 4. c. 72, the principal provisions of which will be found incorporated under the several titles to which they respectively belong.

Newly-created Benefices.] The churches built or acquired under these acts, and appropriated to distinct parishes, (see *ante*, p. 10,) are to be perpetual curacies, and considered as benefices presentative so far only that the license thereto shall operate in the same manner as institution to any such benefice; and the incumbents thereof shall have perpetual succession, and shall be bodies politic and corporate, and may take endowments in lands, or tithes, or any augmentations granted to them; and all such incumbents and persons presenting them, shall be subject to all jurisdictions and laws, and to lapse on neglecting to nominate an incumbent for six months, as in cases of actual benefices. (58 G. 3. c. 45. s. 25.)

The laws relating to marriages, christenings, churchings, and burials, and the registering thereof, and to fees, oblations, or offerings, shall apply to distinct parishes and to *district* parishes, (see *ante*, p. 11,) to be made under the act, when complete, after avoidance of the existing incumbents, and to the churches and chapels thereof, and to the ecclesiastical persons serving them, in like manner as if they had been ancient separate parishes and parish churches. (s. 27.)

Existing Incumbency.] All churches built or acquired under 58 G. 3. c. 45, or 59 G. 3. c. 134. s. 12, whether belonging to parishes completely divided, or to district parishes, shall, after consecration, become distinct benefices and churches for all ecclesiastical purposes. Provided that during the existing incumbency such churches shall be served by stipendiary curates, appointed by the existing incumbent, and subject to all the laws relating to stipendiary curates, except as to assigning salaries to them by the bishop; and such existing incumbent shall, until avoidance, continue to hold all the churches of the divisions of his parish, as if they were one church, unless he shall voluntarily resign one or more of them; any statute against plurality of benefices, or other law to the contrary notwithstanding.

No chapel built or acquired under the 58 G. 3. c. 45, in any district parish, made so for ecclesiastical purposes, under the act, and which shall not be made the *church* of such district, shall be a perpetual curacy or benefice, presentative under said act. (59 G. 3. c. 134. s. 19.)

SECTION II.—CHANCEL.

Whence so called.] Chancel, *cancellis*, seemeth properly to be so called a *cancellis* from the lattice-work partition betwixt the choir and the body of the church, so framed as to separate the one from the other, but not to intercept the sight. (1 Burn. Ec. L. 342.) By the rubric, before the Common Prayer, it is ordained, that the chancels shall remain as they have done in times past; that is to say, distinguished from the body of the church in manner aforesaid; and though, at the Reformation, the King and Parliament yielded so far as to allow the daily service to be read in the body of the church, if the ordinary thought fit, yet they would not suffer the chancel itself to be taken away or altered. (Gibbs 199.)

Chancel inalienable.] Previously to the act for the dissolution of monasteries, the rector could not have alienated any part of the chancel or church without the consent of the ordinary. In that act (31 Hen. 8. c. 13. s. 4.) there is a saving clause, leaving the right as it existed before, and the chancel therefore is still inalienable by the rector, and, consequently, a grant by a lay impropriator of part of the chancel to A his heirs and assigns, is not valid in law. For if the rector might convey in this way to one, he might to fifty persons; it might even enable him to desecrate this part of the church, where particular parts of the service are required to be performed. And it is inconsistent either with the duty of the ordinary or the rector, to alienate any part of the chancel in this manner. (Clifford v. Wicks, 1 Barn. and Ald. 498.)

Seats in Chancel.] Dr. Gibson asserts, that the seats in the chancel are under the disposition of the ordinary in like manner as those in the body of the church. And that in one of our records in Archbishop Grindal's time we find a special licence issued for the erecting seats in the chancel, together with the rules and directions to be observed therein. (Gibs. 200.) And Dr. Watson argues to the same purpose, although the law (he says) seems now to be settled to the contrary. (Wats. c. 39.)

In Hall v. Ellis, Noy R. 133, it was resolved by the court of King's Bench, that the parson or rector impropriate is entitled to the chief seat in the chancel, but that by prescription another parishioner may have it. (See also Johns. 264.)

Vicar's Seat.] In some places where the parson repairs the chancel, the vicar, by prescription, claims a right of a seat for his family, and of giving leave to bury there, and a fee upon the burial of any corpse. (Johns. 242.) Before the Reformation, the hours of the Breviary were to be sung or said in the *chancel*, by the express words of a constitution of Archbishop Winchilsea, on Sundays, festivals, and other days, by the vicar, with the consent and assistance of all the clergymen belonging to the church, which were the ecclesiastical family of the vicar. Hence it is evident that all vicars had a right of sitting there before the Reformation, and, by consequence, must retain this right still, unless it appear that they have quitted it. But if they have not for forty years past used the right, this breeds a prescription against them in the ecclesiastical courts. (Johns. 243.)

So that it is clear the use of the chancel was entirely in the vicar, whoever repaired it; and thus he acquired a right of receiving what fees were due on such occasions, and the Reformation left the rights of parson and vicar as it found them. (Johns. 244.)

Great and lesser Chancels.] It is, therefore, a very groundless notion with impropriators, that they have the same right in the great chancel that a nobleman has in a lesser. These lesser chancels are supposed to have been erected for the sole use of these noble persons. (See Clifford v. Wicks, *ubi supra.*) Whereas it is clear the great chancels were originally for the use of clergy and people, but especially for the celebration of the eucharist, and other public offices of religion, there to be performed by the curate and his assistants.

SECTION III.—AISLE.

Whence so called.] Aisle (ile) is said to proceed from the French word *aile*, (ala,) a wing; for that the Roman churches were built in the form of a cross, with a *nave* and two *wings*. The word *nave* or *naf* is from the Saxon, and signifieth properly the middle of a wheel, being that part in which the spokes are fixed, and is from thence transferred to signify the body or middle part of the church.

Aisle may be private Property.] As the chancel seems to be peculiarly the part of the church in which the incumbent, or parson, has an especial interest, so the aisle is frequently distinguished as belonging either wholly or in part to private families or individuals, or rather to particular estates within the parish; the owners of which, it is presumed, originally erected the aisle for the accommodation of their household, which their successors in the estate claim as appurtenant to the ancient mansion or dwelling-house. But in order to complete this exclusive right, it is necessary, not only that it should have existed immemorially, but that the owners of the mansion, &c. in respect of which it is claimed, should have from time to time borne the expense of repairing that which they claim as having been set up by their predecessors. (3 Inst. 202.) Thus an aisle in a church, which hath time out of mind belonged to a particular house, and been *maintained* and *repaired* by the owner of that house, is part of his frank tenement, and the ordinary cannot intermeddle therewith. And *residence* in the parish is not necessary to this right. (Gibs. 198.)

Seats in Aisle.] It has been held, that a *seat* in an aisle may be prescribed for by an inhabitant of *another* parish. (Gibs. 198, Fuller v. Lane, 2 Add. R. 427; Barrow v. Kew, Siderf, 361.) And it has also been determined, that a seat in an *aisle* may be prescribed for as appurtenant to a *house out of the parish,* (Davis v. Witts, Forrest's, R. 14,) though not for a seat in the nave of a church. *(ib.)*

But it is otherwise if he hath only used to sit and bury in the aisle, and not *repaired* it; for the constant sitting and burying, without reparation, doth not gain any peculiar property therein; but the aisle being repaired at the common charge of the parish, the common right of the ordinary takes place, and he may, from time to time, appoint whom he pleaseth to sit there. (Gibs. 197, Frances and Ley, Cro. Jac. 366-604.)

Remedy upon Intrusion,] It follows, that when any person hath good title to such aisle, if the ordinary doth place another person therein with the proprietor, the proprietor may have his action upon the case against the ordinary; and if he be impleaded in the spiritual court for the same, a prohibition will lie; or if any private person doth sit therein, or keep out him that hath the right or doth bury his dead there without his consent, an action upon the case doth well lie for the proprietor. (Wats. c. 39.) But no such title can be good, either upon prescription, or upon any new grant, by a faculty from the ordinary, to a *man and his heirs,* but the aisle must always be supposed to be held *in respect of the house,* and will always go with the house to him that inhabits it. (Hussey v. Leighton, 12 Co. 106; Crook v. Sampson, 2 Keb. 92, 2 Bulst. 150; Barrow v. Keen, 1 Sid. 88.)

SECTION IV.—PEWS.

Ancient Mode of Worship.] In the construction of churches in former times, the primary object seems to have been to facilitate and display the impressive grandeur of the Roman Catholic ceremonies. The services of religion were regarded as the peculiar province of its ministers, in which the *people* were not invited to participate; and public worship was conducted as a sublime exhibition, calculated to impress the feelings and stimulate the imagination of the spectators, without at the same time diffusing amongst them a consciousness that they were equally interested, and engaged with those ostensibly employed, in one common act of devotion.

No Pews formerly.] This may account for the absence in our cathedrals, and other ancient ecclesiastical edifices, of any fixed and regularly constructed accommodation for the laity, as an essential part of the building. Until about the period of the Reformation, no seats were allowed, nor any distinct apartment in the church assigned to distinct inhabitants, except for the lord of the franchise, or some other eminent persons. The general seats that were provided were moveable, and the property of the incumbent, and thence in all respects at his disposal; and they were frequently bequeathed by incumbents to their successors, or others as they thought fit. This is corroborated by the fact, that the common law books of an earlier period mention but two or three cases upon this subject, and those relating to the chancels and seats of persons of great quality. (See Johns. 175, Ken. Par. Ant. 596.)

By whom Erected and Repaired.] The general charge of erecting seats in churches, and of keeping them in repair, lies upon the parishioners, unless they be relieved by any particular person being chargeable by prescription, to rebuild or repair the same. (Degge, P. 1. c. 12.)

Right to Seats.] By the general law, and of common right, all the pews in a parish church are the common property of the parish: they are for the use, *in common,* of the parishioners, who are *all* entitled to be seated orderly and conveniently, so as best to provide for the accommodation of all. The distribution of seats rests with the churchwardens, as the officers, and subject to the controul of the ordinary. Neither the minister, nor the vestry, have any right whatever to interfere with the churchwardens, in seating and arranging the parishioners, as often erroneously supposed: at the same time, the advice of the minister, and even sometimes the opinions and wishes of the vestry, may be fitly invoked by the churchwardens; and, to a certain extent, may be reasonably deferred to in this matter. The parishioners, indeed, have a claim to be seated according to their rank and station; but the churchwardens are not, in providing for this, to overlook the claims of *all* the parishioners *to be* seated, if sittings can be afforded them. Accordingly they are bound in particular, not to accommodate the higher classes, beyond their real wants, to the exclusion of their poorer neighbours; who are equally entitled to accommodation with the rest, though they are not entitled to equal accommodation; supposing the seats not to be all equally convenient. (Fuller v. Lane, 2 Add. R. 425.) Upon a person quitting the parish, the right to use a seat in the body of the church, whatever was the nature and origin of that right, is at an end, because he has ceased to be a parishioner. (*ib.* 427, Byerley v. Windus, 5. Barn. and Cres. 18.)

Renting or Purchasing Seats.] Every parishioner has a right to a seat in the church without any payment, either as a purchase, or as rent for the same; and if necessary, occupiers of pews, who are not parishioners, having no prescriptive right therein, may be put out by the churchwardens, to enable them to seat parishioners. And though such occupier has *purchased* the seat, and it was erected under a faculty containing a clause, *permitting* the party erecting the same to sell it, this will not avail against the common law right of parishioners, for such permission in the faculty is illegal. The practice of making such sales may have prevailed frequently, but it has *constantly* been discountenanced by the court. (Walter v. Gunner and Drury, 1 Hagg, R. 314.) And it is clear that *extra parochial* persons cannot establish a right to seats in the body of the church, *without* a prescriptive title; and it is doubtful whether they can establish such a claim *by* prescription. (Byerly v. Windus, 5 Barn. & Cres. 1; 7 Dowl. & Ryl. 564.) But in a case decided in the Exchequer before the above, though not published till afterwards, it was held that a pew in the *body* of the church may be prescribed for as appurtenant to a house *out of the parish.* And Macdonald, C. B. observed, it was very probable that the owner of the house, in respect of which the pew was claimed, had built or endowed the church, and that the house, though now not within the present boundaries of the parish, was formerly within the ecclesiastical limits of the church, before they were abridged and narrowed. (Lousley v. Hayward, 1 Younge & J. 583, *post*, p. 26.)

Galleries.] When the number of parishioners increase, so that the seats are insufficient to accommodate all who apply for them, the parish is bound, and may be compelled by ecclesiastical censures, to provide against these inconveniences; and therefore, upon an application for a faculty to erect a gallery in the parish church, the court will consider the grounds of the application, although it is alleged that a great majority of the inhabitants disapprove of it. For the court may refuse the whole parish joined together, or may grant, if it appears necessary, a prayer, upon the application of one against all the rest. But though the court is not bound by the wish of the majority, it will pay great attention to it; and the measure should be regularly submitted to the consideration of the vestry, in the first instance; and if it is then approved, though very few parishioners attend, they have the power of the parish delegated to them; and unless it is afterwards clearly made out that a gallery is unnecessary, or that it is highly inexpedient, the court will decree the faculty. (Groves and Wright v. the Rector of Hornsey, &c. 1 Hagg R. 188.)

But if more pews or galleries be necessary, it is said to be agreed that the churchwardens cannot erect them of their own head; some say it cannot be done without the license of the ordinary; and it is clear if there be a *dispute* whether more pews are necessary, or where they shall be placed, the ordinary is sole judge in that case. But if the incumbent, churchwardens, and parishioners do unanimously agree that more pews are necessary, and that they shall be fixed in such a place, it doth not seem that there is any necessity for the ordinary's interposition: for there can be no need of a judge where there is no controversy. (Johns 163. Ayl. Par. 484.)

Distribution of Seats.] The distribution of seats rests with the ordinary, or bishop, who may place and displace whomsoever he pleaseth. (2 Roll. Abr. 288.) And the churchwardens, as his officers, are to place the parishioners according to their rank and station; (Pettman v. Bridger, 1 Phil. Ec. Ca. 323;) and hence it is, that if any seat, though affixed to the freehold, be taken away by a stranger, the churchwardens, and not the incumbent, may have their action against the wrong-doer. (Wats, c. 39.)

The primary authority of appointing what persons shall sit in each seat, being in the ordinary, (3 Inst, 202,) he is to take care to order all things appertaining to divine service, so that there be no contention in the church, and that all things be done decently, and in order to give precedence to such as ought to have it. (Wats. c. 39.) And his officers for this purpose, the churchwardens, are subject to his control, if any complaint should be made against them. (Pettman v. Bridger, 1 Phil. Ec. Ca. 323.)

Intermixture of Families.] In the *Hornsey* case *(ubi supra)* it was objected against building a gallery to accommodate parishioners who had applied for seats, that the churchwardens might put different families into the same pew, as the pews were not appropriated by any faculty, and would afford more sittings than were then occupied; but Lord Stowell said they might be appropiated by prescription, or by possessory right on allotment by the churchwardens; and a prescriptive title cannot be altered by any authority, nor a possessory title by the churchwardens *alone*, though it may be by the ordinary. And he intimated, that unless there was ample room, it would be improper to put individuals of different families in the same pews, which might produce contention and inconvenience. (See also Tattersall v. Knight, 1 Phil. Ec. Ca. 232.)

Customs as to Ordering Seats.] By custom, the churchwardens may have the ordering of the seats, as in London, which by the like custom may be in other places. (Wats. c. 39.)

So a custom time out of mind of disposing of seats by the churchwardens, and major part of the parish, or by twelve or any particular number of the parishioners, is a good custom, and if the ordinary interpose, a prohibition will be granted. (Gibs. 198.) But the churchwardens must show some particular reason why they are to order the seats exclusive of the ordinary; for a *general* allegation, that the parishioners have used to *build* and *repair* the seats, and that by reason thereof, the churchwardens have used to order and dispose of them, is not sufficient to take away the ordinary's power herein. (Wats, c. 39. Presgrove v. Shrewsbury, 1 Salk. 167, *vide* Gibson, 198. See 2 Rol. Rep. 24.)

Exclusive right to Pew.] But both the ordinary and the churchwardens may be excluded from exercising any right in the disposal of a pew, where an individual has acquired an absolute and exclusive right therein. Still, to exclude the jurisdiction of the ordinary, it is necessary that the person claiming a pew, should shew a *faculty* or a *prescription*, which supposes a faculty, *time out of mind*, the faculty itself being lost. (Tattersall v. Knight, 1 Phil. Ec. Ca. 237.) Still by the general law there can be no *property* in pews. The ordinary may grant a pew to a particular person, while he resides within the parish, or there may be a prescription by which a faculty is presumed; but as to personal property in a pew, the law knows of no such thing. (Hawkins v. Compeigne, 3 Phil. Ec. Ca. 16.) It has been held that the *priority* in the seat, as well as the seat itself, may be claimed by prescription, and that an action on the case lies for it at common law. (Carleton v. Hutton, Noy, 78. Latch, 116.)

By Faculty.] Faculties appropriating certain pews to certain individuals, in different forms, and with different limitations, have been granted in former times with too great facility. The appropriation has sometimes been to a man and his family, "so long as they continue *inhabitants of a certain house* in the parish." The more modern form is, "so long as they continue *inhabitants of the parish.*" The first of these is, perhaps, the least exceptionable form. A third sort of faculty, not unusual after churches have been new pewed, either wholly or in part, appears to have been a faculty for the appropriation of certain pews to certain *messuages* or *farm-houses:* the probable origin of most prescriptive rights to particular pews. Some instances there are, too, of faculties *at large;* that is, appropriating pews to persons, and their families, without any condition annexed of residence in the parish. But such faculties are, so far at least, merely void, that no faculty is deemed either in the spiritual courts or at common law, good, to the extent of entitling any person who is a *non-parishioner* to a *seat* even in the *body* of the church. (Fuller v. Lane, 2 Add. Rep. 426.) But see Lousley v. Hayward, 1 Younge & J. 583.

Ordinaries at the present day are bound not to issue faculties appropriating pews to individuals, but under *special* circumstances. (Woollocombe v. Ouldridge. 3 Add. Rep. 1.)

By Prescription.] To support a prescriptive right to a pew, the mere presumption of a faculty having been anciently granted and since lost, is not sufficient, without some evidence on which a faculty can reasonably be presumed. The strongest evidence of that kind, is the building and repairing time out of mind; for mere repairing for thirty or forty years, will not exclude the ordinary. The possession must be ancient, and going beyond memory, though not the high *legal* memory. (Per Ld. Stowell in Walter v. Gunner and Drury, 1 Hagg. R. 322.) By the united authority of the common and ecclesiastical law, it has been held that a prescription for a seat in the *body* of the church, as appurtenant to a house out of the parish, cannot be supported. See Fuller v. Lane, *(ubi supra.)* Byerley v. Windus, *(ante,* p. 23.) But in a case decided before those last mentioned, though not reported till some time afterwards, it was held, in the Court of Exchequer, that a pew in the body of a church may be prescribed for as appurtenant to a house *out of the parish.* And the chief baron Macdonald is reported to have said, "The boundaries of parishes were settled long after the foundation of churches; and those ecclesiastical districts belonging to churches at their first institution, have been since much varied, and in many cases abridged and narrowed when new churches were built. How, then, can we now say, that the owners of the house or the estate, in respect of which the pew is claimed, did not build or endow the church, or some part of it; or that this house, though now not within the parish, according to its present boundaries, was not formerly within the ecclesiastical limits of the church. Very probably it was so. The distinction between a prescription in a house out of the parish, for a pew in an aisle, but not in the body of the church, is merely made a doubt or question in some of the books; but there is no case in support of it; and there is no distinction in the reason of the thing itself. (Lousley v. Hayward, 1 Younge & J. 583, *ante,* p. 23.)

Occupying and Repairing.] If any repairs have been required within memory, they must be proved to have been made at the expense of the party setting up the prescriptive right. The *onus* and *beneficium* go together. Mere *occupancy* does not prove the right; for though in country parishes the same families occupy the same pews for a long time, they still belong to the parish at large, unless the inhabitants of a particular *house*, (not the owners of particular *lands*) have *repaired* the pew. What might be the effect of a very long occupancy, where no repairs have been *necessary*, seems undecided. (Pettman v. Bridger, 1 Phil. Ec. Ca. 325.) An old entry in a vestry book signed by the churchwardens, stating that a pew had been repaired by A, *in consideration of his using it*, is evidence for a person claiming the pew under A. (Price v. Littlewood, 3 Camp. 288.)

Consideration for Prescription.] If a person prescribe that he and his ancestors, and all they whose estate he hath in a certain messuage, have used to sit in a certain seat in the *nave* of the church for time out mind, in consideration that they have used, time out of mind, to repair the said seat, and the ordinary remove him from this seat, a prohibition lieth; for this is a good prescription, and by intendment there may be a good consideration for the commencement of this prescription, although the place, where the seat is, be the freehold of the parson. But if he prescribe generally, without the said consideration of repairing the seat, the ordinary may displace him. (2 Roll. Abr. 288, Walter v. Gunner and Drury, Pettman v. Bridger, *ubi supra.*)

Seats go with the House.] But the ordinary cannot grant a seat to one *and his heirs*; for the seat does not belong to the person, but to the *house*, for otherwise, when the person goes out of the town to dwell in another place, yet he shall retain the seat, which is unreasonable, (Brabin. v. Tradum, Poph. R. 140, 2 Roll. Abr. 287, Stocks v. Booth, 1 *T. R.* 432. And in Langley v. Sir Thos. Chute, Raym. Rep. 246, a prohibition was refused to a libel for the sole use of a pew, to which the churchwardens would have appointed another person than the person appointed by the ordinary, because (per 3 of 4 J.'s,) the ordinary hath jurisdiction, and the churchwardens cannot justle out his authority, when the privilege is claimed only for defendant *and his family;* and if the plaintiff is grieved by the sentence, he may appeal; for the common law court may determine a point on the canon law, if the party may appeal. (May v. Gilbert, 2 Buls. Rep. 151.)

A seat or pew in the *nave* or *body* of the church may be prescribed for, as belonging to a *house;* and the *occupier* of the house for the time being is entitled to the use of the pew, and not the *owner* of the estate; and it may be transferred with the messuage. (Woollocombe

v. Ouldridge, 3 Add. R. 6.) And Lord Kenyon said he had seen a faculty for exchanging seats in a church, which were annexed to houses. (Stocks v. Booth, 1 T. Rep. 431.)

Reparation pleaded.] The reparation of the pew by the person pleading such prescription, and praying a prohibition, must be alleged in pleading, because the ordinary, in the body of the church, *prima facie* hath the right, and nothing but such private reparation can divest him of that right, notwithstanding possession and use time out of mind. (Woollocombe v. Ouldridge, 3 Add. Rep. 6.) But in Pettman v. Bridger, 1 Phil. Ec. Ca. 327, Sir J. Nicholl thought the defendants plea, that the pew had been, time immemorial, annexed to his house, was sufficient, according to the practice of those courts; as it must be considered as *including* the averment, that the pew had been used, occupied, and repaired from time immemorial.

When not pleaded.] It hath been held, that in two cases reparation need not be particularly pleaded; first, in case of prescription for an *aisle*, because, by the *common law*, the particular persons are *supposed* to repair, and so need not show it; and the foundation of the right may be for other causes than repairing, as for being founder, or having contributed to its building. The second case, (which hath often been declared for law, is where an action upon the case is brought against one who disturbs another in his seat, which disturber being a stranger, and having not any right *primâ facie,* the possession of the other is a sufficient ground of action, and it needs not be alleged that he repairs. (Gibs. 197, 198; 2 Roll. Rep. 24.)

Thus in Kenrick v. Taylor, 1 Wils. R. 326, which was a special action upon the case, against the defendant for disturbing the plaintiff in his pew, which he claimed by prescription, as appurtenant to his messuage in the parish, the Court said, that this being a possessory action against a stranger, and a mere wrong-doer, the plaintiff was not obliged to prove any repairs done by himself or others, whose estate he hath; for it is a rule in law, that one who is in possession need not show any title or consideration for such possession, against a wrong-doer. But it is otherwise, where one claims a pew or an aisle against the ordinary, who undoubtedly hath *primâ facie* the disposal of all the seats in the church; and against him, a title or consideration must be shown in the declaration, and proved. (See Pettman v. Bridger, 1 Phil. Ec. Ca. 325.)

Presumptive Evidence.] Possession for thirty-six years of a pew, claimed as *appurtenant to a messuage in the parish,* was holden to be presumptive evidence of a prescriptive right, in a case where the church had been rebuilt about forty years before. (Rogers v. Brooks,

1 T. R. 431.) Yet, in a later case, it appeared that the seat itself was built thirty-five years before, for the accommodation of the plaintiff, and to put an end to a dispute between two families; this proof was holden to rebut the presumption which would otherwise arise from so long a possession. (Griffith v. Matthews, 5 T. Rep. 296.) And though a possessory right is sufficient to maintain a suit against a mere disturber, it is not as against the churchwardens and ordinary; though if the churchwardens causelessly displace persons in possession, the ordinary will replace them. (Pettman v. Bridger, 1 Phil. Ec. Ca. 316.)

Cannot let to Non-residents.] Individuals having pews appurtenant to their houses, cannot let them to non-resident persons, and thus by contract defeat the general right of the parish. (Walter v. Gunner and another, 1 Hagg. Rep. 317.)

Pulling down Seats.] If any persons shall presume to build any seat in the church without license of the ordinary, or consent of the minister and churchwardens, or in any inconvenient place, or too high, it may be pulled down by order from the bishop, or his archdeacon, or by the churchwardens, or by the consent of the parson; but if any presume, without such authority, to cut or pull down any seat annexed to the church, the parson may have an action of trespass against the misdoer, though he formerly set it up. (Wats. c. 39.)

" All persons ought to understand that the sacred edifice of the church is under the protection of the ecclesiastical laws, as they are administered in these courts; that the possession of the church is in the minister and churchwardens; and that no person has a right to enter it when it is not open for divine service, except with their permission, and under their authority. That pews already erected cannot be pulled down without the consent of the minister and churchwardens, unless after cause shown by a faculty or license from the ordinary." (Sir J. Nicholl in Jarratt v. Steele, 3 Phil. Ec. Ca. 169.)

If any seats annexed to the church be pulled down, the property of the materials is in the parson, and he may make use of them if they were placed in the church by any one, of his *own head,* without legal authority; but for the seats erected by the parishioners, by good authority, it seemeth that the property of the materials, upon removal, is in the parishioners. (Degge, P. 1. c. 12.)

Suits where triable.] The ecclesiastical jurisdiction does not extend to the trial of customs, or prescriptions; and, consequently, in all cases of prescriptions for seats, the matter is solely determinable at common law. (Degge P. 1. c. 12, Wats. c. 39.) And, therefore, where W. was sued for disturbing a person in his seat in the church, it was suggested for a prohibition, that he purchased an ancient house with this seat belonging to it, to him and his heirs, which was pleaded below. *Per curiam.* "This is enough to show the temporal right is in question," and a prohibition was awarded. (Witcher v. Chesham, 1 Wils. 17.)

The spiritual court may proceed for a disturbance in a seat upon libels grounded on prescription, where the prescription is *not denied,* as in cases for a modus or a pension by prescription. (Jacob v. Dalton, 2 Salk. 551, Lord Raym. 755.) So that such suits are not absolutely *coram non judice.* And the reason why a prohibition is granted, where a custom or prescription is denied, seems to be, because the ecclesiastical law allows of different times in creating customs or prescriptions, and generally of less time than is allowed of by the common law, which admits no custom or prescription to be valid, the commencement whereof is shown to be since the reign of Richard the First, or within legal memory. Therefore, the common law will not suffer the spiritual courts to try prescriptions, whereby they might affect and charge persons inheritances, by adjudging them to be good which are no prescriptions. (Wats. c. 39.)

Action against Disturber.] Trespass will not lie for entering a pew, because the plaintiff has not the *exclusive* possession; the *possession* of the church being in the parson. (Stocks v. Booth, 1 T. R. 430; Cross v. Salter, 3 T. R. 639;) and, in Mainwaring v. Giles, Abbott C. J. said, "In no case has a person a right to the possession of a pew analagous to the right which he has in his house or land; for trespass would lie for an injury to the latter, but for an intrusion into the former, the remedy, undoubtedly, is by an action on the case. That furnishes strong reason for thinking, that the action is maintainable only on the ground of the pew being annexed to the house as an easement; because, an action on the case is the proper form of remedy for the disturbance of the enjoyment of an easement annexed to land, as in the case of a right of way, or a stream of water. I am of opinion, that this being a pew in the *body* of the church, and not in a *chancel,* which might be the freehold of an individual, no action at common law can be maintained for a disturbance, because the pew is not annexed to any house." (5 Barn. and Ald. 361.)

SECTION V.—GOODS AND ORNAMENTS OF THE CHURCH.

Ornaments in general.] By the 1 Eliz. c. 2. s. 25, such ornaments of the church, and of the ministers thereof, shall be retained, and be used as was in the Church of England by authority of Parliament in the second year of the reign of King Edward the sixth, until *other order* shall be therein taken.

Pursuant to which clause, in the third year of the same reign, a commission was granted to reform the disorders of chancels, and to add to the ornaments of them, by ordering the commandments to be placed at the east end. (Gibs. 201 ; see also Lind. 52.)

And the statute of *circumspecte agatis*, 13 Ed. 1. St. 4, gives its sanction to the church being *conveniently decked*, and adds, " in which cases the spiritual judge shall have power to take knowledge notwithstanding the king's prohibition." (See 2 Inst. 489.)

Churchwardens care therein.] By canon 85, the churchwardens or questmen shall take care that all things in the church be kept in such an orderly and decent sort, without dust or any thing that may be either noisome or unseemly, as best becometh the house of God, and is prescribed in an homily to that effect. (See " CHURCHWARDENS.")

Communion Table.] The 82d canon appoints, that communion tables shall, from time to time, be kept and repaired in sufficient manner, at the charge of the parish.

In the case of Newson v. Bawldry, the court held, that where the parishioners at a meeting had resolved to repair the *chancel* and rails about the communion table, which had been anciently placed in the chancel, and to replace the table there, and raise the floor some steps higher for the sake of greater decency; that they might do these things, for they are compellable to put things in decent order. And as to the degrees of order and decency there is no rule, but as the parishioners, by a majority, do agree; and a rate for this purpose, it seems, may be enforced. (Far. 70, Burn. Ec. L. 368.)

Pulpit.] In ancient times the bishops preached standing upon the steps of the altar. When afterwards it was found more convenient to have pulpits erected for that purpose.

The churchwardens or questmen, at the common charge of the parishioners, were required to provide a comely and decent pulpit, to be set in a convenient place, within every church, by the discretion of the ordinary of the place. (Ayl. Par. 21. Canon 83.)

Reading Desk.] A convenient seat must also be made at the charge of the parish, for the minister to read service in. (Canon 82.)

Font.] By a former constitution, too much neglected in many places, a font of stone shall be placed in every church and chapel, where baptism is to be ministered in the ancient usual places. (Canon 81. Gibs. 360.)

Chest for Alms.] The churchwardens are required, by Canon 84, to provide, at the charge of the parish, a strong chest with a hole in the upper part thereof, having three keys; of which one shall remain in the custody of the parson, vicar, or curate, and the other two in the custody of the churchwardens for the time being; which chest they shall set and fasten in the most convenient place, to the intent the parishioners may put into it their alms for their poor neighbours. And the keepers of the keys shall yearly, quarterly, or oftener, as need requireth, take such alms, &c. out of the chest, and distribute the same, in the presence of most, or of six chief parishioners, to their most poor and needy neighbours.

Chalice, Wine, &c.] It is also the duty of the churchwardens, at the charge of the parish, to provide a chalice, or more if necessary, (Lind. 252,) a sufficient quantity of fine white bread, and of good and wholesome wine for the communion, which wine is required to be brought to the communion table in a clean and sweet standing pot, or stoop of pewter, if not of purer metal. (Canon 20.)

Books, Bells, Bier, &c.] There must also be provided the largest Bible, and a true printed copy of the [present] book of Common Prayer, (13 & 14 Car. 2. c. 4,) at the costs and charges of the parishioners, of every parish church and chapelry, cathedral church, college, and hall. Gibs. 202.) And the book of homilies may also be provided in like manner, (Canon 80,) and bells and ropes, and a bier for the dead, are likewise to be furnished at the cost of the parish. (Lind. 252.) For bells are not mere ornaments; they are as necessary as the steeple, which is of no use without them. (Woodward v. Makepeace, 1 Salk. 164.)

Table of Degrees.] Canon 99. The table of degrees of marriage prohibited, shall be, in every church, publicly set up at the charge of the parish.

Ten Commandments.] Canon 82. The ten commandments shall be set, at the charge of the parish, upon the east end of every church and chapel, where the people may best see and read the same. And the like is directed with respect to other chosen sentences.

Monuments in Churches.] Although Lord Coke says, in general terms, that it is lawful to build or erect tombs, sepulchres, or monuments, for the deceased, in church, chancel, chapel, or churchyard, in a manner not to the hindrance of the celebration of divine service, (3 Inst. 102—202,) yet this must be intended by license of the bishop, or consent of the parson and churchwardens. (Degge. P. 1. c. 12, Wats, c. 39, Gibs, 453.) The churchwardens can have no absolute uncontrolled authority in this respect; and, therefore, assuming that a custom for them to set up monuments of a *proper description* in the church without the leave of the parson may be good, yet it is too large a proposition to contend for, that, without either the consent of the rector or of their common ecclesiastical superior, they may put up any thing, however unseemly. (Beckwith v. Harding, 1 Barn. and Ald. 508.)

Faculty to erect Monument.] Though a well-established custom, or the authority of the rector and churchwardens may occasionally suffice, yet no practice can absolutely *legalize* the erection of a monument without a faculty; (Seagar v. Bowle, 1 Add. R. 541;) for it is a general rule, that they cannot be set up without the consent of the ordinary; (Palmer v. Bishop of Exeter, 1 Stra. 576; Cart. v. Marsh, 2. ib. 1080.) A faculty is in strictness requisite, though it be omitted under the confidence reposed in the minister. The consent of the incumbent is thus taken on some occasions, and especially for monuments in the chancel. (Maidman v. Malpas, 1 Hagg. R. 208.) But he cannot grant away *vaults;* this can only be done by a *faculty;* and therefore where a rector having agreed, for a *pecuniary* consideration, that the party should make and have the exclusive use of a vault in the church, and afterwards caused it to be opened, and the body of another person interred therein, it was held that an action for disturbing the vault could not be maintained against him, as no faculty had been obtained. (Bryan v. Whistler, 8 Barn. & Cres. 288)

Appeal to Metropolitan.] Though the ordinary is the proper judge in these cases, yet, notwithstanding his allowance, an appeal lies to the metropolitan; because the power of the ordinary in this respect must be exercised according to a prudent and legal discretion, which the superior has a right to look into and correct, (Cart. v. Marsh, Stra. 1080), and the party cannot waive the appeal and apply to the court of K. B. for a *prohibition* instead. (Bulwer v. Hase, 3 East, 217.)

Repairing Monuments.] After monuments have been once erected, they may be repaired, for this is of public consequence, when their importance in tracing family descents, &c. is considered. It may be proper to apply to the churchwardens for leave to do so, but they are bound to grant it as far as their authority extends; and by refusing, may incur the censure of the Ecclesiastical Court; for decency and propriety require that monuments should not remain in a state of ruin and decay. (Barden v. Calcott, 1 Hagg. Rep. 16.)

Defacing Monuments.] The defacing of monuments is punishable at common law; for the property in grave-stones, winding-sheets, coats of arms, pennons or other ensigns, placed or hung up in memory of the dead, remains in the executors, who may have actions against those who break, deface, or carry them away, or an appeal of felony. (Co. Lit. 186, Cro. Jac. 367, 3 Inst. 110;) but if they are put up without the ordinary's consent, he may remove them. (Palmer v. Bishop of Exetèr, 1 Stra. 576.) And according to Godbolt, (279,) the churchwardens may bring an action for defacing a monument. (1 Burn. Ec. L. 373.)

Images and other Things.] If any superstitious pictures are in a window of a church or aisle, it is not lawful for any to break them without license of the ordinary; and the offender may be bound to his good behaviour. (Cro. Jac. 367.) There are also many other articles for which no express provision is made by any special law, and therefore must be referred to the general power of the churchwardens, with the consent of the parishioners, and under the direction of the ordinary; such as the erecting galleries, adding new bells, (and of consequence, as it seemeth, salaries for the ringers,) organs, clock chimes, king's arms, pulpit-cloths, hearse-cloth, mats, vestry furniture, and the like. (1 Burn. Ec. L. 374.) The consent of the parishioners is not indispensable, unless to charge the parish with any expense for *new* ornaments, &c., or for their support after they have been put up. Where no charge is incurred, their approbation is not necessary, nor their disapprobation binding on the ordinary. (St. John's, Margate, 1 Hagg. R. 198; Butterworth v. Walker, 3 Burr. 1689.)

Organs.] In cathedrals organs may be deemed necessary, and the ordinary may compel their erection by the dean and chapter. In parish churches it is otherwise, and it may be proper to discourage them in some particular cases. In a recent instance, Lord Stowell decreed a faculty for accepting and erecting an organ offered to a parish church, without a *clause against future expenses being charged to the parish,* which was rich and populous. (St. John's, Margate, 1 Hagg. R. 198. See Butterworth v. Walker, 3 Burr. 1689.)

Property therein.] A person may give or dedicate goods to the service of religion in such a church, and deliver them into the custody of the churchwardens, by which the property is immediately changed (Degge, p. 1. c. 12.) The goods of the church do not belong to the incumbent, but to the parishioners; and if they be taken away or injured, the churchwardens have their action at common law, or suit in the Ecclesiastical Court: the latter is said to be the most proper remedy, (Welcome v. Lake, 1 Sid. 281, 2 Keb. 22,) unless the thing taken or injured be not strictly church property,—as the title deeds to the advowson,—deposited in a chest in the church, in which case the proceeding at common law may be preferred. (Gardner v. Parker,

4 T. R. 351.) And it would probably be now held, that where property of any kind, taken from a church, is sought to be recovered, or a compensation in respect of it obtained, the same rule must prevail. (See Starky v. Watlmgton, 2 Salk. 547.) And the stealing of articles from a church, though they be not such as are used for divine service, is sacrilege. (R. v. Rourke, Russ. & R. C. C. 386.) So if they be taken from the church tower, having a separate roof, but accessible only from the body of the church, it is a stealing in the church, under 7 and 8 Geo. 4. c. 29. s. 10. (R. v. Wheeler & Ors, 3 Car. & P. 585.)

Alienation of Goods, &c.] By the civil law, the goods belonging to a church are forbidden to be alienated, or pawned, unless for the redemption of captives, relief of the poor in time of great famine, or for paying the debts of the church, if a supply cannot be otherwise raised; or upon other cases of necessity or great advantage to the church. (Wood, liv. L. 142.) But by the law of England, the goods belonging to a church *may be* alienated; yet the churchwardens alone cannot dispose of them without the consent of the parish: and a gift of such goods by them, without the consent of the sidesmen or vestry, is void. (Wats. c. 39, 1 Burn. Ec. L. 376.)

SECTION VI.—REPAIRS OF THE CHURCH.

By Parishioners.] When the bishops had the whole tithes of the diocese, a fourth part in every parish was to be applied to the repair of the church; but afterwards, the duty, as incident to the receipt of this fourth part, was transferred with it to the rectors. (Degge, p. I. c. 12.) But custom, or the common law, has cast the burden upon the parishioners, at least with respect to the *nave* of the church; and in some instances of the chancel also; which the parishioners may be compelled to observe, by proceedings in the spiritual court. (Lind. 53; 2 Inst. 489, 653; 3 Bla. Com. 92.)

Repair of Chancel.] But generally the parson is bound to repair the chancel, if there be no custom for the parish, or the owner of some particular estate, to do it. (Gibs. 199.) And where there are both rector and vicar in the same church, they shall contribute in proportion to their benefice, unless there be a custom or order fixing to which of them it shall appertain.

As spiritual persons, so also impropriators are bound of common right to repair the chancels; but whether in case of neglect the spiritual court may proceed by sequestration, (it is said they can in 3 Keb. 829,) or against the person of the layman, at common law, seems to remain in some doubt, though the latter course appears to have had the sanction of the Court of Common Pleas. (2 Vent. 35; 2 Mod. 257; Wats, c. 39; Gibs. 199.)

Several Impropriators.] Where there are several impropriators, which is not unfrequently the case, and the prosecution is to be carried on by the churchwardens to compel them to repair, it is adviseable to obtain the sanction of the vestry to prosecute at the parish expense. The court in such case will not settle the proportions among the impropriators, but admonish all the parties to the suit to repair the chancel, under pain of excommunication. It is not *necessary* to make every impropriator a party, but only to prove that those against whom the proceedings are taken, have received tithes or other rectorial profits sufficient to repair it; though it may be adviseable to make as many of them parties as can be included with certainty. (1 Burn. Ec. L. 352.)

Mutual Exemptions.] The division of the burden between the parson and the parishioners, is by consequence a mutual release of each other from that part which the other took; and thus, repairing of the chancel is a discharge from contributing to the repairs of the church; though the impropriator is rateable to the church for lands which are *not parcel of the parsonage.* (Serjeant Davie's case, 2 Roll. Rep. 211.) And therefore, when the farmer of an impropriation pleaded exemption from a parish rate, on the ground of his obligation as parson to repair the chancel, and the plea was disallowed in the spiritual court, (Slowman's Case, 2 Keb. 730, 742,) it must probably have been in reference to other possessions in the parish. (Gibs. 199.)

Repairing Chapel no Exemption.] If there be a chapel of ease within a parish, and part of the parishishioners have used, time out of mind, alone to repair it, and there to marry and do all other things, except that they *bury* at the mother church, they are still liable to contribute to the repairs of the latter, even though they prescribe that they have time out of mind used to *repair the chapel;* and by reason thereof have been discharged of the reparation of the mother church. (2 Roll. Abr. 289.) And though the chapel be three miles distant from the church, and they have always repaired the chapel, and married, and *buried* there, and have never within 60 years been so charged, this will not suffice, for they ought to show their exemption, if they have any, upon the *endowment.* (2 Roll. Abr. 290. *l.* 10.) But, if it can be intended, from the facts, that the chapelry is coeval with the church, and *never* contributed to the repairs of the latter, it may be exempt. (Ball v. Cross, 1 Salk. 165.; Hobart, 66.)

A Consideration Exempts.] But if the inhabitants of a chapelry, who repair their own chapel, and perform therein all the solemnities of the church, except burial, claim to be exempt by prescription, and show a good cause or *consideration* for the exemption, as the payment of 30*s.* 4*d.* per annum for the reparation of the mother church, (2 Rolls. Abr. 290; Wise v. Creake, 2 Lev. 186,) or that they have immemorially repaired part of the wall of the churchyard of the parish church at their own cost, the prescription in such case is good, and a prohibition lieth. (ib. *l.* 30, 45.)

No Prohibition.] By the statute of *circumspecte agatis,* 13 Ed. 1, the authority of the spiritual court to punish for neglect to repair or adorn the church is confirmed; and therefore if a suit be there instituted for this cause, a prohibition does not lie; (Com. Dig. Prohibition, G. 2,) and by *the church,*.is intended not only the body thereof, walls, windows, and covering, (Lindw. 53,) but also any *public* chapel annexed to it; but this extends not to any *private* chapel, though it be affixed to the church, for that must be repaired by him that hath the proper (exclusive) use of it, for he that hath the profit ought to bear the burden. (2 Inst. 489.)

Churchwardens' Duty therein.] By the 85th canon, the churchwardens or questmen are enjoined to take care and provide that the churches be well and sufficiently repaired, and so from time to time kept and maintained; and although they are not charged with the repairs of the chancel, yet they are bound to see that it be not permitted to dilapidate and fall into decay; and if any default be made therein, they are to make presentment thereof at the next visitation. (1 Burn. Ec. L. 357.)

Parishioners' Controul.] The churchwardens may make the *ordinary* reparations of the fabric, or ornaments of the church, without the previous sanction of the parishioners, for to this they are bound by their office, and are punishable if they neglect it; but if they propose to erect any thing new and additional, as a new gallery, where there was none before, they must have the consent of the major part of the parishioners, and also a license of the ordinary. (Groves v. Rector, &c. of Hornsey, 1 Hagg. Rep. 188; Rogers v. Davenant, 1 Mod. 237.)

Enlarging or Rebuilding.] If it be necessary to enlarge the church for the accommodation of an increased population, or if it be necessary, from its being greatly dilapidated and out of repair, to pull it down and rebuild, this can only be done by consent of the majority of the parishioners, declared at a meeting duly assembled upon proper notice. (Thomas v. Morris, 1 Add. Rep. 478.) The churchwardens must also take care to obtain the previous concurrence of the parish to a rate for the purpose, as they cannot, after the alterations are made, call upon the parish to reimburse them. (R. v. Bradford, 12 East, 556. Lanchester v. Thompson, 5 Madd. R. 4.—See "CHURCH RATE.")

Demolition of Church.] Where a church was in a state of dilapidation, having been shut up, upon the parish being united to the adjoining parish by act of Parliament, and there were no persons compellable by law to restore and uphold it, though it had been long used by a congregation of French Protestants, who paid rent for it, a faculty for taking it down unconditionally was applied for, and it was said, "The Court is disposed, on the whole, to accede to the present application, unwilling as it is, upon general considerations, to sanction the utter demolition of any building, which has something, at least, of the character of a national church." And the parties were directed to consider whether the building could not be made subservient in some way (for instance, as a national school) to the church establishment, before the faculty actually issued. (Hollah v. St. Martin Orgars, 2 Add. Rep. 255.)

SECTION VII.—PROFANATION OF CHURCHES.

Arrests therein forbidden.] The 50 Edw. 3. c. 5, & 1 R. 2. c. 15, were enacted, as appears from their respective recitals, to suppress the practice of arresting "persons of holy church," against whom process had issued, "whilst they attended to divine service in churches, churchyards, and other places dedicated to God." Under these statutes, though apparently confined to clergymen, (see Tidd, 219,) it would seem, that all persons are protected in the places mentioned; and in the week-days also, if attending religious service. (Pit v. Webley, Cro. Jac. 321. See 3 T.R. 739.) But the privilege applies to civil proceedings only, between party and party, and not to a *warrant* from a justice of the peace. (Id. ibid. Prinsor's case, Cro. Car. 602.) And if, in the case of a civil suit, the party stay in church, with a fraudulent design of eluding the process of the law, the protection ceases.

But so much of both these statutes as relate to the arrest "of persons in holy church," was repealed by 9 G. 4. c. 31; and the protection of clergymen from arrest upon civil process, in going to perform, or during the performance, or returning from the performance thereof, re-enacted by s. 23: and the person making such arrest, is punishable by fine or imprisonmet, or both.

Plays in Churches.] The acting of plays in churches was frequent in this and other nations, till some time after the Reformation. These dramatic exhibitions consisted of representations of remarkable events in Scripture history; or, what was more agreeable to the depraved taste of their auditors, of delineations of the corrupt manners and practices of the clergy. (Gibs, 181.) They were at length suppressed, and the part which the ecclesiastical authorities took in this good work is apparent from the 88th canon, which ordains that churchwardens or questmen, and their assistants, shall suffer no plays, banquets, musters, or any other profane usage, to be kept in the church, chapel, or churchyard.

Brawling.] By the 5 & 6 Ed. 6. c. 4. s. 1, quarrelling, chiding, or brawling, by words only, in any church or churchyard, is punishable by the ordinary, upon the evidence of two witnesses, by suspension of the offender, if he be a layman, from the entrance of the church; and if a clerk, from ministration of his office for so long as the ordinary shall think fit The offence of brawling subsisted at common law before this statute was enacted, and a party may now proceed either on the statute or at common law. (Wenmouth v. Collins, Ld. Raym. 850; ex parte Williams, 4 Barn. and Cres. 313; 6 Dowl. and Ryl. 373.)

What is Brawling.] It appears, that the popular notion of brawling is not very strictly adopted by the courts. Thus, words spoken during divine service by a clergyman, by way of admonition, of a passionate nature, though expressed without any *tone* of passion, amount to this offence, and he was suspended for a fortnight. (Cox v. Gooday, 2 Hagg. R. 138.) So, where the defendant, in answer to a question put to him, exclaimed, "It is a damned lie; I do not say you are a liar, but it is a damned lie;" he was held criminal. (Austen v. Dugger, 3 Phil. Ec. Ca. 122.) It seems also, that reading a "notice of vestry," in church, during divine service, without *due* authority, constitutes the offence. (Dawe v. Williams, 2 Add. R. 130.) If the misconduct is not in a consecrated place, though violent and directed against the minister while presiding at a meeting of his parishioners, it is not an offence within the statute of Ed. 6; but it may still be an ecclesiastical offence, and punishable, especially if it be in a vestry-room, *partly* within the churchyard. (Williams v. Goodyer, 2 Add. Rep. 463.)

Proceedings under the first section of the statute must be supported by *two* witnesses on the specific charge; but by the ecclesiastical law, *one* to the fact and *one* to the circumstance would be sufficient. (Hutchins v. Denziloe, 1 Hagg. Rep. 181.) The Court will consider time and place in these cases; for the same conduct may not amount to this offence in the vestry, which would do so in the church. (1 Hagg. Rep. 184.) Suspension of a parishioner "from the entrance of the church," was limited to a month only, under certain circumstances. (Clinton v. Hatchard, 1 Add. Rep. 96); and in Canning v. Sawkins, (2 Phil. Ec. Ca. 293,) for brawling in a chancel, to three weeks, with notification in the church of such suspension, and costs in both. And in North and Little v. Dickson, (1 Hagg. Rep. N. S. 730,) *provocation* was held no defence to a suit for brawling in a church at a vestry meeting.

Misnomer fatal.] This being a criminal proceeding, the office of the judge wrongly promoted by misnomer of the judge, in a copy of the articles, for this offence, is fatal. (Williams v. Bott, 1 Hagg. 1; Thorp v. Mansell, ib. 4.)

Punishable by Justices.] The 1 M. st. 2. c. 3, and 1 W. & M. c. 18. s. 18, provide, that persons who wilfully and maliciously disturb any minister, or the congregation, during divine service, may be apprehended by the constable, churchwarden, or any other person present, and taken before a magistrate, who may punish the offender. This protection extends to all religious assemblies, authorised by the several acts in favour of non-conformists, &c., (R. v. Hube, 5 T.R. 542,) and the offender, upon conviction at the next quarter sessions, shall suffer the penalty of 40*l.* (52 G. 3. c. 155. s. 12. See Rex. v. Wadley, 4 Maul. and Sel. 508.) But where the parish clerk refused to read in church a notice respecting parish affairs, which was presented to him for that purpose, and the person presenting it read it himself, when no part of the service was actually going on, it was held that though a constable might be justified in removing him from the church, and detaining him till the service was over, yet he could not legally detain him afterwards, in order to take him before a magistrate, as the object of the person did not appear to be *maliciously* to disturb the congregation, or misuse the preacher. (Williams v. Glenister, 2 Barn. and Cres. 699; 4 Dowl. and Ryl. 217.)

Striking in Church.] By the second section of the same statute, (5 and 6 Ed. 6. c. 4,) if any person smite or lay violent hands in any church or churchyard, (which includes cathedrals, Cro. Eliz. 224. 1 Leon, 248,) then, *ipso facto*, the offender shall be deemed excommunicated, and be excluded from the fellowship and company of Christ's congregation. A threatening posture, though an assault at common law, even without a blow, is not held to be *smiting* within the statute. (Jenkins v. Barret, 1 Hagg. Rep. N. S. 15. See Cro. Jac. 367, 1 Haw. 139, Ld. Raym. 850.)

But it hath been holden, that churchwardens, or perhaps private persons, who whip boys for playing in the church, or pull off the hats of those who refuse to take them off themselves, or gently lay hands on those who disturb any part of divine service, and turn them out of the church, are not within the meaning of this statute. (1 Haw. 139; Hall v. Plenner, 1 Lev. 196; Sid. 301; 1 Saund. 14; Comb. 17; Com. Dig. Esglise, F. 2.)

Though the act says, the offender shall be *ipso facto* excommunicated, there must be proper proof of the offence in the spiritual court, before excommunication. (1 Haw. 139; Dier v. East, 1 Vent. 146; Wilson v. Greaves, 1 Burr. 240; Cas. temp. Hardwicke, 190.)

Drawing Weapon.] And if any person maliciously strike another with any weapon, or *draw* any weapon in any church or churchyard, to the *intent to strike* another with it, he shall, on conviction by a jury, or his own confession, or two witnesses, at the assizes or sessions, be adjudged to have one of his ears cut off; and if he have no ears, he shall be burned in the cheek with the letter F., whereby he may be known for a fray-maker and fighter, and be excommunicated. (5 and 6 Ed. 6. c. 4. s. 3. See Sonham v. Trunelle, Cro. Eliz. 919; Penhallo's case, Cro. Eliz. 231.) But if he take up a stone and offer to throw it, or having a hatchet in his hand, offer to strike another with it, the offence is not within the words of the act; for these are not such weapons as may properly be said to be *drawn*, as a sword or dagger. (Wats. c. 34.) In Francis v. Ley, (Cro. Jac. 367,) the Star Chamber resolved that when any one is assaulted or beaten in a church or churchyard, it is not lawful for him to return blows in his own defence, as he may elsewhere

Limitation of Suits.] By statute 27 G. 3. c. 4, no suit shall be brought in any ecclesiastical court for striking or brawling in any church or churchyard, after the expiration of eight calendar months from the time that such offence shall have been committed. The ancient privilege of sanctuary was entirely abolished by the 21st James 1. c. 28. s. 7.

Robbing a Church.] Robbing a church is burglary, for the church is the mansion-house of Almighty God, (3 Inst. 64.) And by the 7 and 8 G. 4. c. 29. s. 10, it is provided, that if any person break and enter any church or chapel, and steal therein any chattel, or having stolen any chattel in any church or chapel, shall break out of the same, every such offender, being convicted thereof, shall suffer death as a felon.

Burning or destroying Churches, &c.] And by another statute passed at the same time, (c. 30. s. 2,) it is provided, that if any person unlawfully and maliciously set fire to any church or chapel, or to any chapel for the religious worship of persons dissenting from the united church of England and Ireland, dulv registered or recorded, every such offender shall be guilty of felony, and being convicted thereof, shall suffer death as a felon. And the 8th section enacts the same punishment against persons riotously assembled, demolishing, or beginning to demolish, any such place of public worship. And by the 7 and 8

G. 4. c. 31. s. 2, the damage done to the building, fixtures, furniture, &c. is to be fully compensated by the hundred or district within which the offence is committed.

SECTION VIII.—CHURCHYARDS.

Originally distant from Church.] It seems to be well established, that at the first erection of churches, no part of the adjacent ground was allotted for interment of the dead; but some place for this purpose was appointed at a farther distance, especially in the case of cities and populous towns.

Land, how obtained.] That this was the fact, is corroborated by the 15 R. 2. c. 5, which after reciting, that by 7 Ed. 1. st. 2, if any religious or other, whatsoever he be, shall buy, or under colour of gift or any other manner of title whatsoever, receive of any man any lands or tenements, which might come to mortmain, it shall be lawful to the king, and to other lords upon the said lands, to enter; and then declares, that "now of late by subtile imagination, and by art and engine, some religious persons, parsons, vicars, and other spiritual persons, have entered in divers lands and tenements which lie adjoining to their *churches*, and of the same, by sufferance and assent of the tenants, have made churchyards, and by bulls of the bishop of Rome, have dedicated and hallowed the same, and in them do make continually parochial burying, without license of the king and of the chief lords; therefore it is declared in this Parliament, that it is manifestly within the compass of the said statute. (See further, as to the manner in which lands were acquired for this purpose, "BURIAL," *post.*)

Repair of Churchyards.] By a constitution of Archbishop *Winchilsea*, the parishioners shall repair the fence of the churchyard at their own charge. (Lind. 253.) And Lord Coke says, they ought to do it, because the bodies of the more common sort are buried there; and for the preservation of the burials of those that were, or should have been, while they lived, the temples of the Holy Ghost. And this they ought to do by custom known and approved; and the conusance of which belonged to the Ecclesiastical Court. (2 Inst. 489.)

Prescription to Repair.] But nevertheless, if the owners of lands adjoining to the churchyard have used, time out of mind, to repair so much of the fence thereof as adjoineth to their ground, such custom is a good custom; and the churchwardens have an action against them at the common law for the same. (2 Roll's Abr. 287, Gibs. 194.)

For the duty rests upon the churchwardens or questman to take care that the churchyards be well and sufficiently repaired and fenced, as they have been in each place accustomed, at the charge of those unto whom by law the same appertaineth. (Canon 85.) Although the statute of *circumspecte agatis*, 13 Ed. 1. st. 4, entitled "Certain cases wherein the king's prohibition doth not lie," directs, that if prelates do punish for leaving the churchyard unclosed, the spiritual judge shall have cognizance thereof, notwithstanding the king's prohibition. Still, if the churchwardens sue a person in the Court Christian, alleging a custom for him, and all those whose estate he hath, to repair the fences of the churchyard next adjoining his estate, a prohibition will lie; for this ought to be tried at the common law, inasmuch as this is to charge a temporal inheritance. (2 Roll. Abr. 287. See Com. Dig. Prohibition, (G. 3.) 13 Co. 41.)

Neglect to Repair indictable.] The duty of repairing the fences of churchyards may also, it appears, be enforced by indictment; as the neglect of it amounts to a misdemeanor. However, where a vicar was indicted for such non-repair, and against whom it was alleged that the vicar had been immemorially bound to repair, and the defendant had neglected to do so, by means whereof cattle broke into the churchyard and injured the tombstones, church porch, &c. to the nuisance of the parishioners, and he was acquitted, the Court refused to grant a new trial, moved for on the ground of the verdict being against evidence; Lord Ellenborough observing, "It is very clear that you may indict the defendant again, if the fences have continued out of repair since the last indictment. (Rex v. Reynell, 6 East, 315.)

Trees and Herbage.] The right of property in the trees and grass of churchyards was formerly a subject of great contention; but, upon the principle that laymen have no power to dispose of things ecclesiastical, it was determined that the parishioners have no right to cut down trees or mow the grass, against the will of the rectors or vicars, or others deputed by them for the custody or care thereof, though such parishioners may even intend to apply the trees so cut down to the use of the church. And it is declared by the council of Stratford, that persons guilty of such contempt shall incur the sentence of the greater excommunication, until they shall make sufficient satisfaction and amends. (Lind. 267.) But if the defendant allege that the trees in dispute grew upon his own freehold, a prohibition lies. (Hilliard v. Jefferson, Ld. Raym. 212.)

Right in Rector or Vicar.] If in the same church there be both rector and vicar, it may be doubted (says Lindwood) to whether of of them the trees or grass shall belong; but I suppose they shall belong to the rector, unless in the endowment of the vicarage they shall be otherwise assigned. (Lind. 267.)

And Rolle seems to make the right, as between rector and vicar, to turn upon this, that they belong to him who is bound to repair; which determination agrees well with what is said in the statute, namely, that the parson shall not cut them down but when the chancel wants reparation. (2 Roll's Abr. 337, Gibs. 207.)

Statute herein.] The 35 Ed. 1. st. 2, intituled *Statutum ne rector prosternat arbores in Camiterio,* which Coke (11 Co. 49) says, is but a declaration of the common law, is as follows: Forasmuch as a churchyard that is dedicated is the soil of a church, and whatsoever is planted belongeth to the soil, it must needs follow, that those trees which be growing in the churchyard are to be reckoned amongst the goods of the church, the which laymen have no authority to dispose; but as the holy Scripture doth testify, the charge of them is committed only to priests to be disposed of; and yet, seeing those trees be often planted to defend the force of the wind from hurting the church, we do prohibit the parsons of the church that they do not presume to fell them down unadvisedly, *but when the chancel of the church doth want necesssary reparations;* neither shall they be converted to any other use, except the body of the church doth need like repairs, in which case, the rectors of poor parishes, of their charity, shall do well to relieve the parishioners with bestowing upon them the same trees; which we will not command to be done, but we will commend it when it is done. (See Gibs. 208.)

Suit against Waste.] And if the person who is entitled to cut them for these purposes is about to do so for any other, a prohibition will be granted to hinder waste. And if the trees be actually cut down by any person, for other use than is here specified, it is thought that he may be indicted and fined upon this statute. (Gibs. 208, 11 Co. 49.) And in Strachy v. Frances, (2 Atk. 217,) upon a motion for an injunction by the patron of the living, to stay waste, Lord Chancellor Hardwicke said, " A rector may cut down timber for the repairs of the parsonage-house or the chancel, but not for any common purpose. Under the statute of 35 Ed. 1, if it is the *custom of the country,* he may cut down underwood for any purpose; but if he grubs it up, it is waste. He may cut down timber likewise, for repairing any old pews that belong to the rectory; and he is also entitled to botes for repairing barns and outhouses belonging to the parsonage." And an injunction was granted accordingly. See also 1 Bos. and Pul. 115, n. An injunction for the like purpose was also granted against the widow of a rector, during vacancy, at the suit of the patroness. (Hoskins v.

Featherstone, 2 Br. C. C. 552.) And the attorney general may, on behalf of the crown, as patron of bishopricks, have the like remedy against a bishop, for opening mines; or to restrain him from felling large quantities of timber. But patrons cannot pray an account for their own benefit. (Knight v. Moseley, Amb. 176.)

Vaults, Tombs, &c.] The rector has the freehold of the church for public purposes, not for his own emolument, to supply places for burial from time to time, as the necessities of his parish require; and not to grant away vaults, which cannot be done unless a faculty be obtained. (Bryan v. Whistler, 8 Barn. and Cres. 288.) And a party who erects a tomb in a churchyard, without due authority, may be proceeded against in the Ecclesiastical Court. (Bardin v. Calcott, 1 Hagg. R. 14.) And where a faculty is sought to be obtained for erecting a vault in a churchyard, the court will scruple to decree it without being satisfied that the proposed erection is not likely to be *generally* prejudicial to the parish—even though the issuing of the faculty be unopposed, either on the part of the parish or of any particular parishioner. (Rosher v. Vicar of Northfleet, 3 Add. R. 14.) And therefore, if the rector permit the erection of a vault, and agree that the party shall have the *exclusive* use thereof for a pecuniary consideration, and he afterwards cause it to be opened for the interment of other persons, no remedy lies against him, as he had no power to make such a grant. (Bryan v. Whistler, *supra*. See Spooner v. Brewster, 2 Car. and P. 34.)

Fees on erecting Vaults, &c.] Ancient *custom* often annexes fees for erecting a stone, or any thing else, by which the grave may be protected, and the memory of the person interred preserved. It is no general common law right; but custom will interpose, and where it is shown to be customary, such practice will be supported. (See Bardin v. Calcott, 1 Hagg. Rep. 14.) And whether this fee, or a portion of it, belongs to the incumbent, seems to rest upon similar authority; though it is observed, that after the soil hath been broken for interring the dead, the grass will grow again, and continue beneficial to the incumbent, but after the erection of a monument, there ceaseth to be any further produce of the soil in that place. And if the incumbent's leave is necessary for the erecting a monument, it seemeth that he may prescribe his own reasonable terms, unless an accustomed fee hath been paid. (1 Burn. Ec. L. 273.)

Tombstone, Owner of.] The possession and right of property in tombstones erected in a churchyard, belong not to the parson, but to those who erected them; and if any one deface or injure them, such owners may have their action of trespass against the wrong doer.

(Spooner v. Brewster, 2 Car. and P. 14.) Though if the parson remove, or cause them to be damaged in the exercise of his general authority over the whole freehold of the church, no remedy lies against him, unless the erection has been made under the sanction of a faculty. (Bryan v. Whistler, 8 Barn. and Cres. 288.)

Churchway, &c.] It is said, that a man may prescribe to have a way through the church or churchyard; (2 Roll's Abr. 265); but he cannot make a private door into the churchyard without the consent of the minister, and a faculty also from the bishop for the same. (Par L. c. 26. s. 29.)

Encroachments.] In the case of St. George, Hanover Square, it is said that the Ecclesiastical Court cannot compel the rector and parishioners to concur in a license to be granted for the erection of a charity school on part of the churchyard; and a prohibition was granted. (2 Burr. 1126.) And where the defendant proceeded against in the Spiritual Court for a nuisance and encroachment, pleaded that the buildings complained of stood upon the old site of former tenements belonging to him, and did not project further, a prohibition was likewise granted; for though interrupting the *use* of a churchyard is properly cognisable in the Ecclesiastical Court, yet the *bounds* of it, which is matter of freehold, ought not to be determined there. (Pew v. St. Mary, Rotherhithe, 2 Stra. 1013.)

Additional Churchyards.] The recent statutes for the erection of additional churches have provided that all such parishes or extra-parochial places as *shall be required* by the commissioners, shall furnish lands for enlarging existing, or making additional churchyards or burial-grounds, as the commissioners shall deem necessary; and the commissioners shall give notice to the churchwardens, to be left at their abodes, of the intention to enlarge the existing, or set out new burial-grounds; and of the extent of ground required for such purpose, and for a proper approach thereto, and of the place in which the same is required to be provided; and the churchwardens shall within fourteen days call a meeting of the vestry, or persons possessing the powers of vestry, for taking all necessary measures for providing the same; and in case the parish or place cannot provide the same without purchase, the vestry, or persons possessing the powers of vestry, are required forthwith to proceed to treat for ground according to such notice, but shall not conclude any bargain without the commissioners' approbation. (59 G. 3. c. 134. s. 36.)

Grant or Purchase of Lands.] All the powers and provisions of the 58 G. 3, or this act, which relate to the grant, sale, conveyance, purchase, and re-sale of lands or heriditaments, from his Majesty, or any corporations, persons under legal disabilities, or any other persons whomsoever, to or by the commissioners, for the purpose of building any additional churches or chapels,—or the issuing, advancing, levying, raising, borrowing, or taking up at interest, money for any such purpose, shall extend to grants, &c. of lands or heriditaments necessary for enlarging, or making any churchyard or burial ground, and approaches thereto, under this act; and for issuing, &c. money required for those purposes, repaying it by instalments or otherwise, as if all such provisions had been re-enacted in this act. (59 G. 3. c. 134. s. 37.) Lands added to any existing churchyard, or burial-ground, or appropriated for a new burial-ground, shall, as soon as convenient, be consecrated for the burial of the dead; and shall for ever be used as an additional burial-ground; and the freehold of the land so consecrated, shall thereupon vest in the person or persons in whom the freehold of the ancient burial ground of such parish or chapelry shall from time to time be vested. (s. 38.)

Churchyard Walls.] The commissioners may, if they think fit, alter, repair, pull down, and rebuild, or order or direct to be altered, &c. the walls or fences of any existing churchyard or burial-ground of any parish or chapelry, and to fence off any additional or new burial-ground, to be provided for by this act; and also to stop up and discontinue, or alter or order to be stopped up, &c. any entrance to any churchyard or burial-ground, and the footways and passages over the same, as to them may appear useless and unnecessary, or as they shall think fit to alter; provided the same be done with the consent of two justices of the peace, and on notice being given as prescribed by 55 G. 3. c. 68 :—(59 G. 3. 134. s. 39.)

Authority to enlarge, &c.] It shall be lawful for the commissioners to *authorise any parish*, chapelry, township, or extra-parochial place, desirous of procuring or adding to any burial-ground, to purchase any land the commissioners may think sufficient and properly situate for that purpose, whether within the parish, place, &c.; and to make and raise rates for the purchase thereof, or repaying with interest any money borrowed for making such purchase; and the churchwardens, or persons authorised to make rates, shall exercise all the powers of said acts for making such purchases, and making and raising such rates; and when any land so purchased shall be situate out of the parish or place for which it was intended, the same shall, after consecration, be deemed part of such parish or place. (3 G. 4. c. 72. s. 26.)

SECTION IX.—BURIAL.

Ancient Burial Places.] It seems to have been the practice of all civilized nations, before the Christian era, to bury their dead at a distance from the temples of their religion, and the places of their habitation. Thus, by the old Roman law, the remains of their deceased fellow-citizens were committed to the silent earth beyond the walls of the city, either by the way side, or, in less remote periods, in some peculiar inclosure dedicated to the purpose. The early Christians continued the same custom, and hence the Augustine Monastery was built without the walls of Canterbury, (as Ethelbert and Augustine in their charters intimate,) that it might be a dormitory to them and their successors, the kings and archbishops, for ever.

Burying in Churches, &c.] In the age of Gregory the Great, however, the monks and priests, who then began to make a profit of their prayers for departed souls, procured leave that the rites of sepulture might be in churches or in places adjoining, by which their income from this source was greatly augmented; and the general practice was introduced from Rome into England about the year 750, by Cuthbert, Archbishop of Canterbury; from which period churchyards may be dated in this island. In the outset it was the *nave* or body of the church that became a repository of the dead, and chiefly under arches by the side of the walls. Lanfranc, Archbishop of Canterbury, seems to have been the first to sanction vaults in chancels, and under the very altars, when he had rebuilt the church of Canterbury, about the year 1075. (Ken. Par. Ant. 592.)

Ministers' authority herein.] The common law hath given the privilege of granting permission to bury in the *church* to the parson only. Accordingly, by a resolution in the case of *Frances* v. *Ley*, (Cro. Ja. 367), neither the ordinary himself nor the churchwardens can grant license of burying to any within the church but the parson only, which right belongs to him in his general capacity of incumbent, and as the person whom the ecclesiastical laws appointed the judge of the fitness or unfitness of this or that person to have this favour; because, when the burying in churches came to be allowed, the canon law directeth, that none but persons of extraordinary merit shall be buried there, of which merit the incumbent was in reason the most proper judge, and was accordingly so constituted by the laws of the church. (Gibs. 453, Wats, c. 39.)

Prescriptive Right.] Upon the like foundation of freehold, the common law hath one exception to this necessity of the leave of the parson: namely, where a burying-place within the church is *prescribed* for, as belonging to a manor-house; the freehold of which, they say, is in the owner of that house, and that, by consequence, he hath a good action at law, if he is hindered to bury there. (Gibs. 463. Harvey's case cited in Dawney v. Dee. Cro. Jac. 606.)

In Churchyards.] The superstition of praying for the dead seems to have been the true original of churchyards, as incompassing or adjoining to the church. Which being laid out, and inclosed for the common burial-places of the respective parishioners, every parishioner hath, and always had, a right to be buried in them. (Gibs. 453.)

But a custom that every parishioner has a right to bury his dead relations in the churchyard, as *near their ancestors as possible*, is bad. (Fryer v. Johnson, 2 Wils. 28.) Though, where the *mode* of burial is not in question, the Court of King's Bench will grant a mandamus to compel the clergyman to inter the body of a parishioner, if he should refuse. (Rex v. Coleridge, 2 Barn. and Ald. 806. 1 Chit. Rep. 588.) And an information was granted against a clergyman in one instance for a similar neglect. (Rex. v. Taylor, Willes R. 538.)

In another Parish.] It seems that a person is not absolutely entitled, as of common right, to be buried in the churchyard of *another* parish. In the case of the churchwardens of Harrow-on-the-Hill, (Perkins 1740,) an admonition was given to the churchwardens not to suffer strangers to be buried in their churchyard; but they, or the parishioners whose parochial right of burial is invaded thereby, may give permission for the purpose, though it should be sparingly granted; (See Bardin v. Calcott, 1 Hagg. Rep. 17;) and the sanction of the incumbent, whose soil is broken, may be necessary. (See 1 Burn. Ec. L. 258.) But where a parishioner dies at a considerable distance from his own parish, being absent on a journey or otherwise, the obvious expediency of interment where the death happens, may supersede this right of exclusion.

Arrest of Corpse.] The vulgar notion, that a dead body may be arrested for debt, and prevented from being buried, which seems to have been imported from the civil law, has now become obsolete, though Lindwood says it at one time prevailed, (Wood. Civ. L. 143, Lind. 278;) and the funeral of Sir Barnard Turner, in 1784, proceeding from London to Hertford, was said to have been stopped by an arrest of his body, till his friends entered into engagements for his debts; and the body of Dryden, the poet, was seized in like manner. But the legality of such a proceeding cannot be supported. Such an arrest cannot be made on mesne process, to compel *an appearance*, from the nature of the thing itself; and that a dead body cannot be taken in execution on a *capias ad satisfaciendum*, should appear from the writ directing the sheriff to have the *body of the debtor* at Westminster on the day of the return, without specifying whether he be dead or living, yet it states the reason to be *in order to satisfy the plaintiff for his debt.*

But by the death of the debtor all his property is vested in others, his heir and personal representatives; he cannot, therefore, satisfy the creditor out of his property, and that his body after death can be no satisfaction, seems to be the opinion of the legislature in the Stat. 21. Ja. 1. c. 24, which provides, that if a debtor die in execution, the persons at whose suit he stands charged may sue out new execution against his lands and goods.

Illegality of such Arrest.] The authority of the case cited by *Hyde*, C. J., in *Quick* v. *Copleton*, (1 Levinz. 161, 1 Sid. 242, 1 Keb. 866,) in which a woman was holden liable on a promise to pay, in consideration of forbearance to arrest the dead body of her son, was thus eloquently contradicted by Lord *Ellenborough*, in Jones v. Ashburnham, (4 East. 460—465): "It is impossible to contend that this last forbearance could be a good consideration for an *assumpsit;* to seize a dead body upon any such pretence would be *contra bonos mores*, and an extortion on the relatives. It is contrary to every principle of law and moral feeling. Such an act is revolting to humanity, and illegal; and therefore any promise extorted by the fear of it could never be valid in law. It might as well be said, that a promise in consideration that one would withdraw a pistol from another's breast, could be enforced against the party acting under such unlawful terror."

Burying in Woollen.] In the earlier periods of the woollen manufacture in this country, laws were passed to compel the burial of the dead in woollen shrouds, as a means of encouraging what was the chief, and considered to be the staple, trade of the kingdom; but the 54 Geo. 3. c. 108, repealed the existing statutes on the subject, and left it to the custom, which had thus been induced, to continue the use of this article for such purposes.

Iron Coffins.] In all cases where the statute law is silent upon the subject, the mode of burying the dead is a matter of ecclesiastical cognizance; and therefore where the question was, whether a parishioner had a right to be buried in the parish churchyard in an *iron* coffin, which was a *new* and unusual mode, the Court of King's Bench refused to grant a mandamus. (Rex v. Coleridge, 2 Barn. and Ald. 806; 1 Chit. Rep. 588. See 3 Inst. 303.)

Bodies cast on Shore.] The 48 G. 3. c. 75, enacts, that the churchwardens and overseers in any parish in which any dead human body is cast on shore from the sea, shall, upon notice thereof given to them, cause such body to be conveyed to some convenient place, and with all speed cause it to be interred, with the customary duties, in the parish churchyard or burial-ground, so that the expenses thereof, and fees, &c. do not exceed the sum allowed by such parish for the burial of persons buried at the expense of the parish; but if such body is cast on shore in any extra-parochial place, where there are no churchwardens, &c. such notice shall be given to the constable or headborough thereof, who shall proceed as before directed in case of churchwardens, &c.

Reward for Notice.] By s. 3, every person finding any such body on the shore, and giving notice within six hours after to such officers, &c., or shall leave such notice at their usual abode, shall be entitled to five shillings for his trouble, but no greater sum shall be given for one notice, though there may be more bodies than one. But the expenses are to be borne by the county; and the act directs, that one justice for the county or place in which such bodies are buried shall, by writing under his hand, direct the treasurer of the county to pay to such churchwardens, constable, &c., such sum for his expenses about the execution of this act, as he may deem reasonable, after the same have been verified on oath.

Penalty for Neglect.] Persons finding bodies, and neglecting to give notice within six hours after, shall forfeit £5, and every churchwarden, &c., neglecting to remove such bodies from the shore for twelve hours after such notice, or to perform the other duties hereby required of them, shall forfeit, for each offence, £5. (ss. 4, 7.)

Penalties how recovered.] All penalties, if not paid on conviction, shall be levied with costs, and paid to the informer, by distress and sale of the offender's goods, by warrant under the hand and seal of any justice for the county or place; which he may grant on confession, or on evidence of one witness on oath. And in default of a distress, the offender may be committed to the county gaol, or house of correction, for not exceeding two calendar months, nor less than fourteen days, unless the penalty and charges be sooner paid.

Appeal.] The party may appeal to the quarter-sessions next after one month after the cause of such appeal arose, on giving ten days' notice of the matter thereof, and entering into recognizance before some justice of the county or place, with sufficient sureties to abide the order and award of the court thereon, who may order costs to either party, mitigate the penalty, or direct further reasonable satisfaction to be made to the party injured, and such, their determination, shall be binding and conclusive.

Manors still liable.] Lords of manors throughout England shall pay to the churchwardens, constables, &c. of such parishes or places, such sums as they were accustomed to pay for placing any such bodies into the ground in the state in which they were found; such sums to go in part discharge of the expenses incurred under this act, and credit to be given for the same by such churchwardens, &c. in their accounts with the county. (s. 13.)

Refusing Burial.] The duty cast upon the clergyman by his office, in respect of burials, is enforced by canon 68, which provides, that no minister shall refuse or delay to bury any corpse that is brought to the church or churchyard, convenient warning being given him thereof, in such manner and form as is prescribed in the book of Common Prayer. And if he shall refuse so to do, except the deceased were denounced, excommunicated, *majori excommunicatione*, for some grievous and notorious crime, and no man able to testify of his repentance, he shall be suspended, by the bishop of the diocese, from his ministry by the space of three months.

But where sufficient evidence has appeared to the bishop of the repentance of the deceased, commissions have been granted, both before and since the Reformation, not only to bury persons who died excommunicate, but to absolve them, in order to Christian burial. (Gibs. 450.)

Dissenters.] The Rubric, confirmed by 13 and 14 Car. 2. c. 4, forbids the use of the customary office in the burial of any that die unbaptized, which was thought to have made *church* baptism essential. But in *Kemp* v. *Wickes, Clerk Arches*, Dec. 11, 1809, *cor* Sir *John Nicholl*, the baptism of a child by a dissenting minister was held a sufficient baptism to entitle the child to Christian burial by a minister of the church of England. The court recognized this important question, as one of disability and exclusion of all dissenting subjects from the general right of burial by the established church, and rested its judgment, 1st, on the canon law, rubrics, and practice affecting lay baptism before the Act of Toleration; 2dly, on the Act of Toleration itself; and generally, on every ground of public and ecclesiastical policy. The court declared, that by the above statute the acts of non-conformists, for the purposes of their own worship, are legalized under certain regulations, and are to be recognized in courts of law Indeed, the baptisms of dissenters have been expressly recognized by stat. 25 G. 3. c. 75, which extended the stamp duty on registers of church of England baptisms to registers of baptisms of Protestant dissenters. (See the *Report of this Case*, published by *Butterworth*. 1810.)

Other Exclusions.] Persons not receiving the holy sacrament, at least at Easter, or such as were killed in duels, tilts, or tournaments, were alike excluded; but at this day, it seems, that these prohibitions are restrained to the three classes of persons: viz. excommunicate,—unbaptized,—and those that have laid violent hands upon themselves. The rubric, before the office of burial, is in this form: "Here it is to be noted, that the office ensuing is not to be used for any that die unbaptized, or excommunicate, or have laid violent hands upon themselves." It seems to be clear, that attainted traitors and felons, who die *before* execution, are entitled to Christian burial; and, as they are admitted to the receiving of the sacrament and other rites of the church, and may be attended by ministers of the church of England in their last extremity, there appears to be no good reason why death by the law should deprive them of this privilege, though by two ancient canons it was denied them. (1 Burn. Ec. L. 261.)

Idiots, Lunatics.] Of the class who have laid violent hands upon themselves, is to be understood not all who have procured death unto themselves, but those only who have done it *voluntarily,* having the capacity to govern themselves; and not idiots, lunatics, or persons otherwise of insane mind.

The proper judges whether persons who died by their own hands were out of their senses are, doubtless, the coroner's jury; or, if the body cannot be viewed, the justices in sessions may inquire, (3 Inst. 55,) though their finding is traversable. But the minister of the parish is neither entitled nor able to judge in the affair, but may well acquiesce in the public determination, without making any private enquiry.

Coroner's Inquest.] The coroner is bound to receive evidence to prove that the deceased was *non compos,* which, if he refuse, the inquisition may be quashed by the King's Bench, who are the sovereign coroners. (3 Inst. 55.) And though there may be reason to suppose that the coroner's jury, from motives of compassion, readily yield to slight evidence of this nature, yet on their returning an acquittal of the crime of self-murder,—the body in that case not being demanded by the law,—it seemeth that a clergyman may and ought to admit that body to Christian burial. (1 Burn. Ec. L. 266.)

Felo-de-se.] By 4 G. 4. c. 52, it is enacted, that it shall not be lawful for any coroner or other officer, having authority to hold inquests, to issue any warrant, or other process, directing the interment of the remains of persons against whom a finding of *felo-de-se* shall be had, in any public highway; but such coroner or other officer shall give directions for the private interment of the remains of such person *felo-de-se,* without any stake being driven through the body of such person, in the churchyard or other burial-ground of the parish or place in which the remains of such person might, by the laws or custom of England, be interred, if the verdict of *felo-de-se* had not been found against such person; such interment to be made within twenty-four hours from the finding of the inquisition, and to take place between the hours of nine and twelve at night. But the act is not to authorise the performing any of the rights of Christian burial in such cases, nor *otherwise* alter the laws and usages relating to the burial of such persons.

Taking Corpse into Church, &c.] It seems to be discretionary in the minister whether the corpse shall be carried into the church or not. And there may be good reason for this, especially in cases of infection.

Ringing at Funerals.] The 67th canon directs, that after the party's death there shall be rung no more but one short peal, and one before the burial, and one after the burial.

Burial Fees.] All the ecclesiastical authorities concur in declaring that payment of fees is not a condition precedent to the right of interment; for burial ought not to be sold, though, if there be a custom to pay, they may be recovered. (Lind. 278, Andrews v. Cawthorne, Willes 536.)

Table of Fees.] Sir Wm. Scott, (Lord Stowell,) in Gilbert v. Buzzard and Boyce, (2 Hagg, R. 355,) after recognizing the above doctrine, says, "But this has not been the way of considering that matter since the Reformation, for the practice goes up at least nearly as far; it appears founded upon reasonable consideration, and is subjected to the proper controul of an authority of inspection. In populous parishes, where funerals are very frequent, the expense of keeping churchyards in an orderly and seemly condition is not small, and that of purchasing new ones, when the old ones become surcharged, is extremely oppressive. To answer such charges, both certain and contingent, it surely is not unreasonable that the actual use should contribute when it is called for. At the same time, the parishes are not left to carve for themselves in imposing these rates; they are all submitted to the examination of the ordinary, who exercises his judgment, and expresses the result, by a confirmation of their propriety, in terms of very guarded caution. It is, perhaps, not easy to say where the authority could be more properly lodged or more conveniently exercised. I shall now direct the parish to compose a table of fees for the consideration of the ordinary." Sir Simon Degge says, that the accustomed fee to the parson for breaking the soil in the churchyard is, for the most part, 3*s.* 4*d.*, and for opening the floor of the chancel, 6*s.* 8*d*. (P. 146.)

Fees on Pauper Funerals.] I am not aware of any instance in which it has been made a question, either in the spiritual or common law courts, whether the clergyman is entitled to the usual fees upon the burial of a pauper who leaves no property whatever, and whose interment is conducted, and the ordinary expenses thereof defrayed, by the parish. I apprehend, however, that his right is not affected by these circumstances, and that it is the duty of the parish officers to pay such dues as are customary upon the burial of persons, in like manner, at the expense of their surviving friends; and that they are entitled to include such disbursements in their accounts, as a legitimate item of parish expenditure. The statute which imposes the duty upon parish officers of burying dead bodies cast on shore from the sea within their parishes, enacts, that the minister, parish clerk, and sexton, shall perform their respective duties in such like manner as is customary in other funerals, and receive, by way of compensation, such and the like sums as in cases of burials *made at the expense of such parishes.* (48 G. 3. c. 75. s. 2.) This obviously refers to the funerals of paupers, and, by a very strong implication, recognizes and confirms the obligation upon parishes to pay the usual fees upon their interment.

Corpse passing through Parish.] In the case of Topsall v. Ferrers, (Hob. 175,) an alleged custom in the parish of St. Botolph's, London, was set up, to the effect that if any person die within that parish and be carried out of the parish to be buried elsewhere, in such case there ought to be paid to the parson of this parish, if he or she be buried elsewhere in the chancel, so much, and to the churchwardens so much, being the sums that they alleged were by custom payable unto them for such as were buried in their own chancel; but it was held to be contrary to reason, that one who is no parishioner, but may pass through the parish, or lie in an inn for that night, should, if he then die, be forced to be buried there, or to pay as if he were, and thus have to pay twice for his burial. (See also Salk. 332.)

Fee where Deceased resided.] But Dr. Gibson saith, a fee for burial belongs to the minister of the parish in which the party deceased *heard divine service and received sacraments,* wheresoever the corpse be buried. And this, he observes, is agreeable to the rule of the canon law, which says, that every one, after the manner of the patriarchs, shall be buried in the sepulchre of his fathers; nevertheless, that if any one desires to be buried elsewhere, the same shall not be hindered, provided that the accustomed fee be paid to the minister of the parish where he died, or at least a third part of what shall be given to the place where he shall be buried. (Gibs. 452.)

Customs as to Fees.] The proportion of fees due for the burial of persons, whether to the incumbent or churchwardens, whether for burying in or out of the parish, depends upon the particular usage and custom of each parish respectively. But although the rule of the canon law is, that in case of denial of the customary fee, justice is to be done by the *ordinary;* yet the temporal courts reserve to themselves the right of determining, first, whether there is such a custom, in case that is denied, and, secondly, whether it is a reasonable custom, in case the custom itself is acknowledged. (Gibs. 453; Fruin v. Dean and Chapter of York, 2 Keb. 778; Andrews and Symson, 3 Keb. 523, 527.)

Fees by whom taken.] By usage about London the churchwardens take the money for burying in the church or churchyard, and the parson has nothing but for burial in the chancel. (*Anon.* 2, Shower. 184.)

Action for Fees.] Where an agreement having existed between the successive vicars and churchwardens of a parish, that certain fees should be taken on the burial of strangers in the churchyard, and divided equally between them, and an in-coming vicar refused to accede to the agreement, and prevailed on the collector of the fees to pay over to him the whole he had in his hands, it was held, that the collector having received one half of these fees to the use of the churchwardens, they were entitled to recover that moiety from the vicar, in an action brought for money had and received. (Littlewood v. Williams. 1 Marsh. Rep. 589, 6 Taunt. 277. s. c.) But an action for money had and received is not maintainable to recover a sum of money paid to a churchwarden for burial dues, which he had paid over to a treasurer of the trustees of a chapel *previous* to the commencement of the action. (Horsfall v. Handley, 2 B. Moore 5.)

Burial in new Churches.] By the 58 Geo. 3. c. 45, no burials are to be permitted in any church or chapel erected under the act, or in the adjacent cemetery, at a less distance than twenty feet from the external walls, except in vaults wholly arched with brick or stone under any church or chapel, and to which the only access shall be by steps on the outside of the external walls, under the penalty of £50 upon conviction before two justices of the peace, one half to the informer, the other to the poor of the parish. (s. 80.)

Exhumation.] A corpse once buried cannot legally be taken up to be deposited in another place, without a license from the ordinary. (Gibs. 454.) But in the case of a violent death, the coroner may order the body to be disinterred, if it has been buried before he has had an opportunity of taking a view for the purposes of his inquest.

It is said, that if the body, after it has been committed to the grave, be disturbed or removed, it is a subject of ecclesiastical cognizance; yet the taking up or disposing of dead human bodies for the purposes of dissection is an indictable offence, as highly indecent, and *contra bonos mores.* (Lynn's case, 2 T. R. 733.)

Stealing Grave-Clothes.] In the Lent Assizes, holden at Leicester, (11 and 12 Ja. 1,) the case was, one William Haines had digged up the graves of three men and one woman in the night, and had taken their winding sheets from their bodies, and buried them again; and it was resolved by the justices of Serjeants Inn, in Fleet Street, that the property of the sheets remained the owner's; that is, in him who had the property therein when the dead body was wrapped therewith, for the dead body is not capable of it; and that the taking thereof was felony. (Haynes's case, 12 Co. 113.) And indictments for this offence have been preferred in more recent times.

SECTION X.—CHAPELS.

Origin of Name.] The etymology of *chapel,* in Latin *capella,* is not very satisfactorily ascertained. Perhaps it may be a diminutive of the word *capa,* which hath been adopted to signify one of the priest's vestments, so called, (saith Lindwood,) *a capiendo,* from its containing or covering the whole back and shoulders; for chapels at first were only tents or tabernacles, sometimes called field-churches, being nothing more than a covering from the inclemency of the seasons. (1 Burn. Ec. L. 295.)

Private Chapels.] Private chapels are such as noblemen and others have, at their own charge, built in or near their houses, for them and their families to perform religious duties in. The chaplains are provided by themselves with honourable pensions; and these anciently were all consecrated by the bishop of the diocese, and ought to be so still. (Degge, P. 1. c. 12.) And though a private chapel may be annexed to the church, the repair thereof belongs to the owner. (2 Inst. 489.)

By canon 71, no minister shall preach or administer the holy communion in any private house, except in times of necessity, upon pain of suspension for the first offence, and excommunication for the second. Provided that houses are here reputed for private houses, wherein are no chapels dedicated and allowed by the ecclesiastical law. And provided also, under the pain before expressed, that no chaplains do preach or administer the communion in any other places but in the chapels of the said houses, and that very seldom, upon Sundays and holidays; so that both the lords and masters of the said houses, and their families, shall at other times resort to their own parish churches, and there receive the holy communion at the least once every year. (Gibs. 210.)

Free Chapels.] These were places of religious worship exempt from all ordinary jurisdiction, except that the incumbents were generally instituted by the bishop, and inducted by the archdeacon of the place. Most of these chapels were built upon the manors or ancient demesnes of the crown, whilst in the king's hands, for the use of himself and retinue, when he came to reside there. When the crown parted with these estates, the chapels went with them, and retained their first freedom. Where this does not appear to have been their origin, such are thought to have been built and privileged by grants from the crown. (Tanner s Notit. Monast. *Pref.* 28.) And the king himself, by the lord chancellor, visits his free chapels and hospitals, and not the ordinary. (Godb. 145.)

By 26 H. 8. c. 3. s. 2, and 1 Eliz. c. 4, free chapels are charged with first fruits; but this the late Mr. Serjeant *Hill* conjectures must mean only such as were in the hands of *subjects.*

Chapels of Ease.] A chapel merely of ease is that which was not allowed a *font* at its institution, and is used only for the ease of the parishioners in prayers and preaching, (sacraments and burials being received and performed at the mother church,) and commonly where the curate is removeable at the pleasure of the parochial minister.

Parochial Chapels.] A parochial chapel hath the parochial rights of christening and burying; and differeth in nothing from a church but in the want of a *rectory* and *endowment.* (Degge, P. 1. c. 12.) If it has parochial rights, as clerk, wardens, &c.; rights of divine service, as baptism, sepulture, &c.; and the inhabitants have a right to them there and not elsewhere; and the curate has small tithes and surplice fees, and an augmentation; it is a *perpetual curacy,* and the curate is not removeable at pleasure. But chapels of ease are merely *ad libitum,* and have no parochial rights; therefore, on the union of the two parishes, one is frequently deemed the parish church, and the other a parochial chapel, but not a chapel of ease. (Att. Gen. v. Breton, 2 Vesey, sen. 425, 427.)

But it has been held, that whether a chapel be a parochial chapel or chapel of ease, is matter of spiritual conusance. Thus, where Keate was libelled against at the promotion of the rector of St. George, Hanover Square, for baptising, marrying, and administering the sacrament, in a chapel in the parish, without a license from the bishop, and for collecting money in the chapel in the offertory, and not paying the said money to the minister or churchwardens of the said parish; the court discharged a rule for showing cause why a prohibition should not go on the above ground. (See Hill's MSS. notes, 1 Burn. Ec. L. 300. See also Ken. Par. Ant. 590.)

Endowment and Dependance.] When parochial bounds became settled, many parishes were still so large that private oratories or chapels were built in remote hamlets, in which a capellane was sometimes allowed by the lord of the manor, or other benefactor, but generally maintained by a stipend from the parish priest, to whom all the rights and dues were entirely preserved. (Ken. Par. Ant. 587.) But to authorise the erecting of a chapel of ease, the joint consent of the diocesan, the patron, and the incumbent, if the church were full, was, and as it seemeth still is, required. (Ken. Par. Ant. 585, 586.)

And at the consecration of a chapel, there was often some fixed endowment, as of lands, or tithes, or voluntary contribution, given to it for its more easy dependance on the mother church. (Degge, P. 1. c. 12.) Hence a chapel may prescribe for tithes. (Saer v. Bland, 4 Leon. 24, Gibs. 209.)

Tributary to Church.] In addition to the obligation upon the inhabitants to resort upon certain festivals to the mother church, the capillane or curate of a chapel was, by a canon still existing, to be bound by an oath of due reverence and obedience to the rector or vicar of the mother church. (Ken Par. Ant. 599, Johns 205.) And the inhabitants of the chapelry, though they repair their own chapel, are nevertheless contributory to the repairs of the mother church, from which they can only be discharged by prescription; for which, it has been said, a consideration ought to appear, as a payment of so much to the repair of the church, or the wall of the churchyard, or the keeping of a bell, or the like compositions, which are clearly a discharge; (Gibs, 197;) and upon which a prohibition may be obtained. (2 Roll. Rep. 265; Aston v. Castle Birnidge Chapel, Hob. 66.) But exemption by custom well established, without proof of consideration, will suffice. (Ball v. Cross, 1 Salk. 164.)

New Chapels of Ease.] Every new church built by the commissioners appointed for building churches, by 58 G. 3. c. 45, and intended as the parish church of any division of a parish, intended to be a *separate* parish, is a chapel of ease *during the existing incumbency* of the original parish church, and shall be served by a curate nominated by such incumbent, licensed by the bishop, and paid by the commissioners. (58 G. 3. c. 45. s. 18; 59 G. 3. c. 134. s. 12.) And a chapel built as above, and situate in a *district* parish, made a parish for ecclesiastical purposes, and which is not made the *church* of such *district,* is not to be deemed a perpetual curacy or benefice, presentative even *after* avoidance by the existing incumbent of the parish. (59 G. 3. c. 134. s. 19. See 58 G. 3. c. 45. s. 25; and "*Existing Incumbency,*" *ante,* p. 18.)

Chapel Repairs.] The repairs of a chapel are to be made by rates on the landholders within the chapelry, in the same manner as the repairs of a church; and such rates are to be enforced by ecclesiastical authority. (Gibs. 209.) Upon an issue whether a certain messuage is situated within a chapelry, a person who occupies a rateable property within the chapelry is a competent witness to prove that it is. (Marsden v. Stansfield, 7 Barn. and Cres. 815.) But all this must be intended of ancient chapels, and where this course hath been used; for if there be land given for the repair of them, or any land or estate charged by prescription to the repairs of them, then the custom must be observed. (Degge, P. 1. c. 12.)

Minister, by whom chosen.] The nomination to a chapel of ease is in the *incumbent* of the mother church; though the chapel was erected and endowed by the lord and freeholders of a manor, and the right was given to the *inhabitants* by the archbishop, in his deed of consecration, and the vicar of the mother church at the time declared he had no right therein. Thus, where inhabitants had repaired the chapel, and nominated for ninety years, it was held that the incumbent can only lose his right by special agreement between patron, parson, and ordinary, which is a general rule of law. (Farnworth v. Bishop of Chester, 4 Barn. and Cres. 555.) And even then, there must be a good consideration, or compensation. A prescription presumes that every thing was proper, and presupposes an agreement by *deed,* not by parol. (Dixon v. Kershaw, Ambler 528.) In Duke of Portland v. Bingham, (1 Hagg. Rep. 168,) Lord *Stowell* says, that the implied right of patronage to a chapel, arising from the right of patronage to the mother church, is considered, since Dixon v. Kershaw, as settled in favour of the incumbent, and against the claim of the mother church. (See Herbert v. Dean and Chapter of Westminster, 1 Peere Williams, 774.) So in Mallet v. Trigg, (1 Vern. 42,) Lord Chancellor Nottingham observed, There was a great difference as to the parson's right of choosing his vicar, where the parson was of a lay fee, and where he had a *cure of souls;* for in the latter case, there was reason he should approve of the man who was to act under him in so high a trust. (1 Vern. 42.)

Government thereof.] The perpetual curate of an augmented parochial chapelry, has a sufficient possession whereon to maintain trespass, for breaking and entering the chapel and destroying the pews.

(Jones v. Ellis, 2 Younge and J. 265.) And according to Degge, (P. 1. c. 12,) chapels of ease have the like officers, for the most part, as churches have, distinguished only in name; and are in like manner visitable by the ordinary. It is said, that if the question be in the Court Christian, whether a church be a parish church, or only a chapel of ease, a prohibition lieth. (2 Roll's Abr. 291; Wats, c. 23.)

But Dr. *Gibson* says, that a chapel or no chapel ought to be tried by the spiritual judge; for, when two spiritual things are to be tried, no prohibition shall be granted. (Gibs. 210.)

But if a question is depending as to the *limits*, whether of a chapel of ease or a parish church, or whether a chapel of ease or a parochial chapel, the same shall be tried, as to the limits, in the temporal court. (Gibs. 213.)

CHAP. III.—MINISTER AND OFFICERS OF THE CHURCH.

SECTION I. *Minister or Incumbent.*
II. *Residence of Incumbent.*
III. *Curates.*
IV. *Lecturers.*
V. *Churchwardens.*
VI. *Parish Clerk.*
VII. *Sexton.*
VIII. *Beadle.*

SECTION I.—MINISTER OR INCUMBENT.

Incumbent.] The appellation *parson,* in the vulgar language of modern times, is applied indiscriminately to every person engaged in conducting public worship; and the word *minister* is liable to a similar objection; there is, consequently, a convenience in the name *incumbent,* which has in a great measure usurped the place of *parson,* to express the individual, whether rector, vicar, or by whatever title he is known, who is the ecclesiastical head of the parish, and temporal representative of his church. The rights and duties of the incumbent, with respect to the various temporalities of his church, will be detailed under the different heads into which the general subject is divided. It may be proper, however, in the first place, to give a brief statement of his privileges and obligations of a merely personal nature, arising from his office and character, so far as they affect others, and particularly his parishioners.

Induction.] Induction is an act of a temporal nature; for by it the incumbent becomes seised of the temporalities of the church: by this ceremony he is put in the *actual* possession of part for the whole, and may afterwards maintain an action for a trespass on the glebe, though he does not actually go upon the glebe itself. (Bulwer v. Bulwer, 2 Barn. and Ald. 470.) He is thus unexceptionably entitled to make grants, or sue, or to plead (as occasion shall require) that he is *parson imparsonee;* and by this the church also is full against all persons, not excepting the king. On which account, induction is compared, in the books of common law, to livery and seisin, by which possession is given to temporal estates. (Gibs 814; 1 Burn. Ec. L. tit. "Benefice.")

Fee Simple of Church.] Although the freehold of the church, churchyard, and glebe, belong to the parson, yet, properly speaking, the fee-simple is not in him, but in abeyance, and therefore he cannot have a writ of right; (Co. Lit. 341, *b;)* but in all other respects, he has the same means of enforcing and defending his interests therein, as the owner of a life interest in a freehold. He may make a lease of the church and churchyard; (2 Rol. 337. l. 10;) shall have the trees growing in the churchyard, for the repair of the church; and can alone give a license for burying in the church; neither the ordinary nor the churchwardens having any authority for this purpose. (Cro. Jac. 367; Com. Dig. tit. "Esglise," G. 1.)

Still it must be observed, that although the freehold of the parish church, with all its appurtenances, rests in the incumbent upon his induction, he is liable to deprivation, unless he confirm his possession by the due observance of the several conditions required by law.

Reading himself in.] By the statutes on this subject, he is bound, within two months after induction, to read the morning and evening prayers at the proper times appointed; and, after such reading, to declare publicly before the congregation assembled, his unfeigned assent to the use of all things therein prescribed, in the form provided by the act.. (See 13 and 14 Car. 2. c. 4. s. 6.) He must also, within the same period, read the Thirty-nine Articles, and make a similar declaration of his assent thereto, or upon default he shall be, *ipso facto,* immediately deprived; (13 Eliz. c. 12. s. 3;) though the 23 G. 2. c. 28, makes an exception, in cases where the omission arises from sickness or other lawful impediment. And he must also, in the same manner, publicly and openly read the ordinary's *certificate* of his having subscribed the declaration of conformity to the liturgy of the church of England, as it is now by law established, together with the *same declaration* or acknowledgment, on some Lord's-day within three months next after such subscription. (13 and 14 Car. 2. c. 4. s. 11.) And these things shall be performed by the incumbent in the same church whereof he shall have cure.

Oaths.] Finally, by the 1 G. 2. st. 2. c. 13, and 9 G 2. c. 26, all ecclesiastical persons shall, within six months after their admission to any ecclesiastical preferment, benefice, office, or place, take the oaths of allegiance, supremacy, and abjuration, in one of the courts at Westminster, or at the general or quarter sessions, on pain of being incapacitated to hold the same, and of being disabled to sue in any action, or to be guardian, or executor, or administrator, or capable of any legacy or deed of gift, or to bear any office, or to vote at an election for members of Parliament, and of forfeiting 500*l.*

When not Arrestable.] There were two statutes, the 50 Ed. 3. c. 5, and 1 R. 2. c. 15, for the protection of clerical persons from arrest, in "churches and churchyards, or while they be intending to divine services." And it hath been adjudged upon this, that if such arrest be made on a Sunday, trespass is the proper form of action against the wrong doer. (Com. Dig. Temps. B. 3.) But if it be on any other day, the action should be in case. (Tarlton v. Fisher, Doug. 671.) But the arrest, if made, is valid; so that if the officer immediately afterwards discharge him, he is liable to an action for an escape; (See Tarlton v. Fisher;) and it will not excuse his contempt in making the arrest. (Wats. ch. 34.) And although the above statutes have been repealed, yet, as the like protection is re-enacted by the same act, the law with respect to clerical persons is still in effect the same. (See 9 G. 4. c. 31. s. 23; *ante,* p. 38.)

But it seems, that if the arrest be upon criminal process, or at the suit of the king, the privilege cannot be claimed. (Cro. Jac. 321.) And for laying violent hands upon a clerk, the offender may be proceeded against in the Ecclesiastical Court; but if a recompense be sought, and not punishment for *sin* merely, or for an assault, the suit ought to be at the common law. (Kelly v. Walker, Cro. Eliz. 655; and see 9 G. 4. c. 31. s. 23.)

Levy on his Goods] No levy can be made by the *sheriff* upon the incumbent's ecclesiastical goods; but the writ must be directed to the *bishop* of the diocese, who grants a sequestration; (2 Inst. 4; Languet v. Jones, 1 Stra. 87; 3 Bla. Com. 418); and an attachment will lie against the chancellor for not returning it. (Rex v. Bishop of St. Asaph, 1 Wils. 332.)

Discharged Insolvent.] The assignees under an Insolvent Act are not entitled to demand and receive the profits of an ecclesiastical benefice which accrue subsequent to the assignment, nor can they maintain an action for the same, though included in the insolvent's schedule. (Arbuckle v. Cowtan, 3 Bos. and Pul. 321.)

Obsolete Privileges.] There are many other regulations for the protection and controul of the clergy, now grown obsolete, and of which it has been well observed, "After all, these distinctions of the clergy are shadows rather than substance; being most of them about matters which are of no significance. The *restraints,* as to the scope and purport of them, are such as the clergy for the most part would choose to put upon themselves; and the *privileges,* such as they are, seem to be scarcely worth claiming, and some of them one would almost imagine to have been calculated to bring disgrace upon the clergy, rather than to be of any real benefit to them; for why should a clergyman be protected from paying his just debts, more than any other person; or be saved from punishment for a crime for which another person ought to suffer death?" (3 Burn's Ec. L. 211.)

SECTION II.—RESIDENCE.

Residence enforced.] By the ancient canon law, if a clergyman deserted his church without just cause, and the leave of the diocesan, he was subject to deprivation; (Gibs. 827.); and it is an intendment of the common law, that he *is* resident upon his cure; and therefore, if he be chosen to a secular office, he may have the king's writ for his discharge. (2 Inst. 625.)

Several statutes were also passed about the period of the Reformation, for enforcing residence, most of which were expressly repealed, and the whole statutory provisions reduced into one entire system, by the 57 G. 3. c. 99. (See R. v. Peterborough, 3 Barn. and Cres. 56.)

Penalty for Absence.] By this latter act, wilful absence, without license or exemption, for three months in the year, unless at some other benefice, parochial chapelry, &c. of which he is possessed, subjects the clergyman to a forfeiture of one-third of the annual value of the benefice, &c. deserted; and if the absence exceed six months but not eight, one half of such value; if above eight months, two-thirds; and for the whole year, three-fourths thereof, to be recovered in the courts of law; and the whole penalty to go to the informer, or person who sues for the same, (s. 5.) As to suing for the penalty, see Com. Dig. *Pleader.* (2 S. 23.) For the purposes of a prosecution, it is sufficient to prove, that the defendant assumed to be, and

and *acted* as parson, without proving admission, institution, and induction. (Bevan v. Williams, 3 T. R. 535, n.)

Wilful Absence.] But the absence must be *wilful;* and therefore, if it be caused by imprisonment without cause, or by the advice of physicians for the recovery of health; or if there be no parsonage-house, or no house of residence provided under this act, (see s. 9,) it is not within the principle of the statute. (See Butler v. Goodall, 6 Rep. 21. b.; Cro. Eliz. 590; 2 Bulst. 18; Gibs. 887.) Residence for nine months in the year within the limits of his benefice, or of the city, place, or parish within which it is situated, provided such residence is not more than two miles from his church, is sufficient. (s. 6.)

Exempt from Penalties.] The exemptions by s. 10 of the act, from the penalties of non-residence are,—every spiritual person being chancellor, vice chancellor, or commissary of Oxford or Cambridge, or warden, or other head of any college, professor, or public reader, within the precincts thereof; and in short, every public officer, or scholar, under thirty years of age, abiding for study, at either university, *bona fide,* and without fraud.

Chaplains exempt.] The exemption also includes every chaplain of the king, or queen, or their children, brethren or sisters, during so long as he shall actually attend in discharge of his duty, as such chaplain in the household to which he belongs. Every chaplain of any archbishop, bishop, peer, &c., the chaplain to the House of Commons, clerk or deputy clerk of the closet of the king, or heir apparent, or chaplain-general of the forces, the royal dock-yards, or the household of any British ambassador abroad.

Others exempt.] To the list thus briefly given are added, no chancellor, vicar-general, archdeacon, minor canon, vicar choral, or priest vicar, or such like officer, in any cathedral or collegiate church, while performing the duties, and during actual residence within the precincts thereof, or of the town, &c.; no dean, sub-dean, priest, or reader, in his Majesty's chapels at St. James's, Whitehall, Windsor, or elsewhere; no preacher of any inn of court; no fellow of either university, during the time he is required to reside and actually residing therein; no warden of, master, or usher in Eton or Winchester colleges; or master of the Charter-house or Westminster school; or principal or professor of the East India college, &c.; shall be liable to any of the penalties of this act for non-residence, during any such period as aforesaid;—but every such spiritual person shall be entitled to account such period as if he had legally resided on some other benefice. (s. 10.) As to the rule to discontinue an action, for a penalty for non-residence, on notification of exemption, see Wright v. Legge, (6 Taunt. 48.)

License for Non-residence.] By s. 15, the bishop may, upon petition, the facts being verified by affidavit if required, grant, in the cases enumerated, a *license* to any spiritual person to reside out of the parish, or proper house of residence, in order to exempt him from the penalty of non-residence.

License to whom granted.] The enumeration includes, first, "any spiritual person prevented from residence in the *proper house of residence* in the parish, by actual illness of himself, wife, or child making part of his family, and residing with him as such." As an incumbent *ought* to reside in the parsonage-house, if he lets it, and dwells elsewhere in the parish, or merely occupies it by a servant, it would be within the penalty of 21 Hen. 8. c. 13, (now repealed,) and doubtless of this statute, if without license. (See Wilkinson v. Allott, 2 Cowp. 429; Butler v. Goodale, Cro. Eliz. 590, Mod. 540, 2 Brownl. 54.)

Where no fit House.] Secondly, "persons holding any benefice wherein *there is no house of residence,* or where it is unfit for residence, such unfitness not being occasioned by default of such person, and the same being kept in repair by him to the satisfaction of the bishop." A license was held unnecessary in this case before this act. (Wynne v. Smythies, 6 Taunt. 198; Law v. Ibbotson, 2 Burr. 2722; Wilkinson v. Clerk, *id.* 2725.) But the want of a parsonage-house was held no excuse for living out of the parish. (Wilkinson v. Allott, Cowp. 429.)

And where the incumbent of two livings, A and B, obtained a license to reside out of the parish of A, for the above cause, on condition of his residing near, and actually performing the duties, this was held not such a residence at A as to excuse him from residing at B, without another license for that purpose. (Wright v. Flamant, 1 Marsh. 368, 6 Taunt. 52. S. C.) But the incumbent of two livings, one with a house of residence on it and the other not, may reside on that in which there is no such house, without a license, and such residence will excuse him from residing on the other living. (Wynne v. Smythies, 1 Marsh 547.)

License to Others.] The catalogue includes almost every beneficed person, who, at the same time, holds any other situation not incompatible with his clerical character, which makes it difficult or impossible to reside, and at the same time discharge the duties of such other situation; particularly as the bishop has a large discretion herein, and may grant a license to reside elsewhere, if he deems it expedient, in any case not enumerated in the statute.

Appeal on refusal.] If the applicant is aggrieved by the refusal of such license, he may apply to the archbishop of the province, who shall forthwith, either by himself or certain commissioners appointed from among the bishops of his province, under his hand, make enquiry into the same, and by writing, signed by himself, confirm such refusal, or grant a license under this act, as seems just; provided that such appellant shall give security to the bishop, to pay such reasonable expenses attending such appeal, as the archbishop or his commissioners shall award.

Curates in such Cases.] The bishop may assign, in cases where stipendiary curates are employed, such salary as he deems fit. He may also grant such license *without application*, where the incumbent is absent from the realm; and appoint a stipendiary curate, where no such curate, duly licensed, is employed in serving such benefice; and may assign or increase the salary, and order the same to be paid by sequestration, provided that the special circumstances of granting the license be forthwith transmitted to the archbishop, who shall, by himself or commissioners appointed from his bishops, examine into the case, and thereupon allow, disallow, or alter such license, as to the period thereof, and the curate's stipend, as seems fit to him, and no such license shall be good unless it is allowed and signed by such archbishop. (s. 16.)

Copy to Churchwardens.] It is further provided by the 21st section, that a copy of every such license shall be transmitted by *the grantee* to the churchwardens of the parish, &c. to which it relates, within one month after the grant thereof; and the bishop shall cause his revocation to be transmitted to the churchwarden, to be deposited in the parish chest.

And the churchwardens must produce a copy of every such license or revocation, to be read at the next visitation. Registrars neglecting to enter licenses or revocations to forfeit £5 for each neglect to the use of the informer, and the files thereof to be inspected by all persons on payment of 3*s*. only.

Report to the King.] A report of every benefice in his diocese shall be made by the bishop—of the number held by each clergyman;—of residents, non-residents, and curates serving for non-residents;—of exemptions, licenses, and revocations, and whether the benefice exceeds 300*l*, a year or not;—such report to be made to his Majesty in Council before the 25th March of every year. The archbishops are likewise to report all licenses granted or approved by them before the 31st January. And non-residents, for any of the temporary causes of exemption enumerated in the act, or from having another benefice on which they reside, shall notify the same to their bishop within six weeks after the 1st January, and whether the benefice on which they *do not reside* is of the yearly value of £300 or not, under a penalty of £20, to be levied by sequestration. (ss. 22, 23, 24.)

Jurisdictions reserved.] The act also reserves the jurisdiction of the ecclesiastical courts in all cases, and the authority of the bishop to issue his monition to reside; and, in case of disobedience, to sequester the profits of the benefice till compliance with the order; and in case the benefice continues under sequestration two years, or three sequestrations are incurred within the like period, and the spiritual person be not relieved therefrom upon appeal, the benefice not resided on shall be void, and the patron may present any other than the same person. (ss. 24, 25, 26. 83.)

Letting House of Residence.] By s. 32, all contracts for letting the house of residence and appurtenances, to which house any spiritual person is required, by order of the bishop, to proceed and reside therein, shall, on serving a copy of such order, &c. on the occupier, be null and void; and a copy of such order shall be transmitted to one of the churchwardens, or such other person as the bishop thinks fit, to be served upon such occupier; and any person continuing to hold the same after the day appointed for such spiritual person to reside, &c., and after service, or leaving such copy at the house, shall forfeit 40*s*. for every day which he continues to hold the same without written permission of the bishop, to be recovered and applied in the same manner as the non-residence penalties under this act.

Justices may give Possession.] It is also provided, that the spiritual person so directed to reside, or any curate to whom such residence is assigned, may, on producing the order, obtain a warrant for taking possession from any magistrate, and possession of such house, &c. may, thereupon, be taken at any hour in the day time, by entering by force, if necessary.

No penalties are incurred for non-residence during the time such tenant shall occupy such house of residence and building, &c. (s. 33.)

Time and Notice.] For the purposes of the act, the year shall commence on the 1st January, and end on the 31st December, both inclusive. And months shall be deemed calendar months, except when they are to be made up of smaller periods, in which case thirty days shall be a month. (s. 39.)

A month before process for penalties is served, notice must be given to the defendant and to the bishop, clearly expressing the cause of action, and the penalty sought to be recovered; and no such notice shall be given *before* the 1st of April in the year next after the penalties have been incurred; and in default of proof of such notice, &c. the defendant shall have a verdict with double costs; (ss. 40, 41, 42;) and the defendant may pay money into court at any time before issue joined, with the same consequences as in other actions.

Staying Proceedings.] Licenses may be pleaded in bar, and if plaintiffs *then* discontinue, defendants shall have double costs; plaintiffs may be ordered to give security for costs. And it seems that if the license do not cover the whole period for which the penalties are demanded, yet if there is not sufficient time left *uncovered* to subject the incumbent to a penalty, the court will interfere to stay the proceedings. (See Wynn v. Kay, 5 Taunt. 843, 1 Marsh 387.)

Monition may be pleaded.] If, before *notice* of action, a monition has been filed, requiring the defendant to reside, or to recover penalties for past non-residence, the action cannot be maintained for penalties incurred before monition issued, or during proceedings had under it. And the monition may be pleaded to the action. (s. 46.)

Taking in Execution.] The defendant cannot be taken in execution whilst he holds any benefice, out of the profits of which the debt, &c. can be levied within three years. (s. 47.)

The remaining clauses of the act relate chiefly to the mode of proceeding in monition; the recovery of penalties, costs, &c. The act does not extend to Ireland.

SECTION III.—CURATES.

Definition of Curate.] The word curate is of ambiguous signification; sometimes, and most properly, it denoteth the incumbent in general, who hath the cure of souls. See "MINISTER OR INCUMBENT," *(ante,* p. 16.) But it is commonly understood to signify a clerk not instituted to the cure of souls, but exercising the spiritual office in a parish under the rector or vicar, (1 Hen. Bla. 424,) and we have now to consider it in this latter sense.

There are two kinds of these curates: first, *temporary,* who are employed under the spiritual rector or vicar, either as assistants or substitutes in his absence, in his parish church, or else in a chapel of ease within the same parish; the other, by way of distinction, called *perpetual,* which is where there is in a parish neither spiritual rector nor vicar, but a clerk is employed to officiate there by the impropriator.

Origin of Curacies.] The origin of perpetual curacies was thus: by the 4 H. 4. c. 12, it is enacted, that in every church appropriated there shall be a secular person ordained vicar perpetual, canonically instituted and inducted, and covenably endowed by the discretion of the ordinary. For the manner in which chapels of ease were erected, see "CHAPELS," (*ante* p. 57.)

But if the benefice was given *ad mensam monachorum*, and by way of union *plesco jure*, it was served by a *temporary* curate of their own house as occasion required. And the like liberty was sometimes granted by dispensation in benefices not annexed to their tables, in consideration of the poverty of the house, or the nearness of the church. But when such appropriations, together with the charge of providing for the cure, were transferred, (after the dissolution of the religious houses,) from spiritual societies to single *lay* persons, who were not capable of serving them by themselves, they were obliged to nominate some particular person to the ordinary for his license to serve the cure; the curates, by this means, became so far perpetual as not to be wholly at the pleasure of the appropriator, nor removable but by due revocation of the license of the ordinary. (Gibs. 819.)

A perpetual curacy is not an ecclesiastical benefice, so as to be untenable with any other benefice; and the acceptance thereof does not make void the living previously held by the clerk, although no dispensation has been obtained, (Weldon v. Green, 2 Burn. Ec. L. 55.) And the grant of a rectory passes a perpetual curacy belonging thereto. (Arthington v. Bishop of Chester, 1 H. Bla. 418.)

Appointment of Curates.] The appointment of a curate to officiate under an incumbent in his own church, must be by such incumbent's nomination of him, under hand and seal, to the bishop, setting forth the stipend for his maintenance, and humbly beseeching the bishop to license him to serve the said cure.

The appointment also of a curate in a *chapel of ease* seemeth most properly to belong to the incumbent of the mother church, who is instituted to the cure of souls throughout the whole parish. (Dixon v. Kershaw and Ors. Amb. 528.) The form of nomination in this latter case, and to a perpetual curacy, is much the same. It of course states the vacancy by death or otherwise, and prays his lordship's license for the curate nominated. (2 Burn. Ec. L. 58.)

Prima facie all parochial duties are committed to and imposed upon the parish incumbent; and all fees and emoluments arising therefrom belong to him; and such rights can only be granted to a chapel, or its officiating minister, by composition with the patron, incumbent, and ordinary; and it has been said, that all three uniting will not be sufficient, without a compensation to future incumbents; though, where nothing is taken from the income of the incumbent, such consent may suffice without any such compensation being provided. (Moysey v. Hillcoat, 2 Hagg. Rep. N. S. 48; Farnworth v. the Bishop of Chester, 4 Barn. and Cres. 568; Dixon v. Kershaw, Ambler. 532.)

Election of perpetual Curate.] The right to nominate to a perpetual curacy is sometimes vested in the parishioners, by custom, the terms and conditions of which must be observed in the exercise of the right; but the courts seem inclined to support a liberal interpretation of such customs, so as to admit the largest number of voters, rather than to abridge the privilege by a rigid construction of the language in which the custom is expressed. Though, if they are required to enforce such rights, the custom must be proved, and the parties must not content themselves with a general allegation of its existence. (R. v. Bishop of Oxford, 7 East. 345; Price v. Doughty, 3 Atk. 576.)

Thus, where it appeared according to the deed of trust, and a decree in the exchequer, that the impropriate rectory was purchased for the use of the parishioners and inhabitants, and that the nomination of the curate had been declared to be in such of them as *paid* to church and poor, the chancellor expressed an opinion that assessment gave the right, though actual *payment* had not been made. (Att. Gen. v. Newcome, 14 Ves. 1.) Though an election made upon the principle, that *payment* should be essential to the right to vote, which was adopted by common consent among other regulations, was established. (Ib. Att. Gen. v. Forster, 10 Ves. 335.)

But in Faulkner v. Elgar, (4 Barn. and Cres. 449, 6 Dowl. and Ryl. 517,) where the right of election to a perpetual curacy was by custom *in the parishioners*, without any other limitation, and at a meeting duly convened, it was decided, before the election began, that parishioners who had not paid *church* rates should not be allowed to vote, and some electors did not, therefore, tender their votes, and the votes of others were rejected, it was held that the election wa void. And it seems that a mode of election otherwise than by show of hands, or by poll, contrived for the purpose of concealing for which candidate the elector votes, is not legal. (Ib.)

Particular Customs to Elect.] By agreement, (of the bishop, patron, and incumbent,) the inhabitants may have a right to *elect* and nominate a curate; and there are instances in which, according to the custom, he is *nominated* by the inhabitants, (as founders and patrons,) to the vicar, and by him presented to the ordinary. In other cases, a curate was to be presented by the patron of the church to the vicar, and by him to the archdeacon, who was then obliged to admit him; in other places, the lord of the manor presented a fit person to the appropriators, who, without delay, were to give admission to the person so presented. (Ken. Par. Ant. 589; see Herbert v. Dean and Chapter of Westminster, 1 P. Wms. 773.)

Where the founder of a chapel by his will directed that his son should, during his life, have the nomination and election of the minister, and might, by will, set down the course of the nomination, and election after his death; and that, if he did not prescribe the course, the nomination, and election, should be in all the householders and heads of families in the township, and his, the founder's, heirs male of his body, and such other of his kindred or blood as should have any land in the township, or the greater number of them; and by the instrument of consecration all tithes, fees, and emoluments whatsoever, on burials, marriages, &c. were reserved to the vicar of the parish; and the son not having set down any order or course, it was held, that the householders and heads of families in the township had no right to present a curate to this chapel without the consent of the vicar. (Farnworth v. the Bishop of Chester, 4 Barn. and Cres. 555; Dowl. and Ryl. 56.)

Lapse.] It is not necessary, in order to prevent a lapse, that the appointment be within six months, unless specially provided for by the founder, (Co. Lit. 344, Serjeant Hill's MSS. notes,) except in the case of having received the augmentation from Queen Anne's bounty. But the bishop may compel the patron, by spiritual censures, to make the appointment. (1 Inst. 344, Gibs. 8, 19.)

This was so held in Fairchild and Gayre, (Cro. Jac. 63,) with regard to donatives; and it holds more strongly in the case of curacies, where both church and patron are subject to the ordinary's jurisdiction, and where, therefore, he may likewise sequester the profits, and appoint another to take care of the cure till the patron shall nominate a fit and proper clerk. (Gibs. 1819.)

Additional Curate.] The general act, (see "RESIDENCE," *ante*, p. 64,) for enforcing the residence of the clergy, and providing curates where it becomes necessary, enacts, that whenever it is made to appear, to the satisfaction of the bishop, that by reason of the number of churches or chapels belonging to any benefice within his diocese, or of their distance from each other, or of the distance of the residence of the clergyman serving the same from them, or any or either of them, or from the negligence of the incumbent, the ecclesiastical duties of such benefice are inadequately performed, the bishop may require the incumbent to nominate to him a fit person or persons, with sufficient stipend, to be licensed to assist in performing such duties; and upon non-compliance for three months, the bishop may, make such appointment, subject to an appeal, by the incumbent, to the archbishop of the province. (57 G. 3. c. 99. s. 50.)

Examination and Admission.] By canon 48, no curate or minister shall be permitted to serve in any place without examination and admission of the *bishop of the diocese*, or ordinary of the place having episcopal jurisdiction, under his hand and seal, having respect to the greatness of the cure and meetness of the party. The object of this canon seems to be, that curates, who are engaged to take *charge of parishes*, either altogether or in part, for a continued time, shall be " examined and admitted " by the diocesan. But a clerical person, who officiates for the rector *occasionally*, if not so licensed by the bishop of the diocese, does not, it seems, incur ecclesiastical censures under this canon; and if he has a *license to preach* under the 50th and 52d canons, which need not be had of the *local* ordinary, it is considered sufficient. (Gates v. Chambers, 2 Add. R. 191.)

It must also appear that he is in deacon's orders at least, if he is to be licensed to be an assistant curate, and of priest's, if he is to be licensed to a *perpetual* curacy; for, by the 13 and 14 C. 2. c. 4. s. 14, no person shall be admitted to *any benefice or ecclesiastical promotion* before he shall be ordained priest. Which words extend to all chapels of ease which have received the augmentation of Queen Anne's bounty, as they are thenceforth to be *perpetual cures and benefices.*

By canon 48, if curates remove from one diocese to another, they shall not be, by any means, admitted to serve, without testimony in writing of the bishop of the diocese, or ordinary of the place, having episcopal jurisdiction, from whence they came, of their honesty, ability, and conformity to the ecclesiastical laws of the church of England. (See Lind. 48, Gibs. 896.)

Serving Two Places.] By 57 G. 3. c. 99. s. 59, no spiritual person shall serve more than two churches or chapels, or one church and one chapel, in one day, unless, from their local situation, or the value of the benefices, or other special causes, the bishop license him to serve three churches or chapels; such churches, &c. not being distant from each other more than four measured miles; provided the reasons for granting such license shall be stated therein, and provided that such person's residence is so placed that he need not travel more than sixteen measured miles in one day to do the several duties.

Non-Residence.] By 57 G. 3. c. 99. s. 48, if any spiritual person, holding any *benefice*, (which means *with cure*, and includes donatives, perpetual curacies, and parochial chapelries, s. 72,) who does not actually reside thereon nine months in the year, (unless he shall do the duty thereof, or has a legal exemption from residence, or a license to reside elsewhere than in the usual house of residence,) shall for exceeding three months absent himself, without leaving a curate duly licensed, or other spiritual person to perform, and who shall duly perform, the ecclesiastical duties of such benefice, or who shall, for three months after the death or removal of any curate who has served his church, neglect to notify the same to his bishop, or to nominate to him a proper curate, then the bishop may appoint and license a curate to serve such church, with such salary as is by this act directed, (see infra.) Provided, that in every such case the license shall specify whether the curate is to reside within the parish or place, or not, and if he is permitted by the bishop to reside out of the parish, &c.; the grounds of such permission shall be set forth therein, and the distance of his residence shall not exceed five statute miles from the church he is to serve, except in cases of necessity approved by the bishop and specified in the license.

Where Curate must reside.] And, by s. 49, it is enacted, that where a curate is appointed to serve the benefice of any incumbent who is lawfully non-resident for more than three months in the year, such curate shall reside within the parish, provided the gross annual value of the benefice amounts to £300, and the population to three hundred persons; or provided the population amount to one thousand persons, whatever be the value of the benefice: provided, that upon urgent reasons the bishop may allow him to reside in some convenient place near to the parish, the circumstances being specified in the license.

And, by s. 64, in the case of an incumbent non-resident four months each year, the bishop may allot for the curate's residence the house of residence, with the appurtenances, during the time he shall serve the cure, or during the incumbent's non-residence, and may sequester the profits of such benefice in any case in which possession shall not be given up to the curate. And the curate must pay the taxes and parish assessments in respect of such house, &c., as if he had been appointed to the benefice, where he occupies the same by direction of the bishop, and is assigned a salary of not less than the gross annual value of the benefice which he serves. (s. 65.)

Curate's Stipend.] When any person shall become incumbent of any benefice after the 20th July, 1813, and shall not duly reside thereon, (unless he do the duty, having an exemption, or license for non-residence,) the bishop shall appoint the salary of the licensed curate, as follows: that is, not less than £80 *per annum*, or the annual value of the benefice, if its gross value does not amount to that sum; nor less than £100 *per annum*, or the whole value as above, if the value shall not amount to £100 *per annum*, where the population of the place amounts to three hundred persons; and not less than £120 *per annum*, or the whole value as above, if it does not amount to £120 *per annum*, where the population amounts to five hundred persons; and not less than £150 *per annum*, or the whole value as above, if it does not amount to £150 *per annum*, where the population amounts to one thousand persons; provided that such annual value shall be estimated from the return made to the governors of Queen Anne's bounty, or in the actual income whereof any considerable variation has taken place either by augmentation by Queen Anne's bounty or otherwise. (57 G. 3. c. 99. s. 55.)

Where it appears that the benefice, clear of all deductions, exceeds £400 *per annum*, the bishop may assign to the curate resident within and serving no other cure, a salary of £100 *per annum*, though the population does not amount to three hundred persons; or where the actual income exceeds £400 *per annum*, and the population amounts to five hundred persons, he may assign him any larger salary not exceeding by more than £50 *per annum* those in s. 55, required to be assigned to any such curate. (s. 56.)

Lesser Stipends.] By s. 57, smaller salaries may be assigned by the bishop to curates, where, by reason of sickness, age, or other unavoidable cause, any incumbent has become non-resident or incapable to perform the duties thereof.

And, by s. 60, the bishop, in certain cases, may license any person holding a benefice to serve as curate of an adjoining or other parish, with a salary less by a sum not exceeding £30 *per annum* than that in the several cases herein specified, (viz. in s. 55, 56.)

By s. 61, all contracts between incumbents and their curates, in fraud or derogation of this act, shall be void at law, and not pleaded or given in evidence; and the curate, or his personal representatives, shall be entitled to the full amount of what remains unpaid of the salary specified in his *license*, and payment thereof, with treble costs, of recovering the same shall be enforced by monition and by sequestration; provided the application by the curate be made twelve months after quitting his curacy, or by representatives within twelve months after his death.

Stipend how recovered.] If the bishop assign the salary, the curate's most effectual remedy for his pay is to apply to the ecclesiastical court, for there, in default of payment, a sequestration may be served on the benefice; but if the curate have no license he cannot sue in that court. (Johns. 87.)

If he sue for his salary at common law, he must prove an agreement betwixt himself and the incumbent; but in such case he may be called upon to prove that he made the subscriptions and declarations before-mentioned, and otherwise qualified himself as the law directs. (Johns. 87.) And if he sue for the salary accrued after dismissal, without just cause duly notified to him, the defendant will not be permitted to show, in answer to the action, that he removed the plaintiff for *fault by him committed;* for the rector ought to have represented his conduct to the bishop, and applied to him to remove him; or if he himself could remove him on that account, he ought to have notified to him that the cause of his removal was his immoral behaviour. But the death of the rector puts an end to such a contract, and the curate cannot insist upon its continuance against his executors. (Martyn v. Hind, Cowp. 440, Doug. 137.)

Stipend recovered by Monition.] But the 53rd section of the statute already mentioned provides, that the bishop, subject to the provisions and restrictions contained in the act, shall appoint to every curate such salary as is allowed and specified in the act, to be specified in the license granted to him; and in case of any dispute touching such stipend, or the payment thereof, the bishop shall summarily hear the same; and in case of neglect or refusal to pay such stipend, or the arrears thereof, he is empowered to proceed by sequestration or monition. The Court of King's Bench held, that this section relates only to licenses granted, and salaries or stipends assigned in some way in conformity to the act. And that, therefore, a curate cannot have the benefit of a proceeding by monition for the recovery of a salary assigned by a bishop without the *consent of the incumbent,* the incumbent being resident on his benefice, and discharging the duties generally, but desirous of the assistance of a curate. (R. v. Bishop of Peterborough, 3 Barn. and Cres. 47; 4 Dowl. and Ryl. 720; 2 Add. R. 194.)

Notice to quit Residence.] The bishop at any time, on three months' notice in writing, may direct any such curate to give up possession of the house of residence, with the appurtenances, which he has been permitted to occupy by order of the bishop under the 64th section of the act. And such curate shall accordingly do so; and in case of refusal shall forfeit to the incumbent of the benefice 40*s.* for each day of such wrongful possession, to be recovered by such rector, &c. in an action of debt in any court of record at Westminster, as any penalties for non-residence under this act may be recovered. (57 G. 3. c. 99. s. 66.)

But the incumbent shall not dispossess the curate without the permission of the bishop and upon the above notice; and, in case the benefice becomes vacant, the curate shall quit the residence within three months after appointment thereto, on being required so to do by the new incumbent, and on having one month's notice to quit. (s. 67.)

And, by s. 68, no curate shall be permitted to quit until after three months' notice given to the person holding such benefice, and to the bishop of the diocese, unless with consent of the latter, upon pain of forfeiting to such incumbent a sum not exceeding six months' stipend.

Registry and Revocation of License.] The bishop may summarily revoke all licenses granted to any curates employed in his diocese, or subject to his jurisdiction; and may remove such curates for reasonable cause, subject to appeal to the archbishop of the province, to be determined in a summary way. (57 G. 3. c. 99. s. 52.)

And copies of licenses and revocations are to be entered in the registry of the diocese, and to be accessible to public inspection on payment of 3*s*. only; and a copy of every such license and revocation shall be transmitted by the registrar to the church or chapel-wardens of the parish, &c. to which it relates, within one month after such grant or revocation, to be deposited in the parish chest; and neglect to make such entry, or transmit such copy, is punishable with a penalty of £5. And he shall have from such wardens a fee of 10*s*., and no more, for every such copy, and such fee shall be allowed in their accounts. (57 G. 3. c. 99. s. 70.)

It would seem by the comprehensive terms of the statute, that power is given to the ordinary to revoke the licenses of *perpetual* curates, as well as those of every other description; and it has been said at common law and in the ecclesiastical courts, his authority extends thus far, as they are licensed by the bishop as well as others, (Powell v. Milbank, 1 T. R. 399, n.) though he seldom or never exercises it in such cases. (Price v. Pratt, Bunb. 273, Johns. 89.) But the point has never been expressly decided; and it has been said, that they are not to be removed but for such cause as would deprive a rector or vicar. (2 Burn. E. L. 74. 76.)

Augmented Curacies.] The 1 G. 1. st. 2. c. 10,—reciting that the late Queen Anne's bounty to the poor clergy was intended to extend to stipendiary preachers or curates,—most of which are not corporations, nor have a legal succession and therefore are incapable of taking a grant or conveyance of such perpetual augmentation as is intended by the said bounty, and in many places it would be in the power of the donor, impropriator, parson, or vicar to withdraw the allowance, which was before paid to the curate or minister,—it is enacted, that all such churches, curacies, or chapels, which shall be augmented by the governors of the said bounty, shall be from thenceforth perpetual cures and benefices; and the ministers duly nominated and licensed thereunto, shall be in law bodies politic and corporate, and have perpetual succession; and the impropriators or patrons of any augmented churches or donatives, and the rectors and vicars of the mother churches, whereunto such augmented curacy or chapel doth appertain, shall be excluded from receiving any profit by such augmentation, and shall pay to the ministers officiating, such annual and other pensions and salaries, which by ancient custom or otherwise, of right, and not of bounty, they were before obliged to pay.

And for continuing the succession in such augmented cures, hereby made perpetual cures and benefices, and that the same may be duly and constantly served, if they shall be suffered to remain void for six months, they shall lapse in like manner as presentative livings. (s. 6.)

It has been decided, that the perpetual curate of an augmented parochial chapelry has a sufficient possession whereon to maintain trespass, for breaking and entering the chapel, and destroying the pews; and that the chapelwarden cannot enter and remove the pews, without his consent. (Jones v. Ellis, 2 Younge and J. 265.)

SECTION IV.—LECTURER.

Origin of Lecturers.] There is another class of ministers of the established religion, called lecturers, whose situation in the church presents somewhat of an anomaly, as they are in many cases, though subordinate, not subjected to the controul of the rector or minister of the church in which they discharge their functions; and in other instances, though they have no superior in the church or chapel to which they are appointed, they have not the enjoyment of all the privileges which usually belong to the person filling the office of chief minister of a church or chapel, of an independent foundation.

Lectureships seem to have originated in the piety of the whole body of parishioners, in some cases; and in others, of benevolent individuals; from a desire to lighten the burthen of the rector, and to secure the due performance of the services of religion. In other instances, they have been founded for the purpose of insuring the promulgation or discussion, at particular periods, of some peculiar doctrines in morals or theology. (See R. v. Bathurst, 1 Bla. Rep. 210.) There are also lecturers in most of our cathedrals, whose labours are of course directed by the ordinary rules of church government

By whom chosen.] It is a general rule, that no person can be a lecturer, endowed or unendowed, without the rector's consent. But there may be a custom to elect without his consent; and where it exists, it is binding on the rector, as it supposes a consideration to him. *Endowment* may be material in such cases, as furnishing an argument in support of the custom, and to show that it had a legal commencement. (Clinton v. Hatchard, 1 Add. Rep. 103.)

The appointment is sometimes vested in trustees, by the will of the founder, or in his heirs, &c.; but it is very doubtful whether such a lectureship is not null and void, although acquiesced in for a series of years, where it was not formally sanctioned by the proper ecclesiastical authorities at the time. (See R. v. Bathurst, 1 Bla. Rep. 210; R. v. Bishop of Exeter, 2 East, 462.) And Lord Ellenborough declared, that it is not competent to any person to engraft a lectureship, by compulsion, on the church. A lectureship, in which the consent of the rector or vicar is not requisite, must have a legal commencement by custom or act of Parliament; and in the former case, any practice originating within legal memory will not suffice. (Id. 466.)

But where there is no fixed lecturer or ancient salary, but the lectureship is to be supported only by voluntary contributions, the ordinary is the proper judge whether or no any lecturer in such place ought to be admitted. And the Court of King's Bench, upon consideration, refused a mandamus to the Bishop of London, to grant a license to a lecturer, under such circumstances. (R. v. Bishop of London, 1 Wils. 11; 2 Stra. 1192.) And in support of the right of the rector in such cases, it has been said by the court, no person can use the pulpit of another, unless he consents; but an immemorial usage may partially supersede his right in this respect, as a good consideration is presumed for it. (R. v. Field, 4 T. R. 125; R. v. Bishop of London, 1 T. R. 331.)

Election by Custom.] The custom must be good at common law, that is, it must have existed immemorially. The right to elect, where such custom prevails, is generally vested in the parishioners; and in some instances, where the lectureship has been founded by the bounty of an individual, the election is directed to be made by them in the will of the founder. (See the Churchwardens of St. Bartholomew's case, 3 Salk. 87.)

But in R. v. the Bishop of Exeter, (2 East, 462,) where the donor devised a rent charge of 50*l.* per annum, payable out of an impropriate rectory, for the use of a lecturer within the same parish for ever; and it appeared, that the lectureship was founded in 1658, and consequently there could be no immemorial usage; and as the episcopal constitution was at that time suspended, there could be no assent of the bishop, rector, and vicar to the endowment; the Court of King's Bench refused a mandamus to the bishop to license a lecturer without the consent of the vicar, although lecturers had been regularly appointed under the grant, from its foundation to the last vacancy.

Bishop's Power herein.] The bishop's power, however, is generally only to judge as to the qualification and fitness of the person, and not as to the right of the lectureship. And therefore, where the bishop of London determined in favour of one of two rival candidates, and granted an inhibition and monition accordingly, Holt, C. J. said, "A prohibition must go to try the right: it is true, a man cannot be a lecturer, without a *license* from the bishop or archbishop; but their power is only as to the qualification and fitness of the person, and not as to the right of the lectureship: and the Ecclesiastical Court may punish the churchwardens, if they will not open the church to the person, or to any one acting under him; but not if they refuse to open it to any other." (3 Salk. 87.)

Must be licensed.] By canon 36, no person shall be received into the ministry, nor admitted to any ecclesiastical living, nor suffered to preach, to catechise, or be lecturer, or reader of divinity in either university, or in any cathedral or collegiate church, city, or market town, parish church, chapel, or any other place within this realm, except he be licensed either by the archbishop or by the bishop of the diocese where he is to be placed, under his hand and seal, or by one of the two universities, under their seal likewise; and except he shall first subscribe to the three articles concerning the king's supremacy, the book of Common Prayer, and the thirty-nine Articles; and if any bishop shall license any person without such subscription, he shall be suspended from giving licenses to preach for the space of twelve months.

The court will not entertain a motion for a mandamus to the bishop to license a lecturer, appointed by the parish, upon the previous refusal of the bishop to do so, for unfitness in the party elected; unless it be shown, that the like application had also been made to, and rejected by, the *archbishop*. (R. v. Bishop of London, 13 East, 419; and 15 East, 117.) The affidavit made by the bishop on the latter occasion, stated, that the party elected had been admitted before him with a view to his being "approved and licensed," (which are the words of the act, imposing that function on the archbishop or bishop, before any lecturer may lawfully preach,) that he had made diligent enquiry concerning his conduct and ministry; and being convinced, from such enquiry, that he was not a fit person to be allowed to lecture, he had conscientiously determined, after having heard him, that he could not approve or license him thereunto. It is equally open to the party to apply against the archbishop, in case of his declining to enquire as to his fitness, with a view to approve or disapprove of him as a proper person to be licensed.

Subscribe to the Articles.] By canon 37, No one licensed as aforesaid, to preach, and lecture, or catechise, coming to reside in any diocese, shall be permitted there to preach, read, lecture, catechise, or minister the sacraments, or to execute any other ecclesiastical function, (by what authority soever he be thereunto admitted,) unless he first consent and subscribe to the three articles before mentioned, in the presence of the bishop of the diocese, wherein he is to exercise such function.

Declaration of Conformity.] By 13 and 14 C. 2. c. 4. s. 19, no person shall be allowed or received as a lecturer, unless he be first approved, and thereunto licensed by the archbishop of the province, or bishop of the diocese, or (in case the see be void) by the guardian of the spiritualities, under his seal; and shall in the presence of the archbishop, or bishop, or guardian, read the Thirty-nine Articles, with a declaration of his unfeigned assent to the same; and every person who shall be appointed or received as a lecturer, to preach upon any day of the week, in any church, chapel, or place of public worship, the first time he preacheth, (before his sermon,) shall openly, publicly, and solemnly read the common prayers, and service appointed to be read for that time of the day, and then and there publicly and openly declare his assent unto, and approbation of the said book; and to the use of all the prayers, rites and ceremonies, forms and orders therein contained; and shall, upon the first lecture-day of every month afterwards, so long as he continues lecturer or preacher there, at the place appointed for his said lecture or sermon, before his said lecture or sermon, openly, publicly, and solemnly read the common prayers and service for that time of the day; and after such reading thereof, shall openly and publicly, before the congregation there assembled, declare his unfeigned assent unto the said book, according to the form aforesaid; and every such person who shall neglect or refuse to do the same, shall from thenceforth be disabled to preach the said or any other lecture or sermon, in the said or any other church,, chapel, or place of public worship, until he shall openly, publicly, and solemnly read the common prayers and service appointed by the said book; and conform in all points to the things therein prescribed, according to the purport and true intent of this act.

In Cathedrals.] Provided, that if the said lecture be to be read in any cathedral, or collegiate church, or chapel, it shall be sufficient for the said lecturer openly, at the time aforesaid, to declare his assent and consent to all things contained in the said book, according to the form aforesaid. (s. 20.)

Common Prayers.] Provided, that at all times, when any sermon or lecture is to be preached, the common prayers and service, in and by the said book appointed to be read for that time of the day, shall be openly, publicly, and solemnly read by some priest or deacon in the church, chapel, or place of public worship, where the said sermon or lecture is to be preached before such sermon or lecture be preached, and that the lecturer then to preach shall be present at the reading thereof. (s. 22.)

Punishment.] And if any person, who is by this act disabled, [or prohibited 15 C. 2. c. 6. s. 7,] to preach any lecture or sermon, shall, during the time that he shall continue so disabled (or prohibited,) preach any sermon or lecture, he shall suffer three months imprisonment in the common gaol; and any two justices of the peace of any county within this realm, and the mayor or other chief magistrate of any city or town corporate within the same, upon certificate from the ordinary made to him or them of the offence committed, shall, and are hereby required, to commit the person so offending to the gaol of the same county, city, or town corporate. (s. 21.)

University Churches.] And provided, that this act shall not extend to the university churches, where any sermon or lecture is preached there as and for the university sermon or lecture; but the same may be preached or read in such sort and manner as the same hath been heretofore preached or read. (s. 23.)

SECTION V.—CHURCHWARDENS.

Sidesmen.] It seems, that soon after the institution of episcopal synods, it was the practice of the bishops to summon some of the most reputable persons from every parish to give information of the state of morals, and to attest the disorders of the clergy and people. They were called *testes synodales,* and became in time a species of inquest jury, consisting of two or more persons in every parish, and thence sometimes called *questmen,* and were bound by oath to present all heretics and other irregular persons. (Ken. Par. Ant. 649.) In process of time they became standing officers,—called *synodsmen,* hence *sidesmen,* and, by canon 90, they were to be chosen yearly in Easter week by the minister and parishioners, or, in case of their disagreement, by the ordinary of the diocese. The office still exists in some parishes, though, in many cases, its whole duties having devolved upon the churchwardens, sidesmen are no longer chosen. But where the office has been preserved, the right of election vests in the minister and parishioners, unless there be a special custom to the contrary, precisely in the same manner as the appointment to the office of churchwarden.

Sidesman's Oath.] The sidesman's oath is as follows: "You shall swear, that you will be assistant to the churchwardens in the execution of their office, so far as by law you are bound. So help you God." (Gibs. 216.)

Churchwardens a Corporation.] Churchwardens are the guardians or keepers of the church, and representatives of the body of the church. They are, in favour of the church, for some purposes, a kind of corporation; being enabled, by that name, to have a property in goods and chattels, and to bring actions for them, (1 Bla. Com. 394; Gibs. 243,) whether the goods were taken in their own time or that of their predecessors. (2 Saund. 47 c.) They may take money or things by legacy, gift, &c., for the benefit of the church. (Attorney General v. Ruper, 2 P. Wms. 125.) But one churchwarden cannot singly dispose of the goods of the parish, (Cro. Car. 234,) nor both without the consent of the parishioners. (1 Roll. Ab. 393; 1 Vent. 89; Yel. 173.) Nor have they *virtute officii* the custody of the title deeds of the advowson, though they are kept in a chest in the church, as they are not the goods of the church. (Gardner v. Parker, 4 T. R. 351.)

Who may be elected.] Churchwardens are usually two in number; and, although it has been said that the parishioners may choose and trust whom they think fit, without limitation, (Morgan v. The Archdeacon of Cardigan, 1 Salk. 166,) yet this doctrine must not be taken to be correct in its largest sense; for, although it is the duty of the ordinary not to make slight objections, he is bound to take care, that an election, in his opinion void in itself, should have no legal effect; and this is a duty which he owes to the parish, and to the general law of the country. (Anthony v. Seger, 1 Hagg. R. 10.)

Therefore, if a parish return an alien, a Papist, or a Jew, or a child of ten years of age, or a person convicted of felony, (none of whom are qualified for the office,) "I conceive the ordinary would be bound to reject." (Sir Wm. Scott, id.) But poverty is not a disqualification; and therefore where, to a mandamus to swear in a churchwarden, the return was, that he was *pauper lactarius, et servus minus habilis*, (a poor dairyman, and unqualified for the office,) the court held the return insufficient, and a peremptory mandamus issued; for it is at the peril of the parishioners who elect him, if he misconduct himself. The ecclesiastical judge cannot controul the election. (1 Salk. 166; Rex. v. Simpson, 1 Stra. 609.)

Who are Exempt.] The exemptions from serving the office include, peers of the realm, members of parliament, and clergymen, (Gibs. 215,) Roman Catholic clergy taking the oath, and subscribing the declaration provided by 31 G. 3. c. 32, and dissenting ministers, (see tit. Dissenters;) barristers and attornies, (Com. Dig. tit. Attorney;) clerks in court, (1 Rol. Rep. 368;) physicians, surgeons, apothecaries, aldermen, dissenting teachers, and persons *living out of the parish,* although they occupy lands within it. (Gibs. 215.) But if they occupy a house of trade there, although they take their meals and sleep in another parish, they are liable. (Stephenson v. Langston, 1 Hagg. R. 379.) In this latter case the defendant was chosen sheriff of another county pending the suit, which the court held would exonerate him, though he was condemned in the costs.

The judgment of the Court of King's Bench in Rex v. Poynder is also to the like effect. In this case it was held, under similar circumstances, that each of three partners in trade was liable to serve the office of overseer as a householder within the 43 Eliz. although no one of them resided on the premises. (1 Barn. and Cres. 178; 2 Dowl. and Ryl. 258.)

When one having privilege is chosen, a writ goes to the ecclesiastical court, that he be not sworn. (Palm. 392.)

Serving by Deputy.] The Toleration Act, (1 W. and M. c. 18. s. 7), provides, that if any person dissenting from the church of England be appointed to the office of churchwarden, or any other parochial office, and scruples to take the oaths, &c., he may execute the same by a sufficient deputy, to be approved in such manner as the officer himself should by law have been allowed and approved; and the same relief is extended to Roman Catholics by the 31 G. 3. c. 32. s. 7.

When and by whom chosen.] The churchwardens shall be chosen the first week after Easter. (Canon 90.) And, by canon 89, the choice shall be made by the joint consent of the minister and the parishioners, if it may be; but, if they cannot agree, the parishioners shall choose one, and the minister another; and a curate may stand in the place of minister for this purpose, (Hubbard v. Penrice, 2 Stra. 1246;) and without such joint or several choice, none shall take upon themselves to be churchwardens. (Gibs. 241.)

In the churchwardens of Northampton's case, (Carthew 118,) Holt, Chief Justice, is reported to have said, "Of common right the choosing churchwardens belongs to the parishioners; 'tis true, in some places, the incumbent chooses one, but that is only by usage; and tke canon concerning the choosing of churchwardens is not regarded by the common law; this was the opinion of Lord Chief Baron Hale, as may be seen in Dawson v. Fowle, Hardres. 378." But in Slocombe v. St. John, tried at the Croydon Summer Assizes, 1829, which was an issue, to ascertain whether the right of election was in the parishioners, in exclusion of the minister, and in support of the affirmative the above decision in Carthew was quoted, and, on the other side (1 Burn. Ec. L. 401;) and the authorities there collected were relied upon, it was held by Park, J., that in general the minister and the parishioners are to choose the two churchwardens, and if they do not concur, then the minister is to choose one and the parishioners the other; and though the evidence established that, generally, for upwards of two hundred years, the minister and parishioners concurred, yet there was no evidence that the minister had ever separately appointed one, still this was not enough to support a supposed custom in exclusion of the minister, because their long concurrence was not sufficient to affect the general right.

Where the right of appointing exists in the parishioners, it is to be exercised in vestry assembled; and the parson cannot intermeddle in the election. (Stoughton v. Reynolds, 2 Stra. 1045.) Where it is the custom for the parson to choose one churchwarden, and he is under sentence of deprivation, the right to elect both results to the parishioners. (Carth. 118.) And, *by custom*, both may be chosen by the parishioners without the parson, (2 Roll. 234. l. 15; Warner's case, Cro. Jac. 532;) or by a select vestry, or a particular number of the parishioners. (Hard. 379; 1 Mod. 181.) But where the custom was for the old churchwardens to choose one of the new ones, the parson choosing the other, and they could not agree, but one of them presented a person of the name of Berwick, and thereupon the parishioners at large chose one named Catten, the court held, that by this disagreement between the old churchwardens, the custom was laid out of the case; and then they must resort to the canon, under which, Catten being duly elected, they decreed for him with costs. (Catten v. Berwick, Stra. 145.)

Chosen by Lord of Manor.] In some places the lord of the manor prescribes for the appointment of churchwardens; but this shall not be tried in the ecclesiastical court. (Godb. 153; 2 Inst. 653.)

Custom in London.] In most of the parishes in London the parishioners choose both churchwardens by custom; yet in all the new-erected parishes, under 9 Ann. c. 22, the *canon* shall take place, (unless the particular act, in virtue of which any church was erected, shall have specially provided that the parishioners shall choose both,) inasmuch as no *custom* can be pleaded in such new parishes. (Gibs. 215; Co. Litt. 113.)

On an issue, whether a churchwarden ought to be elected by the select vestry, a record between a former churchwarden and another person, is admissible evidence. (Berry v. Bonner, Peake 156.)

How chosen in new Churches.] The legislature, in the recent provisions for the erection of additional churches, &c., have framed the enactment upon this subject upon the same principle as the canon which regulates the right to elect in all cases, where there is no custom to the contrary. By the 58 G. 3. c. 45. s. 73, it is provided that two fit persons shall be appointed churchwardens for every church or chapel built or appropriated under the act, at the usual period of appointing parish officers in every year, one by the incumbent, and the other by the inhabitant householders in the district, and shall be admitted and sworn according to law. They shall receive the rents of the pews and seats, pay their stipends to the minister and clerk, and do all acts requisite for the repairs, management, and good order in the church or chapel; and shall continue in office till others be chosen; and, on non-payment of the rents of seats and pews, may enter upon and sell the same, or recover them by action, in the names of "The Churchwardens of the Church or Chapel of," [describing the same,] without specifying their own names; and no such action shall abate by their death or going out of office. And, by section 74, churchwardens of every parish in which any additional chapel shall be built or provided under the act, without making any division thereof into separate parishes or district parishes, shall do all such things as churchwardens to be appointed under the act are authorized and required to do.

Mode of Election.] The churchwardens, whose office is about to expire, are properly the returning officers at such elections; but it is not indispensably necessary that the court should be informed, by this method, where an election is disputed, provided satisfactory information of the election be given in any other way. (Anthony v. Seger, 1 Hagg. R. 9.) If, after a show of hands, a poll is demanded, it destroys the previous voting by a show of hands; and every thing anterior is not of the substance of the election, nor to be so received; and consequently, where one of three candidates had many hands held up in his favour, but afterwards did not poll any votes, he could not be taken as elected, upon one of the persons returned being afterwards found ineligible. (Id.) As to the proper mode of voting, see Faulkner v. Elger, 4 Barn. & Cres. 449, *(ante,* p. 71.) If there be a custom to conclude the poll for the election at a certain time that being a reasonable time, the voters must tender their votes within it. (Rex v. the Commissary of the Bishop of Winchester, 7 East. 573.) The power of adjourning the poll seems to be in the voters. (Stoughton v. Reynolds, 2 Stra. 1045.) And any attempt to disturb the election is punishable in the ecclesiastical court. (Wilson v. M'Math. 2 Barn. & Ald. 48.)

Double Return.] If there be a contest as to the right of making the election, and two sets of churchwardens be chosen in consequence, the commissary or ordinary, it is said, is bound to swear them all; and a mandamus lies to compel him to do so, in order that both parties may be made capable to try the right, (but see *Mandamus to Admit, infra.*) The right can only be determined in an action at law, as they are temporal officers; and a prohibition lies, if the spiritual court entertains such a suit. (Williams v. Vaughan, 1 Bla. Rep. 28; 2 Roll's Abr. 287. Rex v. Harris. 3 Burr. 1420. Evelin's Case, Cro. Car. 551. King's Case, 1 Keb. 517. Warner's Case, Cro. Jac. 532.)

Quo Warranto.] The writ of *quo warranto* will not be granted, as the office does not concern the rights or prerogatives of the crown; for which only the old writ of *quo warranto* lay; and an information in the nature of a *quo warranto* can only be granted in such cases. (Rex v. Shepherd, 4 T. R. 381. Rex v. Dawbeny, 2 Stra. 1196.)

Mandamus to Elect.] If the parishioners and minister neglect to choose churchwardens, the ordinary, nevertheless, cannot interfere. Thus a prohibition was granted to the spiritual court, where it was libelled against the defendant for not appearing to take the office of churchwarden, though thereunto appointed *by the ordinary.* And it was held, that although the parishioners and parson neglect, for ever so long, to choose churchwardens, yet the ordinary hath no jurisdiction; for churchwardens are a corporation at common law. And, by the court, "the proper way is to take a mandamus out of the King's Bench." (Stutter v. Freston, Stra. 52.) Upon the authority of this dictum Mr. Nolan says, "If those persons, who ought to choose churchwardens, neglect to do so at the proper season, they may be compelled to it by a writ of mandamus. (1 Nol. P. L. 44.)

But, in a more recent instance, the Court of King's Bench refused to grant a mandamus to churchwardens to call a vestry in Easter week for the election of churchwardens, saying, there was no instance of such a mandamus; and they could not take notice who had a right to call the vestry, and, consequently, did not know to whom it should be directed. (Anon. 2 Stra. 686. See Com. Dig. Mandamus, (B.)

Mandamus to Admit.] The authorities are somewhat at variance upon the question, whether to a mandamus to *swear* in a churchwarden, a return that the party was not elected, is good; and, as he might try the validity of his election in an action for a *false* return, there does not appear any very strong reason against the decisions, that such a return may properly be made. (See Rex v. White, Ld. Raym. 1379—1405; 2 Salk. 433.)

But all doubt upon the subject may be considered as having been put at rest by the decision in R. v. Williams, (8 Barn. and Cres. 681,) wherein Bayley, J., after an elaborate review of the cases touching the question, held with the full concurrence of the other puisne judges of the court, that a return stating that the party *was not duly elected* is good; and Parke, J., said, "The commissary may deny any material allegation in the writ. He cannot exercise any judicial authority; but he may inquire whether the party has been duly elected, otherwise he would be bound to admit any person who presents himself for admission, even if he knew the fact to be that such person was never elected. The party, who obtains the mandamus, states the foundation of his right in the writ. The commissary may deny it. In this case he has done it, by showing that the party who seeks to be admitted was not duly elected." (See also Anthony v Seger, 1 Hagg. Rep. 10.)

Must be Sworn in.] Churchwardens, immediately after their election, are to take an oath to execute the office truly and faithfully, (Gibs. 243); and they must not enter upon their office till they are sworn. After being duly elected, they may be directed by the spiritual court to take the oath before the proper officer, (Cooper v. Allnut, 3 Phil. Ec. Ca. 166); and they may be excommunicated for refusal, and no prohibition will lie. (Gibs. 216. 243—961.)

By whom Sworn.] The oath is to be administered by the archdeacon or proper ordinary of the diocese. No fee can be demanded for swearing the churchwardens, or taking their presentments. (Goslin v. Ellison, 1 Salk. 330.) By the canon, (1 Jac. 89,) they are to continue in office one year, except they are again chosen in like manner. (Com. Dig. Esglise, F. 1.) But this refers only to the time when others should be appointed in their stead; for when once sworn in, they continue in office until their chosen successors take the oath in like manner. (Canon 188. Burn.; Ec. L. 410.)

The Oath.] The form of the oath is as follows: "You shall swear truly and faithfully to execute the office of a churchwarden within your parish; and, according to the best of your skill and knowledge, present such things and persons as to your knowledge are presentable by the laws ecclesiastical of this realm. So help you God, and the contents of this book." (Gibs, 216. See Hardres Rep. 364. Rex v. Pratt, 3 Keb. 206.) By 13 & 14 W. & M. c. 6. s. 14, & 1 G. 1. st. 2. c. 13. s. 20, churchwardens are exempted from taking the oaths of allegiance, supremacy, abjuration, &c., on entering their offices.

Their Rights in Personal Property.] It has already been observed, that churchwardens are held to be a corporation at common law, for some purposes. They may in that capacity purchase goods for the use of the parish; and may bring actions to recover the goods of the church, or for damages done to them. (1 Burn. Ec. L. 408.) But one churchwarden cannot dispose of such goods without the consent of the other. (Starkey v. Berton, Cro. Jac. 234;) nor both together, without the consent of the parishioners, for the goods belong to them; and the churchwardens can do nothing to the disadvantage of the church. (1 Rol. Ab. 393; 13 H. 7. 10. a.; Yelv. 173; and 2 Brownl. 215.) And the license of the ordinary is also said to be necessary: therefore if it is thought expedient to sell an old bell, towards other repairs, or to dispose of old communion plate to buy new, &c., the churchwardens cannot safely do it without first obtaining the concurrence of the above parties. But although the goods belong to the parishioners, the churchwardens are the corporation in whom they are vested; and consequently, if they improperly dispose of them, the parishioners cannot sue thereupon, either to recover them, or otherwise; but they must tarry till new churchwardens are chosen, who have a right to call their predecessors to account before the ordinary; and to commence suit against them for any damage done the parish, by their violation of the trust reposed in them. (Prid. Direct. 78.) And they may bring their action against their predecessors, for money remaining in their hands; and they are not bound to make all the present or late churchwardens plaintiffs or defendants. (Astle v. Thomas, 2 Barn. and Cres. 271. 3 Dowl. and Ryl. 492.)

Where an *obligation* is made to churchwardens and their *successors*, and they die, their executors shall have action, and not their successors. (Vin. Ab. Churchwardens, D.)

Their Rights in real Property.] But their corporate character does not enable them to purchase lands, or to take by grant, (12 H. 7. 29 a.; 1 Rol. 393. l. 10,) except in London, where they are a corporation for those purposes also, (Gibs. 215; Warner's case, Cro. Jac. 532); and therefore, gifts of land to the parish, for the use of the church, should be to feoffees, in trust to the use intended; which should be from time to time renewed, as the trustees die off; and the churchwardens cannot grant leases of such lands, nor maintain trespass or other action, for entry or taking possession of them. (12 H.

7. 29, a.) Nor can they prescribe to have lands to them and their successors. (Vin. Ab. Churchwardens, A.)

They are however enabled, jointly with the overseers, by the 9 G. 1. c. 7. s. 4, with the consent of the major part of the parishioners or inhabitants in vestry, to purchase houses to lodge and employ the poor in; and the 59 G. 3. c. 12. s. 17, enacts, that churchwardens and overseers shall take and hold, in the nature of a body corporate, for and on behalf of the parish, all buildings, lands, and tenements belonging to the parish. But it was held, that in order to constitute the body corporate intended by this act, there must be two overseers, and a churchwarden or churchwardens; and that where there were two overseers appointed, one of whom was afterwards appointed (by custom) sole churchwarden, the act did not vest parish property in them. (Woodcock v. Gibson and Ors. 4 Barn. and Cres. 462; 6 Dowl. and Ryl. 524.) So a lease of parish land, granted by *churchwardens alone,* is invalid. (Phillips v. Pearce, 5 Barn. and Cres. 433; 8 Dowl. and Ryl. 43.)

Their Ecclesiastical Duties.] Most of the duties of churchwardens will appear incidentally under different heads in the course of the work; for which see the proper titles respectively, and the index. The great changes in the manners and habits of the people, have relieved churchwardens from the invidious task of enforcing the attendance of the people upon the services of religion; and presenting those to ecclesiastical censures who absent themselves from church; as well as preventing the excommunicated from entering within its walls. But they are bound, and may occasionally have to exercise their authority, in preserving due decorum in the time of divine service. Thus, they may justify taking off the hat of a person who refuses to do it himself, upon request. (Hall v. Planner, 1 Lev. 197.) And they are, to a certain degree, the guardians of the moral character, and public decency of their respective parishes. (Griffiths v. Reed and Harris, 1 Hagg. Rep. N. S. 208.)

Their Duty respecting the Minister.] Churchwardens are required by the canons to see that curates are duly licensed by the bishop; and that strangers, unless duly qualified, shall not preach in the church. They are also to present the minister for non-residence, or for irregular and incontinent living, or any other excess or irregularity calculated to bring disgrace upon their sacred office.

If the minister introduces any irregularity into the service, the churchwardens have no authority to interfere; but they may and ought to repress all indecent interruption of the service by others; and they desert their duty if they do not. And if a case could be imagined, in which even a preacher himself were guilty of any act, grossly offensive, either from natural infirmity, or from disorderly habits, it seems, that the churchwardens, and even private persons may interpose, to preserve the decorum of public worship; but that is a case of instant and overbearing necessity, that supersedes all ordinary rules. In cases which fall short of such a singular pressure, and can await the remedy of a proper legal complaint, and a private and decent application to the minister himself, fails in preventing a repetition of the irregularity, the churchwardens may complain to the ordinary. (Hutchins v. Denziloe and Another, 1 Hagg. R. 174.)

Duty as Sequestrators.] It is part of the office of churchwardens to have the care of benefices during their vacancy, whether by death of the incumbent or otherwise. Upon any such avoidance, they are to apply to the Chancellor of the diocese, for the sequestration of the profits thereof; and being thereupon authorised by instrument, under seal, they are to manage the profits and expences, for the benefit of the successor. In this capacity, they are to till the glebe, gather the tithes, and dispose of the produce at the best market; and do every thing for the interest of the next incumbent. They are also to take care that the church be duly served by a curate, and to pay him out of the profits of the benefice, such sum as the ordinary may fix, if applied to for the purpose. They are bound to account to the new minister, when he is instituted; and if he is satisfied, and gives them a discharge, this concludes the matter. (See 28 H. 8. c. 11.)

Although the churchwardens are the proper officers for this business, and are bound to perform it if required, yet the ordinary may confide the trust to others, willing to accept it. (3 Burn. Ec. L. 340.)

Sequestration for Debt.] Benefices are sometimes sequestered though not vacant; as on a suspension, in order to provide for serving the cure; and in the case of dilapidations of the chancel, or the minister's house, for repairing them; sometimes a sequestration is commanded by the King's writ, for the payment of the minister's debts, which is tantamount to a *fieri facias* against a lay person; in all which cases, the same obligation rests upon the churchwardens, unless the ordinary finds other persons whom he judges proper to intrust with the duty. It is customary for the ordinary to take a bond, which may be sued upon at law, in case the sequestrators (who are a kind of bailiff to the bishop) do not give a faithful account of their trust. (See Prideaux on Churchwardens.)

Creditor Sequestrator.] The creditor is the person to whom the sequestration is usually granted, when it is issued for the purpose of levying in satisfaction of a debt, for which a judgment has been obtained; but that is only for the convenience of proceeding under it, and by the authority of the bishop; but such creditor cannot assume a preference, which a third person would not be compellable to allow. (Hubbard v. Beckford, 1 Hagg. R. 312.) But it is the duty of the Court to carry the writ into immediate execution. (Campbell v. Whitehead, id. in note.)

Subsequent Sequestration.] A creditor, who has obtained a subsequent sequestration, whilst a rectory is already under a prior one, is entitled to an account in equity against such first sequestrator; and payment of the surplus, after satisfaction of the first creditor; nor are prior incumbrancers, who have not obtained sequestration, necessary parties to the suit. (Cuddington v. Withy, 2 Swanst. 174.)

Under a sequestration, the landlord is entitled to be paid arrears of rent. (Dixon v. Smith, 1 Swanst. 457.)

Sequestration limited.] In all cases, the sequestrators are not to meddle with any timber, trees, wood, or underwood standing upon the glebes of the living, unless it be for necessary repairs of the church or parsonage; nor commit any other waste thereupon. (9 H. 3. c. 5.) And in the case of a sequestration for dilapidations, all the profits are not to be taken, but a portion is to be left to the minister for his livelihood. (Anon. 2 Vent. 35.) There can be no sequestration of an *impropriate* rectory; for being a lay fee it is out of the jurisdiction of the ecclesiastical courts, and the parties must be proceeded against as laymen, for not repairing the church. (Id.)

Churchwardens' Presentments.] At the Easter visitation, when the churchwardens go out of office, and before their successors are sworn, they must make their presentments of all things amiss within their parish. (4 Burn. Ec. L. 25.)

Passing their Accounts.] At the end of their year, or within a month afterwards, the churchwardens must, before the minister and parishioners in vestry, present their accounts of receipts and disbursements; and if they are allowed, an entry in the church book of accounts should be made to that effect, which should be signed by the parties allowing the same; and the balance of money, if any remains in the hands of the churchwardens, must be delivered over to their successors; with the goods, &c. of the church, according to the inventory, by bill indented. (Canon 89.)

Must produce Accounts.] The Ecclesiastical Court may compel the production of accounts, but cannot dispute the validity of them when produced; for the ordinary is not to *take* the account, but only to give judgment, that the churchwardens do account. (Wainwright v. Bagshaw, 2 Strange, 974; Adams v. Rush, 2 Strange, 1133.) Nor can that Court proceed against them, to account upon oath, after they have passed their accounts before the vestry. (Snowden v. Herring, Bunb. 289.) And a custom to account to a select vestry, or a certain number of persons, having the government of the parish by custom, is good and sufficient. (Gibs. 216.) If the Spiritual Court take any step after the accounts are delivered in, it is an excess of jurisdiction, for which a prohibition will be granted, even after sentence. (Leman v. Goulty, 3 T. R. 3.)

They are bound in common with the overseers, to permit an inspection of their accounts; and upon the party stating *some special reason*, for which he wishes to see the accounts, a mandamus to compel them to allow such inspection will be granted; and it is no answer to such an application to the Court that the statute 17 G. 2. c. 38, imposes a penalty for improperly refusing such inspection. (R. v. Clear, 4 Barn. and Cres. 899; 7 Dowl. and Ryl. 393.)

Proof of Disbursements.] The oath of the churchwardens is generally held sufficient, with respect to all items in their accounts under 40*s*., unless they are suspected to be unfair; but the payment of larger sums must be verified by receipts and vouchers; and if required, *witnesses* should also be produced, who were present at the making thereof, who shall subscribe their names to the vouchers, &c. in proof of the authenticity of the same. (Prid. Direct. 93.)

Disbursing own Money.] Churchwardens should, on no occasion, except for the immediate relief of the poor, in their capacity of overseers, when there is no rate, or during an appeal, (41 G. 3. c. 23. s. 9.) advance their own money for parochial purposes; but should take care that such purposes are provided for by a previous rate, duly made, as a rate cannot legally be imposed subsequently, to *reimburse* them. Nor can a mandamus to compel them to make a rate be granted. (R. v. Wilson, 5 Dowl. and Ryl. 602.) See "CHURCH RATE."

Responsible for Church Goods.] The churchwardens may be cited by the ordinary, to give further account of the church goods, although their accounts have been already allowed in vestry; and if it appear that they have disposed of any of the said utensils or goods, with the approbation of the parishioners, but without his consent, in order to defray any part of the church rates or expences, the ordinary may compel the churchwardens to replace the same out of their own pockets; or inflict such other punishment as he may deem expedient; otherwise, the parishioners might combine to defraud the church of her costly ornaments, plate, and other goods, to relieve themselves from the rates, or for their private emolument. (Godb. 279; Prid. Direct. 94. See Bishop's case, 2 Roll. R. 71.)

Their Agreements valid.] Churchwardens in their corporate capacity, may enter into reasonable agreements, beneficial to the parish, which shall be binding on their successors, and the parishioners. Thus in the case of Dr. Martin and Lady Arabella his wife, v. Nutkin and others, (2 P. Wms. 268,) it appeared that Lady Arabella being of a sickly constitution, was much disturbed by the ringing of the five o'clock bell every morning, as was the custom in the parish; and was about removing elsewhere, but it was agreed between the plaintiffs and the parish, upon a vestry being duly convened for the purpose, that the ringing should cease during the lives of the plaintiffs and the survivor of them, they covenanting, in consideration thereof, to build a cupola to the church, and erect a clock and new bell. The plaintiffs performed their covenants in the deed executed between them and the parish; and the bell was silenced for about two years; when the defendant Nutkin obtained a new order of vestry, for ringing the five o'clock bell, but an injunction was granted by Lord Chancellor Macclesfield, to continue during the lives of the plaintiffs, and the survivor of them; especially as it appeared that the majority and better part of the parish continued willing to abide by the agreement, and protested against the new order.

May bring Actions.] We have already seen, that churchwardens may bring actions for recovery of, or damage done to the goods of the church. See (1 Bac. Ab. 372;) but such actions must be in the *joint names* of both; and if one execute a release, or give a discharge to such action rightly commenced, it is null and void; as are all official acts, where one takes upon himself to act alone, except in presentments, where one may know of offences of which the other is ignorant; or which the other may previously and wickedly refuse to present, though known to both. If the damages for which they sue were done in their *own time*, they may lay the action either *in damnum parochianorum*, or *in damnum ipsorum;* but if in the time of their predecessors, or the action be against their predecessors for defaults in office, it must be *in damnum parochianorum.* (Hadman and Another v. Ringewood, Cro. Eliz. 179; Attorney-General v. Ruper, 2 P. Wms. 125. See 6 Bac. Ab. 565.) And though they cannot commence a suit in their own names, *after* their office has expired, yet if commenced before, they may proceed in it afterwards, *ex necessitate rei.* (Dent v. Prudence and Another, 2 Stra. 852.) And churchwardens *de facto,* may maintain an action against a former churchwarden, for money received by him for the parish, though the validity of the election of the plaintiffs to the office be doubtful, and though they be not the immediate successors of the defendant. (Turner

v. Baynes, 2 H. Bla. 559.) But churchwardens cannot sue at law for a legacy, or a thing never in their possession. (Com. Dig. Esglise, F. 3.)

Proceedings against.] Churchwardens may be removed for misbehaviour, and others chosen before the year expires. (Lamb. Off. Ch. sect. 3;) or they may be sued for neglect of duty in the Ecclesiastical Court. (Welcome v. Lake, 1 Sid. 281.) So an indictment lies against them, if they take money, &c. *corrupte colore officii,* and do not account for it, (Rex v. Eyres, 1 Sid. 307;) but they cannot be sued by their successors; for a thing honestly done *ratione officii.* (Godb. 279.) If a churchwarden be committed for not accounting as *overseer,* it must be expressed in the mittimus, that he is committed in the latter character; for though the latter office is annexed to the former, the justices have no power over him as churchwarden. (Rex v. Pecke, 1 Keb. 574.)

By 9 G. 3. c. 37, churchwardens, for paying the poor otherwise than in lawful money, are to forfeit to the poor not less than 10*s.* nor more than 20*s.* And by 39 & 40 G. 3. c. 99. s. 28, churchwardens and overseers on notice from a justice of the peace, are to prosecute pawnbrokers offending against that act, at the expence of the parish.

Protection when sued.] If an action be brought against churchwardens, or any persons called sworn men, executing the office of churchwarden, for any thing done *virtute officii,* they may plead the general issue, and give the special matter in evidence; and if they obtain a verdict, or the plaintiff be nonsuit, or discontinue, they shall have double costs. (7 J. c. 5. 21 J. c. 12;) but this right of double costs does not extend to actions against them, arising out of their presentments, for matters of favour in the Spiritual Courts; but is confined to temporal affairs, concerning their office. (Kircheval v. Smith, Cro. Car. 285.) And the above statutes do not extend to actions against them for non-feasance, such as the non-payment of money, laid out for the support of one of their paupers by another parish; and for which an action of assumpsit was brought against them. (Atkins v. Banwell, 3 East, 92.) Nor are they entitled to double costs, on judgment as in case of a nonsuit, in an action brought against them, for the price of goods sold and delivered to them for the use of the poor. (Blanchard v. Bramble, 3 Maul. and Sel. 131.)

Decayed Buildings.] By the Metropolis Building Act, if a presentment be made by any jury, duly constituted within the limits of the act, that any house or building is in a ruinous condition, the Court of Mayor and Aldermen within the city and liberties of London, or the *churchwardens* or overseers of the parish or place, not being in the city, on notice of any such presentment being made, and a copy thereof being laid before them or him, are authorised to cause, with all convenient speed, a proper hoard to be put up for the safety of passengers; and to give notice thereof to the owner, or, in case no owner can be found, to affix it on the door or most notorious part of the building, to repair or pull down such building, as the case may require, within fourteen days; and, if this is not complied with, upon proof on oath before the lord mayor in the city, or a justice of the peace elsewhere, of the notice having been so given or affixed as aforesaid, the mayor and aldermen in the city, or the churchwardens and overseers in the other parts of the metropolis, may cause the repairs, &c., to be done, or the premises taken down, &c., out of the parish funds, &c., and may re-imburse themselves from the materials, &c., accounting for the surplus to the owner of the premises; but, if enough is not raised by the sale of such materials to refund all the expenses incurred, the owner must make good the deficiency to the churchwardens, &c., which may be levied by distress and sale of such owner's goods; and, if no owner can be found, then the next person occupying the premises, or the scite thereof, is to deduct it out of the rent. (14 G. 3. c. 78. s. 70, 71.)

SECTION VI.—PARISH CLERK.

Origin of Office.] Parish clerks were heretofore chosen from among the poorer candidates for the clerical office, of whom every minister had at least one to assist under him in the celebration of divine offices. For his better maintenance, the profits of the office of *aquæbajalus,* (an assistant in carrying the holy water,) were annexed to the office of parish clerk; so that in after-times *aquæbajalus* was only another name for the clerk officiating under the chief minister. (Lind. 142.)

His Qualifications.] By canon 91, it is required, that the said clerk shall be twenty years of age at least, known to the minister to be of honest conversation, and sufficient for his reading, writing, and also for his competent skill in singing, (if it may be.)

By whom chosen.] The nomination of clerks, it is said, was at one time vested in all incumbents, by the common law and custom of the realm. (Gibs. 214.) But differences having arisen between ministers and their parishioners about the conferring of such offices, Archbishop Boniface decreed, that the same rectors and vicars, whom it more particularly concerned to know who were fit, should make the choice.

Chosen by Minister.] And, by canon 91, no parish clerk, upon any vacation, shall be chosen within the city of London, or elsewhere, but by the parson or vicar; or, where there is no parson or vicar, by the minister of that place for the time being: which choice shall be signified by the said minister, vicar, or parson, to the parishioners, the next Sunday following, in the time of divine service.

Election by Custom.] Since the making of the above canon, the right hath often been contested between incumbents and parishioners; and wherever it has appeared to be in the latter by custom, a prohibition has issued to the ecclesiastical court, in order that the question might be determined at the common law.

Custom preferred to Canon.] The parish of St. Alphage, in Canterbury, prescribed to have the election of their parish clerk; and, by the canon, the election of the clerk was given to the vicar. It was adjudged, however, that the prescription should be preferred before the canon; because the party chosen is a mere temporal man, and the custom is merely temporal, so as the official cannot deprive him; but upon occasion the parishioners might displace him. (13 Co. 70; Hughes 275.) So in Jermyn's case, where the rector and clerk sued in the spiritual court, to have the said clerk established, having been nominated according to the canon, but disturbed by the parishioners; and the churchwardens and parishioners prayed a prohibition, upon the surmise of a custom for the vestry to elect: after divers motions a prohibition was granted; for they held that it was a good custom, and that the canon cannot take it away. (Cro. Ja. 670; Townsend v. Thorpe, 2 Raym. 1507.) So, though he is in without deed. (2 Salk. 536.)

How admitted.] Parish clerks, after having been duly appointed, are usually licensed by the ordinary. (Johns. 204.) And sworn to obey the minister. (Johns. 205.) And if a parish clerk hath been used immemorially to be chosen by the vestry, and admitted, and sworn before the archdeacon, and he refuse to swear him, but admitteth another, chosen by the parson, a mandamus lies to the archdeacon, commanding him to swear him. (2 Rol. Ab. 234; Vin. Ab. Mandamus H.; Bac. Ab. Mandamus (C.)

Remuneration.] It seems that parish clerks cannot claim any thing by way of a certain allowance or endowment, by reason of their office of *aquebajalus*. But their sustentation ought to be collected and levied according to the manner and custom of the country. And hereunto the parishioners may be compelled by the bishop. (Lindw 143.)

Customary Recompense.] A custom of this kind is good and

laudable; that every master of a family, (for instance,) on every Lord's day, give to the clerk somewhat according to the exigency of his condition; and that, on Christmas day, he have of every house one loaf of bread, and a certain number of eggs at Easter, and in the autumn certain sheaves. Also that may be called a laudable custom, where such clerk, every quarter of the year, receiveth something in way of money for his sustenance, which ought to be collected and levied in the whole parish. (Lind. 143; Gibs. 214.) But, if he sue for these things in the spiritual court, a prohibition lieth. (2 Rol. Ab. 286.)

Clerk's Rate.] In some instances a custom to levy so much money every year for his recompense is set up; and though, by canon 91, it is ordained that he shall have his *ancient wages,* and sue for them in the ecclesiastical court, yet Holt,. C. J., said, a clerk of a parish is neither a spiritual person, nor is this duty in demand spiritual, for it is founded on a custom, and, by consequence, triable at law; and therefore the clerk may have an action on the case against the churchwardens, for neglecting to make a rate, and to levy it, or if it had been levied, and not paid by them to the plaintiff. (Parker v. Clarke, 6 *Mod.* 252; 3 Salk. 87.) So in Pitts v. Evans, a prohibition was granted to a suit by the clerk of St. Magnus, for 1*s.* 4*d.* assessed on the defendant's house, at a vestry in 1672, to be paid to the parish clerk; for, if such a rate is due by custom, he may maintain an *assumpsit,* if not a *quantum meruit,* or a bill in equity. (Strange 1108; 13 Vin. Ab. 155.)

A temporal Officer.] It is said, that a parish clerk may be deprived by him that placed him in his office; but if he is unjustly deprived, a mandamus will lie to the churchwardens to restore him; (Ile's Case. 1 Ventr. 148;) for the law will not suffer the ecclesiastical court to deprive him, but only to correct him for any misdemeanor by ecclesiastical censure. (3 Rol. Abr. 234; Gibs. 214; God. 192.)

But where a parish clerk, pending proceedings to deprive him, in the ecclesiastical court, was indicted, and convicted, and pilloried for the offences alleged against him in the spiritual court, a consultation was granted as to the proceeding to *deprive;* and a prohibition issued as to any other punishment. The court saying, he was an ecclesiastical officer as to every thing but his election. (Townshend v. Thorpe, 2 Str. 776.)

However, in Peake v. Bourne, (2 Stra. 942,) the judges, on being pressed with their own authority in Townshend v. Thorpe, in support of the doctrine that a parish clerk is a spiritual officer, said it was a hasty opinion, into which they were transported by the enormity of the case. And that he is a *temporal* officer, was admitted and confirmed in Tarrant v. Haxby, (1 Burr. 367.)

A freehold Office.] The common law regards parish clerks as belonging to the class of persons who have freeholds in their offices; and therefore, though they may be punished, yet they cannot be deprived by ecclesiastical censures. (2 Rol. Ab. 234.) In R. v. Warren, (Cowp. 370,) it was stated, that the clerk was appointed by the minister; that he had since become bankrupt, and had not obtained his certificate; that he had been guilty of many omissions in his office, was actually in prison at the time of his amoval, and had appointed a deputy who was totally unfit for the office. Yet, after stating an adjournment of the case, the report adds, " and now, on this day, upon reading the affidavits, Lord Mansfield said, it was settled in the case of K. and Dr. Ashton, 28 G. 2, ' That a parish clerk is a temporal officer, and that the minister must show good ground for turning him out.' Now, in this case, there is no sufficient reason assigned in the affidavits that have been read, upon which the court can exercise their judgment; nor is there any instance produced of any misbehaviour of consequence; therefore the rule for a mandamus to restore him must be made absolute."

In new Churches.] The recent acts for building new churches, and making new ecclesiastical districts, provide, that the clerks to such churches and chapels shall be annually appointed by the minister thereof. (59 G. 3. c. 134. s. 29.)

Divided Parishes.] And the 10th section of the same statute enacts, that, when any parish shall be divided, &c., all fees and emoluments, of the clerk and sexton afterwards arising in any division, shall belong to the clerk and sexton of the division to which they shall be assigned. *(post,* 101.)

Incorporated in London.] By a charter of Hen. III., the parish clerks in and about London were incorporated, and authorized to make bye-laws and ordinances for their own regulation; and, by the 10 Anne, for the building of fifty new churches within the bills of mortality, it is enacted, " that the parish clerks of such new erected churches shall be members of the company or corporation of the clerks of the parish churches within the city, and suburbs, and liberties of London, Westminster, and Southwark, and the fifteen out parishes named in the letters patent of the said corporation; and shall make weekly and yearly accounts of the churchings and burials happening in their parishes; and shall, in all respects, be subject to the rules and orders of the said company."

False Entry as to Marriages.] A parish clerk who deceives the clergyman, to make a false entry of the due publication of banns, when none have been published, commits thereby a very serious offence, and may be indicted for the same as a felon; and, if found guilty, transported for life. (See 52 G. 3. c. 146. s. 14; 4 G. 4. c. 76. s. 29.) And, if he make a false entry himself, he is equally guilty, and liable to the same punishment.

Embezzling Alms.] The parish clerk is in some places employed, upon the occasion of administering the Lord's supper, to collect the alms from the communicants; and the purloining or embezzling any portion of the money so received is, doubtless, punishable as a crime; though it seems, from the following case, that he cannot be considered as a *servant* to, nor the money so taken as the *property* of, the minister and churchwardens, or either of them. But these objections would have less force against an indictment at common law, and the offence may be so charged as to ensure conviction and punishment, where the facts are fully established. The case is as follows:

John Burton was tried at the Summer Assizes for the county of Derby, 1829, before Lord Tenterden, and the indictment stated,

That the prisoner on, &c., was employed in the capacity of a *servant* by Richard Wilmot, clerk; and, being employed, did, on, &c., by virtue of such employment, receive into his possession certain money: to wit, two half-crowns in the name, and on account of the said R W; and having so received the said money, did, then and there, fraudulently embezzle the same; and so the indictment concluded, that the prisoner did, on, &c., feloniously steal the said money against the statute, and against the peace, &c.

The second count was similar, only stating the prisoner to be servant to A B and C D. The third similar, only stating the prisoner to be servant to R W and A B and C D. The fourth count was like the first, but stating also that the half-crowns were the *property of* R W. The fifth count was like the second, stating the property in A B and C D. And the sixth, and last, count was like the third, laying the property in R W and A B and C D.

At the trial it appeared, that the Reverend Richard Wilmot, was the curate, and the prisoner parish clerk, of the parish of Chattesden, in Derbyshire; that, on the Sunday mentioned in the indictment, the sacrament was administered in the church, and R W was the minister who performed the church service. The prisoner, on that occasion, carried round the plate to receive the oblations of the communicants; and two half-crowns were, among other monies, put into the plate; which two half-crowns the prisoner fraudulently took out of the plate, and they were afterwards found in his pocket. No specific directions were, on the day in question, given to the prisoner to carry round the plate; but that service had been usually performed by the parish clerk, for the time being, and the prisoner had been parish clerk several years, and as such had performed that service. A B and C D were churchwardens of the parish.—It was objected on behalf of the prisoner,

First, that as there was no proof of the relation of master and servant, having existed between the prisoner and the minister or churchwardens, or both, before the employment in question, that the employment proved, was not of itself sufficient to constitute such relation; and therefore, that the allegation, that he had received the money as a *servant*, was not made out.

Secondly, that the *property* had not been described rightly; that there was no ground whatever for laying it in the minister alone, or the churchwardens alone; and that though the minister, jointly with the churchwardens, had a right to the uistribution of the oblations, yet they had a mere power of appointment; and no property therein, even as trustees; for that in case of their not agreeing, the right devolved upon the ordinary. (See *Alms for the Poor, post* 106.)

The facts of the case were clearly made out by the evidence, and the prisoner was found guilty. Lord Tenterden, without expressing any decided opinion upon the objections taken to the form of the indictment, passed sentence upon the prisoner; stating, at the same time, that he should reserve the objections which had been urged in his favour for the consideration of another tribunal; accordingly, in the following term, the judges met in the Exchequer Chamber, and his lordship then reported the case for their determination. No counsel attended to argue the objections; but it was held by the learned judges, that the prisoner could not be considered as a person employed or entrusted in the capacity of a *servant* to the minister, or to the churchwardens, or either of them, to receive money for, or on account of them, or either of them, as laid in the indictment; and that, therefore, the conviction was wrong. (Michas. Term, 1829.)

This case will, at least, clear away some of the difficulties which were supposed to stand in the way of a prosecution for an offence of this nature. The popular notion, that it is necessary, in all cases, where a person is accused of having obtained the possession of property by crime or dishonesty, that it should be alleged that the property belonged to some *particular and known* person or persons is not correct; and, in the above instance, if the indictment had been for stealing *from the plate*, at common law, it might have sufficed, had the allegation of ownership been omitted. (See 7 & 8 G. 4. c. 29. s. 44; Hickman & Dyer's case, Leach. 358.)

Gains a Settlement.] Serving the office of parish clerk for a year gains a settlement, although he be chosen by the parson and not the parishioners, and have no license from the ordinary; and although he be a certificate man. (1 Salk. 536; 2 Str. 942; 2 Sess. Cas. 182.)

SECTION VII.—SEXTON.

How chosen.] The sexton (*segsten, segerstane,* the keeper of the things belonging to divine worship) is usually chosen by the parish, though sometimes by the minister, where an usage to that effect prevails. His salary depends upon custom, and is paid by the churchwardens. His fees are generally settled by order of the vestry, and a table of them is hung up in the vestry room, or in the church. (Shaw, Par. L. 71.)

Duty of Sexton.] His business is to keep the church clean swept and adorned; to open the pews; to make and fill up the graves for the dead; and to provide, under the direction of the churchwardens, candles and necessaries belonging to the church; to get the linen washed, &c.; to attend during divine service; to keep out excommunicated persons; and to prevent any disturbance in the church. (Ib.)

A Freehold Office.] Sextons are considered by the common law to have freeholds in their offices; and therefore, if they be improperly removed, or for alleged misconduct, a mandamus lies to restore them; (Rex v. Kingscleere, 2 Lev. 18; Salk. 428. Ile's case, 1 Ventr. 153;) for though they may be *punished* they cannot be *deprived* by ecclesiastical censures. (2 Roll. Ab. 234; Bac. Ab. Mandamus, (C.)

But a return to a mandamus that L. C. was not duly elected sexton, according to the ancient custom, and that there is a custom for the inhabitants to remove *at pleasure,* and that L. C. was removed pursuant to such custom, is good. (Rex v. Churchwarden of Taunton, 1 Cowp. 413.) So upon a return to a mandamus, that the sexton held his office *at pleasure,* the court decided this to be sufficient, as there was no certificate that he was chosen for life. (Rex v. the Churchwardens of Thame, 1 Stra. 115.)

Female Sexton.] In the case of Olive v. Ingram, (Stra. 1114,) two points were made: First, whether a woman was capable of being chosen sexton; and, secondly, whether women could vote in the election. As to the first, the court seemed to have no difficulty about it; there having been many cases where offices of greater consequence have been held by women, and there being many women sextons at that time in London. The authorities cited upon this point were—Spelman's Gloss. 497, a woman appointed governor of Chelmsford workhouse, (2 Ld. Raym. 1014;) Lady Broughton's case, who was keeper of the Gatehouse, (3 Keb. 32; 4 Inst. 221; Dy. 285; Hob. 148.) And in Brady's "History of Boroughs" it appears, that Lady Parkington was returning officer for members at Aylesbury; and the Countess of Pembroke, Dorset, and Montgomery, had the office of hereditary sheriff of Westmoreland, and exercised it in person, sitting with the judges on the bench at the assizes at Appleby. (Har. Co. Lit. 326.)

Female Electors.] As to the second point, though women cannot vote for members of Parliament or coroners, yet the court, notwithstanding, held, that this being an office that did not concern the public, or the care and inspection of the morals of the parishioners, there was no reason to exclude women who paid rates from the privilege of voting; and no usage of excluding them was stated which might have altered the case. (Id. ib.)

United Parishes.] Where two parishes were united after the fire of London, and one set of officers, elected at a joint vestry, had served for both, and the office of sexton had been filled in the same way upon nine successive vacancies, and the salary had been paid in equal proportions by both parishes, but afterwards one of the parishes claimed to elect a *separate* sexton, of which they had given notice to the other; in such case, that other parish cannot maintain an action for money paid to the use of the first parish for their quota of the sexton's salary; for this was paid against their *express consent.* Nor can the right of the sexton be tried in such case without his being a party thereto; nor can he bring his action in such case against both parishes on a *joint* obligation, or against one of them only for the *whole* sum. (Stokes v. Lewis, 1 T. R. 20.)

Divided Parishes.] In the recent statutes for the erection of additional churches, provision is made for the protection of the interests of sextons in those cases where it is found expedient to create new parishes. The 59 G. 4. c. 134. s. 10, enacts, that when any parish shall be divided under the provisions of those acts, all fees, dues, profits, and emoluments, belonging to the parish clerk or sexton respectively of any such parish, which shall thereafter arise in any district or division of any parish so divided, shall belong and be recoverable by the clerks and sextons respectively of *each division* to which they shall be assigned in like manner, and after the same rate as they were recoverable by the clerk and sexton respectively of the original parish; and the commissioners may make compensation for any loss of fees or emoluments which any clerk or sexton may sustain by reason of any such division.

Gains a Settlement.] The office of sexton, like that of parish clerk, confers a right of settlement; and if the churchyard lie in *two* parishes, the sexton may gain a settlement in the one in which he resides, although no part of the church lies within that parish. (Rex v. Liverpool, 3 T. R. 118.)

Church Keys.] In a case where, after a contested election for the office of sexton, an application was made for a mandamus to deliver up the keys of the church to the successful candidate, Lord Ellenborough said, "Why did they not get new keys. The keys of the church are not like an emblem of office, or the like. If it will probably prevent any breach of the peace, we will grant it; but you had better get a new key." (2 Chitty, R. 255.)

SECTION VIII.—BEADLE.

Nature of Office.] Beadle (in the Saxon *bydel* from *beodan*, to bid) signifies, generally, a crier or messenger of a court.

How chosen.—Duty.] The beadle of a parish is chosen by the vestry; and his business is to attend the vestry, and give notice to the parishioners when and where it is to meet; to execute its orders as messenger or servant; to assist the constable in taking up beggars, passing vagrants, &c.; for which latter purpose he is sometimes inserted among the overseers of the poor, &c. (Shaw, Par. L. c. 19; 4 Burn. Ec. L. 10.)

His appointment is during pleasure; and he may be dismissed for misconduct, at any time, by the parishioners in vestry assembled.

How far a Peace-Officer.] In some of the wards in the city of London it is customary to swear in the beadle as constable also; and it seems, that whether he has this additional office cast upon him or not, he may, in common with watchmen, by the common law, arrest and detain in prison, for examination, persons *walking the streets* at night, whom there is reasonable ground to *suspect of felony*, without any proof of a felony having been actually committed. (Lawrence v. Hedger, 4 Taunt. 14.) But, unless he is regularly sworn as a peace-officer, he is not entitled, generally, to act as such; and he cannot, in that character, receive into his custody a person charged with a breach of the peace, or other offence. (Cliffe v. Littlemore, 5 Esp. 39.)

CHAPTER IV.—SACRAMENTS.

SECTION I.—THE LORD'S SUPPER.

Number of Sacraments.] There are but two sacraments ordained in the gospel: that is to say, the supper of the Lord, and baptism; but to these have been added five others, commonly so called, viz. confirmation, penance, extreme unction, orders, and matrimony. (3 Burn. Ec. L. 324.) The first two and the last are all that will be treated of in this place.

The Lord's Supper.] The ecclesiastical authorities of earlier times were duly solicitous to have the sacred rite of the Lord's supper administered frequently, and to as large a number of communicants as could be obtained, without admitting those who were unfitted to be received by crimes of a heinous nature,—notorious evil living,—oppression of their neighbours,—or reciprocally cherished malice and hatred. And the churchwardens, as well as the minister, were required, by canon 28, to mark the absentee parishioners from this holy communion. And also, within forty days after Easter, to report the names to the bishop or his chancellor, of all parishioners, men and women, being of the age of sixteen years, receiving not the communion the Easter before. (Canon 112.)

How often Administered.] By the ancient canon law, lay parishioners, qualified by their goodly living, were required to communicate at *least* thrice in the year: viz. at Easter, Whitsuntide, and Christmas; and the secular clergy, not communicating at these times, were not to be reckoned among Catholics. (Gibs. 387.)

And all deans, heads of cathedrals and collegiate churches, vicars, petty canons, and all others of the foundation, shall receive the communion four times in the year, at the least. (Canon 24.)

Notice given.] The minister is to give notice on the Sunday, or on some holiday immediately preceding; and those who intend to be partakers shall signify their intention some time the day before the communion. But if there be not a convenient number to communicate, there shall be no celebration; and there must be four, or three at the least, even where the parish contains no more than twenty persons qualified to receive the communion. (2 Burn. Ec. L. 425.)

Where administered.] In all churches, convenient and decent communion tables being provided, they must be kept in a seemly condition, covered, in time of divine service, with a carpet of silk, or other decent stuff; and, at the time of ministration, they should be covered with a fair linen cloth; at which time the table shall be placed in so good sort within the church or chancel, as thereby the minister may be more conveniently heard, and the greater number of communicants may be accommodated. (Canon 82.) And it is forbidden to administer the holy communion in private houses, except in times of necessity, to the dangerously sick and impotent. But this prohibition does not extend to the *chapels* of private houses, allowed by the ecclesiastical law. (Canon 71.)

Bread and Wine provided.] The churchwardens are to provide a sufficient quantity of fine white bread, and of good wholesome wine, with the advice of the minister; and although, in the case of Franklyn v. the Master and Brethren of St. Cross, the vicar, by the endowment, was to find the sacrament wine, yet the court were of opinion that it should be found by the parish, according to the canon or *rubric*, which is established by act of parliament. (Bunb. 79; 2 Burn. Ec. L. 427.) And if any remain unconsecrated, the curate shall have it to his own use; but the surplus of that which was consecrated shall be eat and drank, after the blessing, *in the church*, by the priests and such communicants as he shall then call unto him.

How administered.] By canon 27, no minister, when he celebrateth the communion, shall wittingly administer the same to any but to such as kneel. But it is declared, that no adoration of the elements is intended or ought to be done, for that were idolatry. And, by the statute 1 Ed. 6. c. 1, it is enacted, that the blessed sacrament be administered unto the people, with the priest, under both the kinds: that is to say, of bread and wine, and not bread only, except necessity require otherwise; as more conformable to the usage of the apostles and the primitive church, than that the priest should receive it alone.

Alms for the Poor.] The ecclesiastical law enjoins the collection of alms for the poor, by the deacons, churchwardens, or other fit persons, during the reading of the offertory; and they are to bring it to the priest, to be disposed of after divine service. The sums thus obtained are to be employed in such pious and charitable uses as the minister and churchwardens shall think fit, or, in case of their disagreement, by the ordinary. (See the last Rubric after the article "Communion" in the Liturgy, and 2 Burn. Ec. L. 427.)

Alms collected in chapels, as well as in parish churches, during the reading of the offertory, are, by direction of the rubric, at the disposal of the incumbent of the parish, and the churchwardens thereof, and not of the minister or proprietors of the chapel. (Moysey v. Hillcoat, 2 Hagg. Rep. N. S. 56.)

Refusing a Communicant.] An action upon the case was brought against a minister for refusing the sacrament to another person; and the jury found for the plaintiff, with damages. And it was moved, in arrest of judgment, that the plaintiff had not set forth in his declaration, that he had given notice according to the statute, nor that he was a parishioner of that parish. But these points seem to have been passed over, as another objection was held fatal; viz. that the plaintiff declared for not administering two Sundays, and had not set forth that, in the second instance, he desired the minister to do it to him; and yet entire damages had been given for both. It was also objected, that this was more properly a matter of spiritual cognizance; upon which also the court gave no opinion. (Clovell v. Cardinall, 1 Sid. 34.)

Penalty for Reviling.] The 1 Ed. 6. c. 1, enacts, that whoever shall deprave, despise, or contemn the Lord's supper, in contempt thereof, by any contemptuous words, or by any words of depraving, despising, or reviling, shall suffer imprisonment of his body; and make fine, and ransom, at the king's will. The information may be laid before *three* justices, upon the oath of two witnesses; and afterwards the accused may be tried at the quarter-sessions; the justices taking bail in the mean time for his appearance. And the justices, at their quarter-sessions, are to issue a writ, requiring the attendance of the bishop or his chancellor at the trial of such person, to *give counsel and advisement* in the matter. Provided, that no person shall be so indicted, but within three months next after the offence committed.

SECTION II.—BAPTISM.

Sponsors.] It is required by the rubric, that there shall be, for every male child to be baptized, two godfathers and one godmother; and, for every female, one godfather and two godmothers. But parents cannot assume this office for their own children. (Canon 29.) The sponsor ought to be of the same station as the person to whom he becomes surety. (Broome. Johns. Dict. "Sponsor.")

Naming the Child.] By a constitution of Archbishop Peccham, the ministers shall take care not to permit wanton names, which, being pronounced, do sound to lasciviousness, to be given to children baptized, especially of the female sex. And if otherwise it be done, the same shall be changed at confirmation. (Lind. 245.) Which, being so changed, shall be deemed the lawful name. (1 Inst. 3.) But now, as the bishop does not pronounce the name of the person to be confirmed, it is said he cannot alter it. (Johns. A. D. 1281. *num.* 3; 1 Burn. Ec. L. 110.) It seems, therefore, doubtful, whether a parent can insist upon the minister baptizing the child, in a name which offends against the above constitution of the archbishop.

Private Baptism.] If the acting minister, being duly informed, without collusion, of the weakness and danger of death of any infant unbaptized in the parish, and being, thereupon, desired to go to its residence to baptize it, shall either refuse, or by gross negligence so defer the time, that it dieth unbaptized through his default, the said minister shall be suspended for three months; and before his restitution, shall acknowledge his fault, and promise, before his ordinary, that he will not wittingly incur the like again. (Canon 69.)

Fees.] No fee is due of *common right* for christening; and where proceedings were taken by the vicar and clerk of the parish against a Frenchman, who had his child christened at the *French* church within the parish, for the recovery of such fees, *Holt*, C. J., said, quoting *Lindwood,* it is simony to take any thing for christening or burying, unless it be a fee due by *custom;* but then a custom for any person to take a fee for christening a child, when he doth not christen him, is not good; if you have a right to christen, you should libel for that right; but you ought not to have money for christening when you do it not. (Bourdeaux v. Lancaster and another, 1 Salk. 332, 12 Mod. 171.)

Papists and Dissenters.] By the 3 Jac. 1. c. 5. s. 14, Popish recusants are required, under a penalty of £100, to cause their children to be baptized by a lawful minister, according to the laws of this realm, within one month after birth; and this must be in the neighbouring church or chapel, where baptism is usually administered, unless prevented by illness. But the liberality of modern times has suffered this harsh provision to become obsolete. And it has been decided, that baptism by Protestant dissenting ministers entitles the party to burial by the church of England. (See tit. "BURIAL;" also REGISTER BOOK.)

SECTION III.—MARRIAGE.

Who may not Intermarry.] It is not intended to detail the various degrees of affinity, either by blood or marriage, within which marriage is prohibited. The subject will be found at large in its more proper place, under title " Marriage," in 2 Burn's Ec. L. (433.)

The prohibited degrees are all those which are under the fourth degree of the civil law, except in the ascending and descending line; and, by the course of nature, it is scarcely a possible case that any one should ever marry his issue in the fourth degree; but, between collaterals, it is universally true, that all who are in the fourth or any higher degree are permitted to marry; as first cousins are in the fourth degree, and therefore may marry; and nephew and great aunt, or niece and great uncle, are also in the fourth degree, and may intermarry; and though a man may not marry his grandmother, it is certainly true that he may marry her sister. (Gibs. Cod. 413.)

The same degrees by affinity are prohibited. Affinity always arises by the marriage of one of the parties so related; as a husband is related by affinity to all the *consanguinei* of his wife; and, *vice versa*, the wife to the husband's *consanguinei*; for the husband and wife being considered one flesh, those who are related to the one by blood are related to the other by affinity. (Gibs. Cod. 42.) Therefore a man, after his wife's death, cannot marry her sister, aunt, or niece, or daughter by a former husband. (2 Phil. Ecc. Ca. 359.) So a woman cannot marry her nephew by affinity, such as her former husband's sister's son. (2 Phil. Ecc. Ca. 18.) So a niece of a wife cannot, after the wife's death, marry the husband. (Noy. Rep. 29.)

But the *consanguinei* of the husband are not at all related to the *consanguinei* of the wife. Hence two brothers may marry two sisters; or father and son, a mother and daughter; or, if a brother and sister marry two persons not related, and the brother and sister die, the widow and widower may intermarry; for though a man is related to his wife's brother by affinity, he is not so to his wife's brother's wife; whom, if circumstances would admit, it would not be unlawful for him to marry. (1 Bla. Com. 435, n.)

Marriage of Jews.] By the ancient law of England, Jews were forbidden to intermarry with Christians, upon pain of death; (3 Inst. 89;) but where both are Jews, their marriage is recognized by the law; and the nullity thereof will be tried by the evidence of the laws of the Jews, as in the case of a foreign marriage. (Lindo v. Belisario, 1 Hagg. Rep. 216.) *Ketuba*, or what a man binds himself to give his wife as a dower, should always precede a Jewish marriage; and *Kedushim*, a betrothment, does not constitute it without *Hupa*, (viz. bringing home the bride, setting her aside for her husband's special use, and being united with her, if marriageable.) The practice among the Jews on marriage is, for the husband to take all the wife's fortune, and to covenant to restore it, with £50. per cent. profit. Choses, in action, falling to the husband in right of the wife, are sometimes taken by him at the same time. (Basevi v. Serra, 3 Meriv. 674; 14 Ves. 313.) Two witnesses to the ceremony are essential, in the Jewish law, to the validity of a marriage; and if such witnesses be incompetent, the marriage is invalid. (Goldsmid v. Bromer, 1 Hagg. Rep. 324.) It also appears, that a Jewish marriage is not sufficiently proved in a civil action, by witnesses present at the ceremony in the synagogue, which is merely a ratification of a previous contract in writing, and that the original contract must be produced. (Flour v. Noel, 1 Comb. 61.) A Jewess married by Christian rites was held within the Marriage Act, requiring consent of parents or guardians. (Jones v. Robinson, 2 Phil. Ec. Ca. 285.)

It is expressly provided by the 31st section of the late Marriage Act, that it shall not extend to marriages where both parties are Quakers, or persons professing the Jewish religion.

The Marriage Act.] The Marriage Act, (4 G. 4. c. 76,) which is a revision of the law as it previously existed, occupied the anxious attention of the legislature for a considerable time; and is sufficiently ample in its details, to render it unnecessary to introduce the various decisions in the spiritual and common law courts, upon questions arising upon the statutes and the canons before that period. The Royal Marriage Act is untouched by the recent statute; and several acts have been passed to confirm the legality of certain antecedent marriages, solemnized under circumstances which left their validity questionable. It can be of no use to refer to them more at large here; the object being to present the law as it now stands, for the guidance in future of those who are interested in its present provisions. The present statute is limited to England, and its enactments are as follow.

Marriages, where solemnized.] It shall and may be lawful for marriages to be, in future, solemnized in all churches and chapels erected since the passing of the 26 G. 2. c. 33, and duly consecrated; in which churches and chapels it has been customary and usual, from the passing of that act, to solemnize marriages: and all marriages hereafter solemnized therein, shall be as good and valid in law as if such marriages had been solemnized in parish churches or public chapels, having chapelries annexed, and wherein banns had usually been published, before or at the time of passing the said act. (6 G. 4. c. 92. s. 2.)

Marriages in Chapels.] The bishop of the diocese, with the consent of the patron and the incumbent of the church of the parish, in which any public chapel, having a chapelry thereunto annexed, may be situated, or of any chapel situated in an extra-parochial place, signified to him under their hands and seals respectively, may authorise, by writing under his hand and seal, the publication of banns and the solemnization of marriages in such chapel, for persons residing within such chapelry or extra-parochial place, respectively; and such consent, together with such written authority, shall be registered in the registry of the diocese. (4 G. 4. c. 76. s. 3.)

Provided, that in every chapel in respect of which such authority shall be given, there shall be placed in some conspicuous part of the interior, notice in the words following: "Banns may be published, and marriages solemnized, at this chapel." (s. 4.)

Parishes having no Church or Chapel.] All parishes where there shall be no parish church or chapel belonging thereto, or none wherein divine service shall be usually solemnized every Sunday, and all extra-parochial places whatever, having no public chapel wherein banns may be lawfully published, shall be deemed and taken to belong to any parish or chapelry next adjoining, for the purposes of this act only; and where banns shall be published in any church or chapel of any parish or chapelry, adjoining to any such parish or chapelry, where there shall be no church or chapel, or none wherein divine service shall be solemnized as aforesaid, or to any extra-parochial place as aforesaid, the parson, vicar, minister, or curate publishing such banns, shall, in writing under his hand, certify the publication thereof, in the same manner as if either of the persons to be married had dwelt in such adjoining parish or chapelry. (s. 12.)

When Church is Rebuilding.] If the church of any parish, or chapel of any chapelry, wherein marriages have been usually solemnized, be demolished in order to be rebuilt, or be under repair, and on such account be disused for public service, it shall be lawful for the banns to be proclaimed in a church or chapel of any adjoining parish or chapelry, in which banns are usually proclaimed, or in any place within the limits of the parish or chapelry, which shall be licensed by the bishop of the diocese for the performance of divine service, during the repair or rebuilding of the church as aforesaid; and where no such place shall be so licensed, then, during such period as aforesaid, the marriage may be solemnized in the adjoining church or chapel, wherein the banns have been proclaimed: and all marriages heretofore solemnized, or *hereafter*, under the like circumstances, (5 G. 4. c. 32. s. 1,) in other places within the said parishes or chapelries than the said churches or chapels, on account of their being under repair, or taken down in order to be rebuilt, shall not be liable to have their validity questioned on that account; nor shall the ministers who have so solemnized the same, be liable to any ecclesiastical censure, or to any other proceeding or penalty whatsoever. (4 G. 4. c. 76. s. 13.)

All banns of marriage proclaimed, and marriages solemnized, according to the provisions of the act, in any place licensed as aforesaid, within the limits of any parish or chapelry, during the repair or rebuilding of the church or chapel of such parish or chapelry, shall be considered as proclaimed and solemnized in the church or chapel of such parish or chapelry, and shall be so registered accordingly. (5 G. 4. c. 32. s. 3.)

Consent of Parent or Guardian.] The father, if living, of any party under twenty-one years of age, such party not being a widower or widow;—or if the father shall be dead, the guardian or guardians of the person of the party so under age, lawfully appointed, or one of them;—and in case there shall be no such guardian or guardians, then the mother of such party, if unmarried;—and if there shall be no mother unmarried, then the guardian or guardians of the person appointed by the Court of Chancery, if any, or one of them;—shall have authority to give consent to the marriage of such party; and such consent is hereby required for the marriage of such party so under age, unless there shall be no person authorised to give such consent. (4 G. 4. c. 76. s. 16.)

Where a marriage was solemnized by license, the man being a minor, whose father was living, and who did not consent to the marriage; it was held that the marriage was nevertheless valid, the above section being directory only. (R. v. Birmingham, 8 Barn. & Cres. 29, 2 Man. & Ryl. 230, Chitty's Statutes, 727.)

Where Parent, &c. Insane.] In case the father or fathers of the parties to be married, or one of them, so under age as aforesaid, shall be *non compos mentis*, or the guardian or guardians, mother or mothers, or any of them, whose consent is made necessary as aforesaid to the marriage of such party or parties, shall be *non compos mentis*, or in parts beyond the seas, or shall unreasonably, or from undue motives refuse or withhold his, her, or their consent to a proper marriage; then it shall and may be lawful for any person desirous of marrying, in any of the before-mentioned cases, to apply by petition to the Lord Chancellor, Lord Keeper, or the Lords Commissioners of the great seal of Great Britain for the time being, Master of the Rolls, or Vice Chancellor of England, who is and are respectively hereby empowered to proceed upon such petition in a summary way; and in case the marriage proposed shall, upon examination, appear to be proper, the said Lord Chancellor, Lord Keeper, or Lords Commissioners of the great seal for the time being, Master of the Rolls, or Vice Chancellor, shall judicially declare the same to be so; and such judicial declaration shall be deemed and taken to be as good and effectual to all intents and purposes, as if the father, guardian or guardians, or mother of the person so petitioning, had consented to such marriage. (4 G. 4. c. 76. s. 17.)

To render a marriage contract valid, the consent of a free and rational agent is an essential ingredient. (Lord Portsmouth's case, 1 Hagg. Rep. N. S. 372.)

Marriage Contracts not enforced.] In no case whatsoever shall any suit or proceedings be had in any ecclesiastical court, in order to compel a celebration of any marriage in *facie ecclesiæ*, by reason of any contract of matrimony whatsoever, whether *per verba de præsenti*, or *per verba de futuro*, any law or usage to the contrary notwithstanding. (4 G. 4. c. 76. s. 27.)

Notice to publish Banns.] No parson, minister, or curate, shall be obliged to publish the banns of matrimony between any persons whatsoever, unless the persons to be married shall, seven days at the least before the time required for the first publication of such banns respectively, deliver or cause to be delivered to such parson, vicar, minister, or curate, a notice in writing, dated on the day on which the same shall be so delivered, of their true Christian names and surnames, and of the house or houses of their respective abodes within such parish or chapelry as aforesaid, and of the time during which they have dwelt, inhabited, or lodged in such house or houses respectively. (Id. s. 7.)

How and when Published.] All banns of matrimony shall be published in an audible manner in the parish church, or in some public chapel,—in which chapel banns of matrimony may now, or may hereafter be lawfully published, of or belonging to such parish or chapelry, wherein the persons to be married shall dwell,—according to the form of words prescribed by the rubric, prefixed to the office of matrimony in the book of Common Prayer, upon three Sundays preceding the solemnization of marriage, during the time of morning service, or of evening service, (if there shall be no morning service in such church or chapel upon the Sunday upon which such banns shall be so published,) immediately after the second lesson. (Id. s. 2.)

Parties not resident in same Parish.] Whensoever it shall happen that the persons to be married shall dwell in divers parishes or chapelries, the banns shall in like manner be published in the church, or in any such chapel as aforesaid, belonging to such parish or chapelry wherein each of the said persons shall dwell; and that all other the rules prescribed by the said rubric, concerning the publication of banns and the solemnization of matrimony, and not hereby altered, shall be duly observed; and that in all cases where banns shall have been published, the marriage shall be solemnized in one of the parish churches or chapels where such banns shall have been published, and in no other place whatsoever. (4 G. 4. c. 76. s. 2.)

Banns of Minors.] No minister, vicar, or curate solemnizing marriages between persons, both or one of whom shall be under the age of twenty-one years after banns published, shall be punishable by ecclesiastical censures for solemnizing such marriages without consent of parents or guardians; unless such parson, minister, vicar, or curate shall have notice of the dissent of such parents or guardians; and in case such parents or guardians, or one of them, shall openly and publicly declare, or cause to be declared, in the church or chapel where the banns shall be so published, at the time of such publication, his, her, or their dissent to such marriage, such publication of banns shall be absolutely void. (Id. s. 8.)

Republication of Banns.] Whenever a marriage shall not be had within three months after the complete publication of banns, no minister shall proceed to the solemnization of the same, until the banns shall have been republished on three several Sundays, in the form and manner prescribed in this act, unless by license duly obtained according to the provisions of this act. (s. 9.)

Register of Banns.] It is also provided, that the churchwardens and chapelwardens of churches and chapels wherein marriages are solemnized, shall provide a proper book of substantial paper, marked and ruled respectively, in manner directed, for the register-book of marriages; and the banns shall be published from the said register-book of banns by the officiating minister, and not from loose papers; and after publication, shall be signed by the officiating minister, or by some person under his direction. (Id. s. 6.)

Marriage by License.] No license of marriage shall be granted by any archbishop, bishop, or person having authority to grant such licenses, to solemnize any marriage in any other church or chapel than in the parish church, or in some public chapel of or belonging to the parish or chapelry, within which the usual place of abode of one of the persons to be married shall have been, for the space of fifteen days immediately before the granting of such license. (Id. s. 10.)

Caveat against License.] If any caveat be entered against the grant of any license for a marriage, such caveat being duly signed by, or on the behalf of, the person who enters the same, together with his place of residence, and the ground of objection on which his caveat is founded, no license shall issue till the said caveat, or a true copy thereof, be transmitted to the judge, out of whose office the license is to issue; and until the judge has certified to the register that he has examined into the matter of the caveat, and is satisfied that it ought not to obstruct the grant of the license for the said marriage; or until the caveat be withdrawn by the party who entered the same. (Id. s. 11.)

Oath before License granted.] For avoiding all fraud and collusion in obtaining licenses, one of the parties shall personally swear before the surrogate, or other person having authority to grant the license, that he or she believeth that there is no impediment of kindred or alliance, or of any other lawful cause, nor any suit commenced in any ecclesiastical court, to bar or hinder the proceeding of the said matrimony, according to the tenor of the said license; and that one of the said parties hath, for the space of fifteen days immediately preceding such license, had his or her usual place of abode within the parish or chapelry within which such marriage is to be solemnized; and where either of the parties, not being a widower or widow, shall be nnder the age of twenty-one years, that the consent of the person or persons, whose consent to such marriage is required under the provisions of this act, has been obtained thereto: provided always, that if there shall be no such person or persons having authority to give such consent, then upon oath made to that effect, by the party requiring such license, it shall be lawful to grant such license, notwithstanding the want of any such consent. (Id. s. 14.)

When new License necessary.] Whenever a marriage shall not be had, within three months after the grant of a license, by any archbishop, bishop, or any ordinary or person having authority to grant such license, no minister shall proceed to the solemnization of such marriage, until a new license shall have been obtained; unless by banns duly published, according to the provisions of this act.

Where License extends.] And that all licenses shall extend to *any place*, within the limits of such parish or chapelry, which shall be licensed by the bishop, for the performance of divine service, during the repair or rebuilding of any church or chapel; or if no such place shall be so licensed, then to the church or chapel of any adjoining parish or chapelry, wherein marriages have been usually solemnized. (5 G. 4. c. 32. s. 2.)

Special Licenses.] Nothing hereinbefore contained shall be construed to extend to deprive the Archbishop of Canterbury, and his successors, and his and their proper officers, of the right which hath hitherto been used in virtue of a certain statute, made in the twenty-fifth year of the reign of the late king Henry the Eighth, intituled *An Act concerning Peter Pence and Dispensations,* of granting special licenses to marry at any convenient time or place. (4 G. 4. c. 76. s. 20.)

Marriage falsely procured.] If any valid marriage, solemnized by license, shall after the said 1st day of November next, be procured by a party to such marriage, to be solemnized between persons, one or both of whom shall be under the age of twenty-one years, not being a widower or widow, contrary to the provisions of this act, by means of such party falsely swearing as to any matter or matters to which such party is hereinbefore required personally to swear, such party wilfully and knowingly so swearing; or if any valid marriage by banns shall, after the said 1st day of November next, be procured by a party thereto, to be solemnized by banns between persons, one or both of whom shall be under the age of twenty-one years, not being a widower or widow, such party knowing that such person as aforesaid, under the age of twenty-one years, had a parent or guardian then living, and that such marriage was had without the consent of such parent or guardian, and knowing that banns had not been duly published, according to the provisions of this act, and having knowingly caused or procured the undue publication of banns, then, and in every such case, it shall be lawful for his Majesty's attorney-general, (or for his Majesty's solicitor-general, in case of the vacancy of the office of attorney-general,) by information, in the nature of an English bill, in the Court of Chancery or Court of Exchequer, at the relation of a parent or guardian of the minor, whose consent has not been given to such marriage, and who shall be responsible for any costs incurred in such suit, such parent or guardian previously making oath as hereinafter required, to sue for a forfeiture of all estate, right, title, and interest, in any property which hath accrued or shall accrue to the party so offending, by force of such marriage. (Id. s. 23.)

Property guarded from the Offender.] And thereupon, the court may order and direct that all such estate, right, title, and interest in any property as shall have then accrued, or shall thereafter accrue to such offending party, by force of such marriage, shall be secured under the direction of such court, for the benefit of the innocent party, or of the issue of the marriage, or of any of them, in such manner as the said court shall think fit, for the purpose of preventing the offending party from deriving any interest in real or personal estate, or pecuniary benefits from such marriage; and if both the parties so contracting marriage shall, in the judgment of the court, be guilty of any such offence as aforesaid, it shall be lawful for the said court to settle and secure such property, or any part thereof, immediately for the benefit of the issue of the marriage, subject to such provisions, for the offending parties by way of maintenance, or otherwise, as the said court, under the particular circumstances of the case, shall think reasonable; regard being had to the benefit of the issue of the marriage during the lives of their parents, and of the issue of the parties respectively by any future marriage, or of the parties themselves, in case either of them shall survive the other. (Id. s. 23.)

Oath before proceedings taken.] But no such information as aforesaid shall be filed, unless it shall be made out to the satisfaction of the attorney or solicitor-general, before he files the same, by oath or oaths, sworn before one of the masters in ordinary in Chancery, or before one of the barons of the Exchequer, and which they are hereby respectively empowered to administer, that the valid marriage to be complained of in such information, hath been solemnized in such manner, and under such circumstances, as, in the judgment of the said attorney or solicitor-general, are sufficient to authorize the filing the information under the provisions of this act; and that such marriage has been solemnized without the consent of the party or parties, at whose relation such information is proposed to be filed, or of any other parent or guardian of the minor married, to the knowledge or belief of the relator or relators so making oath; and that such relator or relators had not known or discovered that such marriage had been solemnized more than three months previous to his or their application to the attorney or solicitor-general. (Id. s. 23.)

When prior Settlements void.] All agreements, settlements, and deeds, entered into and executed by the parties to any marriage, in consequence of or in relation to which marriage such information as aforesaid shall be filed, or by either of the said parties before and in contemplation of such marriage, or after such marriage, for the benefit of the parties, or either of them, or their issue, so far as the same shall be contrary to, or inconsistent with the provisions of such security and settlement as shall be made by or under the direction of such court as aforesaid, under the authority of this act, shall be absolutely void, and have no force or effect. (s. 24.)

Limit of adverse Proceedings.] Provided always, that any original information to be filed for the purpose of obtaining a declaration of any such forfeiture as aforesaid, shall be filed within one year after the solemnization of the marriage by which such forfeiture shall have been incurred, and shall be prosecuted with due diligence; and in case any person or necessary party to any such information shall abscond, or be or continue out of England, it shall be lawful for the court, in which such information shall be filed, to order such person to appear to such information, and answer the same within such time as to such court shall seem fit, and to cause such order to be served on such person at any place out of England, or to cause such order to be inserted in the London Gazette, and such other British and foreign newspapers as to such court shall seem proper; and in default of such person appearing and answering such information within the time to be limited as aforesaid, to order such information to be taken as confessed by such person, and to proceed to make such decree or order upon such information, as such court might have made if such person had appeared to and answered such information: provided always that in case the person at whose relation any such suit shall have been instituted shall die pending such suit, it shall be lawful for the Court of Chancery, if such court shall see fit, to appoint a proper person, or proper persons, at whose relation such suit may be continued. (s. 25.)

Unduly solemnizing,—felony.] If any person shall, from and after the said first day of November, solemnize matrimony in any other place than a church, or such public chapel wherein banns may be lawfully published, or at any other time than between the hours of eight and twelve in the forenoon, unless by special license from the Archbishop of Canterbury, or shall solemnize matrimony without due publication of banns, unless license of marriage be first had and obtained from some person or persons having authority to grant the same, or if any person falsely pretending to be in holy orders shall solemnize matrimony, according to the rights of the church of England, every person knowingly and wilfully so offending, and being lawfully convicted thereof, shall be deemed and adjudged to be guilty of felony, and shall be transported for the space of fourteen years, according to the laws in force for transportation of felons: provided that all prosecutions for such felony shall be commenced within the space of three years after the offence committed. (s. 21.)

Pecuniary Penalties.] And by the 7 and 8 W. 3. c. 35, every parson, vicar, or curate, who shall marry any persons without license, or due publication of banns, or suffer any other minister to do so, in the church or chapel to such parson, &c. pertaining, shall forfeit 100*l.*; (ss. 2, 3;) and the man so married shall forfeit 10*l.*; and the sexton or clerk officiating on the occasion shall also forfeit £5, to be recovered with costs by him who shall sue for the same; (s. 4;) and the man and woman are also liable to be proceeded against in the Ecclesiastical Court. (Middleton et Ux v. Croft, 2 Stra. 1056; 2 Atk. 650.)

Void Marriages.] If any person shall knowingly and wilfully intermarry in any other place than a church, or such public chapel wherein banns may be lawfully published, unless by special license as aforesaid, or shall knowingly and wilfully intermarry without due publication of banns, or license from a person or persons having authority to grant the same, first had and obtained; or shall knowingly and wilfully consent to, or acquiesce in the solemnization of such marriage, by any person not being in holy orders; the marriages of such persons shall be null and void to all intents and purposes whatsoever. (4 G. 4. c. 76. s. 22.)

But where the marriage of a female pauper was brought about by the fraud of parish officers, the marriage was held valid, and it was also held that the fraud did not prevent her from acquiring a settlement by the marriage in the husband's parish. (R. v. Birmingham, 8 Barn. & Cres. 29; 2 Man. & Hy. 230.)

Marriage Fees.] No fee is due to the clergyman of *common right* for performing the marriage ceremony, although it is said in the rubric in the office of matrimony, that at the time of delivering the ring, the man shall also lay down the accustomed duty to the priest and clerk. But it may become payable by custom, upon performance of the duty. And it has been said, that as by ancient custom the marriage ought to take place where the woman was a parishioner, the ecclesiastical law allows a fee, due to the curate of that parish, whether she be married there or not; but this custom has been declared unreasonable, and cannot be supported. (Thompson v. Davenport, Lutw. 1059. See Naylor v. Scott, Ld. Raym. 1558; 3 Bla. Com. 90.)

Pauper Marriages.] The practice, which prevails to a considerable extent among parish officers, of assisting paupers, or indigent persons, between whom an illicit intercourse has ubsisted, to marry, though adopted in many cases from very proper motives, is of questionable policy. The parties, or at least one of them is constrained to enter into the contract, as the means of escaping from the immediate thraldom of a prison; or as the preferable alternative, to binding himself to payments which he feels he cannot make, and will merely put off the hour of his incarceration. The comfort and respectability of the individuals so united, has but a precarious foundation in such cases; and it may be doubted whether any salutary effect is produced upon public morals, among the lower classes of society, by such marriages.

It is presumed to be undeniable, that the money advanced on these occasions is a misapplication of the parish funds; and that if objected to on passing the overseers' accounts, such items must be disallowed. The question has never yet, it is believed, been before the superior courts; but it can hardly be said that expenses so incurred are for the relief of the poor, or can be classed among any of the objects to which those funds are by law applicable. The ordinary inducement with overseers, in these cases, is to protect their funds from a threatened incumbrance; but they may so conduct themselves, upon such occasions, as to become liable to an indictment for a conspiracy, to cast the burden upon another parish.

Conspiracy to marry Paupers.] Several cases have occurred in which the conspiring and contriving, by sinister means, to marry a pauper of one parish to a settled inhabitant of another, in order to bring a charge upon it, has been considered an indictable offence. (Rex v. Tarrant, 4 Burr. 2106; Rex v. Herbert and others, 1 East. P. C. c. 11. s. 11. p. 461; Rex v. Compton and others, Cald. 246, Mod. 320.) It is observed respecting a conspiracy of this kind, that considering the offence as a prostitution of the sacred rites of marriage, for corrupt and mercenary purposes; and that, by artful and sinister means, persons are seduced into a connexion for life without any inclination of their own, and contrary to that freedom of choice which is peculiarly required in forming so close an union, and on which the happiness of them both so entirely depends; and this for the sake of some gain or saving to others, who bring about such marriage; in this light it seems a fit ground for criminal cognizance, not only as being a great oppression upon the parties themselves, more immediately interested, but as an offence against society in general; being an abuse of that institution by which society is best continued and legal descents preserved, and a perversion of the purposes for which it was ordained. (1 East. P. C. c. 11. s. 11. p. 461.) But in a case where, upon an indictment against parish officers for a conspiracy of this kind, it appeared, that a man of one parish having gotten a woman with child belonging to another, the defendants had agreed with the man, (who was of the age of twenty-nine,) with the approbation of his father, to give him two guineas if he would marry the woman; and that he afterwards married her on such condition, and received the money from the defendants immediately after the marriage; and it was also sworn, both by the man and the woman, that they were willing to marry at the time; Buller, J., directed an acquittal, notwithstanding the proof of the money having been given to procure such consent, and this after the putative father had been taken up under a magistrate's warrant, and was in custody of the overseers. And that learned judge held it necessary, in support of such an indictment, to show that the defendants had made use of some violence, threat, or contrivance, or used some sinister means, to procure the marriage without the voluntary consent or inclination of the parties themselves; and that the act of marriage, being in itself lawful, a conspiracy to procure it could only amount to a crime by the practice of some undue means. (Rex v. Fowler and others, cor Buller, J., Taunton, Spr. Ass. 1788; 1 East. P. C. c. 11. s. 11. p. 461.) And the learned Judge said, that this point had been so ruled several times by several judges.

Form of Indictment.] In a case where the indictment stated the marriage to have been procured by threats and menaces against the peace, &c., it was holden to be sufficient, without averring in terms, that the marriage was against the will or consent of the parties, though that must be proved. (R. v. Parkhouse and Tremlet, cor Buller, J., Exeter Sum. Ass. 1792; 1 East. P. C. c. 11. s. 11. p. 462.)

Upon an indictment for conspiring together, and giving the husband money to marry a poor helpless woman who was an *inhabitant* of B, in order to settle her in the parish of A, where the husband was settled, judgment was arrested; because it was not averred that she was last legally settled in B. (Rex v. Edwards and others, 8 Mod. 320.) But it is observed, that it seems to be perfectly immaterial where the woman's settlement was, if it were *not* in A, provided that fact distinctly appeared. (1 East. P. C. c. 11. s. 11. p. 462.) It is further said, however, that it is usual to aver the settlements of the parties in their respective parishes, and also that the woman was chargeable to her own parish at the time; though this latter had never been adjudged to be necessary, nor seems to be required according to the general rules which govern the offence of conspiracy. (Id. ibid.) It should seem, that in such cases, both the purpose and the means used are clearly unlawful. (2 Russell on Crimes, 561.)

Certificate of Marriage.] By the 6 & 7 W. 3. c. 12. s. 2, and 55 G. 3. c. 184, Sched. Part. I. tit. *Certificate of Marriage*, for every certificate of marriage (except the marriage of any common seaman, soldier, or marine) shall be paid a stamp duty of 5*s*. And if any person shall write such certificate upon the same before it be stamped, he shall forfeit £5. (6 & 7 W. 3. c. 12. s. 7. see MARRIAGE REGISTER, *post.* 126.)

Foreign Marriages.] Marriages of British subjects *in foreign countries* are valid, if made according to the laws of those countries.

(Herbert v. Herbert, 1 Roper, 337; The King v. The Inhabitants of Brampton, 10 East, 282; Lantour and P. v. Teesdale and another, 2 Marsh, 243; Lacon v. Higgins and another, 1 Dowl. & Ryl. N. P. Rep. 38.) So a marriage in Ireland, performed by a clergyman of the church of England in a private house, was held valid, although no evidence was given that any license had been granted to the parties. (Smith v. Maxwell, Ryan. & Moody. N. P. Rep. 80; 1 Car. & P. 271.)

CHAP. V.—PARISH BOOKS.

SECTION I. *Parish Registers.*
II. *Parish Library.*
III. *Rate Books, &c.*

SECTION I.—PARISH REGISTERS.

When Registries began.] The very important practice of keeping a church book for the purpose of recording the birth, or, more properly speaking, the date of the christening of all children who underwent that ceremony, and of the death and burial of those who were committed to the grave in the parish, began in the thirtieth year of King Henry the 8th, by the instigation of Lord Cromwell, who at that time, as vicar-general to the king, was vested with all the power that the pope's legates formerly had. As all wills that were above two hundred pounds value, were to be proved in his court, it obviously became a matter of great consequence, to set on foot a register of all persons born, and of all who were buried, in the parish; in order that this rule, with respect to the proof of wills, might be enforced. The duty of keeping such book, and the mode of making the entries, was further enforced by the canon law, in the reigns of Edw. 6 and Queen Elizabeth. (See Bac. Abr. Evidence (F.) 3 Godb. 144; 3 Burnet, 139.)

To be kept by the Minister.] By 6 and 7 W. 3. c. 6. s. 24, every person in holy orders (including bishops, 9 and 10 W 3. c. 35. s. 4) shall within their respective parishes and places, take an exact account, and keep a register of every person married, christened, or born therein, or buried in the common burying places where parishioners are buried; to view which register, all parties concerned shall have free access at seasonable times, without fee; and every minister who shall not keep a true register thereof, as above, shall forfeit £100, recoverable in any court at Westminster, by action of debt or information, without essoin, &c. to go in moieties to his Majesty and the party suing, with full costs to the latter.

And now, by 52 G. 3. c. 146, "*For better regulating and preserving parish and other registers of births, baptisms, marriages, and burials in England,*" it is enacted, that after 31st Dec. 1812, registers of public and private baptisms, marriages, and burials, solemnized according to the rites of the united church of England and Ireland, within all parishes or chapelries in England, whether subject to the ordinary, peculiar, or other jurisdiction, shall be kept by the rector, vicar, curate, or officiating minister of every parish, or of any chapelry where baptisms, marriages, and burials, have usually been performed (s. 1.)

Form of Entries.] The registration is to be in books of parchment, if required by the church or chapelwardens, (s. 2.) of durable paper, to be provided by his Majesty's printer, at the expense of the parish or chapelry; whereon shall be printed, on each side of every leaf, the heads of information herein required to be entered in the registers of baptisms, marriages, and burials respectively; and every such entry shall be numbered progressively, from beginning to the end of each book, and being divided from the next entry by a printed line, according to the forms in schedules A. B. C. (see *post.* 125) every page being numbered progressively at the middle of the top. (s. 1.)

Separate Books.] There shall be a separate book for baptisms, another for marriages, and another for burials, and they shall be respectively proportioned to the population of the several parishes and chapelries according to the last returns; and other like books shall, when necessary, be furnished by the church or chapelwardens, at the expense of the parish, &c. whenever required by the rector, &c. or officiating minister. (s. 2.)

Entries of Baptism or Burial.] Such pastor, &c., or officiating minister, shall, as soon as possible (and never later than seven days, unless prevented by sickness or unavoidable impediment) after the solemnization of every private or public baptism, or burial, enter, in a legible hand-writing in the proper register-book, the required particulars, and sign the same. (s. 3.)

Baptisms, &c. not in Parish Church.] Whenever the ceremony of baptism or burial is performed in any other place than the church or churchyard of a parish; or chapel, or chapel-yard of any chapelry, providing its own distinct registers; by any other minister than the rector, curate, &c., thereof, the minister performing the same shall, on that or the next day, transmit to such rector, &c., or his curate, a certificate of such baptism or burial as in schedule D.; (see *post.* 126;) who shall thereupon enter the same in such book, adding to such entry, "According to the certificate of the Rev. ———, transmitted to me on the — day of ——," &c. (52 G. 3. c. 146. s. 4.)

Custody of Register Books.] The above books of entries, and all register-books heretofore in use, shall belong to every such parish or chapelry, and shall be safely kept by the rector, &c., in a dry, well-painted iron chest, at the expense of the parish, &c.; and which shall be constantly kept locked in some dry and safe place in his house, if resident within the parish, &c., or in the church or chapel; and shall not be removed therefrom, except for making the above entries, and for inspection of persons desirous to search the same, or to obtain copies thereof, or to be produced as evidence in some court, or for inspection into their state, or for the purposes of this act; and immediately after shall be forthwith returned into the chest. (s. 5.)

Copy to be made on Parchment.] At the expiration of two months after every year's end, fair copies of all the entries of baptisms, marriages, and burials, solemnized in the year preceding, shall be made by the officiating minister (or church or chapelwarden's clerk, or other person under his direction,) on parchment, (as in the said schedules,) to be provided by the parishes; and the contents thereof shall be verified by the declaration of such minister, fairly written, without stamp, on the said copy, immediately after the last entry therein, and his signature thereto shall be attested by one, at least, of the church or chapelwardens. (s. 6.)

Copies for Registrar of Diocese.] Copies of such register-books, verified and attested as above, shall be transmitted by the church or chapelwardens, after having been signed by one of them, by the post, to the registrars of the diocese, on or before 1st June in each year. (s. 7.)

Report herein to the Bishop.] The registrar of every diocese in England shall, on or before 1st July in each year, make a report to the bishop, whether such copies have been sent to him, as in ss. 6, 7, is required, and the registrar shall specially state the default herein of any parish, in his report to the bishop. (s. 9.)

In extra-parochial Places.] In all cases of baptism or burial, in any extra-parochial place in England, according to the established church, where there is no church or chapel, the officiating minister shall, within one month after such baptism or burial, deliver to the rector, vicar, or curate of such parish, immediately adjoining to such extra-parochial place, as the ordinary shall direct, a memorandum of such baptism, signed by such parent of the child baptized, or of such burial, signed by the parson employed therein, with two of the persons attending the same, as the case may require, containing the particulars hereinbefore required; which memorandum, so delivered, shall be entered in the parish register. (s. 10.)

All letters containing the copies of such registers to be transmitted as in s. 7, superscribed by the church and chapelwardens, as in schedule E., (see *post.* 126,) shall go postage free. (s. 11.)

Alphabetical Lists by Registrars.] The registrars shall cause the copies of registers transmitted to them, to be safely kept from damage, and to be so arranged as to be resorted to when required; and they shall also cause correct alphabetical lists to be made, in books suitable to the purpose, of the names of all persons and places mentioned therein, which, with the above copies, shall be open to public search, at reasonable times, on payment of the usual fees. (s. 12.)

False Entries or Copies.] Every person who shall knowingly and wilfully insert, or cause or permit to be inserted, in any such register of such baptisms, burials, or marriages, or in any such copy, as in s. 6, or in any writ or declaration, ordered to be transmitted to such registrars, any false entry of any thing relating to any baptism, burial, or marriage, or who shall falsely make, utter, forge or counterfeit, or cause, procure, or wilfully permit to be falsely made, altered, forged or counterfeited, any part of any such register, list, or declaration, or copy of such register; or who shall wilfully destroy, deface or injure, or cause to be destroyed, any such register, or part thereof; or shall wilfully sign or certify any copy of such register, required to be transmitted as in s. 6, which is false in any part thereof, knowing it to be false; shall be deemed guilty of felony, and transported for fourteen years. (s. 14.)

Accidental Errors.] No rector, &c. or officiating minister of any parish or chapel, who shall discover any error to have been committed in the form or substance of the entry, in the register-book of any such baptism, burial, or marriage, respectively by him solemnized, shall be liable to any of the penalties in the act mentioned, if he shall within one calendar month after discovery of such error, in the presence of the parent of the child baptized, or of the parties married, or of two persons who attended at any burial; or in the case of the death or absence of the respective parties, then in presence of the church or chapelwardens (who shall attest the same,) alter and correct the entry which was found erroneous, by *entry in the margin* of such book wherein such erroneous entry is made, without alteration of the original entry; and he shall begin such entry in the margin, and add to such signature the day of the month and year when such correction is made; provided that in the fair copy of the registers transmitted to the registrars of the dioceses, the officiating minister shall certify the alterations so made by him. (54 G. 3. c. 146. s. 15.)

Fees the same.] Nothing herein shall increase or diminish the fees payable to any minister, for performance of any of the above duties, or to him or any registrar, for giving copies of such registrations; but the same, and the power of recovering the same, shall remain as before this act. (s. 16.)

Stamp Duty.] No duplicate or copy of any such register, made under this act, shall be chargeable with stamp duty. (s. 17.)

Application of Penalties.] One half of all fines or penalties, levied under this act, shall go to the informer or party suing for the same; and the remainder of those imposed on any church or chapelwarden, shall go to the poor of the parish or place;—and the remainder of those imposed on any rector, vicar, minister, curate, or registrar, shall be paid and applied to such charitable purposes in the county as the bishop shall direct and appoint. (s. 18.)

This act shall extend, so far as circumstances will permit, to cathedral and collegiate churches, chapels of colleges or hospitals, and the burying-grounds belonging thereto, and to the ministers who shall officiate therein, and shall baptize, marry, or bury any persons, although such churches, hospitals, or burying-grounds, be not parochial, and such ministers officiating therein may not be parochial ministers, and there be no churchwardens thereof; and in all such cases, the books hereinbefore directed to be provided, shall be provided at the expense of the body having right to appoint the officiating minister in every such cathedral, or collegiate church, or chapel of a college or hospital; and copies thereof shall be transmitted to the registrar of the diocese, by such officiating minister, as is herein directed with respect to parochial ministers; and shall be attested by two of the officers of such church, &c. as by s. 6 directed in respect of churchwardens. Provided that nothing in this act shall extend to repeal any part of 26 G. 2. c. 33, for preventing clandestine marriages. (s. 20.)

Schedules provided by 54 G. 3. c. 146.

SCHEDULE (A).

BAPTISMS solemnized in the parish of *St. A.* in the county of *B.* in the year one thousand eight hundred and thirteen.

When baptized.	Child's Christian Name.	Parents' Name.		Abode.	Quality, Trade, or Profession.	By whom the Ceremony was performed.
		Christian.	Surname.			
1813. *1st February* No. 1.	*John Son of*	*William* *Elizabeth.*		*Lambeth.*		
3d March No. 2.	*Ann Daughter of*	*Herry* *Martha.*		*Fulham.*		

SCHEDULE (B).

MARRIAGES solemnized in the parish of *St. A.* in the county of *B.* in the year one thousand eight hundred and thirteen.

A. B. of { *the* / *this* } parish.

and *C. D.* of { *the* / *this* } parish.

were married in this { *church* / *chapel* } by { *banns* / *license* } with consent of { *parents* / *guardians* }

this day of in the year ,

By me, *I. I.* { *rector* / *vicar* / *curate* }

The marriage was solemnized between us { *A. B.* / *C. D.* }

In the presence of { *E. F.* / *G. H.* }

SCHEDULE (C).

BURIALS in the parish of *A.* in the county of *B.* in the year one thousand eight hundred and thirteen.

Name.	Abode.	When buried.	Age	By whom the Ceremony was performed.
John Williams. No. 1.	*Duke Street, Westminster.*	1813. 1st *May.*	62.	

SCHEDULE (D).

I do hereby certify, that I did on the day of baptize according to the rites of the united church of *England* and *Ireland*, son *(or daughter)* of and his wife, by the name of
To the rector [*or as the case may be*] of

I do hereby certify, that on the day of *A. B.* of aged was buried in [*stating the place of burial*], and that the ceremony of burial was performed according to the rites of the united church of *England* and *Ireland*, by me,
To the rector [*or as the case may be*] of

SCHEDULE (E).

To the registrar of the diocese of
at
A. B. } Churchwardens (*or* chapelwardens) of the parish (*or* chapelry) of
C. D. } [*or such other description as the case shall require*].

Marriage Registers.] By 4 G. 4. c. 76. s. 28, in order to preserve the evidence of marriages, and to make the proof thereof more certain and easy, is is enacted, that from and after the 1st November, 1823, all marriages shall be solemnized in the presence of two or more credible witnesses, besides the minister who shall celebrate the same; and that immediately after the celebration of every marriage, an entry thereof shall be made in the register-book, to be kept as by law is now directed; in which entry or register it shall be expressed, that the said marriage was celebrated by banns or license; and if both or either of the parties married by license be under age, not being a widower or widow, with consent of the parents or guardians, as the case shall be; and such entry shall be signed by the minister, with his proper addition; and also by the parties married, and attested by such two witnesses; which entry shall be made in the form, or to the effect following; that is to say,

A. B. of [*the* / *this*] *parish* ———— ———— *and* C. D. *of* [*the* / *this*] *parish* ———————— *were married in this* [*church* / *chapel*] *by* [*banns* / *license*] *with consent of* [*parents* / *guardians*] *this* ———— *day of* ———— *in the year* ———— *By me* J. J. [*Rector* / *Vicar* / *Curate*]

This marriage was solemnized between us [A. B. / C. D.]

in the presence of [E. F. / G. H.]

It will be seen that this form is substantially the same as the one provided by the register act, (*ante* 125, Sched. (B.)

Forging, &c. Marriage Register.] And if any person shall, from and after the 1st day of November, 1823, with intent to elude the force of this act, knowingly and wilfully insert, or cause to be inserted, in the register-book of such parish or chapelry, as aforesaid, any false entry of any thing relating to any marriage, or falsely make, alter, forge, or counterfeit any such entry in such register; or cause or procure the same to be done, or act or assist therein, or utter, or publish as true any such false, altered, forged or counterfeited register as aforesaid, or a copy thereof; or shall wilfully destroy, or cause or procure to be destroyed, any register-book of marriages, or any part of such register-book, with intent to avoid any marriage, or to subject any person to any of the penalties of this act; he shall be deemed guilty of felony, and shall suffer transportation for life, according to the laws in force for transportation of felons. (4 G. 4. c. 76. s. 29.)

Chapel Registers.] The fith section of the act enacts, that the provisions relative to providing and keeping marriage registers in parish churches, shall extend to chapels in which marriages are authorized to be performed by the act as aforesaid; and every thing required to be done relative thereto by churchwardens in the parish church, shall be done by the chapelwarden or other officer exercising analogous duties in such chapel

Baptismal Registers Evidence.] Parish registers are for some purposes considered as public books, and persons interested in them have a right to inspect and take copies of such parts as relate to their interest. (Dormer v. Ekyns, 2 Barnard. 269; Warriner v. Giles, 2 Stra. 954; and see 52 Geo. 3. c. 146. s. 5, *ante*, p. 122.) And a parish register has been received in evidence as an original authentic book, although the constant practice of the parish was to make a memorandum of the christenings in a day-book, from which entries were some time afterwards made into such register. (May v. May, 2 Stra. 1073.)

The question was again considered, in a case where the plaintiff's legitimacy was disputed. By the evidence it appeared, that the practice was to make the entries in the general parish register, once in three weeks, out of a day-book, in which entries were made immediately after the christening, on the same morning; and in the case of illegitimate children, to insert in the entry the letters B. B., signifying "base born." The defendant's counsel then offered in evidence this day-book, in which the letters B. B. were inserted, as the original entry. But a majority of the judges present at a trial at bar were of opinion that such evidence ought not to be received, on the ground that there could not be two registers in the parish, and that the one first produced ought to be taken to be the true register. If, indeed, the entry in the day-book, representing the plaintiff as illegitimate, had been signed by the reputed father or the mother, or made under their direction, such evidence would have been admissible, as the delaration of a deceased parent on a question of legitimacy; for the declarations of deceased persons, supposed to have been married (who might themselves be examined if alive) are admissible to disprove the fact of marriage. (Rex v. Bramley, 6 T. R. 330.) But in the absence of such proof, the entry seems to have been considered merely a private memorandum, kept for the purpose of assisting the clerk to make up the register. And an entry in the register-book by the minister of the parish, of the baptism of a child, which had taken place before he became minister, or had any connexion with the parish, and of which he received information from the parish clerk, is not admissible in evidence, nor is the private memorandum of the fact, made by the clerk who was present at the baptism. (Doe & Warren v. Bray, 8 Barn. & Cres. 813.)

Burial Registers Evidence.] The rules of law which apply to the registration of baptisms, are also applicable to the registry of burials, when produced as evidence. In general, they can only be received in either case, in proof of the single fact which they have been established to record, and are inadmissible to support any collateral circumstances, which are frequently inserted at the same time. (See 1 Stark. Ev. 174.; 3 ib. 1116.)

Marriage Registers Evidence.] The law, which seems more anxious to create and preserve evidence of marriages, than of the other events to which parish registers are devoted, has provided that witnesses shall be present at the ceremony, and that they, with the officiating minister, shall attest the performance thereof, by signing the entry thereof, in the form required by the act. (See *ante*, p. 129.)

And the 6 G. 4. c. 92. s. 3, enacts, that the registers of marriages solemnized, or to be solemnized in the said churches or chapels, (see *antè*, p. 129,) or copies thereof, shall be received, in all courts of law and equity, as evidence of such marriages, in the same manner as the registers of marriages solemnized in parish churches or public chapels are received in evidence; provided nevertheless that in all such courts the same objections shall be available to the receiving such registers or copies as evidence, as would have been available to receiving the same as evidence, if such registers or copies had related to marriages solemnized in such last-mentioned parish churches or public chapels, as aforesaid.

Proof of Residence unnecessary.] After the solemnization of any marriage under a publication of banns, it shall not be necessary, in support of such marriage, to give any proof of the actual dwelling of the parties in the respective parishes or chapelries wherein the banns of matrimony were published; or where the marriage is by license, it shall not be necessary to give any proof that the usual place of abode of one of the parties, for the space of fifteen days as aforesaid, was in the parish or chapelry where the marriage was solemnized; nor shall any evidence in either of the said cases be received to prove the contrary, in any suit touching the validity of such marriage. (4 G. 4. c. 76. s. 26.)

Dissenters' Registers.] Copies of the register of a dissenting chapel shall not be pleaded as evidence, they not being in official custody; but they may be produced at the hearing of the cause, and be made evidence to a certain extent. (Newham v. Raithby, 1 Phil. Ec. Ca. 315; Goodright ex. dem. Stevens v. Moss, Cowp. 594.)

SECTION II.—PARISH LIBRARY.

Parish Libraries Confirmed.] By the 7 Ann, c. 14, whereas in many places in England the provision for the clergy is so mean, that the necessary expense of books for the better prosecution of their studies cannot be defrayed by them; and whereas, several persons of late years have, by charitable contributions, erected libraries within several parishes and districts; but some provision is wanting to preserve the same, and such others as shall be provided in the same manner from embezzlement; it is enacted, that in every parish or place where such a library is, or shall be erected, the same shall be preserved for such uses as the same is and shall be given, and the orders and rules of the founders thereof shall be observed and kept. (7 Ann, c. 14. s. 1.)

Visitation by Ordinary.] And it shall be lawful for the proper ordinary or his commissary, or official, or the archdeacon, or by his direction, his official, or surrogate, if the said archdeacon be not the incumbent of the place where such library is, in their visitation to enquire into the state and condition of the said libraries, and to amend and redress the grievances and defects of and concerning the same, as to him or them shall seem meet; and it shall be lawful for the proper ordinary from time to time, as often as shall be thought fit, to appoint such persons as he shall think fit, to view the state and condition of such libraries; and the said ordinaries, archdeacons or officials, respectively, shall have free access to the same at such times as they shall respectively appoint. (s. 3.)

Locked up during Vacancy.] And to prevent any embezzlement of books upon the death or removal of any incumbent, immediately after such death or removal the library belonging to such parish or place shall be forthwith shut up, and locked, or otherwise secured by the churchwardens, or by such persons as shall be authorized by the proper ordinary or archdeacon respectively; so that the same shall not be opened again till a new incumbent, rector, vicar, minister, or curate, shall be inducted or admitted. (s. 6.)

Provided, that if the place where such library shall be kept shall be used for any public occasion—for meeting of the vestry, or otherwise for the dispatch of any business of the said parish, or for any other public occasion for which the said place hath been ordinarily used,—the said place shall nevertheless be made use of as formerly for such purposes, and after such business is dispatched, shall be again forthwith shut and locked up, or otherwise secured, as is before directed. (s. 7.)

Security by Incumbent.] And for the encouragement of such founders and benefactors, and to the intent they may be satisfied that their pious and charitable intent may not be frustrated, every incumbent, rector, vicar, minister, or curate of a parish, before he shall be permitted to use or enjoy such library, shall enter into such security by bond, or otherwise, for preservation of such library, and due observance of the rules and orders belonging to the same, as the proper ordinaries within their respective jurisdictions in their discretion shall think fit. (s. 2.)

New Catalogues.] And where any library is appropriated to the use of the minister of any parish or place, every rector, vicar, minister, or curate of the same, within six months after his institution, induction, or admission, shall make a new catalogue of all books remaining in or belonging to such library, and shall sign the said catalogue, thereby acknowledging the custody and possession of the said books; which said catalogue, so signed, shall be delivered to the proper ordinary within the time aforesaid, to be kept or registered in his court without any fee or reward for the same. (7 Ann, c. 14. s. 4.)

And where any library shall at any time hereafter be given and appropriated to the use of any parish or place, where there shall be an incumbent, rector, vicar, minister, or curate, in possession, he shall make a catalogue thereof, and deliver the same as aforesaid within six months after he shall receive such library. (s. 5.)

Books not to be Alienated.] And none of the said books shall, in any case, be alienable, or be alienated without the consent of the proper ordinary, and then only when there is a duplicate of such book. (s. 10.)

Books Lost or Detained.] And in case any book or books be taken, or otherwise lost out of the said library, it shall be lawful for a justice of the peace to grant his warrant to search for the same; and in case the same be found, such book or books so found shall immediately, by order of such justice, be restored to the said library. (Id.)

Action for Books.] And in case any book or books belonging to the said library shall be taken away and detained, it shall be lawful for the incumbent, rector, vicar, minister, or curate for the time being, or any other person or persons, to bring an action of trover and conversion in the name of the proper ordinaries, within their respective jurisdictions; whereupon treble damages shall be given with full costs of suit, as if the same were his or their proper book or books, which damages shall be applied to the use and benefit of the said library. (s. 2.)

List of Benefactions.] And for the better preservation of such books, and that benefactions given towards the same may appear, a book shall be kept within the said library for the entering and registering of all such benefactions, and such books as shall be given towards the same; and therein the minister shall enter such benefactions, and an account of all such books as shall from time to time be given, and by whom given. (s. 8.)

New Regulations.] And for better governing the said librraries, and preserving of the same, it shall be lawful for the proper ordinary, together with the donor of such benefaction (if living), and after the death of such donor, for the proper ordinary alone, to make such other rules and orders concerning the same, over and above, and besides, but not contrary to such as the donor of such benefaction shall in his discretion judge fit and necessary; which said orders and rules, so to be made, shall from time to time be entered in the said book, or some other book to be prepared for the purpose, and kept in the said library. (s. 9.)

Excepted from the Act.] But nothing in this act shall extend to a public library erected in the parish of Ryegate, in the county of Surrey, for the use of the freeholders, vicar, and inhabitants of the said parish, and of the gentlemen and clergymen inhabiting in parts thereto adjacent; the said library being constituted in another manner than the libraries provided for by this act. (7 Ann, c. 14. s. 11.)

SECTION III.—RATE BOOKS, &c.

Poor-Rate Book.] It is enacted by statute 17 G. 2. c. 38. s. 13, that true copies of all rates and assessments made for the relief of the poor be entered in a book, to be provided for that purpose by the churchwardens and overseers of the poor of every parish, &c., who shall take care that such copies be entered accordingly, within fourteen days after all appeals from such rates are determined, and shall attest the same by putting their names thereto; and every such book shall be carefully preserved by the churchwardens, &c. for the time being, or one of them, in some public place in every such parish, &c. whereto all persons assessed may freely resort, and shall be delivered over from time to time to the new and succeeding churchwardens, &c. as soon as they enter into their offices, and shall be produced by them at the general or quarter sessions when any appeal is to be heard or determined.

Parish-Indenture Book.] The 42 G. 3. c. 46, enacts, that the overseers of the poor of every parish shall provide and keep a book at the expense of the parish, and enter therein the name of every child who shall be bound out by them respectively as an apprentice, together with the several other particulars, in the manner and form required by this act; and every such entry shall be produced and laid before two justices of the peace, who shall signify their assent to the indenture of apprenticeship, at the time when such indenture shall be laid before them for that purpose; and each entry shall, if approved of, be signed by them, according to the prescribed form. And in the third section it is enacted, that any person may, at all seasonable hours, inspect such book in the hands of the said overseer, and take a copy of such entry; and every such book shall be deemed to be sufficient evidence in all courts of law in proof of the existence of such indentures, and also of the several particulars specified in the register respecting such indentures, in case it shall be proved to the satisfaction of the court that the indentures are lost or destroyed.

Vestry Books.] The 58 G. 3. c. 69. s. 2, directs that the minutes of the proceedings and resolutions of every vestry shall be fairly and distinctly entered in a book, (to be provided for the purpose by the churchwardens and overseers of the poor,) and shall be signed by the chairman, and by such other of the inhabitants present as shall think proper to sign the same.

Custody of, and Access thereto.] The same statute, by section 6, enacts, that as well the books directed to be provided by that act, and kept for the entry of the proceedings of vestries, as all former vestry-books, and all rates and assessments, accounts, and vouchers of the churchwardens, overseers of the poor, and surveyors of the highways, and other parish officers, and all certificates, orders of courts, and of justices, and other parish books, documents, writings, public papers of every parish, except the registry of marriages, baptisms, and burials, shall be kept by such person and persons, and deposited in such place and manner as the inhabitants, in vestry assembled, shall direct; and if any person, in whose hands or custody any such book, rate, assessment, account, voucher, certificate, document, order, writing, or paper shall be, shall wilfully or negligently destroy, obliterate or injure the same, or suffer the same to be destroyed, obliterated, or injured, or shall after reasonable notice and demand refuse or neglect to deliver the same to such person or persons, or to deposit the same in such place as shall, by order of any such vestry, be directed; every person so offending, and being lawfully convicted thereof on his own confession, or on the oath of one or more credible witness or witnesses, by and before two of his majesty's justices of the peace, upon complaint thereof to them made, shall for every such offence forfeit and pay such sum, not exceeding £50, nor less than 40*s.*, as shall by such justices be adjudged and determined; and the same shall be recovered and levied by warrant of such justices, in such manner and by such means as poor-rates in arrear are by law to be recovered and levied, and shall be paid to the overseers of the poor of the parish against which the offence shall be committed, or to some of them, and be applied for and towards the relief of the poor thereof; provided nevertheless that every person who shall unlawfully retain in his custody, or shall refuse to deliver to any person or persons, authorised to receive the same, or who shall obliterate, destroy, or injure, or suffer to be obliterated, destroyed, or injured, any book, rate, assessment, account, voucher, certificate, order, document, writing, or paper belonging to any parish, or to the churchwardens, overseers of the poor, or surveyors of the highways thereof, may in every such case be proceeded against in any of his majesty's courts, civilly or criminally, in like manner as if this act had not been made.

Demand of Inspection.] The 17 G. 2. c. 3. s. 2, enacts, that overseers of the poor shall permit inhabitants of the parish to inspect the rates at all seasonable times; and the third section provides, that if any overseer shall not permit an inhabitant to inspect the rate, such overseer for every such offence shall forfeit and pay to the party aggrieved the sum of £20. In an action to recover this penalty, the judge directed a nonsuit, against his own opinion, upon the authority of the case of Spencely v. Robinson, (3 Barn. & Cres. 658,) in which it was held that, under this act, the party must show that he has *sustained an injury* by the act of the overseer. Liberty was given to move to set the nonsuit aside, and to enter a verdict for the penalty; and after argument at the bar, the court held, that a demand to inspect a rate made on the overseer by a rated inhabitant, in the presence of his attorney, is a lawful demand; that the refusal to produce a rate upon a lawful demand constitutes the inhabitant *a party grieved* within the meaning of the statute; that a demand to see "the rate" is sufficiently specific, there being only one rate in esse at the time; that the overseer, by refusing to show the rate, and referring the party to the select vestry, as a place where he would be allowed to inspect it, incurred the penalty imposed by the 17 Geo. 2. c. 3. (Bennett v. Edwards, 7 Barn. & Cres. 586; 1 Man. & Ry. 482.)

But a new trial was ordered on the ground that the defendant, who was *assistant overseer* only, is not liable to the penalties, unless it be proved that the select vestry have imposed upon him the duty of producing the rate to the inhabitants. And upon the case coming before the court again, after a second trial, the court decided, that if the defendant had the rate in his possession as assistant *overseer*, it might be presumed that it was his duty to produce it when lawfully demanded; and though the declaration did not contain such an averment, as it ought, there was sufficient on the record, after verdict, to warrant a judgment for the plaintiff. (8 Barn. & Cres. 702.)

Assistant Overseer liable.] The above case was afterwards carried to the Exchequer Chamber upon a writ of error; and I have been favoured with a note of the judgment in that, and in another similar case, by Mr. Moore. They will be found at large in the third volume of Moore and Payne's Reports.

Mr. Serjeant Ludlow for the plaintiff in error, and Mr. Campbell for the defendant in error, having recapitulated the arguments adopted in the court below; Lord Chief Justice Tindal, in delivering the judgment of the court, said, that "they were of opinion, *first*, that an assistant overseer was within the provisions of the statute (17 G. 2. c. 3. s. 2,) as he was a person authorized to take care of the poor; he having been nominated and elected by the inhabitants of the parish in vestry assembled, and appointed an assistant overseer by warrant, in writing, under the hands and seals of two justices of the peace, as required by the statute; (59 G. 3. c. 12;) and that thereby a sufficient authority was given to him to execute all the duties of the office of such overseer, as should be expressed in the terms of the warrant. With respect to the objection, that the fourth count of the declaration did not bring the plaintiff in error within the terms of the statute 17 G. 2, yet that count is sufficient after verdict; as it must be now intended that every thing alleged therein was proved at the trial. It was alleged that the plaintiff in error was the assistant overseer of the parish, and that he was requested by the defendant in error, as such overseer, to permit him, the defendant in error, to inspect the rate; and that the plaintiff in error, as such assistant overseer, had the rate then in his possession. The fact of his being assistant overseer must have been proved by the production of the warrant under which he was appointed; and, although he might not have a general authority to take care of the poor at large, yet he might have had a limited authority, by which he was entitled to have the custody of the rate as such assistant overseer. If it had been alleged, that he had authority to take care of the poor, there would have been no doubt. The case of the King v. Everett is distinguishable, as there only three descriptions of persons were authorized to seize goods under a warrant from the officers of the customs; and the seizure was made by a person not falling within either of those descriptions. There too the party was charged with a criminal offence, whilst here he was only liable to a penalty, to be enforced by civil remedy.—*Judgment affirmed.*

Mr. Campbell then moved, that the judgment in Parker v. Edwards might be affirmed, where a demand to inspect the rate had been made by another parishioner upon the defendant upon his own premises, not far from his house, and he refused to allow the inspection; but not on the ground that it was inconvenient to go to his house for that purpose. In an action against him for the refusal, the Court of King's Bench held that this was a reasonable demand.—*Judgment affirmed accordingly.*

Proof of Entries in Registers.] An entry in a parish register, like any other public document, may be proved by means of an examined copy; and it is of course unnecessary to give any proof by means of the subscribing witnesses, or to prove their hand-writing. (Birt v. Barlow, Doug. 173.) The register is no proof of the *identity* of the parties. (Ib. 1 Stark, Ev. 176.)

CHAPTER VI.—DISSENTERS.

SECTION I.—GENERAL RIGHTS OF DISSENTERS.

Christianity part of the Law.] It has been frequently declared in the senate and from the judgment-seat, that Christianity is part and parcel of the law of the land. (Rex v. Taylor, 3 Keb. 607; Rex v. Woolston, 2 Stra. 834.) Its zealous adoption by the princes and people of this country, at a time when their civil institutions were few and in their infancy, facilitated the introduction of its sanctions into the policy of the state; and the far greater influence which it exercised over the hopes and fears of men, even in matters of worldly interest, than had resulted from the visionary promises and denunciations of Paganism, offered a strong inducement to its union with temporal power. Accordingly, every new device for the government of the people, whether decreed by the will of the sovereign or sent forth by the great council of the nation, bore the impress and the sanction of Christianity. And thus the authority of a pure and holy religion, and of an improving system of government, were concentrated in the same institutions, and administered by the same functionaries; and hence the Christian religion became part and parcel of the law of the land.

This maxim of the courts has been sometimes questioned, and its correctness denied; because, in more recent times, the profession of peculiar religious opinions has been discountenanced and condemned by the legislature. But it is presumed, that an answer to this objection will be found in the terms of the proposition, which do not assert any individual creed, or necessarily embrace any particular system of worship to the exclusion of all others. The Christianity which is here represented as interwoven with the constitution, is the comprehensive scheme of moral discipline and improvement, enforced by the belief of an accountability hereafter, for the promulgation and support of which the state exerted its vigilance and pledged its authority.

Origin of Sectarianism.] For several centuries after the Christian religion had been established in Great Britain, no division among its followers into separate sects existed; and the law, therefore, knew nothing of different denominations; but when a reckless spirit of inquiry led to a conviction that the dogmas and practices of Popery were not warranted by the sacred volume from whence they were professedly drawn, and the eye of patriotism saw they were equally inimical to civil liberty, a new system was formed, to which the patronage of the state was transferred; and the faith which had so long predominated was abandoned and proscribed. It was then that the statute-book began to teem with penal enactments and civil disabilities, in restraint of the liberty of conscience; some of them, doubtless, provoked by the machinations of those against whom they were directed, but others originating in an overweening self-confidence, which having asserted the right of private judgment *for itself*, denied it to others; because, as it was practically alleged, all others must come to the same conclusions, or at least *ought to do so*, and therefore it was either unnecessary or dangerous to allow them the exercise of this privilege. The futility of attempts to force the consciences of men, and the vindication of the *law of the land* from this imputation, in contradistinction to the statute law, cannot be more eloquently expressed than by Lord Mansfield, when delivering his judgment in the

House of Lords, upon the question, whether a person elected to a corporate office might plead, in excuse of the fine for refusing to serve, that he was a dissenter, and could not conscientiously take the sacrament as required by the statute.

Freedom of Religious Opinions.] His Lorship said, " The defendant in the present cause pleads, that he is a dissenter within the description of the Toleration Act; that he hath not taken the sacrament in the church of England within one year preceding the time of his supposed election, nor ever in his whole life, and that he cannot in conscience do it. Conscience is not controllable by human laws, nor amenable to hnman tribunals. Persecution, or attempts to force conscience, will never produce conviction, and are only calculated to make hypocrites or martyrs. My lords, there never was a single instance from the Saxon times down to our own, in which a man was ever punished for erroneous opinions concerning rites or modes of worship, but upon some positive law. The common law of England, which is only common reason or usage, knows of no persecution for mere opinions. For atheism, blasphemy, and reviling the Christian religion, there have been instances of persons prosecuted and punished upon the common law; but bare non-conformity is no sin by the common law; and all positive laws inflicting any pains or penalties for non-conformity to the established rites and modes, are repealed by the Act of Toleration, and dissenters are thereby exempted from all ecclesiastical censures. What bloodshed and confusion have been occasioned, from the reign of Henry 4th, when the first penal statutes were enacted, down to the revolution in this kingdom by laws made to force conscience! There is nothing certainly more unreasonable; more inconsistent with the rights of human nature; more contrary to the spirit and precepts of the Christian religion; more iniquitous and unjust, more impolitic, than persecution. It is against natural religion, revealed religion, and sound policy. Sad experience, and an enlightened mind, taught that great man, the President De Thou, this doctrine; let any man read the many admirable things, which, though a Papist, he hath dared to advance upon the subject in the dedication of his History to Henry the Fourth of France, (which I never read without rapture,) and he will be fully convinced, not only how cruel, but how impolitic it is to persecute for religious opinions. As a subject of Great Britain, I should not have been sorry if France had continued to cherish the Jesuits and to persecute the Huguenots. There was no occasion to revoke the Edict of Nantz. The Jesuits needed only to have advised a plan similar to what is contended for in the present case,—make a law to render them incapable of office; make another to punish them for not serving. If they accept, punish them; if they refuse, punish them; if they say yes, punish them; if they say no, punish them. My lords, this is a most exquisite dilemma, from which there is no escaping."

His Lordship concluded with moving that the judgment be affirmed: —and the judgment was immediately affirmed *nemine contradicente.* (Appendix to Furneaux's Letters to Mr. Justice Blackstone, 2d edit.; 2 Burn. Ec. L. 218; 6 Bro. P. C. 181.)

Eligibility to Office.] The earliest statutory interference was directed to the laudable object of enforcing a due observance of the sabbath, a proper attendance upon the ordinances of public worship, and a decorous and befitting demeanor in the sanctuaries of religion. But in the progress of the strife between the repudiated and the adopted faith, it was thought expedient for the safety of the government, and the more certain triumph of the reformed church, to admit none but its members to public office or employment. Still, as in the enactments upon this subject, the principal object of the legislature was to secure the power to persons who outwardly professed the religion of the state; the punishment of non-conformists, by excluding them from power, was the consequence, not the end and purpose, of the law: and agreeably to this principle, those laws have been abrogated or relaxed, with the growing liberality of the times, and the attainment of a better knowledge of the true maxims of civil government. Both the lay and ecclesiastical tribunals were, no doubt, occasionally employed in denouncing peculiar doctrines, and punishing heterodoxy; but the conscientious profession of particular doctrines ceased to be *a crime,* when the Unitarians were admitted within the pale of express statutory toleration, by the 57 G. 3. c. 70.

Privileges and Duties.] Except in those instances where the legislature has expressly interfered to restrain or impose conditions upon Protestant dissenters, they participate, in common with their fellow-subjects of the Established Church, in all the rights and duties, and are alike entitled to the protection and benefit, of the civil institutions of the empire. They are admissible into either house of Parliament; the tests imposed upon the members thereof being no longer incompatible with the religious principles either of Catholics or other dissenters from the established church. (10 G. 4. c. 7; 9 G. 4. c. 17; 1 W. & M c. 1; 8 G. 1. c. 6.)

The right of dissenters to be admitted to the sacrament of baptism, and to the canonical rites of burial, are mentioned elsewhere.

Bequests for the benefit of their communities, are executed in the courts of equity, with a due regard to the probable intentions of the testator; and trusts for the promotion of public worship, according to their peculiar rites, and the inculcation of doctrine at variance with the established faith, if not directly contrary to law, are equally under the protection of the courts of equity. (Attorney General v. Cock, 2 Ves. 273; Walter v. Childs, Amb. 524; 3 Merivale, 399.)

They are exempted from payment of tolls in going to their usual place of worship tolerated by law, on Sundays, or on any day on which divine service is by authority ordered to be celebrated. (3 G. 4. c. 126. s. 32.)

This advantage, however, as well as various others, can be enjoyed by those persons only who are *bonâ fide* dissenters. (Harrison v. Evans, *supra.*)

But it is expressly provided by the Toleration Act, that they shall not be exempt from tithes or any other parochial duties, or any other duties to the church or minister. (1 W. & M. st. 1. c. 18. s. 6.)

The major part of the penal enactments which formerly disfigured the statute-book, having been absolutely or virtually repealed by a succession of remedial statutes, but few remain; and those, in their present mode of administration, deduct, in no very considerable degree, from practical liberty.

The Toleration Act (1 W. & M. s. 1. c. 18) took precedence; and the 52 G. 3. c. 155, & 53 G. 3. c. 160, dispensed still further concessions; to which have recently been added the 9 G. 4. c. 17, which repeals the sacramental test, the great barrier against admission to office and public employment. And lastly the 10 G. 4. c. 7.

SECTION II.—TESTS AND OATHS OF OFFICE.

Sacramental Test.] The mode in which the legislature sought to protect the constitution against the apprehended danger from Popery and sectarianism, was by requiring a pledge in favour and support of the Established Church, from the candidates for municipal offices, and the various employments in the state. By the statutes, as they stood down to the passing of the 9 G. 4. c. 17, no person could be elected, or take upon himself the office of mayor, alderman, recorder, bailiff, town clerk, common councilman, or any other office relating to the government of cities, corporations, boroughs, cinque ports, and other port towns in England, Wales, and Berwick-upon-Tweed; unless he had within one year preceding taken the sacrament of the Lord's Supper, according to the rites of the Church of England. (13 Car. 2. st. 2.

c. 1.) But by the 5 G. 1. c. 6, the time for proceeding against an offender under the above act, was limited to six months after obtaining actual possession of his office; the moving for a rule *nisi* being considered a sufficient commencement of such proceedings. (3 T. R. 514, n.)

Sacramental Test abolished.] The above statute (9 G. 4. c. 17) is entitled, " An act for repealing so much of several acts as imposes the necessity of receiving the sacrament of the Lord's Supper, as a qualification for certain offices and employments;" and recites the Corporation Act, 13 Car. 2. st. 2. c. 1; the 25 Car. 2. c. 2; and the 16 G. 2. c. 30; and repeals so much of them as require the persons therein described to receive the sacrament, as a qualification for civil or municipal offices or employments. It then provides the following declaration, which is to be made and signed in lieu of the sacramental test:

" I, A. B. do solemnly and sincerely, in the presence of God, profess, testify, and declare, upon the true faith of a Christian, that I will never exercise any power, authority, or influence, which I may possess by virtue of the office of [*naming it*], to injure or weaken the Protestant Church, as it is by law established in England; or to disturb the said church, or the bishops and clergy of the said church, in the possession of any rights or privileges to which such church, or the said bishops and clergy, are or may be by law entitled."

Declaration, when and where to be made.] The act provides, that in case of neglect to make the declaration within one calendar month before, or upon admission, to any such corporate office, &c., the election shall be void. And that persons admitted into any office, which before the passing of this act required the taking of the sacrament, shall make the declaration within *six* months after such admission, or the appointment be void. The declaration in cases of appointments to offices under the Crown, may be made and signed in the Court of Chancery or the King's Bench, or at the quarter sessions of the county where the party resides; and in the cases of admission to corporate offices, before the persons who usually administer the oaths; or in default thereof, of two justices of the peace of the county or franchise; and the same shall be preserved among the records of the said court, &c. Naval officers below the rank of rear-admiral, and military officers below the rank of major-general in the army, or colonel in the militia, are exempted from making the declaration in respect of their commissions. And the like exemption extends to commissioners of customs, excise, stamps, or taxes, and the officers under them, or under the postmaster-general. And naval and military officers receiving place or appointment during absence from England, or within three months previous to departure from thence, may make the declaration at any time within six months after their return to England. The act also indemnifies from penalties, and confirms the possession of all persons then in offices which theretofore required the taking of the sacrament, and who had omitted to do so; and provides, that omissions to make the declaration shall not affect the rights of others not privy thereto.

Oaths of Office.] The declaration against transubstantiation, and the declaration against transubstantiation, the invocation of saints, and the sacrifice of the mass, are repealed by the 10 G. 4. c. 7; and therefore, no persons whatever are now required to make them, or either of them. But the oaths of allegiance, supremacy, and abjuration, are still to be administered as before, upon the admission to corporate offices or employments under the crown, unless the individual be a Catholic. And all persons neglecting or refusing to take the said oaths, &c. and make the said declaration, are *ipso facto* and altogether disabled to hold the office or employment, or any profit appertaining thereto, and the same is adjudged void.

These enactments do not extend to any pension or salary granted by the crown for valuable and sufficient consideration, other than those relating to offices or places of trust under the crown, or to pensions of bounty or voluntary pensions. Nor to the office of petty constable, tithing-man, headborough, overseer of the poor, churchwarden, surveyor of the highways, or any like inferior civil office; nor to any office of forester, or keeper of a park, chase, warren, or game; bailiff of a manor or lands, or like private offices; nor to persons having only the before-mentioned or like offices. Nor do they extend to make any forfeiture, disability, or incapacity, by or in non-commissioned officers in the navy, duly subscribing the declaration against transubstantiation; or by or in any person beyond the seas, duly qualifying within six months after his return to England. (See 13 Car. 2. st. 2. c. 1; amended by 1 G. 2. st. 2. c. 13; 5 G. 1. c. 6.)

If the party do not take the oaths, and comply with the other requisitions of the statutes, upon which the validity of his election or appointment depends *whether they be tendered or not*, the election is void. But he may demand to have them administered to him, and the Court of King's Bench will grant a mandamus to compel the proper officer to perform the ceremony, if he refuse. (R. v. Mayor of Oxon, 2 Salk. 428; 5 Mod. 316.; Comb. 419.)

Serving Office by Deputy.] Protestant dissenters appointed to any parochial or ward office, who scruple to take on themselves such offices, in regard to the oaths or other matter or thing required by law to be taken or done, respecting such office, are permitted by the Toleration Act (1 W. & M. st. 1. c. 18. s. 7.) to execute the same by a sufficient deputy, to be provided by them, who will comply with the laws in that behalf; such deputy being allowed and approved in the same manner as the officers themselves should, by law, have been allowed and approved.

Insignia of Office.] By the 5 G. 1. c. 4, it is provided, that if any mayor, bailiff, or other magistrate in England, Wales, Berwick-on-Tweed, or the isles of Guernsey or Jersey, shall knowingly or wilfully resort to, or be present at any public meeting for religious worship, other than of the Established Church, in the gown or other peculiar habit, or attended with the ensigns of office, he shall, on being duly convicted thereof, be disabled to hold his office, and shall be adjudged incapable to bear any public office or employment whatsoever.

A similar provision is contained in the Catholic Relief Bill, which enacts, that if any person holding a civil or judicial office, or any mayor, provost, jurat bailiff, or other corporate officer, shall so offend either in England, or Ireland, or in Scotland against the church of Scotland, he shall forfeit his office, and pay for every such offence the sum of £100. (10 G. 4. c. 7. s. 25.)

Catholic Relief Bill.] The declaration against transubstantiation is repealed generally; the oaths of allegiance, supremacy, and abjuration, still remain on the statute book, but are no longer a bar to the admission of papists to corporate offices or other higher employments in the state, whether civil or military. The only exceptions are, the office of regent of the united kingdom, under whatever name or title such office may be constituted, the office of lord chancellor, lord keeper, or lord commissioner of the great seal of Great Britain or Ireland, or the office of lord lieutenant, or lord deputy, or other chief governor of Ireland, or his majesty's high commissioner to the general assembly of Scotland. (10 G. 4. c. 7. s. 12.)

The act also provides, that Catholic members of lay corporations, are not to vote at, or join in, the election or appointment of any person to any ecclesiastical benefice or office, connected with the united church of England and Ireland, or the church of Scotland, which may be in the gift of such corporation. (s. 15.)

And it is also provided, that the act shall not enable any persons, otherwise than as they were before enabled, to hold any office in the established church, ecclesiastical courts, universities, colleges, or schools, nor to present to benefices, nor to *advise the crown*, or the chief governor of Ireland, touching or concerning the appointment or disposal of any office or preferment in the church, &c.; upon pain of being disabled for ever from holding any office, civil or military, under the crown. (ss. 16—18.)

Jesuits, &c.] Jesuits, and members of other religious orders of the church of Rome, bound by monastic or religious vows, in the kingdom at the passing of the act, and natural born subjects, being jesuits, &c., returning to the kingdom, are to send the necessary particulars to the clerk of the peace where they reside, in order that they may be registered; and if any members of any such society *come into the realm*, they shall be banished; unless such persons come under a license granted by the secretary of state, who is authorised to grant the indulgence for six months, revocable at any time if he shall think fit. (s. 31.)

The 37th section provides, that nothing contained in the act shall extend to affect any religious order, community, or establishment, consisting of females bound by religious or monastic vows.

The Catholic Oath.] The act authorizes the admission of Catholics into parliament, and to all offices and employments, with the exceptions already stated, upon taking and subscribing the following oath, instead of the oaths of allegiance, supremacy, and abjuration.

I, A. B., do sincerely promise and swear, that I will be faithful, and bear true allegiance to his Majesty King *George* the Fourth, and will defend him to the utmost of my power against all conspiracies and attempts whatever which shall be made against his person, crown, or dignity; and I will do my utmost endeavour to disclose and make known to his Majesty, his heirs, and successors, all treasons and traitorous conspiracies which may be formed against him or them. And I do faithfully promise to maintain, support, and defend to the utmost of my power, the succession of the crown; which succession, by an act intituled, *An Act for the further limitation of the Crown, and better securing the rights and liberties of the subject*, is, and stands limited to the princess *Sophia*, electress of *Hanover*, and the heirs of her body, being Protestants; hereby utterly renouncing and abjuring any obedience or allegiance unto any other person claiming or pretending a right to the crown of this realm. And I do further declare, that it is not an article of my faith, and that I do renounce, reject, and abjure the opinion, that princes excommunicated or deprived by the pope, or any other authority of the see of *Rome*, may be deposed or murdered by their subjects, or by any person whatsoever. And I do declare, that I do not believe that the pope of *Rome*, or any other foreign prince, prelate, person, state, or potentate, hath, or ought to have, any temporal or civil jurisdiction, power, superiority, or pre-eminence, directly or indirectly, within this realm. I do swear that I will defend to the utmost of my power the settlement of property within this realm, as established by the laws. And I do hereby disclaim, disavow, and solemnly abjure any intention to subvert the present church establishment as settled by law within this realm. And I do solemnly swear, that I never will exercise any privilege to which I am, or may become entitled, to disturb or weaken the Protestant religion or Protestant government in the united kingdom. And I do solemnly, in the presence of God, profess, testify, and declare, that I do make this declaration, and every part thereof, in the plain and ordinary sense of the words of this oath, without any evasion, equivocation, or mental reservation whatsoever,

So help me God.

SECTION III.—QUAKERS AND MORAVIANS.

Affirmation in lieu of Oath.] The peculiar opinions of Quakers and Moravians upon several matters of municipal government, and the civil institutions of the country, have given rise to certain legislative provisions with respect to them, by which they in some measure become a distinct, *civil*, as well as a separate religious community among their fellow-subjects.

The scruple entertained by both Quakers and Moravians, to take an oath, excludes them from serving on juries. It likewise disables a quaker, except in the Colonies, (13 G. 2. c. 7,) to hold office or place of profit under government.

On the other hand, by a recent act of parliament the solemn affirmation of Quakers or Moravians has become of the same validity to enable them to give evidence, as an oath administered in the usual form, in all cases, whether civil or criminal; and a false affirmation is tantamount to perjury, and punishable in the same manner as the latter crime. (9 G. 4. c. 32. ss. 1, 2.)

They are enjoined, in lieu of the oaths to government, to make a declaration of fidelity, (8 Geo. 1. st. 2. c. 6. s. 1,) an affirmation of abjuration, (Ib. s. 3; as to Moravians, 22 Geo. 2. c. 30,) and a profession of Christian belief, (1 W & M. st. 1. c. 18. s. 13.) These, when lawfully required, must be taken, made, and entered, at the general quarter sessions of the peace for the county, city, or place of residence of the party qualifying; who is thereupon exempted from the penalties of the statutes enumerated in the 13th section of the Toleration Act, and entitled to the full benefit of that act, equally with other Protestant Dissenters. (1 W. & M. st. 1. c. 18. s. 13.)

Payment of Tithes.] The 7 and 8 W 3. c. 34, 1 Geo. 1. c. 6, and 27 Geo. 2. c. 20, amended by 53 Geo. 3. c. 127, provide, on behalf of Quakers objecting to pay or compound for any tithes, rates, customary or other rights, dues, or payments belonging to the established church, that when any such, by law and custom, payable for the stipend or maintenance of any minister or curate, officiating in any church or chapel, amounting to a sum not exceeding £50, are due, any justice of the peace of the county or place, (other than the patron or person interested in the same,) on complaint of any parson, vicar, curate, farmer, or proprietor of, or entitled to receive or collect such tithes, rates, dues, or payments, respectively, may, and is required to summon, by writing, under his hand and seal, with reasonable warning, any Quaker refusing to pay or compound for the same, to appear before any two or more justices of the peace of the county or place aforesaid, and, on his appearance, or in default of his appearance, the warning or summons being proved on oath, they are empowered to examine on oath or affirmation, the truth of the complaint, to ascertain what is due, and, by order, under their hands and seals, to direct its payment: and on refusal to obey the order, it is lawful for one of the said last-mentioned justices, by warrant under his hand and seal, to levy the money by distress and sale of the goods of the offender, his executors or administrators, rendering only the surplus, after deducting the necessary costs and charges of making the distress, not exceeding the sum of 10*s*. Persons aggrieved may appeal to the next general quarter sessions; but these proceedings cannot be removed or superseded by *certiorari*, or other writ whatsoever, unless the title to such tithes, &c., comes in question; and in case of appeal, no warrant of distress may be granted, until after such appeal is determined. A general act of the same import, applying only to small tithes, offerings, oblations, obventions, and compositions, was passed in 7 and 8 Wm. 3. c. 6; made perpetual by 3 and 4 Anne, c. 18. s. 1, and extended to the value of £10 by 53 Geo. 3. c. 127. s. 4. The time for bringing actions to recover penalties for not setting out tithes and instituting suits in an equity or ecclesiastical court, to recover the value of tithes, is limited to six years. (53 Geo. 3. c. 127. s. 6.)

Militia Service.] The mode in which a Quaker is made to contribute to the militia is as follows: if he neglects or refuses to serve, (42 Geo. 3. c. 90. s. 50,) when embodied, or to provide a fit substitute, any two or more deputy lieutenants may provide one for him; and, by warrant under their hands and seals, levy upon him, by distress and sale, such reasonable sum as may be expended in procuring a substitute; and if no goods, or none sufficient can be found, and it satisfactorily appears to the said deputy lieutenants, that the said Quaker is of sufficient ability to pay the sum of £10, being the sum forfeited by other persons for similar instances of neglect and refusal, they may commit him to gaol for the term of three months, or until he pays the expense of procuring a substitute.

In case of supposed oppression in levying the distress, a complaint may be made by the party thinking himself aggrieved, to the next general meeting of the deputy lieutenants, who are authorised finally to determine the same.

Who deemed Quakers.] No person is to be deemed a Quaker within the meaning of these enactments, unless he produces to the deputy lieutenants, at a sub-division meeting, a certificate of that fact, under the hands of two respectable householders, being Quakers, dated within three months of the day of its production; and a similar certificate is required to be produced by householders, being Quakers, to the constable or other officer whose duty it may be to furnish a list of the inhabitants liable to military service. (42 Geo. 3. c. 90. ss. 27. 50, 51; see also 46 Geo. 3. c. 91.)

And if a Quaker is chosen constable, or otherwise appointed for the purposes of the Militia Act, and neglects or refuses to serve; on his producing a similar certificate, it is lawful for two justices to appoint a deputy for him, who shall be invested with the same powers, and liable to the same penalties, as he himself would have been; and on such appointment being made, he is discharged. (42 Geo. 3. c. 90. s. 33.)

Similar provisions are made in the act for the defence of the realm, and includes Moravians; (46 Geo. 3. c. 90. ss. 21, 28;) and likewise in the Local Militia Act, (52 Geo. 3. c. 38. ss. 25, 27.) And by the 20th section of the former act, a Quaker or Moravian balloted under that act, is exempted from service on producing a similar certificate to the proper authorities, who may fine the party in a sum not exceeding £7, nor less than 20*s.*, for the year of the ballot, to be levied by distress; and in case no goods can be found, may imprison him for any time not exceeding fourteen days, unless such sum is sooner paid or satisfied; but this act does not extend to the city of London.

A like provision to the last, is made in the Local Militia Act, but the fines specified in s. 44, being £30, £20, or £10, according to the ability of the party, may be mitigated, at the discretion of the deputy-lieutenants; who possess likewise the power of remitting the imprisonment, which is for one month.

Their Marriages.] Quakers are expressly excepted from the operation of the Marriage Acts, and enjoy the liberty of solemnizing matrimony in their conventicles, where both the contracting parties are of this denomination.

Their conjugal rights are the same as in other cases; nor would the title of the husband, it is presumed, to administer the effects of his deceased wife, be now disputed; as it was before the passing of the Marriage Act, (26 Geo. 2. c. 33,) as that specially exempts them from its operation. (Haydon v. Gould, 1 Salk. 120; see Hutchinson v. Brookebanke, 3 Lev. 376.)

Local Exemptions.] By various acts of parliament, Quakers are locally exempted from offices opposed to their religious scruples; such as that of assessor or collector of a stipend to a rector or vicar; (23 Geo. 2. c. 36; 47 Geo. 3. c. 132;) of collector, treasurer, clerk, or receiver, for building, re-building, or repairing a church, chapel, or steeple; (26 Geo. 2. c. 38; 55 Geo. 3. c. 44;) and of churchwarden or chapelwarden of new churches or chapels. (43 Geo. 3. c. 117; 51 Geo. 3. c. 69; 57 Geo. 3. c. 34.)

They may also compound, in certain specified instances, for parochial and other rates. (50 Geo. 3. c. 14; 56 Geo. 3. c. 56; 58 Geo. 3. c. 22.)

And their charitable foundations and donations are not included in the act for registering and securing charitable donations in general. (52 Geo. 3. c. 102.)

The statutes which more immediately extend the benefits of toleration to Quakers, are the 1 W. & M. s. 1. c, 18, and 10 Anne, c. 2.

SECTION IV.—IMMUNITIES OF DISSENTING MINISTERS.

Preaching in certified Places.] All persons teaching, preaching, or officiating in any congregation or assembly for the religious worship of Protestants, (that is, Dissenters, and not ministers of the church of England, (Trebec v. Keith, 2 Atk. 498,) whose place of worship is *duly certified* according to law, are now as fully exempted, without precedent qualification, (unless they have been legally required to qualify, 52 Geo. 3. c. 155. s. 4,) from the penalties of any acts relating to *religious worship*, as those who take the oaths *mentioned* in the Toleration Act, or any other act amending the said act.

Provided, that if any such person, not having taken the oaths to government, and subscribed the declaration (now abolished, 10 G. 4. c. 7) against transubstantiation, shall, when required by any one justice of the peace, by writing under his hand, or signed by him, continue to teach or preach in any such congregation or assembly, without taking the said oaths, he shall forfeit for each offence a sum not exceeding £10, nor less than 10*s.*, at the discretion of the convicting justice. (52 Geo. 3. c. 155. s. 5.)

But no person is required to go farther than five miles from his place of residence at the time of such requisition, for the purpose of qualifying. (Ibid, s. 7.)

Uncertified Places and locked Doors.] Preaching or officiating in any place of worship, field, or place in the open air, or other place, *not duly certified*, subjects the offender to the penalties incurred by the laity by being present at unlawful conventicles. And on certificate from the ordinary to two justices of a county, or the chief magistrate of a city or town corporate, the offender is liable, under the 13 & 14 Car. 2. c. 4, and 15 Car. 2. c. 6. s. 7, to be imprisoned for three months, —for neglecting to use the book of Common Prayer;—for administering the Lord's supper without episcopal ordination;—or for preaching and lecturing without episcopal license, assent to the thirty-nine Articles, and open reading, or assent to, the Book of Common Prayer.

And preaching in an assembly consisting of more than the lawful number, in any place, without the consent of the occupier thereof, (52 Geo. 3. c. 155. s. 3,) or in any place with the door locked, bolted, barred, or otherwise fastened, so as to prevent any person entering therein during the time of meeting, (s. 11,) the offender incurs, on conviction, by the oath of one or more witnesses, a forfeiture for each offence of the first class, of a sum not exceeding £30, nor less than 40*s.*; and of the second class, of a sum not exceeding £20, nor less than 40*s.*, at the discretion of two or more convicting justices.

It must be also observed, that dissenting ministers are excluded from the provision which exonerates lay Dissenters in general, from the penalties of acts relating to religious worship, on *ex post facto* qualification. (10 Anne, c. 2.)

Dissenting Ministers in Trade.] It is necessary for ministers engaged in trade, although teaching a separate congregation, to qualify under one or other of the following enactments, in order to avail themselves of the subsequent immunities and exemptions.

Every teacher, (1 W. & M. st. 1. c. 18. s. 11, extended to Unitarians by the 53 Geo. 3. c. 160,) or preacher, in *holy orders*, or *pretended holy orders, being preacher, or teacher, of a separate congregation*, (R. v. J. J., Denbighshire, 14 East. 284,) who takes the oaths to government, at the general or quarter sessions for the county or division where he lives, (which such court is empowered to administer, and enter of record, the clerk of the peace being entitled to a fee of sixpence for the same;) and also subscribes the thirty-nine Articles, except the thirty-fourth, thirty-fifth, and thirty-sixth, and these words of the twentieth article, viz. "*the church hath power to decree rites or ceremonies, and authority in controversies of faith and yet:*" or in case he scruples the baptizing of infants, except also, part of the twenty-seventh article touching infant baptism; is exempted from being chosen or appointed to the office of churchwarden, overseer of the poor, or any other parochial or ward office, or other office in any hundred, city, town, parish, or division, whether the same were in being at the time of the passing of this enactment, or has been subsequently created.

By the late Jury Act it is enacted, that none but teachers or preachers of dissenting congregations described in the ninth section of the 52 Geo. 3. c. 155, viz. such as employ themselves *solely* in the duties of preacher, and do not follow any *trade* or *profession* except that of a schoolmaster, shall be exempted from serving on juries; and such persons must produce a certificate of some justice of the peace, of their having taken the oaths, &c., required by law. (6 Geo. 4. c. 50. s. 2. See Kenward v. Knowles, Willes, 463.)

And every such person being a *preacher or teacher of any congregation,* and scrupling (19 Geo. 3. c. 44) to subscribe his assent to any of the articles aforesaid, who makes and subscribes the declaration of Protestant belief, is entitled to the same exemptions from civil service, and from *serving* in the militia: and the justices at the general sessions for the county or place where he lives, are required to administer the said last-mentioned declaration, to such person offering to make and subscribe the same, and thereof to keep a register; and for the entry thereof, with the oaths and other declarations aforesaid, a fee of sixpence only is due; and an additional fee of sixpence for any certificate of the same.

Meaning of Holy Orders, &c.] The exact meaning of the phrases, '*holy orders,*' '*pretended holy orders,*' and '*pretending to holy orders,*' has not been determined; but it has been held not essential to the pretending to holy orders, within the eighth section of the Toleration Act, that a person should be the teacher or preacher of a *separate* congregation; and a *mandamus* will issue to the justices at quarter sessions, to administer the qualification; yet such qualifying will not confer on the individual, who is not a preacher or teacher to a separate congregation, the immunities enjoyed under the eleventh section of the Toleration Act, but merely exempts him from certain *penalties* otherwise incurred by the exercise of the clerical function. (R. v. Justices of Gloucestershire, 15 East, 576.)

The sessions cannot require, that a person applying to qualify as a teacher of a separate congregation, shall produce a certificate from two of his congregation, authenticating such his appointment. (R. v. Justices of Suffolk, 15 East, 590.)

Exemption from serving or *providing a substitute* in the militia is also granted to every teacher of any *separate* congregation, who has been licensed *twelve months,* at the least, before the yearly meeting of the lieutenantcy of the county in October, under the Militia Act. (43 Geo. 3. c. 10.) But there are no exemptions from ballot or service under the *Local* Militia or *Training* acts, in favour of dissenting ministers carrying on trade.

Dissenting Ministers not in Trade.] The 52 Geo. 3. c. 155. s. 9, enacts, that every person who *teaches* or *preaches* in any congregation or assembly for religious worship, whose place of worship is duly certified according to law, and who employs himself solely in the duties of a teacher or preacher, and follows no trade or other employment for his livelihood, except that of a schoolmaster, and who produces a certificate of some justice of the peace of his having taken the oaths to government, &c., shall be exempt from the civil services and offices specified in the Toleration Act, and from serving in the militia or local militia of any place in any part of the United Kingdom. The production of a false certificate, for the purpose of claiming exemption from civil or military duties, subjects the party to a penalty for each offence of £50, recoverable by any person who will sue for the same. But such actions are made local, and must be brought within three months after the offence.

Minster's Right to his Office.] The principle of public policy does not extend to prevent a court of equity from sanctioning the appointment of a minister to a dissenting congregation for a *limited* period; provided such is the usage of the congregation, or the provision of the original trust. (Attorney-General v. Pearson and others, 3 Meriv. 402; R. v. Jotham, 3 T. R. 577.)

Where a minister has been duly elected, or claims title to an *endowed* pastorship, or a function with *emoluments,* which is resisted without a colour of right, and there is no specific legal remedy, the Court of King's Bench will grant a *mandamus* to the trustees to *admit,* even though the other party is in possession: the election and appointment constitute a legal right, which a *mandamus* to admit enables him to try and the use of the meeting-house and pulpit is incident to the clerical function. (R. v. Barker, 3 Burr. 1265, 1043. 1 Bla Rep. 300, 352.) Where a power of removal is not given to any particular part of a body, it rests with the society at large. (Rex v. Faversham, 8 T. R. 356.)

But in a case of endowment, where the minister has a certain interest in his office not depending on the voluntary contributions of the congregation, it is doubtful how far usage would justify a removal without reasonable cause. And a *mandamus* to *restore* an *endowed* minister has been granted in order to enable him to try their right of dispossessing him. (R. v. Jotham, 3 T. R. 577.)

Power of Trustees by Deed.] But where a trust-deed invests certain individuals with authority, *quasi* visitors, to dismiss or suspend a regularly appointed minister, the courts cannot interfere to prevent it; if, however, it is provided, that the same shall be done according to certain *rules, constitutions,* and *regulations* specified in the deed, before the courts will lend their assistance to enforce the sentence, they will be satisfied that those rules, &c., have been complied with.

Devise to Dissenting Ministers.] A devise in trust, "for those persons that are commonly called dissenting ministers," naming some of them, is good as it regards the ministers, notwithstanding the statutes of mortmain. (Lloyd v. Spillet, 3 P. W. 346.) So a legacy to Baptists generally, (Attorney-General v. Cock, 2 Ves. 275;) to Presbyterians, (Attorney-General v. Wansay, 15 Ves. 234;) and to Quakers, (Highmore, 146,) are respectively good. So a bequest in augmentation of a fund for poor dissenting ministers living "in *any county* in England," is held good, notwithstanding its uncertainty; and it being proved that there were three distinct societies of dissenters in England, the bequest was ordered to be distributed among the poor of each society. (Waller v. Childs, Amb. 524.)

A bequest in trust for "nonconforming ministers and dissenters," is good.

So an annuity to the minister of a Baptist meeting-house and his successors, has been held to be good. (Attorney-General v. Cock, 2 Ves. 273)

But a court of equity regards with a jealous eye bequests for the encouragement of *itinerant* preachers. (Attorney-General v. Stepney, 10 Ves. 22.) And a bequest of money to be laid out in land, for the benefit of two preachers at a chapel, although it is to be otherwise invested till an eligible purchase can be made, is void under the statute of mortmain.

Foreign Protestant ministers, domiciled in this country, it seems, are entitled, on the same terms, to the privileges of dissenting ministers. (R. v. Hube, Peake, 132.)

Dissenting Schoolmasters.] Every department of tuition being prohibited to Protestant Dissenters, by various statutes and canons, it is only on condition of qualifying specially, in a similar manner to preachers, that schoolmasters can legally exercise these professions. (See 19 Geo. 3. c. 44. s. 2.) But the better feeling and enlightened liberality of the age affords them a still more extended protection and impunity; from penal enactments, which may be said to have grown obsolete.

But persons so qualifying are not enabled to obtain or hold the mastership of any college or school of royal foundation, or of any other endowed college or school for the education of youth, unless the same has been founded since the 1st year of the reign of William and Mary, for the immediate use and benefit of Protestant Dissenters. (19 Geo. 3. c. 44. s. 3.)

Persons employed in the several departments of tuition, who have neglected or refused to qualify specially for this purpose, are exposed to the penalties and disabilities enumerated in the several statutes upon the subject; but as, for the reasons above suggested, they are not likely to be enforced, it is unnecessary to state them in detail.

SECTION V.—DISSENTING PLACES OF WORSHIP.

Registering Meeting-Houses.] No congregation or assembly for the religious worship of Protestants, at which are present more than twenty persons, in addition to the family and servants of the person on whose premises they assemble, or of Quakers, not more than four persons besides the family, &c., is permitted, if not duly certified under some acts or acts prior to the 52 Geo. 3. c. 155, (under which prior act or acts the Quakers must still certify,) unless and until the place of meeting shall have been, or shall be, certified to the bishop of the diocese, to the archdeacon of the archdeaconry, or to the justices of the peace, at the general or quarter sessions of the peace for the county, division, &c., in which such meeting shall be held; of which places of worship so certified respectively, reciprocal returns shall be made once in the year, between the bishop's or archdeacon's court, and the quarter sessions. And all such places shall be registered in the bishop's or archdeacon's court respectively, and recorded at the general quarter sessions, by the registrar or clerk of the peace, who is required to register and record the same; and the bishop, or registrar, or clerk of the peace, to whom any such place of meeting is certified under this act, must give a certificate thereof, to any person demanding the same, for which no greater fee than 2*s.* 6*d.* shall be taken.

Any Protestant Dissenter may certify a meeting-house under these acts. (Green and others v. Pope, 1 Ld. Raymond, 125.) The duty of registering is purely ministerial, and a *mandamus* issues against the person on whom it devolves, to compel performance. (R. v. Justices of Derbyshire, 1 Bla. Rep. 606; 4 Burr. 1991.)

The penalties incurred by permitting unlawful assemblies to be held, and of officiating at them, either with or without permission of the occupier of the premises, have been already noticed. (*Ante*, 149.)

And also that no assembly for religious worship, requiring a certificate, may be held in any place, with the door locked, bolted, or barred, or otherwise fastened, so as to prevent any persons entering during the time of such meeting. (52 Geo. 3. c. 155. s. 11.)

Disturbing a Lawful Assembly.] The 52 Geo. 3. c. 155. ss. 12. 15. 17, enacts, that any person wilfully and maliciously or contemptuously disquieting or disturbing any meeting, assembly, or congregation of persons authorized by this act, or any former act or acts of parliament, or in any way disturbing or molesting any preacher or person officiating at such meeting, or any person or persons there assembled, on proof thereof before any justice of the peace, by two or more credible witnesses, must find two sureties, to be bound by recognizances in the penal sum of £50 to answer for such offence; and in default of sureties, is to be committed to prison till the next general or quarter sessions; and on conviction there, he incurs a penalty of £40; and this penalty may be levied by distress; one moiety to be paid to the informer, and the other to the poor of the parish where the offence was committed; and in case of no sufficient distress, the justices may commit the offender to prison for any period not exceeding three months; but no penalty can be recovered under this act unless the offence is prosecuted within six months after its commission; and no person who suffers imprisonment for nonpayment of the penalty, is afterwards liable to its payment.

This enactment, however, does not extend to Quakers, (s. 14,) nor to assemblies for religious worship held by them; they are nevertheless within the protection of the 1 W. & M. c. 18. s. 18, by which any person who wilfully, maliciously, or contemptuously comes into any congregation *permitted* by the Toleration Act, and disquiets or disturbs the same, or misuses any preacher or teacher, incurs, on information and conviction thereof, in a manner similar to that abovementioned, a penalty of £20 to the use of the crown. (See cases upon these enactments, R. v. Hube, 5 T. R. 542; Rex v. Wadley, 4 M. & S. 508, 5 East, 294; R. v. Wroughton and others, 3 Burr. 1683.)

The protection of these statutes extends to Lutheran and other

Protestant congregations, composed principally of *foreigners* performing service in a foreign language. (R. v. Hube and others, Peake's Rep. 180.)

Rates, &c., of Places of Worship.] The ground on which a place of worship, or building for a charitable purpose, is erected, is not necessarily thereby exonerated from a land tax, to which it was *previously* liable: but where held on lease, and no *profit* is derived from it by any person, beyond the amount of rent reserved, the rent furnishes the measure of the assessment; and if *no rent* is reserved, or the inheritance is in the trustees, and no profit whatever is derived from it by any person, it is not liable to the tax at all. (46 Geo. 3. c. 133; 49 Geo. 3. c. 67.)

But if a profit is made of a chapel, or other building for charitable purposes, as by letting pews, or in any other way; whoever makes that profit may be considered a beneficial occupier, and is rateable to the poor in respect of the thing occupied. And if pews are let by trustees, in whom the property vests, they are deemed to make a profit of the rent, and are rateable for it, even though the expenditure of the trust exceeds its income; the subsequent disposition of the rent being considered altogether a matter of private arrangement. (R. v. Agar, 14 East, 256; Jones v. Mansell, Doug. 302, 1 Nol. P. L. 182.)

But chapels used solely for religious purposes, and from which no pecuniary advantage is derived by any person, or by mere pew-holders, (R. v. St. Bartholomew's, 4 Burr. 2435; R. v. St. Luke's, 2 Burr. 1053,) founders of a charity who derive no profit from it, (R. v. Agar, *supra;* R. v. Waldo, Cald. 358,) and poor inmates who have no controul over the premises they inhabit, are not rateable. (R. v. Woodward, 5 T. R. 79; Tracey v. Talbot, Salk. 531.)

Window and House Tax.] Windows in any room of a dwelling house, licensed according to law as a chapel for divine worship, and for no other purpose; and hospitals, charity schools, and houses for the reception and relief of poor persons, except the apartments therein which are occupied by the officers or servants of the charity, and which are to be severally assessed as entire dwelling houses, are exempted from the window tax; but they must be stated in the certificate of assessment; and on proof of the several grounds of exemption, may be discharged by the commisssioners. (43 Geo. 3. c. 161. Sch. (A).

Charity schools, hospitals, houses for the reception or relief of poor persons, are exempted from the inhabited house duty. (Ibid.

Sch. (B.) Chapels used exclusively for divine worship, do not come within this description.

Parochial Taxes.] The watch, scavenger, lamp, sewer, and other parochial or ward taxes, depend for their applicability to chapels and charitable institutions, on the several statutes and local provisions, under the authority of which they are respectively levied: (see 7 Ann, c. 9; 10; 10 Geo. 2. c. 22, &c.:) but if the yare taxes on the occupier, beneficial occupation, as in the instances before mentioned, will be the criterion of their rateability.

Grants and Trusts to Dissenters.] A grant of lands, &c., or money to be laid out in the purchase of lands, &c., for the purpose of supporting a chapel for public worship among Protestant Dissenters, is for a charitable use within the meaning of the statute of mortmain. (9 Geo. 2. c. 36. s. 1.)

Hence, the owner of land having, at his own expense, built a chapel, which was used for public worship, and the congregation having subscribed a sum of money for the purpose of enlarging and improving it; he, in consideration that the money so subscribed should be expended for that purpose, demised the premises by lease for twenty-three years, reserving a pepper-corn rent during his life, and £10 per annum after his death. A declaration of trust in favour of the congregation assembling there, was also made by some of the lessees. It was held, that this conveyance was for the benefit of a charitable use, and therefore void; that neither the sum agreed to be expended on the premises, nor the rent reserved at the death of the lessor, was a full consideration for the lease, within the meaning of the second section of the statute; and that a declaration of trust executed by some of the lessees, is evidence against all, of the purpose for which the lease was granted. (Doe dem Wellard and others v. Hawthorn, 2 Barn. & Ald. 96.)

Devises and Bequests.] So a legacy to be applied towards the discharge of a mortgage on a dissenting chapel; and a bequest to enable trustees to complete a contract for the purchase of land; (Corbyn v. French, 4 Ves. 418;) a conveyance of a meeting-house and burial-ground, in trust to permit a society of Quakers, who then held them, to continue to use them so long as they paid certain rent, and kept the same in repair; and also to permit the society to take part of a farm to build a new meeting-house, if necessary; (Doe dem. Thomson v. Pitcher, 2 Marsh. 61, 3 Maul. & Sel. 407, 6 Taunt. 359;) and a trust by will, for building or purchasing a chapel, where it may appear to the executors to be most wanted; if any overplus, to go to the support of a faithful gospel minister, not exceeding £20 a year; and if any further surplus, for charitable uses as the executors should think proper; all these several bequests were held void, and in the last case the whole trust was avoided; the real estate went to the heir at law, and the *personal* to the next of kin. (Chapman v. Brown, 6 Ves. 404; 2 Brown, 428; 3 Ves. 141.)

But a devise to trustees, of a reversion in land to be applied by them and their successors, and the officiating ministers for the time being, of a Methodist congregation, as they shall from time to time *think fit* to apply the same, is not a devise to charitable uses within the statute; the trustees, therefore, are entitled to recover at law, however the court of Chancery may afterwards direct the application of the trust fund. (Doe dem. Toone v. Copestake, 6 East. 328.)

Nor is a legacy for the increase and improvement of Christian knowledge, a legacy within the statute; but the court of Chancery will see to its application. (Attorney General v. Stepney, 10 Ves. 22.) And although a legacy given to Protestants Dissenters, to pay off a mortgage on their chapel, is void, yet if it be previously paid off in the testator's lifetime, by other means, it seems the money may be employed in repairing the chapel, but it can be applied to no other purpose. (Corbyn v. French, 4 Ves. 418.)

Trustees and Congregations.] Where, by a trust for religious worship, it appears to have been the founder's intention (although not expressed) that a particular doctrine should be preached, it is not in the power of the trustees, or of the congregation, to alter the design of the institution. (Attorney General v. Pearson and others, 3 Meriv. 400.)

So, where a fund is raised for the purchase of property to be devoted to religious worship, the property so purchased must be applied to those purposes, according to the principles of the individuals who so acquired that property; provided they are not contrary to law: and those who have contributed towards such fund, have a continued right to exercise a power consistent with the original contract, and the principles of toleration. (Attorney General v. Fletcher and others, M. S.)

Nor can any agreement among the donees of a charity, alter or direct it to other uses than those expressly limited by the donor. (Man v. Ballett, 1 Vern. 42.)

A trust for the benefit of a charity is broken by pulling down a chapel, and converting the burial-ground to other purposes; and on petition, under the 52 Geo. 3. c. 101. s. 12, the court of Chancery will direct a conveyance to new trustees; (Ex-parte Greenhouse, 1

Madd. 92;) yet the court will, in its discretion, permit a departure from the terms of the trust, when its object is substantially preserved; as to build a new chapel, where the trust was for repairing. (Attorney-General v. Foyster and others, 1 Anst. 116.) It has been decided, that a provision in case of the desertion and removal of any of the trustees, that the remaining trustees may, within a limited time, elect others in the room of those so deserting, does not extend to disable a trustee having so deserted, from acting again, where no successor has, in the mean time, been appointed; nor to the case of a trustee, who retired on account of the trust having been converted, against his approbation, to purposes differing from the intent of the founder. (Attorney-General v. Pearson, 3 Meriv. 412.)

Chancery Jurisdiction.] The court, on regular application, will give to dissenting bodies the full benefit of the laws of the country, applicable to their *discipline* and *conduct*, so far as the same are not contrary to law. (Attorney-General v. Pearson and others, ib. 397.)

It will also interpose to prevent an improper person from receiving pew rents, and appoint a receiver during the suit; but it will not, it seems, interfere with a voluntary subscription. (Attorney-General v. Fowler, 15 Ves. 88; Ex-parte Pearson 6 Price, 213.) The question of religious belief is considered by the court as irrelevant, except when called on to execute a trust: but if the parties applying make out that a particular mode of belief was intended by the founder of the trust, still they must show that the meeting-house was for such purposes as the law can sanction, in order to entitle themselves to the assistance of the court. (3 Meriv. 415.)

Mode of construing Trusts.] If land or money be properly given for maintaining " the worship of God," without more, the court will execute the trust in favour of the established religion. If it is clearly *expressed* that the purpose is that of maintaining dissenting doctrines, so long as they are not contrary to law, the court will execute the trust accordingly; and where the intention clearly appears *aliunde*, though *not* expressed in the instrument creating the trust, the court will also carry the manifest design of the founder into execution, so far as it is consistent with law.

In these and similar cases, the court will probably refer it to the Master, to inquire the facts of the case: as for instance, in whom the legal estate is vested; the particular object (with respect to worship and doctrine) for which the trust was created; the usage of Protestant Dissenters as to the election of ministers, and the duration of their office; and whether any agreement or understanding relative thereto subsists between the parties. (3 Meriv. 420.)

In cases of surplus revenue, the court will apply it according to the doctrine of *Cy pres:* as on a bequest made before the stat. 9 Geo. 2. c. 36, to the congregation of Presbyterians to which the testator belonged, for placing out as apprentices two poor boys of such as were members of the congregation, and living in the parish of St. Martin in New Sarum, the fund becoming more than sufficient, the court applied the surplus, first, to place out sons of members within that parish;—secondly, sons of members in other parishes;—thirdly, daughters of members in like manner;—and lastly, sons of Presbyterians generally, previous to building a school and other purposes; and sons of persons of the established religion within the parish were, on a proposal, rejected. (Attorney-General v. Wansey, 15 Ves. 231.)

Burning or destroying Meeting Houses.] The former acts on this subject were repealed, with a multitude of other statutes relating to criminal offences, by the 7 & 8 G. 4. c. 27, for the purpose of consolidating their scattered provisions in new enactments By the 7 & 8 G. 4. c. 30. s. 2, it is provided, that if any person shall unlawfully and maliciously set fire to any chapel for the religious worship of persons dissenting from the united church of England and Ireland, duly registered or recorded, every such offender shall be guilty of felony, and being convicted thereof, shall suffer death as a felon. And the 8th section enacts the same punishment against persons riotously assembled, demolishing, or beginning to demolish, any such place of public worship. And by the 7 & 8 G. 4. c. 31. s. 2, it is enacted, that if any such place of worship shall be feloniously demolished, pulled down or destroyed, wholly or in part, by any persons riotously and tumultuously assembled together; in every such case, the inhabitants of the hundred, or other district in the nature of a hundred, by whatever name it shall be denominated, in which any such offence shall be committed, shall be liable to yield *full compensation* to the person or persons damnified by the offence; not only for the injury to the building, but also for any damage which may at the same time be done to any fixture, furniture, or goods whatever, in any such chapel. (See Pritchet v. Waldron, 5 T. R. 14; 2 Saund. 377; Beatson v. Rushforth, 7 Taunt. 45; 2 Marsh. 362.)

The act requires, that the party injured having knowledge of the circumstances of the offence, or the servants who had the care of the property, shall, within seven days after the commission of the offence, state on oath before a neighbouring justice, the names of the offenders, if known; and submit to examination by such justice on the subject, and become bound to prosecute the offenders, when apprehended.

And no action can be brought, unless it be commenced within three calendar months after the offence committed. (s. 3.)

Process must be served on the high constable, who may, with the approbation of two justices, either defend the same or suffer judgment by default; and he must continue to act in the proceedings, although his office may expire before they are concluded. (s. 4.)

CHAPTER VII.—HIGHWAYS.

SECTION I.—THE SEVERAL KINDS OF HIGHWAYS.

Three kinds of Ways.] There are three kinds of WAYS: first, a foot way, for man alone to pass along, called in Latin *iter;* secondly, a foot and horse-way, *actus ab agendo,* commonly called a pack and prime way; and thirdly, *via* or *aditus,* a road for carriages, horses, and men, including both the former; this last being twofold, viz. *regia via,* the king's highway for all men, &c.; and *communis strata,* belonging to a city, or town, or private persons. (Co. Lit. 56. a.)

In legal acceptation, a *way* comprehends no more than the mere surface upon which it passes; and includes neither the fences on either side (Rex v. Commissioners of Landillo, 2 T. R. 232) nor the minerals or earth under it. (Rol. Abr. 392.) A common street is a public king's highway; (Woodyer v. Hadden, 5 Taunt. 137;) though *communis strata,* and *alta regia via,* were formerly attempted to be distinguished from each other. (Rex v. Hammond, 1 Stra. 44.) A highway may be created by act of Parliament. (Sutcliffe v. Greenwood, 8 Price, 535.) Any of these roads, which are common to all his Majesty's subjects, though leading merely from a hamlet, may be properly termed high or common ways. (Rex v. Harrow, 4 Burr. 2090.)

Thoroughfare or not.] It has not yet been determined whether there can be a public highway which is not a *thoroughfare;* but in two cases where this question was incidentally mentioned, several of the judges seemed inclined to the negative. (See Wood v.

Veal, 5 Barn. & Ald. 454; Woodyer v. Hadden, 5 Taunt. 125.) A passage from one part to another of a street, made originally for private convenience, may become a public highway, notwithstanding it is circuitous. (Rex v. Lloyd, 1 Camp. 260;) or is used by the public occasionally only; and though it does not terminate in a town, or in any other public road. (Rex v. Wandsworth, 1 Barn. & Ald. 63.)

On the contrary, it is not *necessarily* a highway, although it does lead from one market town to another; or although it might be advantageously used by the public, or *is* used by them under certain restrictions. (Rugby Charity v. Merryweather, 11 East, 376.—See "Partial Dedication," post 164.)

Way by Dedication.] Where a man builds a street on his own land, and it is used by the public as a highway, and no bar or other impediment is erected thereon by him, a dedication to the public will be *presumed.* (Lade v. Sheppard, 2 Stra. 1004; Rex v. Lloyd, 1 Camp. 260.) But if a bar, rail, or gate, however slight, be kept across it, although the public be permitted in general to pass, no dedication can be presumed, (Woodyer v. Hadden, 5 Taunt. 135;) and if such bar, &c. erected at first, be afterwards knocked down and not replaced, still the presumption is rebutted, for a dedication must be made openly, and with a deliberate purpose, (Roberts v. Karr, 1 Camp. 262. n.) The circumstance of the street being a *cul de sac,* favours the presumption that no dedication was intended, even should it be determined that there can be a highway which is *not* a thoroughfare. (See Wood v. Veal, & Woodyer v. Hadden, *ubi supra.*)

Where a street, which had been forming for six years, leading from an old public street to a new road across fields, over which fields the way had been used for five or six years, was unfinished; one half only being lighted, the other half being neither lighted nor paved; but the inhabitants had paid the highway and paving rates;—it was held that this was sufficient evidence to go to a jury of a dedication of the street to the public. (Jarvis v. Dean, 11 Moore 354, 3 Bing. 447.)

Dedication, by whom made.] The act of dedication must be by the owner of an estate of inheritance, in the land; and a leaseholder, however long his term, cannot devote any portion of the land to a highway, so as to bind the reversioner. (Wood v. Veal, 5 Barn. & Ald. 454.) In this last mentioned case, it appeared that the road in question was included in a lease of a yard and premises, from 1719 to 1818, and that the road had been used as far back as living memory could go, but there was no evidence of *consent* by the owner of the inheritance, before or since the lease; and it was held, that there was no dedication, although during the lease, the *locus in quo,* which was a *cul de sac,* was paved and lighted by the parish; and was described in 11 G. 3, for paving, &c. as "Little Abingdon-street, Westminster;" and the owner of the inheritance had lived in the neighbourhood for the last twenty-four years. Lord Ellenborough however, held, that where the way had been used for a great number of years over a close, in the hands of a succession of tenants, one of whom frequently *complained* thereof to the landlord's steward, but no action was brought against any trespasser, that a dedication must be presumed; although the landlord was never in the actual possession himself, nor proved to have been near the spot. (Rex v. Barr, 4 Camp. 16.)

Where the owner of the inheritance is aware of the use made by the public, and does not oppose it, *how long* a time shall be sufficient to bind him irrevocably, seems unsettled. In the Rugby Charity case, Lord Kenyon speaks of six years; but Mansfield, C. J., in Woodyer v. Hadden, asks, if six, why not one? why not half a year? In Woodyer v. Hadden (5 Taunt. 135,) Gibbs, J. observes, that "in all the cases where it has been held, that there has been a dedication of a way to the public, there has been a considerable space of time of user as a *material ingredient;* in one of the most leading cases, that of the Foundling Hospital, (11 East, 375, n.) Lord Kenyon treats that as a very material ingredient."

Partial Dedication.] It has not been yet expressly decided, whether there may be a *partial* dedication of a highway to the public. Two of the learned judges of the King's Bench, (Mr. Justice Bayley, and Mr. Justice Holroyd,) said they saw no objection in principle to such a dedication; and were disposed to think it might be made, though Mr. Justice Littledale entertained some doubt on the subject. (See Marquis of Stafford v. Coyney, 7 Barn. & Cres. 260.) However, the court decided in that case, where a landowner suffered the public to use, for several years, a road through his estate for all purposes *except* that of carrying coals, that this was either a limited dedication, or no dedication at all, but only a *license* revocable; and that a person carrying coals along the road, after notice not to do so, was a trespasser; and supposing it to amount to a partial dedication, whether legal or not, it was further observed, that at all events, the right given cannot be more extensive than the gift imports.

Repair of dedicated Road.] It does not follow, that because there is a dedication of the road by the owner of the soil, and the public use it, that the parish is therefore bound to repair. There ought to be evidence that the parish acquiesced in that dedication, in addition to the public user, to make it such a public road as the parish is bound to repair. (Rex v. St. Benedict, Cambridge, 4 Barn. & Ald. 447.)

The dedicating a way to the public, communicates no more than the right of passage; the original owner retains his interest in the soil, with all trees that grow upon it, and mines which may be opened beneath it. (2 Inst. 705.)

Turnpike Roads.] The greatest portion of the highways throughout the kingdom, are what are technically called Turnpike Roads, from their having been either originally formed, or subsequently regulated by acts of Parliament, which have provided the means of keeping them in repair, by the tolls which are taken at the turnpikes erected upon them, for the purpose.

Parishes, however, are not exonerated from *liability* to repair such roads, where they have existed immemorially, though it is not often found necessary to resort to them for such repairs; as the funds vested in the trustees are generally sufficient to meet all the necessary expences of this description. And it is provided by the general Turnpike acts, that materials may be procured for such roads, in like manner as the Highway acts have directed, with regard to the highways more immediately under the care and management of parishes, by their surveyors. The same acts also provide, that the statute duty, to which parishioners are liable, may be ordered to be performed in part upon turnpike roads, or a proportion of the composition paid in lieu thereof, may be directed to be handed over to the treasurer of such turnpike roads. So that turnpike trusts, and the monies which they raise and expend in keeping these roads in good condition, are in fact established in ease and relief of parishes, and not as an absolute discharge of their liability. (See 3 Geo. 4. c. 126. 7 & 8 Geo. 4. c. 24. 9 Geo. 4. c. 77.)

SECTION II.—REPAIRING HIGHWAYS.

Parish primarily liable.] Although the duty of *repairing* highways is charged by the common law upon the parishes through which they pass, it does not impose the obligation of making *new* roads, or *widening* old ones, however necessary, either upon parishes, or upon any person or persons whatever. (Rex v. Devon, 4 Barn. & Cres. 670; 7 Dowl. & Ryl. 147.) These objects are provided for by the General Highway act, the 13 G. 3. c. 78, (which, see *post,*) or by turnpike, or local acts passed from time to time, as the exigencies and convenience of the public may require.

At common law, each parish is liable to repair those portions of a common highway, which lie within its own limits. (H. P. C. b. 1. c. 76. s. 5.) And therefore, where a township or particular district of a parish, is exempted from the whole, or any part of this burden, by an express act of Parliament, it must necessarily fall on the rest of the parish. (Rex v. Sheffield, 2 T. R. 111; 1 Ventr. 90, 183, 189.)

Insolvent or negligent Trusts.] This primary obligation upon the parish is so strong and absolute, that if other persons or public bodies be made chargeable by statute, (as commissioners, trustees, &c.) and they become insolvent (1 Lord Raym. 725,) or neglect to repair when necessary, (Rex v. St. George, Hanover-square; 3 Camp. 222;) the duty of the parishioners revives; unless they are expressly exempted by the statute; and the parish, after making the proper repairs, may seek a remedy over against such commissioners or trustees, &c. The same liability falls upon the parish, in the case of *new* highways, (Rex v. Netherthong, 2 Barn. & Ald. 183;) though if it be a turnpike road, and the trustees are directed to repair it from time to time, with the money arising from the tolls, this is an auxiliary fund, from which the trustees may be required to bear part of the expence, according to the discretion of the court in which an indictment may happen to be preferred against the parish, when the road is out of repair. (13 G. 3. c. 84. s. 33.) And although in every turnpike act, a provision is contained for the repair of the roads out of the money arising by virtue of the act, no case has occurred of an indictment against *trustees* for the non-repair of their roads. And they are not liable by way of indictment; and the only persons who are so liable, are the parishioners or inhabitants. (R. v. Netherthong, *ubi supra.*) Nor can the parish be discharged from its liability, by virtue of an agreement with others; and consequently, a count alleging the defendant's liability upon such an agreement, with the owners of houses alongside the highway cannot be sustained. (Rex v. Liverpool, 3 East, 86.)

The whole Parish liable.] The duty rests *prima facie* upon the *whole* parish; and therefore, if it is actually thrown upon some particular part of it, the precise grounds upon which the liability is thus shifted must be shown. (Rex v. Penderryn, 2 T. R. 513.) So if a parish extend into *two* counties, and one of its roads lying in one county be out of repair, the *whole* parish, and not that part of the parish, or those inhabitants who live in that portion of the parish which is in the same county as the road, must be proceeded against. (Rex v. Clifton, 5 T. R. 498.) On the other hand, if the defective way runs through several parishes, and it is intended to compel the repair of the whole, a *joint* proceeding against all such parishes is not sustainable. (6 Wentw. 409, in notes.)

Roads on Boundaries.] In many instances the boundary of

parishes is in the middle of a highway, and therefore, to prevent any difficulty in determining by whom such highways must be kept in repair, the 34 Geo. 3. c. 60, enables two justices to settle and mark the boundaries, and each parish must then repair the portion thus allotted to it. But where a road is awarded by commissioners of an inclosure act, to a different parish to that in which it has heretofore been situated, and the same parish to which it formerly belonged continues, for some time after the award, to repair the road, the parishioners cannot subsequently avail themselves of the award, to relieve them from the liability, without showing that the previous notices required by the act, under which the award was made, were properly given, that the boundaries were about to be ascertained and settled by the commissioners. (Rex v. Haslingfield, 2 Maul. & Sel. 558.)

Extra-parochial Hamlets, &c.] Though the public have the security in the policy of the common law for the reparation of the highways, in all cases where the direct obligation is not cast upon others, still parishes may be and are relieved, in some instances, from this responsibility with respect, at least, to some of their roads. It seems doubtful whether the inhabitants of an extra-parochial hamlet, (not included in a larger district, the inhabitants of which are bound to repair the whole,) are, in this respect, in the same situation as the inhabitants of a parish; and liable, as of common right, to repair their own roads. The court did not decide that question; as the case was determined upon the form of the pleadings. (See Rex v. Kingsmoor, 2 Barn. & Cres. 190, 3 Dowl. & Ryl. 398.) But it is clear, that a hamlet, or other district than a parish, may be liable by custom or prescription. (Id. Rex v. Great Broughton, 5 Burr. 2700).

Liability by Inclosure.] In ancient times, when roads were frequently made through uninclosed lands, and were not formed with that exactness which the exigencies of society now dictate, it was part of the law, that the public, when the road was out of repair, might pass along the land by the side of the road. This right on the part of the public was attended with this consequence, that although the parishioners were bound to the repair of the road, yet if an owner excluded the public from using the *adjoining* land, he cast upon himself the *onus* of repairing the road. If the same person was the owner of the land on both sides, and inclosed both sides, he was bound to repair the whole of the road. If he inclosed on one side only, the other being left open, he was bound to repair to the middle of the road, and where there was an ancient inclosure on one side, and the owner of lands inclosed on the other, he was bound to repair the whole. (Rex v. Staughton, 1 Hawk. P. C. c. 76. s. 7.)

Hence it followed as a natural consequence, that when a person inclosed his land from the road, he did not make his fence close to the road, but left an open space at the side of the road, to be used by the public when occasion required. This appears to be the most natural and satisfactory mode of explaining the frequency of wastes left at the sides of roads; the object being to have a sufficiency of land for passage by the side of a road, when it was out of repair. (Steel v. Prickett, 2 Stark. R. 469.) This conditional right to go upon the adjacent ground is not restrained by the land being cultivated or sown with grain. (1 Roll. Ab. 390. (B.) pl. 1; Absor. v. French, 2 Show. 28; Taylor v, Whitehead, Doug. 749, 2 Saund. 161. n. (12.)

The owner who so incloses his lands, next adjoining a highway, is bound to make a perfect *good* way, and shall not be excused by merely making it as good as it was at the time of the inclosure, if it were then any way defective. (1 Hawk. P. C. c. 76. s. 6.) And, if the road be insufficient, any of the king's subjects may justify breaking down the inclosure, and passing as before on the adjoining land. (3 Salk. 182.) But the party thus rendered liable, may discharge himself of the burthen by throwing down the inclosure, and restoring the passage to its former condition. (1 Hawk. P. C. c. 76. s. 7.)

Inclosed under Writ or Statute.] But where a highway is altered, changed, or inclosed by a legal course, as by a writ of *ad quod damnum,* or under the authority of the statute 13 Geo. 3. c. 78. s. 19, the owner of the land is not obliged to repair the new road, unless in the case of a writ of *ad quod damnum,* the jury impose such a condition upon him. But if a new road be made in substitution of an old one, upon a writ of *ad quod damnum,* and extend into a parish where no part of the old road existed, then the person who sued out the writ and his heirs ought not only to make it, but to keep that portion in repair which runs into such other parish. (Ex-parte Vennor, 3 Atk. 772.) So, where a highway is inclosed under the authority of an act of Parliament for dividing and inclosing open common fields, the person whose allotment abuts upon the highway, and who incloses, is not bound to repair it. (Rex v. Flecknow, 1 Burr. 465.)

Repair by Prescription.] It is said, that a corporation aggregate may be compelled to repair a road, by force of a general prescription, that it ought and hath used to do it; without showing that it used to do so in respect of the tenure of certain lands, or for any other consideration; because such a corporation in judgment of law never dies; and therefore, if it were ever bound to such a duty, it must needs continue to be always so. Neither is it any plea, that such a corporation have always done it out of charity, for what it hath always done, it shall be presumed to have been always bound to do. (1 Hawk. P. C. b. 1. ch. 76. s. 8.) The inhabitants of a division of a parish may also, by this means, be liable to repair without any peculiar benefit. (2 Saund. 158. d. n. 9.)

But a particular person cannot be bound by prescription, by reason that he and all his ancestors have repaired the road, if it be not in respect of the tenure of his land, taking of toll, or other profit; for the act of the ancestor cannot charge the heir without profit. (13 Co. 33, 2 Saund. 158. d. n. 9; Rex v. Kerrison, 1 Maul. & Sel. 435.) And when the *origin* of a way can be shown, the prescription to repair it is necessarily destroyed. (R. v. Hudson, 2 Stra. 909.)

In order to subject any person, thus liable to repair, to a prosecution, the road must be incommodious, not merely from the season, as in winter, or its own narrowness, but from the want of sufficient reparation. (R. v. Stretford, 2 Ld. Raym. 1169.)

SECTION III.—INDICTMENTS AND PLEADINGS.

Modes of Prosecution.] There are three ways by which parishes, districts, or parties, liable to repair highways, may be prosecuted for suffering them to decay, or neglecting to repair them when necessary, viz. by indictment, information, and the presentment of a judge or justice of the peace.

The proceeding by indictment is now usually adopted, though an information may be granted in the discretion of the Court of King's Bench. (Rex v. Inhabitants of Essex, Sir Thomas Raym. 384.) But the court will not give leave to file an information, except in cases of great importance, or where the grand jury have been guilty of gross misbehaviour in refusing to find the bill of indictment; because the fine on conviction, upon an information, cannot be applied to the repair of the road, as it always is upon an indictment. (See Chitty, Crim. L. 569.)

Road Presentment.] The mode of proceeding by presentment is regulated by 13 Geo. 3. c. 78. s. 24. (see *post* p. 199.) A presentment made according to the act has exactly the same effect as the finding of a grand jury; and it has been held, that the power given by the sixteenth section of the act to two justices to order any highways to be widened, extends to roads repairable *ratione tenuræ;* and that, upon disobedience to such order, the party may either be proceeded against summarily under the statute, or by indictment.

Rex v. Balme, Cowp. 648.) But neither this proceeding, nor that of indictment can be instituted before any other tribunal than that in the jurisdiction of which the cause thereof arises; and no *certiorari* can be allowed to remove the proceedings before traverse and judgment, *unless the duty to repair be denied.* As, however, this clause (s. 24) makes no mention of the crown, and as the traverse can proceed from the other party, it is holden, that the prosecutor, though he merely use the king's name, is not affected by this regulation, but may remove the proceedings whenever he thinks fit; and that it was the delay of defendants only against which the statute was directed. (Rex. v. Bodenham, Cowp. 78.)

So that every defence which could be relied upon in an indictment, will be equally available when the nuisance is *presented* by a judge or justice of the peace. (Rex v. Hornsey, Carth. 212; Rex v. Wiltshire, 3 Burr. 1530.)

Indictment against a Parish.] An indictment or presentment against a parish for not repairing must show three things: that the road in question is *a highway,* that it is situate within the parish, and that it is out of repair.

With respect to the description of the road, though it is often stated in indictments or presentments, that *from time whereof the memory of man is not to the contrary,* or from time immemorial, there was, and is, a common and ancient king's highway, yet it has been adjudged sufficient to state compendiously, both in indictments and in pleas, justifying under a right of way, that it is a highway, without showing *how* it became so, or that it has been so from time immemorial. (Aspindall v. Brown, 3 T. R. 265, 2 Saund. 185. n. 4.) It has also been held, that if the nuisance be laid to all the king's subjects, it is necessarily implied, that the way wherein it is, is a common way for public benefit. (Thrower's case, 1 Vent. 208, Say, 168.)

Averment of Kind of Way.] An averment, that the *locus* was a common and public highway for, &c., "*to pass along at pleasure, paying a certain toll,*" is not inconsistent or contradictory, particularly if it is not said to be *immemorial;* for it may be a highway created by act of Parliament. (Sudcliffe v. Greenwood, 8 Price. 535.) It has been said, that it is not requisite to state whether it is for the use of carriages, horses, or foot passengers; for, by Lord Hardwicke, "the length and breadth of the way, and from whence and whither, are necessary to be ascertained in these indictments; but I do not remember any authority that holds it necessary to say, that it is a highway for this or that particular carriage." (Rex v. Hatfield, Rep. temp. Hardw. 315.) However, as so general a description would be improper, if the road be not a highway, for *all* purposes; as, for instance, if it be a foot way only, it is certainly advisable to insert the more peculiar description. (Allen v. Ormond, 8 East, 4.)

Indefinite Averments.] If the public have only a limited right to use the way, subject to its being occasionally shut up at the will of the owner of the soil, it must be described accordingly, and the averment, that it is used by all the king's subjects, "at their free will and pleasure," would be a fatal variance. (Rex v. Marquis of Buckingham, 4 Camp. 189.)

If the description be too indefinite in another respect, (as, "a certain highway leading from Hammersmith towards and unto Uxbridge,") being equally applicable to *several* highways, the objection cannot be taken advantage of, unless it is specially pleaded, if the description be true in fact. (Rex v. Hammersmith, 1 Stark. R. 357.)

Averment of Termini.] It does not seem *necessary* to state that the highway leads *from one place to another,* for the highways have no other bounds than the sea; therefore, if the *terminus a quo,* and the *terminus ad quem* are omitted, the indictment, or plea, &c., is, nevertheless, good. (Halsey's case, Latch. 183, Palm. 389; Nottingham's case, 2 Roll. Rep. 412, 10 Mod. 382; Rouse v. Barden, 1 H. Bla. 351.) In the King v. Haddock, (Andr. 145,) Lee, C. J., said, that the objection, "that the River T., where the nuisance was committed, being a highway, the *terminus a quo* and the *terminus ad quem* ought to have been set out, has been given up, and not without reason; for it was overruled in the case of the King v. Hammond, (1 Stra. 44, 10 Mod. 382,) which was an indictment for a nuisance in a street; and it was objected, that there were no *termini* stated; and 1 Roll. Rep. was cited in support of the objection; but the court held that it was not necessary, because highways have no bounds; and Parker, C. J., cited the King v. Thompson, (10 W 3,) where it was so determined. And though Mr. Serjeant Hawkins says, (1 Hawk. P. C. c. 76. s. 86,) that it is *safest* to show both the place *from* which, and also the place *to* which, the way supposed to be out of repair doth lead; yet, he says, that exceptions, for want of such certainty, have sometimes been disallowed; and probably he was not aware, at the moment, of the before-mentioned cases.

Averment of Locality.] The highway must be *alleged* to lie in the parish indicted; and, if it be not so alleged, the indictment or presentment is erroneous, and judgment will be reversed. (Rex v. Hartford, Cowp. 111, 2 Saund. 158, n. 5.) And therefore, as the words *from* and *unto* are exclusive, if the allegation be, that the road leads *from* or *to* the parish, though the part out of repair is charged as situate within it, this averment will not aid the defect;

(Rex v. Gamlingay, 3 T. R. 513.) But in a recent case Lord Tenterden said, "My mind is not satisfied with the decision in Rex v. Gamlingay, that the words *from* and *to* are necessarily exclusive:" and as the indictment alleged that the defendants removed a culvert *in the parish*, although it went on to say, in a highway there, *leading from the parish*, to another place it was held, that it sufficiently appeared that the culvert was *in* the parish. (Rex v. Knight, 7 Barn. & Cres. 413.)

So a material *variance* from the description will be fatal; thus an averment, that the highway leads from A to C, and thence to D, will not be satisfied by evidence of a road leading from A *towards* C; but turning off to B *before* it reached C, by a quarter of a mile. (Rex v. Great Caulfield, 6 Esp. 136.) But an indictment describing the way as leading from a hamlet in the parish indicted, is good; because the road may well pass through other parts of the same district. (Rex v. Harrow, 4 Burr. 2090.)

If a parish lie partly in one county and partly in another, and a highway lying in one part is out of repair, an indictment stating that the inhabitants of *that part* of the parish ought to repair, is bad; for it must be against the *whole* parish. (Rex v. Clifton, 5 T. R. 498, overruling Rex v. Weston, under Penyard, 4 Burr. 2507.)

Averment of out of Repair.] The indictment, &c., must also expressly aver that the way is *out of repair*; an allegation that it is narrow and muddy, is insufficient; because there is no obligation at common law to *widen* a way that is narrow; and a road may be made muddy, though in good repair. (Reg. v. Stretford, 2 Ld. Raym. 1169.)

Averment of Length and Breadth.] It is said to be necessary to allege to what part of the highway the nuisance complained of extends, as by showing how many feet in length, and how many feet in breadth it contains. The reason assigned is, that if it be not, the defendant will not know the certainty of the charge against which he is to make his defence, nor will the court be able to judge what will be the proper fine to assess. (Rex v. Hatfield, Cas. temp. Hardw. 106; Rex v. Roberts, 1 Show. 390.) But as the court does not at present estimate the fine, from the length and breadth of the road, as stated in the indictment, perhaps the omission of such statement would not now be considered a fatal objection. (Say. 98. 167.) It has been held, that an indictment alleging, that a certain part of the king's *highway*, between A and B, is in a ruinous condition, is not bad, for not setting out the length and breadth of the nuisance; (Rex v. East Lidford, Say. 301, 2 Saund. 158, n. (7).

But an indictment against a parish for not repairing one side of the road, (the other side lying in another parish,) ought to state that each parish was liable to repair *ad medium filum viæ,* and not merely that a certain part of the road, *in breadth* fifteen feet, was out of repair. (Rex v. St. Pancras, Peakes, R. 219.)

Indictment against a Township, &c.] The inhabitants of a parish being liable, as of common right, it is sufficient, as against them, to allege that they *ought* to repair. But if it be sought to charge the inhabitants of *part* of a parish, as of a township, or other division, or a number of persons in any other capacity, or a private individual, with the burden of repair, that being against common right, it must be shown on the *face of the indictment,* or other pleading, *how* the liability arises, whether by custom, prescription, or ratione tenuræ. (R. v. Kingsmoor, 2 Barn. & Cres. 1933, 3 Dowl. & Ryl. 398; R. v. Penderryn, 2 T. R. 513; R. v. Great Broughton, 5 Burr. 2700.) And though it may be doubtful, whether an extra-parochial hamlet is liable, at *common law,* to repair its own roads, it is necessary to aver, that the inhabitants of the hamlet were immemorially bound to repair, and that the hamlet does not form part of a larger district, the inhabitants of which are bound to repair. (Rex v. Kingsmoor, *ubi supra.)*

Averment of Custom, &c.] Agreeably to the distinction taken in Keilway, (52. pl. 4,) between an obligation to repair by reason of tenure, and of inhabitancy, it has been holden, that an indictment against a *particular part* only of a parish, such as a district, township, division, or the like, for not repairing a highway in the parish, stating that the *inhabitants* of the district from time immemorial *ought* to repair and amend it, is erroneous; it should state, that the inhabitants of such district from time whereof, &c., *have used and been accustomed,* and of right ought to repair and amend it. For the inhabitants of a particular division of a parish are not bound to repair by common law, but their obligation must arise from custom or prescription; and therefore, the indictment ought to show the custom, prescription, or reason of their obligation. (Rex v. Broughton, 5 Burr. 2700; St. Andrew, Holborn, Freem. 522, 3 Keb. 301; Rex v Sheffield, 2 T. R. 111.)

Where a township, or some other district *less* than a parish, is sought to be charged, if a prescriptive obligation to repair all public roads within the township or district be alleged, and it should appear that there is any road within such township or other division, which it is not bound *to repair,* the variance would be fatal, unless the exception be *specially alleged.* But if the exception be alleged, it is not necessary to allege by *whom* such excepted road ought to be repaired. (Rex v. Ecclesfield, 1 Stark. Rep. 393.)

Indictment against an Individual.] It is said, that it is not safe in an indictment against a person for not repairing a highway, which he ought to have done in respect of the tenure of certain lands, barely to say, that he was bound to repair it *ratione tenuræ terre*, without adding *suæ*. (1 Hawk. P. C. c. 76. s. 8 & 9.) But the word *suæ* is omitted in the precedent in 2 Saund. 157, and it has been held not to be necessary; as where in an indictment for not repairing a highway, which the defendant was obliged to do *ratione tenuræ* of a certain house, which, in another part of the indictment, was mentioned to be the mansion house of the defendant, it was objected on the authority of 5 H. 7. 3. pl. 8, that the occupier, and not the owner, was chargeable to the repairs of the highway; and therefore the indictment should have *been ratione tenuræ suæ;* for it might be, that the house was let to another, and Latch. 206. Anon. was cited. But the court, upon consideration, held it not necessary to lay it so; for *ratione tenuræ*, implies it to be such a tenure as makes him chargeable; and so it was held in Rex v. Fanshaw, 1 Vent. 331. But if it were necessary to say *sua*, the court thought that it was impliedly averred, by calling it afterwards his mansion house, so *quacunque viâ datâ*, the indictment was well enough. (Rex v. Corrock, 1 Stra. 187.)

It seems that the occupier, and not the owner, is the proper person against whom the indictment should be brought; for how are the public to know who is the owner of the lands charged with the repair? And it does not seem to be material what estate the occupier has in the lands liable. (Reg. v. Watts, 1 Salk. 357; per Powell, J.; Queen v. Bucknell, 7 Mod. 55. See also Rex v. Kerrison, 1 Maul. & Sel. 435. Rex v. Kent, 13 East, 220. Rex v. Lindsey, 14 East, 317.)

Averment of his Liability.] In many precedents of indictments, or presentments against persons for not repairing a highway, by reason of tenure, it is stated, that the party ought to repair, by reason of his tenure, *as he and all those who held the said lands for the time being, from time whereof the memory of man is not to the contrary, were wont to do;* but the obligation seems to be sufficiently shown, by averring that he ought to repair, by *reason of the tenure of his lands*, without adding, that those who held the lands for the time being, have *immemorially* repaired. So in Co. Ent. 358. as well as in 2 Saund. 158, it is only stated, that the defendant ought to repair, by reason of the tenure of his lands; and it is said in Kielw. 52. pl. 4, that it is not necessary, either in an indictment or plea, to allege any title of *prescription*, because a prescription is *implied* in the estate of inheritance in the land.

Averment ratione tenuræ.] But where a person is bound to repair such a highway by *reason of inhabitancy*, a prescription must necessarily be alleged; and this difference was admitted to be a good one by the whole court. (See 1 Hawk. P. C. 76. pl. 8.) It is true, that Styles, 400, seems at first view to the contrary: there, a motion was made to quash an indictment for not repairing a highway, upon two grounds; one, because it concluded that the party ought to repair it by *reason of his tenements*, which was too uncertain; whereas it should have been, that he and all those whose estate he has in the tenements, used to repair it; and the other, that the indictment should have said, that by reason of the *tenure* of his tenements, he ought to repair, and not by reason of his *tenements;* and for these exceptions, the indictment was quashed. But this authority, when it is considered, appears to be in favour of the proposition; for it seems clear, that the true way of stating the liability to repair, on account of lands or tenements, is to say, that the party is bound to repair, by reason of the *tenure* of them; and even if it could be laid, that he is so bound, by reason of *his tenements*, then it would be necessary to allege, that he and all those whose estate he has used to repair, so that either way the indictment was bad. (2 Saund. 158. e. n. 9. See Rex v. Kingsmoor, 2 Barn. & Cres. 190.)

But an individual cannot be bound by prescription, that he and all his ancestors have repaired a highway or bridge, unless it be in respect of the tenure of his land, taking of toll, or other profit; for the act of the ancestor cannot charge the heir without profit; though a corporation, or a parish, or a part of it, may be charged by prescription to do so. (13 Rep. 33; 1 Hawk. P. C. c. 76. s. 8.)

Lands liable, conveyed severally.] Where lands bound to the repair of a bridge or highway, *ratione tenuræ*, are conveyed to several persons, every grantee being a tenant of any parcel, is liable to the whole repair, and may call upon the tenants of the residue to contribute. They are thus chargeable, although the grantor convey the lands or manor discharged of the repair; and the grantees must have their remedy against the grantor. The reason seems to be, because the whole manor or lands, and every part thereof in the possession of one tenant, being once chargeable with the repair, it shall remain so, notwithstanding any act of the owner; for the law will not suffer him to apportion the charge, and so make the remedy for the public benefit more difficult, or against insolvent persons quite frustrate. And though such lands or manor come into the hands of the crown, yet the duty continues; and any person afterwards claiming the whole or any part, under the crown, will be alike liable. (Reg. v. Duchess of Buccleugh,

1 Salk. 358. See 3 Viner. Apportionment. 5 pl. 9; 2 Saund. 159. n. 9.) The allegations and the evidence should correspond; but the court will not countenance captious objections, where the merits of the case, or the rights of parties cannot be affected, although the indictment is not drawn with a precision which describes every minute peculiarity, &c. of the road indicted. The terms may be more general, so as they are sufficiently definite to mark the particular road or part of the road indicted, and express the obligation upon the defendant to repair, whether by prescription or otherwise. Thus, where an indictment for a nuisance to a highway stated it to be a way for all the liege subjects to go, return, &c. with their "horses, coaches, carts and carriages," the evidence was, that the highway in question passed under an arch gateway, nine feet broad and ten feet high; and that carts of particular description, and loaded in a particular manner, could not pass along this highway. Held, that this was not a mis-description, it not being laid as a highway for *all* carts, carriages, &c. (Rex v. Lyon, Ryan & Moody, 151.)

Indictment upon an Agreement.] An indictment against an individual, or a corporation, for not repairing a highway, which "by virtue of a certain agreement, they are bound to do," is bad. (Rex v. the Mayor of Liverpool, 3 East, 86;) for no *agreement* with any person can take off this charge, which the law lays upon the parish. (1 Vent. 90; 2 Saund. 159. n. 10.) Nor even a fund provided by act of Parliament, although in such cases the parish is not likely to be called upon, unless the funds become inadequate to the necessary repairs, or the trustees who have the management of the funds, neglect to keep the roads in proper condition; in which case, after the parish has been compelled by indictment to repair the road, the trustees may be compelled to re-imburse the parish, according to their means. (R. v. St. George, Hanover-square, 3 Camp. 222; 2 Saund. 159. b. n. *f*.)

Variance.] All the material averments must be proved as they are laid; this observation applies with peculiar force to averments of customs, or prescriptive obligations in discharge of the parish. And where the proceeding is against an individual, care must be taken to state the mode in which the defendant became liable, whether by tenure of his lands, taking a toll, or other profit, &c. (2 Saund. 158. n. 9.)

Plea of guilty.] If the liability to repair is admitted, and also that at the *time charged* the road was out of repair, but has since been amended, the court will not quash the indictment upon affidavits of these facts, as that would destroy the evidence of liability which a conviction affords against the party in future. The proper course is to plead guilty, upon which the court may impose a nominal fine only. (Rex v. Lincombe, 2 Chit. Rep. 214; Rex v. Cheshunt, 1 Bl. Rep. 295.) In such case, there should be the certificate of two justices that the road is in repair and is likely to *continue so*; and the probable continuance in repair, must also be expressly stated in the affidavit. (Rex v. Loughton, 3 Smith Rep. 575.)

Plea of not guilty.] When the obligation to repair is *admitted*, and the fact of the bad state of the road is alone disputed, there can of course, be no other plea than *not guilty*. Under this plea, any *variance* in the description of the highway may be taken advantage of; but if the description be *too indefinite*, being equally applicable to *several* highways, the objection should be taken by plea in abatement, alleging that all these roads are equally well known by the description in the indictment. (Rex v. Hammersmith, 1 Stark. R. 358.)

Not guilty, by Parish.] The parish cannot remove the burthen of repairing a road from themselves, and cast it upon others by pleading not guilty; except where the burthen has been transferred by act of Parliament. (Rex v. St. George, Hanover-square, 3 Camp. 223;) and even in that case, if the parties upon whom the obligation is transferred by statute become insolvent, the justices of the peace may put the charge upon the rest of the inhabitants. (1 Ld. Raym. 725.)

Not guilty, by other Persons.] It is a settled rule, that where a party is charged with the repair of a highway or bridge, *against common right*, he may discharge himself (if not actually liable,) upon *not guilty* to the indictment; and therefore, when a particular division of a parish is charged with the repair by prescription, or a particular person by reason of tenure or the like, which are obligations *against* the common law, they may throw the burthen either on the parish, or even on an individual, on the general issue. (Rex v. City of Norwich, 1 Stra. 180; 2 Saund. 159. a. n. 10;) and the reason seems to be, because upon this issue the prosecutor is bound to prove, that the defendant is chargeable by tenure or prescription, and therefore the defendant may disprove it by opposite evidence.

And if the inhabitants of a township, bound *by prescription* to repair the roads within the township, are expressly exempted by the provisions of a road act from the charge of repairing new roads to be made within the township, the charge must necessarily fall on the rest of the parish. (Rex v. Sheffield, 2 T. R. 106); and therefore, if the fact of any of these roads being out of repair is admitted, but the liability of the parish is disputed, upon an indictment against the parish, the defendants must plead specially the prescription, to which of course the prosecutor must reply the exemption by statute.

But in the case of an indictment of a township bound by a similar prescription to repair, and a local act for similar purposes, contained no such exemption, as in the above instance, it was held that the inhabitants of the township (not the rest of the parish,) were bound to repair; as by the prescription, the township was, as to all roads within it, a parish; and that therefore, when a new highway was brought into it, it became subject to the *lex loci,* as to the repairs. (Rex v. Netherthong, 2 Barn. & Ald. 179.)

Denial of liability by Parish.] If the defence to an indictment against a parish rests upon a denial of the liability to repair, the non-liability must be *specially pleaded;* and the form and substance of the necessary pleas become an important consideration. (R. v. St. Andrews, 1 Mod. 112; Vent. 256; 1 Hawk. P. C. c. 76. s. 9.)

It is said in Mr. Serjeant Williams' note to 2 Saund. 159. (n. 10,) that if a parish is indicted for not repairing a highway, or a county for not repairing a bridge, and they throw the charge upon another, they ought not to traverse their obligation to repair, for it is a traverse of *matter of law;* and such traverse, though very often inserted, is demurrable. But with submission to so great an authority, it may be suggested, that the traverse in such case is of a *mixed* nature, combining *law* and *fact,* (See 2 Bl. Rep. 776;) for whether the parish is liable to the repair of the road, or not, depends upon the *fact* of the " other, upon whom they throw the charge" *not* being liable. And indeed, in Rex v. Ecclesfield, (1 Barn. & Ald. 348,) one of the objections to a plea by a parish was, that the plea did not conclude with a traverse of the obligation of the parish to repair. But the court said, that if such a traverse were necessary, the conclusion of the plea in the words, "and that the inhabitants of the said parish at large ought not to be charged," was a sufficient and effectual traverse. The result probably will be, if ever this point is pressed for the decision of the court, that it will be held immaterial in such a plea whether the traverse be inserted or not.

Pleading a Prescription.] Where different districts or townships of a parish, are bound by prescription to repair the highways within them, and one of these highways is out of repair, and the *parish* at large is indicted, as it may be, care must be taken that this prescription is pleaded; for if judgment is given against the parish, whether after verdict upon not guilty or by default, the judgment will be conclusive evidence afterwards that the *whole* parish is bound to repair unless fraud can be shown. (Rex v. St. Pancras, Peake Rep. 219;) or the other districts can show they had *no notice* of the indictment; in which case, the court will give the other districts leave to plead the prescription, to a subsequent indictment for not repairing the highways in that part of the parish. (Rex v. Townsend, Doug. 421; Rex v. Eardisland, 2 Camp. 494.)

The way of pleading the prescription in such case, seems to be, that *each district* claiming an exemption from repair (in the particular instance,) should state, in a separate plea to the indictment against the parish, " that the parish has immemorially been divided into a certain number of districts or townships, called A. B. C. (naming them;) and that the inhabitants respectively of the several districts of A. and C. (the districts in which the highway lies,) have immemorially been used and accustomed to repair and amend the several and respective highways, situate and lying in their respective districts, independent of each other; and that the said part of the said highway in the said indictment mentioned, lies in that part of the said parish called the district of C.; and by reason of the premises, the inhabitants of the said district ought to have repaired the same, independent of the inhabitants of the said district of A. in the said parish. And this, &c. wherefore, &c." The prosecutor then traverses the prescription, and issue is taken upon it. (See 2 Saund. 159 c. n. 10.)

Plea must be certain.] But where the plea by the parish was that the parish was immemorially divided into seven townships, the inhabitants of which respectively were immemorially bound to repair the highways within their respective townships; and that *part* of the highway indicted was within the township of G. B. &c.; and that the residue was within the township of L. B., &c.; and that the respective parts ought to be repaired by the inhabitants of the respective townships, &c.: this was held bad on special demurrer, for not specifying *what part* of the highway lay within one township, and what part within the other; as the parish, being liable at common law to repair all roads within it, must show with certainty the parties who were bound to repair any part of the highway indicted, and in what right they were so bound. (Rex v. Budekirk, 11 East, 304.)

Special or general Prescription.] It is also material to observe, that there is a difference between cases where the indictment charges a *special* prescription for a township to repair a *particular* road, and a *general* prescription to repair *all* roads within the township. In the former case, the rule is that it is sufficient for the defendants to show that some others are liable, without fixing on the individuals, or showing with certainty what lands are chargeable with the burthen, for such evidence negatives the special liability imposed by custom contrary to common law on the township; but in the latter case, the prescription, if proved, places the inhabitants of the township in the same situation as the inhabitants of a parish. (See Rex v. Netherthong, 2 Barn. & Ald. 179;) and so they must show in their defence with certainty, some other persons bound to repair. (Rex v. Hatfield, 4 Barn. & Ald. 80.)

Pleading unnecessarily.] If defendants do, though unnecessarily, plead the special matter in their discharge, this must be done with the same exactness as in other cases. (2 Saund. 159. a. n. 10.)

Requisites of Pleas.] Every special plea must not only deny that the defendant is bound to repair, but must state on whom the obligation lies, and whence it arises. (Rex v. Yarnton, 1 Sid. 140; Rex v. Hornsey, Carth. 213.) The traverse of liability is said to be improper in a special plea by a parish. (2 Saund. 159. c. n. 10;) but see *(ante,* 178.)

In a late case, where an indictment was brought against a parish for the non-repair of a highway lying within it—a plea that the inhabitants of *another parish* have repaired, and been used and accustomed to repair, and of right ought to have repaired, was held bad, for the plea ought in this case to have shown a consideration. (Rex v. St. Giles, Cambridge, 5 Maul. & Sel. 260.) But where the inhabitants of a parish pleaded that the inhabitants of a particular district *within the parish,* were bound by prescription to repair all common ways situate *within that district,* save and except one common highway, within the said district, it was holden that the plea might be supported; though it appeared, that the excepted highway was of recent date, and it was not averred by whom the excepted highway was repairable; (Rex v. Ecclesfield, 1 Stark. R. 393;) and although the plea did not state any consideration for the liability of the inhabitants of that district. (S. C. 1 Barn. & Ald. 348; Rex v. West Riding of Yorkshire, 4 Barn. & Ald. 623.) The result of which cases is, that if one parish seek to charge another parish with the repair of a road within the former, a consideration must appear on the face of the plea; but if the parish charges a district within its own boundaries, and which is part of the parish, it is not necessary to aver any consideration in pleading.

Replication.] Whenever the plea concludes to the country, the *similiter* may be added, viz. " And A. B. who prosecutes for our lord the king doth the like." (1 Chit. Crim. Law, 477.) If the plea of a *parish* sets out other persons upon whom the obligation rests, and traverses the liability of the parish, the replication, it is said, ought not to take issue upon the traverse, but upon the liability of the parties upon whom the duty is thus attempted to be cast. (1 Saund. 23. n. 5.) This, however, has been doubted; and such a traverse would perhaps not now be held demurrable. (See Rex v. Ecclesfield, 1 Barn. & Ald. 348, *ante* 178.)

Certiorari.] The indictment may be removed by certiorari, upon the usual affidavit, stating that the right or title to repair may come in question. (See 5 W. & M. c. 11. s. 6.) And it may without such affidavit be so removed *pro rege,* at the instance of the prosecutor, notwithstanding the 13 G. 3. c. 78. s. 24; (Rex v. Bodenham, Cowp. 78.) And though a parish plead not guilty only, it may remove the indictment by the above means; as the obligation to repair may come in question upon that plea. (Rex v. Taunton St. Mary's, 3 Maul. & Sel. 465.)

The Evidence.] The facts necessary to be proved will generally appear from the state of the pleadings. Any material variance in proof will be fatal. The proof that the road is a public highway, consists usually in showing that it has been so used without interruption for a considerable space of time. The particular manner in which it has been used for some public purpose, as for conveying materials for the repairs of other highways, (Rex. v. Wandsworth, 1 Barn. & Ald. 63 ;) or upon any occasion likely to attract notice, is very material; for such instances of user would naturally awaken the jealousy and opposition of any private owner, who was interested in preventing the acquisition of any right by the public, and consequently *acquiescence by the owner of the fee,* affords a stronger presumption of right than that which results from possession and use in ordinary cases. (Wood v. Veal, 5 Barn. & Ald. 454. See Stark. Ev. 666.) Proof of repairs by the *parish,* or by a *parishioner* under an agreement with the parish, that he shall therefore be excused his statute duty, is strong evidence to show that it is a public highway. (Rex v. Wandsworth, 1 Barn. & Ald. 63.)

Evidence of reputation is admissible, to prove that the way is public, (1 Vent. 189;) but evidence of this nature arising *post litem motam,* is not admissible. (R. v. Cotton, 3 Campb. 444.) So a verdict, on an issue taken on a public right of way, and finding it to be such, is afterwards evidence, (Reed v. Jackson; 1 East, 355;) although such issue be taken in an action of trespass between private parties, and offered to prove the fact between other parties in a civil action: but it is not conclusive evidence. (Id.) If a prescriptive obligation to repair all public roads within the district be alleged, proof must be given of such repairs within the division; but it is unnecessary to prove that the road in question is an ancient road. (Rex v. Netherthong, 2 Barn. & Ald. 179.)

Upon an indictment against an individual for not repairing a road, which he is bound to do *ratione tenuræ*, the defendant must be proved to be the *occupier* of the lands in respect of which the obligation arises; since the law looks to the visible occupier, and not to the owner; (1 Roll. 390. b. 60;) and the prosecutor must in such case also prove the prescription; or that the former occupiers repaired, &c. (See Rex v. Skinner, 5 Esp. Rep. 219; 2 Saund. 157, 160. n. 12.)

Effect of former Verdict.] An acquittal upon a former indictment, for not repairing a highway, is not conclusive evidence, if it be evidence at all, to discharge the defendant; it concludes nothing as to the general liability, but only shows that the defendant was not liable at the particular time laid in the former indictment. (1 Stark. Ev. 223.) But a conviction in such case is conclusive as to the liability, unless fraud can be shown. (Rex v. St. Pancras, Peake's Rep. 219.) Or want of notice, as where a *parish* consisting of two districts, bound to repair separately, was convicted, and it appeared that the district in which the indicted road lay, defended without any notice of the indictment being given to the other, this was not binding upon the *parish:* but the court considered it as being substantially the conviction of the one district only. (Rex v. Townsend, Doug. 421; 2 Saund. 159. c. n.) So upon an indictment against a parish, consisting of several districts, *one* of which pleaded a custom for the inhabitants of each of the three districts to repair their own roads, independently of each other, which custom was traversed, the prosecutor having upon the trial proved *records of conviction* of the parish at large, upon not guilty pleaded, for not repairing roads lying in the particular districts, the defendants were permitted to adduce evidence that such pleas were pleaded without their knowledge. (Rex v. Eardisland, 2 Campb. 494.) Upon an indictment for non-repairs of a road *ratione tenuræ*, it was held, that an award, made under a submission by a former tenant of the premises, could neither be received as an adjudication, the tenant having no authority to bind the rights of his landlord, nor as evidence of reputation, having been made *post litem motam.* (Rex v. Cotton, 3 Campb. 444.)

Witnesses.] The surveyor of the parish is a competent witness for the prosecution; or for the defendants. (13 G. 3. c. 78. s. 69.) An inhabitant of the parish, even the prosecutor himself, (1 Stark. Ev. 357,) is a competent witness for the prosecution, by the 76th section of the act, and 3 G. 4. c. 126. s. 137; though Lord Ellenborough, in Rex v. Wandsworth, said, that an inhabitant is not a competent witness for the parish; but had the above section of the Highway act been alluded to, he would probably have been of a different opinion. A witness is competent to prove a road to be a highway, though he has agreed to grant, at an annual rent, a way across his own land, which cannot be used unless the disputed road be established. (Pollard v. Scott; Peake Rep. 18.) Upon an indictment against the township of P. charging the inhabitants with the liability to repair all roads within it, an inhabitant of the *adjoining* township of N. is competent to prove, that the road which extended through N. was a public highway. (Rex v. the Inhabitants of Pilling; Stark. on Evid. Appendix to p. 673.)

View by the Jury.] It may frequently be requisite that the jury should have *a view* of the place indicted. This cannot, it seems, be granted by the judges at the assizes, (1 Sess. Cas. 180; 2 Barnard. 214; 1 Chit. Crim. L. 483;) but may be obtained by removing the proceedings into the King's Bench by *certiorari,* which writ the court will grant on proper affidavits.

New Trial.] Although the trial of a prosecution for not repairing highways, is in general a mere contest respecting a *civil* liability; yet, as the proceedings are in form criminal, the court, after verdict for the defendant, will not grant a new trial. But if the nuisance in question continue, the continuance will form a distinct offence, for which he may be again indicted. (Rex v. Reynell, 6 East, 315.) And under very special circumstances, the court will suspend the entry of judgment upon the first verdict, so as to enable the parties to have the question reconsidered upon another indictment, without the prejudice of the former conviction. (Rex v. Wandsworth, 1 Barn. & Ald. 63.)

Judgment.] As the object of this prosecution is not the punishment of the defendant, but the repair of the highway, it is not indispensably requisite that he should be in personal attendance at the time judgment is pronounced. And where a district is indicted, this is of course impossible. (1 Salk. 55, 6; Hawkins, b. 2. c. 48. s. 17.) Where an individual has been found guilty, he may obtain a rule to show cause why his personal appearance may not be excused, on his agent's engaging to pay such fine as the court may assess; and if no sufficient reason to the contrary is shown, the court will make the rule absolute, and give judgment in the defendant's absence. (Id.)

Amount of Fine.] The judgment usually is, that the defendants pay a fine, and repair the nuisance, (Bro. Abr. Nuisance, 49; Rex v. Stead, 8 T. R. 142.) But upon a certificate of a justice of the peace, that the road is in good condition, at the time judgment is about to be pronounced, the court will merely assess a small fine, as 6*s.* 8*d.* And if the certificate state that the way has since been diverted by the order of two justices, and that so much thereof as is retained, is in repair, the sentence will also be for the nominal penalty. (Rex v.

Incledon, 13 East. 166.) And therefore, to give a false certificate is indictable, as obstructing the course of justice; and may be prosecuted as a conspiracy between the magistrates and the persons who procure their assistance. (Rex v. Mawbey and others, 6 T. R. 619.)

Where an individual indicted for not repairing, when bound to do so *ratione tenuræ*, applies to the court to submit to a small fine, on a certificate that the road is put in good repair, which is denied; and afterwards on the trial it appears that the repair has been actually effected between such request and the trial, the court will refuse to set a nominal fine, unless the costs of the prosecutor subsequent to the former application are paid. (Rex v. Wingfield, 1 Bla. Rep. 602.)

It was held by the judges, for whose consideration the question was reserved, that on a conviction of a parish for not repairing a road, if it appear that materials cannot be procured without going to a considerable distance, it must be left to the presiding judge, in each particular case, to determine what to do in passing judgment. (MSS. Parish of Whaplode, Lincolnshire, M. T. 1826.)

Application of Fines.] By the 3 G. 4. c. 126. s. 110, where the *parish*, &c. is indicted for the non-repair of a *turnpike* road, the court are to apportion the fine between the parish and the trustees, or commissioners, &c. The fine is not to be returned into the Exchequer, but is to be paid into the hands of such person as the court shall order, to be applied to the repair of the road in question.

Rate to reimburse Fines.] If the fine be levied on individual inhabitants, they may complain at the special sessions, and the justices there assembled are to cause a rate to be made to reimburse them. (13 G. 3. c. 78. s. 47.) The application for this rate ought to be made within a reasonable time after the levy, and before any material change of the inhabitants. The Court of King's Bench refused a mandamus to the justices, to make such a rate, after an interval of eight years, though applications had been from time to time made to the magistrates below in the interval, who declined to make the rate on the ground that the parish at large had been improperly convicted, the onus of repair being thrown by immemorial custom on an inferior district; and though so lately as the year before the application, the magistrates had ordered an account to be taken of the quantum expended upon the repairs, out of the money levied. (Rex v. Justices of Lancashire. 12 East, 366.)

Fine not conclusive.] The matter is not at an end by the defendants being fined, but writs of *distringas* will be issued *in infinitum*, until the road is put in a state of sufficient repair. (Reg. v. Cluworth, 1 Salk. 359; 6 Mod. 163.)

Awarding Costs.] By the 13 Geo. 3. c. 78. s. 64, (see post 201,) the court may award costs to the prosecutor, to be paid by the defendants, if it appear to the court that the defence was frivolous; or to the defendants, to be paid by the prosecutor, if the court shall think that the prosecution was vexatious. Under this clause, the application must be made to the judge who tries the indictment; and if this be omitted, the King's Bench will not afterwards interfere. (Rex v. Chadderton, 5 T. R. 272.) But no precise form of certificate seems to be necessary; and if it be stated on the back of the record that the defence was frivolous, or that the prosecution was vexatious, this will suffice without formally awarding costs. (Rex v. Clifton, 6 T. R. 344.) And the persons who really instigated the prosecution, may be ordered to pay the defendant's costs upon an acquittal, although they are not the ostensible prosecutors, and their names do not appear upon the back of the indictment; and although the indictment originated in a presentment of A. and B., constables, whose names *are* on the indictment. (Rex v. Commerell, 4 Maul. & Sel. 203.)

The order is good in form, if it be for the payment of the costs to the solicitor of the parish. (Rex v. Commerell, supra.) And it has been holden, that if a justice of the peace indict for non-repair, and the defendant remove the proceedings by *certiorari*, the magistrate upon conviction, will be entitled to his costs under 5 W. & M. c. 11. s. 3, as a party aggrieved. (Rex v. Kettleworth, 5 T. R. 33.) So several persons, prosecutors of an indictment removed by *certiorari*, were held entitled to costs; one as constable of the manor within which the highway lay, the other as parties aggrieved, they having used the way for many years, in passing and repassing from their homes to the next market-town, and being obliged by reason of the want of repair, to take a more circuitous route. (Rex v. Taunton St. Mary, 3 Maul. & Sel. 465.) And upon an indictment for not repairing a highway, removed by the prosecutor, if the judge at *nisi prius* certify that the defence was frivolous, the prosecutor shall have his costs, notwithstanding the defendant hath obtained a rule *nisi*, to arrest the judgment. (Rex v. St. John the Baptist, Margate, 6 Maul. & Sel. 130.)

CHAP. VIII.—HIGHWAY ACTS.

SECTION I.—SURVEYORS OF HIGHWAYS.

13 Geo. 3. c. 78. ss. 1, 2, 3. 5. 54. 70. 85. 12. 4. 50. 68. 48.

The Acts in Force.] The person, or ministerial officer, to whom the law has confided the more immediate duty of putting the enactments for the repair and preservation of the roads in execution, is the surveyor. In the matters of higher importance upon this subject, where a road is to be diverted or stopped up, or any other changes in the highways within the contemplation of these statutes, are to be effected, the power is lodged in the magistracy of the county, under certain regulations and restrictions, for the protection of private interests, and the prevention of an indiscreet exercise of this authority.

It has already been observed, that no means are provided by the common law for making new roads, widening old ones, changing their course, or for stopping up those which have become useless to the public. Acts of Parliament, however, have from time to time been passed to supply this deficiency.

The earliest act to be found in the statute book relating to highways, is 13 Ed. 1. Stat. Wynt. c. 5; many others were passed in the following reigns, till the whole were amended and reduced into one by the 13 Geo. 3. c. 78. Some parts of this latter act have been repealed, and other enactments substituted by subsequent statutes. For the sake of brevity and convenience, only those provisions which are still in force are given in the following pages. It may be expedient, however, in the first place, to state the repealed clauses of the statutes now in existence: the 34th, 35th, 38th, and 39th clauses of 13 Geo. 3. c. 78, are repealed by 34 Geo. 3. c. 74. s. 1, the 3d clause of 34 Geo. 3. c. 74 is repealed by 44 Geo. 3. c. 52. s. 1; the 19th clause of 13 Geo. 3. c. 78, is repealed by the 55 Geo. 3. c. 68. s. 1.

By the 86th section of 13 Geo. 3. c. 78, the parish of St. Mary Matfelon, otherwise Whitechapel, and St. John of Wapping, in Middlesex, are exempt from the operation of the act; and the 87th section provides, that the power of commissioners of sewers shall not be affected by the act.

Appointment of Surveyors.] The 13 Geo. 3. c. 78. s. 1, enacts, "Upon the twenty-second day of September, in every year, unless that day shall be Sunday, and then on the day following, the *constables, headboroughs, tithingmen, churchwardens, surveyors of the highways, and householders,* (see Construction 1, post 190,) being assessed to any parochial or public rate, of every parish, township, or place, shall assemble together at the church or chapel of such parish, township, or place; or if there shall be no church or chapel, then at the usual place of public meetings for such parish, township, or place, at the hour of eleven in the forenoon: And the major part of them, so assembled, shall make a list of the names of at least ten persons living within such respective parishes, townships, or places, who each of them have an estate in lands, tenements, or hereditaments, lying within such respective parish, township, or place, in their own right, or in the right of their wives, of the value of ten pounds by the year; or a personal estate of the value of one hundred pounds; or are occupiers or tenants of houses, lands, tenements, or hereditaments, of the value of thirty pounds: And if there shall not be ten persons having such qualifications as aforesaid, then they shall insert in such list the names of so many of such persons as are so qualified, as above required, together with the names of so many of the most sufficient and able inhabitants of such parish, township, or place, not so qualified, as shall make up the number of ten, if so many can be found; if not, so many as shall he there resident, to serve the office of surveyor of the highways: And the constable, headborough, or tythingman, of such parish, township, or place, shall, within three days after such meeting, transmit a duplicate of such list to one of the justices of the peace within the limit of the county, riding, division, hundred, city, corporation, precinct, or liberty, where such parish, township, or place, shall be, living in or near the same; and shall also return and deliver the original list, made and agreed upon at such meeting, to the justices of the peace, at their *special* sessions to be held for the highways within that limit, in the week next after the *Michaelmas general quarter sessions* (see Construction 2. post 190,) of the peace in every year; and shall also, within three days after making the said list, give personal notices to, or cause notices in writing to be left at the places of abode of the several persons contained in such list, informing them of their being so named, to the intent that they may severally appear before the justices at the said special sessions, to accept such office, if they shall be appointed thereto, or to show cause, if they have any, against their being appointed: And the said justices are hereby authorized and required to hold such special sessions at such convenient place or places within their respective limits, as they, in their discretion, shall judge proper; and to give notice of the time and place where they intend to hold the same to the constables, headboroughs, or tythingmen of every such parish, township, or place, at least ten days before the holding of the said session: And the said justices then and there, from the said lists, according to their discretion, and the largeness of the parish, township, or place respectively, by warrant under their hands and seals, shall appoint one, two, or more of such persons as aforesaid, if he or they shall, in the opinion of such justices, be qualified for the office of surveyor; if not, one, two, or more of the other substantial inhabitants or occupiers of lands, tenements, woods, tithes, or hereditaments, within such parish, township, or place, living within three miles thereof, and within the same county, fit and proper to serve the office of surveyor of the highways for such parish, township, or place, if any such can be found; which appointment shall, by the constables, headboroughs, or tythingmen aforesaid, be notified to every person so appointed by the said justices within three days after such appointment, by serving him with the said warrant, or by leaving the same, or a true copy thereof, at his house or usual place of abode: And every person so appointed, if he accepts the said office, shall be surveyor of the highways for the said parish, township, or place, for the year ensuing, and shall take upon him, and duly execute the office aforesaid; and the said justices shall then and there give such of the said surveyors as shall personally appear before them, a charge for the better performance of their duty, according to the directions of this act: And if any of the said persons so appointed, whose names were contained in such list, and who are served with the said notice, shall refuse or neglect to appear at the said special sessions, and accept the said office, if appointed thereto, in manner aforesaid; or shall not, within six days after being served with such warrant of appointment, signify his acceptance thereof, either in person or by writing, to one of the said justices, he shall forfeit the sum of five pounds: And in case any person so appointed by the said justices, whose name ***was not contained in such lists,*** (see Construction 3, post 190;) shall refuse or neglect to accept the said office, or shall not, within six days after being served with such appointment, show to one of the justices signing snch appointment sufficient cause why he should not serve such office, he shall forfeit the sum of fifty shillings: Provided that no person, who hath been appointed and served the office of surveyor for one year, shall be liable to be appointed surveyor for the same parish, township, or place, within three years from the time of such first appointment and service, unless he shall consent thereto. But if no such list shall be made and returned, or if the said justices shall make such appointment as aforesaid, and the person or persons so appointed shall refuse to serve the said office, the said justices, or any two of them, shall and may, and are hereby required, at the said special sessions, or at some subsequent special sessions, to be held within one month after, to nominate and appoint some other person or persons to be surveyor of such parish, township, or place, whom they shall judge proper to execute that office, and shall and may fix such salary to be paid to such surveyor, to be appointed as herein last before mentioned, out of the said forfeitures, and all other forfeitures, fines, penalties, assessments, and compositions, to be paid, levied, and raised under the authority of this act, within such parish, township, or place respectively, as such justices shall think fit, not exceeding one-eighth part of what shall have been raised by an assessment of sixpence in the pound, for the use of the highways within such parish, township, or place, where any such assessment shall have been raised, aud observing the same restriction as near as they can, from the best information they shall be able to get of the probable amount of such an assessment, where none hath been already made: And the said justices shall and may, if they think fit, require the constables, headboroughs, tythingmen, and surveyor, of every such parish, township, and place, or any of them, to return to them, at such time and place as they shall appoint, an account in writing, of the sum which such assessment of sixpence in the pound hath raised, or will, in his or their opinion, raise within such parish, township, or place: And if the constables, headboroughs, tythingmen, churchwardens, surveyor of the highways, and such householders as aforesaid of any parish, township, or place, shall neglect or refuse to make such list as aforesaid; or if the constable, headborough, or tythingman, of any parish, township, or place, shall not return the said list of names when made, and such duplicate thereof, as aforesaid, and give such notice or notices, and serve such warrant or warrants, as in this act is directed; or if the said constable, headborough, tythingman, and surveyor, or any of them, shall neglect to return such account of the amount of such assessment as aforesaid, when so required as aforesaid, every constable, headborough, tythingman, churchwarden, or surveyor, so neglecting or refusing, in any of the said cases, shall, for every such default, respectively forfeit the sum of forty shillings."

Construction 1, *ante* 187.] Although it has been questioned, whether a parish meeting would be legal, unless composed of the several denominations set forth in the act; yet the court seemed strongly inclined to the opinion, that the legislature only meant it to be a full parish meeting, in the ordinary sense; and that the absence of any of the officers named would not invalidate the proceedings. (R. v. Pettiward and others, 4 Burr. 2452.)

Construction 2, *ante* 188.] By the 54 Geo. 3. c. 84, the Michaelmas quarter sessions are directed to be held in the first week after the eleventh of October, which led to the enactment of the 55 Geo. 3. c. 68. s. 8, empowering justices assembled in *petty* sessions in the week after Michaelmas to do all acts, which theretofore they might legally have done in the *special* sessions, directed to be holden in the week after Michaelmas general quarter sessions. A *special sessions* here means, a sitting convened by *notice* to the other magistrates of the division. (R. v. Worcestershire, 2 Barn. & Ald. 233.) But it is not necessary that the appointment of surveyors should be made at the particular period above stated; as this part of the act has been held to be only *directory;* and the appointment may be made at the next subsequent special sessions. (R. v. Denbighshire, 4 East. 142.)

Construction 3, *ante* 189.] The justices are not *bound* to appoint surveyors from the lists returned to them, if they think the persons named therein are unfit; but they may choose other persons of the parish who are qualified. (R. v. Baldwin, 7 T. R. 169.)

Assistant Surveyor.] The 13 Geo. 3. c. 78. s. 2, provides, "That in all cases where the said justices, upon neglect or refusal of the person so nominated surveyor as aforesaid to accept the said office, shall appoint any other person for such surveyor, with a salary as aforesaid, the said justices shall and are hereby required to appoint one substantial inhabitant of such parish, township, or place, for assistant to such surveyor, in the several matters and for the several purposes hereafter mentioned, until the next annual appointment of surveyors, according to the directions of this act: And if the person so appointed assistant shall, upon notice of such appointment, refuse to accept that office, he shall forfeit the sum of fifty shillings and in that case it shall and may be lawful for such justices to appoint any other substantial inhabitant of such parish, township, or place, for assistant to such surveyor, in manner and for the time aforesaid; and if such second appointed assistant shall decline or refuse to accept the said office, he shall, in like manner, forfeit the sum of fifty shillings; and the said justices shall and may appoint any other person, inhabiting in such parish, township, or place, assistant to such surveyor, who shall be entitled to the said forfeitures herein last before mentioned, and also to some further allowance by way of salary (to be paid as the surveyor's salary is hereby directed to be paid,) if the said justices shall think any such salary necessary, and shall order the same, which they are hereby authorized to do: Provided that no person so appointed assistant for one year shall be liable to be appointed assistant for the same parish, township, or place, within three years next following such first appointment without his consent."

Bond given by Surveyor.] "The surveyor of every parish, township, and place, who shall not reside therein, but shall be appointed with such salary as aforesaid, shall, if required by the churchwarden, overseer of the poor, or any principal inhabitant of the parish, township, or place, for which he shall be so appointed surveyor, at the time of his appointment, or within fourteen days after, give a bond upon paper, without stamp thereupon, to some proper person within such parish, township, or place, to be nominated by the said justices, with sufficient surety to account for the money which shall come to his hands as surveyor, according to the directions of this act; which bond shall be good and effectual in law." (Id. s. 3.)

Surveyor elected, with Salary.] "If two parts out of three of those so to be assembled in any such parish, township, or place, for the nomination of surveyors as aforesaid, shall agree in the choice of any particular person of skill and experience, to serve the said office of surveyor for such parish, township, or place, and in the settling of a certain salary for his trouble therein, and shall return the name of such person, together with the list hereinbefore directed, to the justices of the peace at their said sessions to be held in the week next after the Michaelmas quarter sessions, that then, in every such case, it shall and may be lawful for the said justices, if they shall think proper, to appoint such person to be surveyor for such parish, township, or place, and allow him the salary mentioned in such agreement; which shall be raised and paid in the same manner as the salary hereinbefore mentioned is directed to be raised and paid: And in case any surveyor, to be appointed under the authority of this act, shall die or become incapable of executing that office before such next special sessions for appointing surveyors, the said justices, or any two of them, shall and may, at some special sessions, nominate and appoint such person or persons as they shall think proper to execute the said office, until such next special sessions for appointing surveyors as aforesaid; and if such deceased surveyor had a salary, they may allow the same salary to his successor, in proportion to the time he shall serve the said office; and if the said justices of the peace, at their said special sessions, or at any time afterwards, pursuant to the powers of this act, shall appoint more than one person for surveyor of any parish, township, or place, all and every person or persons so appointed shall be comprehended under the word surveyor, in every part of this act." (Id. s. 5.)

"Provided, That nothing in this act contained shall authorize or empower, or be deemed, construed, or taken to authorize and empower any justice, or justices of the peace, for any city, town corporate, or borough, to fix or allow any salary to or for any surveyor, to be appointed by any such justice or justices, other than and except such salary as shall be settled and agreed upon by two parts out of three of the persons assembled in the parish, township, or place, within such city, town corporate, or borough, for which such surveyor shall be appointed pursuant to the directions of this act." (Id. s. 54.)

Abstract of Act for Surveyors.] And in order to have the contents of this act more generally communicated and known, be it further enacted, That the justices of the peace within their respective limits shall, at every special sessions to be held in the week next after the *Michaelmas* general quarter sessions of the peace, procure and deliver, or cause to be procured and delivered, a printed abstract of the most material parts of this act, to every surveyor, to be then appointed by them respectively, as the charge hereby directed to be given; and shall also, at their said special sessions, to be held in the year one thousand seven hundred and seventy-three, deliver, or cause to be delivered, to every of the said surveyors one other of the said printed abstracts of this act, for the use of the parish, township, or place, for which the said surveyor shall be appointed; which last-mentioned abstract the said surveyors are hereby respectively ordered and required to fix on the church or chapel door, or other public place within their respective liberties, on the next Sunday after they shall so receive the same; and the said surveyors shall severally pay to the said justices' clerks the sum of sixpence for each of the said last-mentioned printed abstracts." (Id. s. 70.)

"Provided, That nothing in this act contained, touching the

making and returning lists of persons qualified to be surveyors of the highways, and the appointment of such surveyors, nor the repeal of part of an act made in the third year of King William and Queen Mary, relating to such surveyors, shall extend, or be construed to extend to the city of Bristol." (Id. s. 85.)

Surveyors' Duties.] The duty of surveyors with respect to the removal of nuisances, encroachments, &c., is set forth in the following sections.

"The surveyors of the highways to be appointed by virtue of this act, shall, at all such times and seasons as they shall judge proper, view all the common highways, trunks, tunnels, plats, hedges, ditches, banks, bridges, causeways, and pavements, within the parish, township, or place, for which they shall be appointed surveyors; and in case they shall observe any nuisances, encroachments, obstructions, or annoyances, made, committed, or permitted in, upon, or to the prejudice of them, or any of them, contrary to the directions of this act, they shall from time to time, as soon as conveniently may be, give, or cause to be given, to any person or persons doing, committing, or permitting the same, personal notice or notices, in writing, to be left at his, her, or their usual place or places of abode, specifying the particulars wherein such nuisances, defaults, obstructions, or annoyances consist: And if such nuisances, obstructions, or annoyances shall not be removed, and the ditches, drains, gutters, and watercourses aforesaid effectually made, scoured, cleansed, and opened, and such trunks, tunnels, plats, and bridges, made and laid, and such hedges properly cut and pruned within twenty days after such notice of the same respectively given as aforesaid, then the said surveyors shall be, and they are hereby fully authorized and empowered forthwith to remove such nuisances, obstructions, or annoyances, and open, cleanse, and scour such ditches, gutters, and watercourses, and make or amend such trunks, tunnels, plats, or bridges, and cut and prune such hedges for the benefit and improvement of the said highways to the best of their skill and judgment, and according to the true intent and meaning of this act: And the person or persons so neglecting to make or open and cleanse such ditches, gutters, or watercourses, or cut or prune such hedges, during the time aforesaid, after such notice given, shall forfeit for every foot in length which shall be so neglected the sum of one penny; and the said surveyors shall be reimbursed what charges and expenses they shall be at in removing such nuisances, obstructions, or annoyances, and making or opening, cleansing, or scouring such ditches, gutters, and watercourses, and in making or amending such trunks, tunnels, plats, or bridges, and in cutting and pruning such hedges respectively, by the person or persons who ought to have done the same, over and above the said forfeiture; and in case such person or persons shall, upon demand, refuse or neglect to pay the said surveyor his charges and expenses occasioned thereby respectively, and also the said forfeiture of one penny per foot, then the said surveyor shall apply to any justice of the peace, and upon making oath before him of notice being given to the defaulter in manner aforesaid, and of the said work being done by such surveyor, and of the expenses attending the same, the said surveyor shall be repaid by such person or persons all such his said charges as shall be allowed to be reasonable by the said justice; or in default of payment thereof on demand, the same shall be levied in such manner as the penalties and forfeitures hereby inflicted are directed to be levied." (13 Geo. 3. c. 78. s. 12.)

Duty of Assistant Surveyor.] "And be it further enacted, That the assistant, so to be nominated and appointed, shall, and is hereby required, to the best of his skill and judgment, to assist the said surveyor, whenever requested by him, in calling in and attending the performance of the statute duty; in collecting the compositions, fines, penalties, and forfeitures; in making and collecting the assessments; in making out and serving the notices authorized by this act; and in such other matters and things as shall be reasonably required of him by the surveyor, in the execution of his office as surveyor, pursuant to this act: And the said assistant shall justly and truly account with, and pay to the said surveyor, or to his order, from time to time, according to the directions of this act, all the money which shall come to his hands, as assistant, by the means aforesaid; and in default thereof he shall forfeit double the value of the money by him so received, and not so paid and accounted for: And if the said assistant shall wilfully neglect or make default in the performance of any of the duty required from him by this act, he shall forfeit for every such offence any sum not exceeding five pounds, nor less than forty shillings, at the discretion of the justice or justices of the limit within which such assistant shall be appointed: And the said surveyor shall, and is hereby required to send orders in writing upon the said assistant, for the payment of all sums due to any person or persons for work or materials, by virtue of this act, which amount to forty shillings, or upwards; and the said surveyor shall not be responsible for any sum or sums of money which shall be received by the said assistant, and shall not be actually paid to such surveyor, or to his order, as aforesaid." (Id. s. 4.)

Fine on Neglect of Duty.] "If any surveyor of the highways, after his acceptance of the said office, shall neglect his duty in any thing required of him by this act, for which no particular penalty is imposed, he shall forfeit, for every such offence, any sum not exceeding five pounds, nor less than ten shillings, at the discretion of the justice or justices having jurisdiction therein." (Id. s. 50.)

May be a Witness.] "The surveyor of any parish, township, or place, shall be deemed, in all cases, a competent witness, in all matters relative to the execution of this act, notwithstanding his salary may arise in part from the forfeitures and penalties hereby inflicted." (Id. s.68.)

A surveyor of turnpike roads is not personally liable to answer the labourers, but they must look to the commissioners or their treasurer. (Pochin v. Pawley, 1 Bla. Rep. 670, Amb. 771.)

Surveyor's Accounts.] "The surveyor of the highways for every parish, township, or place, shall carefully and diligently collect, or cause to be collected, the several assessments, forfeitures, penalties, sums of money, and compositions, directed and allowed to be received and taken within the same, by virtue of this act, within the year for which he is appointed surveyor; and shall keep one or more book or books, in which he shall fairly enter a just, true, and fair account of all such money as shall have come to his hands, or to the hands of the said assistant, in respect of such parish, township, or place, by virtue and for the purposes of this act; and to whom, and on what occasion, he shall have paid or applied the same; and shall also enter in such book or books, a list or lists of all such sums of money as shall then remain due and owing from any person or persons, in respect of the payments, compositions, assessments, penalties, or forfeitures, to be collected, received, or taken, for and in respect of the said highways, by virtue of this act; and the said surveyor shall also enter in the said book or books an account of all tools, materials, implements, and other things provided, or to be provided, by order of the inhabitants, at a vestry or other public meeting, for the repair of the said highways, at the public expense of such parish, township, or place; and shall produce such books, and the assessments made within that year for the purposes of this act, unto the inhabitants of the parish, township, or place to which they belong, at a vestry or other public meeting to be held for that purpose, within fifteen days before the said special sessions so to be held in the week next after Michaelmas quarter sessions as aforesaid, to the intent that the said accounts, assessments, and lists, may be inspected by the inhabitants of such parish, township, or place respectively; and every such surveyor shall, after the said books and assessments shall have been produced at such meeting, take the same to such justice of the peace, (see " Passing Accounts." *post* 197,) for the limit wherein such parish, township, or place, doth lie, and on such day, and at such hour, as shall be agreed upon at such meeting, some day after the said meeting of the inhabitants, and before such last-mentioned special sessions, and then and there verify such account, or any part thereof, upon oath, if required; and such justice may allow such account, if he finds it just, or postpone it until such special sessions, if he finds cause for so doing; in which case it may be settled and allowed at such special sessions, after the parts objected to by such justice shall have been explained and verified by proper evidence, to the satisfaction of the justices at such special sessions; and in case any articles contained in such accounts shall not be explained and proved to the satisfaction of such justices, they may disallow the same; and whenever the said accounts shall be so settled, and allowed or disallowed as aforesaid, all such books and assessments shall be transmitted to the churchwarden or overseer of the poor for such parish, township, or place respectively, or if the place be extra-parochial, then to some principal inhabitant thereof, to be kept for the use of such parish, township, or place; and the said surveyor shall forthwith deliver a duplicate of such book and account, together with all sums of money as shall remain in his hands, and likewise all tools, materials, implements, and other things, as aforesaid, to the succeeding surveyor for such parish, township, or place, in case any new surveyor shall be appointed; or retain the same in his hands, and account for them in his next account, if he shall be continued surveyor of such parish, township, or place, in the succeeding year: and it shall and may be lawful for the succeeding surveyor, and he is hereby authorized and required, to recover, collect, and receive, all such sums of money which shall be due and owing as aforesaid, by all such ways and means as fully and effectually, to all intents and purposes, as the preceding surveyor could, might, or ought to have recovered, collected, or received the same: and in case such surveyor shall neglect to provide such book or books, or to enter such respective accounts and lists therein, or to deliver the said book or books, and such duplicate thereof, and such assessments, tools, materials, implements, and other things, in manner aforesaid, he shall for every such offence forfeit any sum not exceeding five pounds, nor less than forty shillings; and in case he shall make default in the paying or accounting for the money, so remaining in his hands, within the time, and according to the directions aforesaid, he shall forfeit double the value of the money which shall be adjudged by the said justices to be in his hands; (see "Action for Balance in Hand," *post*, 197;)

and in case any such surveyor shall die before such respective accounts and lists shall be made out, or such monies, books, assessments, tools, materials, and implements, shall be so delivered and paid, the executors or administrators of such surveyor shall make out, pay, and deliver the same, in like manner, and under the like penalty, as such surveyor is hereby required and made subject and liable to: and every surveyor shall pay to the justice's clerks, for the appointment and charge, the sum of one shilling, for the bond sixpence, and for the account so to be examined and taken, and for the oath so to be administered, the sum of one shilling, and no more; and if any person or persons shall receive any greater sum or fee for the business aforesaid than hereinbefore mentioned, he shall forfeit the sum of ten pounds for every offence." (13 Geo. 3. c. 78. s. 48.)

Passing Accounts by Justices.] The surveyor's accounts *must* first be laid before *one* justice, and the justices at petty sessions have no original jurisdiction over them; the reference to them being merely of those parts which are not allowed by the single justice. Thus where they allowed accounts which had not previously been submitted to one justice, the court granted a certiorari to remove the order, and quashed it. (R. v. JJ. Somersetshire, 5 Barn. & Cres. 816, 6 Dowl. & Ryl. 469, 8 Dowl. & Ryl. 733.) And even when the magistrate, before whom the accounts were exhibited, declined to investigate them, because the assessments were not also produced, but desired the surveyor to attend, with all the necessary documents, at the petty sessions, by whom the accounts were allowed, it was held that such allowance was invalid. (R. v. JJ. N. R. Yorkshire, 6 Barn. & Cres. 152.)

There is no appeal from the petty to the quarter sessions; the only mode of reviewing the decision of the former is by certiorari. (R. v. JJ. W. R. Yorkshire, 5 T. R. 629, id. 701.)

Action for Balance in Hand.] It seems that the surveyor is the proper party to sue his predecessor, for not paying over the balance declared against him, upon passing his accounts before a justice; but notice of action must be given, stating the precise sum which it is alleged the defendant has in his hands, which he ought to have paid over to his successor, and the double amount of which is sought to be recovered, and to which the evidence to be adduced on the trial applies. (Heudebourck v. Langton and another, 3 Car. & P. 566.)

Where there are two surveyors appointed, and *one only* has received the money, to recover which an action is brought, *both* cannot be sued for money had and received. (Id.)

If a surveyor be guilty of any embezzlement, or breach of duty, he may be indicted. (R. v. Anderson, 1 Chitty's Statutes 455.)

SECTION II.—REPAIR OF HIGHWAYS.

13 Geo. 3. c. 78. ss. 23. 51. 25. 24. 64, 65. 27, 28, 29, 30, 31, 32, 33. 49; 34 Geo. 3. c. 64. ss. 1, 2, 3, 4, 5. 7.

Repair ratione tenuræ.] The common law liability upon individuals or corporate bodies, to repair by reason of their tenure of adjoining property, is aided by the Highway acts.

The 13 Geo. 3. c. 78. s. 23 provides, " That every surveyor shall and may, from time to time, give information upon oath to the said justices, or any two or more of them, of all such highways, and of all bridges, (see "Bridges," *infra*,) causeways, or pavements upon such highways as are out of repair, and ought to be repaired by any person or persons, bodies politic or corporate, by reason of any grant, tenure, limitation or appointment, of any charitable gift, or otherwise howsoever; and the said justices shall limit a time for repairing the same, of which notice shall be given by the said surveyor, to the occupier or occupiers of the lands or tenements, liable to the burthen of such repairs, or to such other person or persons, bodies politic or corporate, as are chargeable with the same; and if such repairs shall not be effectually made within the time so limited, the said justices shall and are hereby required to present such highways, bridges, causeways or pavements, so out of repair, together with the person or persons, bodies politic or corporate, liable to repair the same, at the next general quarter sessions of the peace for the limit wherein such highways shall lie; and the justices at such quarter sessions may, if they see just cause, direct the prosecution to be carried on at the general expense of such limit, and to be paid out of the general rates within the same."

Bridges.] The obligation to repair bridges rests, by law, upon counties, and there are several statutes on the subject from the 22 H. 8. c. 5, down to the 55 G. 3 c. 143, inclusive; for which see Chitty's Statutes. And where the county is liable to repair the bridge, it is also bound to repair the highways, to the extent of three hundred feet at each end of the bridge. (R. v. W. R. York, 7 East, 588; 5 Taunt. 284.) But a parish, township, corporation, or a private individual, may be liable to repair a bridge by prescription, or *ratione tenuræ.* (Hale, P. C. 143; see R. v. Inh. Kent, 13 East, 220; R. v. Inh. of Lindsey, 14 East, 317.) But the obligation to repair does not carry with it the liability to *widen* the bridge, however the public exigencies may require that it should be widened. (R. v. Devon. 4 Barn. &

Cres. 670; 7 Dowl. & Ryl. 147; *overruling* R. v. Cumberland, 6 T. R. 194; 3 Bos. & Pul. 354.) It has been held, that where trustees of a turnpike road built a wider bridge of brick, in the place of an old wooden one, which the parish was bound to repair by prescription, and the public had used the new one for forty years, the liability to repair it was removed from the parish to the county. (R. v. Surrey, 2 Campb. 455.) But where townships have enlarged a bridge, which they were before bound to repair as a foot bridge, they shall be liable *pro rata*. (R. v. W. R. York, 2 East, 353.)

By the 3 Geo. 4. c. 126. ss. 107, 108, parishes liable to repair bridges are enabled to enter into compositions or agreements with the trustees of the roads, or persons acting on behalf of counties, by which they shall be relieved from the repair thereof in future.

Lands for Repair of Ways.] "Where any lands have been, or shall be given for the maintenance of causeways or pavements, highways and bridges, all such persons who are or shall be enfeoffed or trusted with any such lands, shall let them to farm at the most improved yearly value without fine: and that the justices of the peace, in their open sessions, shall and may inquire, by such ways and means as they shall think fitting, into the value of all such lands so given, or to be given, and order the improvement and employment of the rents and profits thereof, according to the will and direction of the donors of such lands, if they find that the persons so intrusted have been negligent or faulty in the performance of their trust; (except such lands have been given for the uses aforesaid to any college or hall in either of the universities of this kingdom which have visitors of their own) any law, statute, usage, or custom, to the contrary notwithstanding." (13 Geo. 3. c. 78. s. 51.)

What Ways shall be first repaired.] "The said justices of the peace, at any special sessions to be held by virtue of this act, may, by writing under their hands and seals, order and appoint those highways (not being turnpike road) which in their opinion do most want repair within their jurisdiction, to be first amended, and at what time and in what manner the same shall be amended; according to which order, if such there be, all and singular the respective surveyors of the said highways, are hereby required to proceed within their respective liberties." (Id. s. 25.)

Presentments by Justices.] "Every justice of assize, justices of the counties Palatine of Chester, Lancaster, and Durham, and of the great sessions in Wales, shall have authority by this statute, upon his or their own view; and every justice of the peace, either upon his own view, or upon information upon oath to him given by any surveyor of the highways, to make presentment, (see "Presentments," *infra,*) at their respective assizes or great sessions, or in the open general quarter sessions, of such respective limit of any highway, causeway, or bridge, not well and sufficiently repaired and amended; or of any other default or offence committed and done, contrary to the provision and intent of this statute; and that all defects in the repair thereof shall be presented in such jurisdiction where the same do lie, and not elsewhere; and that no such presentment, nor any indictment for any such default or offence, shall be removed, by *certiorari* or otherwise out of such jurisdiction, till such indictment or presentment be traversed, and judgment thereupon given; except where the duty or obligation of repairing the said highways, causeways, or bridges may come in question; and that every such presentment made by any such justice of assize, counties palatine, great sessions, or of the peace, upon his own view, or upon such information having been given to such justice of the peace upon the oath of such surveyor of the highways, as aforesaid, shall be as good and of the same force, strength, and effect in the law, as if the same had been presented and found by the oaths of twelve men; and that for every such default or offence so presented as aforesaid, the justices of assize, counties palatine, and great sessions, at their respective courts, and the justices of the peace at their general quarter sessions, shall have authority to assess such fines as to them shall be thought meet: saving to every person and persons that shall be affected by any such presentment, his, her, or their lawful traverse to the same presentment, as well with respect to the fact of non-repair, as to the duty or obligation of repairing the said highways, as they might have had upon any indictment of the same presented and found by a grand jury; and the justices of the peace at their general quarter sessions, or the major part of them may, if they see just cause, direct the prosecutions upon such presentments as shall be made at the quarter sessions as aforesaid, to be carried on at the general expense of such limit, and to be paid out of the general rates within the same." (13 Geo. 3. c. 78. s. 24.)

Road Presentments.] Although the 24th section authorizes a justice of the peace upon his own view, or upon "information upon oath to him given by *any surveyor* of the highways," to make presentment, &c., yet this expression must be construed with reference to the known duties of a surveyor, and they are limited to the district for which he is appointed; and therefore, when a magistrate presented a road in the township of F. upon the information of the surveyor of *another* township, it was held in arrest of judgment, that the presentment was bad; for the presentment cannot be made upon the information of any other surveyor than the surveyor appointed for the particular parish, township, or place where the road lies. (R. v. Fylingdales, 7 Barn. & Cres. 438; 1 Man. & Ryl. 176.)

A magistrate is justified in presenting, upon his own view, only such highways as are *really* out of repair; and he is liable to an action, if he certify falsely and maliciously. (Keen v. Wightwick, Chitty's Statutes, 448.) And when he proceeds upon the oath of a surveyor, it must also appear, upon the presentment itself, that the information on oath, was given to the magistrate who makes the presentment. (R. v. Fylingdales, *supra.*) If the presentment be of a smaller district than a parish, it must state expressly how the liability arises. (R. v. Penderryn, 2 T. R. 513.) A high constable cannot make presentment of a nuisance in a highway, in this manner; but he must go before the grand jury, and give his evidence upon oath. (R. v. Bridgewater and Taunton Canal Co. 7 Barn. & Cres. 514.) And where a justice presents a *nuisance* in a highway, it must be expressly alleged to be *against the form of the statute.* (R. v. Winter, 13 East, 258.)

It seems, that a justice may allow another person to prosecute a presentment in *his name*; but the justice is responsible for costs, if the presentment turn out to be improper, in the same manner as if he had conducted the proceedings himself. (R. v. Penderryn, *supra.*)

Court may award Costs.] "It shall and may be lawful for the court before whom any indictment or presentment shall be tried for not repairing highways, to award *costs* to the prosecutor, to be paid by the person or persons so indicted or presented, if it shall appear to the said court that the defence made to such indictment or presentment was frivolous; or to award costs to the person indicted or presented, to be paid by the prosecutor, if it shall appear to the said court that such prosecution was vexatious." (13 G. 3. c. 78. s. 64.)

Certificate for Costs.] If the judge on the trial certify that the defence was frivolous, without awarding costs in express terms, the prosecutor is entitled to receive them under this section. (R. v. Clifton, 6 T. R. 344, *ante,* 184.)

Expenses of Prosecuting, &c. how paid.] "If the inhabitants of any parish, township, or place, shall agree, at a vestry or public meeting, to prosecute any person by indictment for not repairing any highway within such parish, township, or place, which they apprehend such person was obliged by law to repair, or for committing any nuisance upon any highways; or shall agree, at such vestry meeting, to defend any indictment or presentment preferred against any such parish, township, or place, it shall and may be lawful for the surveyor of such parish, township, or place, to charge in his account the reasonable expenses incurred in carrying on or defending such respective prosecutions, after the same shall have been agreed to by such inhabitants at a vestry or public meeting, or allowed by a justice of the peace within the limit where such highways shall be; which expenses, when so agreed to, or allowed, shall be paid by such parish, township, or place, out of the fines, forfeitures, compositions, payments, and assessments authorised to be collected and raised by virtue of this act." (13 G. 3. c. 78. s. 65.)

Repair of Boundaries.] "Whereas the common highways in this kingdom are to be maintained and kept in repair (except in certain cases) by the inhabitants of the several parishes in which such common highways are situated; but it frequently happens that the boundaries of such parishes pass through the middle of such common highways, and one side of such highways is situated in one parish, and the other side of such highways is situated in another parish, whereby great inconveniences have often arisen to such parishes in settling the time and manner of repairing and amending the same, and great detriment has arisen to the public from the want of the due repair of such highways; for remedy thereof, Be it enacted, That it shall and may be lawful for any two justices of the peace for any county, riding, or division, upon complaint or application to them by any surveyor, or any one of the surveyors of the highways, of any parish, (stating to such justices in writing, and by a plan thereunto annexed, that there is situated in the said parish, and also in some other parish adjoining thereto, specifying the same, a certain common highway, particularly describing the same by metes, bounds, and admeasurement thereof, one side of which common highway ought to be made or repaired by one of such parishes, and the other side thereof by the other of such parishes), to issue their summons, with a copy of such writing and plan thereunto annexed, to the surveyor or one of the surveyors of the highways of such other parish, to appear before them on a day to be mentioned in such summons, not more than fourteen days, nor less than seven days from the day of the date of such summons; and that in case the parties shall then appear before such justices, they may then proceed finally to decide the matter in the manner hereinafter mentioned, in case all the parties shall consent thereto: but in case the surveyor summoned shall not appear on such first summons, or appearing, shall require further time, the said justices shall adjourn the further consideration of the matter for any further time, not more than twenty-one days, nor less than fourteen days from the day of such adjournment, of which the surveyor not appearing shall have notice; on which day the said justices shall proceed to hear the parties and their witnesses, and whether the party summoned does or does not appear, shall proceed to examine and finally determine the matter in form following: (that is to say,) That it shall and may be lawful for such justices, and they are hereby required to divide the whole of such common highway, by a transverse line crossing such highway, into two equal parts, or into two such unequal parts and proportions as, in consideration of the soil, waters, floods, the inequality of such highway, or any other circumstances attending the same, they, in their discretion, shall think just and right; and to declare, adjudge, and order, that the whole of such highway, on both sides thereof in one of such parts, shall be maintained and repaired by one of such parishes, and that the whole of such highway on both sides thereof in the other of such parts shall be maintained and repaired by the other of such parishes; and shall cause such their order, and a plan of such highway, and the allotment thereof as before mentioned, to be fairly delineated on paper or parchment, and filed with the clerk of the peace of the county in which such highway shall happen to lie; and shall also cause such posts, stones, or other boundaries, to be placed and set up in such highway as in their judgment shall be necessary for ascertaining the division and allotment aforesaid." (34 G. 3. c. 64. s. 1.)

Parishes to repair parts allotted.] "And, that from and after such order and plan shall be so filed with the clerk of the peace as aforesaid, such parishes, and the inhabitants thereof respectively, shall be bound, as of common right, to maintain and keep in repair such parts of such common highway so allotted to them as aforesaid; and shall be liable to be prosecuted and indicted for neglect of such duty, and shall in all respects whatsoever be liable and subject to all the provisions, regulations, and penalties contained in any act or acts of Parliament for the repair of the highways which are or shall be in force, in like manner as they are liable and subject to with respect to the repair of any other common highway within such parishes respectively, and also shall be discharged from the repair of such parts of such highway as shall not be included in their respective allotments." (Id. s. 2.)

How Costs defrayed.] "All costs, charges, and expenses to be incurred by reason of any of the proceedings before mentioned, shall be borne and defrayed by such two parishes, the same being settled and ascertained by such two justices; and in case the said parties shall refuse or neglect to pay and discharge their respective share of such costs and expenses, it shall and may be lawful for either of such justices, or any other justice of the peace for the said county, riding, or division, to levy the same by distress and sale, with the costs of such distress, on the goods and chattels of any surveyor of the highways of the parish, so refusing or neglecting to defray such costs and charges as aforesaid." (34 Geo. 3. c. 64. s. 3.)

Boundaries not otherwise changed.] "Nothing in this act contained shall extend, or be construed to extend, to affect, change, or alter, in any manner whatsoever, any boundaries of counties, lordships, hundreds, manors, or any other division of public or private property, nor the bonndaries of any parishes, otherwise than for the purpose of amending and keeping in repair such particular portion of the highways, in the manner hereinbefore mentioned." (Id. s. 4.)

Bodies Politic, &c. may adopt the Act.] "Nothing herein contained shall relate, or be construed to relate, to any highways, the repair of any part of which belongs to any bodies politic or corporate, township, or other such place, or to any private person or persons, by the reason of tenure of any lands, or otherwise howsoever, but that the same shall be construed to relate to such highways, the repair of which belongs to parishes only: Provided always, that in case any such body politic or corporate, township, or other such place, or any private person or persons as aforesaid, or any other person or persons who shall be bound by law to repair one side of any part of any common highway, shall be desirous that the same should be placed under the regulations of this act, and that a division or allotment thereof should be made, according to the provisions thereof, and the parties who are bound to the repair of the other side of the said highway shall consent thereto, it shall and may be lawful for such two justices to make an order for the division and allotment of such highway, and such order, when filed with the clerk of the peace, shall have the like force and effect, to all intents and purposes whatsoever, as is herein directed with respect to the like order when parishes only are concerned." (Id. s. 5.)

Appeal to Quarter Sessions.] "It shall and may be lawful for either of the two parishes, between whom any such allotment of any highway shall be made by virtue of this act, by an order in vestry, specially called for that purpose, to appeal to the quarter sessions of the peace for the county where such parishes shall lie, to be holden next after the time when such order and plan shall be filed with the clerk of the peace as aforesaid, and not otherwise; and that upon the hearing of such appeal, the justices at such quarter sessions shall make such order as shall appear to them to be just, either by affirming, quashing, or amending the order of the two justices, and shall allow costs to either party, as in their discretion they shall think right; which order of the quarter sessions shall not be removed by writ of *certiorari* or otherwise, but shall be final to all intents and purposes whatsoever." (Id. s. 7.)

Materials how procured.] "For the better repairing, and keeping in repair, the said highways, and providing of materials for that purpose, be it enacted, That it shall and may be lawful to and for every surveyor, to be appointed as aforesaid, to take and carry away, or cause to be taken and carried away, so much of the rubbish or refuse stones of any quarry or quarries lying and being within the parish, township, or place where he shall be surveyor, (except such as shall have been got by the surveyor of any turnpike road,) without the license of the owner or owners of such quarries, as they shall judge necessary for the amendment of the said highways; but not to dig or get stone in such quarry without leave of the owner thereof: And also, that it shall and may be lawful for every such surveyor, for the use aforesaid, in any waste land or common ground, river or brook, within the parish, township, or place for which he shall be surveyor, or within any other parish, township, or place wherein gravel, sand, chalk, stone, or other materials are respectively likely to be found, (in case sufficient cannot be conveniently had within the parish, township, or place, where the same are to be employed, and sufficient shall be left for the use of the roads in such other parish, township, or place,) to search for, dig, get, and carry away the same; so that the said surveyor doth not thereby divert or interrupt the course of such river or brook, or prejudice or damage any building, highway, or ford, nor dig or get the same out of any river or brook within the distance of one hundred feet above or below any bridge, nor within the like distance of any dam or wear; and likewise to gather stones lying upon any lands or grounds within the parish, township, or place where such highway shall lie, for such service and purpose, and to take and carry away so much of the said materials as by the discretion of the said surveyor shall be thought necessary, to be employed in the amendment of the said highways, without making any satisfaction for the said materials; but satisfaction shall be made for all damages done to the lands or grounds of any person or persons by carrying away the same, in the manner hereinafter directed, for getting and carrying materials in inclosed lands or grounds: but no such stones shall be gathered without the consent of the occupier of such lands or grounds, or a license from a justice of the peace for that purpose, after having summoned such occupier to come before him, and heard his reasons, if he shall appear and give any, for refusing his consent." (13 G. 3. c. 78. s. 27.)

Not to collect Beach.] "Provided, That nothing in this act contained relative to the gathering or getting of stones, shall extend to any quantity of land (being private property) covered with stones thrown up by the sea, commonly called beach." (13 Geo. 3. c. 78. s. 28.)

Materials got from Inclosed Grounds.] "That it shall and may be lawful for every such surveyor, for the use aforesaid, to search for, dig, and get sand, gravel, chalk, stone, or other materials, if sufficient cannot conveniently be had within such waste lands, common grounds, rivers, or brooks, in and through any of the several or inclosed lands or grounds of any person or persons whomsoever, within the parish, township, or place where the same shall be wanted; or by license from two justices of the peace, at a special sessions, within any other parish, township, or place, adjoining or lying near to the highway for which such materials shall be required; if it shall appear to such justices that sufficient materials cannot be conveniently had in the parish, township, or place, where such highways lie, or in the waste lands, or common grounds, rivers, or brooks, of such adjacent parish, township, or place, and that a sufficient quantity of materials will be left for the use of the parish, township, or place where the same shall be, (such lands or grounds not being a garden, yard, avenue to a house, lawn, park, paddock, or inclosed plantation;) and to take and carry away so much of the said materials as by the discretion of the said surveyor shall be thought necessary to be employed in the amendment of the said highways: the said surveyor making such satisfaction for the damage to be done to such lands or grounds by the getting and carrying away the same, as shall be agreed upon between him and the owner, occupier, or other person interested in such lands or grounds respectively, in the presence, and with the approbation of two or more substantial inhabitants of such parish, township, or place; and in case they cannot agree, then such satisfaction and recompense shall be settled and ascertained by order of one or more justice or justices of the peace of the limit where such land or ground shall lie: (see "Recompense for Damage," *infra*:) and in such places where, from the want of other materials, burnt clay may be substituted in the place thereof, it shall and may be lawful for the surveyor to dig clay in such places as he is hereby authorized to dig chalk or gravel, and to dry the same upon the lands adjoining, and to burn the same upon any waste lands or common grounds, and to carry such clay in such manner as other materials are allowed to be carried by this act, upon making such satisfaction for the damages within the several inclosed lands or grounds, where such clay shall be placed or carried, as herein directed with regard to other materials: Provided, that when the owner of any such inclosed lands, shall have occasion for any such materials lying within the same for the repair of any highway, or other roads or ways upon his estate, or which he shall be under obligation to repair, and shall give notice to such surveyor that he apprehends there will not be sufficient for those purposes, and also for the use of the public highways, then, and in every such case, the surveyor shall not be permitted to dig or take such materials without the consent of such owner, or an order of two justices of the peace, after having summoned and heard the said owner or occupier, or his steward or agent; which justices are hereby authorized to inquire into the nature and circumstances of the case, and to permit or restrain such power in such manner, and under such directions, as to them shall seem just." (Id. s. 29.)

Recompense for Damage.] The amount must be ascertained in the mode prescribed by the above section. Thus where surveyors broke a new way over plaintiff's land, in order to carry such materials, though an old but circuitous road existed before, and after an action of trespass brought against them, paid money into court by way of amends, under the 79th section, it was held, that the sufficiency of such amends could not be questioned at Nisi Prius, the statute having referred the quantum of amends, if not agreed upon between the parties, to the decision of the justices. But it seems to be competent to the plaintiff in such action to show, that the making of such new road was *maliciously* and *wantonly* done, and not for the necessary or convenient carriage of the materials over the land; and in such case he would not be concluded by the amends tendered, or paid into court. (Boyfield v. Porter, 13 East, 200.) See also the decision upon similar provisions, in a local Turnpike act. (R. v. Manning, 2 Kenyon's Rep. 561; 1 Burr. 377.)

Pits, &c. to be filled up.] "That if any surveyor, or person employed by him, shall, by reason of the searching for, digging, or getting any gravel, sand, stones, chalk, clay, or other materials for repairing any highways, make, or cause to be made, any pit or hole in any such lands or grounds, rivers or brooks, as aforesaid, wherein such materials shall be found, such surveyor, person or persons, shall forthwith cause the same to be sufficiently fenced off, and such fence supported and repaired, during such time as the said pit or hole shall continue open; and shall, within three days after such pit or hole shall be opened or made, where no gravel, stones, or materials shall be found, cause the same to be forthwith filled up, levelled, and covered with the turf or clod which was dug out of the same; and where any such materials shall be found, within fourteen days after having dug up sufficient materials in such pit or hole, cause the same to be filled up, sloped down, or fenced off, and so continued; and every surveyor shall, within twenty days after he shall be appointed to that office, cause all the said pits and holes which shall then be open, and not likely to be further useful, to be filled up, or sloped down, in manner aforesaid; and if they are likely to be further useful, he shall secure the same by posts and rails, or other fences, to prevent accidents to persons or cattle: and in case such surveyor, person or persons, shall neglect to fill up, slope down, or fence off, such pit or hole, in manner and within the time aforesaid, he or they shall forfeit the sum of ten shillings for every such default; and in case such surveyor, person or persons, shall neglect to fence off such pit or hole, or to slope down the same as hereinbefore directed, for the space of six days after he or they shall have received notice for either of those purposes from any justice of the peace, or from the owner or occupier of such several ground, river, or brook, or any person having right of common within such common or waste lands as aforesaid, and such neglect and notice shall be proved upon oath before one or more of the said justices of the peace, such surveyor, person or persons, shall forfeit and pay any sum not exceeding ten pounds, nor less than forty shillings, for every such neglect, to be determined and adjudged by such justice or justices, and to be laid out and applied in the fencing off, filling up, or sloping down, such pit or hole, and toward the repair of the roads in the parish, township, or place, where the offence shall be committed, in such manner as the said justice or justices shall direct and appoint; which forfeiture, in case the same be not forthwith paid, shall be levied as other forfeitures are hereinafter directed to be levied." (13 G. 3. c. 78. s. 31.)

Materials dug for other Parish.] "That no stone, gravel, or materials, to be dug for the use of any other parish, township, or place, than that wherein the same are found, shall be removed or carried from the place where they shall be so dug at any other time than between the first day of April and the first day of November, or in the time of hard frost in the winter season." (Id. s. 32.)

Damaging Mills, &c. Penalty.] "That if any person shall dig, or cause to be dug, materials for the highways, contrary to the direction of this act, whereby any bridge, mill, building, dam, highway, ford, mines, or tin works, may be damaged or endangered, every offender therein shall forfeit, for every such offence, any sum not exceeding five pounds, nor less than twenty shillings, at the discretion of the court or justices before whom complaint thereof shall be made." (Id. s. 33.)

Contracts for getting Materials.] "That in every parish, township, or place, where a sufficient quantity of stone, gravel, chalk, or other materials, cannot be provided and carried by the labourers and teams required by this act to perform statute duty within such parish, township, or place, the said surveyor shall and is hereby required to contract for the getting and carrying thereof (in the presence of the said assistant, if any such shall be appointed), at a meeting to be held for that purpose, of which ten days' notice in writing shall be given, by fixing the same upon the door of the church or chapel of such parish, township, or place, or if there be no church or chapel, at the most public place there; which notice shall specify the work to be done, and the time and place for letting thereof: And if any surveyor shall have any part, share, or interest, directly or indirectly, in any such contract, or in any other contract or bargain for work or materials, to be made, done, or provided, upon, for, or on account of any of the highways, roads, bridges, or other works whatsoever, under his care or management, or shall upon his own account, directly or indirectly, let to hire any team, or sell or dispose of any timber, stone, or other materials, to be used or employed in making or repairing such roads, bridges, or other works as aforesaid, (unless a license in writing for the sale of any such materials, or to let to hire any such team, be first obtained from some justice of the peace within that limit,) he shall forfeit for every such offence the sum of ten pounds, and be for ever after incapable of being employed as a surveyor with a salary under the authority of this act." (Id. s. 49.)

SECTION III.—WIDENING AND DIVERTING HIGHWAYS.

13 G. 3. c. 78. ss. 15, 16, 17, 18. 20, 21, 22;
55 G. 3. c. 68. ss. 2, 3, 4, 5.

Width of Cartways, &c.] "Surveyors of the highway shall, and they are hereby required to make, support and maintain, or cause to be made, supported and maintained, every public cartway leading to any market town twenty feet wide at the least; and every public horseway or driftway, eight feet wide at the least, if the ground, between the fences inclosing the same, will admit thereof." (13 G. 3. c. 78. s. 15.)

Roads widened or diverted.] "That where it shall appear upon the view of any two or more of the said justices of the peace, that the ground or soil of any highway between the fences thereof, is not of sufficient breadth, and may be conveniently widened and enlarged; or that the same cannot be conveniently enlarged, and made commodious for travellers, without diverting and turning the same; such justices shall, and they are hereby empowered, within their respective jurisdictions, to order such highways respectively to be widened and enlarged, (see "Widening Roads," *post*, 212.) or diverted and turned, in such manner as they shall think fit; so that the said highways, when enlarged and diverted, shall not exceed thirty feet in breadth; and that neither of the said powers do extend to pull down any house or building, or to take away the ground of any garden, park, paddock, court, or yard: and for the satisfaction of the person or persons, bodies politic or corporate, who are seised or possessed of, or interested in their own right, or in trust for any other person or persons, in the said ground that shall be laid into the said highways, respectively so to be enlarged, or through which such highway, so to be diverted and turned, shall go; the said surveyor, under the direction and with the approbation of the said justices, shall and is hereby empowered to make an agreement with him, her, or them, for the recompense to be made for such ground, and for the making such new ditches and fences as shall be necessary, according and in proportion to their several and respective interests therein, and also with any other person or persons, bodies politic or corporate, that may be injured by the enlarging, altering, or diverting such highways respectively, for the satisfaction to be made to him, her, or them respectively, as aforesaid. And if the said surveyor, under the direction and with the approbation of the said justices, cannot agree with the said person or persons, bodies politic or corporate, or if he, she, or they, cannot be found, or shall refuse to treat, or take such recompense or satisfaction as shall be offered to them respectively by such surveyor; then the justices of the peace, at any general quarter sessions to be holden for the limit wherein such ground shall lie, upon certificate in writing, signed by the justices making such view as aforesaid, of their proceedings in the premises, and upon proof of fourteen days' notice in writing having been given by the surveyor of such parish, township, or place, to the owner, occupier, or other person or persons, bodies politic or corporate, interested in such ground, or to his, her, or their guardian, trustee, clerk, or agent, signifying an intention to apply to such quarter sessions for the purpose of taking such ground, shall impannel a jury of twelve disinterested men out of the persons returned to serve as jurymen at such quarter sessions: and the said jury shall, upon their oaths, to the best of their judgments assess the damages to be given, and recompense to be made, to the owners and others interested as aforesaid in the said ground, for their respective interests, as they shall think reasonable, not exceeding forty years' purchase, for the clear yearly value of the ground so laid out; and likewise such recompense as they shall think reasonable, for the making of new ditches and fences on the side or sides of the said highways that shall be so enlarged or diverted, and also satisfaction to any person or persons, bodies politic or corporate, that may be otherwise injured by the enlarging or diverting the said highways respectively; and upon payment or tender of the money so to be awarded and assessed to the person or persons, bodies politic or corporate, intitled to receive the same, or leaving it in the hands of the clerk of the peace of such limit, in case such person or persons, bodies politic or corporate, cannot be found, or shall refuse to accept the same, for the use of the owner of, or others interested in the said ground, the interest of the said person or persons, bodies politic or corporate, in the said ground, shall be for ever divested out of them; and the said ground, after such agreement or verdict as aforesaid, shall be esteemed and taken to be a public highway, to all intents and purposes whatsoever: saving nevertheless to the owner or owners of such ground all mines, minerals, and fossils lying under the same, which can or may be got without breaking the surface of the said highway; and also all timber and wood growing upon such ground, to be fallen and taken by such owner or owners within one month after such order shall have been made, or in default thereof, to be fallen by the said surveyor or surveyors within the respective months aforesaid, and laid upon the land adjoining, for the benefit of the said owner or owners. And where there shall not appear sufficient money in the hands of the surveyor or surveyors, for the purposes aforesaid, then the said two justices, in case of agreement, or the said court of quarter sessions, after such verdict as aforesaid, shall order an equal assessment to be made, levied, and collected, upon all and every the occupiers of lands, tenements, woods, tithes, and hereditaments, in the respective parishes, townships, or places where such highways shall lie, and direct the money to be paid to the person or persons, bodies politic or corporate, so interested, in such manner as the said justices or court of quarter sessions respectively shall direct and appoint; and the money thereby raised shall be employed and accounted for according to the order and direction of the said justices, or court of quarter sessions, respectively, for and towards the purchasing the land to enlarge or divert the said highways, and for the making the said ditches and fences, and also satisfaction for the damage sustained thereby; and the said as-

P 2

sessment, if not paid within ten days after demand, shall, by order of the said justices, or court of quarter sessions respectively, be levied by the said surveyor in the manner hereinafter mentioned: Provided, That no such assessment to be made in any one year, shall exceed the rate of sixpence in the pound of the yearly value of the lands, tenements, woods, tithes, and hereditaments so assessed." (Id. s. 16.)

Widening Roads, &c.] The authority given by the above section to order any highway to be widened, extends to roads repairable *ratione tenuræ*, and disobedience in such case may be proceeded against summarily under the act, or by indictment at common law. (R. v. Balme, Cowp. 648.) This is the only enactment which gives justices any authority to divert and turn a road, without the consent of the owner of land through which the new road is to be carried; and it is doubted whether the order need specify the names of such owners, although the form, No. 21 in the schedule, contains blanks for the purpose. (R. v. Casson, 3 Dowl. & Ryl. 40.) As, however, the 19th section is no longer operative, being in part repealed, and in part obsolete, (see Waite v. Smith, 8 T. R. 133;) the proceedings for *diverting* and *turning* roads, will in most cases be conducted under the 55 Geo. 3. c. 68, subject of course to the exceptions and conditions in the other sections of the former act.

Old Highway to be sold.] "That when any such new highways shall be made as aforesaid, the old highway shall be stopped up, and the land and soil thereof shall be sold by the said surveyor, with the approbation of the said justices, to some person or persons whose lands adjoin thereto, if he, she, or they, shall be willing to purchase the same; if not, to some other person or persons for the full value thereof: but if such old road shall lead to any lands, house, or place, which cannot, in the opinion of such justices respectively, be accommodated with a convenient way and passage from such new highway which they are hereby authorized to order and lay out, if they find it necessary, then and in such case, the said old highway shall only be sold subject to the right of way and passage to such lands, house, or place respectively, according to the ancient usage in that respect; and the money arising from such sale, in either of the said cases, shall be applied towards the purchase of the land where such new highway shall be made: and upon payment or tender of the money so to be agreed for as aforesaid, and upon a certificate being signed by the said two justices, or by the chairman of the said court of quarter sessions, in case the same shall be determined there, describing the lands so sold, and expressing the sum so agreed for, and directing to whom the same shall be paid, and upon the purchasers taking a receipt for such purchase-money from the person entitled to receive the same, by an indorsement on the back of such certificate, the soil of such old highway shall become vested in such purchaser and his heirs; but all mines, minerals, and fossils, lying under the same, shall continue to be the property of the person or persons who would from time to time have been entitled to the same if such old highway had continued there." (13 Geo. 3. c. 78. s. 17.)

Costs, by whom payable.] "That in case such jury shall give in and deliver a verdict for more monies as a recompense for the right, interest, or property of any person or persons, bodies politic or corporate, in such lands or grounds, or for the making such fence, or for such damage or injury to be sustained by him, her, or them respectively, as aforesaid, than what shall have been proposed and offered by the said surveyor, before such application to the said court of quarter sessions as aforesaid; that then and in such case the costs and expenses attending the said several proceedings shall be borne and paid by the surveyor of the said highway out of the monies in his or their hands, or to be assessed and levied by virtue and under the powers of this act: but if such jury shall give and deliver a verdict for no more, or for less monies than shall have been so offered and proposed by the said surveyor, before such application to the said court of quarter sessions; that then the said costs and expenses shall be borne and paid by the person or persons, bodies politic or corporate, who shall have refused to accept the recompense and satisfaction so offered to him, her, or them, as aforesaid." (Id. s. 18.)

Lands between Old Road Fences.] "That no common land, lying between the fences of any old highway to be stopped up or inclosed by virtue of this act, shall be inclosed; and where the land lying between the fences of such highway, not being common land, shall, upon a medium, exceed thirty feet in breadth, and not extend to fifty feet in breadth, the same shall not be stopped up or inclosed, until satisfaction shall be made to the owner of such land, for so much thereof as shall exceed the said breadth of thirty feet; and if the parties cannot agree in the satisfaction so to be made, the same shall be adjusted by the said justices, or the jury, if a jury shall be impanelled; and if the land between the fences inclosing such highways, not being common land, shall exceed fifty feet in breadth upon a medium, or if the said old road, so to be diverted or turned, shall lie through the open field or ground belonging to any particular person or persons, such person or persons, and also the person or persons entitled to the land between the fences on the side of such highway, shall respectively hold and enjoy the land and soil of such old highway, and pay to the surveyor for the use of the highways so much money as shall be agreed upon between the parties; or if they cannot agree, so much as shall be deemed and adjudged by the said justices or jury, if such jury shall be impanelled, as aforesaid, to be adequate to the purchase of it, estimating such highway at thirty feet in breadth upon an average." (Id. s. 20.)

Satisfaction for Old or New Footways.] "And be it further enacted, That where any footway shall be diverted by virtue of this act through the land belonging to the same person who owned the land through which such old footway lay, the same shall be adjudged and deemed an exchange only, and no satisfaction or compensation shall be made, unless the land to be used for such new footway shall be of greater length, and of greater value, than the land used for such old footway; and where the said footway shall not be turned through the lands belonging to the same person, the damage occasioned by such old footway to the lands through which it lay, if the parties interested shall not agree in adjusting the same, shall be adjudged by two indifferent persons, the one to be named by the owner of the land, and the other by the said two justices; and if the persons so to be nominated cannot agree therein, they shall choose some third person to adjudge the same, whose determination shall be final and the money at which such damages shall be so assessed, shall be applied in making satisfaction to the owner or owners of the land through which such new footway shall be made." (Id. s. 21.)

Unnecessary Highways stopped.] "That if in any parish, township, or place, where any highway shall be diverted and turned by virtue of this act, it shall appear to the justices, who are hereby authorized to view or inquire into the same, that there are other highways within such parish, township, or place, besides that so to be diverted and turned, which may, without inconvenience to the public, be diverted into such new highway hereby authorized to be made, or into any other highway or highways within such parish, township, or place, and the charge of repairing such highway or highways, may be thereby saved to such parish, township, or place, it shall and may be lawful for such justices to order such highway or highways, which shall appear to them unnecessary, to be stopped up, and the soil thereof sold in such manner, and subject to such restrictions, and such right of appeal to the party or parties aggrieved thereby, as are hereinbefore respectively directed and given concerning the highways to be stopped up or inclosed." (Id. s. 22.)

Highways turned by Justices at Sessions.] "That when it shall appear, upon the view of any two or more of the said justices of the peace, that any public highway, or public bridleway, or footway, may be diverted, so as to make the same nearer, or more commodious to the public, and the owner or owners of the lands and grounds through which such new highway, bridleway, or footway, so proposed to be made, shall consent thereto by writing under his or their hand and seal, or hands and seals, (see "Consent of Owner," *post*, 216.) it shall and may be lawful, by order of such justices at some special sessions, to divert and turn and to stop up such footway, and to divert, turn, stop up, and inclose, sell and dispose of such old highway or bridleway, and to purchase the ground and soil for such new highway, bridleway, or footway, by such ways and means, and subject to such exceptions and conditions, in all respects, as in the said recited act mentioned with regard to highways to be widened or diverted: and also when it shall appear, upon the view of any two or more of the said justices of the peace, that any public highway, bridleway, or footway, is unnecessary, it shall and may be lawful, by order of such justices, or any two of them, to stop up, and to sell and dispose of such unnecessary highway, bridleway, or footway, by such ways and means, and subject to such exceptions and conditions, in all respects, as in the said recited act is mentioned in regard to highways to be widened and diverted, (see "Public Right in New Highways," *post*, 217.) except that the money to arise from such sale, where, by the said act, it would be applicable to the purchase of the ground and soil of the new highways or bridleways therein mentioned, shall be paid to the surveyor or surveyors, and be applied towards the general repairs of the highways and bridleways of the parish, township, or place within which the said highway, bridleway, or footway, so stopped up shall be situate: Provided, That in the several cases before mentioned, a notice, in the form or to the effect of schedule (A) to this act annexed, shall be affixed in legible characters at the place, and by the side of the said highway, bridleway, or footway, from whence the same is directed to be turned, diverted, or stopped up, and also inserted in one or more newspaper or newspapers published, or generally circulated, in the county where the parish, township, or place, in which the highway, bridleway, or footway, so ordered to be diverted and turned, or stopped up, (*as the case may be,*) shall lie, (*or in case no such newspaper shall be so published or circulated in such county, then in any newspaper or newspapers published or circulated in the nearest adjoining county,*) for three successive weeks after the making of such order; and a like notice shall be affixed to the door of the church or chapel of every parish, township, or place, in which such highway, bridleway, or footway, so ordered to be diverted, turned, or stopped up, or any part thereof, shall lie, on three successive Sundays subsequent to the making of such order; and the said several notices having been so published, the said order shall, at the quarter sessions which shall be holden within the limit where the highway, bridleway, or footway, so diverted and turned, or stopped up, shall lie, next after the expiration of *four weeks*, (see "Confirming Order," *post*, 217,) from the first day on which such notices shall have been published as aforesaid, be returned to the clerk of the peace in open court, and lodged with him; and the said order shall at such quarter sessions *be confirmed*, and by the clerk of the peace enrolled amongst the records of the said court of quarter sessions." (55 Geo. 3. c. 68. s. 2.)

Diverting, stopping up, &c.] The 19th section of the former act being repealed, the directions in the above section must be pursued. It has, however, been doubted whether commissioners authorized by an Inclosure act to stop up ways, &c. are bound to give the notices required by this statute. (R. v. Townsend, 5 Barn. & Ald. 424.)

There are other decisions upon Inclosure acts, some of which it may be expedient to notice. Thus, where a public footway passed over a common and across a farm-yard, and the commissioners were not to stop up any old road leading over land *not to be inclosed* without the concurrence of two magistrates, (see 41 Geo. 3. c. 109. s. 8;) and they stopped up the footway without such concurrence, it was held, that the right of way over the farm-yard was not extinguished. (Logan v. Burton, 5 Barn. & Cres. 513; 8 Dowl. & Ryl. 299; Harber v. Rand, 9 Price, 58.) But where a *discretion* is vested in commissioners, by a local act, as to stopping up roads, &c., though roads of a particular kind are excepted from the general operation of the act, they may stop up any of them as they may deem proper. (De Beauvoir v. Welch, 7 Barn. & Cres. 266.)

Consent of Owner; ante, 215.] Where a highway is proposed to be made through private property, there must be a consent of the person who is owner of the estate at the *time when the order is actually made;* and therefore where an order recited that the justices had received evidence of the consent of J. T. "in his lifetime," and it appeared that another person was owner at the time the order was made, it was held insufficient. (R. v. Kirk, 1 Barn. & Cres. 21; 2 Dowl. & Ryl. 52.) So an order signed and sealed, in his own name, by the *attorney* of the party, is alike invalid, though authorized by power of attorney; but which was not enrolled at the quarter sessions. (R. v. Crewe, 3 Dowl. & Ryl. 6; 1 Barn. & Cres. 622.) And the inquisition of damages by a jury under a similar provision in a Local act, authorizing trustees to turn roads through private lands, was quashed by the Court of King's Bench, because it did not appear on the face of the proceedings that any notice had been given to the owners. (R. v. Bagshaw, 7 T. R. 363.)

Public Right in New Highways; ante, 215.] By the 17th section of 13 Geo. 3, (*ante,* 212,) justices have power to stop up an old highway only when the *new highway* shall be made, and it ought to appear that the whole of the new road substituted for the old one, is a highway over which the public have as good and permanent a right, as they had over the old one. It follows therefore, if the new or substituted way be a new line of turnpike road, which may be made so for a term of years only, it must be shown, that the public have secured to them, by the order of the magistrates, a right of using the new road, co-extensive with that which they had over the old road; and whether this right be given to the public in such case by a Local act, creating the new turnpike road, or if the road has been diverted under the General Turnpike act, (3 G. 4. c. 126;) and the new line substituted, that ought to be shown. (R. v. Winter, 8 Barn. & Cres. 785.)

It is questionable, whether the magistrates can divert a road partially, so as to vary the line of road for carriages, but continue it for foot passengers. It may be open to the objection, that the parish will be thus bound to keep two roads in repair instead of one. (Id.)

Confirming Order; ante, 216.] The computation of the four weeks must be made from the first day of giving that description of notice which is last published; and therefore, where the notice of the order for diverting a path was given on the 20th of December, and the order was confirmed on the 17th of January, it was held irregular and quashed. (R. v. Crewe, 3 Dowl. & Ryl. 6; 1 Barn. & Cres. 622.) Although the order ought to state, on the face of it, that it was made at a *special* sessions, yet, where the quarter sessions confirmed an order, without proof that it was previously made at a special sessions, the Court of King's Bench refused to interfere, as the question was within the cognizance of the quarter sessions, and had been determined by them. (1 Chitty's R. 164.)

Requisites of Order.] It must distinctly appear, on the face of an order for stopping up an unnecessary way, in what parish, &c. the way is situate; and the order must also describe the length and breadth of the way to be stopped up. And *semble* that the order must be for the *sale,* as well as the stopping up of such way. (Rex v. Kenyon, 6 Barn. & Cres. 640; Davison v. Gill, 1 East, 64.) It must also be *stated on the order,* according to the fact, that it was made at a special sessions. (R. v. Sheppard, 3 Barn. & Ald. 414.) And in an order for stopping up a highway as unnecessary, under this act, it must be stated, that it appeared to the justices *on view*, that the way was unnecessary; and, therefore, where the justices in an order merely stated that, " having upon view found," or it " having appeared to us" that the way was unnecessary, the court held the order insufficient; for by this statement, the justices say, they had done that which the legislature required, *or something else*; and it cannot be said, that by this form of words it appears that the justices had jurisdiction. (R. v. J. J. Worcestershire, 8 Barn. & Cres. 254; R. v. Rogers 2 Maul. & Ryl. 289.)

An order of justices for turning a road, reciting that they had viewed the *new* road, and found it to be in good condition and repair, was held to be a sufficient certificate thereof, under the 19th section of 13 Geo. 3. c. 78; and of course will be so under the 55 Geo. 3. c. 68. s. 2: and if the certificate be deposited with the clerk of the peace, that is an enrolment of it within the same section. Where a road is stopped up by order of justices, and a new one is substituted partly over the ground of a stranger, and partly over an accustomed road, that is a sufficient compliance with the act, provided the new road convey the public to the same place as the old one did. (De Ponthieu v. Pennyfeather, 1 Marsh. 261; 5 Taunt. 634.)

Appeal by the aggrieved.] "That where any such highway, bridleway, or footway, shall be so ordered to be stopped up or inclosed, and such new highway, bridleway, or footway, set out and appropriated in lieu thereof, as aforesaid, or where any unnecessary highway, bridleway, or footway, shall be so ordered to be stopped up as aforesaid, it shall and may be lawful for any person or persons *injured or aggrieved* by any such order or proceeding, or by the inclosure of any road or highway, by virtue of any inquisition taken upon any writ of *ad quod damnum*, to make his or their complaint thereof, by appeal to the justices of the peace at the said quarter sessions, upon giving ten days' notice in writing of such appeal to the surveyor of the highways of the parish, township, or place wherein such highway, bridleway, or footway shall be situated, and also affixing such notice to the door of the church or chapel of such parish, township, or place; and the said court of quarter sessions is hereby authorized and empowered to hear, and finally determine such appeal." (55 Geo. 3. c. 68. s. 3.)

Appeal against stopping up a Way.] The right of appeal against an order for diverting a footway, seems to depend upon this section, and not on the 80th section of the 13 Geo. 3; (R. v. Wing, 4 Barn. & Cres. 184; 6 Dowl. & Ryl. 323.) But if the proceedings be under an Inclosure act, it is doubtful whether the notices required by the general statute must be given; at all events, if such order be appealed against, on the ground that the notices have not been given, the appeal must be brought within the period prescribed by the *general act*, although the local statute may give a longer time. (R. v. Townsend, 5 Barn. & Ald. 420.) Where the proceeding to stop up a road is by writ of *ad quod damnum*, the notices required by the above act must be given. (R. v. J. J. Essex, 1 Barn. & Ald. 373.)

The appellant in his *notice* must state himself to be "*injured*" or "*aggrieved*," pursuant to the language of this section, or he is not entitled to be heard; as the privilege of appeal is given to those who have sustained some special and peculiar injury, and not to any captious person whomsoever. (Rex v. J. J. Essex, 5 Barn. & Cres. 431; 7 Dowl. & Ryl. 658.) The correctness of the rule laid down in this last case being questioned in a subsequent case, the court upon consideration said, "We think that if the question had now arisen for the first time, we should have been bound to decide, that the party appealing against an order for stopping up a footway, must, on the face of his notice, show that he is injured." (R. v. W. R. Yorkshire, 7 Barn. & Cres. 678; 1 Man. & Ryl. 547.)

The same rule applies to local acts, authorizing trustees to stop up old roads, and which give the right to appeal to parties injured or aggrieved, (R. v. J. J. W. R. Yorkshire, 7 Barn. & Cres. 678;) and, in short, in all such-like cases, where the appeal is given in terms, to the party aggrieved.

If an order be made to *divert* a road, and at a subsequent time another order be made for stopping up the old road—a party aggrieved may appeal against the latter, though he is too late to appeal against the former order. (R. v. J. J. Hertfordshire, 3 Maul. & Sel. 459.)

If Order confirmed, Proceedings conclusive.] "That if no such appeal be made, or, being made, such order and proceedings shall be confirmed by the said court, the said inclosures may be made, and the said ways stopped; and the proceedings thereupon shall be binding and conclusive to all persons whomsoever; and the new highways, bridleways, and footways, so to be appropriated and set out, shall be and for ever after continue a public highway, bridleway, or footway, to all intents and purposes whatsoever: but no inclosures of such old highways, bridleways, or footways (except in the case of stopping up such useless highways, bridleways, or footways, as hereinbefore mentioned) shall be made, until such new highway, bridleway, or footway shall be completed and put into good condition and repair, and so certified by two justices of the peace upon view thereof; which certificate shall be returned to the clerk of the peace, and by him enrolled amongst the records of the court of quarter sessions, next after such order as aforesaid shall have been confirmed, or enrolled pursuant to the directions herein before contained: but from and after the enrolment of such order and certificate, such old highway, bridleway, or footway, shall be stopped up, and the soil of such old highway or bridleway sold in the manner, and subject to the reservations and restrictions in the said recited act mentioned, with respect to highways to be diverted by virtue of the said recited act." (Id. s. 4.)

SECTION IV.—STATUTE DUTY.

34 Geo. 3. c. 74. ss. 4. 2. 6; 13 Geo. 3. c. 78. ss. 36, 37. 43.

Proportions of Statute Labour.] The 34 Geo. 3, provides, "That the surveyor to be appointed by the 13 Geo. 3, together with the inhabitants and occupiers of lands, tenements, woods, tithes, and hereditaments, within each parish, township or place, shall at proper seasons in every year use their endeavours for the repair of the highways, and shall be chargeable thereunto as followeth: (that is to say,) Every person keeping a waggon, cart, wain, plough, or tumbrel, and three or more horses or beasts of draught used to draw the same, shall be deemed to keep a team, draught, or plough, and be liable to perform statute duty with the same in the parish, township, or place, where he resides, and shall six days in every year, (if so many days shall be found necessary), to be computed from Michaelmas to Michaelmas, send on every day and at every place to be appointed by the surveyor, for the amending the highways in such parish, township, or place, one wain, cart, or carriage, furnished after the custom of the country, with oxen, horses, or other cattle, and all other necessaries fit to carry things for that purpose, and also two able men with such wain, cart, or carriage; which duty so performed shall excuse every such person from his duty in such parish, township, or place, in respect of all lands, woods, tithes, tenements, or hereditaments, not exceeding the annual value of fifty pounds, which he shall occupy therein: and every person keeping such team, draught, or plough, and occupying in the same parish, township, or place, lands, tenements, woods, tithes, or hereditaments, of the yearly value of fifty pounds over and beyond the said yearly value of fifty pounds in respect whereof such team duty shall be performed; and every such person occupying lands, tenements, woods, tithes, or hereditaments, of the yearly value of fifty pounds in any other parish, township, or place, besides that wherein he resides; and every other person not keeping a team, draught, or plough, but occupying lands, tenements, woods, tithes, or hereditaments, of the yearly value of fifty pounds, in any parish, township, or place, shall in like manner respectively, and for the same number of days, find and send one wain, cart, or carriage, furnished with not less than three horses or four oxen, and one horse or two oxen, and two horses and two able men to each wain, cart, or carriage, and in like manner for every fifty pounds per annum respectively, which every such person shall further occupy in any such parish, township, or place respectively: such wains, carts, or carriages, to be employed by the surveyor in the repairing and amending the highways within the parish, township, or place, where such lands, tenements, woods, tithes, or hereditaments shall respectively lie."

When Money to be paid in lieu thereof.] "And every person who shall not keep a team, draught, or plough, but shall occupy lands, tenements, woods, tithes, or hereditaments under the yearly value of fifty pounds in the parish, township, or place, where he resides, or in any other parish, township, or place, and every person keeping a team, draught, or plough, and occupying lands, tenements, woods, tithes, or hereditaments, under the yearly value of fifty pounds in any other parish, township, or place, than that wherein he resides, shall respectively contribute to the repair of the highways, and pay to the surveyor of such parish, township, or place respectively, in lieu of such duty, the sums following: *videlicet,* For every twenty shillings of the annual value of such lands, tenements, woods, tithes, or hereditaments respectively, the sum of one penny for every day's statute duty which shall be required and called for by the surveyor of such parish, township, or place respectively, in every year, not exceeding six days' duty in the whole, as aforesaid; and every such person respectively shall in like manner pay the sum of one penny for every twenty shillings of the annual value of the lands, tenements, woods, tithes, and hereditaments, which he shall occupy in any such parish, township, or place respectively, above the annual value of fifty pounds, and less than one hundred pounds, and so for every twenty shillings that each progressive and intermediate annual value of twenty shillings of the lands, tenements, woods, tithes, and hereditaments which he shall so occupy, shall fall short of the further increase of fifty pounds in every parish, township, or place, where such lands, tenements, woods, tithes, and hereditaments shall respectively lie, for every day's statute duty so to be required as aforesaid: Provided that no person keeping such team, draught, or plough, and performing duty with the same as aforesaid in the parish, township, or place, where he resides, and not occupying lands, tenements, woods, tithes, or hereditaments, within the same, of the yearly value of thirty pounds, shall be obliged to send more than one labourer with such team, draught, or plough: Which said several sums shall be considered as compositions, and shall be paid to the surveyor of the parish, township, or place in which they are charged, for the use of the highways therein, at the time such compositions are to be paid under the authority of the said act, or within ten days after; or in default of such payments, the said surveyor shall make application to a justice of the peace, acting for the limit or district wherein such default shall be made, and the justice, to whom such application shall be made, shall summon the party so making default to appear at some special or other petty sessions, to be holden for such limit or district, and at which two justices at the least shall be present, to show cause why he has refused or neglected to pay such composition money; and in default of appearance, or if on appearance he shall not make it appear to the satisfaction of the said justices that he is poor and indigent, and as such is an object deserving relief, such money shall be levied by distress and sale of the goods and chattels of the person or persons refusing or neglecting to pay the same, in such manner as the forfeitures for the neglect in performing the statute duty are hereby authorized to be levied, and raised: Provided always, that when, on application as above mentioned, the justices shall think proper to discharge any poor and indigent person from payment of the rate or composition money, such person shall at the same time be discharged from any expenses which may arise in consequence of such summons and appearance." (34 Geo. 3. c. 74. s. 4.)

Liability to Statute Duty.] In an action of trespass, for levying penalties upon a conviction for default in performing statute duty, upon complaint of the surveyor appointed for the whole parish, it was held, that the conviction being good upon the face of it, and being unreversed and *unappealed* against, was a sufficient answer to the action. And that the plaintiff could not in such action try the question whether an occupier in one of several townships within the parish was exempt from the burden of repairing the roads in *other parts* of the parish. The proper course would be to appeal against the appointment of *one surveyor* for the *whole* parish. (Fawcett v. Fowlis, 7 Barn. & Cres. 394.) In the same case it appeared that the surveyor called upon the plaintiff to do certain statute duty, *or* compound for it. The conviction stated, that he was an occupier of land in the parish, and had neglected to do the work, but did not notice the composition. Held, that it was unnecessary to do so, or to state that the plaintiff kept a team; for that if he did not keep a team, or had compounded, that was matter of defence which ought to have been urged by him in answer to the complaint.

The inhabitants of a parish into which a road is turned by turnpike trustees, are not bound under these acts to do statute work there. (Wheeler v. Cooper, 1 Bla. Rep. 603;) though the General Turnpike acts authorize magistrates to direct it to be done on turnpike roads, when found necessary.

Persons keeping a Cart or Coach, &c.] "That from and after the said twenty ninth day of September, every person who shall not keep a team, draught, or plough, but shall keep one or more cart or carts, and one or two horses, or beasts of draught, only used to draw in each of such carts upon the highways, shall be obliged to perform his statute duty for the like number of days with such cart or carts, and horse or horses, or beasts of draught, and one labourer to attend each cart, or to pay for the lands, tenements, woods, tithes, and hereditaments, which he shall occupy, according to the rate hereinafter mentioned, at the option of the surveyor; and every person who shall keep a coach, postchaise, or chair, or other wheel carriage, and not keep a team, draught, or plough, nor occupy lands, tenements, woods, tithes, or hereditaments, of the annual value of fifty pounds in the parish, township, or place, where he shall reside, shall pay to the surveyor one shilling in respect of every such day's statute duty for every horse which he shall draw in any such carriage, or shall pay according to the value of the lands, tenements, or hereditaments which he shall occupy, according to the rate hereinafter mentioned, at the option of the surveyor: And if the said teams, draughts, or ploughs, or any of them, shall not be thought needful by the surveyor on any of the said days, then every such person who should have sent any such team, draught, or plough, according to the directions aforesaid, shall, according to the notice to be given as hereinafter directed, send unto the said work for every one so spared three able men, there to labour as aforesaid, or pay to the said surveyor the sum of four shillings and sixpence in lieu thereof, at the option of the surveyor: and all such persons as aforesaid shall respectively have and bring with them such shovels, spades, picks, mattocks, and other tools and instruments as are useful and proper for the purposes aforesaid; and all the said persons and carriages shall diligently perform the work and labour to which they shall be appointed by such surveyor, for eight hours in every of the said days, within such parish, township, or place, or in getting and carrying materials in and from any other parish, township or place, to be employed in the repair of the highways of the parish, township, or place, for which they shall be required to perform such duty and labour as aforesaid: and if any person, sending a team as aforesaid, shall not send a sufficient labourer besides the driver (except as before mentioned), or if any such labourer or driver, or the driver of any cart required to perform statute duty as aforesaid, shall refuse to work and labour during the time above mentioned, according to the directions of the surveyor, or if any driver shall refuse to carry proper and sufficient loads, it shall and may be lawful for such surveyor to discharge every such team, cart, or labourer, and to recover from the owner of every such team or cart the forfeiture which every such person or persons would have incurred, by virtue of the said act, in case no such team, cart, or labourer respectively, had been sent." (34 Geo. 3. c. 74. s. 2.)

Half Team, Cart, or Waggon.] "The surveyor, where the employment for teams is of such sort that two horses will be sufficient for one cart, or where a stand cart with one horse shall be necessary, may call upon any person liable to send a team, or draught, or plough, by virtue of this act, who keeps one or more cart or carts, and three or more horses, to send such cart or carts, horse or horses, to perform his statute duty as the surveyor shall find most convenient, and shall direct; and the surveyor shall allow every such stand cart and one horse as half a team, and every cart and two horses as two-thirds of a team: and if a waggon shall be found necessary for any particular business, the surveyor may require the duty, or any part thereof, to be performed with such waggon, by any person who keeps one; which directions of the surveyor shall be observed, or the person liable to perform such duty shall forfeit such sum as the duty so required of him shall bear in proportion to the forfeiture hereby inflicted for every neglect in performing duty with a team, draught, or plough." (13 Geo. 3. c. 78. s. 36.)

Statute Duty.] "Every surveyor shall, from time to time, give to or cause to be left at the house or usual place of abode of every person or persons so liable to perform such duty or labour as in this act directed, four days' notice at the least of the day, hour, and place, upon which each of the said day's duty shall be required to be performed: And every person or persons making default in finding and sending each wain, cart, or carriage, furnished as aforesaid, and such able men with the same as herein required, or in performing the said duty at the time and place, and in the manner by this act directed, shall for every such default or neglect in sending such wain, cart, or carriage, with such men as aforesaid, forfeit the sum of ten shillings; and for every default in sending every cart with one horse and one man, three shillings; and for not sending every cart with two horses and one man, five shillings: and every person or persons making default in sending any such labourer, and every person making default in performing such labour at the time and place, and in the manner directed by this act, or in paying such composition money for the same as herein mentioned, shall for every such neglect forfeit the sum of one shilling and sixpence; all which forfeitures shall be applied for the use of the highway within the parish, township, or place, where the same shall arise: And the said surveyor shall fairly and equally demand and require such duty and labour from every person or persons liable to perform the same according to the directions of this act, without favour or partiality to any person or persons whomsoever; and if in any parish, township, or place, it shall not be necessary to call forth the whole duty in any year, it shall be abated in a just and equal proportion amongst all persons liable to the same: and the said surveyor may and shall, and he is hereby required, with all convenient speed, after default made in performance of such duty or labour as aforesaid, to proceed for the recovery of the penalties or forfeitures hereby inflicted for the same respectively, in manner hereinafter directed, so that the same may be recovered before he makes up his accounts, in the manner directed by this act." (Id. s. 37.)

Team and Personal Duty in kind.] If it shall appear to the justices, at their special sessions, to be held in the week next after Michaelmas quarter sessions, or at any other special or petty sessions held within the limits of any parish, township, or place, at which two or more justices shall be present, that from the directions hereinbefore given for the performing and compounding the statute duty, there will be difficulty in procuring the necessary carriage, or a sufficient number of labourers, for the repair of the highways in any particular parish, township, or place, within their respective limits, without paying high and extravagant prices for the same, it shall and may be lawful for such justices to order and direct the team duty, or so much thereof as they shall think fit, to be performed in kind within every such parish, township, or place, except in respect of such teams as belong to persons who do not occupy lands, tenements, woods, tithes, or hereditaments, of the annual value of thirty pounds within the same; and also to order all such persons as shall gain their living by the wages of daily labour, or such part of them as they shall think fit, to perform six days' labour upon such highways in kind, either by themselves or other sufficient labourers, in case so many days' duty shall be required, upon being paid for such labour the usual and customary wages given to labourers in such parish, township, or place:

Provided that if part of such teams or labourers only are required, it shall be directed by the said order of the justices, in some given proportion, as one half, third, or fourth part thereof; and the surveyor shall, in that case, at a public vestry for such parish, township, or place, put the names of all the persons liable by this act to send such teams into one hat or box, and the names of all the persons liable to perform such labour into another hat or box, and some inhabitant then present shall draw out such number from each as shall be equal to the proportion so ordered by the said justices, and the persons so drawn shall perform such duty in kind for that year: and that if any such order shall be made or continued in the subsequent year, the same method shall be observed, but the names drawn in the preceding year shall not be put into such hat or box; and in every succeeding year such method and regulation shall be observed by such surveyor, as to render the duty so required to be performed in kind, as equal amongst the several persons liable thereto as may be; which order of the said justices, so far as the same shall be extended, shall supersede the said power or liberty of compounding, and shall be binding and effectual to all intents and purposes whatsoever, and shall continue in force until it shall be discharged or varied by the justices at some subsequent special sessions for the highways within such limit, to be held in the week next after Michaelmas quarter sessions; any thing herein contained to the contrary thereof in any wise notwithstanding." (34 Geo. 3. c. 74. s. 6.)

Fixing Seed Time and Harvest.] "And in order to prevent as much as possible any inconvenience to the persons liable to perform statute duty, be it enacted, That it shall and may be lawful for the inhabitants of every parish, township, or place, at some vestry, or other public meeting or meetings to be held pursuant to this act, to appoint three months in every year within which no statute duty shall be performed, viz. one month in the spring to be called *the seed month;* one month in the summer for the hay harvest; and one other month in the summer for the corn harvest. Provided that notice in writing be given of the times so appointed, to the surveyor of such parish, township, or place respectively, and also to the surveyor of every turnpike road, lying within the same, within three days after every such meeting, and fourteen days at least before the beginning of each of such months." (13 Geo. 3. c. 78. s. 43.)

SECTION V.—STATUTE DUTY COMPOSITION.

44 Geo. 3. c. 52. s. 2. 13 Geo. 3. c. 78. ss. 41, 42. 44. 40.
54 Geo. 3. c. 109. ss. 4, 5, 6, 7.

Compounding for Statute Work.] "Any person or persons liable to perform statute duty, by sending one or more team or teams, draught or draughts, plough or ploughs, with men, horses, or oxen, in manner in the 34 Geo. 3. mentioned, may compound for the same, if he, she, or they shall think fit, by paying to the surveyor of the highways, at the time and in the manner in the 13 Geo. 3. mentioned, such sum or sums of money as the justices of the peace for the limits wherein the parish, township, or place, for which the said duty is liable to be performed, is situate, or the major part of them, at their special session to be held in the first week after Michaelmas quarter sessions in every year, shall adjudge and declare to be reasonable, not exceeding twelve shillings, nor less than three shillings, for each team, draught, or plough, for each day; and in default of their adjudging and declaring the same, the sum of six shillings for and in lieu of every day's duty for each team, draught, or plough: and for each cart with two horses, or beasts of draught, not exceeding eight shillings nor less than three shillings; and in default of their adjudging and declaring the same, the sum of four shillings: and for each cart with one horse, or beast of draught, not exceeding six shillings, nor less than two shillings; and in default of their adjudging and declaring the same, the sum of three shillings." (44 Geo. 3. c. 52. s. 2.)

Notice of Compounding.] "The surveyor of every parish, &c., shall, on some Sunday in November in every year, cause ten days' notice at the least to be given in the church or chapel of such parish, township, or place; and if there be no church or chapel, or no service performed therein, then at the most public place there, and repeat the like notice, in such church, chapel, or place, on the next succeeding Sunday, of the time and place when and where the persons permitted under the authority of this act, and inclined to compound for the said duty in manner aforesaid, may signify to such surveyor their intention to compound; and all and every person or persons signifying the same, who shall then, or within the space of one calendar month afterwards, pay to such surveyor the composition authorized and allowed by this act, shall be discharged from the performance of such duty, which composition money shall be employed by the surveyor for the use of the highways; and that no composition shall be permitted, unless the same shall be paid at the day, or within the time aforesaid: but in cases where the occupation of any lands, tenements, woods, tithes, or hereditaments, shall be changed, or any new occupant or inhabitant shall come to reside in such parish, township, or place, after the time appointed for such composition, then the person or persons occupying such lands, tenements, woods, tithes, or hereditaments, or so residing in such parish, township, or place, shall be allowed to compound in manner aforesaid: Provided he, she, or they, shall pay the said composition money to the said surveyor within fourteen days after he, she, or they, shall enter upon such lands, tenements, or hereditaments, or shall come to reside in such parish, township, or place; and every tenant or occupier of any lands, tenements, woods, tithes, or hereditaments, who intends to quit the possession thereof within six calendar months from the time fixed for making such composition, shall and may compound for half the duty hereby required, and the succeeding tenant or occupier shall and may, in that case, compound or perform the duty in kind for the other half thereof; and if the surveyor shall receive from any person or persons a composition for more duty than shall be required from the other inhabitants and occupiers within the same parish, township, or place, for the same year, he shall repay such extraordinary composition money to such person or persons, so as to bring the duty to an equality amongst all such inhabitants and occupiers." (13 Geo. 3. c. 78. s. 41.)

Draught or Plough Horses.] "In every parish, township, or place, where any person shall keep a draught or plough and no carriage, he shall pay to the surveyor the sum of one shilling for every horse, or pair of oxen, or neat cattle, used in such draught or plough, for every day's statute duty on the day such duty is required to be performed; or pay according to the rate aforesaid, for the lands, tenements, woods, tithes, and hereditaments, which he shall occupy in such parish, township, or place, at the option of the surveyor." (Id. s. 42.)

Composition to Turnpike Road, &c.] "And whereas by several acts of Parliament concerning turnpike roads, a certain part of the duty called ***statute duty*** is or may be directed to be performed on such roads, and it may happen in some places that the several persons liable thereto may have compounded for the same: be it therefore further enacted, That in all such cases, the surveyor of the highways of the parish, township, or place, where such composition shall have been made, shall pay to the treasurer or surveyor of such turnpike roads a certain part of the composition money so received, to be proportioned according to the number of days' duty which such person or persons was or were liable to perform on such turnpike road: which money shall be laid out and expended, on such part of the said turnpike road as lies within the parish, township, or place, from which it was received, and not elsewhere; and if such surveyor of the highways shall refuse or neglect to pay to the treasurer or surveyor of such turnpike road, such part of the said composition money so received by him, within twenty days after he shall have received the same, upon demand made by such treasurer or surveyor, the same shall and may be levied upon the goods and chattels of such surveyor, in such manner as penalties and forfeitures are by this act authorized to be levied." (Id. s. 44.)

" And whereas by, &c." (34 Geo. 3. c. 74,) " it is enacted, That it shall be at the option of the surveyor either to require the statute duty in kind, or a composition in money in lieu thereof, at certain rates which are therein fixed: And whereas by, &c., (44 Geo. 3. c. 52,) the rates for such statute duty have been increased so far as respects teams, draughts, ploughs, and carts, with one or two horses: And whereas the actual wages of labour, and the actual rate of hiring teams, carts, horses, or oxen, vary at different times, and in different parts of England; be it therefore further enacted, That in all cases in which it shall *be made to appear* to two or more justices of the peace acting within the district, by the surveyors of the highways, or of any turnpike road, that the maintenance and repair thereof can be more effectually carried on by a composition in money, than by a performance of the statute duty in kind, he or they shall be at liberty to require such composition in money, upon receiving an authority under the hands and seals of the said justices for that purpose, in lieu of either the whole or of any certain part of the statute duty, from the several persons who are bound by law to perform such statute duty; and the justices of the district, at their special sessions for the highways held in the week next after Michaelmas yearly, shall fix such rates as they shall adjudge reasonable, as a composition in lieu of the teams, carts, horses, oxen, or labour, which such persons are bound in the proportions now fixed by law to provide and perform; which rates the said justices are hereby authorized and required annually to make known at such special sessions, due regard being had to the actual wages of labour, and to the actual rate of hiring teams, draughts, ploughs, carts, horses, or oxen, in the parish, place, or district, in which such composition is required; and such composition shall be paid in the same manner, and within the same period, and subject to the same regulations and provisions, as are now by law established for enforcing the payment of compositions in lieu of statute duty: Provided always, that in case where the whole composition in money shall not be required in lieu of the whole of the duty in kind, such composition shall be demanded in fair and equal proportions from each and every person liable to pay the same, unless any of the said persons shall prefer to pay a composition for the whole of their statute duty, according to the rates fixed in the manner herein directed." (54 Geo. 3. c. 109. s. 4.)

Rate of Composition.] "All persons who are liable under any of the provisions of any of the hereinbefore recited acts, to contribute to the repair of the highways, by a payment of money in lieu of statute duty, shall contribute thereto in lieu of every day's statute duty, for every twenty shillings of the actual annual value, at the time of making the said assessment of the lands, tenements, woods, tithes, and hereditaments, which such persons shall respectively occupy in the parish, township, or place, where they reside, or in any other parish, township, or place, a sum equal to one-fiftieth part of the sum fixed by the justices, at the time and in the manner by this act directed, as the composition for one day's labour of a cart, wain, or carriage, furnished with three horses and two able men, omitting any fractional part of the said sum which does not amount to one farthing; and all persons occupying more than fifty pounds per annum in the parish, township, or place wherein they reside, or in any other parish, township, or place, and less than one hundred pounds per annum, shall contribute to the repairs of the highways, in lieu of every day's statute duty, for every twenty shillings of the actual annual value, at the time of making the said assessment of the lands, tenements, woods, tithes, and hereditaments, which such person shall respectively occupy over and beyond the said sum of fifty pounds per annum, and under one hundred pounds, a sum equal to one-fiftieth part of the sum fixed by the said justices, at the time and in the manner by this act directed, as the composition for one day's labour of a cart, wain, or carriage, furnished with three horses and two able men, omitting any fractional part of the said sum which does not amount to one farthing; and so on progressively for every twenty shillings of the actual annual value of the lands, tenements, woods, tithes, and hereditaments, which they shall respectively occupy over and beyond every additional fifty pounds per annum; and the said sum or sums shall be paid in the same manner and within the same period, and subject to the same regulations and provisions, as are now by law established for enforcing the payment of composition in lieu of statute duty." (Id. s. 5.)

Composition how Estimated and Authorized.] Before magistrates grant their warrant for the collection of a composition, it ought to be ascertained, by persons having competent authority for that purpose, *how many days'* statute duty would be required to put the road in question into a complete state of repair, and it should be *notified to the inhabitants,* that the amount demanded is calculated upon this principle, and that, in the judgment of the surveyor, the composition in lieu of so many days' teamwork was advisable, in order that the inhabitants may have an opportunity of contesting the claim made upon them. If, therefore, magistrates proceed without having such evidence before them, they are liable to an action of trespass for goods seized under their warrant to levy a distress for such composition. (Stanley v. Fielden, 5 Barn. & Ald. 425.)

And *semble,* that in order to justify two magistrates in granting an authority to collect a composition in lieu of statute duty, it should be made to appear *upon oath,* to both the magistrates present, that the road can be more effectually repaired by such composition; and also *semble,* that where the composition is to be collected in *several* townships, it ought to appear on the face of the authority itself, that, in the judgment of the magistrates, a composition in lieu of statute duty is advisable in *each* particular township. (Id. ibid.)

The proceedings to recover compensation money, duly assessed in lieu of statute duty, must be by distress, according to the provisions of these statutes; and *cannot* be by action. For, wherever the legislature has given a claim, or imposed a charge upon the inhabitants, and prescribed a particular remedy for enforcing it, no other can be resorted to. (Underhill v. Ellicombe, 1 M'Clel. & Y. 450.)

Liability by keeping Carriages.] " Every person who shall keep a coach, postchaise, chair, or other wheel carriage, and not keep a team, draught, or plough, nor occupy fifty pounds per annum in the parish, township, or place, where he resides, shall pay to the surveyor or surveyors in respect of every day's statute duty, for every horse which he or she shall use in drawing such carriage, such a sum as the justices shall at the time and in the manner by this act directed fix, as the composition for one day's work of a horse; or shall, at the option of the surveyor or surveyors, pay in lieu of every day's statute duty, for every twenty shillings of the actual annual value of the lands, tenements, woods, tithes, and hereditaments, which he or she shall respectively occupy, a sum equal to one-fiftieth part of the sum fixed by the justices, at the time and in the manner by this act directed, as the composition for one day's labour of a cart, wain, or carriage, furnished with three horses and two able men, omitting any fractional part of the said sum which does not amount to one farthing; and the said sum or sums shall be paid in the same manner, and in the same period, and subject to the same regulations and provisions, as are now by law established for enforcing the payment of compositions in lieu of statute duty." (54 Geo. 3. c. 109. s. 6.)

Enforcing Duty, Forfeitures, &c.] "All persons who shall refuse or neglect to perform any part of their statute duty in kind, on being regularly summoned by the surveyor for that purpose, shall forfeit and pay a sum equal to twice the amount of the composition for such statute duty as they shall have so neglected or refused to perform according to the rates fixed by the justices under the provisions of this act; and the said persons shall also be liable to perform the said statute duty which they have so neglected or refused to perform, either in the same or in the following year; the payment of such forfeitures and the arrears of such statute duty to be enforced, and applied to the benefit of the highway or turnpike road, as the case may be, to which the original neglected duty was due or owing, by the surveyor or surveyors for the time being, and under the same regulations and in the same manner as other forfeitures may be levied, and statute duty may in other cases be enforced by any of the provisions of any of the said hereinbefore recited acts." (Id. s. 7.)

Mitigating Composition.] "If any person or persons who shall keep a team, draught, or plough, and shall not occupy lands, tenements, woods, tithes, or hereditaments, to the value of thirty pounds per annum, in the parish, township, or place where he shall reside, but shall in part maintain his horses and beasts of draught used in such team upon or from lands which he shall occupy in one or more adjacent parish or parishes, it shall and may be lawful for the said justices, at some special sessions, to mitigate and reduce the duty or composition so required to be performed or paid by such person or persons, in such manner and to such sum as they shall think just and reasonable." (13 Geo. 3. c. 78. s. 40.)

SECTION VI.—NUISANCES TO HIGHWAYS.

13 Geo. 3. c. 78. ss. 6. 9, 10, 11. 52. 62. 8. 14. 63. 7. 13.

Trees near Highways.] "No tree, bush, or shrub, shall be permitted to stand or grow in any highway within the distance of fifteen feet from the centre thereof, (except for ornament or shelter to the house, building, or court-yard of the owner thereof,) or hereafter to be planted within the distance aforesaid; but the same shall respectively be cut down, grubbed up, and carried away, by the owner or occupier of the land or soil where the same doth or shall stand or grow, within ten days after notice to him, her, or them, or his, her, or their steward or agent, given by the said surveyors, or any of them, on pain of forfeiting, for every neglect, the sum of ten shillings." (13 Geo. 3. c. 78. s. 6.)

Rubbish, &c., in Highways.] "If any person or persons shall lay in any highway any stone, timber, straw, dung, or other matter, or in making, scouring, or cleansing the ditches or water-courses, shall permit the soil or earth dug out of such ditches, drains, or water-courses, to remain in such highway, in such manner as to obstruct or prejudice the same, for the space of five days after notice thereof given by the surveyor of the highways, every person or persons offending in any of the said cases, shall, for every such offence, forfeit and pay the sum of ten shillings." (Id. s. 9.)

Timber, Manure, Stone, &c.] "If any stone or timber, or any hay, straw, stubble, or other matter for the making of manure, or on any pretence whatsoever, not tolerated by this act, shall be laid in any highway within the distance of fifteen feet from the centre thereof, and shall not, within five days after notice given by the surveyor, or some person aggrieved thereby, be removed; it shall and may be lawful for the owner or possessor of the lands adjacent, or any other person or persons whomsoever, by order from some justice of peace, to clear the said highways, by removing the said stone, timber, hay, straw, dung, or other matter, and to have, take, and dispose of the same to his and their own use." (Id. s. 10.)

Obstructions in Highways.] "And for preventing obstructions in the said highways, be it enacted, That if any person shall wilfully set, place, or leave any waggon, cart, or other carriage, or any plough or instrument of husbandry, in any of the said highways, (except only with respect to such waggon, cart, or carriage, during such reasonable time as the same shall be loading and unloading, and standing as near the side of such highway as conveniently may be,) so as to interrupt or hinder the free passage of any other carriage, or of his Majesty's subjects; every person so offending shall forfeit the sum of ten shillings for every such offence." (Id. s. 11.)

Damaging Posts or Causeways.] "And whereas in some places it hath been and may be found necessary, and the surveyors are hereby authorized and required, to secure horse causeways and foot causeways, by posts, blocks, or great stones, fixed in the ground, or by banks of earth cast up, or otherwise, from being broken up and spoiled with waggons, wains, carts, or carriages; and forasmuch as several evil-disposed persons do or may wilfully or wantonly pull up, cut down, and remove or damage the said posts, blocks, and great stones, so fixed or to be fixed as aforesaid, and drive carriages upon such banks and causeways, or against the sides thereof, and also dig or cast down the said banks, which are the securities and defence of the said causeways, whereby the causeways or banks are often ruined and destroyed; and such evil-disposed persons do or may break, damage, or throw down the stones, bricks, or wood, fixed upon the parapets or battlements of bridges, and do or may pull down, destroy, obliterate, or deface any mile-stone or post, graduated or direction-post or stone, erected or to be erected upon any highway; For prevention thereof, be it enacted, That every person who shall be guilty of any such offence, shall, upon complaint thereof made to any justice of the peace of the limit where the same shall be proved to be done, by the oath of any one credible witness, or upon view of the justice himself, forfeit for every of the said offences any sum not exceeding five pounds, nor less than ten shillings; and in default of payment thereof, shall be committed to the house of correction of such limit, there to be whipped, and kept to hard labour for any time not exceeding one calendar month, nor less than seven days, at the discretion of such justice." (Id. s. 52.)

No Ale-Houses on Toll Bridges.] "And for preventing obstructions, which frequently happen by stopping of carriages on or near public bridges, be it further enacted, That if any person or persons collecting any tolls payable for passing over any public bridge with carriages, or cattle of any kind, shall keep any victualling-house, ale-house, or other place of public entertainment, or shall sell, or permit to be sold therein, any wine, beer, ale, cider, spirituous liquors, or other strong liquors by retail, he, she, or they, being lawfully convicted of such offence, by the oath of one or more credible witness or witnesses, or by his own confession, before any justice of the peace of the limit wherein such offence shall be committed, shall for every such offence forfeit the sum of five pounds." (Id. s. 62.)

Ditches, Drains, &c.] "Ditches, drains, or water-courses, of a sufficient depth and breadth for the keeping all highways dry, and conveying the water from the same, shall be made, scoured, cleansed, and kept open, and sufficient trunks, tunnels, plats, or bridges, shall be made and laid where any cartways, horseways, or footways, lead out of the said highways into the lands or grounds adjoining thereto, by the occupier or occupiers of such lands or grounds; and every person or persons who shall occupy any lands or grounds adjoining to, or lying near such highway through which the water hath used to pass from the said highway, shall, and is hereby required from time to time, as often as occasion shall be, to open, cleanse, and scour the ditches, water-courses, or drains, for such water to pass without obstruction; and that every person making default in any of the matters or things aforesaid, after ter days' notice to him, her, or them, given of the same by the said surveyor, shall, for every such offence forfeit the sum of ten shillings." (Id. s. 8.)

Where new Ditches, &c., may be made.] "Where the aitcnes, gutters, or water-courses which have been usually made, or which are hereinbefore directed to be made, cleansed, and kept open, shall not be sufficient to carry off the water which shall lie upon and annoy the highways, that then and in every such case it shall and may be lawful for the said surveyors, by the order of any one or more of the said justices, to make new ditches and drains in and through the said lands and grounds adjoining or lying near to such highways, or in and through any other lands or grounds, if it shall be necessary, for the more easy and effectually carrying off such water from the said highways, and also to keep such ditches, gutters, or water-courses, scoured, cleansed, and opened; and the said surveyors and their workmen are hereby authorized to go upon the said lands for the purposes aforesaid; provided that the said surveyors make proper trunks, tunnels, plats, bridges, or arches, over such ditches, gutters, or water-courses, where the same shall be necessary, for the convenient use and enjoyment of the lands or grounds through which the same shall be made, and from time to time keep the same in repair; and do also make satisfaction to the owner or occupier of such lands which are not waste or common, for the damages which he, she, or they shall sustain thereby; to be settled and paid in such manner as the damages for getting materials in several or inclosed lands or grounds are hereafter directed to be settled and paid." (Id. s. 14.)

Encroaching on Highways.] "And whereas inconveniences have arisen from making hedges or other fences, and from ploughing or breaking up the soil of lands or grounds near the middle or centre of highways; For remedy thereof, be it enacted, That if any person shall encroach by making, or causing to be made, any hedge, ditch, or other fences, on any highway, not being turnpike road, within the distance of fifteen feet from the middle or centre thereof; or shall plough, harrow, or break up the soil of any land or ground, or in ploughing or harrowing the adjacent lands, shall turn his plough in or upon any land or ground within the distance of fifteen feet from the middle or centre of any highway, where the breadth of such highway is formed and marked or described with certainty, and does not exceed in breadth thirty feet, every person so offending shall forfeit, for every such offence, forty shillings to such person who shall make information of the same; and it shall be lawful for the surveyor, who hath the care of any such road, to cause such *hedge, ditch, or fence to be taken down*, or *filled up*, at the expense of the person or persons to whom the same shall belong; and it shall and may be lawful for any one or more justice or justices of the peace for the limit where such offence shall be committed, upon proof to him or them made upon oath, to levy as well the expenses of taking down such hedges as aforesaid, as the several and respective penalties hereby imposed, by distress and sale of the offender's goods and chattels, in such manner as distresses and sales for forfeitures are authorized and directed to be levied by virtue of this act." (Id. s. 63.)

Removing Fence.] Neither this nor the sixth section of the act, (see "Trees near Highways," *ante* 232,) authorizes the surveyor to widen a road to thirty feet by removing a fence, unless it stand upon land which had anciently been road, and is actually *on* the highway. (Lowen v. Kaye, 4 Barn. & Cres. 3. 6 Dowl. & Ryl. 20.)

Pruning Hedges.] "The possessors of the land next adjoining to every highway shall cut, prune, and plash their hedges, and also cut down or prune and lop the trees growing in or near such hedges or other fences, (except those trees planted for ornament or shelter as aforesaid, [see s. 6,]) in such manner that the highways shall not be prejudiced by the shade thereof respectively, and that the sun and wind may not be excluded from such highway to the damage thereof; and that if such possessor shall not, within ten days after notice given by the surveyor for that purpose, cut, prune, and plash such hedges, and cut down or prune, and lop such trees, in manner aforesaid, it shall and may be lawful for the surveyor, and he is hereby required, to make complaint thereof to some justice of the peace of the limit where such highway shall be, who shall summon the possessor of the said lands to appear before the justices at some special sessions for that limit, to answer to the said complaint; and if it shall appear to the justices at such special sessions, that such possessor had not complied with the requisites of this act, it shall and may be lawful for the said justices, upon hearing the surveyor and the possessor of such land, or his agent, (or in default of his appearance, upon having due proof of the service of such summons,) and considering the circumstances of the case, to order such hedges to be cut, plashed, and pruned, and such trees to be cut down or pruned, in such manner as may best answer the purposes aforesaid; and if the possessor of such lands shall not obey such order within ten days after it shall have been made, and he shall have had due notice thereof, he shall forfeit the sum of two shillings for every twenty-four feet in length of such hedge which shall be so neglected to be cut and plashed, and the sum of two shillings for every tree which shall be so neglected to be cut down or pruned and lopped; and the surveyor, in case of such default made by the possessor, shall and is hereby required to cut, prune, and plash such hedges, and to cut down or prune and lop such trees, in the manner directed by such order; and such possessor shall be charged with, and pay over and above the said penalties, the charges and expenses of doing the same; or in default thereof, such charges and expenses shall be levied, together with the said forfeitures, upon his or her goods and chattels by warrant from a justice of peace, in such manner as is authorized for forfeitures incurred by virtue of this act." (13 Geo. 3. c. 78. s. 7.)

Times of cutting Hedges, &c.] "No person or persons shall be compelled, nor any surveyor permitted, by virtue of this act, to cut or prune any hedge at any other time than between the last day of September and the last day of March; and that nothing herein contained shall extend or be construed to oblige any person or persons to fell any timber-trees growing in hedges at any time whatsoever, except where the highways shall be ordered to be enlarged, as hereinafter mentioned, or to cut down or grub up any oak-trees growing within such highway, or in such hedges, except in the months of April, May, or June; or any ash, elm, or other trees, in any other months than in the months of December, January, February, or March." (Id. s. 13.)

SECTION VII.—GENERAL REGULATIONS.

13 Geo. 3. c. 78. ss. 26. 60. 55, 56, 57, 58, 59.

Direction Posts.] "For the better convenience of travellers where several highways meet, the said justices, at some special sessions to be held for the purposes of this act, shall issue their precept to the surveyor of the highways for any parish, township, or place, where several highways meet, and there is no proper or sufficient direction post or stone already fixed or erected, requiring him forthwith to cause to be erected or fixed, in the most convenient place where such ways meet, a stone or post, with inscriptions thereon, in large legible letters painted on each side thereof, containing the name or names of the next market town or towns, or other considerable place or places to which the said highways respectively lead; and also at the several approaches or entrances to such parts of any highways as are subject to deep or dangerous floods, graduated stones or posts denoting the depth of water in the deepest part of the same, and likewise such direction posts or stones as the said justices shall judge to be necessary for the guiding of travellers in the best and safest track through the said floods or waters; and the said surveyor shall be reimbursed the expenses of providing and erecting the same respectively out of the monies which shall be received by him or them pursuant to the directions of this act; and in case any surveyor shall, by the space of three months after such precept to him directed and delivered, neglect or refuse to cause such stones or posts to be fixed as aforesaid, every such offender shall forfeit the sum of twenty shillings." (13 Geo. 3. c. 78. s. 26.)

Drivers punishable.] "And whereas many bad accidents happen, and great mischiefs are frequently done upon the streets and highways, by the negligence or wilful misbehaviour of persons driving carriages thereon; be it therefore further enacted, That if the driver of any cart, car, dray, or waggon, shall ride upon any such carriage in any street or highway, not having some other person on foot, or on horseback, to guide the same, (such carriages as are conducted by some person holding the reins of the horse or horses drawing the same excepted;) or if the driver of any carriage whatsoever on any part of any street or highway, shall, by negligence or wilful misbehaviour, cause any hurt or damage to any person or carriage passing or being upon such street or highway; or shall quit the highway, and go on the other side the hedge or fence inclosing the same, or wilfully be at such distance from such carriage whilst it shall be passing upon such highway, that he cannot have the direction and government of the horses or cattle drawing the same; or shall, by negligence or wilful misbehaviour, prevent, hinder, or interrupt the free passage of any other carriage, of his Majesty's subjects, on the said highways; or if the driver of any empty or unloaded waggon, cart, or other carriage, shall refuse or neglect to turn aside and make way for any coach, chariot, chaise, loaded waggon, cart, or other loaded carriage; or if any person shall drive, or act as the driver of any such coach, post-chaise, or other carriage, let for hire, or waggon, wain, or cart, not having the owner's name, as before required, painted thereon, or shall refuse to discover the true Christian and surname of the owner of such respective carriages, every such driver so offending in any of the cases aforesaid, and being convicted of any such offence, either by his own confession, the view of a justice of peace, or by the oath of one or more credible witness or witnesses, before any justice of the peace for the limit where such offence shall be committed, shall, for every such offence, forfeit any sum not exceeding ten shillings, in case such driver shall not be the owner of such carriage; and in case the offender be owner of such carriage, then any sum not exceeding twenty shillings: and in either of the said cases shall, in default of payment, be committed to the house of correction for any time not exceeding one month, unless the same shall be sooner paid: and every such driver, offending in either of the said cases, shall and may, by authority of this act, with or without any warrant, be apprehended by any person or persons who shall see such offence committed, and shall be immediately conveyed or delivered to a constable or other peace-officer, in order to be conveyed before some justice of the peace, to be dealt with according to law; and if any such driver, in any of the cases aforesaid, shall refuse to discover his name, it shall and may be lawful for the justice of the peace before whom he shall be taken, or to whom any such complaint shall be made, to commit him to the house of correction for any time not exceeding three months, or to proceed against him for the penalty aforesaid, by a description of his person and the offence, and expressing in such proceedings that he refused to discover his name." (Id. s. 60.)

Number of Horses to Waggons, &c.] "And whereas the highways, not being turnpike roads, are much prejudiced by the narrowness of the wheels of the several carriages travelling thereon, and by the excessive burthens loaded in such carriages; be it enacted, That no waggon, having the sole or bottom of the fellies of the wheels of the breadth of nine inches, shall go or be drawn with more than eight horses; and that no cart, having the sole or bottom of the fellies of the wheels thereof of the breadth of nine inches, shall go or be drawn with more than five horses; and that no waggon, having the sole or bottom of the fellies of the wheels of the breadth of six inches, and rolling on each side a surface of nine inches, shall go or be drawn with more than seven horses; and that no such waggon, rolling a surface of six inches only, shall go or be drawn with more than six horses; and that no cart, having the sole or bottom of the fellies of the wheels of the breadth of six inches, shall go or be drawn with more than four horses; and that no waggon, having the sole or bottom of the fellies of the wheels of less breadth than six inches, shall go or be drawn with more than five horses; and that no cart, having the sole or bottom of the fellies of the wheels of less breadth than six inches, shall go or be drawn with more than three horses, upon such highways, under the pains, penalties, and forfeitures hereinafter mentioned; (that is to say,) that the owner of such waggon or cart respectively shall forfeit the sum of five pounds, and the driver, not being the owner, the sum of ten shillings, for every horse or beast which shall be so drawing above the number hereby so respectively limited as aforesaid, to the sole use and benefit of the informer; but carriages moving upon wheels or rollers of the breadth of sixteen inches on each side thereof, with flat surfaces, are hereby allowed to be drawn with any number of horses or other cattle." (Id. s. 55.)

Time limited for Prosecution.] "No prosecution shall be commenced before a justice of peace, by way of information, for any forfeiture incurred by the owner or driver of any carriage having a greater number of horses therein than are allowed by this act, unless such information be laid within three days after the offence committed; and that no action shall be commenced for any such offence, unless the same be commenced within one calendar month after the offence committed; and that neither such information or action shall be laid or commenced, unless notice shall be given by the informer to the driver of every such carriage, on the day upon which the offence shall be committed, of an intention to complain of such offence; and if it shall appear to the justice, before whom such complaint shall be made, that the offender lives so remote as to make it inconvenient to summon him to appear before such justice, the justice may dismiss the complaint, and leave the informer to his remedy by action at law." (Id. s. 56.)

Drawing up Hills.] "The justices of the peace, at their respective general quarter sessions of the peace held in the week after Michaelmas, may license in such manner, and for such time, as they shall think fit, an increase of the number of horses to be drawn in carriages up any steep hill, or on any road not turnpike, within their respective jurisdictions, over and above the number hereinbefore limited, if upon inquiry into the state and condition of such roads they shall find any additional number of horses necessary; and from time to time, at any Michaelmas quarter sessions, to revoke, alter, or vary the same as they shall think fit." (Id. s. 57.)

When may stop Legal Proceedings.] "Provided, That if it shall appear, upon the oaths of credible witnesses, to the satisfaction of any justice or justices of the peace, or any court of justice authorized to enforce the execution of this act, that any waggon, cart, or carriage, could not, by reason of deep snow or ice, be drawn by the number of horses or beasts of draught hereby respectively allowed; then, and in every such case, it shall and may be lawful for such justice or justices of the peace, or court respectively, and they are hereby respectively required, to stop all proceedings before them respectively, for the recovery of any penalty or forfeiture which may have been incurred by drawing with a greater number of horses or beasts of draught, than are hereby allowed; any thing herein contained to the contrary notwithstanding: Provided also, That the regulations hereinbefore mentioned, concerning the number of horses and wheels of carriages, shall not be deemed or construed to extend to carts, waggons, or other carriages, employed only in carrying any one stone, block of marble, cable, rope, or piece of metal, or piece of timber; or to such ammunition or artillery as shall be for his Majesty's service; and that two oxen or horned cattle shall, for all the purposes of this act, be considered as one horse." (Id. s. 58.)

Owner's Name on Waggons, &c.] "And for the better discovery of offenders against this present act, be it enacted, That the owner of every waggon, wain, or cart, and also of every coach, post-chaise, or other carriage, let to hire, shall paint, or cause to be painted, upon some conspicuous part of his waggon, wain, or cart, and upon the pannels of the doors of all such coaches, post-chaises, or other carriages, before the same shall be used upon any public highway, his or her Christian and surname, and the place of his or her abode, in large legible letters, and continue the same thereupon so long as such waggon, cart, coach, post-chaise, or other carriage, shall be used upon any such highway; and the owner of every common stage-waggon, or cart, employed as travelling stages from town to town, shall over and above his or her Christian and surname paint, or cause to be painted, on the part and in the manner aforesaid, the following words, "*Common Stage Waggon*" or "*Cart*," as the case may be; and every person using any such carriage as aforesaid upon any highway, without the names and descriptions painted thereon respectively as aforesaid, or who shall paint, or cause to be painted, any false or fictitious name or place of abode on such waggon, wain, cart, coach, post-chaise, or other carriage, shall forfeit, for every such offence, a sum not exceeding five pounds, nor less than twenty shillings." (13 Geo. 3. c. 78. s. 59.)

SECTION VIII.—PENALTIES AND HOW RECOVERED.

13 Geo. 3. c. 78. ss. 71. 47. 72, 73, 74, 75, 76, 77, 78, 79. 81.

Resistance or Disobedience.] In case any person or persons shall resist or make forcible opposition against any person or persons employed in the due execution of this act, or make any rescue of the cattle or other goods distrained by virtue of this act; or if any constable, headborough, or tithingman, shall refuse or neglect to execute or obey any warrant or precept granted by any justice of the peace pursuant to the directions of this act; every such person offending therein, and being convicted thereof by a justice of the peace, shall, for every such offence, forfeit any sum not exceeding ten pounds nor less than forty shillings, at the discretion of the justice before whom he or she shall be so convicted, to be paid to the surveyor of the highways for the parish, township, or place where the offence was committed, to be laid out in the repair of the highways; and in case he or she do not forthwith pay, or secure to be paid, the said forfeiture after such conviction, then it shall and may be lawful for such justice of the peace to commit such person or persons to the common gaol or house of correction, of the limit where such offence shall be committed, there to remain for any time not exceeding three months, unless the said forfeiture shall be sooner paid." (13 Geo. 3. c. 78. s. 71.)

Fines, &c., to whom paid.] "That no fine, issue, penalty, or forfeiture, for not repairing the highways, or not appearing to any indictment or presentment for not repairing the same, shall hereafter be returned into the Court of Exchequer or other court, but shall be levied by, and paid into the hands of, such person or persons residing in or near the parish, township, or place, where the road shall be, as the court imposing such fines, issues, penalties, or forfeitures shall order, and direct, to be employed towards the repair and amendment of such highways; and the person or persons so ordered to receive such fine shall, and is hereby required, to receive, apply, and account for the same, according to the direction of such court, or in default thereof shall forfeit double the sum received; and if any fine, issue, penalty, or forfeiture to be imposed on any such parish, township, or place for not repairing the highways, or not appearing as aforesaid, shall hereafter be levied on any one or more of the inhabitants of such parish, township, or place, that then such inhabitant or inhabitants shall and may make his or their complaint to the justices of the peace, at their special sessions; and the said justices are hereby empowered and authorized, by warrant under their hands and seals, to cause a rate to be made, according to the form and manner herein last before prescribed, for the reimbursing such inhabitant or inhabitants the monies so levied on him or them as aforesaid; (see "Rate to Reimburse," *infra;*) which rate so made, and confirmed by any two justices, shall be collected and levied by the surveyor of the highways of such parish, township, or place, so presented or indicted as aforesaid; and the said surveyor shall, within one month next after the making and confirming the rate aforesaid, collect, levy, and pay, unto such inhabitant or inhabitants the money so levied on him or them as aforesaid." (Id. s. 47.)

Rate to reimburse.] An application, under the 47th section, for a rate to reimburse two inhabitants of a parish, on whom a fine for the non repair of a highway had been levied, after a conviction upon an indictment against the parish for non-repair, ought to be made within a reasonable time after such levy, before there is any material change of inhabitants; and the Court of King's Bench refused a mandamus for such rate after an interval of eight years, though applications had been, from time to time, made to the magistrates below, in the interval, who had declined to make the rate, on the ground that the parish at large had been improperly convicted; the onus of repair being by immemorial custom on an infer or district; and though so lately as the year before the application, the magistrates had ordered an account to be taken of the *quantum* expended upon the repairs out of the money levied. (Rex v. Lancashire, 12 East. 336.)

Fines to whom payable.] Fines for not repairing roads *ratione tenuræ* are payable to the surveyor of the parish highways. (Rex v. Wingfield, 1 Bla. Rep. 602.)

Penalties how recovered.] "All penalties and forfeitures by this act imposed for any offence against the same, and all costs and charges to be allowed and ordered by the authority of this act, (the manner of levying and recovering of which is not hereby otherwise particularly directed,) shall be levied by distress and sale of the goods and chattels of the offender, or person liable or ordered to pay the same respectively, by warrant under the hand and seal of some justice of the peace for the limit where such offence, neglect, or default, shall happen, or such order for payment of such costs or charges shall be made, rendering the overplus of such distress (if any be) to the party or parties, after deducting the charges of making the same; which warrant such justice is hereby empowered and required to grant, upon conviction of the offender by confession, or upon the oath of one or more credible witness or witnesses, or upon order made as aforesaid; and the penalties and forfeitures, when so levied, shall be paid, the one half to the informer, and the other half to the surveyor of the highway where such offence, neglect, or default, shall happen, to be applied towards the repair thereof, unless otherwise directed by this act; but in case the surveyor shall be the informer, then the whole shall be employed towards the repair of such highway: and in case such distress cannot be found, and such penalties and forfeitures, or the said costs and charges, shall not be forthwith paid, it shall and may be lawful for such justice, and he is hereby authorized and required, by warrant under his hand and seal, to commit such offender or offenders, or person or persons liable to pay the same respectively, to the common gaol, or house of correction, of the limit where the offence shall be committed, or such order as aforesaid shall be made, for any time not exceeding three months, unless the said penalty, forfeiture, costs, and charges, shall respectively be sooner paid; and if such offender or offenders, or person or persons liable or ordered to pay the same respectively, shall live out of the jurisdiction of the justice hereby authorized to grant such warrant, it shall and may be lawful for any justice of the peace of the limit wherein such person shall inhabit, and every such justice is hereby required, upon request to him for that purpose made, and upon a true copy of the conviction whereby such forfeiture or penalty was incurred, and of the order for the payment of such costs and charges, produced and proved by a credible witness upon oath, by warrant under his hand and seal, to cause the penalty or forfeiture mentioned in such conviction, and the costs and charges mentioned in such order, or so much thereof as shall not have been paid, to be levied by distress and sale of the goods and chattels of such offender or offenders, or person or persons liable or ordered to pay the same respectively as aforesaid; and if no sufficient distress can be had, to commit such offender or offenders, or person or persons liable as aforesaid, to the common gaol, or house of correction, of such limit for the time and in manner aforesaid." (13 Geo. 3. c. 78. s. 72.)

Mode of Recovery.] If a statute prohibits the doing of a thing under a penalty to be paid to the party grieved, or without saying to whom it shall be paid, and does not prescribe any mode of recovery, debt lies for the party grieved. (Underhill v. Ellicombe, 1 M'Clel. & Y. 450.) But where the statute prescribes a particular remedy, that must be followed; and therefore surveyors cannot maintain debt to recover composition money assessed in lieu of tithes, as the proceeding is directed to be by distress and sale. (Underhill v. Ellicombe, 1 M'Clel. & Y. 450.)

Distress stayed Six Days.] "That no warrant of distress, unless otherwise directed by this act, shall be issued for levying any penalty or forfeiture, costs or charges, until six days after the offender shall have been convicted, and an order made and served upon him or her for the payment thereof." (13 Geo. 3. c. 78. s. 73.)

Proceedings by Information or Action.] "Every prosecutor or informer may, at his election, sue for and recover any forfeiture or penalty imposed by this act, which shall amount to the sum of forty shillings or upwards, (the manner of recovery thereof not being particularly directed by this act,) either in the manner herein before directed, or by action at law to be brought by such informer or prosecutor in any of his Majesty's courts of record, in manner following: (that is to say,) where any person shall be liable to any such pecuniary penalty, it shall and may be lawful to sue for and recover the same by action of debt, in which it shall be sufficient to declare that the defendant is indebted to the plaintiff in the sum of , being forfeited by an act passed in the thirteenth year of the reign of his present Majesty, intitled, '*An act to explain, amend, and reduce into one act of Parliament, the Statutes now in being for the Amendment and Preservation of the Public Highways, within that part of Great Britain called England, and for other purposes;*' and the plaintiff, if he recovers in any such actions, shall have double costs." (Id. s. 74.)

Action and Notice thereof.] "There shall not be more than one recovery for the same offence; and that ten days' notice, in writing, be given to the party offending, previous to the commencement of such action; and that the same be brought and commenced within one calendar month after the offence, for which such action is brought, shall have been committed." (Id. s. 75.)

Inhabitant's Witnesses.] "No conviction shall be had or made by virtue of this act, unless upon confession of the party accused, or upon the oath of one or more credible witness or witnesses, or upon the view of a justice of the peace, in the cases before mentioned; and that any inhabitant of any parish, township, or place, in which any offence shall be committed contrary to this act, shall be deemed a competent witness, notwithstanding his or her being an inhabitant of such parish, township, or place." (Id. s. 76.)

"It shall and may be lawful for any justice of the peace to administer an oath to any witness or witnesses, or other person or persons, for the better discovery and execution of the several matters or things herein before authorized or directed to be examined, inquired into, or performed by such justice." (Id. s. 77.)

Special Damages recoverable.] "Where any distress shall be made for any sum or sums of money to be levied by virtue of this act, the distress itself shall not be deemed unlawful, nor the party or parties making the same be deemed a trespasser or trespassers, on account of any default or want of form in any proceedings relating thereto; nor shall the party or parties distraining be deemed a trespasser or trespassers *ab initio*, on account of any irregularity which shall be afterwards done by the party or parties distraining; but the person or persons aggrieved by such irregularity may recover full satisfaction for the special damage in an action on the case." (Id. s. 78.)

Tender of Amends, &c.] "No plaintiff or plaintiffs shall recover in any action for any irregularity, trespass, or wrongful proceedings, if *tender of sufficient amends* shall be made by or on the behalf of the party or parties who shall have committed, or cause to be committed, any such irregularity, trespass, or wrongful proceedings, before such action brought; and in case no such tender shall have been made, it shall and may be lawful for the defendant in any such action, by leave of the court where such action shall depend, at any time before issue joined, to pay into court such sum of money as he or they shall see fit, whereupon such proceedings or orders and judgment shall be had, made, and given, in and by such court, as in other actions where the defendant is allowed to pay money into court." (Id. s. 79.)

Tender inconclusive.] It seems the plaintiff in such action may show, that the making of a *new* road over his land was maliciously or wantonly done by the surveyors, and not for the necessary or convenient carriage of materials over the land for the purposes of the act; and in such case he would not be concluded by the amends tendered or paid into court. (Bayfield v. Porter, 13 East. 200.)

Limitation of Actions.] "If any action or suit shall be commenced against any person or persons for any thing done or acted in pursuance of this act, then and in every such case, such action or suit shall be commenced or prosecuted within three calendar months after the fact committed, and not afterwards; and the same and every such action or suit shall be brought within the county where the fact was committed, and not elsewhere; and the defendant or defendants in every such action or suit shall and may plead the general issue, and give this act and the special matter in evidence, at any trial to be had thereupon, and that the same was done in pursuance and by the authority of this present act; and if the same shall appear to have been so done, or if any such action or suit shall be brought after the time limited for bringing the same, or be brought or laid in any other place than as afore mentioned, then the jury shall find for the defendant or defendants; or if the plaintiff or plaintiffs shall become nonsuit, or discontinue his, her, or their action, after the defendant or defendants shall have appeared, or if upon demurrer judgment shall be given against the plaintiff or plaintiffs, the defendant or defendants shall and may recover treble costs, and have the like remedy for recovery thereof as any defendant or defendants hath or have in any other cases by law." (13 Geo. 3. c. 78. s. 81.)

Limitation how construed.] Surveyors having, in the execution of their office, undermined a wall adjoining to the highway, it fell in consequence thereof, but not till *more* than three months afterwards; upon which, the proprietor brought an action *on the case* against them *within* three months after the *wall fell*, and it was held, that if the action had been trespass, it must have been brought within three months after the *act of trespass* complained of; but being an action on the case for the consequential damage, it could not have been brought till the specific wrong had been suffered. (Roberts v. Read, 16 East. 215; Sutton v. Clarke, 1 Marsh. 437, 6 Taunt. 37.)

SECTION IX.—EXECUTION OF THE ACTS.

13 Geo. 3. c. 78. ss 66. 53. 61. 69. 80. 54 Geo. 3. c. 109. s. 8.
55 Geo. 3. c. 68. s. 6.

Notice of Public Meetings.] "In all cases where a vestry or public meeting of the inhabitants of any parish, township, or place, is authorized or directed by this act, there shall be public notice given of the day, hour, and place, of holding the said meeting, at the church or chapel of such parish, township, or place, on the *Sunday* next preceding such meeting, and also notice thereof in writing, specifying the purpose of such meeting, fixed at the same time upon the door of such church or chapel, and the same shall not be held till three days at least after such notice given; and if there be no church or chapel, the like notice of such meeting shall be given in writing, and put up at the most public place therein, three days at least before such meeting." (13 Geo. 3. c. 78. s. 66.)

Justices of Cities, &c., to execute the Act.] "The justices of the peace of all cities, corporations, boroughs, and other places, are hereby required to put in execution every part of this act within their respective jurisdictions." (13 Geo. 3. c. 78. s. 53.)

"The justices of the peace and magistrates of all cities, corporations, boroughs, precincts, liberties, and other separate jurisdictions, are hereby authorized and required to put in execution every part of this act within their respective jurisdictions, so far as the provisions thereof are applicable, in as full and ample a manner as the justices of any county or of any division thereof." (54 Geo. 3. c. 109. s. 8.)

Special Sessions and Adjournments.] "Any two or more justices of the peace, within their respective limits, are hereby empowered, from time to time, whenever they shall judge proper, to hold any special sessions, besides that which is hereinbefore directed, for executing the purposes of this act, and to adjourn the same from time to time, as they shall think fit, causing notice to be given of the time and place of holding such special sessions, and of the adjournment thereof, to the several justices acting and residing within such limits, by the high constable or other proper officer within the same." (13 Geo. 3. c. 78. s. 61.)

Power in Special Sessions.] "And whereas, by the 54 Geo. 3. c. 109, it is among other things enacted, That two or more justices of the peace, at their special sessions to be holden in the week next after Michaelmas yearly, shall fix such rates as they shall adjudge reasonable as a composition in lieu of teams, carts, horses, oxen, or labour; and whereas certain other matters relative to the highways are directed to be done by justices of the peace, at their special sessions to be holden in the week next after the Michaelmas quarter sessions; and whereas the time for holding the Michaelmas quarter sessions has been altered by 54 Geo. 3. c. 84, be it therefore enacted, That it shall and may be lawful for the justices of the peace assembled in their special sessions in the week after Michaelmas, to do and perform every act which they might heretofore legally have done in the special sessions directed to be holden in the week after the said Michaelmas general quarter sessions of the peace." (55 Geo. 3. c. 68. s. 6.)

Special Sessions, Notice of.] Though the proceeding be under the 55 Geo. 3. c. 68, reasonable notice of holding the special sessions, at which an order for diverting a way, &c., is made, must be given as required by the 13 Geo. 3. c. 78. s. 61, and unless such notice has been given to the justices residing within the division, the quarter sessions ought not to confirm and enrol such order, even though there be no appeal against it. (Rex v. JJ. Worcestershire, 2 Barn. & Ald. 228.) The notices should be served by the high constable; but if signed by him, and *served* by a person under *his* authority, it is sufficient. (Rex v. JJ. Suffolk, 6 Barn. & Cres. 110, 9 Dowl. & Ryl.) But where they were served by the magistrate's clerk, it was held that the proceeding was irregular. (Rex v. JJ. Surrey, 5 Barn. & Cres. 241, 9 Dowl. & Ryl. 857.)

Appeal, and Notice thereof.] "If any person shall think himself or herself aggrieved by any thing done by any justice or justices of the peace or other person in the execution of any of the powers given by this act, and for which no particular method of relief hath been already appointed, every such person may appeal to the justices of the peace at any general quarter sessions of the peace, to be held for the limit wherein the cause of such complaint shall arise; such appellant giving, or causing to be given, notice in writing of his or her intention to bring such appeal, and of the matter thereof, to the justice or other person or persons against whom such complaint shall be made, within six days after the cause of such complaint arose; and within four days after such notice entering into recognizance before some justice of the peace within such limit, with one sufficient surety, conditioned to try such appeal at, and abide the order of and pay such costs as shall be awarded by the justices at such quarter session; and every justice of the peace and other person, having received notice of such appeal as aforesaid, shall return all proceedings whatsoever had before them respectively, touching the matter of such appeal, to the said justices at their general quarter sessions aforesaid, on pain of forfeiting five pounds for every such neglect; and the said justices at such session, upon due proof of such notice being given as aforesaid, and of the entering into such recognizance, shall hear and finally determine the causes and matters of such appeal in a summary way, and award such costs to the parties appealing or appealed against as they the said justices shall think proper, to be levied and recovered as hereinbefore directed; and the determination of such quarter sessions shall be final and conclusive to all intents and purposes; and that no proceedings to be had or taken in pursuance of this act shall be quashed or vacated for want of form, or *removed by certiorari*, or any other writ or process whatsoever (except as hereinbefore mentioned,) into any of his Majesty's Courts of Record at *Westminster*, any law or statute to the contrary notwithstanding; provided that no such appeal shall be made against any conviction for any penalty or forfeiture incurred by virtue of this act, unless the person convicted shall, at the time of such conviction if he or she shall be then present, if not, within six days after, give notice of his or her intention to appeal, and at the same time enter into recognizance with sufficient sureties to pay such penalty or forfeiture, in case such conviction shall be affirmed upon such appeal; and upon his or her giving such security, the further proceeding for such penalty or forfeiture shall be suspended until such appeal shall be heard and determined." (13 Geo. 3. c. 78. s. 80.)

Appeal, generally.] The above section relates to appeals generally, whatever may be the supposed grievance resulting from enforcing any of these statutory provisions. But some of the more recent statutes contain similar provisions; and it seems, that appeals against stopping up or diverting highways depend upon, and ought to be regulated by, the 55 Geo. 3. c. 68. s 3, (see "Appeal against Stopping up a Way," *ante* 218,) and not upon the 13 Geo. 3. c. 78. s. 80. At all events, if a party is anxious to avail himself of this latter enactment in preference to the former, for the purpose of obtaining costs if he ultimately succeeds, he must take care to give his notice within six days after the cause of complaint arises, according to the condition of this latter statute. (R. v. Wing. 4 Barn. & Cres. 184, 6 Dowl. & Ryl. 323.)

Notice of Appeal.] In an appeal upon a distress for nonpayment of a highway rate, the notice of appeal may be given within six days after the *levy*, and need not be within six days after the granting the warrant of distress. The notice need not disclose the grounds on which the appellant objects to the regularity of the distress. (The King v. Justices of Devon, 1 Maul. &. Sel. 411.)

And where, under the general turnpike act, 4 Geo. 4. c. 95, which gives a right of appeal upon notice within six days after the cause of complaint arises, two justices made an *order* upon the surveyors to perform a certain part of the statute duty on a turnpike road, it was held that the cause of complaint did not arise until a copy of the order in writing had been served; and that notice of appeal within six days from that time was valid. (Rex v. Lancashire, 8 Barn. & Cres, 593.)

Certiorari.] Even if the order of justices, made under *this* statute, for diverting a road is informal, still it cannot be removed by certiorari. (The King v. Casson, 3 Dowl. & Ryl. 36.)

Forms of Proceedings.] "The forms of proceedings relative to the several matters contained in this act, which are set forth and expressed in the schedule hereunto annexed, shall be used upon all occasions, with such additions or variations only as may be necessary to adapt them to the particular exigencies of the case; and that no objection shall be made, or advantage taken, for want of form in any such proceedings, by any person or persons whomsoever." (13 Geo. 3. c. 78. s. 69.)

It may here also be observed, that if a magistrate proceeds with an intention to convict for an offence committed in his own view, he must carefully pursue the act. Thus, where the driver of a waggon was riding thereon, contrary to the statute, (13 Geo. 3. c. 78. s. 60, *ante* 238,) and not only refused to tell his name, but placed himself so as to conceal his master's name on the waggon, whereupon the justice stopped the horses, and forcibly removed the driver, and thereby informed himself of the owner's name; it was held, that he was not justified in so doing. The court observed, that the magistrate might have convicted the offender on his own view, either for the riding on the waggon, or for refusing to give his name; or he might, as a private individual, have apprehended him, to be dealt with according to law: he had taken neither of these courses, but, on the contrary, laid violent hands upon the driver, *to remove him from the waggon*, which the act did not sanction, and was an assault in law. (Jones v. Owen, 2 Dowl. & Ryl. 600.)

Variance.] It has been held, that the forms *must* be observed, and that a material variance is fatal, and may be taken advantage of in a collateral proceeding. (Davison v. Gill, 1 East. 64; Goss v. Jackson, 3 Esp. Rep. 198.) But it seems that the order for diverting and turning a road, need not set out the *names of the owners* of the lands through which it is proposed to be carried, the form XXI. being merely *directory* in this respect. (Rex v. Casson, 3 Dowl. & Ryl. 36.)

CHAPTER IX.—PARISH VESTRIES.

SECTION I.—VESTRY MEETINGS.

Vestry what, and whence the Name.] A vestry, properly speaking, is the assembly of the whole parish, met together in some convenient place for the dispatch of the affairs and business of the parish; and this meeting being commonly held in the vestry adjoining to, or belonging to the church, it thence takes the name of vestry, as the place itself doth from the priest's vestments, which are usually deposited and kept there. (Shaw's Par. L. c. 17.)

It is not essential to the validity of the meeting that it should be held in the vestry of the church, and it may be convened in the church itself; but, if it be held in either of those places, the Ecclesiastical Court has jurisdiction *ratione loci,* (see 2 Ld. Raym. 850.) over any misconduct or disorder committed therein, (Wilson v. M'Math, 3 Barn. & Ald. 241;) though more license is permitted in the vestry room, than would be considered excusable in the church, as the vestry is the place for parish business; and the court would not interpose in such case, further than might be necessary for the preservation of due order and decorum. (Hutchins v. Denziloe, 1 Hagg. R. 185.)

Vestry, how often held.] These meetings are usually assembled according as the exigencies of the parish require; and though it was formerly considered fit and proper, if any thing peculiar was to be done, that notice should be given of the specific purpose for which a vestry was called, it was also held not to be absolutely necessary to give such notice, (Clutton v. Cherry, 2 Phil. Ec. Ca. 384 ;) but now it is provided, that what was formerly adjudged fit and proper to be done in this respect, shall be observed and performed. (See *infra.*)

Notice of Vestry Meeting.] It is also said in the older authorities, that notice ought to be given publicly, on the Sunday before the meeting is to take place, either in the church after divine service is ended, or else at the church door as the parishioners come out. (Wats. c. 39.) And it has been decided, that proclamation *during* divine service for the *meeting* of a vestry, or of the *purport* of such meeting, is convenient and proper, though it would be indecorous to announce the *result* of a meeting in the same way. (Thompson v. Tapps, MSS.; Cas. 17; 4 Burn. Ec. L. 8.) And that in whatever way the notice is given of such meeting, the time and place of the assembling of it should be stated, and it will be *fairest* then also to declare for what business the said meeting is to be held, that none may be surprised, but that all may have full time before, to consider of what is to be proposed at the said meeting. (Wats. c. 39.)

Notice required by Statute.] All doubt, however, upon this subject is now determined by the 58 Geo. 3. c. 69. s. 1, passed for the regulation of parish vestries, but extending only to England and Wales; by which it is enacted, " That from and after the first day of July, 1818, no vestry or meeting of the inhabitants in vestry of or for any parish, shall be holden until *public notice shall have been given* of such vestry, and of the *place* and *hour* of holding the same, and of the *special purpose* thereof, three days before the day to be appointed for holding such vestry, by the publication of such notice, in the parish church or chapel, on some Sunday during, or immediately after, divine service; and by affixing the same on the principal door of such church or chapel."

It is stated to be usual, for half an hour before the meeting begins, for one of the church bells to be tolled to give the parishioners notice of their assembling together. (Shaw's Par. L. c. 17.)

By whom called.] Vestries for church matters regularly are to be called by " the churchwardens, with the consent of the minister." The above act of Parliament neither altered the general authority under which, nor the persons by whom, vestries are to be called; it only adds some farther formalities in the mode of calling, or rather makes the preliminary announcements essential, which were before considered expedient by the spiritual and ecclesiastical courts. It therefore follows, that a private parishioner has no right given him by the act, and he had none before, during the time of divine service, and of his own authority, to publish a notice for a vestry to choose new church-wardens, or any other notice in the church. (Dawe v. Williams, 2 Addams' Rep. 138.)

An allegation in an indictment, "that A. was duly elected treasurer of the said parish," is supported by an entry in the parish book, stating the election to have been at a vestry duly held in pursuance of notice. (Rex v. Martin, 2 Camp. 100; see Thomas v. Morris, 1 Addams' Rep. 470.)

Who may attend a Vestry.] Anciently, at the common law, every parishioner who paid to the church rates, *or* scot and lot, and no other person, had a right to come to these meetings. But this must not be misunderstood of the minister who hath a special duty incumbent on him in this matter, and must be responsible to the bishop for his care herein; and therefore in every parish meeting he *presides* for the regulating and directing this affair; and this equally holds, whether he be rector or vicar. (Shaw's Par. L. c. 17.)

Qualification to Vote.] Residence within the parish is not a necessary qualification, as all out-dwellers occupying land in the parish, have a vote in the vestry, as well as the inhabitants, (Johns. 19.) Nor is the payment of church rates essential to entitle a person to vote at vestry meetings. And although at a meeting of the parishioners, in whom, by the custom, the right of electing to a perpetual curacy was vested, such meeting being duly convened for the purpose of choosing a fit person to fill the perpetual curacy, it was resolved, before the election began, that parishioners who had not paid, (not having been assessed to) *church* rates, should not be allowed to vote, and in consequence, several persons, legally qualified to vote, did not tender their votes; and the votes of others were rejected, because they had not paid the church rate, though they had paid poor rates; it was held by the Court of King's Bench, that the election was not according to the custom; and that it was not competent to the parishioners assembled to narrow the custom by passing a bye-law, which would have the effect of making it depend upon the will of particular persons whether a person had a right to vote or not, by inserting, or omitting to insert, the names of any particular parishioners in the church rate, and demanding payment thereof. (Faulkner v. Elger, 6 Dowl. & Ryl. 517; 4 Barn. & Cres. 449.)

Inhabitancy not necessary.] By the 59 Geo. 3. c. 85, passed to amend the act of the preceding session, it is enacted, "That any person who shall be assessed and rated for the relief of the poor, in respect of any annual rent, profit, or value, arising from any lands tenements, or hereditaments, situate in any parish in which any vestry shall be holden under the said recited act, although such person shall not reside in, or be an inhabitant of such parish, shall and may lawfully be presented at such vestry; and such person shall have and be entitled to give such and so many vote or votes at such vestry, in respect of the amount of such rent, profit, or value, as by the said act any inhabitant of such parish present at such vestry might or ought to have, and be entitled to give in respect of such amount, and to all intents and purposes, as if such person were an inhabitant of such parish, any thing in the said recited act to the contrary, in any wise notwithstanding." (s. 1.)

Rateability necessary.] The 58 Geo. 3. c. 69. s. 4, provides, that when any person shall have become an inhabitant of any parish, or become liable to be rated therein, since the making of the last rate for the relief of the poor thereof, he shall be entitled to vote for and in respect of the lands, tenements, and property for which he shall have become liable to be rated, and shall consent to be rated, in like manner as if he should have been actually rated for the same.

Payment, if demanded, necessary.] No person who shall have refused or neglected to pay any rate for the relief of the poor, which shall be due from, and shall have been demanded of him, [" *and*"] shall be entitled to vote or to be present in any vestry of the parish, for which such rate shall have been made, until he shall have paid the same. (Id. s. 5.)

The 59 Geo. 3. c. 85, which was passed to amend the above act, recites, that the word "*and*," was inserted in the above place by mistake; and to correct the ambiguity, re-enacts the provision as it would stand without that word. And with respect to the votes of companies, &c. (see *post*, 255,) by their clerks, &c. goes on to enact, "That no such clerk, secretary, steward, or agent, shall be entitled to be present, or to vote, nor shall be present or vote at any vestry in such parish, unless all rates for the relief of the poor which shall have been assessed and charged upon, or in respect of the annual rent profit or value, in right of which any such clerk, secretary, steward, or agent, shall claim to be present and vote, which shall be due, and which shall have been demanded at any time before the meeting of such vestry, shall have been paid and satisfied." (Id. s. 3.)

SECTION II.—PROCEEDINGS IN VESTRY.

Chairman of Vestry.] It has already been stated, that the minister has a right to preside at all vestry meetings; for a minister is not a mere individual of vestry; on the contrary, he is always described as the *first*, and as an integral part of the parish; the form of citing a parish being, "the *minister*, churchwardens, and parishioners;" and that he and any other individual should be put in competition for the office of chairman, would be placing him in a degraded situation, in which he is not placed by the *constitutional* establishment of this country. In sound legal principle he is the head and *praeses* of the meeting. (Wilson v. M'Math. 3 Phill. Ec. Ca. 87. 3 Barn. & Ald. 246, *notis.*) The vestry act provides, that in case the rector or vicar, or perpetual curate, shall not be present, the persons so assembled shall forthwith nominate by plurality of votes, to be ascertained as is directed by the act (see infra. s. 3.,) one of the inhabitants to be chairman, which is nearly tantamount to a declaration, or by necessary implication declares, that if the rector, vicar, or curate *be present*, he shall preside; and the legislature must evidently have considered, that by law and usage he was entitled to preside. (See 58 Geo. 3. c. 69. s. 2.)

Plurality of Votes.] The vestry act has also made some important regulations with respect to the right of voting, transferring the right in effect from the person to the property; or at least giving to property a direct influence in these matters which it did not possess under the former system. It is provided by the third section of the act, "that in all such vestries, every inhabitant present, who by the last rate made for the relief of the poor shall have been assessed in respect of any annual rent, profit, or value, not amounting to £50, shall give one vote and no more; if assessed for any such annual rent, &c. amounting to £50, or upwards (whether in one or more than one charge) shall be entitled to give one vote for every £25, in respect of which he shall have been assessed, so that no inhabitant shall give more than six votes; and where two or more of the inhabitants present shall be jointly rated, each shall vote according to the proportion which shall be borne by him of the joint charge; and where only one of the persons jointly rated shall attend, he shall vote according to the whole of the joint charge." (58 Geo. 3. c. 69. s. 3.)

Votes of Companies, &c.] And be it further enacted, "That in all cases where any corporation, or body politic, or corporate, or company, shall be charged to the rate for the relief of the poor of such parish, either in the name of such corporation, or of any officer of the said corporation, it shall and may be lawful for the clerk, secretary, steward, or other agent, duly authorized for that purpose, of such corporation or body politic, or corporate, or company, to be present at any vestry to be holden in the said parish, under the said recited act;

and such clerk, secretary, steward, or agent, shall be entitled to give such and so many vote or votes at such vestry, in respect of the amount of the rent, profit, or value of such lands, tenements, or hereditaments, as by the said act, any inhabitant assessed to such rate, present at such vestry, might or ought to have, and be entitled to, in respect of such amount, any thing in the said recited act to the contrary, in any wise notwithstanding. (59 Geo. 3. c. 85. s. 2.)

Plurality of Votes denied.] Where, however, in the parish of St. M. the poor rates had according to an ancient custom been always assessed without regard to the annual value of property in the parish, but according to the supposed ability of the party assessed, it was held, that persons so rated were not entitled to the benefit conferred by the vestry act, as to the plurality of votes, although assessed in respect of property exceeding the annual value of £50. (Nightingale v. Marshall, 2 Barn. & Cress. 313.; 3 Dowl. & Ryl. 549.)

And where feoffees of a charity were directed to do certain acts, only in a vestry or meeting of the said feoffees, and of ten of the inhabitants of the parish, which should be vestrymen in the said parish, and not feoffees, it was held, that the votes were to be taken *per capita*, and not according to this act, giving a plurality of votes. (Atto. Gen. v. Wilkinson, 3 Brod. & Bing. R. 266. 7 Moore, 187.)

Mode of Voting.] The *mode* of voting may also be of importance to the validity of the proceedings. The common law mode of election is by show of hands, or by poll; and the party electing is then said to have a voice in the election. It is clear that, at common law, where parties have the right of voting, the restriction of voting by ballot cannot be imposed; it presents an insurmountable difficulty to a scrutiny because no person can tell for whom a particular individual voted; (See Faulkner. v. Elger, 4 Barn. & Cres. 449.; 6 Dowl. & Ryl. 517;) besides, under the vestry act, where one person may have any number of votes to the amount of six, other objections might present themselves to voting by ballot. It is therefore evident, that the common law mode of voting ought to be adhered to. These reasons are equally cogent against voting by proxy. (See 17 State Trials, 822.)

Casting Vote.] The same section also provides, that in all cases of equality of votes, the chairman shall (in addition to such vote or votes as he may by virtue of the vestry act be entitled to give in right of his assessment,) have the casting vote. It is also provided, that the chairman *shall* sign the proceedings.

Signing the Proceedings.] It is also provided, that such of the inhabitants present as shall think proper, *may* also sign the proceedings. (Id.) But they incur no separate or individual responsibility for any thing which may be done in pursuance of a resolution of vestry so signed by them. It has been determined, that vestrymen, who signed a resolution, ordering the parish surveyor to take steps for defending an indictment for not repairing a road, were not to be responsible for the payment of the attorney employed by the surveyor (Spratt v. Powell, 3 Bing. 478.); for in signing the resolution, they act merely as vestrymen, without any intention of becoming individually responsible. (Lanchester v. Tricker, 1 Bing. 201, 8 Moore, 20.; Lanchester v. Frewer, 2 Bing. 361, 9 Moore, 688.)

SECTION III.—POWER OF VESTRIES.

Controul in Parish Matters.] The popular spirit which pervades the constitution of our national government, exists also in these local assemblies, and has of late been excited, in many instances, with similar energy for the correction of real or supposed abuses. The vestry has the right to investigate and restrain the expenditure of the parish funds, to determine the expediency of enlarging or altering their churches and chapels, or of adding to or disposing of the "goods and ornaments" connected with those sacred edifices. The election of some of the parish officers is either wholly, or in part, to be made by the vestry, and it has either directly or indirectly, a superintending authority in all the weightier matters of the parish.

Acts of Vestry binding.] If a vestry is called, every parishioner is bound to attend, or, if he do not, he is bound by the acts of those who do. (Clutton v. Cherry, 2 Phil. Ec. Ca. 380.) It seems, therefore, both reasonable and just, that whoever impedes or obstructs them in the exercise of this right should be held responsible, as for a personal injury. And to this effect is the case of Phillybrown v. Ryland, (as reported in Stra. 624,) as follows, (though in Ld. Raym. 1388, and And. 235, it is said the court gave no opinion upon this point.) "The plaintiff brought a special action on the case, for excluding him from the vestry-room, and upon demurrer the court made no difficulty but that such an action was maintainable; however in this case they gave judgment for the defendant, it not being averred that the parish had any property in this room, or right to meet there, so that for aught appears it might be the defendant's own house, and then he might let in whom he pleased, and refuse the rest. And this was a fault in substance, and need not to be shown for cause of demurrer. (See also Vin. Abr. tit. Vestry.)

Adjourning Vestry.] In Stoughton v. Reynolds, it was adjudged, that the right of adjourning the vestry is not in the minister or any other person as chairman, nor in the churchwardens, but in the whole assembly, where all are upon an equal footing; and the same must be decided (as other matters there) by a majority of votes. (Str. 1045.)

Review by next Vestry.] The acts of one vestry are not absolutely binding on a succeeding vestry, and they may be confirmed or rescinded by such succeeding vestry; but the confirmation of the succeeding vestry is not *necessary* to make the acts of the preceding one valid. (Mawley v. Barbet, 2 Esp. 687.)

Distributing Pews.] The vestry, as such, has no authority whatever in the distribution of pews—the churchwardens are not bound to follow their directions; at the same time the sense and opinion of the vestry ought to have weight with them. The vote of the vestry is of itself of no authority as to the question of right; but it marks the opinion of the parish. (Sir John Nichol in Pettman v. Bridger, 1 Phil. Ec. Ca. 316.)

Extent of Vestry Act.] The provisions of the 58 Geo. 3. c. 69, are expressly extended by the 7th section, "to all townships, vills, and places, having separate overseers of the poor, and maintaining their poor separately; and that all its directions and regulations in regard to vestries shall extend and be applied to all meetings which may by law be holden of the inhabitants of any parish, township, vill, or place for any of the purposes in the act expressed, and that the notices of vestry meetings may, in places where there is no parish church or chapel, or divine service is not performed in such church or chapel, be given and published in such manner as notices of the like nature are there usually published, or as shall be most effectual for communicating the same to the inhabitants thereof."

"Provided also, that nothing in this act contained shall alter the time of holding any vestry, parish, or town meeting, which is by the authority of any act required to be holden on any certain day, or within any certain time in such act prescribed and directed; nor shall any thing in this act contained, extend to take away, lessen, prejudice, or affect the powers of any vestry or meeting holden in any parish, township or place, by virtue of any special act or acts, of any ancient and special usage or custom, or to change or affect the right or manner of voting in any vestry or meeting so holden." (Id. s. 8.)

"Provided always, and be it further enacted, that nothing in this act contained shall extend to any parish within the city of London, or any parish in the borough of Southwark." (Id. ss. 9, 10.)

VESTRY CLERK.

Election and Duty.] The vestry clerk is chosen by the vestry, and he acts as registrar or secretary thereto, but he has no vote upon, or right to take part in, the questions submitted to the vestry. His business is to attend at all parish meetings, and to draw up and copy all orders and other acts of the vestry, and to give out copies thereof when necessary; and therefore he hath the custody of all books and papers relating thereto. (Shaw's Par. L. c. 18.)

Custody of the Books.] But although it is his duty to produce such books and papers, and permit copies to be taken for the ordinary parish purposes, or when they are wanted for the purpose of advancing any parochial right, he cannot be compelled to furnish such documents if they are required for any personal object. The court therefore refused to compel a vestry clerk to produce documents in the parish chest in his custody, it being in effect to furnish evidence against himself, in an action of libel brought against him by an inhabitant of the parish. (May v. Gwynne, 4 Barn. & Ald. 301.) But if the parish books be in the custody of any other person, it seems the vestry clerk may have a mandamus to compel the delivery of them to him. (Rex v. Croydon, 5 T. R. 713.) Though in a later case, where the application was against a churchwarden, Lord Ellenborough said, "If the muniments belong to the vestry clerk as annexed to his office, he may bring an action of detainer or trover; and his lordship refused the rule. (2 Chit. R. 255.) And by the 58 Geo. 3. c. 69. s. 6, it is provided, that the vestry books, rates and assessments, accounts and vouchers, of churchwardens, overseers of the poor, and surveyors of the highways, and other parish officers, and all certificates, orders of justices, and of courts, and all other parish books, writings, and papers, shall be kept by such person, and in such place and manner, as the inhabitants in vestry shall direct. (See *ante*, "Vestry Books," 133.)

Duration of Office.] The office of vestry clerk is not fixed and permanent, for which a mandamus will lie. It depends altogether on the will of the inhabitants, who may elect a different clerk at each vestry. Neither is any salary annexed to this situation. With regard to any supposed agreement made by the parishioners, that this should be an annual office, it could not be obligatory longer than the parties chose to fulfil it; for it might be revoked at the next vestry. (Per Lord Kenyon in Rex v. Croydon, 5 T. R. 714.)

CHAPTER X.—SELECT VESTRIES.

SECTION I.—SELECT VESTRIES BY CUSTOM.

How they originated.] Select vestries seem to have grown from the practice of choosing a certain number of persons yearly to manage the concerns of the parish for that year; which by degrees came to be a fixed method, and the parishioners lost not only their right to concur in the public management as oft as they would attend, but also in most places, if not in all, the right of electing the managers. And such a custom, of the government of parishes by a select number, hath been adjudged a good custom, in that the churchwardens accounting to them was adjudged a good account. (Gibs. 219.)

Fallen into disrepute.] In some parishes these select vestries having been thought oppressive and injurious, great struggles have been made to set aside and demolish them. (Shaw's Par. L. c. 17.)

And no wonder that it hath been so in such parishes where by custom they have obtained the power to choose one another; for it is not to be supposed, but if they are guilty of evil practices, they will choose such persons as they think will connive at or concur therein. (4 Burn. Ec. L. 10.)

Such is the language employed by writers upon the subject, more than half a century ago; and the history of select vestries, in more recent times, affords no sufficient grounds for believing that the censure is no longer applicable. All experience demonstrates that governing bodies, whose powers are wielded in the secret conclave, uncontrolled by a higher authority, or the influence of public opinion, become in time corrupt; not always from bad motives actuating the conduct of the members of such bodies, but from that very *love of ease,* (and the consequent neglect of duty) which is considered as the counterpoise of that *love of power* which induces men, in the first instance, to take upon themselves gratuitously, the burthen of administering public affairs. The propriety, therefore, of inquiring into the foundation of such institutions, in order to ascertain the just limits of their authority, and the responsibility under which it is exercised, is obvious.

Founded in immemorial usage.] Until the recent act of parliament, commonly called Mr. Sturges Bourne's act, select vestries existed by custom or prescription alone; and as that statute merely relates to the maintenance of the *poor,* wherever a select vestry assumes to itself the management of the affairs of *a parish,* its authority must rest upon the foundation of special usage, from time immemorial; and none other, except those established under the above, or some local, statute, can have any other legal origin. For it is quite settled that a select vestry cannot be constituted by a faculty from the bishop; (Berry v. Banner, Peake, Rep. 156); and being in derogation of the common rights of parishioners, can only be sustained by immemorial usage, or by act of parliament. (Goodall and Gray v. Whitmore and Fenn, 2 Hagg. Rep. N. S. 374.) Wherever a select vestry, therefore, of the latter kind, is proved to exist, the next inquiry is into the legality of it; for if it is not a good custom, it ought to be no longer used. "*Malus usus abolendus est,*" is an es ablished maxim of law. (Litt. s. 212, 4 Inst. 274.)

Requisites of such Custom.] It has been already stated that a custom, to be valid, must have existed immemorially. But the growing interest which has been excited respecting the validity and constitution of select vestries supported by custom, renders it expedient to explain what are the requisites of a legal and well-established custom.

If any one can show the beginning of a custom, it is no good custom; for which reason no custom can prevail *against* an express act of parliament, since the statute itself is a proof of a time when such a custom did not exist.

The memory of man is taken in law to run to the beginning of the reign of Richard I.; consequently, if it can be shown that the custom *commenced* at any period *since,* or, did not exist *before* that period, it is invalid. But a regular usage for twenty years, *unexplained and uncontradicted,* is sufficient to warrant a jury in finding an immemorial custom. (Rex v. Joliffe, 2 Barn. & Cres. 54.; 3 Dowl. & Ryl. 240; 2 Saund. 175 a. d. Peake's Evid. 336.)

Must be Continuous.] It must have been *continued.* Any interruption would cause a temporary ceasing: the revival gives it a new beginning, which will be within time of memory, and thereupon the custom will be void. But this must be understood with regard to an interruption of the *right;* for an interruption of the *possession* only for ten or twenty years, will not destroy the custom. As, if the inhabitants of a parish have a customary right of watering their cattle at a certain pool, the custom is not destroyed, though they do not use it for ten years, it only becomes more difficult to prove.

In like manner, where a select vestry existed by custom, but a faculty was obtained naming forty-nine persons, together with the vicar and churchwardens, to constitute that body in future, and appointing that number to be kept up by election, to be made by ten at least, together with the vicar and churchwardens; and in a few years afterwards, another faculty was obtained, reducing this number of ten to seven; and these faculties had been constantly acted upon for upwards of sixty years, yet it was held that the custom was not thereby destroyed: because, in the first place, these faculties, though acted upon, had no validity in law; and next it appeared, that ten out of the fourteen vestrymen, who were present at the vestry holden immediately before the promulgation of the first faculty, were part of the forty-nine *named in that faculty;* and lastly, the vestry, as appointed by the faculty, and as it had since continued, was not inconsistent with the vestry previously existing by the custom; and therefore there was not, either in fact or in law, any discontinuance. (Golding *v.* Fenn, 7 Barn. & Cres. 781; 1 Man. & Ryl. 647.)

But if the *right* be any how discontinued, even for a day, the custom is at an end. (1 Bla. Com. 77.)

Must be acquiesced in.] It is also requisite to the legality of a custom, that it shall have been *peaceable,* and acquiesced in, not subject to contention and dispute; for as customs owe their original to common consent, their being *immemorially* disputed, either at law or otherwise, is a proof that such consent was wanting. (1 Bla. Com. 77.)

Must be reasonable.] Customs must be *reasonable,* or rather, taken negatively, they must not be unreasonable, which is not always, as Sir Edward Coke says, (1 Inst. 62,) to be understood of every unlearned man's reason, but of artificial and legal reason, warranted by authority of law. Upon which account a custom may be good, though the particular reason of it cannot be assigned; for it sufficeth, if no good reason can be assigned against it. Thus a custom in a parish that no man shall put his beasts into the common, till the 3d of October, would be good, and yet it would be hard to show the reason why that day in particular is fixed upon, rather than the day before or after. But a custom that no cattle shall be put in till the Lord of the Manor has first put in his, is unreasonable, and therefore bad; for, peradventure, the lord will never put in his, and then the tenants will lose all their profits. (Co. Copyh. s. 33.)

The above shows the principle upon which the *reasonableness* of an alleged custom is to be determined. The application of the principle to select vestries is illustrated in the case of Golding v. Fenn, before cited. It was there held, that a custom by which a select vestry should consist of an *indefinite* number of members, to be filled up at its own choice, without either *maximum* or *minimum* being fixed by the custom, is not unreasonable, overruling the dictum of Lord Kenyon in Berry v. Banner, Peake's R. 156. The Court said, "There is obviously no weight in the objection, that without a *maximum* being fixed, the vestry may consist of *too many* persons; and that although no numerical *minimum* be fixed by the custom, it by no means follows as a consequence, that the number may be reduced to two or three, as the objection supposes: the law may consider it as *part of the custom,* that there shall be a *reasonable* number, with reference to long-established usage, and to the population of the parish. That number which might not be too small and not *unreasonable,* three or four centuries ago, in a parish in which there might not be more than a dozen substantial householders, or even fewer, might not be *reasonable,* on a change of circumstances, when, by covering fields with houses, the number might be increased more than a hundred fold." (Golding v. Fenn, 7 Barn. & Cres. 780.)

Must be Compulsory.] Customs, though established by consent, must be (when established,) *compulsory,* and not left to the option of every man, whether he will use them or no. Therefore, a custom that all the inhabitants shall be rated toward the maintenance of a bridge, will be good; but a custom that every man is to contribute thereto at his *own pleasure,* is idle and absurd, and indeed no custom at all.

Must be Consistent.] Lastly, customs must be *consistent* with each other; one custom cannot be set up in opposition to another. For if both are really customs, then both are of equal antiquity, and both established by mutual consent: which to say of contradictory customs, is absurd. Therefore, if one man prescribes that by custom he has a right to have windows looking into another's garden, the other cannot claim a right by custom to stop up or obstruct those windows, for these two contradictory customs cannot both be good, nor both stand together. He ought rather to deny the existence of the former custom. (1 Bla. Com. 77. *per tot.*)

Vestries, how governed, &c.] The ordinary rules and principles of law which relate to vestries generally, (see *ante,*) are also applicable to select vestries. It may be observed, that if there be any inherent imperfection in their constitution, from which the evils, at any time complained of, necessarily flow, the remedy is in the hands of the legislature. Courts of justice can only administer the law as it exists, and are not responsible for suggested improvements, however salutary, nor at liberty to depart from the settled maxims of jurisprudence, however beneficial it might be in the particular instance.

Custom where triable.] The legality of a select vestry *may*, it seems, be tried incidentally to the principal matter of a suit in the ecclesiastical courts. Thus in questions of subtraction of church-rate, the court having jurisdiction on the subject matter, is bound, unless stopped by prohibition, to proceed to the trial of a select vestry, by which the rate was made, and it must be a prohibition in the *particular* suit; for if other parties before the court upon the same question have been stopped by prohibition, this will not authorise the refusal of the court to proceed with the cause. (Goodall & Gray v. Whitmore & Fenn, 2 Hagg. Rep. N. S. 369.)

Prohibition.] But wherever a custom is in dispute, the proper tribunal is a court of common law, and a prohibition will in all such cases be granted, if sufficient appears in proof of the alleged custom, and that the matter in dispute in the inferior court depends upon the custom. Thus where the suggestion set forth that the parish of Masham in Yorkshire was an ancient parish, and that time out of mind there were twenty-four of the chief parishioners, who all along had been called the four-and-twenty; and that during time immemorial, as often as any one of the said four-and-twenty parishioners happened to die, the rest surviving of the four-and-twenty did choose, and during all the same time used to choose, one other fit parishioner to be one of the four-and-twenty, in the room of him so deceased; and that within the said parish there is, and during time immemorial there always hath been, a custom, that the said four-and-twenty for the time being have been used and accustomed, as often as there was occasion, to make rates, and to assess reasonable sums upon the parishioners for the repairs of the church; and that the churchwardens of the said parish, during all the time aforesaid, have used to receive all duties and dues for burials in the body or aisles of the said church; and if any of the inhabitants refused to pay the said rates or dues for burials as aforesaid, then the churchwardens, *by warrant from the twenty-four* for the time being, were used to distrain the goods of the said parishioners; and that the said twenty-four, with the consent of the vicar or curate, have used to repair the body and aisles of the said church; and that the churchwardens for the time being have always used to give up their accounts to the said four-and-twenty, who allowed or disallowed them as they saw expedient; and that on the allowance of such account, the churchwardens have always been discharged from giving any other account in any other place: that the plaintiffs were churchwardens for the year 1680; and after this year was ended, they gave in their accounts to the four-and-twenty; and that though all pleas concerning prescriptions and customs ought to be determined by the common law, yet the defendant hath drawn and cited them into the Spiritual Court, yet the said defendant hath refused to admit or to receive the said plea. Upon great debate of this case at several times, the court was of opinion that the custom was good and reasonable, and a prohibition was granted. (Batt v. Wilkinson, Lutw. 1027.)

So that prescription and constant immemorial usage seem to be the basis and only support of this select vestry. And pursuant hereunto, upon the same foundation and for the same reasons, was the select vestry of the parish of St. Mary-at-Hill in London, confirmed and established in the King's Bench not many years ago. And since that time, the select vestries of St. Saviour's and St. Olave's in Southwark, for want of proof of such prescription and immemorial usage, have been set aside and demolished. (Shaw's Par. L. c. 17.)

One cannot elect another.] A select vestry for the management of parochial affairs, existing by ancient custom, cannot elect another select vestry for the management of the poor, within the stat. 59 Geo. 3. c. 12; (Rex v. Woodman, 4 Barn. & Ald. 507.)

SECTION II.—SELECT VESTRIES BY STATUTE.

Particular Provisions.] By the act of 10 Anne, c. 11, for building fifty new churches, it is provided, that five or more of the commissioners, with the consent of the bishop or ordinary of the place, shall appoint a convenient number of sufficient inhabitants of each new parish created by the act, to be vestrymen; and from time to time, upon the death, removal, or other voidence of any such vestrymen, the rest or majority of these may choose another, being an inhabitant and householder in the parish. (s. 20.)

In several private acts for building particular churches, provision is made for the appointment of select vestries. In some instances, the minister, churchwardens, overseers of the poor, and others who have served, or paid fines for being excused from serving those offices; in others, the minister, churchwardens, overseers of the poor, and all who pay to the poor rate;—and there are some in which all who rent houses of so much a year, are appointed to be vestrymen within such parishes, and no other persons.

Vestries in new Districts.] The legislature has also, in the measures recently adopted for building and promoting the building of churches in populous parishes, provided that the system of *select* vestries shall be included, for the management of the ecclesiastical affairs in the new districts or parishes created by those statutes. The provisions on this subject are as follow:—

Vestry, how constituted.] In every district, parish, or division of a parish, or district chapelry, or consolidated chapelry, in which any church or chapel shall be built, acquired, or appropriated under the said act (58 G. 3. c. 45,) or this act, in which there shall not be a distinct vestry, a select vestry of so many persons as the commissioners shall direct, shall be appointed by the commissioners, with the advice of the bishop, out of the substantial inhabitants, for the care and management of the church or chapel, and all matters relating thereto; and such select vestry shall annually elect the church or chapelwardens on the part of the parish or chapelry; and shall elect new members of such vestry, as vacancies shall arise by death, resignation, or ceasing to inhabit the parish and proper pews, shall be provided for the use of the church or chapelwardens. (59 Geo. 3. c. 134. s. 30.)

Former Vestrymen to continue.] Where any parish or place shall be divided into separate parishes, for ecclesiastical purposes, or into separate districts or chapelries, in which select vestries shall be appointed by the commissioners, all members of the select vestry of the original church or chapel, shall continue to act as the vestry of such district or division, in all matters relating to such church or chapel, and the repairs thereof, or to any other ecclesiastical matters or things, or in the distribution of any proportion of any bequests, gifts, or charities, which may, under this act, be assigned to any such district or division; provided that no member of any select vestry shall, after such division, act in any manner relating to any church or chapel, or any other ecclesiastical matters or things, except such as relate to the division in which he shall reside; and if by reason of such division, a sufficient number of such members of select vestry shall not remain resident in the division within which the original church or chapel shall be situate, according to the proportion fixed by the commissioners, (regard being had to the population of such division, and its relative population to that of the whole parish or place,) all such deficiencies shall be filled up as vacancies have before been filled up therein; provided that no person shall vote in supplying such deficiencies, unless resident within the division for which the members are to be chosen; provided that the persons chosen shall not thereby be members of the vestry for any other purposes than such as relate to the division for which they shall be chosen, or for the distribution of any charitable gifts therein; provided that all the members of the select vestry of any such parish or place, resident in any other divisions thereof, shall be members of such vestries as shall be appointed under the acts for the divisions in which they shall reside." (3 Geo. 4. c. 72. s. 10.)

The court refused to compel a vestry to appoint a surveyor to certify, that a newly-formed road had been properly constructed, drained, &c., which the vestry had the power of doing under their local act, as that would cast the burden of repairing the road on the parish; and it appeared that it would not be so much for the benefit of the public as of the proprietors, during the time their buildings were completing. (R. v. Paddington Vestry, 9 Barn. & Cres. 456.)

SECTION III.—VESTRIES FOR AFFAIRS OF THE POOR.

How constituted.] "For the better and more effectual execution of the laws for the relief of the poor, and for the amendment thereof, it is enacted, That it shall be lawful for the inhabitants of any parish (in England) in vestry assembled, and they are hereby empowered, to establish a select vestry for the concerns of the poor of such parish, and to that end, to nominate and elect in the same or in any subsequent vestry, or any adjournment thereof respectively, such and so many substantial householders or occupiers within such parish, not exceeding the number of twenty nor less than five, as shall, in any such vestry, be thought fit to be members of the select vestry; and the rector, vicar, or other minister of the parish, and, in his absence, the curate thereof, (such curate being resident in and charged to the poor's rates of such parish,) and the churchwardens and overseers of the poor for the time being, together with the inhabitants, who shall be nominated and elected as aforesaid, (such inhabitants being first thereto appointed by writing, under the hand and seal of one of his Majesty's justices of the peace, which appointment he is hereby authorized and required to make,) shall be, and constitute, a select vestry, for the care and management of the concerns of the poor of such parish, and any three of them, (two of whom shall neither be churchwardens nor overseers of the poor,) shall be a quorum." (59 Geo. 3. c. 12. s. 1.)

Select, supersedes ancient, Vestry.] Wherever a select vestry is appointed, the right of the common law vestry has always, in practice, been considered as *de facto* superseded; and the language of this act of Parliament appears to confer upon that body the authority relative to the care and management of the poor which the parishioners at large were before in the habit of exercising. It is optional with the parishioners, whether they will or will not proceed upon the old law, or upon the provisions of this statute, by the appointment of a select vestry; but if they pursue the latter course, they delegate their authority to that body. It follows, that the consent of a select vestry, constituted under this act, is sufficient to render valid a contract under the 9 Geo. 1. c. 7. s. 4, for the lodging, keeping, and maintaining the poor of a parish. (Clarke v. King, 2 Younge & J. 525.)

Ancient cannot elect Select Vestry.] Where a select vestry, which had existed immemorially, assumed to elect a select vestry for the concerns of the poor under this act, and the magistrates made an order appointing the persons, so chosen, as a select vestry accordingly, upon the order being removed into the King's Bench, it was said by Abbott, C J., "I am clearly of opinion, that the sixteen persons who constituted the ancient select vestry cannot be considered the inhabitants of the parish in vestry assembled, within the meaning of the 59 Geo. 3. c. 12. The power to appoint a select vestry is expressly given to the *inhabitants* in vestry assembled; and here it was exercised, not by the inhabitants in vestry assembled, but by certain persons possessing some of the powers of the inhabitants in vestry assembled. It is not necessary in this case to decide what the inhabitants may do, but I have no difficulty in saying, that, in my opinion, the inhabitants at large may assemble and appoint a select vestry for the care and management of the poor, not interfering with any of the rights of the ancient select vestry." The order was accordingly quashed. (Rex v. Woodman and others, 4 Barn. & Ald. 507.)

Vacancies how supplied.] "When any inhabitant, elected and appointed to serve in any such select vestry shall, before the expiration of his office, die or remove from the parish, or shall become incapable of serving, or shall refuse or neglect to serve therein, the vacancy which shall be thereby occasioned shall, as soon as conveniently may be, be filled up by the election and appointment in manner aforesaid of some other substantial householder or occupier of such parish, and so from time to time, as often as any such vacancy shall occur; and every such select vestry shall continue and be empowered to act from the time of the appointment thereof, until fourteen days after the next annual appointment of overseers of the poor of the parish shall take place, and may be from year to year, and in any future year, received in the manner hereinbefore directed." (59 G. 3. c. 12. s. 1.)

Vestry Meetings.] "Every such select vestry shall meet once in every fourteen days, and oftener if it shall be found necessary, in the parish church, or some other convenient place within the parish, and at every such meeting a chairman shall be appointed by the majority of the members present, who shall preside therein; and in all cases of equality of votes upon any question there arising, the chairman shall have the casting vote." (59 Geo. 3. c. 12. s. 1.)

Duties of Vestries.] "Every such select vestry is hereby empowered and required to examine into the state and condition of the poor of the parish, and to inquire into and determine upon the proper objects of relief, and the nature and amount of the relief to be given; and in each case shall take into consideration the character and conduct of the poor person to be relieved, and shall be at liberty to distinguish, in the relief to be granted, between the deserving and the idle, extravagant and profligate poor; and such select vestry shall make orders in writing for such relief as they shall think requisite, and shall inquire into and superintend the collection and administration of all money to be raised by the poor's rates, and of all other funds and money raised or applied by the parish to the relief of the poor." (Ibid.)

Overseers to obey Vestry.] "Where any such select vestry shall be established, the overseers of the poor are required, in the execution of their office, to conform to the directions of the select vestry, and shall not, (except in cases of sudden emergency or urgent necessity, and to the extent only of such temporary relief as each case shall require, and except by order of justices in the cases hereinafter provided for,) give any further or other relief or allowance to the poor, than such as shall be ordered by the select vestry." (Ibid.)

Relief refused, &c. by Vestry.] "When any complaint shall be made to any justice of the peace of the want of adequate relief by, or on behalf of, any poor inhabitant of any parish, for which a select vestry shall be established by virtue of this act, or in which the relief of the poor is or shall be under the management of guardians, governors, or directors, appointed by virtue of special or local acts; such justice shall not proceed therein, or take cognizance thereof, unless it shall be proved on oath before him, that application for such relief hath been first made to, and refused by, the select vestry, or by such guardians, governors, or directors; and in such case the justice, to whom the complaint shall be made, may summon the overseers of the poor, or any of them, to appear before any two of his Majesty's justices of the peace to answer the complaint; and if, upon the hearing thereof, it shall be proved on oath, to the satisfaction of the justices who shall hear the same, that the party complaining, or on whose behalf the complaint shall be made, is in need of relief, and that adequate relief hath been refused by the select vestry, or by such guardians, governors, or directors, or that such select vestry shall not have assembled as by this act directed, it shall be lawful for such justices to make an order under their hands and seals for such relief as they, in their just and proper discretion, shall think necessary, (reference being also had by such justices to the character and conduct of the applicant,) provided, that in every such order the special cause of granting the relief thereby directed, shall be expressly stated, and that no such order shall be given for, or extend to any longer time, than one month from the date thereof, provided, that it shall be lawful for any justice to make an order for relief in case of urgent necessity to be specified in such order, so as such order shall remain in force only until the assembling of the select vestry of the parish, or of such guardians, governors, or directors, as aforesaid, to which such case shall relate." (59 Geo. 3. c. 12. s. 2.)

Minutes of Proceedings.] "Every select vestry to be established by the authority of this act shall cause minutes to be fairly entered in books, to be for that purpose provided, of all their meetings, proceedings, resolutions, orders, and transactions, and of all sums received, applied, and expended by their direction; and such minutes shall, from time to time, be signed by the chairman, and shall, together with a summary or report of the accounts and transactions of the select vestry, be laid before the inhabitants in vestry assembled, in the month of March and the month of October, and at such other times as the select vestry shall think fit; and the minutes, proceedings, accounts, and reports of every select vestry shall belong to the parish, and be preserved with the other books, documents, accounts, and public papers thereof." (Ibid, s. 3.)

Notice of Vestry Meetings.] "Provided, that the churchwardens and overseers of the poor shall cause ten days' notice, at the least, to be publicly given, in the usual manner, of every vestry to be holden for the purpose of establishing any select vestry, or of nominating and electing the members, or any member thereof, and of every vestry to be holden for the purpose of receiving the report of the select vestry, and every notice of any such vestry shall state the special purpose thereof." (Ibid, s. 4.)

Relief where no Select Vestry.] "Every order to be made for the relief of any poor person by the churchwardens and overseers of the poor of any parish, not having a select vestry under the authority of this act, shall be made by two or more justices, who shall, in making every such order, take into their consideration the character and conduct of the person applying for relief, provided, that in every such order the special cause of granting the relief thereby directed shall be expressly stated, and that no such order shall be given for, or extend to, any longer time than one month from the date thereof; provided also, that in cases of emergency and urgent distress, it shall be lawful for one justice to order such relief as the case shall require, stating in his order the circumstances of the case; but no such last-mentioned order shall entitle any person to claim relief by virtue thereof more than fourteen days from the date of the order, nor shall the same have any force or effect after the next petty session to be holden within the hundred or other division or district, in which the parish to which the same shall apply shall be situated." (59 Geo. 3. c. 12. s. 5.)

Townships, Justices, &c.] "All powers and authorities by this act given to, and vested in, justices of the peace, shall be exercised and executed by such justices within the limits of their respective commissions and jurisdictions, and not elsewhere; and that all provisions, clauses, authorities, and directions in this act contained, in relation to parishes, shall extend, and be construed to extend, to all townships, vills, and places, having separate overseers of the poor, and maintaining their poor separately; and that all acts and duties required or authorized by this act to be done and executed by churchwardens and overseers of the poor, may, in every parish, be performed, exercised, and executed by the major part of the churchwardens and overseers of the poor thereof; and that in townships, vills, and places, which have no churchwardens, the same may be performed, exercised, and executed by the overseers thereof, or the major part of them; and that all the powers, provisions, and clauses in this act contained, which relate to vestries, or to the inhabitants of any parish in vestry assembled, shall be construed to extend to all meetings of the inhabitants of any township, vill, or place, having separate overseers of the poor, and maintaining its poor separately, to be held after due and legal notice for carrying into execution the laws for the relief of the poor, as fully as if, in every such provision and clause, they were severally and respectively named and repeated." (s. 35.)

Saving Powers by other Acts.] "Nothing in this act contained shall extend, or be construed to extend, to take away, abridge, alter, prejudice, or affect, further than is hereby expressly enacted, any of the powers, directions, provisions, or regulations contained in the 22 Geo. 3. c. 83, for the better relief and employment of the poor in, or with respect to, such parishes, townships, and places as have adopted, or shall adopt, and become subject to, the provisions of that act, nor to take away, abridge, alter, prejudice, or affect any of the powers or provisions of any special or local act or acts for the maintenance, relief, or regulation of the poor, in any city, town, hundred, district, parish, or place; so, nevertheless, that in every city, town, hundred, district, parish, or place, such of the clauses, directions, and powers in this act contained, as are not repugnant to, nor incompatible with, the provisions of the said act of the 22 Geo. 3, or of such respective special or local acts, shall have the like force and effect, and may be adopted and applied in like manner as in other parishes and places; provided also, that nothing in this act contained shall extend, or be construed to extend, to alter, affect, or disturb any select vestry which in any parish has been established and acted upon by virtue of any ancient usage or custom." (s. 36.)

CHAPTER XI.—JUSTICES OF THE PEACE.

SECTION I.—APPOINTMENT AND QUALIFICATION.

Different kinds of Justices.] Justices of the peace are of three sorts; *first,* by act of Parliament, as the bishop of Ely and his successors, the archbishop of York, and the bishop of Durham: *secondly,* by charter or grant, made by the king under the great seal, as the mayors and chief officers in corporate towns; and, *thirdly,* by commission. (27 Hen. 8. c. 24; 2 Hawk. P. C. 40.)

Antiquity of the Office.] The officer to whom the accumulated duties of justice of the peace are now confided, was in the times of our Saxon kings, and for a long period afterwards, chosen by the freeholders of counties, in the same manner as coroners are still elected. They were then known under the appellation of *conservatores pacis,* and it was not till about the year 1327, that justices, or commissioners of the peace, were created, the earliest statute on the subject to be found in the parliamentary rolls being the 1 Edw. 3. c. 16.

By whom appointed.] "No person, of whatever estate, degree, or condition soever he be, shall have any power or authority to make any justices of peace; but that they shall be made by letters patent under the king's great seal, in the name and by authority of the king, and his heirs, kings of this realm, in all shires, counties, counties palatine, and other places of this realm, Wales and the marches of the same, or in any other his dominions, at their pleasure and wills, in such manner and form as justices of peace be commonly made in every shire of this realm; any grants, usages, prescriptions, allowances, act or acts of Parliament, or any other thing or things to the contrary thereof notwithstanding." (27 Hen. 8. c. 24.)

It seems very doubtful, whether since this statute the crown can delegate to a subject the power of appointing a justice of the peace. And therefore, where by the charter of a borough, the aldermen for the time being were to be justices of the peace, and they were empowered to execute, in their absence, by *their deputies*, the offices of aldermen of the said borough, it was held, that the deputy had not the power of a justice of the peace vested in him: and that at all events, if the crown can delegate the power of appointing a justice in this manner, such a delegation can only be made in the most clear and express language, and not by implication merely. (Jones v. Williams, 2 Barn. & Cres. 762; 5 Dowl. & Ryl. 654.)

In County Palatine, &c.] The 5th section of the act provides, "That justices of the peace, to be made and assigned by the king's highness within the county palatine of Lancaster, shall be made and ordained by commission under the king's usual seal of Lancaster, in manner and form as hath been accustomed." Section 6 provides, "That all cities, boroughs, and towns corporate within this realm, which have liberty, power, and authority to have justices of peace, or justices of gaol delivery, shall still have and enjoy their liberties and authorities in that behalf, after such like manner as they have been accustomed, without any alteration by occasion of this act." (27 Hen. 8. c. 24.)

Form of the Commission.] The form of the commission was revised by the judges in 1590; and being presented to the Lord Chancellor, he commanded the same to be adopted, which continues, with very little alteration, to be still used. (Lamb. c. 9.) It is as follows:—

"George the Fourth by the grace of God of the united kingdom of Great Britain and Ireland, King, Defender of the Faith, to A, B, C, D, &c. greeting.

"Know ye, that we have assigned you jointly and severally, and every one of you, our justices to keep our peace in our county of S. And to keep and cause to be kept all ordinances and statutes for the good of the peace, and for preservation of the same, and for the quiet rule and government of our people made in all and singular their articles in our said county (as well within liberties as without), according to the force, form, and effect of the same; and to chastise and punish all persons that offend against the form of those ordinances or statutes, or any one of them, in the aforesaid county, as it ought to be done according to the form of those ordinances and statutes, and to cause to come before you, or any of you, all those who to any one or more of our people concerning their bodies, or the firing of their houses, have used threats, to find sufficient security for the peace, or their good behaviour, towards us and our people; and if they shall refuse to find such security, then them in our prisons, until they shall find such security, to cause to be safely kept."

(*In Sessions.*] The commission then proceeds to explain their power and duty in sessions thus:)—

"We have also assigned you, and every two or more of you (of whom any one of you, the aforesaid A, B, C, D, &c. we will shall be one,) our justices, to inquire the truth more fully by the oath of good and lawful men of the aforesaid county, by whom the truth of the matter shall be the better known, of all and all manner of felonies, poisonings, enchantments, sorceries, arts magic, trespasses, forestallings, regratings, ingrossings, and extortions whatsoever; and of all and singular other crimes and offences, of which the justices of our peace may or ought lawfully to inquire, by whomsoever and after what manner soever in the said county done or perpetrated, or which shall happen to be there done or attempted; and also of all those who in the aforesaid counties, in companies against our peace, in disturbance of our people, with armed force, have gone or rode, or hereafter shall presume to go or ride; and also of all those who have there lain in wait, or hereafter shall presume to lie in wait, to maim, or cut, or kill our people; and also of all victuallers, and all and singular other persons who, in the abuse of weights or measures, or in selling victuals against the form of the ordinances and statutes, or any one of them, therefore made for the common benefit of England, and our people thereof, have offended or attempted, or hereafter shall presume in the said county to offend or attempt; and also of all sheriffs, bailiffs, stewards, constables, keepers of gaols, and other officers, who, in the execution of their offices about the premises, or any of them, have unduly behaved themselves, or hereafter shall presume to behave themselves unduly, or have been or shall happen hereafter to be careless, remiss, or negligent in our aforesaid county: and of all and singular articles and circumstances, and all other things whatsoever, that concern the premises of any of them, by whomsoever and after what manner soever in our aforesaid county done or perpetrated, or which hereafter shall there happen to be done or attempted in what manner soever; and to inspect all indictments whatsoever so before you, or any of you, taken or to be taken, or before others, late our justices of the peace in the aforesaid county, made or taken, and not yet determined; and to make and continue processes thereupon against all and singular the persons so indicted, or who before you hereafter shall happen to be indicted, until they can be taken, surrender themselves, or be outlawed; and to hear and determine all and singular the felonies, poisonings, enchantments, sorceries, arts magic, trespasses, forestallings, regratings, engrossings, extortions, unlawful assemblies, indictments aforesaid, and all and singular other the premises, according to the laws and statutes of England, as in the like case it has been accustomed or ought to be done; and the same offenders, and every of them, for their offences, by fines, ransoms, amerciaments, forfeitures, and other means, as according to the laws and custom of England, or form of the ordinances and statutes aforesaid, it has been accustomed or ought to be done to chastise and punish.

"Provided always, that if a case of difficulty upon the determination of any of the premises before you, or any two or more of you, shall happen to arise, then let judgment in nowise be given thereon, before you or any two or more of you, unless in the presence of one of our justices of the one or other bench, or of one of our justices appointed to hold the assizes in the aforesaid county.

"And therefore we command you, and every of you, that to keeping the peace, ordinances, statutes, and all and singular other the premises, you diligently apply yourselves, and that at certain days and places which you or any such two or more of you, as is aforesaid, shall appoint for these purposes, into the premises ye make inquiries, and all and singular the premises hear and determine, and perform and fulfil them in the aforesaid form, doing therein what to justice appertains according to the law and custom of England, saving to us the amerciaments and other things to us therefrom belonging.

"And we command, by the tenor of these presents, our sheriff of S. that at certain days and places, which you or any such two or more of you, as is aforesaid, shall make known to him, he cause to come before you, or such two or more of you, as aforesaid. so many and such good and lawful men of his bailiwick (as well within liberties as without), by whom the truth of the matter in the premises shall be the better known and inquired into.

"Lastly, We have assigned to you the said A. B. keeper of the rolls of our peace in our said county; and therefore you shall cause to be brought before you and your said fellows, at the days and places aforesaid, the writs, precepts, processes, and indictments aforesaid, that they may be inspected, and by a due course determined, as is aforesaid.

"In witness whereof we have caused these our letters to be made patent. Witness ourselves at Westminster," &c.

Who may be Justices.] By stats. 13 R. 2. st. 1. c. 7; and 2 H. 5. st. 2. c. 1, The justices shall be made within the counties, of the most sufficient knights, esquires, and gentlemen of the law.

By stat. 1 Mary, sess. 2. c. 8. s. 2, No *sheriff* shall exercise the office of a justice of the peace during the time that he acts as sheriff; and the reason seems to be, because he cannot act at the same time both as judge and officer, for so he would command himself to execute his own precepts. Also, if he be made a *coroner*, this, by some opinions, is a discharge of his authority of justice. (Dalt. c. 3.)

By stat. 1 Edw. 6. c. 7. ss. 3, 4, If he be created a *duke, archbishop, marquis, earl, viscount, baron, bishop, knight, judge,* or *serjeant at law,* this taketh not away his authority of a justice of the peace.

Also, by stat. 5 Geo. 2. c. 18. s 2. No *attorney, solicitor,* or *proctor,* shall be a justice of the peace for any county, during the time he shall continue in the practice of that business; but this does not extend to cities or towns counties of themselves, or to cities, towns, cinque ports, or liberties, having justices of the peace by charter, commission, or otherwise, (s. 4;) nor to peers of Parliament, or to eldest sons or heirs apparent of such, or of persons qualified to serve as knight of the shire, (s. 6;) nor to heads of colleges or halls in either of the universities. (s. 7.)

Mayor when a Justice.] Though a man be a *mayor,* it doth not follow that he is a justice of the peace, for that must be by a particular grant in the charter. (R. v. Langley, 2 Ld. Raym. 1030.) But although he be not a justice of the peace by the charter, yet there are many cases wherein he hath the same power as a justice of the peace given unto him by particular statutes; as, for instance, with regard to the customs, alehouses, Lord's day, swearing, gaming, weights, servants, &c.

Oath of Office.] By the 1 Geo. 3. c. 13. s. 2, Power is given to the clerk of the peace of every county, riding, or division in England and Wales, to administer the oaths to justices. And by the 7 Geo. 3. c. 9, it is provided, that justices, who have already taken the oaths, shall not be required to go through that ceremony again, upon the issuing of a new commission, during the same reign. The oath of office is as follows:—

"Ye shall swear, that as justice of the peace in the county of S., in all articles in the king's commission to you directed, you shall do equal right to the poor and to the rich, after your cunning, wit, and power, and after the laws and customs of the realm, and statutes thereof made; and ye shall not be of counsel of any quarrel hanging before you; and that ye hold your sessions after the form of the statutes thereof made; and the issues, fines, and amerciaments that shall happen to be made, and all forfeitures which shall fall before you, ye shall cause to be entered without any concealment (or embezzling), and truly send them to the king's exchequer. Ye shall not let for gift or other cause, but well and truly ye shall do your office of justice of the peace in that behalf; and that you take nothing for your office of justice of the peace to be done, but of the king, and fees accustomed, and costs limited by statute; and ye shall not direct, nor cause to be directed, any warrant (by you to be made) to the parties, but ye shall direct them to the bailiff of the said county, or other the king's officers or ministers, or other indifferent persons, to do execution thereof. So help you God."

Qualification of Justices.] The 18 Geo. 2. s. 1, after reciting, That whereas by many acts of Parliament of late years made, the power and authority of justices of the peace is greatly increased, whereby it is become of the utmost consequence to the commonweal to provide against persons of mean estate acting as such: it is enacted, that from and after the twenty-fifth day of March, one thousand seven hundred and forty-six, no person shall be capable of being a justice of the peace, for any county, riding, or division in England, or the principality of Wales, who shall not have either in law or equity, to and for his own use and benefit in possession, a freehold, copyhold, or customary estate for life, or for some greater estate, or an estate for some long term of years, determinable upon one or more life or lives, or for a certain term originally created for twenty-one years or more, in lands, tenements, or hereditaments, lying or being in England, or the principality of Wales, of the clear yearly value of one hundred pounds, over and above what will satisfy and discharge all incumbrances that affect the same, and over and above all rents and charges payable out of, or in respect of the same; or who shall not be seised of or entitled unto, in law or equity, to and for his own use and benefit, the immediate reversion or remainder of and in lands, tenements, or hereditaments, lying or being as aforesaid, which are leased for one, two, or three lives, or for any term of years determinable upon the death of one, two, or three lives upon reserved rents, and which are of the clear yearly value of three hundred pounds, and who shall not before the said twenty-fifth day of March, or before he takes upon himself to act as a justice of the peace after the said twenty-fifth day of March, at some general or quarter sessions for the county, riding, or division, for which he does or shall intend to act, first take and subscribe the oath following :—

Qualification Oath.] "I, A. B. do swear, that I truly and *bonâ fide* have such an estate in law or equity to and for my own use and benefit, consisting of [*specifying the nature of such estate, whether messuage, land, rent, tithe, office, benefice, or what else*], as doth qualify me to act as a justice of the peace for the county, riding, or division of , according to the true intent and meaning of an act of parliament made in the eighteenth year of the reign of his majesty king George the Second, intituled, '*An Act to amend and render more effectual an act passed in the fifth year of his present majesty's reign, intituled, "An act for the further qualification of justices of the peace;"*' and that the same [*except where it consists of an office, benefice, or ecclesiastical preferment, which it shall be sufficient to ascertain by their known and usual names*] is lying or being or issuing out of lands, tenements, or hereditaments being within the parish, township, or precinct of , or in the several parishes, townships, or precincts of , in the county of , or in the several counties of , [*as the case may be.*"]

Which oath so taken and subscribed as aforesaid, shall be kept by the clerk of the peace among the records of the sessions, who shall upon demand, deliver a true and attested copy thereof to any person paying two shillings for the same, which shall be admitted in evidence in any action, suit, or information to be brought upon this act. (s. 2.)

Unqualified person acting.] Any person who shall act as a justice of the peace for any county, &c. without having taken and subscribed the said oaths, or without being qualified according to the true intent and meaning of this act, shall for every such offence forfeit one hundred pounds, one moiety to the poor of the parish in which he most usually resides, and the other to the person who shall sue for the same, to be recovered with full costs by action of debt, bill, plaint, or information in any of his majesty's courts of record at Westminster, in which no essoign, protection, wager of law, or more than one imparlance shall be allowed; and in every such action, &c. the proof of his qualification shall lie on such person against whom the same is brought. (s. 3.)

Defendant to specify Lands.] If the defendant in any such action, &c. shall intend to insist upon any lands, &c., not contained in such oath as his qualification in part, or in the whole, at the time of the supposed offence wherewith he is charged, he shall, at or before the time of his pleading, deliver to the plaintiff, or informer or his attorney, a notice in writing, specifying such lands, &c., (other than those contained in the said oath), and the parish, or place, wherein the same are respectively situate, (offices and benefices excepted, which it shall be sufficient to ascertain by their known and usual names; and if the plaintiff or informer in any such action, &c., shall think fit thereupon not to proceed any further, he may, with the leave of the court, discontinue such action, suit, or information, on payment of such costs to the defendant as the court shall award. (s. 4.)

Lands omitted not allowed.] Upon the trial of any such action, &c., no lands, &c., which are not contained in such oath and notice as aforesaid, or one of them, shall be allowed to be insisted upon by the defendant as any part of his qualification. (s. 5.)

Lands incumbered.] Where the lands, &c., contained in the said oath or notice are, together with other lands, &c., belonging to such person, liable to any charges, rents, or incumbrances, that within the true intent and meaning of this act, the lands, &c., contained in the said oath or notice shall be deemed and taken to be liable and chargeable only so far as the other lands, tenements, and hereditaments so jointly charged, are not sufficient to pay, satisfy, or discharge the same. (s. 6.)

Qualification by Rent.] Where the qualification required by this act or any part thereof consists of rent, it shall be sufficient to specify in such oath or notice as aforesaid, so much of the lands, tenements, or hereditaments, out of which such rent is issuing, as shall be of sufficient value to answer such rent. (s. 7.)

Action discontinued.] In case the plaintiff or informer in any such action, suit, or information, shall discontinue the same otherwise than as aforesaid, or be nonsuit, or judgment be otherwise given against him, that then and in any of the said cases, the person against whom such action shall have been brought, shall recover treble costs. (s. 8.)

Only one penalty.] Only one penalty of one hundred pounds shall be recovered from the same person by virtue of this act, or of

5 Geo. 2. c. 18., for the same or any other offence committed by the same person before the bringing of the action, &c., upon which one penalty of one hundred pounds shall have been recovered, and due notice given to the defendant of the commencement of such action, &c., any thing in this or the same act to the contrary notwithstanding. (s. 9.)

Subsequent Action for prior Offence.] Where an action, &c., shall be brought, and due notice given thereof as aforesaid, no proceeding shall be had upon any subsequent action, &c., against the same person for any offence committed before the time of giving such notice as aforesaid; but the court, where such subsequent action, &c., shall be brought, may, upon the defendant's motion, stay proceedings upon every such subsequent action, &c., so as such first action, &c., be prosecuted without fraud and with effect, it being hereby declared, that no action, &c., which shall not be so prosecuted, shall be deemed or construed to be an action, suit, or information, within the intent and meaning of this act. (s. 10.)

Limitation of Actions.] Every action, &c., given by this or the said former act, shall be commenced within the space of six calendar months after the fact, upon which the same is grounded, shall have been committed. (s. 11.)

Places excepted.] This act shall not extend to any city or town being a county of itself, or to any other city, town, cinque port, or liberty, having justices of the peace within their respective limits and precincts by charter, commission, or otherwise, but that in every such city, town, liberty, and place, such persons may be capable to be justices of the peace, and in such manner only, as they might have been if this act had never been made. (s. 12.)

Persons excepted.] Nothing in this act or in stat. 5 Geo. 2. c. 18. contained shall extend to any peer, or to the lords or others of his majesty's privy council, or to the judges, the attorney or solicitor-general, the justices of great sessions for Chester, or Wales, within their respective jurisdictions, or to the eldest son or heir-apparent of any peer or lord of parliament, or of any person qualified to serve as a knight of a shire by stat. 9 Ann. c. 5., or the officers of the board of green cloth within the verge of his majesty's palaces, the commissioners and principal officers of the navy, or the two under secretaries in each of the offices of the principal secretary of state, or the secretary of Chelsea college, or any of the heads of colleges or halls in either of the two universities of Oxford and Cambridge, the vice-chancellor of either of the said universities, the mayor of the city of Oxford, or of the town of Cambridge, but they may be and act as justices of the peace, as fully and freely in all respects as heretofore they have lawfully used to execute the same. (ss. 13, 14, 15.)

Other Oaths, &c.] A justice of the peace must also, within six months, take the oaths of allegiance, supremacy, and abjuration, in one of the courts at Westminster, or at the general or quarter sessions, of the place where he shall be or reside, as other persons qualifying for offices. But the recent statute, the 10 Geo. 4. c. 7, for the relief of his majesty's Roman Catholic subjects, has substituted another oath in the place of those above named, to be taken by persons professing the Roman Catholic religion. And the sacramental test is repealed in all cases, and a declaration to be made in lieu thereof is provided by 9 Geo. 4. c. 17. (See *ante* p. 141.)

Act of Indemnity.] It is the practice to introduce an indemnity in some act of parliament every session, and to give further time to justices of the peace to take the oaths of allegiance, &c., provided they take the same within the time therein specified, and qualify according to stat. 18 Geo. 2. c. 20. And provided also, that the same shall not extend to any person against whom final judgment shall have been given; nor to exempt any such justice from such penalties who shall act without being duly qualified. (See 10 Geo. 4. c. 12.)

Becoming disqualified.] In an action of debt, brought upon the stat. 18 Geo. 2. c. 20, to recover the penalty for acting as a justice of the peace in the county of York, the defendant not being duly qualified; it appeared that the defendant had taken the benefit of an insolvent act in January, one thousand eight hundred and fourteen, subsequently to which time he had repeatedly acted as a magistrate without acquiring any new qualification. He had qualified originally in one thousand eight hundred and two. No notice of action had been given, according to the provisions of the 24 Geo. 2. c. 44, and Wood B. ruled that the defendant was not within the act, and therefore not entitled to notice. It was contended, that if the defendant could show that when he was discharged from prison, there was a fair probability that his estate would pay his debts, and leave a sufficient surplus to uphold the qualification of a magistrate, the action would not lie. Upon which Wood B. said, all the defendant's estate is now vested in the clerk of the peace; his legal and equitable rights are equally transferable to his creditors. We cannot take an account here, and declare a surplus in his favour. The defendant may ultimately be entitled to qualify; but at present he has not the title which the act of parliament requires, and the plaintiff had a verdict. (Wright v. Horton, Holt R. 458.)

Acts of unqualified Justice.] But the acts of a justice of the peace who has not duly qualified, are not absolutely void, and therefore persons seizing goods under a warrant of distress, signed by a justice who had not taken the oaths at the general sessions, nor delivered in his certificate as required, are not trespassers. And Abbott C. J. in delivering the judgment of the court, said, "It is obvious, that if the act of the justice issuing a warrant be invalid, on the ground of such an objection as the present, all persons who act in the execution of the warrant will act without an authority: a constable who arrests, and a gaoler who receives a felon, will each be a trespasser; resistance to them will be lawful, every thing done by either of them will be unlawful, and a constable, or persons aiding him, may, in some possible instance, become amenable even to a charge of murder, for acting under an authority which they reasonably considered themselves bound to obey, and of the invalidity whereof they are wholly ignorant. An exposition of these statutes, pregnant with so much inconvenience, ought not to be made if they will admit of any other reasonable construction. 'Acts of parliament,' says Lord Coke, 'are to be so construed, as no man that is innocent, or free from injury or wrong, be, by a literal construction, punished or endamaged.' We think these acts do most reasonably admit of another construction. We think the *restraining* clauses are only prohibitory upon the justice. By the particular act upon which this question has arisen, Mr. Dyson having been named in the commission, is declared to be a justice, and invested with power and authority as such. The proper effect, therefore, as it seems to us, of the third section, is only to make it unlawful in him to act as such; but not to make his acts invalid. Many persons acting as justices of the peace, in virtue of offices in corporations, have been ousted from their offices from some defect in their election or appointment; and although all acts properly corporate and official done by such persons are void, yet acts done by them as justices, or in a judicial character, have in no instance been thought invalid. This distinction is well known. The interest of the public at large requires that the acts done should be sustained: sufficient effect is given to the statutes by considering them as penal upon the person acting." (Margate P. C. v. Hannam, 3 Barn. & Ald. 266.)

Office how determinable.] By stat. 1 Ann. st. 1. c. 8. s. 2., "No patent or grant of any office or employment shall determine by the king's death or demise, but shall continue in force for six months after, unless in the mean time superseded, determined, or made void by the successor."

The king may also determine the commission at his pleasure,

and that either expressed, as by writ under the great seal, or by implication, by making a new commission, and leaving out the former justices' names. But until notice or publishing of the new commission, the acts of the former justices are good in law. (Dalt. c. 3.)

Officers in corporations.] But to mayors and chief officers in corporations, who have the authority of justices of the peace, or of conservators of the peace, by grant under the king's letters patent to them and their successors, the authority remaineth notwithstanding the king's death or demise. (Dalt. c. 3.)

SECTION II.—THEIR JURISDICTION.

Limits of their jurisdiction.] It is said, that recognizances and informations, voluntarily taken before justices in any place, are good. (2 Hawk. P. C. c. 8. s. 28.) And although it be generally true, that a justice of the peace has no jurisdiction over offences committed *out* of his county, yet there are cases, where the presence of an offender *within* his county, gives him authority to proceed against such offender.

Thus, it has been long settled, that if a man commit felony in the county of C., and goes into the county of W., a justice of the peace of the latter county may take the examinations there, commit him and bind over the witnesses to give evidence at the trial, and proceed as if the offence had been committed within his jurisdiction. (2 Hale, P. C. 51.)

And he hath a like authority with respect to a man coming into his county, after having committed a felony on the high seas; and if the offence be bailable before either one or more justices, the requisite number of justices may take a valid recognizance for the appearance of the person accused at the next session of oyer and terminer, &c., there to answer to such matters as shall be objected against him. (See 1 Chit. Crim. L. 94, 7 Geo. 4. c. 64.)

Justices, either of the county from which tenants fraudulently remove goods, or of that in which they are concealed, may convict the offenders in their respective counties. (Rex. v. Morgan, Cald. 156.)

May grant Warrants, &c., at their Dwellings.] By stat. 9 Geo. 1. c. 7. s. 3. " If any justice of the peace for any county shall happen to dwell in any city, or other precinct that is a county of itself, situate within the county at large, for which he shall be appointed justice of peace, although not within the same county, it shall and may be lawful for any such justice of peace to grant warrants, take examinations, and make orders for any matters which any one or more justice or justices of the peace may act in, at his own dwelling-house, although such dwelling-house be out of the county where he is authorized to act as a justice of peace, and in some city or other precinct adjoining, that is a county of itself, and that all such warrants, orders, and other act or acts of any justice of peace, and the act or acts of any constable, &c., in obedience to any such warrant or order, shall be as valid, good, and effectual in the law, although it happen to be out of the limits of the proper precinct or authority: provided that nothing in this act contained shall extend to give power to justices of the peace for the counties at large, to hold their general quarter sessions of the peace in the cities or towns which are counties of themselves, nor to empower justices of the peace, constables, &c., or any other peace-officers of the counties at large, to act or intermeddle in any matters or things arising within cities or towns which are counties of themselves, but that all such actings and doings shall be of the same force and effect in law, and none other, as if this act had never been made. (See also 28 Geo. 3. c. 49. s. 4.)

The 15 Geo. 2. c. 24, empowers justices of a liberty or corporation to commit offenders to the house of correction of the county, riding, or division in which such liberty or corporation is situate.

May enforce Rates, &c., though chargeable Themselves.] "It shall and may be lawful to and for all and every justice or justices of the peace for any county, riding, city, liberty, franchise borough, or town corporate within their respective jurisdictions, to make, do, and execute all acts, matters, or things appertaining to their office as justice or justices of the peace, so far as the same relates to the poor laws, vagrants, highways, or to any other laws concerning parochial taxes, levies, or rates, notwithstanding any such justice or justices of the peace is or are rated to or chargeable with the taxes, levies, or rates within any such parish, township, or place affected by any such act or acts of such justice or justices aforesaid." (16 Geo. 2. c. 18.)

But the statute is not to empower them to act in the determination of any appeal to the quarter sessions for any such county or riding from any order, matter, or thing relating to any such parish, township, or place where they are so charged, taxed," &c. (Ibid. s. 3.)

Warrant against Persons escaped.] By 24 Geo. 2. c. 55. s. 1. "In case any person against whom a warrant shall be issued, escape, reside, or be in any other county, riding, &c., out of the jurisdiction of the justice granting such warrant, any justice where such person resides or is, must, upon proof being made upon oath of the hand-writing of the justice granting such warrant, indorse his name on such warrant, which shall be a sufficient authority to the person or persons bringing such warrant, and to all other persons to whom such warrant was originally directed, to execute such warrant in such other county, riding, &c., out of the jurisdiction of the justice or justices granting such warrant as aforesaid; and such justice of such other county may, on the offender being brought before him, take bail, as in other cases, for his appearance," &c. (See Rex v. Kynaston, 1 East. 117.)

Escapes to Ireland or Scotland.] The 13 Geo. 3. c. 31, authorizes the arrest of any person, against whom a warrant has issued in Scotland, by a justice indorsing the same, under which the offender may be apprehended within the county, &c., in England where such indorsement is made, and carried to the county in Scotland where the offence was committed, if on the borders, and if not, then to such border county of Scotland as is nearest to the place where the offender is taken, there to be dealt with according to the Scottish law, and a like power is given in cases of offenders escaping from Ireland either into England or Scotland, by 44 Geo. 3. c. 92. Both these statutes have been amended by 45 Geo. 3. c. 92, which provides, that in case any person or persons shall be apprehended, in one of the said parts of the United Kingdom, for an offence which was committed, or charged to have been committed, in either of the other parts of the same, under any warrant indorsed in such manner as in that respect is provided by virtue of either of the said recited acts, such person or persons shall and may be taken before the judge or justice who indorsed the said warrant, or before some other justice or justices of the county or place where the same was indorsed, and in case the offence be bailable in law, may take bail according to the exigence of the said warrant.

The recognizance or bail-bond must be taken in duplicate; one to be given to the constable or other officer, who shall deliver, or cause to be delivered, such recognizance or bail-bond to the clerk of the crown, or clerk of the peace, or other proper officer for receiving the same, belonging to the court in which, by such recognizance or bail-bond, such offender or offenders shall be bound to appear, and the said judge or justice so taking bail as aforesaid, shall transmit the other of such duplicates to the court of exchequer, of such part of the United Kingdom in which such bail shall be taken, there to be kept of record: Provided always, that if such offence be not bailable, or such offender shall not give bail, the said judge or justice, before whom such offender shall be brought, shall remand him to the custody of the constable or other officer, who shall proceed to convey such offender into that part of the United Kingdom, wherein the offence was committed.

The 2d section of the act directs, that such judge or justice granting such warrant, shall, upon the face of such warrant, write the words "not bailable;" and in all cases in which such words shall not have been so written, it shall and may be lawful for the judge or justice or justices before whom any offender or offenders may be brought, under such warrant so indorsed, to admit such offender or offenders to bail.

Warrants acted upon in either Country.] "All warrants issued in England, Scotland, or Ireland, respectively, may and shall be indorsed and executed, and enforced and acted upon, in any part of the United Kingdom, in such and the like manner as is directed by the act of the thirteenth year of the reign of his present Majesty, in relation to warrants issued or granted in England and Scotland respectively, as fully and effectually, to all intents and purposes, as if all the provisions of the said act were in this act severally and separately repeated and re-enacted, and made part of this act, as to every part of the United Kingdom, and as to all justices of the peace, sheriffs' officers, constables, or other officer or officers of the peace in Ireland, as well as in England and Scotland respectively." (54 Geo. 3. c. 186. s. 2.)

Offences at Sea.] "It shall and may be lawful to and for any one or more of the commissioners for the time being, named or to be named in the commission of oyer and terminer for the trying of offences committed within the jurisdiction of the admiralty of England, and also to and for any one or more of the commissioners for the time being, named or to be named in any commission made or granted under or by virtue of the act of the forty-sixth year of king George the third, and also to and for any one or more of his Majesty's justices of the peace for the time being, for any county, riding, division, or place, in the United Kingdom, and they are hereby respectively authorized, empowered, and required, from time to time to take any information or informations of any witness or witnesses upon oath, which oath they and each of them are hereby respectively authorized to administer, touching any treason, piracy, felony, robbery, murder, conspiracy, or other offence, of what nature or kind soever, committed upon the sea, or in any haven, river, creek, or place, where the admiral or admirals hath or have power, authority, or jurisdiction; and thereupon, (if such commissioner or commissioners, justice or justices of the peace, shall see cause,) by any warrant or warrants under his or their hand and seal, or hands and seals, to cause the person or persons charged in such information or informations to be apprehended and committed to safe custody, to remain in such custody until discharged in due course of law, or until bailed, in cases in which bail may by law be taken." (7 Geo. 4. c. 38.)

Exclusive, or concurrent Jurisdiction.] "It has been adjudged, that a charter, granting jurisdiction to borough magistrates over a district not within the borough, does not exclude the county justices from having a concurrent jurisdiction, without express words in the charter; and though such charter contain words of reference to former charters, in which exclusive jurisdiction is given to the borough justices within the borough, and add, that they shall have jurisdiction within the new district *in tam amplo modo et formâ, &c.*, yet if there be in the latter charter a saving clause of the rights of the crown, and of all other persons, the borough magistrates have only a concurrent jurisdiction with the county justices." (Blankley v. Winstanley, 3 T. R. 279, 2 Hale 47.)

So, by charter, the mayor and some of the aldermen of London have jurisdiction in Southwark: but, as the charter contains no *non intromittant* clause as to the justices of the county of Surrey, the latter have a concurrent jurisdiction with the former. (Rex v. T. Sainsbury, 4 T. R. 451.)

Where two sets of magistrates have a concurrent jurisdiction, and one appoints a meeting to grant ale licences, their jurisdiction attaches so as to exclude the others from appointing a subsequent meeting; but they may all meet together on the first day. But if, after such appointment, the other set of magistrates meet on a subsequent day and grant other licences, their proceeding is illegal, and the subject of an indictment. (Rex v. Sainsbury, 4 T. R. 451.)

The justices of a borough had exclusive jurisdiction within the borough itself, but jurisdiction concurrent with that of the county justices, over certain places called the liberties of the borough: held, that for an offence committed within the liberties they might commit to the county gaol, and cause the prisoner to be brought before them for trial at the borough sessions. (Rex v. Musson, 6 Barn. & Cres. 74; 9 Dowl. & Ryl. 172; Rex v. Amos, 2 Barn. & Ald. 533; 15 Geo. 2. c. 24.)

By the 60 Geo. 3. and 1 Geo. 4. c. 14, justices have power within their respective limits, to commit any person duly charged before them, with any capital offence committed within such limits, to the gaol of the county, to be tried at the next sessions of oyer and terminer, or general gaol delivery for such county; and they may bind over parties and witnesses by recognizance to prosecute and give evidence, and must transmit such recognizance and depositions to the clerk of the crown, clerk of assize, or other proper officer. (s. 2.)

The expenses to which the county may be put shall be borne and paid by the said town or place within which such offence shall have been committed.

And by several statutes, the last of which amends the former ones, it is enacted, " that it shall be lawful for any justice acting for any county at large, or for any riding or division of a county in which there are several and distinct commissions of the peace, to act as justice *for such county* at large, riding, or division, in sessions or otherwise, *at any place* within any city, town, or other precinct, having *exclusive* jurisdiction, but not being a county of itself, and situate within, surrounded by, or adjoining to, any such county at large, riding, or division; such act and acts, matters and things, which shall be done, or which may heretofore have been done, by any such justice or justices of the peace for the said county at large, riding, or division, within such city, town, or other precinct, shall be as valid and effectual in the law as if the same had been done within the same county, riding, or division, to all intents and purposes whatsoever: Provided that nothing in this act contained shall give power to county justices, not being justices for such city, town, or other precinct, or any constable or other officer, to intermeddle in any matters arising within such city, town, or precinct, in any manner whatsoever." (1 & 2 Geo. 4. c. 63.)

SECTION III.—THEIR MINISTERIAL DUTIES.

The multifarious duties of justices of the peace may be divided into two parts; the first, consisting of such acts as they are required to perform in confirmation of, or to compel obedience to, the obligations imposed by some other authority, as in the case of warrants to levy distresses, &c.; to which may be added their inquisitorial functions in cases of alleged crime, which are afterwards to be submitted to a higher tribunal; and these may be classed under the denominations of their ministerial duties. The other division comprehends the power, reposed in them, of adjudicating in questions arising upon penal statutes, which they are directed to enforce; and upon charges of minor offences and the breaches of prohibitory enactments, which it is the policy of the law to restrain by summary punishments.

Their authority, in some cases, partakes of both qualities, but whether the instances are stated under the first division or the second, is not very material, where the duty assumes this twofold character. It is also to be observed, that the same rules and principles of conduct will be generally applicable in both; though where they have to exercise the province of determining upon the guilt of the accused, which usually belongs to a jury, and afterwards that of judge in the same case, more circumspection, and a nearer adaptation of their proceedings to the model afforded in the practice of the superior courts, is required.

Land-Tax Commissioners.] By the 45 Geo. 3. c. 48. s. 3, it is provided, that all persons who shall act as justices of the peace of or for any county, riding, shire, or stewardry in Great Britain, being duly qualified, may act as commissioners for the land tax, although not specially named in the act.

Turnpike Trustees.] And the 3 Geo. 4. c. 126. s. 61, enacts, that all his Majesty's justices of the peace for the time being, acting for the county or counties through which any turnpike road now does, or hereafter shall pass, shall be added to and joined with the trustees or commissioners for making, repairing, or maintaining every such turnpike road, and shall, on qualifying themselves as hereafter mentioned, (but this is dispensed with by 4 Geo. 4. c. 95,) have all the same powers and authorities, to all intents and purposes, as if the said justices had severally been named, or elected trustees or commissioners, in or under any act or acts of Parliament, under which such roads shall be made, repaired or maintained.

Quorum Justices.] The practice of nominating but few justices in the commission to be of the quorum, has declined in modern times, as it was found to produce inconvenience and delay, in those cases, where it was required, that a justice of the quorum should be present, and take part in the proceedings.

The inconvenience is further obviated by the 4 Geo. 4. c. 27, which recites, that whereas by the 7 Geo. 3. c. 21, it was enacted, that in all such cities, boroughs, towns corporate, franchises, and liberties as have only one justice of the peace of the quorum, that all acts, orders, adjudications, warrants, indentures of apprenticeship, or other instruments which shall be made, done, or executed by two or more justices of the peace within such cities, boroughs, towns corporate, franchises, and liberties, though neither of the said justices are of the quorum, shall be valid and effectual in law: and whereas it is expedient, that the provisions of the said act should be extended to such cities, and other jurisdictions, as have two, or any other limited number, of justices of the quorum qualified to act within the same:

be it therefore enacted, That from and after the passing of this act, in all cases where the number of justices of the peace for any city, borough, town corporate, franchise, liberty, or other local jurisdiction, is limited, and any one, two, or more of such justices only are of the quorum, all acts, orders, adjudications, warrants, indentures of apprenticeship, or other instruments which shall be made, done, or executed either in or out of the general quarter-sessions or petty sessions, or any adjournment thereof, by virtue of any charter or grant, or by virtue of any act of Parliament made or to be made, by any two or more justices of the peace acting within the same, though neither of the said justices be of the quorum, shall be valid in law, to all intents and purposes, as if the said justices had been of the quorum; any grant, charter, law, or custom to the contrary thereof in anywise notwithstanding. (4 Geo. 4. c. 27.)

When should not Act.] It is obvious, for the sake of justice and the dignity of their office, that magistrates ought not to execute their functions in their own case. Thus, where a justice of the peace was also surveyor of the highway, and a matter which concerned his office coming in question at the sessions, he joined in making the order, and his name was put in the caption, the order was quashed. So it was determined that on an appeal to the sessions against an order of removal, those justices who are rated to the relief of the poor in either of the contending parishes, have not a right to vote. (Rex v. Yarpole, 4 T. R. 71.) And in a still later case it was held, that if he be a rated inhabitant of the parish, he cannot vote either on the determination of an appeal against the allowance of overseers' accounts, or on a question as to granting a case for the opinion of the Court of King's Bench. And Abbott, C. J., said, "We think it the safer course to hold that magistrates should not interfere in cases where they are interested." (Rex v. Gudridge, 5 Barn. & Cres. 459, 8 Dowl. & Ryl. 217.) But if a justice be assaulted or grossly insulted in his office, and no other magistrate be present, it seems he may commit the offender till he find sureties. (Dalt. c. 173. Rex v. Revel, 1 Stra. 420.)

Summons, when proper.] In all legal proceedings, the person complained of ought to have notice of the charge laid against him, and to have an opportunity of being heard in his own defence. Consequently, where a person is accused before justices, they ought to summon the party to appear, or issue their warrant to bring him before them. The manner of conveying the parties, is sometimes directed by the acts of Parliament, creating the respective offences, which therefore ought to be pursued, accordingly. In other cases, where it is left discretionary in the justice, it seemeth most agreeable to the mildness of our laws, to put the party to no more inconvenience than needs must; and therefore, where the case will bear it, a summons seems more apposite than a compulsory process. If a justice proceed against a person without summoning him, so that he may be heard, in a case of summary conviction, it would be a misdemeanour; for which an information would be granted, upon such conviction being removed before the court. (Rex v. Allington, 2 Stra. 678; Rex v. Dyer, 1 Salk. 181.)

In the summons it is usual, and upon many accounts convenient, to fix a day and hour for the appearance of the party; but if he attends at the time, and the justice is not there, he is not to go away, but must wait during the remainder of the day; for many things may happen to hinder the justice's immediate attendance.

It has been made a question in some cases, whether the service of the summons must be *personal?* It seems, in general, necessary that it should be so, unless where personal service is dispensed with by the statute. (5 Burn's J. 295.)

Warrant when proper.] In cases of sureties of the peace, larceny, and other felonies, and generally where the proceeding is in the name of the king, and also in cases between party and party, where the body of the offender is liable, a warrant is the regular process.

Where a statute gives a justice jurisdiction over an offence, it impliedly gives him power to apprehend any person charged with such offence. A magistrate may therefore issue his warrant, to apprehend a person charged with an offence under the malicious trespass act, (1 Geo. 4. c. 56,) especially after the offender had neglected a summons. (Bane v. Methuen, 2 Bing. 63, 9 Moore 161.)

It was formerly doubted, whether one justice could legally make out a warrant, for an offence against a penal statute, or other misdemeanour cognizable only by a sessions of two or more justices; on the ground, that as the offence could only be heard and determined by *two,* those only who have jurisdiction over a cause, can award proceedings concerning it; yet the long, constant, and uncontrolled practice seems to have altered the law in this respect, and to have given justices an authority in relation to such arrests, not now to be disputed. (2 Hawk. P. C. c. 13. s. 16.) And by the 3 Geo. 4. c. 23. s. 2, one justice, &c., may receive original information, &c., where two or more justices, &c., are empowered to hear and determine.

Warrant against Libeller.] A justice of peace has authority to issue his warrant, for the arrest of a party charged with having published a libel; and upon the neglect of the party so arrested to find sureties, may commit him to prison, there to remain till he be delivered by due course of law. (Butt v. Conant, 1 Brod. & Bing. 548, 4 Moore, 195.)

Power to administer Oaths.] Stat. 15 Geo. 3. c. 39. An act to empower justices of the peace to administer oaths, where any penalty is to be levied, or distress to be made, in pursuance of any act of Parliament wherein the same is not expressly directed.—" Whereas it is frequently necessary for justices of the peace to administer oaths or affirmations where penalties are to be levied or distresses to be made in pursuance of acts of Parliament, which they have no power to administer unless authorized so to do by such acts respectively; be it therefore enacted, that in all cases where any penalty is directed to be levied or distress to be made by any act of Parliament now in force or hereafter to be made, it shall and may be lawful for any justice or justices acting under the authority of such acts respectively, and he and they is and are hereby authorized and empowered to administer an oath or oaths, affirmation or affirmations, to any person or persons for the purpose of levying such penalties or making such distresses respectively."

There hath been much doubt how far a justice of the peace has power to administer an oath, unless it is expressly given by the statute he has to put in force. (See 3 Burn's Justice, 583.) And the aforesaid act of 15 G. 3. c. 39, being a parliamentary declaration in *one instance*, so far as it goes, decides against a general power of the justices in this respect. It certainly appears very desirable that some legislative declaration should be made upon the subject.

Voluntary Affidavits.] The practice, which still prevails to some extent, of administering oaths in cases where justices of the peace have no jurisdiction, ought not to be followed. It is much to be questioned how far any magistrate is justifiable in taking a *voluntary affidavit* in any extra-judicial matter; since it is more than possible, that by such idle oaths, a man may frequently in *foro conscientiæ* incur the guilt, and at the same time evade, the temporal penalties of perjury. (4 Bla. Com. 137.)

Lord Coke says, " Oaths that have no warrant by law, are rather *nova tormenta, quam sacramenta,* and it is a high contempt to minister an oath without warrant of law, to be punished by fine and imprisonment. (3 Inst. 165.) And the Court of King's Bench has often reprehended the taking of voluntary affidavits, by justices of the peace in extra-judicial matters.

Taking Depositions.] The depositions are of course written down by the magistrate's clerk, at the time of the examination or inquiry into the matter of complaint; and it is, perhaps, impossible to narrate the facts in a proper and intelligible form, *precisely* in the language of the party making the deposition. But it is the duty of the magistrate to see that this is done as nearly as can be conveniently. In a case under the malicious trespass act, the words of the act of Parliament, (7 & 8 Geo. 4. c. 30,) describing the offence, were imported into the deposition of the witness; upon which Tindal, C. J., said, (the case coming before the court upon motion for a new trial, of an action of trespass and false imprisonment,) "Undoubtedly it was not correct to take the depositions in the precise words of the act, because such could not have been the language of the witnesses; but that alone will not make the defendants' conduct malicious." Park, J., added, "I reprobate the framing depositions in the words of acts of Parliament;" and Burrough, J., observed, "The depositions ought not to have been taken in the terms of the act of Parliament. That is not the language of witnesses." (Mills v. Collett, 6 Bing. 92.)

Commit for Re-examination.] Nothing is more common than for magistrates, upon proof that a crime has been committed, and the suspected offender is apprehended and brought before them for examination, to send him to prison till further evidence can be collected, or it is made to appear that he cannot justly be required to answer the charge, before a higher tribunal. It is obvious that this power may, in its exercise, work great and unmerited hardship, and is liable to be abused either by the negligence, or the improper motives of those to whom it is confided. It is not, however, left entirely without limit or control. In the recent case of Davis v. Capper, determined in Michaelmas term, 1829, it was declared by the Court of King's Bench, after much discussion and consideration, that magistrates can only commit a party for further examination, for a *reasonable time;* and in an action against a magistrate, founded on such an imprisonment, it is a question for the jury to determine, what is a reasonable time, under all the circumstances; and that if the commitment, though in form for re-examination, be in fact to obtain an admission from the prisoner of a particular fact in dispute, an action of trespass and false imprisonment may be supported against him (Davis v. Capper, MSS. E. T. 1829, 9 Barn. & Cres., 3 Man. & Ryl. See "Illegal Commitments," *post* 319.)

Taking Bail in Felony.] The law on this subject has been much improved by the 7 Geo. 4. c. 64. which,—reciting that the technical strictness of criminal proceedings might in many instances be relaxed so as to ensure the punishment of the guilty without depriving the accused of any just means of defence, and the administration of justice in England might in other respects be rendered more effectual,—enacts, that where any person shall be taken on a charge of felony, or suspicion of felony, before one or more justice or justices of the peace, and the charge shall be supported by positive and credible evidence of the fact, or by such evidence as if not explained or contradicted shall, in the opinion of the justice or justices, raise a strong presumption of the guilt of the person charged, such person shall be committed to prison by such justice or justices, in the manner hereinafter mentioned; but if there shall be only one justice present, and the whole evidence given before him, shall be such as neither to raise a strong presumption of guilt, nor to warrant the dismissal of the charge, such justice shall order the person charged to be detained in custody, until he or she shall be taken before two justices at the least; and where any person so taken, or any person in the first instance taken before two justices of the peace, shall be charged with felony, or on suspicion of felony, and the evidence given in support of the charge shall, in their opinion, not be such as to raise a strong presumption of the guilt of the person charged, and to require his or her committal, or such evidence shall be adduced, on behalf of the person charged, as shall in their opinion weaken the presumption of his or her guilt, but there shall, notwithstanding, appear to them in either of such cases, to be sufficient ground for judicial inquiry into his or her guilt, the person charged shall be admitted to bail by such two justices, in the manner hereinafter mentioned : provided always, that nothing herein contained shall be construed to require any such justice or justices to hear evidence, on behalf of any person so charged as aforesaid, unless it shall appear to him or them to be meet and conducive to the ends of justice to hear the same.

Must certify the Bailment.] That the two justices of the peace before they shall admit to bail, and the justice or justices before he or they shall commit to prison, any person arrested for felony, or on suspicion of felony, shall take the examination of such person, and the information upon oath of those who shall know the facts and circumstances of the case, and shall put the same, or as much thereof as shall be material, into writing, and the two justices shall certify such bailment in writing; and every such justice shall have authority, to bind by recognizance all such persons as know, or declare any thing material touching any such felony, or suspicion of felony, to appear at the next court of oyer and terminer, or gaol-delivery, or superior criminal court of a county palatine or great sessions, or sessions of the peace, at which the trial thereof is intended to be, then and there to prosecute or give evidence against the party accused; and such justices and justice respectively shall subscribe all such examinations, informations, bailments, and recognizances, and deliver or cause the same to be delivered to the proper officer of the court, in which the trial is to be, before or at the opening of the court. (s. 2.)

Bail in Misdemeanors.] That every justice of the peace before whom any person shall be taken on a charge of misdemeanor, or suspicion thereof, shall take the examination of the person charged, and the information upon oath of those who shall know the facts and circumstances of the case, and shall put the same, or as much thereof as shall be material, into writing before he shall commit to prison or require bail from the person so charged, and in every case of bailment shall certify the bailment in writing, and shall have authority to bind all persons by recognizance to appear to prosecute or give evidence against the party accused, in like manner as in cases of felony, and shall subscribe all examinations, informations, bailments, and recognizances, and deliver or cause the same to be delivered to the proper officer of the court in which the trial is to be, before or at the opening of the court, in like manner as in cases of felony. (s. 3.)

Justices offending herein.] If any justice shall offend in any thing contrary to the true intent and meaning of these provisions, the court to whose officer any such examination, information, evidence, bailment, recognizance, or inquisition, ought to have been delivered, shall, upon examination and proof of the offence, in a summary manner, set such fine upon every such justice as the court shall think meet. (s. 5.)

All these provisions relating to justices shall apply to the justices, (and coroners, s. 4.) not only of counties at large, but also of all other jurisdictions. (s. 6.)

SECTION IV.—THEIR JUDICIAL DUTIES.

Nature of their Judicial Authority.] The judicial authority of magistrates is derived partly from their commission, but chiefly from acts of Parliament. The proceedings before them, in some instances, assume the character of an inquiry before a civil tribunal; as where they have to adjudicate in the disputes between master and servant, &c., or to enforce the payment of rates, fines, penalties, &c. In other cases they act as criminal judges, either with summary power to determine the guilt or innocence of the accused, by their own impressions of the evidence, and to punish the offender; or in the graver offences within their jurisdiction, by the assistance of a jury in the court of quarter sessions.

It is laid down, that where an act of Parliament gives power to two justices finally to hear and determine any offence, or when they are to do any other *judicial* act, as making an order of bastardy, (Billings v. Prinn, 2 Bla. Rep. 1017,) adjudging the settlement of a pauper, (R. v. Coln. St. Aldwin's, Burr. S. C. 136), appointing overseers of the poor, (R. v. Forrest, 3 T. R. 38), allowing the indenture of a parish apprentice, (R. v. Hamstall Ridware, 3 T. R. 380), they should be together to hear the evidence, and consult together. And where a special authority is given to justices out of sessions, it ought to appear in their orders that such authority was exactly pursued. (Chittinston v. Penhurst, 2 Salk. 475; Rex. v. York, 5 Burr. 2686.)

How far Judges of Record.] Justices of the peace are judges of record when made so by act of Parliament, and in matters comprehended within their commission (Dalt. c. 2); and therefore a record or memorial made by a justice of the peace, of things done before him judicially, in the execution of his office, shall be of such credit, that it shall not be gainsaid. (Lamb. 63, Basten v. Carew, 3 Barn. & Cres. 653; 5 Dowl. & Ryl. 558.)

In all cases where justices may hear and determine out of sessions (viz. on their own view, or confession, or oath of witnesses), the justices ought to make a record, in writing, under their hands, of all the matters and proofs. (Dalt. c. 115.)

To estreat Fines.] If upon a conviction the offender is to be fined to the king, then the justices are to estreat such fine, and to send the estreat into the Exchequer, whereby the barons of the Exchequer may cause the said fine or forfeiture to be levied, for the king's use. (Dalt. c. 115. And see stat. 3 Geo. 4. c. 46, post 307.)

And in all cases of convictions, the justices should return the convictions to the next sessions. (See stat. 7 Geo. 4. c. 64; 7 and 8 Geo. 4. c. 29, 30.)

Assuming Jurisdiction.] Although in many instances, if the proceedings before magistrates, when returned into the Court of King's Bench, are *prima facie* correct and legal, the court will not inquire into the facts, yet magistrates cannot *make facts* by their determination, in order to give to themselves jurisdiction, contrary to the truth of the case. Therefore, if an order of sessions state as a fact, that a *new* road has been set out in lieu of an old one, which has been stopped up, when in truth that which is so called new, is merely an old one widened in different parts, the termini remaining the same, this may be shown in contradiction to such order. (Welsh v. Nash, 8 East. 403.) So the calling a party to a contract to perform certain work, *a labourer* cannot give a magistrate jurisdiction over such party, by virtue of the acts relating to masters and servants. (Lancaster

v. Greaves, MSS. E. T. 1828; see "Disputes of Masters and Servants," post 301.)

In malicious Injuries.] In a recent case it was contended in argument, that a magistrate has no power, under the 7 and 8 Geo. 4. c. 30, for the summary punishment of malicious injuries, to convict a person who cuts down a tree, upon premises in his own occupation; upon which Tindal, C. J. said, "I cannot accede to the proposition, that the circumstance of the party's being the occupier of the premises on which the tree is cut, necessarily takes a case out of the statute. Suppose the tree excepted in a lease, the tenant would be a trespasser; and if liable in trespass, I am not prepared to say he might not be liable criminally." And the court held unanimously, that a justice convicting a person charged, under such circumstances, with such an offence, is not liable to an action, though he should be mistaken in the law, he having jurisdiction over the matter of complaint, and no improper motive being found against him. (Mills v. Collett, 6 Bing. 85; Davis v. Russell, 5 Bing. 354.)

Jurisdiction over Smugglers.] By 6 Geo. 4. c. 108. s. 3. If any vessel therein described shall be found on the high seas, within 100 leagues of any part of the coasts of the United Kingdom, or shall be discovered to have been within the said distance, having on board the goods therein specified, the goods and the vessel shall be forfeited. By s. 49, every person who shall be found or discovered to have been on board any vessel liable to forfeiture under that act, for being found or discovered to have been within any of the distances or places mentioned in the act from the United Kingdom, shall forfeit £100., and may be detained and taken before two justices, to be dealt with as thereinafter mentioned. By s. 74, any offence within the act shall, for the purpose of prosecution, be taken to have been committed, and the penalties incurred at the *place on land* in the United Kingdom into which the person committing such offence, or incurring such penalty, *shall be taken, brought, on carried;* and in case such place or land is situate within any city, &c., the justices of the peace for the city, &c., as well as those for the county within which such city is situate, shall have jurisdiction to try all offences committed upon the high seas against the act. A vessel, liable to forfeiture under this act, was first seen on the high seas, making towards the harbour, but was not seized till she had arrived in a part of the river Orwell, where the justices of Ipswich had jurisdiction. A person found on board the vessel was taken to Harwich, and prosecuted before two justices of that place, who convicted him in a penalty of £100 for having been *found on the high seas* on board a vessel liable to forfeiture: it was held, that the justices of Harwich, being justices at the first place on land to which the party was carried, had jurisdiction to try the offence. (In re Nunn, 8 Barn. & Cress. 644.)

Proceedings in Convictions.] The power of justices to convict is given by the particular statutes which describe the offences, and affix the penalties or other punishment. The statutes are very numerous, and comprehend various infractions of the laws relating to the preservation of the game, to matters of excise and customs, highways, rates, vagrancy, assaults, reciprocal obligations of masters and servants, malicious trespasses, &c. &c. In all cases the parties accused may be either summoned or brought before the magistrates by warrant, according to the nature of the case, (see *ante*, p. 290), whose proceedings will be the more safe and unexceptionable, the nearer they are assimilated to the practice of the superior courts.

Proceedings on Appearance.] It is obviously the duty of the justice to take the examination of the witnesses formally in writing; for since the passing of the 3 Geo. 4. c. 23, which gives a general form of conviction (see post 304,) the magistrate is bound to set out the evidence on the record of conviction, as nearly as possible in the words used by the witnesses; and if he neglects so to do, a mandamus lies to enforce his compliance with the requisites of that statute. (In re Rix, 4 Dowl. & Ryl. 352; R. v. Marsh, Id. 260.) In a recent case, upon it being suggested by counsel that it was not usual for justices to take down the evidence of the witnesses in a formal manner, the court said it was the duty of the justices to take minutes of the evidence of the witnesses, in order that if called upon they should be enabled to set forth the evidence with accuracy. (R. v. Warnford, 5 Id. 489.)

When Defendant Absent.] If due formality be requisite in the proceedings before justices when the defendant is actually present, *a fortiori*, it ought to be observed in his absence. The justice then sitting in his judicial capacity, is bound to take care that the case is duly and properly made out. Ignorance, incapacity, or other circumstances may be the cause of a defendant's non-appearance, and in such case reason and justice require that all matters of form, as well as substance, should be strictly observed. (Paley on Convictions, by Dowling, 26.)

Defending by Counsel or Attorney.] An opinion has obtained rather generally, that justices may at their discretion exclude whatever persons they please from their presence, in the course of their summary proceedings. Upon due attention, however, to the marked distinction between the ministerial and judicial duties of magistrates, the groundlessness of such an opinion seems to be apparent. It has, indeed, been intimated by Mr. Justice Bayley; (R. v. The J. J. Staffordshire, 1 Chitty's Rep. 217,) "that an attorney has no right to be present, assisting a defendant charged with an information on the game laws." But it is due to that learned judge to observe, that the *dictum* imputed to him was perfectly *obitur*, and made *alio intuitu*. Indeed, so little is this point to be considered as settled by R. v. The J. J. of Staffordshire, that when that case was cited on the argument in Cox v. Coleridge, 2 Dowl. & Ryl. 113, 1 Barn. & Cres. 37, as an authority to show that in proceedings under penal statutes an attorney has no right to be present in the justice's room, Mr. Justice Bayley himself immediately interposed and said, "That case is not to be considered as the solemn decision of the court. The opinion there expressed upon this point was merely the *obitur dictum* of a single judge, to which I pay no respect;" and the lord chief justice added, with reference to the same point, "An observation thrown out by a judge merely in the course of argument is not to be considered as conclusive of the case, and ought not to be urged as a solemn decision." And Mr. Justice Bayley, in delivering his judgment in the principal case, again adverts to what he is reported to have said in R. v. the J. J. of Staffordshire, and observes, "This (Cox v. Coleridge,) is not a question upon a summary conviction, and not any question where the decision of the magistrates will be conclusive against the party; and whenever a question of that kind shall arise, I hope I shall not be bound conclusively by any *obitur dictum* which may have fallen from me in R. v. the J. J. Staffordshire. Whenever that point shall be distinctly raised, my mind shall be open upon it, and I shall be ready to hear it discussed on the one side and the other, and deliver my opinion upon deliberate consideration."

If in his ministerial capacity, a justice is taking examinations upon a charge of felony, it may be essential to the ends of public justice, that the examination should be private, and not interrupted by the interference of any person on the part of the prisoner. This point was certainly determined in Cox v. Coleridge, where it was held, that an attorney retained to attend a prisoner charged with felony, and give advice and assistance, might be forcibly turned out of the justice-room, and excluded during the investigation of the case. In R. v. Borron, 3 Barn. & Ald. 432, it was also held, that in the investigation of a charge of felony before a magistrate, an attorney is only as a matter of courtesy permitted, but has no right to be present. These cases determine that the justices have a discretion to exercise upon the subject; but in practice, counsel and attornies are frequently permitted to be present, to advise and protect the interests of prisoners; and it is consistent with the spirit of our laws that it should be so, except where paramount considerations of public policy dictate the opposite course. On the same principle, it has been held unlawful to publish in a newspaper the *ex-parte* proceedings before justices. (R. v. Fisher, 2 Camp. 563; Duncan v. Thwaites, 3 Barn. & Cres. 556; 5 Dowl. & Ryl. 447.) But these authorities are wholly inapplicable when a magistrate is acting *judicially;* the accused *must then* make his defence, as the magistrate has to decide upon his guilt, and award the punishment; and there is no principle of reason or justice which forbids him the advantage of the same facilities and assistance, which would be his indisputable right before a higher tribunal. In the language of Lord Kenyon in R. v. Stone, 1 East, 469, " Justice requires that he should be duly summoned and *fully heard.*" But this full hearing is not to be limited to the personal hearing of the party accused: it must be understood to comprehend a hearing by counsel or attorney, who, by his skill in the law, is competent to afford him such complete defence as the law permits.

In courts of justice in general, a defendant, upon a charge of any offence not amounting to felony, has a right to appear and *defend* by attorney. (Bac. Ab. Attorney. B.;) and it has been adjudged, that a defendant may be convicted in his absence, and upon an appearance by an attorney appointed by him to defend him. (R. v. Simpson, 1 Str. 44.) Upon the validity of this conviction being questioned, in consequence of the non-appearance of the defendant in person, the court said, " We think that it is certainly good, for the offender may entrust his defence to another, and the justice cannot enforce him to appear in person." If in the superior courts, and even at quarter sessions, a defendant has a right to the benefit of legal advice and assistance *a multo fortiori,* he is entitled to such advice before the justices, when they are judges both of law and fact, and have not the assistance of a jury in arriving at a sound and satisfactory conclusion. (See Basten v. Carew, 3 Barn. & Cres. 649; 5 Dowl. & Ryl. 558; 2 Bla. Rep. 1146; Paley on Convictions, by Dowling, 27.)

Form of Conviction.] Where an act of Parliament gives the form of conviction for the offence to which the act relates, that form must be followed; and it has been said, that a warrant drawn up in any other form is illegal; and that the justice, and those acting under him, are trespassers. (Goss v. Jackson, 3 Esp. R. 198.)

Drawing up Conviction.] Where a criminal information was moved for against a magistrate, for returning to a writ of *certiorari* a conviction of a party, in another and more formal shape than that in which it was originally drawn up, and of which a copy had been delivered to the party convicted, by the magistrate's clerk—Lord Kenyon observed, that it was the constant practice for magistrates to take minutes of their proceedings, without attending to the precise form of them at the time when they pronounced their judgment, to serve as memoranda for them to draw up a more formal statement of them afterwards, to be returned to the sessions; and that it was by no means unusual to draw up the conviction, in point of form, after the penalty had been levied; nor was there any legal objection to this method, provided the facts warranted them in stating what they did: this is not only legal but laudable. (R. v. Baker, 1 East, 186.)

Disputes between Master and Servant.] There are a great many statutes, referring the quarrels, and disputed rights, between masters and servants, to the summary determination of magistrates. It behoves them to ascertain, in all such cases, by the particular statute itself, whether the legislature has confided this power to them or not, because, if they assume and exercise an authority not warranted by the statute, they render themselves liable to an action.

General Statutes as to Labourers, &c.] The acts of a *general* nature, under this title, are 20 Geo. 2. c. 19, for adjusting, and for the more easy recovery of wages of servants, handicraftsmen, and labourers; and the regulation of such servants and apprentices as therein expressed and provided:—the 27 Geo. 2. c. 6, extending the provisions of the former act to Devon and Cornwall, which places were before excepted:—the 31 Geo. 2. c. 11. s. 3, extending the provisions to *all servants* in husbandry, though hired for less than a year:—the 6th Geo. 3. c. 25, authorizing justices to grant warrants against, and to commit, subject to appeal, artificers, handicraftsmen, colliers, potters, labourers, &c. to the house of correction for three months, who absent themselves from the service before they have completed the term of their contracts, or for any other misdemeanor:—the 58 Geo. 3. c. 51, which authorizes masters to pay their workmen, labourers, &c. in local, or bank of England *notes;* if they consent to be so paid; so far altering the previous enactments, (12 Geo. I. c. 34; 22 Geo. 2. c. 27; 57 Geo. 3. c. 22,) which forbade the payment in any other way than in the lawful *coin* or money of the realm, in order to suppress the practice of masters paying their workmen, &c. in goods, or by truck, under penalties to be recovered before justices of the peace:—the 4 Geo. 4. c. 34, for enlarging the powers of justices in such matters; and authorizing them to hear complaints against servants, &c. made by stewards or *agents* on behalf of their principals, or against bailiffs, managers, agents, &c., where masters reside at a distance, or are absent, and to abate wages, or discharge the servant; and to order payment of wages to apprentices; and to distrain in case of refusal, &c.:—the 5 Geo. 4. c. 96, for consolidating the laws relative to the arbitration of disputes between masters and *workmen* relative to wages, hours of work, delays in finishing the work, badness of materials, construction of contracts, &c. &c. The act provides, that the complaints by workmen as to bad materials, shall be made within three weeks of his receiving the same; and all other complaints, within six days after the cause thereof arises; upon which the justices may decide, if the parties so agree; or referees may be appointed as therein provided.

Servants, &c. within the Acts.] Although the 20 Geo. 2. c. 19, has been construed to extend to every description of *labourers*, (Lowther v. Earl Radnor, 8 East, 113;) yet these acts do not extend to *menial* or *domestic* servants, (R. v. Hullcott, 6 T. R. 583,) nor to a person employed by an attorney to keep possession of goods seized under a *fieri facias*, (Branwell v. Penneck, 7 Barn. & Cres. 536; 1 Man. & Ryl. 409;) and consequently, magistrates have no jurisdiction over them. And the 20 Geo. 2, seems only to extend to those labourers with reference to whom the justices had power to make a rate of wages, before the passing of that statute. (Id. See Wilson v. Weller, 1 Brod. & Bing. 57.)

The relation of master and servant must subsist between the parties, in order to give the magistrate jurisdiction under these acts. (Hardy v. Ryle, Lancaster v. Greaves, *post.*) In Lancaster v. Greaves, 24 April, 1828, the court held, that the 4 Geo. 4. c. 34, as to *labourers* and *servants*, does not apply to a person who has entered into a written contract to do certain work on a road, within a certain time, for a certain sum, he not being a servant working for *wages;* and further that a magistrate could not commit for punishment; and *also* discharge from service, as he is only authorized to discharge from service in *lieu* of the punishment. (Chitty's Statutes, 874.)

To bring a person within the jurisdiction of a magistrate, under the 4th section of this latter act, he must have contracted to serve under a written contract, or must have actually entered the complainant's service before the time of the complaint; and in such a manner as will create the relation of master and servant: therefore, a silk-weaver, who had agreed to work up at his own house certain materials for a master manufacturer, was held to have been improperly convicted under the above statute. (Hardy v. Ryle, T. T., 1829. MSS.; 9 Barn. & Cres.; 3 Man. & Ryl.)

Expenses in Cases of Riot.] The 41 Geo. 3. c. 78. s. 2, authorizes two justices to make an order of allowance to high constables, for extraordinary expenses incurred by them in case of riot, such order to be afterwards submitted, on oath of such constables, to the next general quarter sessions to be allowed wholly or in part, who may direct the treasurer of the county, city, division, &c. to pay the same. Where the high constable of a borough, by direction of the justices, employed and paid a number of special constables to suppress riots at an election; and the ordinary constables were also constantly employed by him during the same period, in endeavouring to keep the peace, for which service he made them a compensation, it was held, that the justices were warranted in considering the monies so expended as "extraordinary expenses incurred by the high constable in case of riot," within the meaning of the above statute; and that the sessions were right in making an order upon the treasurer to re-imburse him those expenses. (R. v. Justices of Leicester, 7 Barn. & Cres. 6.)

Fining Officers, &c.] It shall be lawful for any two or more justices assembled at any special or petty sessions, upon complaint made upon oath before them of any neglect of duty, or disobedience of any lawful warrant or order of any justice or justices of the peace, by any constable, overseer of the poor, or other peace or parish officer, (such constable, overseer, or other officer having been duly summoned to appear and answer such charge or complaint,) to impose upon conviction any reasonable fine or fines not exceeding the sum of forty shillings, upon such constable, overseer, or other officer, and by warrant under the hands and seals of any two or more of such justices assembled at any such special or petty sessions as aforesaid, to direct such fine or fines, if not paid, to be levied by distress and sale of the goods of the person so offending, rendering the overplus (if any), after deducting the fine and the charges of such distress and sale to such offender; and such fine shall be applied and disposed of for the relief of the poor of the parish, or place where the offender resides, at the discretion of the justices imposing the same; and if any person shall be aggrieved by any such proceeding, he may appeal to the next general or quarter sessions of the peace, upon giving ten days' notice; and for want of such distress, such person shall be committed to the house of correction for not exceeding ten days. (33 Geo. 3. c. 55. s. 1.)

Justices out of Session may award Costs.] Where any complaint shall be made before any justice of the peace for any county, city, or liberty, and any warrant or summons shall issue in consequence of such complaint, that then it shall be lawful for any justice or justices of the peace, who shall have heard and determined the said complaint, to award such costs to be paid by either of the parties, and in manner and form as to him or them shall seem fit, to the party injured; and in case any person so ordered to pay such money as aforesaid, shall not forthwith pay or give security for the same, it shall be lawful for the said justice or justices, by warrant under hand and seal, to levy the said sum by distress and sale of the goods and chattels of such person so refusing or neglecting; and where goods and chattels of such person cannot be found, to commit such person to the house of correction for the county or liberty wherein such person shall reside, there to be kept to hard labour for not exceeding one month, nor less than ten days, or until such money, together with the expenses attending the commitment of such person to such house of correction, be first paid. (18 Geo. 3. c. 19.)

Costs out of Penalty.] Provided, that upon the conviction upon any penal statute, where the penalty or penalties shall amount to or exceed the sum of five pounds, the said costs shall be deducted according to such justice's discretion, out of the penalty or penalties, so that the deduction do not exceed one-fifth of the said penalty or penalties; and the remainder of the said penalty or penalties shall be paid to, or divided among, the person or persons who would have been entitled to the whole of the penalty or penalties in case this act had not been made. (Ibid. s. 2.)

General Form of Conviction.] The 3 Geo. 4. c. 23, provides, that in all cases wherein a conviction shall have taken place, and no particular form for the record thereof hath been directed, justices, deputy-lieutenants, or other persons, duly authorized to proceed summarily therein, and before whom the offender or offenders shall have been convicted, shall and may cause the record of such conviction to be drawn up in the manner and form following, or in any words to the same effect, *mutatis mutandis;* (that is to say,)

County (or as the case may be) of | Be it remembered, that on the day of in the year of our Lord at in the county of A. B. of in the county of labourer, [*or as the case may be*] personally came before me [*or* before us, &c.] C. D. one [*or* more, *as the case may be*] of his majesty's justices of the peace for the said and informed me [*or* us, &c.] that E. F. of in the county of on the day of at in the said did [*here set forth the fact for which the information is laid*] contrary to the form of that statute in such case made and provided; whereupon the said E. F. after being duly summoned to answer the said charge, appeared before me [*or* us, &c.] on the day of at in the said and having heard the charge contained in the said information, declared he was not guilty of the said offence [*or as the case may happen to be*] did not appear before me [*or* us, &c.] pursuant to the said summons [*or* did neglect and refuse to make any defence against the said charge]: whereupon I [*or* we, &c. *or* nevertheless I, *or* we, &c.] the said justice [*or* justices] did proceed to examine into the truth of the charge contained in the said information, and on the day of aforesaid, at the parish of aforesaid, one credible witness, to wit, A. W. of in the county of upon his oath deposeth and saith [*if E. F be present, say,* in the presence of the said E. F.] that within months [*or as the case may be*] next before the said information was made before me [*or* us, &c.] the said justice, by the said A. B., to wit, on the day of in the year the said E. F. at in the said county of [*here state the evidence, and, as nearly as possible, in the words used by the witness, and, if more than one witness be examined, state the evidence given by each*] [*or if the defendant confess, instead of stating the evidence, say*] and the said E. F. acknowledged and voluntarily confessed the same to be true; therefore it manifestly appearing to me [*or* us, &c.] that he the said E. F. is guilty of the offence charged upon him in the said information, I [*or* we, &c.] do hereby convict him of the offence aforesaid, and do declare and adjudge that he the said E. F. hath forfeited the sum of of lawful money of Great Britain for the offence aforesaid, to be distributed [*or* paid, *as the case may be*] according to the form of the statute in that case made and provided. Given under my hand [*or* our hands, &c.] and seal the day of in the year of our Lord

Merits, Defects of Form.] In all cases where it appears by the conviction that the defendant has appeared and pleaded, and the merits have been tried, and that the defendant has not appealed against the said conviction, where an appeal is allowed, or if appealed against the conviction has been affirmed, such conviction shall not afterwards be set aside or vacated in consequence of any defect of form whatever, but the construction shall be such a fair and liberal construction as will be agreeable to the justice of the case. (s. 3.)

Recovery of Penalties.] The 5 Geo. 4. c. 18, reciting the difficulty of recovering penalties and forfeitures, and that, on conviction of an offender, no power is given to magistrates to detain him, till return of the warrant of distress against his goods, by which means he frequently escapes punishment, goes on to provide, that wherever a penalty is directed to be recovered before justices, and on default of payment, they may distrain on the offender's goods; and in case, upon a valuation being taken of such goods, sufficient distress for the penalties and other costs and charges, cannot be found, or in case it shall appear, either by the confession of the offender, or otherwise, that he has not sufficient goods whereupon the same may be levied, within the jurisdiction of such justice or justices, no sale shall take place of the goods of such offender, but it shall be lawful for such justice or justices, to commit such offender to the common gaol or house of correction, for such time and in such manner as in such acts respectively mentioned and directed; then and in every such case it shall be lawful for such justice, &c., at his or their discretion, to order the offender to be detained in custody until return shall be made to such warrant or warrants of distress, unless such offender or offenders shall give sufficient security, to the satisfaction of such justice, &c., for his appearance before him or them on such day as shall be appointed for the return of such warrant, not being more than eight days from the time of taking such security; or in case it shall appear to the satisfaction of such justice, &c., by the confession of the offender or otherwise, that he hath not goods within the jurisdiction of such justice, &c., sufficient whereon to levy all such penalties, &c., such justice, &c., may at his or their discretion, without issuing any warrant of distress, commit the offender or offenders for such period of time, and in such and like manner, as if a warrant of distress had been issued, and a *nulla bona* returned thereon. (s. 1.)

The 2nd section provides, that in cases where penalties are directed to be recovered by distress, but no remedy is provided by the particular statutes where sufficient distress cannot be found, justices may proceed in such and the like manner as if a warrant of distress had been issued, and a *nulla bona* returned thereon; and may issue their warrant for committing such offender or defendant to the common gaol for any term not exceeding three calendar months, unless the sum adjudged to be paid, and all costs and charges of the proceeding, shall be sooner paid: Provided always, that the amount of such costs and expenses shall be specified in such warrant of commitment.

Offender discharged on Payment.] In case any offender committed to the common gaol or house of correction for default of payment of such penalty or forfeiture, together with the reasonable costs and charges attending the conviction of such offender or offenders, shall, at any time during the period of his imprisonment, pay or cause to be paid to the governor or keeper of the prison the full amount of such penalty, together with the costs and charges, it shall be lawful for such governor or keeper of such prison, and he or they are hereby required forthwith, to discharge such offender or offenders from his or their custody. (s. 3.)

May commit instead of Distraining.] "And whereas, cases may occur where the recovery of such penalty or forfeiture by distress and sale of the goods and chattels of the offender or offenders may appear to the justice or justices of the peace, or magistrate or magistrates for any county, riding, soke, city, division, or place, to be attended with consequences ruinous, or in an especial manner injurious to the offender or offenders, and their family or families, be it enacted, that the justice or justices, and magistrate or magistrates aforesaid shall be empowered, and they are hereby authorized in all cases and upon all such occasions as to them shall seem fit, and where such consequences are likely to arise, to cause to be withheld the issue of any warrant or warrants of distress, and to commit the offender or offenders aforesaid immediately after conviction, and in default of payment of the penalty or forfeiture with costs and charges, to the common gaol or house of correction for such time and in such manner as are in such acts respectively mentioned and directed: Provided always, that it be by the desire, or with the consent in writing, of the party or parties upon whose property the penalty or forfeiture is to be levied." (s. 4.)

Certifying Fines, &c.] The collection, recording and certifying fines, issues, and amerciaments, are matters upon which a variety of acts of Parliament have been passed at different periods. Several of them were repealed by the 3 Geo. 4. c. 46, which enacts, at the place of some of the repealed provisions, that "all fines, issues, amerciaments, forfeited recognizances, sum or sums of money paid or to be paid in lieu or satisfaction of them, or any of them (save and except the same shall by virtue of any act or acts of parliament made or to be made, be otherwise directed to be levied, recovered, appropriated, or disposed of), which already are or hereafter shall be set, imposed, lost, or forfeited by or before any justice or justices of the peace in that part of the United Kingdom called England, shall be and are hereby required to be certified by the justice or justices of the peace by or before whom any such fines, issues, amerciaments, forfeited recognizances, sum or sums of money paid or to be paid in lieu or satisfaction of them, or any of them, shall be set, imposed, lost, or forfeited to the clerk of the peace of the county, or town clerk of the city, borough, or place, in writing, containing the names and residences, trade, profession, or calling of the parties, the amount of the sum forfeited by each respectively, and the cause of each forfeiture, signed by such justice or justices of the peace, on or before the ensuing

x 2

general or quarter-sessions of such county, city, borough, or place respectively; and such clerk of the peace, or town clerk, shall copy on a roll such fines, issues, amerciaments, forfeited recognizances, sum or sums of money paid or to be paid in lieu or satisfaction of them, or any of them, together with all fines, issues, amerciaments, forfeited recognizances, sum or sums of money paid or to be paid in lieu or satisfaction of them, or any of them, imposed or forfeited at such court of general or quarter-sessions, and shall within such time as shall be fixed and determined by such court, not exceeding twenty-one days after the adjournment of such court, send a copy of such roll, with a writ of *distringas* and *capias*, or *fieri facias* and *capias*, according to the form and effect in the schedule, marked (A), annexed to this act, to the sheriff of such county, or the sheriff, bailiff, or officer of such city, borough, or place, having execution of process therein respectively, as the case may be, which shall be the authority to such sheriff of such county, or the sheriff, bailiff, or officer, as the case may be, for proceeding to the immediate levying and recovering of such fines, issues, amerciaments, forfeited recognizances, sum or sums of money to be paid in lieu or satisfaction of them, or any of them, on the goods and chattels of such several persons, or for taking into custody the bodies of such persons, in case sufficient goods and chattels shall not be found whereon distress can be made for recovery thereof, and every person so taken shall be lodged in the common gaol until the next general or quarter sessions of the peace, there to abide the judgment of the said court." (s. 2.)

Notice to Sureties.] "And that each and every justice of the peace, before whom any recognizance shall be entered into or taken, shall, and is hereby required to give or cause to be given at the time of entering into such recognizance to the person or persons, surety or sureties so entering into the same, and to each of them, a written or printed paper or notice in the form or to the effect stated in the schedule marked (B) to this act annexed, adapting the same to the particular circumstances of the case, and each and every such justice shall in such recognizance state and particularly specify, not only the profession, art, mystery, or trade of every person so entering into such recognizance, together with their Christian name and names and surnames, but also the parish, township, or place of his or her residence, and in case such residence shall be in any city, town, or borough, shall also state, and particularly specify the name of the street, and number of the house (if any) in which such person shall reside, and also whether owner or tenant thereof, or lodger therein."

" Schedule (B.)

To wit. } Take notice, that you of are bound in the sum of pounds, and your sureties in the sums of pounds each, to appear at the quarter or general sessions of the peace for the county of to be holden at on the day of next, and unless you personally make your appearance accordingly, the recognizances entered into by yourself and securities will be forthwith levied on you and your bail.

Dated this day of one thousand eight hundred and twenty Justices of the peace."

Binding to keep the Peace.] Persons who have used threats, or conducted themselves in a way to excite a reasonable alarm of serious bodily injury, may be bound to keep the peace towards the complainant, or to be of good behaviour. This is done by requiring them to enter into recognizance to that effect, a power exercised by a reasonable intendment of law, more than by any especial law in that case provided. (Cromp. 125.)

Lord Hale says, this is not intended to be perpetual, but in nature of bail, viz. to appear at such a day at their sessions, and in the mean time to be of good behaviour. (2 Hale, 126.)

But in a recent case it was held, that a justice of the peace is authorized to require surety of the peace for a limited period (e. g. two years) according to his discretion, and that he is not limited to bind the party to the next sessions only. (Willes v. Bridges, 2 Barn. & Ald. 278.)

Superseding their own Order.] Where two justices having made an order of removal, and within three days, reciting that they had been surprised, superseded it, and commanded the churchwardens to return the former order to be cancelled; the court held that the supersedeas was well sent by the justices, and proper to prevent the expense of an appeal. (Pancras v. Rumbald, 1 Stra. 6.)

In bailable Offences.] Mr. J. Ashurst said, the legality of supersedeas in bailable offences is very doubtful, and that at any rate it cannot hold where the party is convicted in the first instance as a rogue and vagabond, and committed in execution, for there he is clearly not bailable. (R. v. Brooke, 2 T. R. 195.)

Dividing Court at Sessions.] The great increase of the business at quarter sessions, induced the legislature to provide for the dispatch of it by two courts being employed at the same time. The act provides, that whenever and as often as any court of quarter session, or general session of the peace shall be assembled for the dispatch of business, the justices then present may, on the first day of their being so assembled, take into their consideration the state of the business likely to be brought before them; and if it shall appear to them that such business, if heard by the whole court, is likely to occupy more than three days, including the day of their being so assembled, it shall be lawful for the said justices to appoint two or more justices, one of whom shall be of the quorum, to sit apart from themselves in some place in or near the court, there to hear and determine such business as shall be referred to them, whilst others of the justices are at the same time proceeding in the dispatch of the other business of the same court; and that the proceedings so had by such two or more justices so sitting apart, shall be as good and effectual in the law, as if the same were had before the court in its ordinary place of sitting, and shall be recorded accordingly. (59 Geo 3. c. 28.)

The 2nd section provides, that regulations made for the apportionment of business need not be renewed at each succeeding session.

And the 3rd section directs the clerk of the peace to appoint a person to record the proceedings of such separate court; and the quarter sessions may order the county treasurer to remunerate the clerk of the peace, and to appoint an additional crier, and to grant him a reasonable remuneration.

Crimes within their Cognizance.] The commission enumerates almost all the various classes of offences, and gives justices the cognizance of them; and although it does not mention murder or manslaughter, yet, under the general word felony, they may exercise the power to hear and determine upon those crimes. However, in practice, they very properly abstain from trying homicide, or any other offence to which a capital punishment is assigned. And it hath been of late settled that they have no jurisdiction over forgery or perjury at the common law. (2 Hawk. c. 8. s. 38.)

SECTION V.—PROTECTION AND LIABILITY.

Not to be slandered or abused.] A justice of the peace is strongly protected by the law in the just execution of his office. He is not to be slandered or abused. (1 Stra. 617—2. Ld. Raym. 1396.) Thus where upon a *colloquium* of him, and the execution of his office, the defendant said, *You are a rascal, a villain, and a liar,* it was moved in arrest of judgment that these words are not actionable. After consideration, Pratt C. J. delivered the opinion of the court, that though *rascal* and *villain* were uncertain, yet being joined with *liar*, and spoken of a justice of the peace, they did import a charge of acting corruptly and partially, and therefore there ought to be judgment for the plaintiff. (Aston v. Blagrave, 1 Stra. 617, Ld. Raym. 1396.)

So an indictment lies for saying of a justice, in the execution of his office, "you are a rogue and a liar." (R. v. Revel, 1 Stra. 420.)

Words spoken of a Justice.] An information was moved for against the defendant on account of the words, *If he is a sworn justice, he is a rogue and a forsworn rogue,* spoken of Mr. Kent, a justice of the peace, in a conversation about a warrant granted by him. To this it was objected, that the words were not spoken *to* him in the *execution of his office.* And the court, on refusing the information, said, it is not the same insult and contempt as if spoken to him in the execution of his office, which would make it a matter indictable. (R. v. Pocock, 2 Stra. 1157.)

But the words are actionable; and, in point of fact, Mr. Kent afterwards recovered against the defendant in an action. (Kent v. Pocock, 2 Stra. 1168.)

Committing for Contempt.] It is doubtful whether a magistrate, not sitting as chairman of the court, but in his private office, can commit for a contempt. (Peake's R. 62.)

But such a commitment (if legal) must be by warrant, in writing. In an action for false imprisonment, the defendant pleaded the general issue. Upon the trial it appeared that the defendant was a magistrate, and that the plaintiff, who was a constable, having been engaged till evening in executing a warrant, signed by the defendant, inquired of him whether any thing was allowed for his service, and being answered in the negative, said to the defendant, *If you have any more warrants to serve, do not send them to me, for I will not serve them.* The defendant mildly replied, *What is that you say, Mayhew?* The plaintiff repeated, *If you have any more warrants to serve, do not send them to me, for I will not serve them; you may serve them yourself.* The defendant immediately gave a verbal order that the plaintiff should be taken away to the cage in the town of Farnham, which was done, and he was confined until the next morning. Gibbs C. J. (C. P.), in delivering the opinion of the court, said, "As to the merits, without considering whether the words spoken were or were not a sufficient cause of commitment by the magistrate, we are of opinion that this commitment, which was clearly by way of punishment, and was made by word of mouth only, without warrant, in writing, cannot be supported; for it is clearly laid down in 2 Hawk.

c. 16. s. 3, and by Lord Hale, (2 Hale, 122,) that such a commitment by a magistrate must be made by a warrant in writing. (Mayhew v. Locke, 7 Taunt. 63, 2 March, 377.)

Must be for a time certain.] Where the defendant was committed under the following warrant—"Receive into your custody the body of T. James, sent by us, and charged by us, upon view for insulting behaviour towards us, by telling us that we were biassed and prejudiced in our conduct towards him as magistrates, in the due execution of our office as magistrates of the county of C., and keep him in custody until he shall be discharged by due course of law;" it was contended upon motion for a habeas corpus, that as this was a commitment for punishment, it ought to have been for a *time certain,* and as there was no course of law by which the defendant could be discharged, such a commitment, if valid, amounted to perpetual imprisonment. *Abbott,* C. J., "Without giving any opinion upon the power of a justice of peace to commit for a contempt, this warrant appears to us to be bad, for not committing for a time certain; take the writ." And the defendant, upon being brought up, was discharged. (R. v. James, 5 Barn. & Ald. 894.)

Notice of Action against.] To render justices more safe in the execution of their office, it is enacted by the 24 Geo. 2. c. 44. s. 1, "That no writ shall be sued out against, nor any copy of any process at the suit of a subject shall be served on, any justice of the peace for any thing by him done in the execution of his office, until notice in writing of such intended writ or process shall have been delivered to him, or left at the usual place of his abode, by the attorney or agent for the party who intends to sue, or cause the same to be sued out or served, at least one calendar month before the suing out or serving the same, in which notice shall be clearly and explicitly contained the cause of action which such party hath, or claimeth to have, against such justice of the peace, on the back of which notice shall be indorsed the name of such attorney or agent, together with the place of his abode, who shall be entitled to have the fee of twenty shillings for the preparing and serving such notice, and no more."

When Notice necessary.] It has been deemed sufficient to entitle a justice to the benefit of this statute, that he thinks he is acting in the execution of his office, though what he did was not properly within his official duty. (Bird v. Gunston, 2 Chit. Rep. 459; Graves v. Arnold, 3 Campb. 242.)

One magistrate who commits the mother of a bastard to custody, for not filiating the child, is entitled to notice of action under the above statute. And in that case Lord *Ellenborough,* C. J. said, "It is not denied, that the defendant had authority to act as a magistrate upon the subject matter of the complaint brought before him, though he could not act *alone*. The very object of the legislature, in requiring the notice to be given, was to enable the magistrate to tender amends as for the wrong done, contemplating him as a wrong doer." (Weller v. Toke, 9 East, 365.)

And accordingly the lord of the manor, who is also a justice of the peace, is entitled to notice of an action brought against him for taking away a gun in the house of an unqualified person, for it will be presumed that he acted as a justice. (Briggs v. Evelyn, 2 H. Blac. 114.) And when a magistrate acts upon a subject matter of complaint, over which he has authority, but which arises out of his jurisdiction, he is also entitled to this notice. (Prestidge v. Woodman, 1 Barn. & Cres. 12.)

But no notice is necessary to support an action against a person for the penalty given by stat. 18 Geo. 2. c. 20, for acting as a justice without a proper qualification. (Wright v. Horton, Holt, R. 458.)

Form of the Notice.] The notice to a justice of the peace must express the nature of the *writ* or *process* intended to be sued out, as well as of the cause of action. Where the notice did not state what particular writ or process the plaintiff intended to sue out, it was held a fatal objection; for this is required by the act of parliament alluded to. (Lovelace v. Curry, 7 T. R. 631.)

The plaintiff having sued a magistrate, gave notice of his cause of action, that the magistrate had unlawfully convicted him of not paying wages, and had issued a warrant for seizing his goods, directed to J. Bark, under which they were seized accordingly. The warrant having been directed to the constable of Halifax, and not to J. Bark: held, that the notice was insufficient. (Aked v. Stocks, 4 Bing. 509, 1 Moore & P. 346.)

But the notice need not specify the *form*, though it must state the *cause*, of action for which the party sues. (Sabin v. De Burgh, 2 Campb. 196.)

And in stating the *cause of action* it is sufficient to inform the defendant substantially of the ground of complaint. (Jones v. Bird 5 Barn. & Ald. 837, 1 Dowl. & Ryl. 497.)

Indorsement of Notice.] Some attention is necessary in this respect; thus where the notice was not indorsed with the place of abode of the attorney, but concluded thus:—" Given under my hand, at Durham, this day of ," it was deemed insufficient. (Taylor v. Fenwick, 7 T. R. 635, 3 Bos. & Pul. 553.)

It is sufficient, in indorsing the attorney's name upon the notice, to put the initial only of his *Christian name*, with his surname and place of abode in words at length. (James v. Swift, 4 Barn. & Cres. 681.)

In Crook v. Curry, (1 Tidd's Prac. 9 ed. p. 30,) Durham Summer Assizes, 1789, *Thompson*, B., held, that the attorney's name and place of abode being in the body instead of on the back of the notice was sufficient, on the grounds of the intent of the statute being that the justice might be able to tender amends to the party, or his attorney, and of the case of Rex v. Bigg, (1 Str. 18, 3 P. Wms. 419,) in which a writing on the inside of a bank-note was holden to be properly described as an indorsement even in an indictment for forgery. (Sed quære.)

The attorney, giving the notice, may describe himself generally of the town in which he resides, as of "Birmingham," (Asborn v. Gough, 3 Bos. & Pul. 551,) or "Bolton-en-le-Moor." (Crook v. Curry, *supra.)* But *Thompson*, B., then said, "London, Manchester," or other such large town generally would not be sufficient. And where he described himself in the notice as of a place in London, which in fact was in Westminster, it was holden to be fatal. (Stears v. Smith, 6 Esp. Rep. 138.)

Tender of Amends.] By s. 2, of the same statute, it is further enacted, "that it shall and may be lawful to and for such justice of the peace, at any time within one calendar month after such notice given as aforesaid, to tender amends to the party complaining, or to his or her agent or attorney; and in case the same is not accepted, to plead such tender in bar to any action to be brought against him, grounded on such writ or process, together with the plea of not guilty, and any other plea with the leave of the court; and if upon issue joined thereon, the jury shall find the amends so tendered to have been sufficient, then they shall give a verdict for the defendant; and in such case, or in case the plaintiff shall become nonsuit, or shall discontinue his or her action, or in case judgment shall be given for such defendant or defendants upon demurrer, such justice shall be entitled to the like costs as he would have been entitled unto, in case he had pleaded the general issue only; and if, upon issue so joined, the jury shall find that no amends were tendered, or that the same were not sufficient, and also against the defendant or defendants on such other plea or pleas, then they shall give a verdict for the plaintiff, and such damages as they shall think proper, which he or she shall recover, together with his or her costs of suit."

May pay Money into Court.] By s. 4, it is further enacted, "that in case such justice shall neglect to tender any such amends, or shall have tendered insufficient amends before the action brought, it shall and may be lawful for him, by leave of the court where such action shall depend, at any time before issue joined, to pay into court such sum of money as he shall see fit, whereupon such proceedings, orders, and judgments shall be had, made, and given in and by such court as in other actions, where the defendant is allowed to pay money into court."

In an action against a magistrate for an assault and false imprisonment, after the general issue pleaded, the court will permit the defendant to withdraw his plea, and pay money into court, and plead *de novo.* (Devaynes v. Boys, 7 Taunt. 33, 2 Marsh. 356.)

So in trespass against a magistrate for an act done in the execution of his office, the court, after issue joined, and notice of trial given, allowed the defendant to withdraw his plea, pay money into court, and plead the general issue *de novo.* (Nestor v. Newcome, 3 Barn. & Cres. 159)

Proof of Notice.] By s. 3, of the same act, " No plaintiff shall recover any verdict against such justice in any case where the action shall be grounded on any act of the defendant, as justice of the peace, unless it is proved upon the trial of such action, that such notice was given as aforesaid; but in default thereof, such justice shall recover a verdict and costs as aforesaid."

By s. 5, it is further enacted, "That no evidence shall be permitted to be given by the plaintiff, on the trial of any such action as aforesaid, of any cause of action except such as is contained in the notice hereby directed to be given."

Certificate, and double Costs.] Section 7 provides, " That where the plaintiff, in any such action against any justice of the peace, shall obtain a verdict, in case the judge before whom the cause shall be tried shall, in open court, certify on the back of the record that the injury for which such action was brought was wilfully and maliciously committed, the plaintiff shall be entitled to have and receive double costs of suit."

Limitation of Actions.] " No action shall be brought against any justice of the peace for any thing done in the execution of his office, or against any constable, headborough, or other officer or person acting as aforesaid, unless commenced within six calendar months after the act committed." (s. 8.)

These months, it seems, are to be reckoned inclusive of the day of committing the act; (Clarke v. Davey, 4 Moore, 465;) but in the case of a continued imprisonment. the magistrate is liable to answer, in an action, for such part of the imprisonment, suffered under his warrant, as was within six calendar months before the action commenced against him. (Massy v. Johnson, 12 East, 67.)

The 7 & 8 Geo. 4. c. 29. s. 75, (the larceny act,) and c. 30, s. 41, the malicious injuries act, contain similar provisions in favour of magistrates and their officers, against whom actions may be brought.

Time, how computed.] In computing the six months limited by 24 Geo. 2. c. 44. s. 8, for bringing an action against a magistrate for false imprisonment, the day of discharge from imprisonment is to be reckoned *exclusively*. Therefore, where a party discharged on the 14th of December sued out a writ on the 14th of June following, it was held that the action was commenced in time. (Hardy v. Ryle, T. T. 1829, MSS., 9 Barn. & Cres., 3 Man. & Ryl.)

Damages limited to Twopence.] And to render justices of the peace more safe in the execution of their duty, it is enacted by stat. 43 Geo. 3. c. 141, that "in all actions which shall be brought against any justice or justices of the peace in the United Kingdom of Great Britain and Ireland, for or on account of any conviction by him or them had or made under or by virtue of any act or acts of Parliament in force in the said United Kingdom, or for or by reason of any act, matter, or thing whatsoever done or commanded to be done by such justice or justices for the levying of any penalty, apprehending any party, or for or about the carrying of any such conviction into effect, in case such conviction shall have been quashed, the plaintiff or plaintiffs in such action or actions, besides the value and amount of the penalty or penalties which may have been levied upon the said plaintiff or plaintiffs, in case any levy thereof shall have been made, shall not be entitled to recover any more or greater damages than the sum of twopence, nor any costs of suit whatsoever, unless it shall be expressly alleged in the declaration in the action wherein the recovery shall be had, and which shall be in an action upon the case only, that such acts were done maliciously and without any reasonable and probable cause."

To what Cases the Act extends.] But this statute does in no instance extend to protect justices of the peace in the execution of their office, unless done on account of some conviction made by them of the plaintiffs in such actions by virtue of any statute, &c. (Massey v. Johnson, 12 East, 67.)

But if a conviction be good upon the face of it, the production and proof of it at the trial will justify the convicting magistrates, under the general issue, as well in respect of such facts stated therein as are necessary to give them jurisdiction, as upon the merits of the conviction. (Gray v. Cookson, 16 East, 13.)

If, however, the conviction do not pursue on the face of it the provisions of the statute, under which it purports to be made, nor show that any offence has been committed, it is bad; and although it has not been quashed, its invalidity may be taken advantage of on the trial of an action of trespass, for a distress taken under a warrant grounded thereon. (Gimbert v. Coyney, 1 M'Clel. & Y. 469.)

In an action against a magistrate for a malicious conviction, it is not sufficient for the plaintiff to show that he was innocent of the offence of which he was convicted; but he must also prove, from what passed before the magistrate, that there was a want of probable cause.

In an action against a magistrate for false imprisonment, proof of a conviction of the plaintiff for an offence differing from that recited in the commitment, is no justification of the imprisonment. Nor is the defendant, in order to deprive the plaintiff of his costs under 43 Geo. 3. c. 141, at liberty to show that the offence mentioned in the conviction had actually been committed by the plaintiff; as that statute applies only to cases where convictions have been quashed. *Quære* whether it is admissible in mitigation of damages? (Rogers v. Jones, 3 Barn. & Cres. 409.)

In trespass against magistrates for taking and detaining a vessel, a conviction by the defendants under the bum-boat act (no defect appearing on the face of the conviction) is conclusive evidence that the vessel in question is a boat within the meaning of the act, and properly condemned. (Brittain v. Kinnaird, 1 Brod. & Bing. 432, 4 Moore, 50.)

If a warrant of commitment does not show an offence over which the magistrate who issued it has jurisdiction, an action lies against him for the commitment, although there might have been a previous regular conviction. (Wickes v. Clutterbuck, 2 Bing. 483, 10 Moore, 63.)

Venue and double Costs.] By 7 Jac. 1. c. 5, (made perpetual by 21 Jac. 1. c. 12. s. 2,) if any action, bill, plaint, or suit upon the case, trespass, battery, or false imprisonment, is brought in any of his Majesty's courts at Westminster, or elsewhere, against any justice of the peace, mayor, or bailiff of any city or town corporate, headborough, port-reeve, constable, tythingman, collector of subsidy or fifteens, for or concerning any matter, cause, or thing, by them or any of them done by virtue of his or their offices the action, &c., shall be laid within the county where the trespass or fact is done and committed, and not elsewhere, (21 Jac. 1. c. 12. ss. 3. 5,) and every defendant may plead the general issue not guilty, and give in evidence the special matter, which being pleaded had been good in law to have discharged defendant of the trespass or other matter laid to his charge; and if on the trial plaintiff shall not prove that the cause of action accrued within the county in which it is laid, the jury shall find the defendant not guilty, without regard to any other evidence for plaintiff (21 Jac. 1. c. 12. ss. 3. 5.); and if a verdict pass for defendant, or if plaintiff discontinues, or is nonsuit, defendant shall have his double costs which he shall have sustained by wrongful vexation in defence of the said action, &c. (See Money v. Leach, 3 Burr. 1742.)

To entitle a defendant (an officer) to double costs under this statute, there must be a certificate of the judge who tried the cause (which may be granted either at the trial or afterwards,) that the defendant was such an officer, and that the action was brought against him for something done by him in the execution of that office. (Harper v. Carr, 7 T. R. 448.)

Justices misbehaving in Office.] If a justice will not, on complaint to him made, execute his office, or shall misbehave in his office, the party grieved may move the Court of King's Bench for an information, and afterwards may apply to the Court of Chancery to put him out of the commission. (Cromp. 7; Ex parte Rook, 2 Atk. 2.)

The Court of King's Bench will not grant a mandamus commanding justices of the peace to do that which may render them liable to an action. (Rex v. Dayrell, 1 Barn. & Cres. 485.)

Not punishable for a mere Error in Judgment.] A justice is not punishable at the suit of the party, but only at the suit of the king, for what he doth as judge in matters which he hath power by law to hear and determine, without the concurrence of any other; but in cases where he proceeds ministerially rather than judicially, if he act corruptly he is liable to an action at the suit of the party, as well as to an information at the suit of the king (2 Hawk. P. C. c. 13. s. 20.)

Error or Mistake excusable.] Where a criminal information is applied for against a magistrate, the question is not whether the act done be strictly right, but whether it proceeded from an unjust, oppressive, or corrupt motive (amongst which fear and favour are generally included,) or from mistake and error only. In the latter case the court will not grant the rule. (Rex v. Borron, 2 Barn.& Ald. 432.)

In Rex v. Young and Pitts, 1 Burr. 556, *Lord Mansfield*, C. J., declared, that the Court of King's Bench hath no power or claim to review the reasons of justices of the peace upon which they form their judgments in granting licenses, by way of appeal from their judgments, or overruling the discretion in that behalf intrusted to them. But if it clearly appear that the justices have been partially, maliciously, or corruptly influenced in the exercise of this discretion, and have (consequently) abused the trust reposed in them, they are liable to prosecution by indictment or information; or even possibly by action, if the malice be very gross and injurious.

And in Rex v. Holland and Forster, (1 T. R. 692,) it appeared, that the defendant Forster had been present at a general meeting at the time when the license was refused; but he had afterwards told the other defendant, Holland, who was not present at the general meeting, that the only reason why a license had not been granted then was, that they might have an opportunity of inquiring into the character of Harrison, and he accordingly prevailed upon Holland, at a private meeting held by those two only, to join in granting a license. The court were clearly of opinion that an information should be granted against a justice as well for granting a license improperly as for refusing one in the same manner. And as it appeared in this case, that Holland, though not altogether blameless, had been deceived by Forster, they discharged the rule as to the former, upon his paying the costs of the application, as against himself; and as to Forster they granted the information. (See also Rex v. Sainsbury, 4 T. R. 451.)

Illegal Commitments.] A commitment of a person who is ultimately found to be entirely innocent of the charge, is not, therefore, necessarily illegal. In an action of trespass and false imprisonment against a constable, under such circumstances, Mr. J. Gaselee told the jury to consider whether the circumstances, under which the arrest was made afforded the defendant reasonable ground to suppose that the plaintiff had committed the felony, and whether, in his situation, they would have acted as he had done. This direction was afterwards held substantially correct by the court. (Davis v. Russell, 5 Bing. 354; see Beckwith v. Philby, 6 Barn. & Cres. 637.)

This rule is equally applicable to magistrates. But if a magistrate commit a prisoner for re-examination, stating that he does so in the hope that the prisoner would admit a fact then in dispute; and the jury should be of opinion, that the commitment, though in point of form for re-examination, was intended to force an admission from the prisoner of the particular fact, the magistrate is liable to an action of trespass and false imprisonment, in respect of that commitment. (Davis v. Capper, MSS. E. T. 1829, 9 Barn. & Cres., 3 Man. & Ryl.)

Committing for unreasonable Time.] An action of trespass and false imprisonment was brought against a magistrate for having committed a party for re-examination for a period of fourteen days, which it was alleged was an unreasonable length of time, occasioned by an improper motive influencing the mind of the magistrate. The jury found that the commitment was made *bona fide* without any improper motive on the part of the magistrate, but that *the time was unreasonable*, and gave a verdict with damages for the plaintiff. Upon a motion for a new trial, it was contended, among other objections, that the form of action was improper, as the magistrate had jurisdiction over the matter of inquiry, and that it ought to have been a special action on the case. The Court of King's Bench, however, held, that the form of action chosen was proper; for to have had a special action on the case, there must have been an improper motive for its foundation. And as to the validity of the commitment on the warrant, which it was urged must be wholly good or wholly bad, as it was found that the time was unreasonable, an action for false imprisonment might be sustained. Whether it was considered void from the beginning on account of its unreasonableness, or as good in the beginning, and bad for so much of it as the imprisonment was beyond the reasonable time, made no difference, for the continuance of imprisonment beyond that reasonable time was a trespass. It appeared, however, to the court as a principle, that the commitment should be considered void from the beginning; for if a magistrate be only authorized by law to commit for a reasonable time, and he commit for an unreasonable time, that is an act for which by law he has no authority. The court, therefore, refused to disturb the verdict. (Davis v. Capper, MSS., see 9 Barn. & Cres., 3 Man. & Ryl.)

Not to be punished criminally and civilly.] But a justice shall not be liable to be punished both ways, that is, both criminally and civilly; but before the court will grant an information, they will require the party to relinquish his civil action, if any such is commenced. And even in the case of an indictment, and though the indictment be actually found, yet the attorney general (on application made to him) will grant a *nolle prosequi* upon such an indictment, if it appear to him that the prosecutor is determined to carry on a civil action at the same time. (Rex v. Fielding, 2 Burr. 719.)

Statements on Oath.] In an action of trespass brought against the defendants, for having, as justices, issued a warrant of distress against the goods of the plaintiff, for a cause which, upon the face of the order, appeared to be within their jurisdiction. Upon the trial, in order to prove the justices to have been trespassers, other facts than those stated before them when they made their order were proved. A verdict was found for the plaintiff, subject to the opinion of the court. And it was held by Lord *Ellenborough*, C. J., that the magistrates could not be affected as trespassers, if the facts stated to them upon oath by the complainant were such whereof they had jurisdiction to inquire, and nothing appeared in answer to contradict the first statement.—And *Lawrence*, J., said, if the magistrates made an order against the evidence laid before them, the party injured would have another sort of remedy against them. But the plaintiff cannot make them trespassers by showing that the real facts of the case will not support the complaint, unless such facts were proved before them. (Lowther v. Earl Radnor, 8 East, 113.) So, trespass does not lie against a magistrate for any thing done in the discharge of his duty, unless he is made acquainted with all the circumstances under which he is called upon to act. (Pike v. Carter, 3 Bing. 78, 10 Moore, 376.)

Acting under Statute.] In trespass against two magistrates, for giving plaintiff's landlord possession of a farm, as a deserted farm, they produced in evidence a record of their proceedings under the act, which set forth all such circumstances as were necessary to give them jurisdiction, and by which it appeared, that they had pursued the directions of the statute. Held, that this was a complete answer to the action. The record unappealed against is conclusive as to the magistrates; for it is their duty to act on the request of the landlord. (Basten v. Carew, 3 Barn. & Cres. 649, 5 Dowl. & Ryl. 558; see Fawcett v. Fowlis, 7 Barn. & Cres. 394, 1 Man. & Ryl. 102.)

Misconduct in Sessions.] Lord *Kenyon* said, he believed there were instances in which a criminal information had been granted against magistrates acting in sessions. (Rex v. Seton, 7 T. R. 374.) But in Rex v. Skinner, (Lofft. 55,) on motion to quash an indictment against ——— Skinner, Esquire, one of his Majesty's justices of the peace of the town of Poole, for scandalous words spoken by him in a general sessions of the county, in which he said to the grand jury, "You have not done your duty; you have disobeyed my commands; you are a seditious, scandalous, corrupt, and perjured jury." Lord *Mansfield*, C. J., said, neither party, counsel, jury, nor judge, can be put to answer civilly or criminally for words spoken in office. If the words spoken are opprobrious or irrelevant to the case, the court will take notice of them as a contempt, and examine on information. If any thing of *mala mens* is found on such inquiry, it will be punished suitably.

Striking in his Office.] An information being moved for against the defendant for assaulting and beating the mayor of Yarmouth, being a justice of the peace, in the execution of his office, the question was, Whether the defendant could justify, the mayor having struck him first?—By Lord *Hardwicke*, C. J. "He may justify it; for though a magistrate is protected by the law whilst he is in the execution of his office, yet in this instance he hath forfeited that protection, by beginning a breach of the peace himself." (Rex v. Symonds, Cas. Temp. Hardw 240.)

Criminal Information against.] It is required by the practice of the court, that complaints against justices should be made promptly, and so as they may come forward without delay to answer them. Thus a rule *nisi* for a criminal information may be obtained at the *end* of a term against a magistrate for malpractices *during the term*, but not for any misconduct before the term began; (Rex v. Smith, 7 Durnf. & East, 80;) or where no assizes have intervened, it may be moved for in the second term: (Rex v. Herries, 13 East, 270:) though it cannot be moved for so late in that term, as to preclude the magistrate from the opportunity of showing cause against it the *same* term. (Rex v. Marshall, 13 East, 322.)

But by refusing a criminal information on the ground of its being moved too late, the court does not shut the door to an inquiry, for a bill of indictment may still be preferred against the defendant. (See Rex v. Bishop, 5 Barn. & Ald. 612.)

A Justice convicted must appear in Person.] The defendant, being a justice of the peace, was convicted on an information for a conviction by him made of an alehouse-keeper, who was never summoned or heard. It was moved, as of course, to dispense with his appearance. This was opposed, unless there was some reason given or affidavit made. And, upon debate, the court resolved, it was not of course, and the defendant afterwards appeared in person.

The general doctrine laid down by the court, and agreed by the counsel on both sides was, that though such a motion was subject to the discretion of the court, either to grant or refuse it, where it was clear and certain that the punishment would not be *corporal;* yet it ought to be denied, in every case where it was probable or possible that the punishment would be corporal. And Mr. Justice Wilmot and Mr. Justice Aston thought, that even when the punishment would most probably be only pecuniary, yet, in offences of a very gross and public nature, the persons convicted should appear in person. (Rex v. Harwood, 2 Str. 1088; Rex v. Hann. & Price, 3 Burr. 1786.)

SECTION VI.—FEES OF THEIR CLERKS.

Justice's Wages.] In the oath of office before mentioned are these words: *and that you take nothing for your office of the peace to be done, but of the king, and fees accustomed, and costs limited by statute.*

And by statute their fees in many cases are limited and ascertained.

Every of the said justices shall take for their wages four shillings the day for the time of their said sessions, and their clerk (the clerk of the peace) two shillings, of the fines and amerciaments rising and coming of the same sessions, by the hands of the sheriffs. (12 R. 2. c. 10.)

And the estreats of the said justices shall be doubled, and the one part delivered by the said justices to the sheriff to levy the money thereof rising, and thereof to pay to the justices their wages by the hand of the said sheriff by indenture betwixt them thereof to be made; and that no duke, earl, baron, or banneret, albeit they be assigned justices of the peace, and hold their sessions with the other justices, shall take any wages for the said office; and that the justices put their names in the same estreats, together with the number of the days of their sessions, to the intent that the sheriffs may know to whom to pay the wages, and to whom not. (14 R. 2. c. 11.)

Table of Fees.] The justices of the peace throughout that part of Great Britain called England, at their respective general quarter sessions of the peace to be held next after the 24th day of June, 1753, shall, and they are hereby required to make and settle a table of the fees, which shall be taken by clerks to justices of the peace within the county, city, or other division for which such respective general quarter sessions shall be held, and such respective tables of fees, being approved by the justices of the peace at the next succeeding general quarter sessions of the peace for such county, city, or other division, with such alterations as such justices of the peace so assembled shall think proper, shall be laid before the judges at the next assizes, or at the great sessions for the principality of Wales and counties palatine of Chester, Lancaster, and Durham, for the respective county, city, or other division, and the said judges are hereby authorised and required to ratify and confirm such respective tables of fees, in such manner and form as the same shall be made, settled, and approved of by the said justices, or with such alterations, additions, or abatements, as to such judges shall appear to be just and reasonable; and it shall and may be lawful for the said justices of peace, in their respective quarter sessions assembled, from time to time, to make any other table of fees to be taken, instead of the fees contained in the table which shall have been ratified and confirmed by the judges of assize, and after the same shall have been approved by the justices of the peace, at the next succeeding general quarter sessions, in manner as aforesaid, to lay such new table of fees before the judges at the next assizes, or at the great sessions for the principality of Wales, and counties palatine of Chester, Lancaster, and Durham, who are hereby empowered and authorised to approve and ratify the same in manner as aforesaid, if they think fit; but no table of fees to be made and settled by the said respective justices of peace, shall be of any validity or effect whatsoever, until the same shall be ratified and confirmed by the said judges. (26 G. 2. c. 14.)

Table for Middlesex.] By 27 G. 2. c. 16. s. 4, (after reciting the above act) it is enacted, that the table of fees to be taken by the clerks to justices of the peace for the county of Middlesex, which is or shall from time to time be made, settled, and approved by the said justices for the said county, at their general or quarter sessions, shall be laid before the lord chief justice of the King's Bench, the lord chief justice of the Common Pleas, and the lord chief baron of the Exchequer, or any two of them, who are hereby authorised and required to ratify and confirm such table of fees, in such manner and form as the same shall be so made, settled, and approved of, or with such alterations, additions, or abatements, as to the said lord chief justice of the King's Bench, the lord chief justice of the Common Pleas, and the lord chief baron of the Exchequer, or any two of them, shall appear to be just and reasonable; and the said justices of the peace for the said county are hereby empowered and required to make a table of such fees at their next general or quarter sessions to be held for the said county, after the 24th day of June, 1754, and to approve or alter the same at the next succeeding general or quarter sessions, and from time to time, and in like manner, to make and approve any other table of such fees.

Penalty on taking other Fees.] By 26 Geo. 2. c. 14. s. 2, it is enacted, that if, at any time, after the space of three calendar months from the time that such table of fees shall be made and ratified as aforesaid, any clerk or clerks to any justice or justices of the peace, or any person or persons acting as such, shall under pretence of any matter or thing done, transacted, or performed by such justice or justices in the execution of his or their office or offices, or done, transacted, or performed by such person or persons, as clerk or clerks to such justice or justices, demand or receive any other or greater fee than shall have been ascertained, ratified, and confirmed in manner as aforesaid, such person shall for every such offence forfeit and pay twenty pounds to any person who shall sue for the same, by action of debt, bill, plaint, or information in any of his majesty's courts of record at Westminster, wherein no essoign, privilege, protection, wager of law, or more than one imparlance, shall be granted or allowed.

Tables of Fees to be put up in Court.] Sec. 3 enacts, that all the tables of fees which shall be made, and settled, and ratified, and confirmed from time to time as aforesaid, shall be deposited with the clerk of the peace for the respective county, city, or other division; and each of the said clerks of the peace shall cause true and exact written or printed copies of the said tables to be placed, and to be kept constantly, in a conspicuous part of the room or place where the general or quarter sessions shall be held, under pain of forfeiting the sum of ten pounds for each offence, to be recovered by action of debt, bill, plaint, or information in any of his majesty's courts of record at Westminster, wherein no essoign, privilege, protection, wager of law, or more than one imparlance, shall be granted or allowed.

Limitation of Actions.] Provided always, that all suits and actions which shall be brought or commenced by virtue of this act, shall be brought before the end of three months after the offence committed, and not otherwise. (s. 4.)

Fees to be taken at Public Offices only.] It is enacted, that no justice of the peace for the county of Middlesex, county of Surrey, city and liberty of Westminster, or the liberty of the Tower of London, or his clerk, or any person on their behalf, elsewhere than at the said police offices, shall, directly or indirectly, upon any pretence or under any colour whatever, take or receive any fee, reward, gratuity, or recompense for any act by him or them done, or to be done, in the execution of his or their office or employ as justice of the peace or clerk as aforesaid, within the limits of the weekly bills of mortality, or within the parishes of Saint Mary-le-bone, Paddington, Saint Pancras, Kensington, and Saint Luke, Chelsea, in the said county of Middlesex, upon pain of forfeiting the sum of one hundred pounds for every such offence, one moiety thereof to the said receiver, to be applied to the purposes of this act, and the other moiety thereof, with full costs of suit, to the person who shall sue for the same in any of his majesty's courts of record at Westminster, by action of debt, bill, plaint or information, wherein no essoign, privilege, wager of law, or more than one imparlance, shall be allowed. Provided always, that nothing in this act contained shall be construed to extend to any fees taken at any general or quarter sessions of the peace, or at any meeting of justices, for the purpose of licensing ale-houses, or to any fees taken at the said public office in Bow Street, or to any fees taken by the vestry clerk of any parish, for the purpose of enforcing the payment of any taxes or assessments arising within the same parish, or for the purpose of hearing and determining any offence, cognizable before justices of the peace by virtue of any statute made and provided for the special regulation or government of such parish. (3 Geo. 4. c. 55. s. 7.)

Surrey Table of Fees.] The following is the table of fees allowed to be taken by the clerks to the justices of the peace, within the county of Surrey :—

	s.	*d.*
All informations, or examinations on oath, or confessions, whereon any warrant or summons shall issue, or whereon any commitment, or order for punishment, or for payment of money shall be made, not being cases of felony, nor hereinafter provided for	1	0
Every warrant or summons, not including more than five names	1	0
For every name above five	0	6
Every commitment, or order for punishment, or for payment of money, not being cases of felony . . .	1	0
Every liberate or discharge of a person in custody . .	1	0
For indorsing every warrant and oath . . .	1	0
Every recognizance (except to prosecute or give evidence in cases of felony, or for a victualler's good behaviour) whatever number of names may be included therein . .	2	6
Every supersedeas	2	6
Every examination (taken in writing) in settlement, or in bastardy cases, and oath	3	0
Every order of removal and duplicate . . .	3	6
Every indorsement of suspension of such order, duplicate and oath	2	0
Every order taking off such suspension, including the order to refund the expenses of maintenance during the suspension and oath	2	0
Every order allowing certificate of settlement and oath .	2	0
Every order allowing the expense of maintaining and removing certificated persons	1	0
Every precept to give notice of nominating overseers, and serving same on high-constable . . .	2	6
Every appointment of surveyors of highways, and charge as per stat.	1	0
Printed abstract of the act, as per stat. . .	0	6
Bond if taken from the surveyor as per stat. . .	0	6
Every warrant to appoint overseers of the poor, whatever number of names may be included therein .	3	0
Duplicate of appointment, if required . . .	1	6

	s.	d.
Every appointment of inspectors of weights and measures .	1	0
Allowing and signing a parish or other rate (each book) and oath	2	0
Every warrant of distress and oath . . .	2	0
Every commitment for want of distress . . .	2	0
Every notice of giving landlord possession of premises deserted by his tenant, and serving same . . .	2	6
Giving possession of same . . .	2	6
Every abjudication in bastardy . . .	3	0
Duplicate thereof	2	6
Allowing and registering a pair of parish indentures .	2	0
Allowing the account of every surveyor of highways, examination and oath as per stat.	1	0
Every order for an additional assessment for repair of the highways, and oath	2	6
Every other order relative to the business of a surveyor .	2	6
Every certificate of a justice of the repair of a road, or abatement of a nuisance, which has been indicted or presented .	5	0
Every privy search-warrant . . .	2	6
Return thereof to the petty-session . . .	2	0
Swearing every affidavit in any case where the magistrates have legal power to administer an oath . .	1	0
Precept to the high-constables to give notice of time and place of licensing victuallers, and serving same . .	1	6
Every licence of a victualler, including 1*s.* for the recognizance, and 1*s.* for the clerk of the peace . .	7	0
Drawing every information on penal stats. and oath . .	3	6
Drawing and ingrossing every conviction, where the form is given by the stat.	2	0
Ditto where the form is not given . . .	5	0
Attesting every soldier	1	0
Every warrant to press baggage-waggons . . .	1	0
Every commitment of a deserter, letter thereon to the secretary at war, and warrant for paying the reward for apprehension	2	6
Every order for paying the reward for apprehending a vagrant	1	0
Every order concerning masters and servants in husbandry .	2	0
Every discharge of an apprentice made out of session .	3	0
Swearing constables to lists of freeholders, or of persons liable to serve in the militia	1	0
Every oath of office	1	0
Every order to seize the estate and effects of a person running away and leaving a family chargeable to parish .	2	0
Every examination of a vagrant, pass thereon, and duplicate .	3	0
Certificate thereon . . .	1	0
Allowing the account of treasurer, or overseers, respecting money advanced for relief of militia-men's families .	1	0
Record of forcible entry and detainer . . .	5	0
Record of writ on view . . .	2	6
Precept to the sheriff to return a jury . . .	2	6
Inquisition on a forcible entry or riot . . .	2	6

	s.	d.
Imposition, or record of fine set	2	6
Warrant to the sheriff to make restitution . .	2	6
Certificate of rioters continuing together after proclamation made	2	6
Order allowing special constables' expenses to be submitted to the session	2	0

CHAPTER XII.—CONSTABLES.

SECTION I.—APPOINTMENT.

High-Constable.] A high-constable is appointed for a larger district than a petty constable, as a hundred, wapenstake, or other similar division; and he is usually considered an officer of greater dignity. In some places there is a custom to appoint more than one such officer. And though a town or other place formerly under the general jurisdiction of the county has been erected into a separate jurisdiction as a county of itself, within time of memory, and it had no high-constable before, yet such an office is incident to such a newly-created district, and the magistrates may appoint a high-constable; (James v. Green, 6 T. R. 232; Weatherhead v. Drewry, 11 East. 168;) and, by analogy, a petty constable may be so appointed where the necessity for such an office arises, by a place becoming, by the increase of population, a township, or vill, though it has been said this officer can only be newly created by statute. (Rex v. Hewson, 12 Mod. 180, Dolting a. Stocklane, Fortesc. 219, 1 Salk. 176.)

By whom appointed.] The high-constable was, at common law, elected by the homage at the leet or view of frankpledge, and appointed by the sheriff or other officer of the town, leet, or franchise. But there may be a custom for the sheriff or lord to nominate as well as appoint him. (R. v. Genge, Cowp. 16; R. v. Adlard, 4 Barn. & Cres. 779, 2 Haw. x. 37, Anon Salk. 175.) But when not so appointed, he may be appointed by the county justices in their quarter sessions, or by the justices of the division in which the hundred lies. (1 Bla. Com. 355, Constable of Stepney, 1 Bul. 174, Com. Dig. Leet. M. 5.)

Petty Constable.] A petty constable is appointed for a vill, township, or tithing, and not for a parish, and the number in each depends upon the custom of the place. (Rex v. Hewson, 12 Mod. 180, Constable of Homeby's case, 1 Mod. 13.) He is elected by the homage or jury, and appointed by the lord or steward of the court leet of the manor in which his precinct lies; but there may be a custom for the officer of the leet to appoint, without any election by the jury. (Rex v. Routlege, Doug. 537, Rex v. Stevens, Sir T. Jones, 212, Com. Dig. Leet, M. C.) And, when not so chosen, he may be appointed by two justices within whose jurisdiction his precinct lies, in pursuance of the statute 14 & 15 Car. 2. c. 12. s. 15. (1 Bla. Com. 355.)

A corporation has no common-law right to appoint a constable. By custom they may, but then they must prescribe for it; for by the common law this power is vested in the leet or sheriff's torn. (Rex v. Barnard, Comb. 416, 1 L. Ray. 94.)

Who are liable to serve.] No one is liable to serve the office of high-constable who is not an inhabitant, that is, a *resident* within the hundred; nor is any one liable to serve the office of constable who is not such an inhabitant, residing within the precinct for which he is appointed. A mere occupier of a tenement for which he pays the rent, rates, and taxes, within such district, if he be not *resiant* is not liable, because these are offices which require personal attendance within the district, and that the person should be well known to the inhabitants. (Rex v. Adlard, 4 Barn. & Cres. 778.) And if there be a parish, and a leet within that parish, not equally extensive with it, a resident in the parish cannot be appointed constable of the leet unless he resides in that part of the parish which is within the leet. (Rex v. Adlard, 4 Barn. & Cres. 777.)

It has been held, although there is a former decision to the contrary, that it is a good custom for the inhabitants of a town to serve the office of constable in rotation, according to the situation of their houses; and that if it come to the turn of a woman, instead of serving personally, she shall be bound to provide a substitute. (Rex v. Stubbs, 2 T. R. 406, 2 Haw. x. 37, Prouse's case, Cro. Car. 389.)

Persons incompetent.] Some persons are not capable of serving, although willing to discharge the office. As justices of the same place, and by the 3 Geo. 4. c. 77, which has expired, licensed victuallers and alehouse-keepers, were rendered incompetent to the office, and a penalty of £10 imposed upon every such person undertaking to act as deputy. And though the recent act for consolidating the laws relating to licensing taverns, alehouses, &c. omits the above provision, yet it enacts that no sheriff's officer, or officer executing the legal process of any court of justice, shall be capable of receiving or using any such licence, (see 9 Geo. 4. c. 61. s. 16,) which, with the obvious policy of rejecting publicans from the office of constable, will in effect be tantamount to a declared incompetency.

Persons exempt.] Other persons, although not disqualified, may claim an exemption from serving the office. As every teacher or preacher in holy orders, or pretended holy orders; that is, a minister, preacher, or teacher of a congregation, that shall take the oaths, make and subscribe the declaration, and subscribe certain articles of the Church of England as required by this act, is exempt from serving any office in any hundred, or any shire, city, town, parish, ward, division or wapenstake. (1 W. & M. c. 18. s. 11.) And the same privilege is extended to priests, preachers, &c. of the Roman Catholic religion, complying with the act 31 Geo. 3. c. 32. s. 8.

No president or fellow of the corporation of the Faculty of Physic, or warden or fellow of the Mystery of Surgeons, of London, shall be chosen constable of the city of London or its suburbs; (32 Hen. 8. c. 40. s. 1; Pordage's case, 1 Mod. 22, 2 Keb. 578, 2 Haw. x. 42;) and practising physicians and surgeons are considered to be exempt throughout the kingdom, except where there is a custom for the inhabitants to serve in rotation, according to the situation of their houses. (Id. ibid. 2 Haw. x. 41, 43.) But members of the Barber's Company, who have not been approved and admitted to practice surgery, by the Bishop of London or the Dean of St. Paul's, are not exempt by the statutes. (3, 5, & 32 Hen. 8, Rex v. Chapple, 3 Camp. 91.)

Apothecaries exempt.] Every person using the art of an apothecary in London, and within seven miles thereof, being free of the Society of the Apothecaries of London, and approved for his skill in that mystery; so long as he shall use the art, and no longer, shall be exempt from the office of constable, and all other parish and leet offices; (6 & 7 W. 3. c. 4, made perpetual by 9 Geo. 1. c. 8. s. 1;) and all persons using that art in other parts of the kingdom, who have served an apprenticeship for seven years, shall likewise be exempt from these offices so long as they shall exercise that art, and no longer.

Militia, &c., exempt.] No militia-man, from the time of his enrolment until he shall be regularly discharged, shall be compelled to serve as a peace officer; (42 Geo. 3. c. 90. s. 174;) nor any officer or effective member of any yeomanry corps, or volunteer cavalry during the period of his continuing enrolled. (57 Geo. 3. c. 44. s. 3.) But it is said, that a captain of the King's guard is not exempt from serving this office, where there is a custom for the inhabitants to serve in rotation, according to the situation of their houses, for he may appoint a deputy. (2 Hawk. x. 41; Sir Walter Franc's case, 1 Lev. 233, 1 Sid. 355.)

Naturalized Foreigner.] If the act, by which a foreigner is naturalized, declare that he shall not be capacitated to take any office or place of trust, either civil or military, he cannot be appointed constable. (Rex v. Mierre, 5 Burr. 2788.)

Superannuated.] And no person within the city or liberty of Westminster, who is of the age of sixty-three years, shall be liable to serve or to find a deputy. (31 Geo. 2. c. 17. s. 13.)

Charter Exemptions.] Exemptions by charter or special custom are construed with great strictness, and cannot be permitted, where sufficient persons would not be left in the place liable and capable to serve the office.

It has been decided, that a younger brother of the Trinity-house is not exempted by the charter of that corporation, or at least not unless he is alleged and proved to be a shipman or mariner. (Rex v. Clarke, 1 T. R. 635, 2 Inst. 129, 2 Haw. x. 40.)

Servants of Colleges.] Servants of the colleges of the University of Oxford, named in the statutes, with an ancient fee and duties which require personal attendance, although not residing within the college, are exempt from the office for the city; such as a barber matriculated in the university, and entered on the buttery books of a college, although residing and keeping a barber's shop in one of the wards of the city. (Rex v. Routlege, Doug. 538.)

Other Exemptions.] Aldermen of the city of London are exempt from serving the office wherever they reside. (2 Haw. x. 40, Alderman Abdy, Cro. Car. 585.) So are practising barristers. Sworn practising attornies, and the officers of all the courts of Westminster Hall, and their servants, but not their tenants. (2 Haw. x. 39; Pordage's case, 2 Keb. 578, Com. Dig. Leet, M. 7.)

And Dissenters and Roman Catholics are allowed to serve by an approved deputy; (1 W. & M. c. 18. s. 7;) the same privilege is extended to all persons professing the Roman Catholic religion. (31 Geo. 3. c. 72. s. 7.)

Persons not exempt.] There are some persons who have claimed to be, but are not, exempt. Thus, resiants of a *private leet* lying within the hundred, whereby they are liable to serve office therein, are not exempt from serving the office of constable of the hundred; but they cannot be appointed to *both* offices during the same period. (Rex v. Genge, Cowp. 13; Constable of Stepney, Bulstr. 174; Reg. v. Jennings, 11 Mod. 215.)

An inspector of the lottery office is not exempt, although regularly appointed by the commissioners, and his serving as constable would interfere with the discharge of the duties of his office of inspector, for he may execute the office of constable by deputy. (Rex v. Wood, 1 Esp. 359.) And it is doubtful whether justices of the peace are exempt, except within their own jurisdiction. (Delamotte's case, Stra. 698.)

Nor are officers or watchmen of the custom-house. (Rex v. Clarke, 1 Keb. 933.) Nor tenants in ancient demesne. (Rex v. Bettsworth, 2 Show. 75.)

SECTION II.—OFFICE OF CONSTABLE.

Mandamus to swear in.] If after a person properly qualified has been duly elected or chosen, the justices or persons who ought to swear him into office refuse to administer the oath, the Court of King's Bench will grant a mandamus to compel them to do so. (Davenport v. Israel, Comb. 285, 2 Haw. x. 47, 1 Rol. Abr. 535.)

Oath by whom administered.] A petty constable may take the oath of office before the court leet, or justice before whom he is elected, or if elected at a court leet, he may take the oath before a justice of the jurisdiction; and it has been held, that if the officer of the leet refuse to swear in a petty constable, duly elected by the homage or jury, a justice may administer the oath to him, and so constitute him a legal officer, although the officer of the leet has sworn in another person who was not duly elected. But the high-constable must be sworn either before the justices in quarter sessions, or the justices who appointed him under a warrant from the quarter sessions. (2 Haw. x. 49; Fletcher v. Ingram, 1 Salk. 175, Com. Dig. Lect. M. (6.)

The Form of the Oath.] "You shall well and truly serve our sovereign lord, the King, [and the lord of the leet, *if sworn at a leet*, in the office of constable for the township,] [*or other place for which he is chosen*,] of —— for the year ensuing, or until another be sworn in your stead, according to the best of your skill and knowledge. So help you God."

The Substitute.] In certain cases, by the provisions of acts of Parliament, as well as by the common law, the person appointed is allowed to excuse himself from service by providing a sufficient *substitute*, to be approved and sworn in his stead; the same thing is allowed by the agreement of all parties among themselves, though it seems the appointee cannot substitute a deputy of his own authority *alone*. (Rex v. Adlard, 4 Barn. & Cres. 780.) In either case the person substituted is to all intents and purposes the constable, and the principal is altogether exonerated from the office for that turn, and cannot be called upon to serve or appoint another, although the substitute die, run away, or be removed for misconduct or inability. (Underhill v. Witts, 3 Esp. 56; Sir W. Vane's case, 2 Keb. 309.)

And if the principal have contracted with his substitute to pay him a certain sum for undertaking the office, it seems that it may be recovered in an action, even before the expiration of the service. (Id. ib.)

Refusal of Office.] If a person elected be present at the court leet, and refuse the office without good cause, the steward may impose a reasonable fine upon him, which may be levied by distress. (Fletcher v. Ingram, 1 Salk. 175, 1 Ld. Raym. 70, Com. Dig. Leet, M. 68, Griesley's case, 8. Co. 38.) Though in Fletcher v. Ingram, which was an action of replevin, it is said a custom so to levy it, should be alleged; but, according to Gresley's case, a custom is not necessary; the right to levy being incident at common law to the right to impose the fine.

If he is absent when elected, the steward may give him notice of a time and place at which to appear before a justice, and take the oath of office; and if he disregard the notice, he may be presented, and a fine imposed at the next court, which may be recovered as aforesaid, or by action; (Moseley v. Stonehouse, 7 East, 181 ;) or the steward may certify his election to the justices, who may thereupon summon him before a justice to take the oath, which, if he refuse to do without good cause, he may be indicted for a misdemeanour at the sessions or assizes. (Rex v. Lone, Str. 920; Rex v. Derbyshire, 2 Burr. 1182.) But the justices cannot fine him for refusing to be sworn. (Crawley's case, Cro. Car. 567.)

Form of Appointment.] If the appointment merely state, that the person elected is an inhabitant of the *parish*, in which the leet or other district for which he is appointed happens to lie, omitting to state that he is an *inhabitant* of such *leet* or other *district*, it is bad, for not sufficiently showing his liability to serve; unless, perhaps, it appear on the face of the appointment, that the leet or district embraces the whole parish. (Rex v. Derbyshire, 2 Burr. 1184; Rex v. Davis, Cas. Temp. Hard. 283.)

Indictment for refusing.] In an indictment, or declaration for the fine or amerciament, for refusing to serve the office, should be set forth the authority to appoint, the manner of the election or appointment, notice thereof and refusal, and before whom the court was holden. It is not sufficient to aver generally that the defendant was duly elected, or legally elected, without showing the *special* circumstances of the appointment and *notice*. (Rex v. Vaws, 1 Mod. 24; Rex v. Harpur, 5 Mod. 96, 2 Haw. x. 46.)

Temporary Deputy.] Though a constable cannot alone appoint a *permanent* substitute, *(ante* 333,) he may, when sick, or necessarily absent, appoint a deputy to do a ministerial act; and it may be by verbal direction, though it had better be done in writing.

Therefore a high-constable may appoint a deputy to billet soldiers on an alehousekeeper, (Midhurst v. Waite, 3 Burr. 1262,) and if the warrant of a justice is directed to a constable, as a constable he may appoint a deputy to execute it, but the deputy cannot empower a third person to do so in his stead. (2 Hawk. xiii. 29.) And though a constable may himself execute it *elsewhere*, he cannot empower a deputy to do so. Constables should beware of appointing deputies where any discretion is to be exercised; as to make arrests, or break open doors, &c., a power reposed in the recognized officer alone. (2 Haw. x. 36, 1 Rol. 274, 1 Sid. 355.)

Substitute or Deputy.] The distinction between a substitute and a deputy should be observed; the former must be sworn and approved, and then becomes the officer and acts in his own name, the person in whose stead he serves having no authority; but a deputy is one employed by the person holding the office, and a return made by him must be in the name of his principal, who is responsible for the act of the deputy. (Phelps v. Winchcombe, 3 Buls. 78.)

Quaker's Deputy.] It is provided by the local militia act, that if any chief or other constable, headborough or tithingman, or overseer, be a quaker, certified to be so by two quakers, and neglect or refuse to perform the duties of this act, any two justices acting for that division shall, when expedient, by an order under their hands and seals, appoint a fit person to be deputy to him for the purpose only of carrying this act into execution; and every such deputy shall have and exercise all the powers, authorities, and jurisdictions given by this act to such officer for whom he shall act, and shall do and perform the like duties and offices, under the like pains, penalties, and forfeitures hereby imposed for neglect of duty of any such officer, in like manner in every respect as the person for whom he shall so act; and the principal shall be discharged from all duty required by this act, and penalties incurred for neglect thereof, after the time of such appointment. (52 Geo. 3. c. 38. s. 27.)

Determination of Office.] The office of constable, though determinable at the end of the year, or at any time by removal for misconduct, is not actually determined until there is a formal removal, or a successor is appointed and sworn; for the district ought not to be without an officer; (Anon. 12, Mod. 2. 56;) and the 13 & 14 Car. 2. c. 12. s. 15, reciting that lords of manors do not in some instances keep court leets every year for making constables, enacts, " that in case any constable, headborough, or tithingman shall die or go out of the parish, any two justices may make and swear a new constable, headborough, or tithingman, until the lord of the manor shall hold a court leet, or until the next quarter sessions, who shall approve of the said officers so made and sworn as aforesaid, or appoint others, as they shall think fit; and if any officer shall continue above a year in his office, the justices in their quarter sessions may discharge him, and put another fit person in his place until the lord of the manor shall hold a court as aforesaid.

But if the quarter sessions discharge old constables and appoint others, on a suggestion that the former have served a year, the appointment must contain an adjudication of such service. (Rex v. Davis, Cas. Temp. Hardw. 282, Stra. 1050.)

Removal from Office.] The sheriff, steward, justices, or others, who have appointed a high-constable, or constable, have power to remove him for misconduct in office, or other good cause, (2 Hawk. x. 38:) but if removed, the Court of King's Bench, upon complaint made, and good cause not being shown, will award a mandamus to restore him to the office, (id. 49,) or a rule of court for the purpose may be obtained, but not a writ of restitution, according to the Constable of Stepney's case. (1 Buls. 174.)

The justices cannot, either out of quarter sessions or at quarter sessions, remove a constable elected, appointed, and sworn at the leet, until after the expiration of the year; and therefore, if a constable chosen by the leet be discharged at the sessions, and another sworn, the King's Bench will issue a mandamus, or grant a rule to the justices to discharge the party chosen by them, and swear him who was chosen at the leet. (Id. Constables of Limington, 2 Stra. 798, Com. Dig. Leet. M. 6.)

If a constable has been unduly appointed, an information, in the nature of quo warranto, may be granted to try the validity of his title. (Rex v. Goudge, Stra. 1213.) But the affidavits on which such an application is made, should state that there is, as the deponents believe, an immemorial custom to elect in the manner in which the party was chosen, and it is not sufficient to state facts from whence that conclusion may be drawn. (R. v. Lane, 5 Barn. & Ald. 488.)

Removal after Year.] Where there is a custom that the constable shall, at the end of his year, present another to be sworn; and he having presented such an one, the officer refuse to swear him, the Court of King's Bench will grant a mandamus to swear the successor, and so to discharge the former; and if the person nominated be unfit, or there be other good cause for the refusal, the officer must rely on it, as his reason and excuse in his return to the writ. (1 Rol. 536. Com. Dig. Leet. M. 5, 7.) "For the constable elected ought to be *homo idoneus*, viz. honest, and of competent knowledge, sustance and ability of body." (Id.)

SECTION III.—POWERS AND DUTIES.

Whence derived.] The powers and duties of the constable are derived from the common law, from several acts of parliament, and from long and well-established usage.

It has been held that a *high*-constable is within the words of the mutiny act, "constable, tything-man, headborough, or other officer;" and it may be concluded, that when the words "constable or other officer" are used in a statute, the high-constable is included, and that in his ministerial capacity he has the same duties to discharge in all parts of his hundred, as well within, as out of the precincts of petty constables, as each petty constable has within his precinct. But he has no jurisdiction over the petty constables whose precincts lie within his hundred; and whether he has concurrent authority with them as a conservator of the peace within their districts, has been questioned, or only in those parts of his hundred which lie within no petty constablewick. (Midhurst v. Waite, 3 Burr. 1261; Rex v. Wyatt, 2 Ld. Raym. 1192, Com. Dig. Leet, M. 5.)

His Duty in Quarrels.] A constable is not justified in taking parties into custody who are merely insulting each other in his presence; but he may admonish them to refrain. If, however, either party strike the other, or offer to strike, or threaten personal violence, the constable may take the offender into custody, and detain him till the affray is over; or he may carry him before a magistrate, (Churchill v. Matthews, 2 Sel. N. P. 911,) or, according to the old books, he may detain him till he finds surety of the peace, (2 Haw. xiii. 8; 2 H. P. C. 88;) or till he can take him before a magistrate, which is the most correct mode of proceeding. But in modern usage the constable, if the affray be in the night, sometimes takes bail for the appearance of the parties, before the magistrate on the morrow.

If private persons deliver one in charge to a constable for having committed an affray in their presence, he must receive him. (1 Haw. lxiii. 17 Hale, 135.)

Arrest when Affray over.] But no arrest, without warrant, can be made either by a private person or a constable, for an affray after it is *over*, although he were present during its continuance; unless a dangerous wound has been inflicted, or there be sufficient ground for supposing that a felony is likely to ensue. Nor would a warrant of a justice, *subsequently* obtained, justify such an arrest. (Sharrock v. Hannemer, Cro. Eliz. 375; Coupey v. Henley, 2 Esp. R. 540, Hale, 92. 136.)

But if a constable is endeavouring to prevent a breach of the peace, and any person stand in his way, purposely to obstruct him in so doing, he may take such person into custody; but he must not give him a blow. (Levy v. Edwards, 1 Car. & P. 40.)

And if one of the affrayers fly from him, he may instantly pursue and take him; so if one opposes and assaults him in the execution of his duty. (1 Haw. lxiii. 15, 16, Hale 135, 4 Inst. 177.)

Breaking open Doors.] If persons are committing an affray in a house, or if there be a noise or disorderly drinking therein, at an unseasonable time of the night, a constable, after declaring the cause of his coming, and having previously demanded admission in vain, may break open the doors, if the affray or the disorder continue. (2 H. P. c. 95.) The same rules apply to rioters, whom it is the constable's duty to apprehend during the time of the ferment, though not afterwards, without a warrant of a justice. (See Clifford v. Brandon, 2 Camp. 358.)

Felony being committed.] Any person may apprehend an offender in the act of committing a felony, or may pursue and take him, if such person saw him committing the offence, although it may not be a breach of the peace; such as exposing an infant in a public place, or a cheat in the act of using false dice, &c. (2 Haw. xii. 1. 4, 2 H. P. C. 90.)

So any person may break open doors to apprehend a person who is endeavouring to commit murder; (Handcock v. Baker, 2 Bos. & Pul. 264 ;) and it is the duty of all persons so to act in such like cases. The practice of levying the hue and cry in pursuit of felons, has been superseded by an improved system of police; but if it be resorted to, all persons are bound to aid and assist, upon pain of fine and imprisonment, in pursuing and securing the offender. (2 Haw xii. 56, Hale 90, 91, 3 Inst. 116, 3 Edw. 1. c. 9.)

And private persons, acting *bona fide*, may arrest a suspected felon, at the risk of an action, in which they must prove the party has been actually guilty of a felony, or pay damages. (Lidwith v. Catchpole, Cald. 291; Adams v Moore, 2 Sel. N. P. 910.)

Felon resisting, killed.] Constables may break open the doors of a house in which a person charged with felony has taken refuge, after informing the inmates of their object. And if the felon resist, and they cannot *otherwise* take him, they are justified in using force, although he is killed in the attempt. But if in such case he make no resistance, the officer is guilty of murder. (1 Haw. xviii. 17. 18. 20; xxix. 16. 2. Haw. xiv. 7.) But without a warrant, no *private* person can justify breaking open the doors of a house to take one suspected of felony, though it is said that if it prove in the event that he was guilty, the person is justified. (2 H. P. C. 82, 83.)

Complaint made to Constable.] If a dangerous wound have been inflicted, the constable, though not present, is bound on complaint, to take the offender into custody, or to receive him from others who have taken him, and forthwith carry him before a magistrate. (Coupey v. Henley, 2 Esp. R. 540; 1 Haw. lxiii. 17.) And on a direct and positive charge of felony being made before him, however false it may ultimately prove, it is his duty to take or receive the accused into custody, unless it is reasonably apparent that the charge is unfounded, in which case he may release him. (White v. Taylor, 4 Esp. R. 80; Rose v. Wilson, 8 Moore, 364; M'Cloughan v. Clayton, Holt. Rep. 478.)

Arrest on Suspicion.] There is a distinction, material to be observed, between a private person and a constable arresting on suspicion. A constable, having reasonable cause to suspect that an individual has committed a felony, may detain him until he can be brought before a justice of the peace to have his conduct investigated; but in order to justify a private person in so doing, he must not only make out a reasonable ground of suspicion, but he must prove that a felony has *actually* been committed. (Beckwith v. Philby, 6 Barn. & Cres. 635.) It, therefore, is evident, that a private person incurs great hazard in arresting another upon suspicion. Nor does the law extend impunity to constables in like cases, unless they act *bonâ fide* upon reasonable grounds. Their experience, and indeed the common sense of mankind, will readily point out what circumstances, as they arise, will justify the taking another person into custody. (See Samuel v. Payne, Doug. 360.) But in the discharge of this very important duty, Mr. Peel's acts afford great facilities, in enumerating a variety of offences for which an arrest may be made.

Arrest without Warrant.] The 7 and 8 Geo. 4. c. 29. s. 63, provides, that any person *found committing* any of the offences punishable under that act, except the offence of angling in the day time, may be immediately apprehended without a warrant, by any peace officer, or the owner of the property injured, or with respect to which the offence is committed, or by his servant or any person authorized by him, and forthwith taken before some neighbouring justice of the peace, to be dealt with according to law; and a similar provision is enacted with respect to offences punishable under the 7 and 8 Geo. 4. c. 30. (see s. 28.) By the 63rd section of the former of these acts, any person, to whom any property is offered to be sold, pawned, or delivered, having reasonable cause to suspect that any such offence has been committed on, or with respect to such property, is authorized, and, if in his power, is required to apprehend, and forthwith carry before a justice, the party offering the same, together with such property, to be dealt with as aforesaid.

For Felony or Larceny.] The offences are as follows, as contained in the sections to which the figures refer, in the 7 and 8 Geo. 4. c. 29.—Stealing securities for money or warrants for goods (5); robbing, or stealing from the person, assaulting with intent to rob, demanding property with menaces or force (6); obtaining property by threatening to accuse of an infamous crime (7); sending letters containing menacing demands, or threatening to accuse of an infamous crime to extort money (8); sacrilege (10); burglary (11); housebreaking and stealing in a house (12); robbery in a building in the same curtilege with, but not part of the house (14); robbery in a shop, warehouse, &c. (15); stealing silk, woollen, linen, or cotton goods in process of manufacture (16); stealing goods in a vessel, barge, &c., in a port, river or canal, &c. (17); plundering a vessel, wrecked, stranded, &c. (18); being in possession of shipwrecked goods without a satisfactory account of them (19); offering such shipwrecked goods for sale, without showing a lawful possession thereof (20); stealing records and other proceedings of a court of law or equity (21); stealing or concealing, &c. wills (22); stealing writings relating to real property (23); stealing horses, cows, or sheep (25); stealing deer (26); being found, upon search warrant, in possession of part of a stolen deer or snares, &c. (27); setting engines for taking deer, or pulling down park fences (28); resisting keepers of deer in the execution of their duty (29); killing hares or conies in a warren or place where they are usually kept (30); stealing dogs or domestic beasts or birds, not the subjects of larceny at common law (31); being in possession of such, or their skins, plumage, &c. (32); unlawfully killing pigeons (33); unlawfully taking fish in *private* property, in the night time, or day, except by angling (34); stealing or dredging for oysters or their brood in a private bed (36); stealing ore, or produce of any mine (37); stealing or destroying trees, shrubs, &c. (38, 39); stealing or destroying live or dead fence, wooden fence, style or gate, or being in possession of such when stolen (40, 41); stealing fruit, or cultivated vegetables (42, 43); stealing glass, wood-work, or fixtures of any kind from a building, or metal fixtures from grounds (44); stealing by tenants or lodgers, of any property let to them with their houses or apartments (45); stealing by clerks and servants, of their masters' property (46); embezzlement by such of money received on their masters' account (47); embezzlement by agents of money, goods, or valuable securities, intrusted to them for safe custody or any specific purpose (49, 50); pledging by factors for their own purpose, of goods, or document, or documents, relating to goods intrusted to them for sale, for more than the amount of their lien upon them (51); obtaining money on false pretences (53); receiving stolen property, knowing it to be stolen (54, 55, 56); taking a reward for helping to the recovery of stolen property, without bringing the offender to justice (58); advertising a reward for the return of stolen property, with impunity to the offender (59); being accessory to a felony, or abetting a misdemeanor (61); abetting any offence named in this act (62).

For Malicious Injuries.] The other statute passed for the purpose of suppressing malicious injuries to property, enumerates the following offences: but it must be borne in mind, that a *malicious intention* is an essential ingredient in the offence. Setting fire to a church, chapel, house, or other building (2, 8); destroying silk, woollen, cotton, or linen goods, in the loom, or the machinery for manufacturing them, or machines for manufacturing other goods, or threshing machines (3, 4, 8); firing coal mines (5); drowning or filling in mines, shafts, &c., with intent to destroy them (6); destroying engines, erections, &c., belonging to mines (7, 8); firing, destroying, or damaging any ship (9, 10, 11); exhibiting false lights to destroy a ship (11); destroying or damaging any sea-bank, or works on a river or canal, or obstructing the navigation of a river or canal (12); destroying or injuring a public bridge (13); destroying or injuring a turnpike-gate or toll-house (14); breaking down the dam of a mill or fishery, &c. (15); killing or maiming cattle (16); firing a stack of corn, grain, straw, hay, &c., or a crop, plantation, or heath (17); destroying hop-binds (18); destroying or damaging trees, shrubs, &c. (19, 20); destroying, &c., fruit or cultivated vegetables (21, 22); destroying, &c., fences, walls, styles, gates, &c. (23); committing any other malicious injury to property (24); aiding or abetting in any of these offences (26). (7 and 8 Geo. 4. c. 38.)

County Rate Accounts.] The chief constables are directed by the statute, at the general or quarter sessions, if thereto required to account for the general county rate by them received, on pain of being committed to gaol until they shall account and pay over the money in their hands, according to the order of the said court, on the like pain. And all the accounts and vouchers shall, after having been passed at the said sessions, be deposited with the clerk of the peace, to be kept among the records, and inspected by the justices without fee. (12 Geo. 2. c. 29. s. 8; 55 Geo. 3. c. 51. s. 12.)

Actions against the Hundred.] The relation in which the high-constable stands to parties bringing actions against the hundred, for injuries by riots, &c. will appear by the following sections of the 7 and 8 Geo. 4. c. 31.

Every process for appearance in such case shall be served on the high-constable, who shall, within seven days after, give notice thereof to two justices of the county or division in which such hundred or district shall be situate, residing in, or acting for the hundred or district, and such high-constable may enter an appearance, and defend the action on behalf of the inhabitants of the hundred or district, as he shall be advised, or instead thereof it shall be lawful for him, with the consent of such justices, to suffer judgment by default, and shall, notwithstanding the expiration of his office, continue to act for all purposes of this act, until the termination of all proceedings consequent upon such action; but in case of his death the succeeding high-constable shall act in his stead. (s. 4.)

And two justices may order him to be reimbursed by the treasurer of the jurisdiction. (s. 7.)

When Damage of small Amount.] Where the damage alleged to have been sustained shall not exceed thirty pounds, the party damnified shall not bring an action, but, within seven days after the commission of the offence, give notice in writing of his claim for compensation to the high-constable, who shall, within seven days after the receipt of the notice, exhibit the same to some two justices of the peace of the county or division in which such hundred or district shall be situate, residing in or acting for such hundred or district; and they shall thereupon appoint a special petty sessions of all the justices of the peace of the county, riding, or division, acting for such hundred or district, to be holden within not less than twenty, nor more than thirty days next after the exhibition of such notice, for the purpose of hearing and determining any claim which may be then and there brought before them on account of any such damage; and such high-constable shall, within three days after such appointment, give notice in writing to the claimant, of the day, and hour, and place appointed for holding such petty session, and shall within ten days give the like notice to all the justices acting for such hundred or district. (s. 8.)

Process to be served on Constable, &c.] In every action to be brought, or summary claim to be preferred under this act, against the inhabitants of a county, of a city, or town, or of any exempt liberty, franchise, city, town, or place, the process for appearance in the action, and the notice required in the case of the claim, shall be served upon some one *peace officer* of such county, liberty, franchise, city, town, or place; and all matters which by this act the high-constable of a hundred is authorized, or required to do in either of such cases, shall be done by the peace officer so served, who shall have the same powers, rights, and remedies, as such high-constable has by virtue of this act, and shall be subject to the same liabilities. (s. 12.)

Duty in case of Fire.] On the breaking out of a fire in London or Westminster, all constables and beadles, upon notice thereof, shall immediately repair to the place where it shall happen, with their staves, and other badges of authority, and assist in extinguishing the fire, and shall apprehend all ill-disposed persons that they find stealing from the inhabitants, and afford their utmost assistance to help the inhabitants to remove their goods. (6 Anne, c. 31. s. 5.)

To assist Excise Officers.] A constable is bound to assist the officers of excise in executing, in the night time, the warrant of a justice, if to search for any concealed still, or other vessel for illicit distillation, or for low wines, spirits, &c., preparing for distillation; and he shall be present at the request of such officer, who is authorized in his presence to break into any distillery after admission has been demanded, and not given: and any person may seize and detain persons hawking, selling, or exposing to sale, spirits, &c., for a reasonable time, till notice can be given to a constable, headborough, or other peace officer, who is to carry such offenders before a justice of the peace where the offence is committed. (6 Geo. 4. c. 80.)

To assist Officers of Customs.] Constables, &c., are likewise to aid the officers of the customs authorized by writ of assistance, under seal from the exchequer, in entering any house, warehouse, cellar, &c., in the day time, by force in case of resistance, and carrying away any prohibited goods, chests, packages, &c., to the custom-house of the nearest port; and a constable may so act in pursuance of this statute, as well beyond the limits of the parish or place of which he is officer, as within it. (6 Geo. 4. c. 108. s. 40.)

To assist Distress for Rent.] Constables shall assist landlords in the day time, in breaking open any house, barn, &c., where the goods of a tenant are clandestinely removed, or fraudulently concealed, for the purpose of levying a distress; but in case the place in which they are suspected to be concealed is a dwelling-house, oath must have been first made before a justice, of a reasonable ground of suspicion. (11 Geo. 2. c. 19. s. 7.) And they are required to aid in the appraisement of goods distrained for rent, and to administer an oath to two appraisers to appraise the same, truly to the best of their understandings. (2 W. & M. Sess. 1. c. 5. s. 2.) And if the premises extend into two hundreds or districts, the constable of the district or place in which they are impounded, should administer the oath for the appraisement. (Walter v. Rumball, 1 Ld. Raym. 53.)

May seize Swearer.] If a person unknown to him profanely swear or curse in the presence of any constable, he may seize and take him before the next justice of the jurisdiction; and if a person *known* to a constable curse or swear in his presence, he shall speedily *give information* of the offence to a justice, under the penalty of 40*s*. (19 Geo. 2. c. 21. s. 3 & 7.)

Unlicensed Hawkers and Pedlars.] Any constable or other officer of the peace who shall neglect, on notice, or his own view, to be aiding and assisting in carrying hawkers and pedlars, trading without a licence, or otherwise than according to their licences, or refusing to show their licences before a justice, or in executing the warrants of justices against such offender, shall forfeit for each offence £10. (50 Geo. 3. c. 41. s. 21.)

May seize Night Walkers.] At night a constable may arrest suspicious persons, and secure them until the morning, unless they can give a good account of themselves; so he is bound to keep in safe custody, a common street walker for the purpose of prostitution, if delivered into his custody, for wandering about at an unseasonable hour of the night; and he is indictable for permitting such a person to escape. (Lawrence v. Hedger, 3 Taunt. 15; Rex v. Bootie, 2 Burr. 864.)

Executing Justices' Warrants.] Any person, whether he be an officer or not, is *justified* in executing the warrant of a justice directed to him by name, any where within the jurisdiction of that justice, but he is not compellable to do so. (Attorney-Gen. v. Jeffrey, M'Clel. R. 288.) A constable, however, is *bound* to execute the warrant of a justice within his own precinct, whether the warrant be directed to him by his *proper name,* or generally to *the constable* or peace officer of that precinct; and such a direction may extend to the officers of a county, in which case the instrument must be construed *reddendo singula singulis,* and the authority delegated to such officer is limited to the district for which he is appointed. (Rex v. Weir, 1 Barn. & Cres. 292, 2 Dowl. & Ryl. 444.)

Where may execute Warrant.] Formerly, if a warrant was directed to constables or peace officers *generally,* no constable was justified in executing it *out of his own precinct,* though, if directed to him by his proper name, he might execute it any where within the jurisdiction of the magistrates granting it. But it is provided, by a recent statute, that any constable or other peace officer *may* execute any warrant of a justice, in *any place* within the jurisdiction for which the justice was acting at the time he granted or *indorsed* the warrant, in the same manner as if it had been addressed to him by his proper name, notwithstanding such place is not within his own precinct. (5 Geo. 4. c. 18. s. 6.)

However, he is not *compellable* to execute it out of his own precinct, whether addressed to him in his own name or in his official character. (Gimbert v. Coyney, 1 M'Clel. & Yo. 469.)

When Offender in other Jurisdiction.] The inconveniences arising from the doctrine, that a warrant could not be executed out of the jurisdiction in which it was granted were remedied by the 24 Geo. 2. c. 55. s. 1, which provides, that if any person, against whom a warrant has been issued in one jurisdiction, be out of such jurisdiction, any justice of the jurisdiction in which the person is, upon proof on oath of the hand writing of the justice granting the warrant, shall indorse his name on it, which shall be sufficient authority for him who brings the warrant, and all others to whom it was originally directed, to execute it in such other jurisdiction, and to carry the offender before the justice who indorsed it, or some other justice of the jurisdiction where it is indorsed; and if the offence be bailable, the justice before whom he is brought shall take such bail to appear at the assizes or sessions where the offence was committed, and shall deliver the recognizance, and all the other proceedings, to the constable apprehending such person, to deliver them over to the clerk of the assizes, or clerk of the peace of the jurisdiction where the offender is so required to appear, under the penalty of £10. And if the offence shall not be bailable, or bail be not to the satisfaction of the justice before whom the offender is so brought, the constable shall carry him before one of the justices of the jurisdiction where the offence was committed.

And by the 13 Geo. 3. c. 31, a similar provision is made for the execution of English warrants against persons in Scotland, and of Scotch warrants in cases where the offender is in England, with this difference, that the offender is to be carried to the adjoining county of England, if it be an English warrant executed in Scotland, there to be dealt with according to the 24 Geo. 2. c. 55, and *vice versâ*, if a Scotch warrant. (See *ante* 285.)

Levying Fines, &c., elsewhere.] It has also been provided, for the purpose of extending the above rule to warrants of distress, that where any penalty or other money may, by the warrant of a justice, be levied by distress and sale, if sufficient distress cannot be found within the jurisdiction of the justice granting the warrant, a justice of another jurisdiction upon oath by one witness, certified by indorsement on the warrant, such penalty, &c., or the residue thereof, shall be levied by distress and sale of the goods and chattels of such person in such other jurisdiction, by the officer to whom the warrant was originally addressed. (33 Geo. 3. c. 55. s. 3; vide 5 Geo. 4. c. 18. s. 1.)

Executing illegal Warrants.] For the protection of constables, &c., against the consequences of executing warrants, the legality of which cannot be sustained, the legislature has provided, by 24 Geo. 2. c. 44, that no action shall be brought against a constable or any person acting in his aid for any thing done in *obedience* to any warrant under the hand and seal of a justice, until a demand hath been made or left at his place of abode by the party intending to bring the action, or his attorney or agent, in writing, signed by the party demanding the same, of the perusal and copy of the warrant, and the same hath been refused or neglected for the space of six days after such demand.

Taking Copy of Warrant.] And if, after such demand and compliance therewith, by showing the warrant to, and permitting a copy to be taken by, the party demanding it, any such action be brought without making the *justice defendant;* on producing and proving such warrant the jury shall give a verdict for the defendant, notwithstanding any defect of jurisdiction in such justice; and if such action be brought jointly against such justice and officer, or other person, on proof of the warrant the jury shall find for such officer or other person, notwithstanding such defect of jurisdiction. (24 Geo. 2. c. 44. s. 6; see Price v. Messenger, 2 Bos. & Pul. 158; Milton v. Green, 5 East, 236.)

An overseer executing a warrant of distress for a poor's rate is within the act; (Nutting v. Jackson, B. N. P. 24; Harpur v. Carr, 7 T. R. 270;) and the constables assisting him, (Clark v. Davey, 4 Moore, 465.)

Notice of Action.] The notice of action is sufficient, if it inform the defendant substantially of the ground of complaint, without setting forth the mode or manner in which the injury has been sustained. (Jones v. Bird, 5 Barn. & Ald. 844, 1 Dowl. & Ryl. 497.) But it is not vitiated by being in the form of a declaration, and unnecessarily ample, if it express the cause of action with sufficient clearness. (Gimbert v. Coyney, 1 M'Clel. & Y. 469.)

When Warrant no Justification.] But a constable, &c., is not protected unless he act in obedience to the warrant; therefore, where a constable, having a warrant to search for certain specified goods, took them and *certain others*, also supposed to have been stolen, but which were not mentioned in the warrant, nor likely to furnish evidence of the identity of those which were so mentioned, he was held liable to an action *without* any demand of the warrant. (Crozier v. Cundey, 6 Barn. & Cres. 232.) The like doctrine was held where a constable in order to levy a poor rate under a warrant of distress, broke and entered the house, and broke the windows, &c. (Bell v. Oakley, 2 Maul. & Sel. 259.) And a constable, who delivers a copy of his warrant to the party grieved, cannot thereby discharge himself, unless the party has thereby a right of action, (supposing the warrant illegal,) against the magistrate under whom he acts. (Sly v. Stevenson, 2 Car. & Pa. 464.) It may be observed, that the constable in this case had acted very improperly in obtaining the warrant.

Verbal Warrant.] A constable may arrest a person in the *presence* of a justice by his *verbal* warrant, although no charge is made known to the constable; but a verbal authority is insufficient, if the justice be not present. And in executing a warrant in writing, under the hand and seal of a justice, he should take care to have it *with him* at the time he executes it. (Hall v. Roche, 8 T. R. 187, 2 Hawk. XIII. 14--21.)

Executing beyond Jurisdiction.] If the warrant, issued by a justice of the county, direct the execution to be in a certain parish, one part of which lies within the jurisdiction of the county justices, and the other part within an exclusive franchise, where they have no jurisdiction, and he executes it beyond the jurisdiction of the justice granting it, in an action against him it is neither necessary to join the justice, nor to demand a copy of the warrant. (Milton v. Green, 5 East, 236.)

General Warrants.] General warrants have been declared illegal; and when magistrates either leave a blank to be filled up afterwards with the name of the person apprehended, or they direct a search for felons or stolen goods generally, or to apprehend the authors, printers, or publishers of a certain seditious and treasonable paper, without *naming* or particularizing them, the constable is liable to an action, if, in execution of such a warrant, he arrest an innocent person, or search a place where no such goods are found; and he is not protected by delivering a copy of the warrant (Money v. Leach, 3 Burr. 1766; Rex v. Wilks, 2 Wils. 151, 2 Haw. xiii. 10—18.)

Warrant a Justification.] But if the warrant direct a particular act to be done, and within six days after the demand the officer allow a perusal and copy of the warrant, he is altogether indemnified, if he have strictly executed it according to its literal directions. For in this case the justice is responsible for the wrong. (Parton v. Williams, 3 Barn. & Ald. 330; Jones v. Vaughan, 5 East. 447.) And the officer is equally safe if he give an inspection and *copy* after the six days have elapsed, if the action is not actually commenced; but if he be sued after the six days have past, and *before* the copy has been delivered, the constable is not entitled to the benefit of this clause of the statute, and must rely upon the sufficiency of the warrant in the same manner as any other person. (Id.)

And where the warrant is directed to overseers, and they employ a constable to assist them in the execution of it, inasmuch as it is neither directed to him nor in his custody; if after demand he so inform the party, and refer him to the overseers, the constable is entitled to a verdict in an action in which he is joined with the overseers. (Clarke v. Davey, 4 Moore, 468.)

When he may break Doors.] An officer is justified in breaking open outer doors or other parts of a house after, *but not before*, he has declared his business, demanded admission, and allowed a reasonable time for opening them, (Radcliff v. Burton, 3 Bos. & Pul. 228,) when he has to execute a capias from the Court of King's Bench or Chancery, or a warrant of a justice, to compel a man to find sureties of the peace, or for good behaviour, (2 Haw. xiv. 3;) or a warrant to apprehend him on a charge of felony, (1 H. P. C. 579;) or a capias founded on an indictment for any crime. (2 Haw. xiv. 312, Co. 131, 4 Inst. 177.)

So he may break open outer doors, if not admitted on demand, in the day time, upon a warrant to search for stolen goods, if accompanied with a direction to bring the person in whose custody they are found before the justice on suspicion of the felony; but if the warrant be *merely to search,* the officer cannot enter *unless the doors are open.* (2 H. P. C. 113, 114.)

He may also, in like manner, resort to the like means to execute a capias utlagatum pro fine in any action; (2 Haw. xiv. 6;) or a warrant of justices for levying a fine in execution of a judgment or conviction, grounded on a statute which gives all or part of the penalty to the king; (Conventicles, Sir T. Jones, 233;) and if an officer has entered a house to execute any warrant, or even civil process, in a legal manner, and others fasten the outer doors upon him, he, and also others in his aid, are justified in breaking them to set him at liberty. (Id.)

When may not break Doors.] But he is not justified in breaking open outer doors, &c. to execute a warrant of distress for a poor-rate, (Bell v. Oakley, 2 M. S. 259;) or for a church-rate, (Theobald v. Crichmore, 1 B. A. 229;) or for bringing a person before a justice to take certain oaths prescribed by a statute, empowering a justice to require persons to come before him for that purpose; for such warrant is not grounded on a precedent offence. (2 Haw. xiv. 11.)

Must show Warrant.] It appears to be settled that not only a private individual, but a known officer, at least beyond the limits of his own precinct, is *bound,* and he ought in *all places* to show the warrant which he is about to execute, on the demand of the party on whom it is to be executed. (Hall v. Roche, 8 T. R. 188, 2 Haw. xiii. 28, 1 H. P. C. 583; Countess of Rutland's case, 6 Co. 54; Mackalley's case, 9 Co. 69.) And the officer should afterwards retain the warrant for his own justification, and he need not deliver it, but should certify what he has done upon it to the justice, or in default thereof he may be amerced by the court, of which he is an officer, or the quarter sessions. (Rex v. Wyatt, 1 Salk. 381; Morley v. Slacker, 6 Mod. 83, 1 East, P. C. 319.)

Duty under Militia Acts.] The regulations established with respect to raising the men for the militia service, require that special constables, aiding in the execution of the act, shall be above the age of thirty years. (52 Geo. 3. c. 38. s. 25.)

Two deputy lieutenants within a division, or one deputy lieutenant and one justice, may issue their warrant, requiring the attendance of the constable or other officer of any place, for the purpose of the act, at a time and place therein mentioned; and if such constable, &c. refuse or neglect to comply with the orders and directions which he shall receive, or be guilty of any fraud or gross neglect in his duty, they may commit the offender to the common gaol for one month, or fine him in any sum not above £20, nor under £2. (Ib. s. 26.)

The deputy lieutenants may add together any two or more parishes or tithings, or add any extra parochial place to any parish, &c. adjoining thereto, for the purposes of this act; and the constables of these places shall act together herein, as if they were respectively officers of one and the same precinct. (Ib. s. 28.)

And the chief constable of each hundred is to direct the constables of the precincts to give notice to every man balloted to serve, to appear at the appointed meeting seven days before such meeting; and such constables shall attend such meeting, and make return upon oath of the days when such notice was served. (Ib. s. 32.)

Billeting the Militia.] All mayors, and other chief magistrates, and constables of cities, towns, &c., and in their absence a justice inhabiting near, shall billet the officers and private men serving in the local militia, when called out to annual exercise, in inns, livery stables, alehouses, victualling-houses, and all houses of persons selling brandy, strong waters, cider, wine, or metheglin by retail, upon application to them by his majesty's lieutenant, or by the commanding officer of the local militia of the county, riding, or place where they shall be called out; and when the local militia is not embodied, all mayors, &c. shall order and provide convenient lodging, with fire and candle, in such houses, for the serjeants, corporals, and drummers thereof in permanent pay. (Ib. s. 100.)

No soldier shall be billeted in the house of any duly accredited foreign consul; (7 Geo. 4. c. 10. s. 88;) nor any marine officer or marine. (7 Geo. 4. c. 11. s. 40.)

Baggage Waggons.] When the local militia shall be called out to be trained, or for the suppression of riots, a justice of the peace of the place, on the requisition of the lieutenant, or a deputy lieutenant of the county, or of the officer, commanding the regiment or detachment, may issue his warrant tc the chief constables of hundreds, or constables of precincts, from, through, near, or to which such body of militia shall march, requiring them to provide sufficient carriages to convey the arms, stores, &c.; and if sufficient cannot be thus provided, any justice for an adjoining county or place may make a like order within his jurisdiction to make up the deficiency, and the officer requiring such carriages and men shall at the same time pay the constables, for the use of the owners, for every mile which they shall travel, one shilling for a waggon with five horses, or a wain with six oxen, or with four oxen and two horses; nine-pence for a cart with four horses; and so in proportion for carriages drawn by a less number, for which sums the constables shall give a receipt; and they shall appoint the persons having carriages within their precincts as they think proper, to furnish such carriages and men, who are required to furnish the same, for one day's journey, and no more. And if the constables, &c. are at any charges herein, over and above the money which shall be so received by them, they shall be repaid to them by the treasurer of the county, riding, or place, in which they are incurred. (52 Geo. 3. c. 38. s. 101.)

Notice of embodying Militia.] The lieutenant of every county, &c. to whom his majesty's order is directed, shall issue a warrant to the constables of hundreds, who are to forward the same to the constables of the precincts, and such constables shall forthwith cause notice in writing to be given to the several local militia-men to attend at the time and place mentioned in such order. (Ib. s. 126.)

And the constables of precincts shall, before the 14th of November in every year, return to the clerk of the subdivision a true account of all persons serving for such precinct in the local militia, specifying such as shall have died or left their residence, and the place to which those have gone, if that can be ascertained, subject to a penalty of £5 for making a false, or neglecting to make any return. (Ib. s. 174.)

Remuneration to Constables.] Every high-constable, petty constable, &c. who shall act in raising the money assessed for deficiency in the number of men who ought to serve for each place, shall be paid, as a recompense for their trouble therein, one penny in the pound on the money raised by the clerk of the subdivision. (Ib. s. 186.)

Militia Deserters.] It is the duty of all constables, and other persons, to apprehend defaulters or deserters from the local militia, and to deliver them into custody at any military head-quarters or gaol, near where they shall be apprehended; and for so doing shall receive twenty shillings for each offender, over and above any reward given under any act for punishing mutiny or desertion. (43 Geo. 3. c. 50. s. 5.) A similar power to apprehend deserters, &c. from the army or marines is given by the annual mutiny acts.

Lists for Ballot.] The constables, within fourteen days after direction, shall leave notice in writing for every occupier of every dwelling-house, or part of a dwelling-house, to produce, within fourteen days after the day of giving that notice, a list in writing of the Christian and surname of every man resident therein between the ages of eighteen and forty-five; and the notice shall contain the day and place appointed for appeals by those claiming exemption. (42 Geo. 3. c. 90. s. 26.)

Army travelling.] The annual mutiny act gives the like general authority to magistrates and constables, in cases of the troops of the regular army removing from town to town, as they exercise with respect to the militia, when embodied. The order for the supply of carriages, horses, &c. must specify whence and where they are to travel, and the distance, not exceeding twenty-five miles. (10 Geo. 4. c. 6. s. 54.)

Extra Carriages for Army.] In cases of emergency, the justices, on such order, shall issue their warrants to such constables, requiring them to provide, not only waggons, &c., but saddle-horses, coaches, chaises, and four-wheel carriages, usually let or kept for hire; and boats, barges, and other vessels, used for the carriage of all manner of goods and merchandize upon any canal or navigable river, on payment of such reasonable sums of money, not exceeding the usual hire, as the justices in the warrant direct. (Ib. s. 56.)

Billeting Soldiers.] Constables, &c. shall quarter and billet the officers, and soldiers, and persons receiving pay in the army, in inns, &c., except of freemen of the company of vintners of London, by right of apprenticeship or patrimony, and in no private house, or the house of any foreign consul. (Id. s. 53.)

The constable, or others appointed to billet soldiers, may billet them equally in the adjoining county with that for which he acts, within one mile from the place mentioned in their route. (Id. s. 49.)

Billeting in Westminster, &c.] The high-constable shall issue his precept to the several constables in their divisions to billet the soldiers of the foot-guards in such houses in Westminster, and the places adjacent in Middlesex, Surrey, and the Borough of Southwark, as are subject thereto in other places, but not in London. And the said constables of Westminster, Middlesex, Surrey, and the Borough of Southwark, at every general quarter sessions, shall deliver to the justices upon oath, true lists, signed by them, of such houses, and the people inhabiting them within their precincts, and the names and rank of the officers and soldiers there quartered, for the inspection of all persons, without fee or reward. (Id. s. 50.)

Marines.] There is also an annual provision, directing that warrants for conveying marines, when on shore, shall be granted in the same manner as for conveying detachments of the regular army, and to be executed by constables in the same manner.

To attend Sessions.] The constables, as well of the hundreds as of parishes, are bound to attend the quarter sessions. (Dalt. 185.) The constables of hundreds, or chief constables, must appear to make return of the warrants directed to them previous to the sessions, to receive the instructions of the justices, and to report the state of the king's peace within the division. Such at least are the *general* duties assigned to them *by* the *nature* and from the original *foundation* of their office. Besides these, however, many others have from time to time been imposed upon them by statute, of an amount too considerable to be distinctly enumerated to any profitable purpose here, as many of them, although more or less connected with their *attendance* upon the sessions, are to be executed out of them.

The petty constables are called over, and fined by the court if they do not answer. Their duties relative to their parishes are in a great degree similar to those of the chiefs respecting the hundreds, with some additional ones, such as reporting the state of their parish stocks, giving evidence respecting the execution of warrants wherewith they may have been charged, and all other matters pertaining to their office, both as conservators of the peace, and as ministers of the justices.

SECTION IV.—TREATMENT OF PERSONS APPREHENDED.

Carrying Offenders before a Justice.] The only case in which a constable can set a person free, seems to be where he has taken him into custody for a mere trivial affray, which he may do when the heat is over; but in all other cases it is his duty to take the person he has in custody, with all convenient speed, before a justice of the jurisdiction, where the offender is apprehended, to be dealt with according to law.

And if he detain his prisoner in custody for an unreasonable period, as to give time to collect witnesses, or treat him with unnecessary harshness, as handcuffing him, unless there is danger of an escape or rescue, which must be averred in pleading, he is liable to an action. But he cannot release him upon bail, or the undertaking of others for his appearance. (Coupey v. Henley, 2 Esp. R. 540; 2 Haw. xv. 26; Wright v. Court, 4 Barn. & Cres. 596; Com. Dig. Impris. H. 4, 5.)

Taking through adjoining Counties.] By the 28 Geo. 2. c. 29. s. 2, " Any constable, or other peace officer, or other persons apprehending any offender whom they ought to apprehend, may convey him to any justice *acting* for the said county, and *resident* in an *adjoining* county; and the said constables, &c., in all such cases, shall act in all such things as if the said justice was resident within the said county to which they respectively belong; and every person obstructing or hindering them in the said adjoining county, shall be liable to the same pains and penalties as if the same had been committed in the county for which the said constables, &c., were appointed to act. And the third section of the same act empowers officers or other persons to carry their prisoners through adjoining counties on their way to gaol, and an escape or rescue shall subject the parties to the like pains and penalties as if the escape had happened, or such rescue made, in the county wherein such offence was committed.

May confine Offender.] The officer may, until he can, with convenient despatch, take the offender before a justice, confine him in a house, or, if necessary, in the stocks, or common gaol, of the place. And therefore a *night* constable may commit one charged with felony to the compter for the night, but not by way of *punishment*, nor for *trial*, for this is the office of the justices of the peace. (2 Haw. xvi. 3; xiii. 8; 2 H. P. C. 81. 120; White v. Taylor, 4 Esp. R. 80; see Rose v. Wilson, 8 Moore, 364.)

And a constable may require a gaoler to take an offender into temporary custody, until he can carry him before a justice, (4 Ed. 3. c. 10. 1 H. P. C. 595,) or if he secure him in the stocks, or the house of a constable, or even of a private person, he is, in contemplation of the law, in a prison; for imprisonment is nothing else but a restraint of liberty. (2 Haw. xviii. 4.)

Suffering Prisoner to go.] If a constable, having arrested a person in execution of a warrant, suffer him to go at large on his promise to return at a certain time and bring sureties, he cannot *retake* him under the *same* warrant. But it seems, that if he do return and surrender himself, the constable may lawfully detain him, and carry him before a justice in pursuance of the same warrant. (2 Haw. xiii. 9.)

Arresting sick Person.] If the person arrested be sick, and cannot be removed without danger of death, he may be detained in his own house, till the officer can reasonably bring him to a justice. (2 H. P. C. 81.)

When a constable conveys a person in his custody before a justice, he is still, in law, in his custody, until the justice have either discharged or bailed him, or committed him to gaol. (Ib. 120.)

SECTION V.—PRIVILEGE.

Exempt from other Office.] Generally, if a person is serving one civil office, it exempts him from being chosen to any other for the same period. (See Price's Case, Sir T. Jones, 46; Abdy's Case, Cro. Car. 585.) But a seafaring man, although appointed and serving as headborough, is not exempt from being impressed in the navy. (Fox's Case, 5 T. R. 276.)

Gains a Settlement.] A person being legally placed in, and who serves the office of constable for a township or other place, and tithingmen, borsholders, and wardens, being officers of the same character as constable, and serving a public annual office in a parish during an entire year, gain a settlement in the parish in which they reside, though they reside under a certificate from another place; (1 Nolan, P. L. 617; Rex v. Wingham, 2 Stra. 1199;) although a constable, after being appointed and sworn, employ another to serve for him as a deputy. (Rex v. Hope, Mansell, Cald. 252.)

But the deputy does not gain a settlement. (Rex v. Winterbourne, Burr. S. C. 520; Rex v. Allcannings, 634.) And if the constable, &c., become actually chargeable, and be removed before the expiration of the year, though more than forty days after entering on his office, he gains no settlement. (Rex v. Fittleworth, Burr. S. C. 238.) Nor if he serve one half year, and then go out of office for an interval, and afterwards serve another half year, for that were not an *annual*, but a semi-annual office. (Rex v. Coldashton, Burr. S. C. 446.) Nor although he be irregularly discharged from the office shortly after he has been duly elected and acted, for he has not executed the office for a year. (Rex v. Holy Cross, 4 Barn. & Ald. 619.)

The settlement is gained in the parish where he resides the last forty days of the year's service, but no settlement is acquired unless the parish or township in which he lives, or some part of it, lies within the precinct of which he is the officer. (Rex v. Liverpool, 3 T. R. 118; St. Mary v. St. Lawrence, 2 Bott. 156.)

Protection in Office.] Every person is bound, in the day-time, to recognize a constable, or other known or sworn officer, when acting within his *own precinct* in the discharge of his duty. Therefore, if he interfere to arrest an affrayer or a felon, or any one violating the peace within his district, to oppose him, or any one whom he calls to his assistance, is a misdemeanor; and if he, or such assistant, be killed, it is murder.

But at night persons are not bound to recognize him as the proper officer, unless he give them some notification of the fact, as by declaring himself to be the constable, or commanding the peace to be kept in the king's name, &c. (2 Haw. xvii.; Kendal's Case, 5 Mod 78; Rex v. Tooley, 2 Ld. Raym. 1296.)

Showing the Warrant.] It is an equal offence to kill, hurt, or obstruct a constable, or a private person, in the execution of a legal warrant, though it may have some latent or technical defect, (1 H. P. C. 460; Rex v. Winwick, 8 T. R. 455,) whether within or beyond his precinct, after he has made known the purpose of his coming, and, if required, shown his warrant. But a refusal to show the warrant on demand, reduces the killing to manslaughter, and the assaulting him may be justified, by showing that it was necessary in defence of one's self or others. For no one is bound to submit to the aggression of a person under the pretext of a warrant, which he asserts to be in his possession, but which he refuses to show. (Countess of Rutland's Case, 6 Co. 54; Mackalley's Case, 9 Co. 69; Hall v. Roche, 8 T. R. 188.)

Assaulting to prevent Arrest.] By the recent act for the consolidation of the laws relating to offences against the person, it is provided, that persons convicted of any assault upon any peace officer, or any other person, with intent to resist the lawful apprehension or detainer of offenders under this act, may be sentenced to imprisonment, with or without hard labour, for any time not exceeding two years, and may also be fined and required to find sureties to keep the peace, if the court shall so think fit. (9 Geo. 4. c. 31. s. 25.)

SECTION VI.—EXPENSES AND REMUNERATION.

Delivering Accounts.] By the 18 Geo. 3. c. 19. s. 4, it is provided, "that every constable, headborough, or tithingman, shall, every three months, and within fourteen days after he shall go out of office, deliver to the overseers of the place a just account, fairly written in a book kept for that purpose, and signed by him, of all sums expended in his office on account of the parish, township, or place, in all cases not otherwise provided for by law, and of all sums received by him on account of the parish, &c.; and the overseers, or their successors, shall, within the following fourteen days, lay the same before the inhabitants, and, if approved by the majority, shall pay out of the poor rate such money as shall appear to be due; but if the account, or any part thereof, be disallowed, they shall give it back to the constable,

&c., who may produce it before one justice or more of that jurisdiction, giving reasonable notice thereof to the overseers; and the justice shall examine the account, and determine on any objection made to it, and settle what sum appears to him due, enter the same on the account, and sign his name thereto, and the overseer shall pay such sum out of the poor rate.

Appeal against Accounts.] If the overseers find that the parish, &c., is aggrieved by any thing done or omitted by the constable, &c., or by any justice of the peace, or have any material objection to the account, or to the justice's determination, they, on giving reasonable notice to the justice or constable, &c., may appeal to the next general or quarter sessions. But if it appear to them, that reasonable notice was not given, they shall adjourn the appeal to the next quarter sessions, then to be determined; and they may award reasonable costs, as in appeals concerning the settlement of the poor. (Id. s. 5.) But it has been decided, that the appeal only lies in case the majority of the overseers concur in it. (Rex v. Lancashire, 5 Barn. & Ald. 757.)

Expenses not allowed.] The constable can only charge for expenses in doing the *business of the parish;* it therefore behoves him to take care how he incurs expense, as it may turn out that he is not entitled to be reimbursed; thus, where a constable took an offender before a magistrate, who had, in his presence, grossly violated the decorum of a chapel, in which divine service was beginning, and he was bound over to prosecute, it was held, that the sum expended in the prosecution was not chargeable to the parish, as monies expended by him in doing the business of his township, though it might have been different had he, previously to the prosecution, received from the inhabitants some authority to proceed. (Rex v. Saville, 5 Barn. & Ald. 180.)

So, in a prosecution for an assault made upon a parish officer, although the proceeding was directed by a justice, and approved by the *court* which tried it; and even though the expenses had been allowed by the vestry, afterwards by two justices, and that allowance was confirmed by the sessions, on appeal, the Court of King's Bench quashed the order. (Rex v. Bird, 2 Barn. & Ald. 526.)

Expenses of conveying Offenders.] Every person committed to the common gaol for any offence, if he have the means, shall bear his own reasonable expenses of conveying him there, and the charges of such as are appointed to guard him; and if he refuse, or do not defray the same, the justice shall give a warrant to the constable, &c., where such person dwells, or whence he is committed, or where he has goods, to sell so much thereof as in the discretion of the justices will satisfy such charges. (3 Jac. 1. c. 10 s. 1, made perpetual by 16 Car. 1. c. 4.)

And if he have not sufficient within the county where he is taken to bear these charges, then, on the application of the constable or other officer who conveyed him, any justice of the same county shall, upon oath, ascertain the reasonable expenses of the constable or officer, and, without fee or reward, by warrant under his hand and seal, order the treasurer of the county or place to pay the same. (27 Geo. 2. c. 3. s. 1.)

Expenses in Riots.] Any two justices within their jurisdiction may, by writing under their hands, order any reasonable and necessary allowances to be made to high-constables for extraordinary expenses incurred in the execution of their duty in cases of tumult, riot, or felony, subject to the approval of the next general quarter sessions, who may order the treasurer of the county, &c., to pay the high-constables such sums as they deem reasonable. (41 Geo. 3. (U. K.) c. 78. s. 2.)

It has been decided, that the expenses which the high-constable is entitled to have paid him, are not such as are merely personal; but if he necessarily employs special constables in cases of riot and tumult, and pays them for their services, he is in like manner to be reimbursed. (Rex v. Justices of Leicester, 7 Barn. & Cres. 6.)

Reward for stolen Goods.] It is no very uncommon practice for parties who have been robbed, to offer a reward to police officers, or others, for the recovery of the property. It seems, by a case recently determined, that such a promise, at least if made to a constable or police officer, is against the policy of the law, and not binding.

The defendant in the case alluded to, having lost some silk dresses and other property, promised the plaintiff (who was a constable,) ten guineas, if he could find out the thief, and obtain the restoration of her property. The plaintiff (who had no magistrate's warrant for the purpose,) accordingly exerted himself, and apprehended the thief with the property in his possession. The thief was tried and convicted, and the property restored. This action was brought to recover the above reward.

Lord Tenterden held, that the action would not lie. A constable has no right to receive or recover a reward for doing his duty, for which he is paid by the public; or if the reward was meant to be given for procuring the restoration of the property, without reference to a prosecution of the thief, it was illegal, and not the subject of an action. The plaintiff was therefore nonsuited. (Harrison v. Hewson Middlesex Sittings, 18th July, 1829.)

The case was mentioned in the following term, but the court intimating a strong opinion against the application for a new trial, upon the above ground, as well as to the insufficiency of part of the proof, the motion was not persisted in. (MSS.)

SECTION VII.—PROTECTION AGAINST ACTIONS.

Plea and Costs.] In any action against any headborough, constable, or tithingman, concerning any thing done by virtue of his office, he and any other person acting *in his aid*, or *by his command*, may plead the general issue, not guilty, and give any special matter in evidence on the trial, which would, if pleaded, have been sufficient in law to discharge the defendant of the matter laid to his charge; and if the defendant shall have a verdict, or the plaintiff be nonsuit, or suffer a discontinuance, the justice or judge, who shall try the cause, shall allow the defendant double costs, recoverable as in other cases. (7 Jac. 1. c. 5.)

Venue.] And such action shall be laid within the county where the trespass or fact was committed, and if, on the trial, it shall *not be proved* to have occurred in that county, the jury shall find for the defendant, not guilty, without regard to any other evidence. And the defendant, on a verdict for himself, or a nonsuit, or a discontinuance, shall have double costs, and all the other advantages and remedies of the aforesaid statute. (21 Jac. 1. c. 12.)

The militia act, 52 Geo. 3. c. 38. s. 206, gives the like protection, as does the 53 Geo. 3. c. 127. s. 12, relating to church rates for any thing done under either of these acts respectively.

Officers not within these Acts.] Borsholders, and other officers similar to constables, are within the meaning of these acts, but not king's messengers, and such persons unknown in the law, who are mere volunteers in executing the warrants of justices. (Money v. Leach, 3 Bur. 1761; Waldron v. Roscarit, 1 Vent. 170.) But a deputy constable is within the act. (See Phelps v. Winchcomb, 3 Buls. 77.)

Pleading a Justification.] In an action for arrest and false imprisonment, against a constable, if a justification be pleaded, though unnecessarily, the plea must show the specific grounds on which the defendant's suspicions were founded, the same as though the action were against a private person. But if there were several grounds, they may be all stated, for the replication *de injuria* puts them all in issue. In such a plea, if the plaintiff is known to have committed the crime, that he did so, may be averred without setting forth particulars; but if he be arrested on suspicion, then, in *addition* to the circumstances raising a suspicion against him, it must be averred that the crime *was committed*. (M'Cloughan v. Clayton, Holt. Rep. 478, 2 Haw. xii. 18. 2 H. P. C. 78.)

Certificate for Costs.] A certificate is not necessary when a *special* verdict is found, showing that the defendant acted in the discharge of his office; for, as it appears on the record, the master must tax double costs. (Grindley v. Holloway, Doug. 308, n. 82.)

But when the verdict is general, there must be a certificate from the judge who tried the cause, which he is bound to give any time before the costs are taxed, and not necessarily at the time of the trial. (Id. Harper v. Carr, 7 T. R. 448.)

The certificate that the defendant acted by virtue of his office, to entitle him to double costs under this act, need not be granted immediately after the trial of the cause. And where the plaintiff is nonsuited, the judge before whom the cause was tried, may, after an interval of four years, upon an affidavit that the defendant was within the provisions of the statute, grant such certificate. (Norman v. Danger, 3 Younge & Jer. 203.)

Limitation of Actions.] It is provided by 24 Geo. 2. c. 44. s. 8, that no action shall be brought against any constable for any thing done in the execution of his office, or any headborough or other officer, or person acting as aforesaid, unless commenced within *six months* after the act committed. And it appears that he is within the protection of this section of the statute in all cases, when acting with the *intention* of discharging his office, in the execution of a warrant, or of his ordinary common law authority, though he, through ignorance or inadvertency, does an act which he is not authorized or justified in doing. (Parton v. Williams, 3 Barn & Ald. 332; Theobald v. Crichmore, 1 Barn. & Ald. 229.)

But if he has not reasonable ground for supposing that the act done is within his authority, he is not so protected. (Cook v. Leonard, 6 Barn. & Cres. 851.)

When Action not maintainable.] In Davis v. Russel and others, the judge directed the jury to consider whether the circumstances proved, afforded the defendant reasonable ground to suppose the plaintiff had committed a felony, and whether in his situation they would have acted as he had done. The jury returned their verdict for the defendants, and the court, upon a motion for a new trial, held, that this direction was substantially correct. (5 Bing. 354.)

A party cannot maintain trover against a constable, for a wrongful taking of goods under a justice's warrant, without joining the justice as a defendant, if perusal and copy of the warrant have been given under the 24 Geo. 2. c. 44. s. 6; Lyons v. Golding, 3 Car. & Pa. 586.

When not Protected.] But where a constable, having in vain searched a house, under a warrant to search for *black* cloth which had been stolen, took cloth of other colours, and carried it before a magistrate, and on being asked by the owner of the house, refused to inform him whether he had a warrant or no, it was held that the action ought to have been brought within six months. (Smith v. Wiltshire, 2 Bro. & Bing. 621; 5 Moore, 322.) But if he take other goods which are not likely to furnish evidence of the identity of the goods stolen and mentioned in the warrant, although such other goods are claimed as having been stolen also, he is not within the protection of the statute. (Crosier v. Cundey, 6 Barn. & Cres. 233.) But he is not protected, even after the expiration of the six months, against an action for an injury, arising from an act done merely under *colour or pretence* of his office, and which is beyond his authority. (Alcock v. Andrews, 2 Esp. R. 542. n.; Postlewaite v. Gibson, 3 Esp. R. 226.) Nor it would seem from the language of the judges, in Theobald v. Crichmore *(supra)*, where he appears to have acted from malice or evil motives; and not bona fide, though ignorantly, with the intention of executing his duty.

When Time begins to run.] The six months is to be calculated from the period at which the fact was done, and not from the determination of any proceedings instituted to try the legality of the act. (Godin v. Ferris, 2 Hen. Bla. 14.) But if the fact be an imprisonment, he is in time if he bring his action at any period within six months after he is liberated, for the whole imprisonment is one entire trespass. (Pickersgill v. Palmer, Bul. N. P. 24; Coventry v. Apsley, 2 Salk. 420.) And the day of discharge is to be reckoned exclusively. (Hardy v. Ryle, *ante*, p. 316.)

Cases not within the Act, &c.] The statute applies only to actions of tort, and does not extend to an action, if brought against the constable, to recover back money which he has levied on the plaintiff, on the conviction of a justice of the peace, where the conviction has been quashed. (Bul. N. P. 24; see Wallace v. King, 1 H. Bl. 13.)

Arrests for Malicious Injuries, &c.] It is also provided, that all actions and prosecutions against any person for any thing done in pursuance of the 7 & 8 Geo. 4. c. 29, and c. 30, shall be laid and tried in the county where the fact was committed, and shall be commenced within six months after the fact committed, and not otherwise, and notice of such action shall be given to the defendant, one calendar month at least before its commencement; and the defendant may plead the general issue, and give either of these acts and the special matter in evidence; and no plaintiff shall recover, if tender of sufficient amends have been made before action brought, or a sufficient sum of money have been since brought into court by the defendant; and if he gain a verdict, or the plaintiff be nonsuit, or discontinue after issue joined, or judgment shall be given against the plaintiff, the defendant shall receive his full costs as between attorney and client; and though a verdict be given for the plaintiff, he shall not have costs against the defendant, unless the justice before whom the trial shall be, certify his approbation of the action and verdict. (ss. 75. 41.)

Arrest of disorderly Persons, &c.] And in all cases where an action shall be brought against any justice, constable, or other person, on account of any thing done or commanded by him in the execution of his office, under the 5 Geo. 4. c. 83, as to disorderly persons, it is provided by the act, that if he have judgment in his favour, he shall have treble costs awarded him by the court, unless the judge shall certify that there was a reasonable cause for such action.

SECTION VIII.—PUNISHMENT.

Neglect to apprehend Felons.] If a constable neglect his duty to endeavour to suppress an affray or riot, or to apprehend a felon, &c., he is guilty of a misdemeanor, for which he may be indicted and punished with fine and imprisonment, and he is equally punishable for neglect of any duty imposed on him by statute, when no other punishment is particularly appointed. (2 H. P. C. 85. Rex v. Wyat, 1 Salk. 381.)

And if other persons being called upon by a constable to aid him in the execution of his duty, refuse to do so, they are alike answerable. (Id. see 1 Bla. Com. 356.)

Escape of Offender.] But a constable is not responsible for the escape of an offender, unless he has had him in *actual* custody, that is, so far in his power, he having surrendered, as to have been able to lay hands upon him. (2 Haw. xix. s. 1—27.)

Cannot divide Responsibility.] Where there are two constables appointed for a precinct, they are both officers throughout the whole, although there may have been a long-continued usage for each of them to superintend one district, and the other the other, and if there be any neglect of duty in any part of the precinct, it wou excuse for one to say, it arose in my colleague's district. Taunton, 3 Maule & Sel. 471.)

May be Fined.] Any two or more justices, at a special or petty sessions, upon complaint upon oath of any neglect of duty, &c., by a constable or other peace-officer, he having been duly summoned, may impose on him, upon conviction of such offence, a reasonable fine, not exceeding 40*s*., to be levied, if not paid, by distress and sale of his goods and chattels; and if any person be aggrieved by such judgment, or any thing done in the execution of the warrant, he may appeal to the next general or quarter sessions, giving ten days' notice thereof at the least. And for want of such distress, the offender shall be committed to the house of correction for any time not exceeding ten days. (33 Geo. 3. c. 55. s. 1.)

It is also provided, that no person acting under such warrant of distress, shall be deemed a trespasser, *ab initio*, by reason of any irregularity in the warrant or proceedings thereon; but the person aggrieved may recover special damages, for the injury sustained, in an action of trespass, or on the case, in any of his Majesty's courts of record. (Ib. s. 21.)

Neglect under Jury Act.] If the high constable, for fourteen days after the warrant of the clerk of the peace shall be served on him, or left at his usual place of abode, neglect to issue his precept to the churchwardens, &c., or to supply a competent number of forms, &c., or if he shall neglect his duty as set forth in this act, or make any alterations in the jury lists, after receipt thereof, he shall for every such offence forfeit not more than £10, nor less than £2. (6 Geo. 4. c. 50. s. 44; See Rex v. Pugh, Doug. 188.)

Neglects as to County Rate.] And if any constable neglect to make the returns of rateable property within the parish, when required for the purposes of assessing the county rate, he is liable to a penalty not exceeding £20 to be fixed by the general or quarter sessions, and to be levied by distress. (55 Geo. 3. c. 51. s. 4.)

Or if he neglect to produce assessment books in his hands, or to give evidence on oath respecting the same, on the requisition of the general quarter or petty sessions of the division, he shall for every offence forfeit not more than £10. (Id. s. 9.)

As to disorderly Houses.] So if he be negligent in the proceedings instituted against disorderly houses, he shall forfeit £20 to each of the inhabitants giving the formal notice of such disorderly houses. (25 Geo. 2. c. 36. s. 7. See "DISORDERLY HOUSES," *post*, 376.)

Other Neglects.] And in nearly all the acts which impose particular duties upon constables, penalties are also provided for their neglect, in the discharge of such duties.

And in some cases, as in the raising assessments under the militia act, (52 Geo. 3. c. 18. s. 189,) the forfeiture is £50; for neglecting to return the lists; £20; for neglecting to assist the excise officers under 6 Geo. 4. c. 80, £20; for neglecting to apprehend &c., vagabonds, £5, (5 Geo. 4. c. 83;) for neglecting to make or return lists, or to give notices, serve warrants, &c., under the highway act, (13 Geo. 3. c. 78,) 40*s.*; and for neglecting to exhibit or give notices in cases of actions against the hundred, under the 7 & 8 Geo. 4. c. 31, the party damnified thereby, may sue such constable for the amount of damages sustained, and recover the same with full costs.

SECTION IX.—SPECIAL CONSTABLES.

In what Cases appointed.] By the 1 Geo. 4. c. 37, it is provided; "That where it shall appear to any two justices, by the information on oath of five respectable householders within their jurisdiction, that any tumult, riot, or felony, has taken place, or is likely to take place, such justices may nominate and appoint by precept, under their hands, any householders or other persons not legally exempt from serving the office of constable, residing within their respective divisions, or the neighbourhood thereof, to act as special constables for such time, and in such manner, as to the same justices shall seem fit, for the preservation of the public peace, and the prevention or suppression of any tumult, &c., such persons to take the usual oath administered by law to all special constables.

"And if any person not so exempt, so appointed as aforesaid, shall refuse or neglect to act as such special constable, he shall be liable to the same penalties and punishments as a person who refuses the office of constable is legally subject to. And the justices assembled at the general or quarter sessions holden for such jurisdiction, may direct reasonable allowances for trouble and expenses to be made to such special constable, to be paid by the treasurer of the jurisdiction." (1 Geo. 4. c. 37; see R. v. Leicester, 7 Barn. & Cres. 6.)

Street Constables.] By the Metropolis act, 6 Geo. 4. c. 21, it is provided, "That it shall be lawful for two of the justices appointed under the said recited act, (3 Geo. 4. c. 55,) to any of the police offices thereby established, upon the application of five of the inhabitants of any street or square, or the proprietors of any place of public resort within the limits of the bills of mortality, and the parishes therein enumerated, to appoint a competent number of persons recommended by such inhabitants, or such proprietor respectively, and approved of by such justices, to be constables, to keep the peace within such street or square, or such place of public resort, and the avenues leading thereto, for such period of time as such justices shall deem fit and necessary, and to administer an oath to every such constable, duly to execute that office within the limits, and for the period of time for which he shall be appointed; and every constable so sworn, shall, within the limits, and during the period for which he shall serve, have all such powers and authorities, privileges and advantages, as any constable, duly appointed, hath or shall have within his constablewick, and shall be paid by the inhabitants or proprietor respectively, on whose application he shall be appointed, such wages as shall be deemed reasonable and adequate by the justices, by whom he shall be appointed.

Metropolis New Police.] The recent police act (the 10 Geo. 4. c. 44,) which establishes an entirely new system in the place of the nightly watch; embracing also the means of protection to persons and property in the day time, is founded, in its details of the duty, obligations, and protection of those officers, upon the law relating to constables, as explained in this chapter. A partial experiment only has yet been made of the system, in a few of the many parishes for which it is intended. The statute occupies too much space to be included in this work.

SECTION X.—WATCHMEN.

Their Appointment.] Since the repeal of the statute of Winton, and some other early statutes on the subject by the 7 & 8 Geo. 4. c. 27, we have no general law concerning the appointment of watchmen, whether they are to be sworn, what is the precise extent of their authority, or how long their charge is to continue. There are several acts of parliament which recognize the office of watchman, but these must be referred to the watch appointed under the statute of Winton, or by special acts of parliament. But notwithstanding the repeal of these acts, the usage of particular places to appoint watchmen may doubtless be continued with propriety; they are a species of special constable for the preservation of the peace, and the protection of property by night. And they might, without any great violence to the letter or the spirit of the 1 Geo. 4. c. 37, be appointed *eo nomine* special constables, under that statute to act by night.

Power and Duty.] A watchman duly appointed has precisely the same power and protection as a constable in preventing breaches of the peace, and apprehending suspicious persons, offenders, and felons; and probably in all cases, although he may not derive his office from an appointment under a local act of parliament, or an immemorial custom, if his appointment has been confirmed by the justices in sessions, the superior courts would recognize his authority when acting within the due limits of such office. When a constable is appointed to keep watch, the watchmen ought to carry those whom they apprehend before the constable, to determine the propriety of detaining or setting them at large. If, however, the constable is not at his post, and cannot be conveniently found, a watchman is justified in delivering a street-walker, or other justly suspected person, into the custody of the gaoler, to be kept to answer his charge in the morning, which must be made known to the gaoler at the time of delivering the prisoner into custody. (Lawrence v. Hedger, 3 Taunt. 15, Rex v. Bootie, 2 Bur. 865, 2 H. P. C. 96, 97, 1 H. P. C. 460, 461.)

Not to execute Warrants.] A watchman is not the officer of the justices to execute warrants; and if a warrant be directed to him, he may refuse to execute it, and if he do execute it, he acts only as a private person, and has not the same protection as a constable under 24 Geo. 4. c. 44.

No person can act as a peace-officer, with all the immunities and rights belonging to that office, unless he has been regularly sworn into the office; and, therefore, a person employed by a parish as a patrol to preserve good order, and who has not been sworn into any legally recognized office, has no more authority than a private individual, not even that of a watchman, and cannot take or receive into his custody a person who has committed an assault, though as a private individual he may interfere to prevent a breach of the peace. (Cliffe v. Littlemore, 5 Esp. Rep. 39.)

CHAPTER XIII.—JURY LISTS.

It is not within the scope and object of this work to state more of the law respecting juries, than relates to the duties to be performed by certain parish and other local officers, in preparing and returning the lists from which juries are ultimately to be summoned.

Warrants of Clerk of Peace.] The *clerks of the peace* in *England* and *Wales* shall, within the *first week in July* in every year, issue their *warrants* to the high-constables, commanding them to issue their precepts to the churchwardens and overseers, requiring them to prepare, before the *first day of September,* lists of all men residing within their parishes and townships, liable to serve on juries. (6 Geo. 4. c. 50. s. 4.)

Precept of Constable.] Every *high constable* shall, within *fourteen days* after the receipt of the warrant, issue his *precept,* with a competent number of printed forms, to the churchwardens and overseers of the poor, or the churchwardens alone where there are no other overseers, requiring them to prepare a list of all men residing within their parishes and townships, liable to serve as jurors, &c. And, where there shall be *more than one high constable,* the clerk of the peace shall issue his warrant to every one of them, each of whom shall be liable for the performance of the matters commanded in the warrant, throughout the whole district. And, where any parish or township shall *extend into more than one hundred,* or other like district, either in the same or different counties, it shall be taken for all the purposes of this act to be within that hundred, &c. in which the *principal church* shall be situate. (Id. s. 6.)

Extra-parochial Places.] The justices of the peace of any division in *England or Wales,* at a *special petty sessions* to be holden for that purpose before the *first day of July,* in any year, may make an order for annexing any *extra-parochial place* to any parish or township adjoining thereto, for the purposes of this act, and shall cause a copy thereof to be served on the churchwardens and overseers of such parish or township. (Id. s. 7.)

Lists, by whom made.] The churchwardens and overseers, upon receiving the precept, are required to make out a list of all men liable to serve on juries, residing in the parish or township, and the *extra-parochial place* thereto annexed; according to the form sent to them by the high-constable, which he receives from the clerk of the peace. (Id. s. 8.)

The lists of men resident in each ward of the city of *London*, shall be made out by the parties who have been heretofore used to make out the same; and the shop, warehouse, counting-house, chambers, or office, occupied by such person, shall, for the purpose of this act, be taken to be his place of abode. (Id. s. 50.)

Lists on Church-doors.] The churchwardens and overseers shall, on the *three first Sundays* in the month of *September*, fix a copy of the list upon the principal door of every *public place of religious worship* within their parishes or townships, with a *notice* stating when and where objections to the list will be heard by the justices of the peace. And shall keep the *original list*, or a copy, to be perused by any inhabitant at any reasonable time during the *three first weeks of September*, without fee or reward, that improper omissions or insertions may be corrected; and they may cause a sufficient number of copies of the lists for these purposes, to be *printed* at the expense of their parishes or townships. (Id. s. 9.)

Sessions for correcting Lists, &c.] The justices of the peace in every division shall hold a *special petty sessions* within the last *seven days of September* in every year, of which notice shall be given before the *twentieth* day of *August* next proceeding, to the high-constable, churchwardens, and overseers, at which the churchwardens, &c. shall *produce the list* of men liable to serve on juries within their parishes or townships, and shall answer upon oath such questions respecting the same as shall be put to them by the justices then present; and the justices may strike out names of persons exempt, and insert the name of any man omitted, and reform any errors or omissions in respect to names, qualifications, &c. upon the application of, or notice to the parties immediately interested. The justices present, or two of them, shall then sign the lists with their allowance, and the high constable shall receive every list so allowed, and *deliver* the same to the court of quarter sessions next holden for the county, or division, on the first day of its sitting, upon oath. (Id. s. 10.)

Inspection of Tax-books.] The churchwardens, &c. shall, upon request made at a reasonable time between the *first of July* and the *first of October*. in every year, to any officer having the custody of any duplicate or *tax-assessment* for such parish or township, have free liberty to inspect the same, and make extracts, as may appear to them to be necessary or useful; and every court of *petty sessions* and justice of the peace shall, upon the like request, have the like free liberty to *inspect*, &c. (Id. s. 11.)

Any constable, churchwarden, or overseer, offending against the act by neglect of duty, or otherwise, may be fined, not more than ten pounds, nor less than forty shillings, at the discretion of the justice before whom he is convicted. (Id. ss. 44. 45.)

CHAP. XIV.—WEIGHTS AND MEASURES.

Section I. *Standard Weights and Measures.*
II. *False Weights and Measures.*

SECTION I.—STANDARD WEIGHTS AND MEASURES.

Two Kinds of Weights.] There are two kinds of weights used in England, and both warrantable; the one by law, the other by custom; they are troy weight and avoirdupois. (Dalt c. 112.)

Troy Weight.] Troy weight is by law, and thereby are weighed silk, gold, silver, pearl, and precious stones; and hath twelve ounces to the pound. (Ib.)

Avoirdupoise.] We evidently derive this weight from the French, and the name imports,—to have full weight. By this are weighed all kinds of grocery wares, flesh, butter, cheese, wax, pitch, tallow, wool, hemp, iron, steel, lead, and all other commodities which bear the name of garbel, that is which are garbled, sifted, parted, and whereof issueth a refuse or waste. This hath sixteen ounces to the pound, and twelve pounds over are allowed to every hundred. (Ib.)

Divers Measures.] Though measures, in point of fact, differ in different places, the law only recognizes the legal measure, and consequently a custom in a particular place to sell eighteen ounces to the pound is bad. But Lord Kenyon said, that he did not mean in deciding that question, that a custom to sell butter in *lumps* of any number of ounces was not good; and Buller J. added, that he had not seen any thing in the acts of parliament requiring persons not to sell more or less than a pound. But the question here is, whether, when a person is selling under the specific denomination of a *pound*, he shall be compellable to sell more than a pound. (Noble v. Durrell, 3 T. R. 271; see Hockin v. Cooke, 4 T. R. 314, 6 T. R. 338.)

Statute Weights and Measures.] It has for centuries been an object with the legislature, to establish one uniform standard of weights and measures throughout the kingdom. The last statute on this subject, which repeals all the former ones, so far as they relate to the ascertaining or establishing any such standards, is the 5 Geo. 4. c. 74, which defines the standards of weights and measures by the originals in the custody of the clerk of the House of Commons, and prescribes the mode in which others shall be made in case those originals are lost, destroyed, or injured.

Models for Counties, &c.] The act provides, that copies and models of the standard of length, weight, and measure, shall be made and verified, under the direction of the lords of the treasury, to be deposited in the office of the chamberlains of the Exchequer at Westminster, and verified copies thereof are to be sent to the Lord Mayor of London, the chief magistrate of Edinburgh and Dublin, and to such other persons and places as the lords of the treasury may direct. And the magistrates of every county, division, city, &c. in England, Ireland, and Scotland, shall, within six months after the passing of the act, purchase for their respective counties, &c. a verified model and copy of each of the aforesaid standards, to be placed by them, for custody and inspection, with such persons as they shall appoint, to be produced by such keepers thereof, upon reasonable notice, at such time and place, as any person by writing under his hand shall require, such person paying the reasonable charges of the same. (5 Geo. 4. c. 74. ss. 11, 12.)

Expenses thereof, how paid.] The expenses of procuring such models and copies are to be paid out of the county rates in England, the assessments under grand jury presentments in Ireland, and of the land-tax in Scotland. (Id. s. 13.)

Standard Gallon ascertained.] The act provides, that where reference cannot readily be had to the standard, in disputes respecting the correctness of any measure of capacity, any magistrate, having jurisdiction in the place, may ascertain the content of such measure by direct reference to the weight of pure or rain water, which such measure is capable of containing; ten pounds avoirdupois weight of such water, at the temperature of sixty-two degrees by Fahrenheit's thermometer, being the standard-gallon ascertained by this act, the same being in bulk equal to two hundred and seventy-seven cubic inches, and two hundred and seventy-four one-thousandth parts of a cubic inch, and so in proportion for all parts or multiples of a gallon. (Id. s. 14.)

Existing Weights may be used.] The 16th section enacts, that existing weights and measures, established either by local custom, or founded on special agreement, may be used, provided that the ratio or proportion which they bear to the said standard weights and measures, is painted or marked upon them respectively; but no new weights or measures are to be made, except in conformity with the standard established by this act. (By 6 Geo. 4. c. 12, the act is to take effect from 1st January, 1826.)

SECTION II.—FALSE WEIGHTS AND MEASURES.

Examiners, by whom appointed.] The recent statute, 5 Geo. 4. c. 74. s. 21, enacts, that the powers and regulations, in force under the prior acts, for seizing and destroying weights, balances, and measures, not conformable to the standards, shall be applied to this act. One of these acts, 37 Geo. 3. c. 143, directs that the justices, at their respective *petty sessions,* (instead of in their *quarter* sessions, as provided by 35 Geo. 3. c. 102,) may appoint one or more person or persons, as examiners of the weights and balances within their respective districts.

Nominated by Inhabitants.] If the majority of the inhabitants of any parish, &c. shall be desirous that any person or persons should be specially appointed to examine the weights and balances within the parish, &c. the inhabitants, at a vestry holden for that purpose, may nominate one or more substantial householder or householders, to be approved of, and appointed by the justices at petty sessions, for the division or district in which the parish, &c. shall lie; which person or persons so nominated, approved, and appointed, shall have the same powers and authorities within the parish, &c. as are vested in the person or persons appointed for any district or place. (37 Geo. 3. c. 143. s. 4.)

Standards to be first procured.] But no such appointment shall be made until the inhabitants have procured the proper weights, according to the standard in the Exchequer, (as directed by 5 Geo. 4. c. 74,) for the use of the parish, &c. to be deposited in the custody of the person or persons so to be appointed; and the justices in the respective petty sessions are authorized to order and direct the costs and charges of procuring such weights, and the recompence and satisfaction to be allowed to such examiner or examiners, for his or their time and trouble in the execution of such office within the parish, &c. to be paid out of the poor's rates. (37 Geo. 3. c. 143. s. 5.)

Seizing false Weights, &c.] The person or persons so appointed are required, (having been first sworn, duly and faithfully to execute the office,) as often as the justices shall direct, in the daytime, to enter the shop, mill-house, outhouses, and other premises near such shop, &c. and into the stall or standing place of any person who sells by retail and weight any wares, provisions, goods, or chattels whatsoever; and then and there to search for, view, and examine, all weights and balances in such shops, &c. and to seize any weight or weights not being according to the standard in the Exchequer, or any false or unequal balance or balances which on any such search be found therein, and to detain the same to be produced before the justices in petty sessions aforesaid, upon the hearing of the information or informations after mentioned. (Id. s. 2.)

Penalty for false Weights, &c.] The person in whose shop, &c. any such defective weight or weights, or any false or unequal balance or balances shall be found, (against whom for such offence or offences an information or informations is and are hereby directed to be preferred,) shall, upon conviction thereof, in petty sessions as aforesaid, upon view or confession, or on the oath of one or more credible witness or witnesses, forfeit and pay for every such offence any sum not exceeding 20*s.* nor less than 5*s.* as the justices shall order and adjudge, together with the costs and charges attending the conviction; such forfeiture, together with the costs and charges to be levied by warrant, under the hands and seals of the said justices, by distress and sale of so much of the goods and chattels of the offender, as shall be sufficient to pay the penalty and the expenses of the distress. (Id. s. 2.)

False Weights to be broken.] On the conviction of the offender, the justice shall cause such defective weights, or false or unequal balances, to be forthwith broken and rendered useless, and the materials thereof to be sold, and the money arising from the sale, together with the amount of the forfeiture or forfeitures, to be paid to the treasurer of the county, riding, or division, towards carrying the acts into execution, and the residue, if any, on account of the public stock of the county. (Id. s. 3.)

Obstructing Examiners.] "If any person shall wilfully obstruct, hinder, resist, or in any wise oppose, such examiners, to view and examine such weights and balances in the due execution of their office; or if any person, selling or retailing by weight, shall refuse to produce his weights and balances to be examined, he shall forfeit for every offence, on being duly convicted on oath before any one or more justices of the peace, any sum not exceeding forty shillings, nor less than five shillings, as the convicting justice or justices shall adjudge, to be levied and applied as before directed." (35 Geo. 3. c. 102. s. 3.)

False Measures.] The 55 Geo. 3. c. 43, makes similar provisions with regard to the examination and seizure of false measures, and gives the inhabitants in vestry power to nominate five or more examiners, to be approved by the justices, and inflicts a penalty not exceeding £5, nor less than 40*s.*, upon those who obstruct them, or refuse to produce their measures to be examined. This act also authorizes justices to commit persons, convicted of having false or deficient measures, to prison for any time not exceeding a month, unless the penalties, &c., be sooner paid.

Limitation of Proceedings.] It is provided that no offence against the acts shall be prosecuted, unless information on oath be given within one month after the offence committed, and that persons convicted shall not be otherwise punished by virtue of any other law. Nor shall the proceedings be removed by certiorari or otherwise. (35 Geo. 3. c. 102; 37 Geo. 3. c. 143.)

And the 5 Geo. 4. c. 74. s. 24, enacts, that nothing in that act contained, shall extend to repeal 31 Geo. 2. c. 17, which empowers the dean and high steward of Westminster, &c., to appoint a proper officer to size and seal weights and measures, to be used within the said city and liberties. And the authority of persons appointed at any court leet of any hundred or manor, for examining, seizing, and breaking false weights or balances, is preserved. (35 Geo. 3. c. 102. s. 6.)

Districts intended by the Acts.] The 37 Geo. 3. c. 143, in directing examiners to be appointed for the districts, divisions, and other places of the several counties of England, must be construed to mean the divisions and districts known and recognized at the time the act passed. And therefore such appointment made by two justices at a petty sessions for a district which they had, without the consent of the other magistrates, created within the last five or six years, was held to be illegal. And a rule nisi for a mandamus to the justices of the county, to allow a compensation out of the county rate, to an examiner of weights and measures so illegally appointed, was discharged with costs. (Rex v. Justices of Devon, 1 Barn. & Ald. 588.)

CHAPTER XV.—DISORDERLY HOUSES.

SECTION I. *Theatres, Music-Rooms, &c.*
II. *Gaming-Houses, &c.*

SECTION I.—THEATRES, MUSIC-ROOMS, &c.

The several Kinds.] Disorderly houses are of three kinds: viz. houses kept for music, dancing, or dramatic exhibitions, without being duly licensed—gaming-houses—and bawdy houses. They are all nuisances in the eye of the law; and although, perhaps, those of the first class are not essentially detrimental to the public welfare, yet it cannot be doubted, that the others have a most pernicious effect upon the public morals, by promoting dissipation, corrupt practices, and open profligacy among the people.

License to Theatres, &c.] To prevent the evils likely to result from the establishment of places of this description, for the resort of all sorts of persons at all hours, under such regulations only as the cupidity and avarice of the proprietors might suggest, the theatres, or other places of public entertainment, in and about the metropolis, not sanctioned by letters patent, the license of the crown, or the lord chamberlain, are placed under the immediate controul of the local magistracy; and they cannot be opened without their license. The words of the act are as follows:—

"Which said license shall be granted at the last preceding Michaelmas sessions, and shall be signed and sealed by four justices in open court, and afterwards be publicly read by the clerk of the peace, with the names of the justices subscribing the same; and no such license shall be granted at any adjourned sessions, nor shall any fee be taken for the same. And there shall be affixed and kept up, in some notorious place, in large capital letters over the door or entrance of every such licensed house or place, '*Licensed pursuant to Act of Parliament of the Twenty-fifth of King George the Second,*' and it shall not be opened for such purposes before five in the afternoon. And the affixing and keeping up such inscription, and the said limitation in point of time shall be inserted in, and made conditions of, such license; and, in case of a breach of either of the said conditions, the license shall be forfeited and revoked by the justices at the next sessions, and shall not be renewed, nor shall any new license be granted." (25 Geo. 2. c. 36. s. 3, made perpetual by 28 Geo. 2. c. 19. s. 1.)

Unlicensed Dancing-Rooms, &c.] " Any house, room, garden, or other place kept for public dancing, music, or other public entertainment of the like kind, in London and Westminster, or within twenty miles thereof, without license from the last preceding Michaelmas quarter sessions, under the hands and seals of four or more justices there assembled, (except the theatres of Drury Lane, Covent Garden, and Hay-Market, and other entertainments exercised by letters patent, or license of the crown, or of the lord chamberlain, s. 4,) shall be deemed a disorderly house or place, and the keeper thereof shall forfeit £100, with full costs to him who shall sue, (in six months,) in any of the courts at Westminster, and be otherwise punishable as in cases of disorderly houses. And it shall be lawful for any constable, or other person, being authorized by warrant under the hand and seal of one justice, to enter such house or place, and to seize every person found therein, that they may be dealt with according to law. (Id. s. 2.)

What within the Statute.] In the first class of disorderly houses is comprised, houses or rooms where persons of both sexes meet for the purpose of dancing, upon paying for their admission. The act of Parliament was made to regulate all places of public resort; and such places, if not properly regulated, may become the resort of the vicious of both sexes. (Clarke v. Searle, 1 Esp. R. 25.)

It is not necessary, in order to subject a party to the penalty, that he should take money for admission; and therefore, where a publican allowed his house to be used in this way every Monday evening, and the sums paid for admission were for the use of a person who, it appeared, professed to teach dancing, the publican was held liable to the penalty. (Archer v. Willingrice, 4 Esp. R. 186.) But a room kept by a dancing master for the instruction of his scholars and subscribers, and to which persons are not *indiscriminately* admitted, is not within the act. (Bellis v. Burghall, 2 Esp. R. 722.) Nor will the mere temporary use of a room in a public-house, for the purpose of dancing on a particular festival or occasion, subject the owner to the penalty. (Shutt v. Lewis, 5 Esp. R. 128.) But a room in which musical performances are *regularly* exhibited, though it is not kept or used *solely* for that purpose, is within the statute, and requires a license. (Bellis v. Beal, 2 Esp. R. 592; see also Gallini v. Laborie, 5 T. R. 242; Rex v. Handy, 6 T. R. 286.)

SECTION II.—GAMING-HOUSES, &c.

Gaming-Houses.] The keeping of a common gaming-house is an offence at common law, as a public nuisance. (Rex v. Dixon, 10 Mod. 336.) The statute provides more certain means for abating the evil. (See Rex v. Rogier, 1 Barn. & Cres. 272; 2 Dowl. & Ryl. 431.) And it has been adjudged, that a *feme covert* may be indicted for this offence. (1 Russ. 299.) An indictment against a defendant, for that he did keep a common, ill-governed, and *disorderly* house, and in the said house, for his lucre, &c., certain persons of ill name, &c., to frequent and come together, did cause and procure, and the said persons in the said house, to remain, *fighting of cocks, boxing, playing at cards, and misbehaving themselves,* did permit, has been held good. (Rex v. Higginson, 2 Burr. 1233.) It is not necessary to prove who frequents the house; but if any persons are proved to be there behaving disorderly, it is sufficient. (1 Russ. 302.)

Bawdy-Houses.] It is fully agreed, that keeping a bawdy-house is a common nuisance. (1 Russ. 299.) And if a lodger, who has only a single *room,* will therewith accommodate lewd people for such purposes, she may be indicted for keeping a bawdy-*house,* as well as if she had the whole house. (Rex v. Pierson, 1 Salk. 382.) A wife may be indicted with her husband for this offence, it being in its nature joint and several. (Rex v. Williams, id. 384.)

Any number of persons may be included in the same indictment for keeping different disorderly houses, stating, that they *severally* kept, &c. (Rex v. Kingston and others, 8 East, 47, 2 Hale, 174.)

Constable to prosecute.] To facilitate the suppression of these nuisances, the fifth section of the same act provides, that if any two inhabitants of any parish or place, paying scot and lot, *give notice in writing to the constable,* or other peace officer of the place, of any person keeping a bawdy-house, gaming house, or other disorderly house therein, he shall go with them to a justice of that jurisdiction; and on their making oath before him that they believe the contents of the notice to be true, and entering into a recognizance in the penal sum of £20 each, to give or produce material evidence of the offence, the constable shall enter into a recognizance in £30, to prosecute such offender at the next general or quarter sessions of the peace, or next assizes for the county in which the parish lies, as to the justice shall seem meet. And such constable shall be allowed the reasonable expenses of such prosecution, as shall be ascertained by two justices of the jurisdiction where the offence was committed, to be paid by the overseers; and, in case such person is convicted, the overseers shall pay £10 each to such inhabitants, or forfeit double the sum to the party grieved.

Notice to the Overseers.] "A copy of the above notice shall also be served on the overseers, or one of them, who shall be summoned, or have reasonable notice, to attend before the justice, before whom the constable has notice to attend; and if the overseers then and there enter into such recognizance to prosecute, the constable shall not be required to do so; but if they do not attend, or attending refuse, the constable must enter into the recognizance as above, (58 Geo. 3. c. 70. s. 7,) or failing therein, or being wilfully negligent in the prosecution, shall forfeit £20 to *each* of such inhabitants." (25 Geo. 2. c. 36. s. 7.)

"When the recognizance to prosecute has been entered into, the justice shall make out his warrant to bring the accused before him, whom he shall bind over to appear at the sessions or assizes, there to answer such indictment as may be found against him, and may take security for such person's good behaviour in the mean time." (25 Geo. 2. c. 36. s. 6.)

Apparent Proprietor responsible.] "Any person, who appears to act as master or mistress, or manager, of any such disorderly house, shall be liable, though not the real owner. (Id. s. 8.) And indictments shall not be removed by certiorari, unless the court, on cause shown, shall adjourn the same. (Id. s. 10.) But no action shall be brought by virtue of this act, unless commenced within six calendar months after offence committed." (Id. s. 14.)

Recovery of Reward.] In an action founded upon the above statute, by one of two inhabitants, who had given information to the parish constable, of A. B. keeping a bawdy-house, in consequence whereof A. B. was prosecuted to conviction, it being necessary, in order to entitle the plaintiff to recover the reward of £10 from the overseers, that the prosecution should have been conducted by the parish constable; and therefore, where the two inhabitants had conducted it, the court held that they were not entitled to the reward; and that a demand upon the overseer, stating the prosecution to have been so carried on, was insufficient to entitle them to an action for the double penalty, given by the act, in case of a neglect or refusal by the overseer to pay such sum of £10 on demand. (Clarke v. Rice, 1 Barn. & Ald. 694.)

CHAPTER XVI.—VAGRANTS.

SECTION I. *Classification of Vagrants.*
II. *Apprehension and Conviction.*

SECTION I.—CLASSIFICATION OF VAGRANTS.

Their Classes.] The legislature, in providing for the security of the public against profligate and dissolute persons, who have no visible or honest means of subsistence, have divided them into three classes: 1st. Idle and disorderly persons; 2dly, Rogues and vagabonds; and, lastly, Incorrigible rogues. The degrees of punishment follow the degrees of turpitude in the same order; and the statute which repealed all the former acts on this subject, the 5 Geo. 4. c. 83, has defined the individuals who belong to each of the classes respectively

Idle and disorderly Persons.] Within this denomination are comprehended: Every person who, being able wholly or in part to maintain himself or herself or family, refuses and neglects so to do, by which he or she, or any of the family which he or she is bound in law to maintain, shall become chargeable as poor. Any person returning to and becoming chargeable in any parish, township, or place from which he has been legally removed, without a certificate from some other parish, &c., acknowledging him to be settled there: Every petty chapman or pedlar wandering abroad and trading without a license or other legal authority: Every common prostitute wandering in the public streets or highways or any place of public resort, and behaving in a riotous or indecent manner: Every person wandering abroad or placing him or herself in any public place to beg or gather alms, or causing or encouraging any child so to do.

Punishment.] The offender. being convicted before any justice, upon his own view, or on the oath of one or more credible witnesses, or the offender's confession, to be imprisoned and kept at hard labour for not more than one calendar month. (s. 3.)

Rogues and Vagabonds.] Within this class are included every person guilty of the foregoing offences, after a conviction of the same: every person pretending to tell fortunes, or using any subtle craft, means, or device, by palmistry or otherwise, to deceive or impose upon others; or wandering abroad and lodging in any barn, outhouse, deserted or unoccupied building, or in the open air, or under a tent, or in any cart or waggon, not having any visible means of subsistence, and not giving a good account of him or herself: Every person wilfully exposing to view, in any public place, any obscene print, picture, or other indecent exhibition; or wilfully, openly, lewdly, and obscenely exposing his person in any street, road, or public highway, or in the view thereof, or in any place of public resort, with intent to insult any female; or wandering abroad, and endeavouring by the exposure of wounds or deformities to obtain or gather alms; or endeavouring to procure charitable contributions of any kind under any false or fraudulent pretence: Every person running away, and leaving his wife, or his or her child or children chargeable, or which shall become chargeable, to any parish, township, or place: Every person playing or betting in any street, road, highway, or other open and public place, at or with any table or instrument of gaming, at any game or pretended game of chance: Every person having in his or her custody or possession any picklock key, crow, jack, bit, or other implement, with intent feloniously to break into any dwelling-house, warehouse, coachhouse, stable, or out-building, or being armed with any gun, pistol, hanger, cutlass, bludgeon, or other offensive weapon, or having upon him or her any instrument with intent to commit any felonious act; or being found in or upon any dwelling-house, warehouse, coachhouse, stable, or outhouse, or in any inclosed yard, garden, or area, for any unlawful purpose: Every suspected person or reputed thief, frequenting any river, canal, navigable stream, dock, basin, or any quay, wharf, or warehouse near or adjoining thereto, or any street, highway, or avenue leading thereto, or any place of public resort, or any avenue leading thereto, or any street, highway, or place adjacent, with intent to commit felony: Every person apprehended as an idle and disorderly person, violently resisting any constable or other peace-officer so apprehending him or her, and being subsequently convicted of the offence for which he or she shall have been so apprehended.

Punishment.] Offenders of this description are punishable by imprisonment and hard labour, for any time not exceeding three months, and forfeiture of the offensive weapons, or other instrument so found upon the offenders. (s. 4.)

Incorrigible Rogues.] These are: persons breaking or escaping out of any place of legal confinement, before the expiration of the term for which they have been committed, or ordered to be confined under this act: Every person committing any offence against this act, which shall subject him or her to be dealt with as a rogue and vagabond, such person having been at some former time adjudged so to be, and duly convicted thereof: Every person apprehended as a rogue and vagabond, and violently resisting any constable or other peace-officer so apprehending him or her, and being subsequently convicted of the offence for which he or she shall have been so apprehended.

Punishment.] Such offenders, upon conviction as aforesaid, may be committed and kept to hard labour till the next general or quarter sessions of the peace, (s. 5,) who may order a further imprisonment, with hard labour, for not exceeding one year, with whipping, except females, according to their discretion. (s. 10.)

SECTION II.—APPREHENSION AND CONVICTION.

Who may apprehend them.] Any person may apprehend an offender against this act, and take him before a justice, or deliver him to a constable or peace officer of the place. And if a peace officer refuse or wilfully neglect to take him into custody and carry him before a justice, or use not his best endeavours to apprehend and carry before a justice, any person that he shall find offending against this act, he shall be liable to a penalty not exceeding £5, to be levied, if necessary, upon his goods and chattels. (ss. 6 & 11.) And complainants shall be reimbursed their expenses out of such penalties. (s. 12.)

Their Property seized.] Persons apprehended and adjudged offenders under this act, may be searched, their money taken from them, and their bundles, packages, &c., shall be inspected before a magistrate, and any horse, mule, ass, cart, caravan, or other vehicle, or goods or effects found in their possession, may be sold, if necessary, to defray the expenses of apprehending and maintaining them during commitment, and the surplus, if any, shall be returned to them. (5 Geo. 4. c. 83. s. 8.)

Recognizance to Prosecute.] Justices may bind persons by recognizance to prosecute vagrants at sessions, who shall, with the necessary witnesses, be reimbursed their expenses, upon application to the justices in sessions; and if such persons refuse to become so bound, the magistrate may commit them to the county gaol. (Id. s. 9.)

Searching Lodging-Houses.] Upon oath being made before any justice, that any rogue, vagabond, &c. (described in this act) is suspected to be harboured in any lodging-house, such justice may grant a warrant to search the same at any time, and bring before him any such offender found therein. (Id. s. 13.)

Appeal.] Section 14 gives an appeal to the sessions to all persons aggrieved by any thing done under the act, upon notice being given, and recognizances and sufficient sureties being entered into, to try the appeal; and the parties in the mean time are to be discharged out of custody. (Id. s. 14.)

Offenders deemed Paupers.] Offenders convicted under this act as vagabonds, &c., shall be deemed chargeable to the parish in which they reside, and shall be liable to be removed to the place of their last legal settlement, by order of two justices. (Id. s. 20.)

Commitment upon Conviction.] The warrant of commitment ought to show that the person convicting had authority to convict: "the not showing before whom they were convicted is a gross defect," (per Ld. Mansfield), and the defendants were therefore discharged. (Rex. v. York, and another, 5 Burr. 2684.) The commitment (see the corresponding words of 17 Geo. 2. c. 5.) must be for a definite time, which must be specified in the warrant. (Baldwin v. Blackmore, 1 Burr. 596.)

And if it be for deserting a family, the warrant must state that they were chargeable, (R. v. Hall, 3 Burr. 1636;) it must also state that the defendant had been convicted, and not merely that he had been charged with the offence. (R. v. Rhodes, 4 T. R. 220; R. v. Hooper, 6 T. R. 225.)

Upon the same principle, where an offender was committed for having upon him picklock keys, and other implements, with an intent feloniously to break into a dwelling house at Wantey, and objection was taken that the commitment did not state that he had those implements upon him *when he was apprehended;* Ld. Kenyon, C. J. said, "I yield with great reluctance to the objection, but I am afraid it is well founded," and the prisoner was discharged. (R. v. Brown, 8 T. R. 26.)

The present lord chancellor, when attorney general, gave his opinion that a person convicted of any offence under this new vagrant act, which subjects him to be dealt with as a rogue and vagabond, and who has also been convicted as a rogue and vagabond under any former act, is by the statute 5 Geo. 4. c. 83, to be deemed an *incorrigible* rogue, and subject to be punished as such. (See 5 Burn's Justice, 560.)

To what Place committed.] The commitment in all these cases, for the offence of vagrancy, must be to houses of correction, and not to common gaols. (See 4 Geo. 4. c. 64. s. 7.)

Vagrant Children.] By the 17 Geo. 2. c. 5. s. 24, it was enacted, that if the child of any vagrant, above the age of seven years, shall be committed to the house of correction, the justices in sessions, if they saw convenient, at any time before such child should be discharged, might order such child to be placed out as a servant or apprentice to any person who was willing to take such child, till such child should be of the age of twenty-one years, or for a less time; and if any offender who was found wandering with such child, should be again found with the same child, which was so placed out, he should be deemed an incorrigible rogue.

But no similar clause, since the repeal of the laws relating to vagrants, by 3 Geo. 4. c 40, was introduced by that statute (now expired,) or in the existing vagrant act, 5 Geo. 4. c. 83.

Vagrants as Soldiers.] Persons committing acts of vagrancy under pretence of being soldiers, but not being really such, are subject to be punished as vagrants. But soldiers in a state of vagrancy from accident or necessity, and their wives, are relieved against the provisions of the vagrant acts by the annual mutiny acts.

By 43 Geo. 3. c. 61, soldiers, sailors, mariners, and the wives of soldiers, who, not being permitted to embark with their husbands, have to return to their homes or respective settlements, from the place of embarkation, and who ask alms, &c., upon the road, are declared free and exempt from the pains and penalties of vagrancy, upon obtaining a certificate from a neighbouring magistrate, stating the route and destination, and time allowed for the journey, upon which the person shall be entitled to ask relief upon her progress.

Certificate to ask Alms.] Justices and visitors of prisons, and houses of correction, are not to be restrained by this act from giving certificates to prisoners about to be discharged, to enable them to have or receive alms or relief on their way to their place of settlement. But if such persons act contrary to the provisions of such certificate, or loiter or deviate from their route, they shall be deemed rogues and vagabonds, within the provisions of the act. (5 Geo. 4. c. 83. s. 15.)

Actions, Costs, &c.] The act also provides, that actions against magistrates, constables, or other persons, for any thing done in pursuance of this act, shall be commenced within three months, and not afterwards, and that such defendants may plead the general issue, and give the special matter in evidence, and that if they obtain the verdict they shall have treble costs, unless the judge certify there was reasonable cause for such action. (ss. 18, 19.)

Form of Conviction.] The 17th section provides, that proceedings under the act shall not be quashed for want of form; that justices shall transmit their convictions to the next general or quarter sessions;

and that copies certified by the clerk of the peace shall be evidence. It also provides, that convictions under the act shall be in the form, or to the effect following, or as near thereto as circumstances will permit.

To wit. } Be it remembered, that on the day of in the year of our Lord at in the county of A. B. is convicted before me, C. D., one of his majesty's justices of the peace, in and for the said county of being an idle and disorderly person, [or a rogue and vagabond, or an incorrigible rogue] within the intent and meaning of the statute made in the fifth year of the reign of his majesty king George the fourth, entituled, An act [here insert the title of this act] that is to say, for that the said A. B. on the day of at in the said county [here state the offence proved before the magistrate] and for which said offence the said A. B. is ordered to be committed to the house of correction at there to be kept to hard labour for the space of [or until the next general or quarter sessions] Given under my hand and seal, the day, year, and at the place first above written.

CHAPTER XVII.—CHURCH RATE.

Rate by whom made.] Rates for the reparation of the church are to be made by the churchwardens, together with the parishioners assembled, upon public notice given in the church. The specific purpose of the meeting should be stated in the notice. (58 Geo. 3. c. 69. See tit. VESTRY.)

The major part of them that appear at the meeting shall bind the parish, or, if none appear, the churchwardens alone may make the rate, because they, and not the parishioners, are to be cited and punished for defect of repairs.

And if a rate be illegally imposed by a commission from the bishop, which he has no authority to direct, (Gibs. 196, 1 Bac. Abr. 373,) or otherwise, without the parishioners' consent, yet if it be afterwards assented to, and confirmed by the major part of the parishioners, that will make it good. (Wats. c. 39.)

Mandamus to make a Rate.] The Court of King's Bench will not grant a mandamus to churchwardens to compel them to *make* a church rate, it being a subject purely of ecclesiastical jurisdiction. (Rex v. Thetford, 5 T. R. 361.) Yet it lies to the churchwardens of two united parishes, under stat. 10. Ann, c. 11, to *assemble* a *meeting* pursuant to s. 24, for the purpose of ascertaining and agreeing whether it be fit that a rate should be made. (Rex. v. St. John & St. Margaret, 4 Mau. & Sel. 250.)

Rate when to be made.] The rate should be made before the expense is incurred, because the propriety and extent of the repairs should be determined before they are undertaken. And no church rate can be legally made for the reimbursement of a churchwarden, because that would be to shift the burthen from the parishioners at the time, to future parishioners. (R. v. Chapelwardens of Bradford, 12 East, 556; Dawson v. Wilkinson, Rep. temp. Hardw. 381, Andrews, R. 11.) And the circumstance of the repairs being authorized by a vestry meeting, does not absolve churchwardens from the consequences of neglecting to make a *prospective* rate to discharge the expense; and although where the parishioners who attended such vestry signed the resolutions for the repairs, it was held, that would not make them individually liable, as they merely acted in their character of vestrymen, without any intention to render themselves personally liable, or separately from the rest of the parishioners. (Lanchester v. Tricker, 1 Bing. 201, 8 Moore, 20.) And although one who attended, and signed afterwards, directed the mode in which certain parts of the repairs should be effected, this was held not sufficient to imply a contract by him. (Lanchester v. Frewer, 9 Moore, 688, 2 Bing. 361.) And a bill filed by the churchwarden, praying that an account might be taken of all sums paid by him, and to which he had become liable for the repairs, and that a vestry might be called to make a rate for the payment thereof, was dismissed with costs; because it was not a *prospective* rate, and a court of equity will not decree a rate to be made to reimburse a former churchwarden monies laid out, whilst in office, in pursuance of a vestry order. (Lanchester v. Tricker & Ors. 5 Madd. R. 4.) And although the spiritual court may compel a church rate for the purpose of repair, it must follow the law, and cannot compel a rate for reimbursement. (Id. 12.)

Rates a personal Charge.] These levies are not chargeable upon the realty, but upon the person in respect of the realty; in some places therefore the rate will be assessed upon the amount of the land, and in others, as in cities and large towns, upon the houses, where of course there is no land which can be specifically so charged.

(Degge, P. 1, c. 12, Lutw. 1019, Hetl. 130.) And the assessment must be estimated according to the value of the rent. (Lindw. 255.)

Whether separate Rate for Ornaments.] In some of the earlier authorities it is contended, that a separate rate must be made for the *ornaments* of the church, and that it is purely a personal charge, not referable to the land occupied, (2 Rolls. Abr. 291,) and that therefore persons having land in the parish, but residing out of it, are not liable to contribute towards the ornaments of the church. (Lindw. 255, Gibs, 196.) But Sir Simon Degge says, that the foreigner who holds lands in the parish, is as much obliged to pay towards the bells, seats, and ornaments, as to the repair of the church.

And he hath seen (he says) a report under the hand of Mr. *Latch*, that it was resolved in *Millymot's* case, H. 6. *Ja.*, and in *Chester's* case in the 10 *Ja.* that a foreigner that held lands in another parish wherein he did not reside, was as much chargeable to the ancient ornaments of the church, as bells, seats, and the like, as those that lived in the parish, but that such landholders could not be charged to new bells, organs, or such like. (Degge p. 1, c. 12; and see 1 Bulstr. 20, to the like effect.)

Lands and Houses equally rated.] No custom by which the rate is sought to be fixed upon lands only, and not upon houses, or upon particular kinds of lands, to the exemption of other kinds, can be good, for by the law all lands and houses are to be equally rated. (Hetl. 130; Latch, 203.)

To this rule there is one exception, viz. possessions, farms, or rents, which are of the glebe or endowment of the churches *to be repaired;* (Lindw. 255;) but if there be lands, &c., within the parish, belonging to another church, it seems they are not exempt. (Ib.)

Not chargeable for Land in other Parish.] But a person cannot be charged in the parish where he inhabiteth, for land which he hath in another parish, to the reparation of that church where he inhabiteth, for then he might be twice charged, for he may be charged for this in the parish where the land lieth. (2 Roll's Abr. 289.)

And therefore the rate shall be laid upon all lands within the parish, although the occupiers *inhabit* in another parish, which point was first fully settled in *Jeffrey's* case, (5 Co. 66,) when it was also resolved (pursuant to the opinion of divers civilians, under their hands,) that such occupation of land maketh the person occupying a *parishioner,* and entitles him to come to the assemblies of the same parish, when they meet together for such purposes: and it was said that if such lands were not liable to be rated, a person who inhabiteth in one parish might occupy the greatest part of the lands in another parish, and so churches might come to ruin. And, although seven years after this, in the case of Paget and Crumpton, (Cro. Eliz. 659,) a prohibition was obtained upon a surmise that the person rated lived not in the parish; yet, upon sight of this precedent, Popham, Chief Justice, changed his opinion, and it was resolved by him, and the whole court, that a consultation should be granted; and now, Lord *Coke* says, this is generally allowed and received for law. (Gibs. 196.)

Residence or Occupancy.] In Woodward v. Makepeace, (1 Salk. 164,) it was resolved that the plaintiff was an inhabitant where he occupied the land, as well as where he personally resided. Secondly, that although he doth not personally live in the parish, yet, by having lands in his hands, he is taxable: and whereas it was pretended that the bells, for the recasting of which the rate was imposed which he had refused to pay, were but ornaments, Holt, Chief Justice, said, "if he be an inhabitant as to the church, which is confessed, how can he not be an inhabitant as to the ornaments of the church?"

Tenant, not Owner, chargeable.] Where such lands are in farm, the tenant shall pay. For (as it was determined in Jeffrey's case, before cited,) there is an inhabitant and parishioner, who may be charged, and the receipt of the rent doth not make the lessor a parishioner. And so it was resolved in Anonymous. (4 Mod. 148.)

Patron, &c. exempt.] It is said that the patron of a church, as in right of the founder, may prescribe that in respect of the foundation he and his tenants have been freed from the charge of repairing the church. (Degge. P. 1. c. 12.)

Rector, &c. exempt.] The rectory, or vicarage, which is derived out of it, are not chargeable to the repair of the body of the church, steeple, public chapels, or ornaments; being at the whole charge of repairing the chancel. (Degge, P. 1. c. 12.)

But an impropriator of a rectory or parsonage, though bound to repair the chancel, must contribute to the reparations of the church, in case he hath lands in the parish which are not parcel of the rectory. (Gibs. 197.)

How far Chapelry exempt.] The inhabitants of a precinct having a parochial chapel which they repair, are nevertheless of common right contributory to the repairs of the mother church.

If they have seats in the mother church, to go thither when they please, or receive sacraments, or sacramentals, or marry, christen, or bury at it, there can be no pretence for a discharge. Nor can any thing support that plea, but that they have time out of mind been discharged, (which also is doubted, whether it be of itself a full discharge,) or that, in consideration thereof, they have paid so much to the repairs of the church, or the wall of the churchyard, or the keeping of a bell, or the like compositions, which are clearly a discharge. (Gibs. 197, 1 Burn. Ec. L. 383.)

Hall of a Company.] The hall of a company being rated to the repairs of a church, the spiritual court may proceed against the master and wardens of such company for non-payment. For the spiritual court hath no other process than by citation, which cannot be executed upon an aggregate corporation, and therefore the officers of the corporation are to be cited, to whom it belongs to pay the tax; and the rate paid by them is to be allowed in their accounts. (Thursfield v. Jones; Sir T. Jones, R. 187.)

Stall in a Market.] If a petty chapman take a standing for rent to be paid by him, in the waste of the manor within the market, for two or three hours every market day, to sell his commodities, the market being holden there one day every week, but he inhabiteth in another parish, he may not be rated to the reparation of the church for this standing. (2 Roll's Abr. 289.)

Rule of Assessment.] A taxation by the pound rate is the most equitable way, and not according to the quantity of the land. (Wood's Inst. b. 1. c. 7.)

The assessors are not to tax themselves, but to leave the taxation of them to the residue of the parish. (Godb. Appendix, 10, 11.)

Customs to be observed.] If a parish consist of several vills, and there is a custom to levy the rate in certain proportions, they must pursue it; for such a custom may be, or may have been, in its commencement, reasonable. (Burton v. Wileday, Andrews, 32.)

Appeal to Ecclesiastical Judge.] If any person find himself aggrieved at the inequality of any such assessment, his appeal is to the ecclesiastical judge, who is to see right done. (Degge, P. 1. c. 12.)

Enforcing Payment.] Parishioners refusing to pay their rates, being demanded by the churchwardens, they are to be sued for in the ecclesiastical courts, and not elsewhere. (Degge, P. 1. c. 12.) For the cognizance of rates made for the reparation of churches and churchyards, in consequence of the 13 Ed. 1, belongs to the spiritual court. (Paget v. Crumpton, Cro. Eliz. 659.)

Where Custom pleaded.] If a suit is instituted in the ecclesiastical court for a church rate, and a custom pleaded of a certain sum, or of something done in the room of it, and that plea is admitted, they may proceed to try that custom in the same manner as a modus; but if the custom is denied, it will be a proper ground for a prohibition; for the trying of the custom is the province of the common law. (1 Atkyns. 289.) So if the party assessed aver that the land for which he is assessed lies in another parish, and not in the parish where it is assessed, he may have a prohibition, and try it at common law. (Degge, P. 1. c. 12.)

Subtraction of Church Rate.] In a suit instituted by churchwardens for subtraction of church rate, (that is, a refusal to pay the sum to which the party has been assessed,) the ecclesiastical court will not, at the prayer of the defendant, issue a monition to the party imposing the rate, for the production of parish books, which are not shown to apply immediately to the question in issue: and if, on the merits, the rate be pronounced for, the court will condemn the defendant in costs, for they are almost universally so decreed in suits for church rates, where the rate is confirmed. (Goodall & Gray v. Whitmore & Fenn, 2 Hagg. Rep. N. S. 369.)

Justices' Authority herein.] By statutes 53 Geo. 3. c. 127. s. 7, for England, and 54 Geo. 3. c. 68. s. 7, for Ireland, when any person rated to church or chapel rate, (the validity of which has not been questioned in any ecclesiastical court,) refuses payment, any justice of the county, city, &c., on complaint of the churchwardens, may convene, by warrant, such person before two or more justices, and examine, on oath, into the merits of the complaint, and may order, under their hands and seals, payment of any sum so due, *not exceeding* £10, besides costs, to be recovered, if payment is not made, by distress and sale of the goods of the offender, his executors or administrators, under the warrant of any one of such justices.

Appeal to Sessions.] An appeal is allowed to the next quarter sessions for the county, &c. wherein the church, &c. for which the rate was made is situate; and if the justices present, or a majority, affirm the judgment, it shall be decreed by order of session, with costs to be levied by distress and sale of appellant's goods. Provided that when such appeal is made as above, no distress warrant shall be granted till after its determination.

Ecclesiastical Jurisdiction saved.] Provided that nothing herein shall alter the jurisdiction of ecclesiastical courts to hear and determine causes, touching the validity of any such church or chapel-rate, or from enforcing payment thereof, if exceeding £10, from the party proceeded against. If the validity of such rate, or liability of the person from whom it is demanded, be disputed, and the party give notice thereof to the justices, they shall forbear giving judgment thereon, and the persons demanding the same may proceed to recovery of their demand by due course of law as before accustomed.

But nothing herein shall affect parliamentary regulations respecting church or chapel rates of any particular parishes or districts.

Distress made out of District.] And by 54 Geo. 3. c. 170. s. 12, the goods and chattels of any person neglecting to pay any sum legally assessed on him for any poor rate, *church cess*, or highway cess of any district, parish, &c. for seven days, after demand made, may be distrained, not only within the parish, district, &c. in which it is made, but also within any other district, parish, &c. within the same county or jurisdiction; and if sufficient distress cannot be found within such county, &c., then, on oath thereof made before any justice of the peace of any other county, &c. in which any of the goods of such person shall be found; which oath such justice shall certify by indorsing his name on the warrant granted to make such distress, such goods, &c. shall be liable to such distress and sale in such other county, &c., and may, under such warrant and certificate, be distrained and sold as if found within the district, parish, &c. in or for which the rate was due.

Preliminaries to issuing Warrant.] Under the 53 Geo. 3. c. 127. s. 7, the justice cannot issue his warrant unless it be made *affirmatively* to appear before him, that the amount does not exceed £10, and that *no question* is made on the rate in the ecclesiastical court.

If neither of these preliminary exceptions exist, the party may give notice to the two justices that he disputes the validity of the rate, or his liability to pay it, though no proceeding is actually commenced in the ecclesiastical court: and any expression by him, manifesting that he disputes the rate *bonâ fide*, will be a sufficient notice to put a stop to the proceedings before the justices. Thus where a parishioner, upon being brought before two justices for not paying the rate, declared in their presence, "that he would bring an action against any person who ventured to levy the rate, as he thought he had no right to pay, because he had no claim to, or seat in the chapel," this was held a sufficient notice for this purpose. (Rex v. the Chapel-wardens of Milnrow, 5 Maul. & Sel. 248.)

Exceeding Authority of Warrant.] Where a constable, having a warrant of distress under 53 Geo. 3. c. 127. s. 7, broke the outer door of, and entered plaintiff's dwelling-house, it was held that although he acted *illegally*, yet as it was not shown that he acted with any other intention than that of executing the authority delegated to him by the warrant, no action could be maintained after the expiration of three calendar months, (the limitation in the statute, s. 12) from the fact committed. (Theobald v. Crichmore, 1 Barn. & Ald. 227.)

Improved Wastes, Parish disputed.] By the 17 Geo. 2. c. 37, where there shall be any dispute, in what parish or place improved wastes, and drained and improved marsh lands lie, and ought to be rated, the occupiers of such lands or houses built thereon, tithes arising therefrom, mines therein and saleable underwoods, shall be rated to this, and all other parish rates within such parish and place as lies nearest to such lands: and, if on application to the officers of such parish or place, to have them rated as aforesaid, any dispute shall arise, the justices of the peace at the next sessions after such application made, and after notice given to the officers of the several parishes and places adjoining to such lands, and to all others interested therein, may hear and determine the same on the appeal of any person interested, and may cause the same to be equally assessed, whose determination therein shall be final.

Rate on Quakers.] The church rate charged upon quakers may be sued for in the ecclesiastical court, as in the case of other parishioners; but it is also recoverable before the justices of the peace, in the same manner as their tithes, which is the preferable mode of proceeding. (See DISSENTERS, *ante* 146.)

CHAP. XVIII.—COUNTY RATE.

Consolidation of Rates.] There are various expenses to which parishes, as integral portions of counties, are liable, for which it was the custom formerly to make separate rates,—as for the maintenance of gaols, support of prisoners, reparation of bridges, &c.; but the great inconvenience of assessing the parishes, and collecting distinct rates for these several purposes, induced the legislature to provide that one general fund for the whole should be raised, called the county rate, under the direction of the county magistrates. Accordingly, the 12 Geo. 2. c. 29, was passed, which has been amended in some of its provisions by subsequent statutes, the object of which is not to impose any new species of rates, but to facilitate the assessing, collecting, and levying those with which the public were previously chargeable, and for which purpose, instead of separate rates for the several purposes for which rates under former acts were imposed, there is to be one general rate to answer all the ends and purposes of the former acts. (See Bates v. Winstanley, 4 Maul. & Sel. 437.)

Charges on County Rates.] The purposes to which the county rates are now principally applicable by different acts of Parliament, are as follows: The paying one moiety of the charges of prosecuting masters for ill treating their parish apprentices. (32 Geo. 3. c. 57. s. 11.) Charges of carrying parish apprentices bound to the sea service to the port to which the master belongeth. (2 & 3 Ann, c. 6.) Repairing county bridges and highways adjoining, salaries for the surveyors thereof, and purchase of lands adjoining. (22 H. 8. c. 5; 1 Ann, st. 1. c. 18; and 52 Geo. 3. c. 110; 14 Geo. 2. c. 33.)

The coroner's fee of 9*d.* a mile for travelling to take an inquisition, and 20*s.* for taking it. (25 Geo. 2. c. 29.) Relief of prisoners in the county gaol. (14 Eliz. c. 5.) Salary of the chaplain thereof, and house of correction, and setting prisoners to work. (4 Geo. 4. c. 64.) Care of their health, (14 Geo. 3. c. 59,) and carrying persons to the gaol or house of correction. (27 Geo. 2. c. 3.) Allowance to discharged prisoners. (5 Geo. 4. c. 85. ss. 22. 25.) Gaolers clerks of assize, clerks of the peace, or clerks of court's fees, upon the acquittal or discharge of prisoners. (55 Geo. 3. c. 50. s. 6; 56 Geo. 3. c. 116.)

For building, enlarging, repairing, and fitting up county gaols, and houses of correction. (4 Geo. 4. c. 64.) Salary of the master of the house of correction, and relieving the weak and sick in his custody. (7 J. 1. c. 4.) Charges of bringing insolvent debtors before the travelling commissioner, in order to their discharge, if the prisoners are not able to pay. (5 Geo. 4. c. 61. s. 2.) For the relief of the prisoners in the King's Bench, Fleet, and Marshalsea prisons, and of Bethlem Hospital, &c. (53 Geo. 3. c. 113.) Expenses of providing, &c., county lunatic asylums, under the direction of visiting justices, &c., by a special rate. (See 9 Geo. 4. c. 40, post 472.) Prosecuting felons. (58 Geo. 3. c. 70. s. 4.) Transporting felons, or conveying them to the places of labour and confinement. (6 Geo. 1. c. 23. s. 3.)

The treasurer's salary, by 55 Geo. 3. c. 51. s. 17. Charges of prosecuting vagrants or incorrigible rogues, or of constables, &c., for neglect of duty. (5 Geo. 4. c. 83.) Expenses of procuring and transmitting models and copies of the standard weights and measures, (5 Geo. 4. c. 74,) and allowance to examiners thereof. (55 Geo. 3. c. 43. s. 5.) Charges of prosecuting and convicting persons plundering shipwrecked goods, (26 Geo. 2. c. 19,) and burying dead bodies cast on shore in England. (48 Geo. 3. c. 75. s. 6.) Charges of the soldiers' baggage-waggons, &c., over and above the officers' pay for the same. (Annual mutiny acts; and militia act, 42 Geo. 3. c. 90. s. 95.)

Sessions make the Rate.] The 12 Geo. 2. c. 29, provides, that the magistrates, in quarter sessions assembled, shall have power to make a rate, to be assessed upon every town, parish, or place within the respective limits of their commissions, to be collected by the high constables of the hundreds, &c. (Id. s. 1.)

To be paid by the Overseers, &c.] Upon which the churchwardens and overseers shall pay the sum rated on their parishes, &c., within thirty days after demand, in writing, to be given to them or any of them, or left at their house, or affixed to the church door by the high constable, (which demand the high-constable must make at the time directed by the justices in sessions,) for which the receipt of the high-constable shall be a discharge; and on neglect of payment by the churchwardens and overseers, the high-constable shall levy the same by distress and sale of the goods and chattels of such churchwardens and overseers, or either of them so neglecting, by warrant under the hands and seals of two or more of the justices. (Id. s. 2.)

When payable by petty Constable.] Where there are no poor rates, the justices shall direct the county rate to be assessed and levied by any petty constable, or other peace officer of the place. And if any petty constable or other peace officer pay the sum to the high-constable before he shall have rated and levied it, he may *afterwards* rate and levy it, or may be reimbursed the same out of any constable's or other rate, as the justices in sessions shall direct. (s. 3.) And in parishes, &c., where high-constables have no jurisdiction, the constable of the parishes, &c., shall perform this duty. (57 Geo. 3. c. 94. s. 5.)

The high-constable shall, at or before the next general or quarter sessions, after receiving such sums, pay the same into the hands of the treasurer appointed by the justices in sessions. (12 Geo. 2. c. 29. s. 6.)

Neglect punishable.] And shall at the general or quarter sessions account for the same before the justices, if required, in the same manner as the treasurer, or shall be committed to the common gaol, without bail or mainprize, until he shall have caused the rates to be demanded or levied, and shall have rendered such accounts; and if he neglect or refuse to pay over to the treasurer the amount remaining in his hands, being required to do so by order of the justices, they may commit him to the common gaol until he shall pay it. (Id. s. 8.) The receipt of the treasurer shall be a discharge to the high-constable. (Id. s. 9.)

Justices may compel an Account.] The justices in sessions may oblige, by their order, the respective high-constables, petty constables, or any other persons empowered to levy or receive any such monies, to account for the sums by them collected, or in their hands, by committing them until they conform. (Id. s. 17.)

Rates in Liberties, &c.] The justices of liberties and franchises having exclusive jurisdictions, and which did not pay the several county rates before the passing the above act, are invested with the same powers for raising a rate, in the nature f a county rate, as the justices of the counties at large, by the 13 Geo 2. c. 18. s. 7.

Returns by which to make Rate.] The better to enable justices to make fair and equal county rates, they may, at any general or quarter sessions, or adjournment thereof, issue precepts signed by the chairman or clerk of the peace, to high-constables, constables, overseers, &c., requiring them to make returns to the justices of their respective divisions in petty sessions, verified on oath at the time of delivery before two justices, of the total amount of the full annual value of the several estates and rateable property within their respective precincts, charged to the poor's rate, or charged or liable to be charged to any other rate. (55 Geo. 3. c. 51. s. 2.)

New Assessments.] By the 12 Geo. 2. c. 29. s. 1, the county rates were to be assessed in such proportions as any of the rates by the former acts had been usually assessed; under that statute, therefore, they had no authority to vary the proportions, notwithstanding any change of circumstances. But by the 55 Geo. 3. c. 51. s. 1, the justices, in general or quarter sessions, are empowered to make a *fair and equal county* rate whenever circumstances shall appear to require it. And by the 14th section of this latter act, an appeal is given against any rate made in pursuance of that or any of the acts in force, to the persons acting on behalf of any parish, township, &c., aggrieved thereby; and therefore where a rate was made in fixed proportions, the same as had been invariably adopted for a series of years, this was held to be a good ground of appeal under this section; and the court considered that such a power of appeal was the most convenient construction that the statute can receive. (R. v. Justices of York, 2 Barn. & Cres. 771.)

Order to levy new Rates.] The justices of any county in general or quarter sessions, or at any adjournment thereof, may order warrants to be issued (in the same manner as for collecting the former county rates) to the high-constables, requiring them to issue their warrants to the overseers within their divisions, to levy and pay to them, within a time limited in the warrant of the justices, the rate to be made under this act upon all rateable property according to its full annual value, which the high-constable shall pay, at a time limited in the same warrant, to the treasurer of the county, and it shall be recoverable by the high-constable by distress on the overseers or other collectors. (55 Geo. 3. c. 51. s. 12.)

High Constables to give Security] The justices may demand, whenever they think fit, good and sufficient security, to be approved by them in general or quarter sessions, from the high-constables employed in levying the county rates; and if the high-constable neglect or refuse to give such security, they may order the churchwardens and overseers, or other persons appointed to levy these rates, of any parish, township, or place, to pay the quota assessed thereupon to the treasurer of the county, division, or place, whose receipt shall be their discharge. (Id. s. 19.)

Section 24 gives the like power to justices of exclusive jurisdictions. And the rate is to be raised notwithstanding any appeal is pending against it; and upon the determination of such appeal, if the rate be set aside or lowered, the money which ought not to have been charged thereon, shall be returned. (57 Geo. 3. c. 94. s. 2.)

Jurisdiction of Justices.] All constables, churchwardens, overseers, &c., of any parish, township, hamlet, or other place, which extends into two or more counties, or divisions, having distinct commissions of the peace, shall be subject to the precepts, warrants, and directions of the justices of the respective divisions or parts thereof, as far as relates to the returns required by the preceding acts, and the levying of the proportion of the county rate for such respective divisions or parts thereof, or otherwise in the execution of these acts within the parts of such parish, township, hamlet, or other place, situate within the jurisdiction of the justices making such precepts, &c.; and shall be subject to the same fines, penalties, and forfeitures, for the neglect and disobedience of such precepts, &c., as such constables, &c., would be subject and liable to if they had resided within the jurisdiction of the justices making them. But this shall not authorize any justice, in any of those cases, to act beyond the limits of his own jurisdiction. (1 & 2 Geo. 4. c. 85. s. 1.)

Rate to reimburse.] The justices have no right, except by following the provisions of particular acts of Parliament, to anticipate the county rates, and so to make the expense of public county works ultimately fall on different persons from those who are by law liable at the time it is incurred. An order of sessions, therefore, for levying and paying to the treasurer of the county, a sum to enable him to reimburse certain persons for an antecedent debt, although such debt had been incurred for county purposes, is bad. (R. v. Justices of Flintshire, 5 Barn. & Ald. 761; 1 Dowl. & Ryl. 470.)

By an act for building a gaol, the justices at sessions were authorized to assess a *special* county rate upon every parish in the county, for the payment of the expenses of building such gaol, and that rate was made payable out of the monies collected in the parishes for the relief of the poor; and there was a proviso, that every tenant might deduct out of his rent one half the amount of the rate. It was held that commissioners under a local act for paving and lighting the town, and managing the poor, could not make a *retrospective* rate, in order to *reimburse* themselves in one year, money which they had paid in a former year on account of such special county rate for building the gaol. (Cortis v. Kent Water Works Co. 7 Barn. & Cres. 314.)

County Fines, &c.] But if a fine be imposed on a county, which the justices at the sessions think illegal, they may order the expense of litigating the question to be defrayed out of the county stock, or the expense of litigating questions between two counties, as to repair of bridges, &c., or the purchase of land adjoining such bridges. (Rex v. Essex, 4 T. R. 591.) But they cannot order the costs of a prosecution for a misdemeanor, carried on under the direction of the magistrates, to be allowed out of the county rates. (Rex v. W. R. Yorkshire, 7 T. R. 377.)

Berwick-upon-Tweed.] A rate in the nature of a county rate may be levied in Berwick-upon-Tweed, under the 55 Geo. 3. c. 51. s. 24, that being a place not subject to the commission of the peace of any county in England, and never having contributed to a rate made for any county, although it does not lie within the body of an English county, and although no rate had ever been levied there before; the corporation having defrayed out of their own funds the charges to which the sums raised by a county rate are applicable. (R. v. Berwick-upon-Tweed, 8 Barn. & Cres. 327; 2 Maul. & Ryl. 378.)

CHAPTER XIX.—HIGHWAY RATES.

13 Geo. 3. c. 78. ss. 30. 45. 46. 67. 54 Geo. 3. c. 109. ss. 1. 2. 3.

Assessments for Materials.] The 13 Geo. 3. c. 78. s. 30, recites, That in some parishes, &c., the surveyor of the highways may be forced to buy materials, there being none in the wastes, rivers, &c., and to make recompense to the owner or occupier of inclosed lands for damage done by getting and carrying thereof: and also recites, that no provision is made for reimbursing the expenses thereof, and the expenses of erecting guide-posts, &c., making or repairing trunks, tunnels, plats, bridges, or arches, and rendering satisfaction for damages done to lands by the making of new ditches or drains, nor for the salary to be paid to such surveyor as aforesaid:

" Be it therefore enacted, That upon application by such surveyor to the justices of the peace, at their special sessions, and oath made of the sum or sums of money which he hath *bonâ fide* laid out and expended, or which will be required for the purposes aforesaid, the said justices, or any two or more of them, shall and they are hereby empowered, by warrant under their hands and seals, to cause an equal assessment to be made, for the purposes aforesaid, upon all occupiers of lands, tenements, woods, tithes, and hereditaments within such parish, township, or place where such money shall be so expended or laid out, and the same shall be made and collected by such person or persons, and allowed in such manner, as the said justices, by their order at such sessions, shall direct and appoint in that behalf; and the money thereby raised shall be employed and accounted for according to the direction of the said justices, for the purposes aforesaid; and the said assessments shall be levied in such manner as herein-aftermentioned: provided nevertheless, that no such assessment to be made for those or any of those purposes, in any one year, shall exceed the rate of sixpence in the pound of the yearly value of the lands, tenements, woods, tithes, and hereditaments so to be assessed."

Assessment for Repairs, &c.] "That if upon application of the surveyor of the highways for any parish, &c., to the justices for the limit, at their general or quarter sessions of the peace, or at some special sessions for the highways, the said justices shall be fully satisfied, by proof upon oath, that the duty hereby directed to be performed, and the money hereby authorized to be collected and received, has been performed, applied, and expended according to the directions of this act, or shall be fully satisfied that the common highways, bridges, causeways, streets, or pavements, belonging to such parish, &c., are so far out of order that they cannot be sufficiently amended and repaired, paved, cleansed, and supported, by the means herein-before prescribed, (notice being first given of such intended application at the church or chapel of such parish, township, or place, on some Sunday preceding such quarter or special sessions, or if the place be extra-parochial, notice in writing being first given of such intended application to some of the principal inhabitants residing in such extra-parochial place, a week at least before such general or special sessions,) that then and in any of the said cases an equal assessment upon all and every the occupier of lands, tenements, woods, tithes, and hereditaments within any such parish, &c., shall, or may be made and collected by such person or persons, and allowed in such manner as the said justices by their order at such general or special sessions shall direct and appoint in that behalf; and the money thereby raised shall be employed and accounted for according to the orders and directions of the said justices, for and towards the amending, repairing, paving, cleansing, and supporting such highways, causeways, streets, pavements, and bridges, from time to time as need shall require." (Id. s. 45.)

Maximum of Rates.] "That the assessment herein last before authorized, and the assessment herein-before authorized for buying materials, making satisfaction for damages, erecting guide-posts, and paying the surveyor's salary, shall not together in any one year exceed the rate of ninepence in the pound of the yearly value of the lands, tenements, woods, tithes, and hereditaments so to be assessed." (Id. s. 46.)

Sums assessed may be levied.] "That if any person shall refuse or neglect to pay the sum or sums assessed upon him by any assessment to be made in pursuance of this act, within ten days after demand thereof made, the same shall and may be levied by the surveyor, or any other person or persons authorized by warrant under the hand and seal of one justice of the peace having jurisdiction therein, by distress and sale of the goods and chattels of the person so refusing or neglecting, rendering the overplus to the owner or owners thereof, the necessary charges of making such distress and sale being first deducted; and in default of such distress, it shall be lawful for any such justice to commit the person so refusing or neglecting, to the common gaol, there to remain until he shall have paid the sum so assessed, and the costs and charges occasioned by such neglect or refusal." (13 Geo. 3. c. 78. s. 67.)

Additional Assessment.] The 54 Geo. 3. c. 109. s. 1, reciting that the assessments which are authorized by the former act are not sufficient for the purposes to which the same are therein directed to be applied goes on; "be it therefore enacted, that if upon the application of the surveyor of the highways of any parish, &c., to the justices at their general or quarter sessions, or at a special sessions for the highways, the said justices shall be fully satisfied that the common highways, bridges, causeways, streets, or pavements, belonging to such parish, township, or place, are so far out of order that they cannot be sufficiently amended and supported by the means in the said therein-before recited act of the thirteenth year of his present Majesty's reign prescribed, and by the assessments therein authorized to be made and collected, it shall and may be lawful for the said justices to authorize, order, and direct an additional assessment to be made on such parish, &c. (over and above all the assessments by the said act authorized to be made and collected); which said additional assessment shall be levied and collected by the same means, and in the same manner and form, as is directed for the levying and collecting the assessments made under the authority of the said herein-before recited act, and upon the same persons as are therein declared to be liable to be rated to the said assessments."

Notice of Application to be given.] "Provided that notice of such intended application shall be first proved before the said justices, upon the oath of the surveyor making such application, to have been given at the church or chapel, on two Sundays preceding such general or quarter sessions, or special sessions for the highways; or in townships or places where there are no churches or chapels, to have been stuck up, in writing, in two or more conspicuous places within the said townships or places, for one week at least previous to such general or quarter sessions, or special sessions for the highways; or in extra-parochial places, to have been given, in writing, to some of the principal inhabitants residing in such extra-parochial place, a week at least before such general or quarter sessions, or special sessions for the highways; in order that any person or persons liable to be rated to the assessment intended to be applied for, may attend at such general or quarter sessions, or special sessions, if they shall think fit, there to state to the said justices any objections which he, she, or they, may have to the making and collecting of such assessment." (Id. s. 2.)

Limit of Amount of Assessment.] "Provided that the assessment herein authorized shall not exceed the rate of one shilling and ninepence in the pound, on the actual value at the time of making such additional assessment." (54 Geo. 3. c. 109. s. 3.)

Tithes, let or compounded.] It has been doubted whether a rector who lets his tithes by parol from year to year, to the *occupiers of the lands* whereon the tithes are produced, and receives a half-yearly composition in the nature of rent, can be treated as an occupier of tithes within these acts, and rateable to the repair of the highways. (Rex v. Bucks. 1 Barn. & Cres. 485, 2 Dowl. & Ryl. 689.) But in a later case it was said, per Holroyd, J. "It is clear, as a general proposition, that not only tithes, but also compensations in lieu of them, are rateable;" and per Bayley, J., "The money payment is liable to the same burdens as the tithes for which it is substituted; it is indeed called a rent, but is in fact nothing more than a sum of money paid annually in lieu of tithes." (Rex v. Boldero, 4 Barn. & Cres. 467, 6 Dowl. and Ryl. 557.)

Upon this principle it was determined, where an inclosure act directed that all great tithes should be extinguished, and that the commissioners should ascertain their *net value*, and affix a *fair clear annual rent* or sum of money per acre in lieu thereof, as an adequate compensation for the same to the rector, that the rector was, in respect of such *rents*, rateable to the repair of the highways. (Rex v. Lacey, 5 Barn. & Cres. 702; 8 Dowl. & Ryl. 457.) A tithe *farmer* is rateable in respect of the tithes. (Rex v. Lambeth, 1 Stra. 525; see also Cortis v. Kent Water Works, 7 Barn. & Cres. 314.)

Balance of Rates.] It is provided, that in case the outgoing surveyor make default in paying over the balance to his successor, he shall forfeit double the amount *adjudged* to be in his hands. (See s. 48, *ante* 195, 197.) It has been held, that all the forms prescribed by that section for passing the accounts and ascertaining the balance, must be observed before any action can be maintained for the recovery of the *double* amount, or even of the balance, which cannot be sued for as money had and received to the use of the succeeding overseer; but the action must be for the penalty. And that the right of action is not given to him *as* surveyor, though he may sue, like any other common informer. (Heudebourck v. Langton, H. T. 1830, K. B. MSS.; see 9 Barn. & Cres. 3 Man. & Ryl.)

CHAPTER XX.—POOR RATES.

SECTION I.—HOW MADE AND AUTHORIZED.

Statutes authorizing Rates.] The funds for the relief of the poor are supplied by the "poor's rate," which is levied in *parishes*, within the jurisdiction of *county* magistrates, by 43 Eliz. c. 2. s. 1, in corporate towns, places, and cities, including the city of London, (by s. 8,) and for extra-parochial townships, and subdivisions of parishes, under 13 & 14 Car. 2. c. 12, s. 22.

Rates, by whom made.] The power of *making* a rate is vested exclusively in the majority of the churchwardens and overseers, (Tawney's case, Salk. 531,) and the Court of King's Bench will compel them to do so by mandamus if necessary, (Rex v. Edwards, 1 Bla. Rep. 637,) or to rate a particular description of property improperly omitted; but they will not interfere with the equality of the rate or assessment, these matters being in the jurisdiction of the quarter sessions. (Rex v. Barnstaple, 1 Barnard, 137; Hull's case, Carth. 14; Rex v. Weobly, 1 Bott. 124.)

Justices allowing Rate.] The act requires the consent of two or more justices, dwelling in or near the parish, &c. whereof one is to be of the quorum, which is called "their allowance," and the rate is taken to them for the purpose. In this they act ministerially merely, (not, as in sessions, judicially,) and they have no discretion to refuse the allowance, though they may think the rate improperly made, (Rex v. Dorchester, 1 Stra. 393, 1 East. 118,) and they may make their allowance separately. (Rex v. Hamstall Ridware, 3 T. R. 380.) But it must be for a place within their jurisdiction, though they need not state that it is so, in their allowance. (Rex v. Folly, 1 Bott. 76, 16 Vin. Ab. 425.)

Alteration of Rate.] After it has been thus allowed, it should not be altered by inserting the names of others, even with the magistrate's approbation. (Doug. 465.) But by 54 Geo. 3. c. 170. s. 11, two or more justices in petty sessions may, upon application, and with the consent of the overseers or other parish officers, and proof of the party's inability from poverty to pay such rate, excuse the payment, and strike out the name of such party from the rate.

Publication of Rate.] The 17 Geo. 2. c. 3. s. 1, requires that the overseers, &c. shall give public notice of the rate on the *next Sunday* after it has been allowed by the justices, otherwise it is null and void. This must be done in the church, and in large towns it is usually published also in the dissenting places of worship. Where notice was not given till the third Sunday, it was held a radical defect in the rate itself, which nothing could cure. (Rex v. Newcombe, 4 T. R. 368.) But in a special case for the opinion of the court above, respecting a rate, it is sufficient to state that the rate was *duly* made, without showing the publication. (Rex v. Aire and Calder Navigation, 2 T. R. 660.)

Rate, for what Time.] The statute of Elizabeth directs the rate to be made "weekly or *otherwise*." Lord Holt was of opinion that they ought to be made monthly, as that is the period at which parish officers are directed to meet in vestry under the act. (Tracey v. Talbot, Salk, 532.) But the Court of King's Bench has determined that a rate may be made prospectively for a quarter of a year, (Rex v. Middlesex, 2 Bla. Rep, 694,) or even half a year, according to the exigencies of the parish. (Durrant v. Boys, 6 T. R. 580.) A standing rate cannot be made, but it must be varied as circumstances change; for the old rate, however just at first, may become very unequal in process of time. (Rex v. Audley, 2 Salk. 526, 1 Bott. 110. 272.)

SECTION II.—PURPOSES OF THE POOR RATE.

Statutes on the Subject.] The statutes declaring the purposes for which a poor rate may be made are many, though the principal one is the 43 Eliz. c. 2, by which it will be seen that the purposes for which a rate may be made are:—for setting to work the children of parents who are not themselves able to keep them; and also for setting to work all persons, married or unmarried, having no means to maintain them, and using no ordinary trade of life to get their living by;—for the necessary relief of the lame, impotent, old, blind, and poor persons not able to work, and also the putting out poor children apprentice.

The 18 Geo. 3. c. 19, relates to repayment to constables, out of these rates, of the money expended by them in the relief and removal of, poor persons, and of vagrants.

Law Expenses on Appeals, &c.] In Rex v. Inhabitants of Essex, (4 T. R. 595, 1 Nol. P. L. 63,) it was said by Ashurst, J. to have been the constant practice to allow the expenses of litigating the questious of settlement, consequent upon the removal of paupers, to be defrayed out of the parish stock; the legality of which had never been disputed.

Reimbursing Overseers.] In Tawney's case, (2 Salk. 531, 1 Nol. P. L. 68, 69,) Tawney being overseer, laid out his money in the relief of the poor, and being turned out of office before the end of the year, by which means he lost the opportunity of making a rate to reimburse himself; upon this he applied to the Court of King's Bench for a *mandamus* to the churchwardens and overseers to make a rate to reimburse him. By Holt, C. J.—"We cannot order the parish or overseers to make a rate to reimburse an overseer, but only to raise money for the relief of the poor, nor can they make a rate otherwise. The act of Parliament is expressly so, and must be pursued. An overseer is not bound to lay out money till he have it; if he do, he must make a new rate for the relief of the poor, and out of that he may retain to pay himself." And by the whole court, "The mandamus lies not."

Nor can an overseer appointed for four successive years, who does not make any rate in the three first years to reimburse himself, make one in the fourth for that purpose, for all the items of the accounts should be confined to that year when the accounts are directed by the act to be passed. (Rex v. Goodcheap, 6 T. R. 159; 1 Bott. 115.)

But the court will grant a *mandamus* to commissioners, entrusted by act of Parliament with the regulation of the expenditure of a parish, to compel them to levy a rate for the purpose of paying off a sum borrowed on the rates by former commissioners without pledging their personal responsibility, where the liabilities created under the former act are reserved by the new act, although the latter directs that the commissioners shall be *sued* in the name of their clerk, and no interest has been paid for twenty years. (1 Man. & Ryl. 591.)

When may reimburse Predecessors.] But now, by statute 41 Geo. 3. c. 28. s. 9, it is enacted, that the churchwardens and overseers, out of any rates they shall collect for the relief of the poor, may reimburse their predecessors such sums as they have heretofore advanced or expended for the relief of the poor, during the time that no rate or assessment for the relief thereof has been made, or during the time that any appeal has been depending which affected the whole of such rate or assessment, or upon hearing of which the whole might be quashed; and in default of payment of such money so advanced and expended within fourteen days next after demand, in writing, such preceding churchwardens and overseers, or guardians, or any of them, may apply to the then next general or quarter sessions, giving due notice in writing of such application to the then churchwardens and overseers, or any two of them; and such court shall examine the parties and witnesses upon oath, and shall make an order upon the then churchwardens and overseers, or any of them, out of the rate collected, or to be collected by them, to pay such sum to such predecessors as the said court shall think fit, and such sums, so ordered to be paid, may be levied by distress, and by all such other means as the poor rate may.

Rate to repay Loans.] On a rule to show cause why a rate for the relief of the poor of Effingham, in Surrey, and an order of sessions confirming the rate, should not be quashed, it appeared that the sessions had refused to state a special case, but the counsel for the appellants being of opinion that the rate would appear to be bad from the title of it, they removed it by certiorari, and obtained the present rule. The title of the rate was as follows: "Surrey to wit: An assessment on all and every the occupiers of lands and houses in the parish of Effingham, for the necessary relief of the poor, and towards *payment of money borrowed* for repairing and rebuilding the workhouse,

Willes, J., said, " Can we reject as surplusage what is a material part of the title of the rate? If we cannot, is a rate good to repay money borrowed? Tawney's case, (*ante* 400,) is in point. The rate cannot be supported." Ashurst, J., of the same opinion. Buller, J., " This rate imports to be made for two purposes, and we are desired to consider it as only made for one. I conceive that a rate cannot be made for money borrowed, even though within the year. Tawney's case goes that length, for it is not confined to the mandamus." The rule for quashing was made absolute. (Rex v. Wavell, Doug. 116, 1 Bott. 112.)

Assistant Overseer's Salary.] By 59 Geo. 3. c. 12. s. 7, assistant overseers of the poor, for such purposes as are named in the act, may be appointed, and with such salary as shall have been fixed by the inhabitants in vestry; and such salary shall be paid out of the money raised for the relief of the poor, at such times and in such manner as shall have been agreed upon between the inhabitants in vestry, and the respective persons so to be appointed.

Constable's Expenses.] The expenses which are to be allowed a constable out of the parish rates, are those necessarily incurred by him on behalf of the parish, as in relieving or conveying vagrants, &c., within 18 Geo. 3. c. 19. s. 4; but the expenses of indicting a party for assaulting him in the execution of his duty are not expenses so incurred, although the prosecution was directed by a magistrate. (See *ante* 356, 357.)

SECTION III.—PERSONS RATEABLE.

The poor rate is to be made by taxation of every inhabitant, parson, vicar, and other, and upon every occupier of lands, houses, tithes impropriate, propriations of tithes, coal mines, or saleable underwoods, in the parish. (43 Eliz. c. 2. s. 1.)

Every Inhabitant, or Other.] The meaning of which is, in this statute, a *resident* inhabitant. (Rex v. North Curry, 4 Barn. & Cres. 953, 7 Dowl. & Ryl. 424.)

In considering the liability to the poor rate, arising from inhabitancy as connected with certain property, the word inhabitant must be understood to mean a person resident permanently and sleeping in the parish. (Rex v. Nicholson, 12 East, 330.) And therefore a person, who is lessee of a stall in a market, and comes there on market days to sell his wares, is not rateable. (Holledge's case, 1 Bott. 123.)

Partners.] Partners resident in one parish, but holding premises and carrying on business in another parish, by means of a servant who resides on the premises, are not inhabitants of the latter parish within the meaning of the statute, and are not rateable to the poor of the parish, in respect of their personal property situate within it. (Rex v. North Curry, ubi supra.)

For what rateable.] The assessment must be made according to the *visible* estate of the inhabitant, both real and personal, *within* the parish, but he shall not be rated in that parish for any property he may have elsewhere, (Sir Anthony Earby's case, 1 Bott. 124,) nor is he rateable by reason of money he has out at interest, or in the funds, (Rex. v. St. John's, Maddermarket, 1 Bott. 239,) or by reason of his salary as clerk, or pay as an officer in the navy, &c., (Rex v. Shalfleet, 4 Burr. 2011;) nor in respect of the profits of his profession, as attorney; (Rex v. Startifant, 7 T. R. 60, 1 Bott. 217;) nor for household furniture merely. (Rex v. White, 4 T. R. 771.)

But he is rateable for his stock in trade, within the parish, of which he makes a profit, (Rex v. Macdonald, 12 East, 324, Bott. 75,) whether there be a custom in the parish to that effect, (Rex v. Hill, Cowp. 613,) or not. (Rex v. Ambleside, 16 East, 380.)

But silk-throwsters, working up in their mills the silk of their employers, sent to them for that purpose, and others in the like circumstances, are not liable to be rated in that respect as for their stock in trade. (Rex v. Sherborne, 8 East, 537, Bott. cont. 67.) Nor is a farmer liable to be rated for his farming stock, because the annual profits of the land being rated, the profits of the stock are included therein. (Rex v. Barking, 2 Ld. Raym. 1280.) A ship-owner is liable to be rated for a ship of which he makes profit, if its principal port, and the residence of such owner, be within the parish, (Rex v. Jones, 8 East, 451,) though the ship is not, at the time of making the rate, actually within the parish. (Rex v. Shepherd, 1 Barn. & Ald. 109.) But if it has *never* been locally within the parish it cannot be rated. (Ib.)

Ambassador, or his Servant.] A rate on a foreign ambassador cannot be levied by distress, nor can any of his suite be rated, if they be clearly within the meaning of the Stat. 7 Anne, c. 12. But where this privilege was claimed by a servant of an ambassador, whose goods had been distrained for a poor rate, he being the tenant of the house, part of which he let out in lodgings, and was a teacher of languages, and also prompter at the opera-house, it was said by the court that such a privilege in this case would be absurd in itself, and not at all within the reason upon which the rights of ambassadors are founded. (Novello v. Toogood, 1 Barn. & Cres. 354, 2 Dowl. & Ryl. 833.)

Parson and Vicar.] The parson and vicar, whether resident in the parish or not, are liable to be rated for their tithes in the parish, (Rex v. Turner, 1 Stra. 77,) although they let them to their parishioners respectively, (16 Vin. Abr. 427,) and also with respect to oblations and other offerings. (Rex v. Carlyon, 3 T. R. 386, 1 Bott. 186.) They are also liable to be rated for other property in their possession or occupation in precisely the same manner as other persons. But if they let the tithes to a *tithe farmer*, the farmer only shall be rated for them. (Rex v. Lambeth, 1 Bott. 127.) But where, upon an inclosure of lands in the parish under a local act of Parliament, it is provided, that the tithes shall be extinguished, and the value thereof shall be estimated, and an *annual rent*, or sum of money per acre, shall be paid in lieu thereof, the rector will be rateable in respect of such rents, unless they are specially exempted by the act. (Rex v. Lacy, 5 Barn, & Cres. 702, 8 Dowl. & Ryl. 467; Chatfield v. Ruston, 3 Barn. & Cres. 863.)

Thus where an inclosure act provided, that a certain corn rent, " free from all taxes and deductions whatsoever, except land-tax," should be issuing out of the lands to be inclosed, and other lands in the parish, and to be paid to the rector in lieu of all great and small tithes, &c.; it was held, that this corn rent was not rateable to the poor. (Mitchell v. Fordham, 6 Barn. & Cres. 274.)

Tithes impropriate, &c.] See the cases under the last preceding title. Where it appeared, that the appellants were the proprietors of the tithe-sheaf of the parish of St. Paul, and also one-tenth of all the fish caught and brought on shore within the parish, they were held rateable for them. (Rex v. Carlyon, 3 T. R. 385, 1 Bott. 186.)

Every Occupier, &c.] The tenant, and not the landlord, is the occupier within the meaning of the statute. (Rex v. Parrot, 5 T. R. 593, 1 Bott. 202.) But where the owner occupies by his servants, he is rateable, for residence is not essential to occupancy, (Rex v. Aberystwith, 10 East, 354;) but a person occupying merely as a servant is not to be rated. (Rex v. Terrot, 3 East, 506, 1 Bott. 230.) Corporations may be rated where they occupy by themselves or servants. (Rex v. Gardner, 1 Bott. 143; Rex v. Mayor, &c. of Sudbury, 2 Dowl. & Ryl. 651, 1 Barn. & Cres. 389.)

What Kind of Occupancy.] To render parties liable to be rated as occupiers, it must be a profitable occupancy for which they are rated; and therefore the persons who erect, or the trustees or governors of an hospital, almshouse, or other charitable institution, are not rateable in respect of such institution, (Rex v. St. Bartholomew's, 4 Burr. 2435, 1 Bott. 139; St. Luke's Hospital, 2 Burr. 1053, 1 Bott. 132;) nor are the persons who reside therein as *menial* servants. (See Rex v. Woodward, 5 T. R. 79, 1 Bott. 205.) But an officer of such an institution is rateable, in respect of a messuage or rooms appropriated separately to his own use; as a schoolmaster upon a charitable foundation, by which a dwelling is provided for him rent free, and without any charge whatever. (Rex v. Catt. 6 T. R. 332, 1 Bott. 213.) And lands given to any such like charitable institution, and from which it *derives a profit*, are rateable. (Ib. 1 Bott. 125, and see 48 Geo. 3. c. 96. s. 26.)

Occupiers of Chapels, &c.] The trustees of a chapel or meeting-house are not rateable, if no emolument be made therefrom, the people being admitted gratuitously, and preachers being provided without receiving anything; (Rex v. Woodward, 5 T. R. 79, 1 Bott. 205;) but if a pecuniary advantage be made by letting out the pews, (Robson v. Hyde, 1 Bott. 164,) although the money thus raised be expended in paying the clergyman's salary, rent, repairs, &c., it is liable to be rated, as the rate is substantially on the clergyman, especially where he takes the surplus, after paying expenses, through the medium of the trustees who receive the profits in the first instance. (Rex v. Agar, 14 East, 256, Bott. 88.)

Occupiers by Gas-pipes.] Pipes in the ground for the conveyance of gas to light a town, is a rateable occupation of land within this act, and the occupiers are rateable to the extent of the increased value of the land so used. (Rex v. Brighton Gas Co. 8 Dowl. & Ryl. 308. 5 Barn. & Cres. 466.)

Occupiers of Alms-houses, &c.] The distinction as to where charities are rateable, and where they are not so, seems to depend upon this—whether there is any body who can be rated as *beneficial occupier.* The objects of a charity, therefore, in the actual occupation of alms-houses, paying no rent for the same, and removeable at the pleasure of the patrons of the charity, are rateable to the relief of the poor in respect of such occupation, although they are themselves described as poor persons, and have no land attached to their dwellings, out of which they may make a profit, (Rex v. Green & Ors. 9 Barn. & Cres. 203.) See also Rex v. Munday, (1 East, 584, 1 Bott. 223,) where it was also held, that the objects of a charitable foundation in the actual occupation of the alms-house and land for their own benefit, in the manner prescribed by the rules of the institution, and liable to be dismissed for any breach of such rules, are rateable in respect of such occupation.

Corporation rateable.] Where a local act for the relief of the poor authorized the commissioners to rate all and every person or persons who occupied or possessed land in the parish, it was held that a corporation was liable to be rated, although, by a clause giving an appeal to the quarter sessions to any party aggrieved, such party was bound to enter a recognizance, and it has been said, (though this is doubted,) that a corporation cannot enter into a recognizance. (See Moore, 68.) For the part of the clause which requires a recognizance to be entered into, may be said to apply only to those persons who are capable of entering into a recognizance, but is inapplicable to those who are not. (Cortis v. Kent Water Works Co. 7 Barn. & Cres. 314.)

Rating Landlords.] In many parishes in large towns, the payment of the poor's rates was heretofore evaded, by reason of houses being let out in separate apartments, or for short terms, or to poor tenants; and in many instances the landlords thereof, availing themselves of this exemption, obtained higher rents upon this very ground, that the occupiers would not be required to pay such rates. To remedy this evil, the 59 G. 3. c. 12 provides, that it shall be lawful for the inhabitants of any parish, in vestry assembled, to direct that the owners of all houses, apartments, or dwellings, being the immediate lessors of the actual occupiers, let at a rent or rate *not exceeding* 20*l.* nor *less* than 6*l.* by the year, or on any agreement by which the rent shall be made payable at any shorter period than three months, shall be assessed to the poor's rates in respect of such houses, &c. instead of the *actual occupiers;* and the inhabitants so assembled in vestry, may from time to time vary and amend their resolutions in these matters, as they see occasion, and the churchwardens and overseers of the poor are required, to carry into effect all such resolutions and directions of the inhabitants in vestry assembled.

Distraining for Landlord's Rate.] Upon non-payment of the sums so assessed, the same may be levied upon the goods and chattels of such landlords, &c. in like manner as poor's rates may by law be levied upon actual occupiers on whom the same are charged. (59 Geo. 3. c. 12. s. 19.) The goods of the occupier are also liable to be distrained, for such rates as shall have become due during his occupancy, to be ascertained in a summary way by the justices granting the warrant of distress; so that the sum so raised does not exceed the amount *then* actually due for the *rent* of the premises on which the distress is made. And which payment shall be a sufficient discharge for so much of the rent payable by him, as he shall have paid, or as shall have been so levied on his goods and chattels, for the rates and the costs of levying of the same. (Ib. s. 20.)

Who is deemed Landlord.] The person receiving the rent of any such house, &c. for his own use, or for any corporation, or of any landlord who is a minor, under coveture, or insane, or for the use of any person not usually resident within twenty miles of the parish, shall for this purpose be taken to be and shall be rateable as the owner thereof. (Ib. s. 21.) And such person shall have the right of appeal, and to be present and vote in every vestry or meeting of the inhabitants for the consideration of any matter or question relating to the poor laws, in like manner as the inhabitants of the parish. (Ib. s. 22.)

It is provided, that the act shall not extend to any city, borough or town corporate, in which the right of *voting* for the election of members to serve in Parliament shall depend upon the assessment of the *voter*, to the poor's rate. (Ib. s. 23.)

SECTION IV.—PROPERTY RATEABLE.

Land, Houses, &c.] The occupiers of lands, whether for pleasure or the ordinary purposes of cultivation, and the occupiers of houses, are liable to be rated by reason of their occupancy, even though they derive no real profit from the occupancy. (Rex v. Hull Dock Company, 5 Maul. & Sel. 394; Rex v. Attwood, 6 Barn. & Cres. 277.) But as the profit arising therefrom, either actual or assumed, is the ground of the assessment, if the annual value of the land or house be enhanced by any collateral circumstances,—as by a mineral spring, (Rex v. Miller, 2 Cowp. 619, 1 Bott. 155,) or a spring of plain water being upon the land,—the rate must be according to its improved value. (Rex v. New River Company, 1 Maul. & Sel. 503, Bott. 96.) The same principle applies, if a dock (Rex v. Hull Dock Co., 1 T. R. 219, 1 Bott. 171,) or waterworks be erected upon the land, (Atkins v. Davis, Cald. 3; Rex. v. Bath, 14 East, 609, Bott. 91,) or if its value be increased by the main pipes from water, or gas works, being laid in it, (Rex v. Rochdale Waterworks Co., 1 Maul. & Sel. 634, Bott. cont. 106,) the rate must be to the extent of the increased value of the land in consequence of its being so used: (R. v. Brighton, 5 Barn. & Cres. 466:) so if a sluice or cut of a navigated river, (Rex v. Milton, 3 Barn. & Ald. 112,) or a canal pass over the land. (Rex v. Grand Junction Canal Co., 1 Barn. & Ald. 289.) The same principle applies if a barge-way or towing-path run over it. (Rex v. the Mayor, &c. of London, 4 T. R. 21.

1 Bott. 196,) or gas works be erected thereupon, or lime works, (Rex v. Alberbury, 1 East, 534,) slate works, (R. v. Woodland, 2 East, 164,) or a potter's clay-pit (Rex v. Brown, 8 East, 528,) be upon it. In like manner, the profits of a steelyard of a weighing machine erected in a house, (Rex v. Gloucester, Cald. 262, 1 Bott. 163,) or of a carding machine, or the like, are rateable, (Rex v. Hogg, Cald. 266, 1 T. R. 721, 1 Bott. 177,) or where a building is let to be used as a canteen (Rex v. Bradford, 4 Maul. & Sel. 317): in all these cases the land or house is liable to be rated according to its value thus improved, unless otherwise provided by some act of Parliament. (See Rex v. Birmingham Gas Light Co., 1 Barn. & Cres. 506, 2 Dowl. & Ryl. 735.)

But lands, converted into drains merely for the purpose of draining other lands, *out* of the parish, and from which the commissioners of the drainage derived no pecuniary advantage whatever, were holden not liable to be rated, (Rex v. Sculcoates, 12 East, 40, Bott. cont. 72:) but the owners of the lands benefited would be liable to be rated at their improved value, in consequence of the drainage, in their respective parishes. (Ib.)

Houses not rateable.] Houses built on land embanked from the Thames, in pursuance of the statute 7 Geo. 3. c. 37, which vests those lands in the owners, "free from all taxes and assessments whatsoever," are not liable to be rated for the relief of the poor. The legislature, in passing this act, clearly contemplated a benefit arising to the public from the embankment on the one hand, and a benefit arising to the persons making the embankment, namely, an exemption from taxes, on the other, (Rex v. London Gas Company, 8 Barn. & Cres. 54, 2 Man. & Ryl. 12.)

Corporation Lands, &c.] A corporation siezed of lands used as common lands by the burgesses, is rateable for the same; (Rex v. Watson, 5 East, 480, 1 Bott. 237;) or if the afternath of certain lands is vested in the corporation as trustees for the burgessses, (Rex v. Tewkesbury, 13 East, 155.) So, where a farmer let his cows, depastured on his own lands, to a tenant at a certain rent per cow, it was holden that *either* the farmer or the dairyman might be rated for the profits arising from the dairy; but as the farmer in this instance was rated for the *whole* farm, the profits of which arose chiefly from the dairy, the dairyman was exempt; and it is obviously most convenient to rate the farmer for the whole, than to lay a proportionate rate upon each. (Rex v. Brown, 8 East, 528.) So a person having the *exclusive* use of a way, (Rex v. Bell, 7 T. R. 598,) and not merely a right of way over the land of another, (Rex v. Jolliffe, 2 T. R. 90, 1 Bott. 181,) is, it seems, rateable for it.

Fishings, Quit-rents, Tolls, &c.] The lessee of the fishings of a river, if connected with any right to the soil, is also rateable. (Rex v. Ellis, 1 Maul. & Sel.) But the lord of a manor is not rateable for the quit rents and casual profits of the manor, (R. v. Vandewale, 2 Burr. 991; see Carth. 14, Comb. 264,) for in that case the property would be rated twice, once in the hands of the landlord, and again in the hands of the tenant. (Rex. v. Alberbury, 1 East, 534.)

Land covered with Water.] It is now settled that only such occupiers as have an exclusive occupation of land, &c. so as to enable them to maintain an action of trespass, in respect of any injury done to the land, are rateable as occupiers of such land. (Rex v. Mersey & Irwell Navigation, 9 Barn. & Cres. 95.) Where therefore the occupancy amounts to no more than an *easement* in the soil of another, as in the case of trustees of turnpike roads or navigable rivers, they are not rateable as *occupiers* of the lands over which such roads or rivers pass, although they are authorized by act of Parliament to keep the former in repair, and cleanse, scour, open, enlarge, and remove all obstructions to the navigation of the latter, and to receive tolls or dues from those passing along the same. But if such trustees make additional cuts or canals, upon lands purchased by them, and erect locks, sluices, or other works for the more profitable enjoyment thereof, then, according to all the authorities, they are rateable in respect of the occupation of such cuts, locks, wears, dams, &c., although the profits are earned chiefly by the passing along the navigable river. (Rex v. Thomas, 9 Barn. & Cres. 114.) In which case the question is very fully discussed, and all the authorities collected.

Rent, Criterion of Value.] Rent is the criterion of the value of the occupation, and the same principle of rating must be adopted, whether the party be owner and occupier, or occupier only. The proprietors of a canal, therefore, are rateable for the sum at which it would let, and not for their gross receipts, minus their expenses. (Rex v. Trustees of Duke of Bridgewater, 9 Barn. & Cres. 68.)

Rating by different Proportions of Rent.] The sessions are in general the proper judges of value, but if they fix the proportions in the rating by a wrong rule, the Court of King's Bench will interfere. But where the rate estimating the value according to the net yearly rent, fixed the rate according to *two-thirds* of the rent in the case of lands, tithes, market-tolls, and waterworks, whilst it fixed it according to *one-half* only in the case of houses, collieries, and coal mines, the court said that, there may properly be a difference in the proportion of annual rent upon which houses and lands are to be rated; it belonging to the sessions to fix the precise proportion. The court also said, " that houses and collieries may be classed together. In the case of houses, the annual profit or value is always a *part* only of the annual rent paid to the landlord. Some portion of that rent ought to be set apart to form a fund for repairing or rebuilding, when necessary; in other words, to maintain or reproduce the subject of occupation: a much less part, if any, of the annual rent of land is wanted for either of those purposes, and the whole in some cases, or nearly the whole in others, is annual profit or value. This difference is mentioned by Lord Mansfield in Rex v. Brograve. (4 Burr. 2491.) In the case of collieries also, a part of the annual rent must be appropriated to repair and replace the works and engines, and in that respect they are in the same situation with houses. The sessions, therefore, were warranted in making a difference in the proportion of rating, with reference to annual rent, between houses and collieries on the one hand, and land on the other; and it is impossible for us to say, that the proportion which they have fixed is not the right one." (Rex v. Tomlinson, 9 Barn. & Cres. 163.)

Rating regulated by Canal Act.] By a canal act it was provided, that lands, whether covered with water or not, and also all dwelling-houses, wharfs, &c., belonging to the company, should be rateable to the maintenance of the poor in the several parishes where they were respectively situated, the lands according to their quantity and quality, and the dwelling-houses, wharfs, &c., according to the nature and respective uses thereof; and should be assessed in like manner as lands of a like quality, and dwelling-houses, wharfs, &c., of a like and similar size or nature, in the respective parishes where the same should be situate, should be assessed; and that the rates, duties, and other personal property of the company, liable to be rated to the poor, should be assessed in like manner, and in the same proportion, as other personal property should be assessed. Held, that land of the company used by them for the purpose of the canal was rateable quâ land, not in respect of its improved value, but in respect of that which would have been its value, if it had not been used for the purposes of the canal.

The company had, on the margin of a large basin, a piece of land adjoining the private yard of a timber merchant. This piece of land next the basin consisted of natural ground; it was not faced with brick or timber, and the ground below the water gradually sloped down to the bottom of the basin. The timber merchant landed his timber upon this piece of land, and it was there marked and measured by the revenue officers. No acknowledgment or rent was paid to the company for this privilege of landing the goods there, but their rates and duties were increased, a greater number of ships entering the basin in consequence of this privilege. Held, that this piece of land was not a wharf within the meaning of the act of Parliament, and was not liable to be rated as such to the relief of the poor. (Rex v. Regent's Company, 6 Barn. & Cres. 720.) But unless there is some clause of exemption in the act of Parliament, land taken for the purpose of a canal will be rateable, not according to the value of the land when it was taken for the purposes of the canal, but according to that value which it has acquired from its having been used for the purposes of the canal. But canals are supposed to be of public benefit, and therefore some canal acts have clauses of exemption, so as to leave land on the same footing in this respect as it was when first taken for the purposes of the canal. (Rex v. St. Peter the Great, Worcester, 5 Barn. & Cres. 478, 8 Dowl. & Ryl. 331.)

Tolls how made rateable.] Tolls *per se* are not rateable, (Rex v. Eyre, 12 East, 416,) as of a ferry, (Rex v. Nicholson, 12 East, 330; Williams v. Jones, 12 East, 346; Rex v. Bell, 5 Maul. & Sel. 221;) but when tolls are connected with *local visible property*, as a *towing-path* or *toll-gate*, they are liable to the rate. (Rex v. Mayor of London, 4 T. R. 21, 1 Bott 196.) So, if they arise out of, wholly or in part, or are *connected* with the *lock* of a canal, (Rex v. Macdonald, 12 East, 324, Bott. cont. 75;) or a *sluice* upon a navigable river, (Rex v. Cardington, 2 Cowp. 581, 1 Bott. 154; Rex v. Salter's Load Sluice, 4 T. R. 730, 1 Bott. 201;) or result, though in part only, from an occupation of real property, they are rateable. (See Rex v. Trent and Mersey Navigation, 1 Barn. & Cres. 545, 2 Dowl. & Ryl. 752.)

Tolls and Dock Dues, when not rateable.] Where the surplus tolls of a river navigation were directed by act of Parliament to be expended in repairing public bridges and highways, it was held, that as those were public purposes, and as no part of the monies received could be applied to private purposes, those monies were not rateable in the hands of the trustees. (Rex v. Trustees of Weaver Navigation, 7 Barn. & Cres. 70.) And where dock dues were to be applied in paying off the debt incurred in making the docks, and in keeping them in repair, and that then the dues should be lowered, reserving sufficient only to keep the docks, &c., in repair, it was held, that as no person had a *beneficial* occupation in any of these works, they were not rateable. (Rex v. Liverpool, id. 61.)

Lighthouse Duties.] Where a poor rate was imposed upon " a lighthouse, together with the duties and contribution-money payable in respect of ships passing by the same;" and the lighthouse was occupied by a servant of the owner, and was situated in the parish, but the duties were collected out of the parish; it was held, that these *duties* did not constitute part of the annual profits of the house or land where the light was placed, and were not rateable to the poor; but the lighthouse is rateable for the sum at which it may be valued. (Rex v. Coke, 5 Barn. & Cres. 797, 8 Dowl. & Ryl. 666.)

Crown Lands.] Lands or houses in the possession of the Crown, or of the *public*, [the nation], are not rateable, (L. Amherst v. L. Somers, 2 T. R. 372, 1 Bott. 184;) nor are persons residing upon them, merely as the *servants* of the Crown, rateable for them. (Rex v. Terrot, 3 East, 506, 1 Bott. 230.) But persons allowed to occupy them *beneficially*, as part of the consideration for their services, or the like, may be rated for such part as they appropriate to their own use. (Old Windsor v. Matthews, Cald. 1, 1 Bott. 151; Rex v. Hurdis, 3 T. R. 497, 1 Bott. 187.)

Coal Mines.] The owner, who is also the occupier of a coal mine, is rateable to the poor at the sum for which the mine would *let*, subject to outgoings. The lessee of coal mines is rateable for the amount of royalty or rent which he pays; and in neither case is any allowance to be made for money expended in rendering the mines productive. (Rex v. Attwood, 6 Barn. & Cres. 277.)

A lessee of a coal mine, being the occupier, having erected a steam engine for working the mine, and thereby improved its annual value, was held liable to be rated for such improved value. It is immaterial, with reference to rateability, whether the landlord or tenant erect an engine, or lay down a railway. The bargain between the landlord and tenant may be varied on that account, but the occupier of the property is rateable in respect of its improved annual value. (Rex v. Lord Granville, 9 Barn. & Cres. 188.)

The occupiers of coal mines are liable to be rated for them as long as they continue to *work* them, whether they produce a profit or not, (Rex v. Parrot, 5 T. R. 593, Bott. 209;) but they are not rateable for them *before* they are worked and productive; (Rex v. Bishop of Rochester, 12 East, 353;) nor *after* they cease to be worked. (Rex v. Bedworth, 8 East, 837.)

Other Mines.] *Coal* mines alone are named in the statute; it has been holden that other mines are not within it, and cannot be rated; (Lead Company v. Richardson, 3 Burr. 1341, 1 Bla. Rep. 389, 1 Bott. 137;) and therefore the occupiers of lead mines, or iron mines, (Rex v. Cunningham, 5 East, 478, 1 Bott. 235,) are not rateable either for them or for engines erected to draw the water from such mines, if used for no other purpose, (Rex v. Bilston, 5 Barn. &

Cres. 851, 8 Dowl. & Ryl. 734;) nor are the landlords, who let such mines to the occupier, liable to be rated for the *money rent*, (Rex v. Bishop of Rochester, 12 East, 353; Rex v. Wellbank, 4 Maul. & Sel. 222;) or rent paid in the smelted metal of the mines. (Rex v. Earl of Pomfret, 5 Maul. & Sel. 139.) But the owners of mines are holden to be rateable for the *portion of the ore* raised, which they receive by agreement from those who work in the mines. This kind of contract is called *lot and cope* in lead mines; (Rowls. v. Gell, 2 Cowp. 451, 1 Bott. 149,) and in tin mines, *toll tin*, and *farm tin*, (Rex v. St. Agnes, 3 T. R. 480, 1 Bott. 188; Rex v. St. Austell, 5 Barn. & Ald. 693;) and although the owner receive, by compromise, from the tenants, not the *ore itself*, but the estimated value of it, in money, the liability remains, as he is so far an *occupier of land*, (Rex v. St. Austell, supra;) for here is a reservation of part of the *thing demised*, which operates not as a render, but as an exception out of the demise. (See Co. Lit. 47 a, 142 a.)

Quarries, Pits, &c.] It is not every excavation of the earth which is a mine, and therefore stone-quarries, lime-works, (Rex v. Alberbury, 1 East, 534, 1 Bott. 223,) slate-works, (Rex v. Woodland, 2 East, 164, 1 Bott. 228,) a potter's clay-pit, (Rex v. Brown, 8 East, 528,) and the like, do not belong to the denomination of *mines*, but are considered merely, for this purpose, as land rendered additionally productive by a particular mode of working it, and the occupiers are rateable in respect thereof accordingly.

Saleable Underwoods.] The word *saleable*, as applied to underwood, has not a very precise and definite meaning, but it has been construed, for the purposes of the poor rate, to mean, not such underwoods as are in a *fit state* for sale *only*, but such as are *intended* for sale; and therefore where an occupier cut and sold his underwoods every *twenty-one* years, they were holden to be rateable *every* year, (Rex v. Mirfield, 10 East, 219, Bott. cont. 68,) in the proportion to the profit which might be made of them when sold. The value in such cases may be estimated, among other ways, according to their worth to rent for a lease of the duration of their intended growth. But firs and larches, planted merely for the purpose of sheltering young oak-trees, and cut from among them, (the roots or boles being left to die in the ground,) from time to time, as the oaks grew stronger, and required more space, though *some* of them returned a profit by sale, have been holden not to be saleable underwood within the meaning of this statute, the primary object of planting them being to protect the young oaks, and not to derive a profit from them, *per se* by sale. (Rex v. Ferrybridge, 1 Barn. & Cres. 375, 2 Dowl. & Ryl. 634.)

Where rateable.] It has already been observed, and the words of the statute are to that effect, that property, whatever may be its kind, if it is rateable, shall be rated in the parish where it is situated. Thus all who occupy real property within the district, though dwelling elsewhere, come within the act. So that if a man occupy lands in the several parishes of A. B. and C. and reside himself in the parish of D., he is liable to be rated in all the *four* parishes; in A. B. and C., for the land he occupies in each respectively, and in D. as an inhabitant. (Jeffrey's case, 5 Co. 66, 1 Bott. 122.)

Canals, &c. locally rateable.] A canal company is rateable to the poor in every parish through which the canal passes, in proportion to the profits which the land occupied by them in such parish yields; and, therefore, where a canal passed through several parishes, in which the tonnage dues varied, it was held that the company were rateable to the relief of the poor of each parish for the amount of tonnage dues actually earned *there,* and not for part of the *whole* amount earned along the whole line of the canal, in proportion to the length of the canal in that parish. (Rex v. Inhabitants of Kingswinford, 7 Barn. & Cres. 236.) It was formerly holden, that navigations and canals were rateable in those parishes only in which the *tolls were payable,* but it is now settled that they are rateable in every parish through which they pass, and in each parish upon the principle above stated. (See Rex v. Milton, 3 Barn. & Ald. 112; Rex v. Earl of Portmore, 1 Barn. & Cres. 551, 2 Dowl. & Ryl. 798.)

So the proprietors of waterworks are now holden to be rateable, not only in the parish in which their reservoirs and works are situate, but also in the several parishes through which their main pipes are laid, (Rex v. Mayor, &c. of Bath, 1 East, 609, Bott. cont. 91; Rex v. Rochdale W. Co., 1 Maul. & Sel. 634, Bott. cont. 106,) so the proprietors of a dock, situate in several parishes, are liable to be rated for it in each parish, in the proportion of the space of it within each parish. (See Rex v. Hull Dock Company, 1 T. R. 219, 1 Bott. 171.)

Conjoint rating.] If a man be rated in respect of two things conjointly, one of which is *not* rateable, the whole is bad. As for instance, if he be rated for an *iron* and coal mine, (an iron-mine not being rateable, Rex v. Cunningham, 5 East, 478, 1 Bott. 235,) or for *rent* received by him for a mine, and also as occupier of certain moors, &c. the rent not being rateable, the rate is bad as to both. (Rex v. Welbank, 4 Maul. & Sel. 222.)

SECTION V.—APPEAL AGAINST A RATE.

Who may Appeal.] Any person *aggrieved* by a rate, or having any material objection to any person being put in, or left out of the rate, or to the sum charged on any person therein, or by any thing done or omitted by the overseers, may appeal to the next sessions upon giving *reasonable notice;* or if reasonable notice have not been given, the justices may adjourn the appeal to the next sessions. (17 Geo. 2. c. 38. s. 4.)

To what Tribunal.] There are some instances in which the general management of the parish matters, including the maintenance of the poor, is vested in commissioners specially appointed by local acts, and appeals are directed to be made to them in the first instance, and afterwards to the sessions, if their determination is not satisfactory. These directions must be strictly pursued. Thus, where, by a local act the management of the parish poor was vested in the churchwardens, overseers, governors, and directors of the poor; and an appeal to them was given, to any person thinking himself aggrieved by any thing to be done, by virtue of the act, and if the appellant should be dissatisfied with their *determination,* then an appeal was given into the quarter sessions; a parishioner having applied for relief against a rate, to the churchwardens, overseers, governors, and directors, upon which, at a meeting, regularly held, a resolution was moved, seconded, and carried, that no further notice of his application should be taken, against which resolution he appealed to the sessions;—it was held, that as the churchwardens, &c. had not come to any *determination* on the subject matter of his complaint, the parishioner could not appeal to the quarter sessions, but that he ought to have first applied for a mandamus to compel the churchwardens, &c. to hear the appeal. (Rex v. JJ. of Kent, 9 Barn. & Cres. 283.)

To what Sessions.] The appeal must be to the sessions of the county, riding, division, or franchise, in which the parish, &c. is situate, (17 Geo. 2. c. 38. s. 4,) except that in corporations or franchises, not having more than six justices, nor having jurisdiction over two or more whole parishes or wards, contained within such corporation, &c. the appeal may then be to the next general or quarter sessions of the *county,* &c. if the party appealing shall think fit. (1 Geo. 4. c. 36.)

It must be to the *next* general quarter sessions, (Rex v. JJ. of London, 15 East, 632,) that is, to the next *practicable* sessions, (Rex

v. Coode, 1 Bott. 281 2 Bott. 727; Rex v. JJ. of Sussex, 15 East, 206,) after allowance. (Rex v. Atkins, 4 T. R. 12, 1 Bott. 287.)

The practice of entering, and respiting an appeal against a poor-rate at the next session after its allowance, as a matter of course, without any notice, is not warranted by 17 Geo. 2. c. 38. s. 4. But where that practice prevails, and an appellant has acted upon it, and the justices at the second sessions refuse to hear the appeal, the Court of King's Bench will issue a mandamus to them to do so. (Rex v. JJ. of Wilts, 8 Barn. & Cres. 380, 2 Man. & Ryl. 401.)

Notice of Appeal.] A week's notice is usually considered "reasonable," and will satisfy the statute, unless there be peculiar circumstances which may induce the justices to adjourn the appeal to the next sessions.

The notice must be given by the *party grieved*, or objecting, &c.; but if several suffer the like grievance, they may join in giving the notice. (Rex v. JJ. of Sussex, 15 East, 206; Bott. cont. 1.) It must be given to any two of the churchwardens and overseers, (41 Geo. 3. c. 23. s. 4,) and when the appeal is on the ground that another person is or is not rated, or rated at more or less than he ought, or for any other cause which may require any alteration in the rate with respect to any other person, notice must be served on every such person also. (Ib. s. 6.)

Form and Contents of Notice.] The notice must be in writing, signed by the appellant, or his attorney in his behalf, and the particular causes of appeal must be stated in it, (41 Geo. 3. c. 23. s. 4,) with the names of the persons with respect to whom the rate is required to be altered, &c. (Rex v. Berkshire, 1 Bott. 274.)

By consent of both parties the appeal may be heard although no notice has been given; and, with the like consent, grounds of appeal not stated, or mis-stated, may be heard and decided by the court. (Id. s. 5.)

But the court of quarter sessions has no power to quash a poor's rate for a defect not pointed out in the notice of appeal, though it be apparent on the face of the rate. The court has never decided that the omission to specify the property in respect of which the rate is made, renders the rate illegal, though if pointed out as a cause of appeal, it would be a ground for quashing the rate. (Rex v. Bromyard, 8 Barn. & Cres. 240; 2 Man. & Ryl. 280.)

Grounds of Appeal.] The several grounds of appeal may be classed as follows:—1. That the appellant should not have been rated at all. 2. That the rate is unequal by reason of the appellant being over-rated,—other persons being under-rated,—other persons being omitted. 3. That the rate is bad on the face of it. 4. That the rate is not made by proper persons. 5. That the rate is not made for a proper purpose. 6. That the rate is not made for a proper period.

Appellant not Rateable.] If a person included in the rate do not come within the description of those upon whom this "taxation" is to fall, (see *ante* 402,) he may of course appeal upon the first of the several grounds above stated.

Appeal, being over-rated.] If the overseers in calculating the proportion in which each of the parishioners ought to be assessed, estimate the rateable means of any one parishioner by a different scale from the rest, so as in effect to charge him with a higher rate than his neighbours, in respect of the same kind of property, the rate is bad. For instance, if the rate be regulated by the *rental,* and one of the parishioners be assessed on a rent of £100, when in fact he pays only £50, and which is the actual annual value, or when a rate is proportioned to the rent *actually paid* by the occupiers, and one pays a *rack* rent, and another a *low* rent for land, the value of which he has much enhanced by improvements, this is an incorrect criterion; or the same principle of rating, according to the present annual value, whatever the rent may be, should be applied in all cases. (See Rex v. Mast. 6 T. R. 154; 1 Bott. 211.) In these, and the like instances, the party over-rated may appeal; but the court of King's Bench will not presume a rate to be unequal, unless it appear manifestly upon the face of it to be so. (Rex v. Brograve, 4 Burr. 2491, 1 Bott. 112. 115.)

Appeal.—Others under-rated.] If any one parishioner be under-rated with reference to the rest, it being the same in effect as if the others were *over*-rated, the rate is thereby unequal and bad, and any of the other parishioners may appeal against it. (R. v. Skingle, 7 T. R. 549.)

Appeal.—Persons omitted.] If any person who ought to be rated either as an inhabitant or occupier, be omitted in the rate, as this has the effect of throwing a greater burthen upon those who are rated, than they should fairly be charged with, the rate ought to be amended, but not quashed, as the 41 Geo. 3. c. 23, was passed, to enable the justices to amend in such cases. Any of the parishioners may appeal against the rate in such case. (R. v. Ambleside, 16 East, 380.)

Appeal.—Rate, prima facie bad.] The rate must show upon the face of it, in respect of what property the assessment is made upon each individual charged by the rate, so that if a person wishes to appeal, on the ground that another is under-rated, he may see in respect of what property the rate is imposed, (R. v. Aire and Calder Navigation, 2 Barn. & Cres. 713; 4 Dowl. & Ryl. 253;) and if this is not observed, the rate is bad on the face of it.

The following Form may be safely used.

"An assessment for the necessary relief of the poor, and for other purposes, in the several acts of parliament relating to the poor for the parish of in the county of made and assessed the day of (being the first [*or second, &c.*] rate, at sixpence in the pound for lands, &c., occupied, and of one penny in the pound on personal property) for the present year:

Names of inhabitants and occupiers.	Description of the property for which they are rated.	Value.			Sums assessed.		
		£.	*s.*	*d.*	£.	*s.*	*d.*
A. B.	A house and garden, annual value.	5	0	0	0	2	6
C. D.	Stock in trade, value.	100	0	0	0	8	4
E. F.	A Ship, value	200	0	0	0	16	8

Assessors A. B. } Churchwardens.
C. D. }
E. F. } Overseers of the poor.
G. H. }

Form of the Allowance of the Rate.

We, two of his majesty's justices of the peace, in and for the said county and dwelling, in [or near] the said parish, one whereof is of the quorum, do consent unto and allow of this assessment. Witness our hands, the day of 18 ,

Witness, I. J.
K. L.

Rate made by improper Persons.] The 43 Eliz. c. 2. s. 1, directs, that the rate shall be made by the churchwardens and overseers of the poor of the parish, or the greater part of them, and therefore, if other persons exercise this power, the rate is bad. And it is no excuse that the proper persons have neglected to make a rate, as the court of King's Bench, upon application, founded on an affidavit that a rate is wanting, will grant a mandamus to compel them to make one. (R. v. Barnstable, 1 Barnard, 137, 1 Bott. 78, 112.)

But the court will not command them to make an *equal* rate, for if they make one that is *un*equal, it is the province of the sessions upon appeal to set that right. (R. v. Barnstable, *supra.*)

Rate made for improper Purpose.] The 43 Eliz. also defines the purposes for which the rate is to be levied; which are for raising "a convenient stock of hemp, wool, thread, iron, and other ware and stuff, to set the poor on work, and also competent sums of money for and towards the necessary relief of the lame, impotent," &c.

And subsequent statutes have authorized the payment of various other charges upon parishes, out of the poor rates. (See *ante*, "Purposes of the Poor Rates," 400.)

Rate made for improper Period.] It has already been stated, that a rate may be made "weekly or otherwise;" (43 Eliz. c. 2. s. 1;) but if made for six months prospectively, it is not on this account bad. (See *ante*, "Rate for what time," 399.)

Proceedings at the Hearing.] If the appeal be on the ground that the party making the appeal ought not to be rated *at all*, having no rateable property in the parish, the respondents begin, if on the ground that he is over-rated, or that another is not rated, &c., the appellant begins. (R. v. Newbury, 4 T. R. 475, 1 Bott. 289.) If on *both* grounds, the respondents begin, and prove not merely that the appellant has rateable property within the parish, but must show some probable ground for the amount at which they charge the party in the rate; the mischief of any other rule would be enormous, for a small occupier might then be rated at once, in the round sum of £1000, and be left to struggle his way out of that charge as he could. (R. v. Topham, 12 East. 549.)

The appellant on his part states and proves the case set forth in his notice of appeal, and it is irregular for him to state, or to offer proof of, any other grounds of objection to the rate, than those contained in his notice.

Inhabitants are competent witnesses, whether rated or holding office or not, or whether supported by the parish, wholly, or in part, or not. (54 Geo. 3. c. 170. s. 9.)

Judgment.] The court of sessions shall amend the rate, so as to give relief, without altering it as to other persons mentioned in the same; but if, upon an appeal against the *whole* rate, it be necessary to quash or set it aside, the court may order the churchwardens and overseers to make a new equal rate, who must make the same accordingly. (17 Geo. 2. c. 38. s. 6.) And they may amend it by inserting or striking out any name, or by altering the sums, &c., or in any other manner necessary to give relief, without quashing the rate. Or if they deem it necessary, to give relief to the appellant, they may quash the same. (41 Geo. 3. c. 23. s. 1.) If the rate be quashed, the court may order any sum in the rate not to be paid, &c.; and if proceedings have been commenced to recover the same, such proceedings shall be no further prosecuted. (Ib. s. 3.) If the sum be increased, it may be recovered, &c., (Ib. s. 7.) and if a name be struck out, the money which has been paid by the person under such rate, may be ordered to be repaid. (Ib. s. 8.)

Costs.] The court may award costs for those in whose favour the appeal is determined, (17 Geo. 2. c. 38. s. 4.) provided the appeal have been entered and terminated. (R. v. Essex, 8 T. R. 583, 2 Bott. 757.)

One Parish contributory to another.] It is provided by 43 Eliz. c. 2. s. 3, that if two justices of the district perceive that the inhabitants of any parish, are not able to raise sufficient for the relief of their poor, they may assess "any other of the other parishes within the hundred;" or if the hundred is too poor, any other of the county in such sums as the justices shall think fit. This rate may be made on particular persons only, or the whole parish. (Knightley's Case, Comb. 309, 1 Vent. 350, Foley, 29.)

But this rate cannot be made by justices of a county, upon a borough having exclusive jurisdiction. (R. v. Holbeche, 4 T. R. 778.)

And though they may order such sums to be paid in this manner, as they shall think fit, yet an order "as long as we the said justices shall think proper," is bad; (St. Mary's, in Marlborough, 2 Stra. 700;) but a sum in gross for a year is good; (Comb. 309;) or to raise the sum of £60; (St. Peter and St. Paul, in Marlborough, 2 Stra. 1114;) but if the rate be to levy a certain sum in the pound, it is bad. (R. v. Telescombe, 1 Stra. 314.)

The sessions may charge parishes *out of* the hundred, towards the maintenance of the poor within the hundred, before two justices have adjudged that the hundred is not able, as it will be presumed that the sessions is satisfied upon that point before the order is made. (R. v. Percivall, 1 Stra. 56.)

SECTION VI.—DISTRAINING FOR POOR RATE.

The 43 Eliz. c. 2. s. 4, declares, that it shall be lawful as well for the present as subsequent churchwardens and overseers, or any of them, by warrant from any two justices, one whereof is of the quorum, to levy all arrearages according to the assessments, by distress and sale.

It seems doubtful whether, in strictness, a rate due from a person who dies before it is paid, may be levied upon his representative. But at all events before this can be done, the latter must be summoned, for he may be able to show good cause against such a demand, as want of assets, &c. (Stevens v. Evans, 2 Burr. 1152.)

Where Distress may be made.] And by 17 Geo. 2. c. 38. s. 7, the goods may be levied by warrant of distress, not only in the same parish or place, but in any other place within the same county; and if sufficient cannot be found there, then on oath being made before some justice of any other county, and certified on the said warrant, the defaulter's goods may be levied in such other county or precinct, subject to an appeal to the next general or quarter sessions of the peace, for the county or precinct where such assessment was made.

The 54 Geo. 3. c. 170. s. 12, is to the same effect, including the right so to distrain for poor rates, church or highway cesses.

Rates levied, though quashed.] By 41 Geo. 3. c. 23. s. 1, if the sessions should quash the rate, all the sums of money by such rate charged on any person, shall *nevertheless be levied* in the same manner as if no appeal had been made against such rate, and such sums when levied or recovered, shall be taken as payment on account of the next effective rate, made for the relief of the poor of the same parish, township, vill, or place.

The second section of the act provides, that the sums rated may be levied by distress, notwithstanding the person so rated, or any other person, shall have given notice of appeal against such rate, provided always, that if any person rated shall give due notice of appeal, then from and after the giving of such notice, and until the appeal shall have been determined, no proceedings shall be commenced to recover any greater sum from such person, than the sum at which he, or any occupier of the same premises, shall have been assessed in the last effective rate which shall have been collected, in such parish or place.

By s. 3, if the court order any rate to be quashed, they may order the sum charged on any person, or any part of it, not to be paid, which shall be a bar to any proceedings for the recovery of such sum, so ordered not to be paid.

And by s. 7, if the sessions order any person to be inserted in the rate and assessed, or the amount of the rate on any persons to be increased, the same shall be recoverable in the same manner as if they had so stood originally in the rate.

What may be distrained.] Money may be distrained for the poor rate, as well as goods. (E. I. Company v. Skinner, 1 Bott. 257.)

Averiæ carucæ are distrainable for the poor rate. (Hutchins v. Chambers, 1 Burr. 579, and working tools in a shop, 2 Show, 126.)

Wherein Distress improper.] A distress for a poor rate for lands not in the occupation of the plaintiff, may be replevied, notwithstanding the sessions on appeal have confirmed the rate, the determining that a man may be assessed for what he does not occupy, being an excess of jurisdiction. (Milward v. Caffin, 2 Bla. Rep. 1330.)

And if the landlord tender the rent for his tenant, the overseers must receive it, and a warrant ought not to be granted to distrain upon the tenant. (Rex v. Cosens, 2 Doug. 426.)

Oath and Summons, before Distress.] The distress cannot be made under a general warrant made before the rate, but there ought to be a special warrant for the purpose. That is to say, the nonfeasance of the party shall not be left to the judgment of the officer, who may, out of private resentment, sell his neighbour's goods without sufficient cause; but oath of the refusal must be made before the justices. And it is reasonable that the party should be heard in his defence, for he may show cause variously, why a distress should not be granted. (Tracey v. Talbot, 2 Salk. 532; 1 Nol. P. L. 258.) And a previous summons must be issued before any such warrant is granted. (Harper v. Carr, 7 T. R. 270.)

Mandamus to grant Warrant.] Against a rule for a *mandamus* to the defendants, justices for Cumberland, to grant warrants of distress to levy a poor rate, it was contended, that there should have been a previous summons. In support of the rule, the case of Rex v. Justices of Middlesex, 1 Bott. 262, in which it was held, that a previous summons was not necessary. But Lord Kenyon said, "I confess I cannot subscribe my assent to the decision in the case cited. The payment of a poor rate, unless it be set aside, must be enforced; and if the magistrates will not issue a summons to the person who refuses to pay the rate, the court will grant a mandamus to compel them to do it; but a summons must precede a warrant of distress, which is in the nature of an execution. On the summons the party may show a sufficient reason to the magistrates why a warrant of distress should not issue.

It is an invariable maxim in our law, that no man shall be punished before he has had an opportunity of being heard; whereas, if a warrant of distress were to be issued without any previous summons, the party would have no opportunity of showing cause why the execution should not issue against him. But the next day the court granted a rule for a mandamus to the magistrates, "to receive such informations and complaints as shall be laid before them, against persons refusing to pay the sums assessed upon them for the relief of the poor of the township of Whitehaven, and to proceed thereupon to levy the same." (R. v. Benn and Church, 6 T. R. 198; 1 Bott. 269.)

Distress illegally executed.] The parties executing a distress for a poor rate, are liable as trespassers, if they commit any excess, not excused by the law.

Thus, where the defendants went to the house of the plaintiff, carrying with them a warrant directed to some of them as churchwardens and overseers, to distrain the plaintiff's goods for a poor's rate, and being informed at the next house that the plaintiff was from home, one of the defendants tried to get in at the cellar, but failed, and in the attempt some windows were broken. They then took the fastening out of a window, and got into the washhouse, but having found nothing there, they returned and took away some planks and other articles which were lying in the garden. A verdict was found for the plaintiff, damages seven guineas, with leave for the defendants to move to enter a nonsuit, on the ground of there not being any proof of a demand of the copy of the warrant, as required by stat. 24 Geo. 2. c. 44. s. 6. Upon the question coming on to be argued, Lord Ellenborough said, the case of Money v. Leach, (3 Burr. 1742; 1 Bla. Rep. 555,) decides, that a defendant, in order to avail himself of the objection upon the statute, must show that he acted in obedience to the warrant. Here the defendants, so far from showing that they acted in obedience to the warrant, commence by an unauthorized course of proceeding; it was a trespass in them, *ab initio*, and I do not see how, after the case of Money v. Leach, they can stir this objection. That was a case of much public interest, and was decided upon great deliberation, and the matter was upon the record. If this had been a distinct subsequent trespass of the offenders, it might have presented a different question. And the other judges concurring the rule to enter a nonsuit was discharged.

CHAPTER XXI.—OVERSEERS OF THE POOR.

SECTION I.—APPOINTMENT OF OVERSEERS.

For what Places appointed.] It has already been observed, that a churchwarden is *ex virtute officii* an overseer; and it must always be understood that they are included under that general name in treating of the duties, &c., of the office. The 43 Eliz., in directing the appointment of overseers, applied only to *parishes;* but by the subsequent statute of 13 & 14 Car. 2. c. 12, overseers may be appointed for a *township, village,* or *hamlet,* (Rex v. Morris, 4 T. R. 550;) and parishes of inconvenient magnitude may be subdivided, and extra-parochial *towns* and *vills* may have separate overseers. (Dolting v. Stokelane, Fort. 219, N. P. L. 10.) But an appointment of overseers for an extra-parochial *place,* or for a *precinct,* is bad. (Ib.)

The town or vill must be actually, or by reputation, of that denomination, and not merely constructively so, from the number of houses contained within the limit. (Rex v. Standard Hill, 4 Maul. & Sel. 378; Rex v. Eyeford, Cald. 542.) And to authorize the division of a parish into districts with separate overseers, it must consist of two or more distinct townships or vills; and it must also appear that the parish cannot otherwise have the full and ordinary benefit of the 43 Eliz. (Rex v. Walsall, 2 Barn. & Ald. 161; Peart v. Westgarth, 3 Burr. 1610.)

And although there may have been a continued appointment of overseers for such separate townships for forty years, and the same has been recognized, (though not *particularly considered,)* by the court of King's Bench; yet this division of the parish is not thereby confirmed, and may be abrogated, unless it appear that it cannot otherwise reap the benefit of the 43 Eliz. (Rex v. Newell, 4 T. R. 266; Rex v. Uttoxeter, Doug. 246) Still such a long separation of districts, vills, &c., is strong evidence of the propriety of the division. (N. P. L. 26.)

Division of Parish, how made.] The quarter-sessions has no power to divide a parish by an original order, but the mode of proceeding is by the magistrates appointing overseers for the divisions, the validity of which may be tried by appeal against the appointment; (Rex v. Morris, 4 T. R. 550,) or by certiorari, (Rex v. Great Marlow, 2 East, 244;) by mandamus, (Rex v. Middlesex, 1 Bott. 34; Rex v. Watts-Horton, 1 T. R. 374;) indictment against the appointee on refusing to take the office, (Rex v. Warner, 8 T. R. 375;) or collaterally, by appeal against an order of removal, (Rex v. Denham, Burr. S. C. 35,) or against a poor's rate, (Rex v. Watson, 7 East, 214; Rex v. Leigh, 3 T. R. 746;) or by action of trespass or replevin when the rate is attempted to be enforced by distress. (Hilton v. Pawle, Cro. Car. 92; Rudd v. Foster, 4 Mod. 157; Lord Bute v. Grindall, 1 T. R. 338.)

When a parish has been subdivided, the separate divisions are to be considered, with respect to the poor laws, as separate parishes. (Rex v. Kirkby Stephen, Burr. S. C. 664.)

Reunion of Districts.] A parish, with the consent of all its districts, may reunite; and that reunion will be valid in law. (Rex v. Palmer, 8 East, 416.) But it seems that such consent is necessary, especially where the division has existed for a long period, (Rex v. Walsall, 2 Barn. & Ald. 157;) and the legislature has, by a recent act, provided, that where towns corporate or franchises have been assessed to the poor, and have been separated from the parish in which they are situate for sixty years from the passing of the act, such separation shall be lawful, although originally made without sufficient authority. (59 Geo. 3. c. 96.)

Overseers, when appointed.] The appointment is directed by the 54 Geo. 3. c. 91, to be made on the 25th of March, or within fourteen days afterwards; and a forfeiture of £5 is imposed upon the magistrate in whom the appointment lies, if he make default, by the 43 Eliz. But an appointment subsequently made seems valid; (Rex v. Sparrow, 1 Bott. 21, 2 Stra. 1123;) and in the case of death, removal to another place, or insolvency of an overseer, two justices may, on oath thereof, appoint another in his stead till new ones are appointed. (17 Geo. 2. c. 38. s. 3.) The court of King's Bench would probably grant a mandamus to compel an appointment where it is neglected beyond the proper time. (1 N. P. L. 46.)

By whom appointed.] The appointment must be made by two or more justices of the county, except in corporate towns and cities, wherein the duty vests in the mayors, bailiffs, &c., being justices of the peace. But it cannot be made by the head officer *alone*, if there are *two* corporate justices; the signature of two being necessary in that case as well as in others. (Rex v. Butler, 1 Bla. Rep. 649.)

To enable the justices to make a fit selection, the existing overseers usually, towards the close of their year, form a list of substantial householders proper to succeed them. And where this is neglected the justices generally issue a precept to the high-constable, who issues his warrant to the petty constables, requiring them to give the overseers notice to deliver the list forthwith. (1 N. P. L. 46.)

Number of Overseers.] More than four, (Rex v. Harman, 1 Bott. 16,) or less than two overseers, cannot be appointed; (Rex v. Morris, 4 T. R. 550; Rex v. Clifton, 2 East, 168;) though the appointment of one is not bad on the face of it, unless it appear that no other is appointed by some other order. (Id) But an appointment of five is void for the whole, for none of them is entitled to preference. (Rex v. Wymondham, 6 T. R. 552.) If a local act direct, that two shall be appointed, without saying that more shall not be appointed, this does not prevent a greater number being appointed under 43 Eliz. (Rex v. Pinney, 2 Barn. & Cres. 322.)

Who may be appointed.] They are to be *householders;* but neither personal residence or payment of rent and taxes is essential. Thus every partner in a firm, carried on in a dwelling-house, though only a servant reside there, is a householder for this purpose, (Rex v. Poynder, 1 Barn & Cres. 178;) and a woman may be appointed overseer. (Rex v. Stubbs, 2 T. R. 395.) The act also requires that they shall be *substantial* householders; but this is a relative term, and therefore labourers, being householders, have been held sufficient, where there were no more competent persons in the township. (Id.) And by the 59 Geo. 3. c. 12. s. 6, residents within two miles of the parish church, or one mile of the boundary of the parish, may be appointed, by their own consent, and the request of the parish in vestry assembled, although they be non-resident *in* the parish, if they are assessed to the poor thereof. But the appointment of residents for *part* of the year only, though they are eligible, is discouraged. (Rex v. Moor, Carth. 161, 1 Bott. 9.)

Exemptions.] The persons exempt from serving other parish offices, are also exempt from the office of overseer. (See tits. "Churchwardens," "Dissenters," "Constables," &c., and 1 N. P. L. 51, 52.)

Form of Appointment.] The *order* of appointment must be in writing, and under hand and seal of the two justices, executed in the presence of each other, (Rex v. Great Marlow, 2 East, 244,) and should appoint the persons named " overseers " *eo nomine*, or it is bad (Rex v. St. George Fort, 320 :) it must state them to be " substantial householders " in the parish; describing them as *principal inhabitants* is bad; (Rex v. Sheringbroke, 2 Lord. Raym. 1394; Overseers of Weobly, 2 Stra. 1261;) and it must state that the appointment is for a parish, township, &c., as the case may be, (Rex v Morris, .4 T. R. 550;) and show that it is within the magistrates' jurisdiction. (Rex v. Houlditch, 1 Bott. 4.) It should express the time for which the appointment is made; (Rex v. Burder, 4 T. R. 778;) and if made on a Sunday, will be bad, unless under peculiar circumstances, and done *bonâ fide*, without any sinister object. (Rex v. Butler, 1 Bla. Rep. 649.) If two sufficient appointments are made on the same day, the last is void, for when the appointment is once legally made, the magistrates' jurisdiction ceases. (Rex v. Searle, 1 Bott. 21.)

Nor can other justices make a new appointment, even though one already appointed applies, upon sufficient cause, to have another substituted in his place, but he must appeal to the sessions. (Rex v. Great Marlow, 2 East, 244.)

Appeal against Appointment.] *Persons aggrieved* by the appointment, whether the *appointee*, or the parishioners at large, may appeal to the next quarter sessions, and the want of jurisdiction in the magistrates making the appointment, or the impropriety of their choice, are good grounds for quashing their order. (Albrighton v. Skipton, 1 Stra. 301; Rex v. Stotfield, 4 T. R. 601; Rex v. Forrest, 3 T. R. 38.)

And the order of the sessions thereon may be removed by certiorari, for the judgment of the court of King's Bench, (Rex v. Gayer, 1 Burr. 245,) or the original order of justices may be so removed, without previous appeal to the sessions, and the court will quash it for any prima facie defects, or for any of the above causes shown by affidavit. (Rex v. Walsall, 2 Barn. & Ald. 157; Rex v. Standard Hill, 4 Maul. & Sel. 378.) But a certiorari cannot be granted pending an appeal to the next sessions, previously lodged, (Warwick, 2 Stra. 991. 1146;) though, if notice be given that the appeal is *abandoned*, it seems the certiorari may be obtained. (Rex v. Bradbury, 1 N. P. L. 58.)

Refusing Office punishable.] Persons appointed overseers, and having had notice thereof, may be indicted where they refuse to undertake, or execute the duty, having taken no steps to get free from the office, or if, having done so, the order has been confirmed. (Rex v. Poynder, 1 Barn. & Cres. 178, 2 Dowl. & Ryl. 258.)

SECTION II.—POWERS AND GENERAL DUTIES.

Their Jurisdiction.] The overseers of a parish or township are duly to execute their office, without dividing themselves, in all places within the parish, in all things to them belonging, although the parish may extend into two or more counties or franchises, &c. (43 Eliz. c. 2. s. 9.) All acts which the whole body are competent to perform, may be properly done by a majority. (Doe d. Grundy v. Clarke, 14 East, 488.)

And where there are no churchwardens, the overseers are to exercise all the powers, and under the same responsibilities, as overseers and churchwardens may do, by any of the statutes relating to the poor. (17 Geo. 2. c. 38. s. 15; 59 Geo. 3. c. 12. s. 25.)

The overseers have by law the custody of the instruments by which they are appointed. (Rex v. Stoke Golding, 1 Barn. & Ald. 173.)

Two overseers, one of whom is also sole churchwarden, do not constitute a body corporate within the meaning of the 59 Geo. 3. c. 12. s. 17, and the parish property does not vest in them. (Woodcock v. Gibson, 4 Barn. & Cres. 462.)

Their Duties.] The care of the poor, in conjunction with the guardians, &c., is entrusted to them, the major part having power to act for the whole; and they are to continue in office till others are elected. They are to make poor's rates, to remove paupers not belonging to their parish, &c., and to inspect and administer to the wants of their proper poor; and, on going out of office, to make up and pass their accounts, and deliver any balance in their hands to their successors, with all the property and documents of the parish, &c. And for these purposes they are required by the 43 Eliz. to meet at least once a month in the church, on Sunday, after divine service in the afternoon.

Must set able Poor to Work.] It is the bounden duty of overseers to endeavour to find work, either in or out of their own parishes, for able-bodied poor persons, who are unable to obtain employment at their usual work themselves; and it seems, that it is only in the event of the former being unable to procure such employment, that they are authorized in giving pecuniary relief. (Rex v. Collett, 2 Barn. & Cres. 324.)

It is a general principle, that the public are not bound to find food for those who are able, but unwilling to work, and persons who are unable, as paupers, or not at liberty, as prisoners, to *find* work for themselves, must accept that which is provided for them, whilst subsisting upon the public. (See Rex v. JJ. of N. R. Yorkshire, 2 Barn. & Cres. 286, 3 Dowl. & Ryl. 510.)

Not to borrow Money.] The borrowing of money is no part of the duty, nor is it within the authority of an overseer. (Massey v. Knowles, 3 Stark. Rep. 65.) Therefore, in an action against a surety on a bond conditioned for the overseer's faithfully accounting for all sums which should arise, or come into his hands *by virtue of his office of overseer*, the surety is not liable for a sum *lent* to the overseer, and applied by him to parochial purposes. If, indeed, the money had been borrowed by the direction of the parishioners, there might be ground for saying that it came into his hands in his character of overseer; but where that does not appear to have been the case, it must be considered as a loan to him *individually*, and not in his character of overseer; and if it was not money received by him by virtue of his office, it is not within the condition of the bond, and the surety is consequently not liable under such circumstances. (Leigh v. Taylor, 7 Barn. & Cres. 491.)

Borrowing when Rate suspended.] If, on a dispute respecting a rate for the relief of the poor, the matter be referred, and in the meantime the overseer borrows money, on his own notes, for the relief of the poor, and make no rate to reimburse the money, the lender may recover it against him, in an action for money had and received to his own use. (How v. Keech, 1 Bott. 381.) Where a payment has been made by a party, at the sole request of one overseer of a parish, and without the knowledge of the others, and no demand is made upon them till after they are out of office, it is a question for the jury to say, whether, under these special circumstances, the party ought not to be considered as having relied on the sole responsibility of that overseer, at whose request the payment was made. (Malkin v. Vickerstaff, 3 Barn. & Ald. 89.)

Surgeon attending casual Poor.] A deputy overseer, or even a mere stranger, directing a surgeon to attend a pauper, is liable to pay the surgeon's bill. But it is doubtful whether an overseer is liable to pay such surgeon who attends a pauper without a retainer, and it seems to be clear, that a deputy overseer is not. (Watling v. Walters, 1 C. & P. 132.)

A pauper having casually met with an accident in the parish of W., the surgeon of that parish attended him; and, in the progress of the cure, one of the overseers of the parish, to which the pauper belonged, called on the surgeon, and desired him "to take care of the pauper, and do what he could for him;" and added, "that he would see him paid;" and on a subsequent application by the parish officers of W. after the pauper was removed to his own parish, the overseer said "if it was right that they should pay the surgeon's bill they would." Held in an action against the overseer by the surgeon for the amount of his bill, that there was no legal obligation on the part of the former to pay such amount. (Gent. v. Tompkins, 1 Dowl. & Ryl. 541.)

SECTION III.—RECOVERING PARISH HOUSES AND LANDS.

Possession, how given to Overseers.] By 59 Geo. 3. c. 12. s. 24, after reciting, "that whereas difficulties have frequently arisen, and considerable expenses have sometimes been incurred, by reason of the refusal of persons who have been permitted to occupy, or who have intruded themselves into parish or town houses, or other tenements, or dwellings, built or provided for the habitation of the poor, or otherwise belonging to such parishes, to deliver up the possession of such houses, tenements, or dwellings when thereto required, and it is expedient to provide a remedy for the same, it is enacted, that if any person, who shall have been permitted to occupy any parish or town house, or any other tenement, or dwelling belonging to, or provided by, or at the charge of, any parish for the habitation of the poor thereof, or who shall have unlawfully intruded himself or herself into any such house, tenement, or dwelling, or into any house, tenement, or hereditament belonging to such parish, shall refuse or neglect to quit the same, and deliver up the possession thereof to the churchwardens and overseers of the poor of any such parish, within one month after notice and demand in writing, for that purpose signed by such churchwardens and overseers, or the major part of them, shall have been delivered to the person in possession, or, in his or her absence, affixed on some notorious part of the premises, it shall be lawful for any two of his majesty's justices of the peace, upon complaint to them made by one or more of the churchwardens and overseers of the poor of the parish, in which any such house, tenement, or dwelling shall be situated, to issue their summons to the person against whom such complaint shall be made, to appear before such justices at a time and place to be appointed by them, and to cause such summons to be delivered to the party against whom the complaint shall be made, or, in his or her absence, to be affixed on the premises seven days, at the least, before the time appointed for hearing such complaint; and such justices are hereby empowered and required, upon the appearance of the defendant, or upon proof on oath, that such summons hath been delivered or affixed as is hereby directed, to proceed to hear and determine the matter of such complaint; and if they shall find and adjudge the same to be true, then, by warrant under their hands and seals, to cause possession of the premises in question to be delivered to the churchwardens and overseers of the poor of the parish, or to some of them.

Possession of Lands, how given.] By s. 25, " If any person to whom any land appropriated, purchased, or taken under the authority of this act, for the employment of the poor of any parish, or to whom any other lands belonging to such parish, or to the churchwardens and overseers thereof, or to either of them, shall have been let for his or her own occupation, shall refuse to quit and to deliver up the possession thereof, to the churchwardens and overseers of the poor of such parish, at the expiration of the term for which the same shall have been demised or let to him or her, or if any person or persons shall unlawfully enter upon, or take or hold possession of any such land, or any other land or hereditaments belonging to such parish, or to the churchwardens or overseers, or to either of them, it shall be lawful for such churchwardens and overseers of the poor, or any of them, after such notice and demand of possession as is by this act directed in the case of parish houses, to exhibit a complaint against the person or persons in possession of such land, before two of his majesty's justices of the peace, who are hereby authorized and required to proceed thereon, and to hear and determine the matter thereof; and, if they shall find and adjudge the same to be true, to cause possession of such land to be delivered to the churchwardens and overseers of the poor, or some of them, in such and the like course and manner, as are by this act directed with regard to parish houses."

Recovering Possession at Common Law.] The statute was not intended to take away a right, which the owner of property had at common law, to enter and take possession, if it could be done peaceably, but to provide an expeditious mode, whereby parish officers might obtain possession where it was obstinately withheld; and that they might not do that which had before been sometimes done, viz. might not turn occupiers out vi et armis, which led to further expense and litigation. Where, therefore, a pauper had been permitted to occupy a parish house, but having gone from home, leaving three children there, for whose support she received an allowance from the parish, the overseers on the second day afterwards entered, took the children to the workhouse, and put locks upon the doors. She having returned in about ten days, and, by breaking the locks, resumed possession of the house, the overseers went there, and, upon her refusal to open the door, broke it open, and carried away the furniture, which belonged to the parish. In an action of trespass by her, it was held, that the overseers might lawfully enter, and resume possession, without giving any notice to quit, and were not bound to pursue the mode pointed out by the 59 Geo. 3. c. 12. s. 24. (Wildbor v. Rainforth, 8 Barn. & Cres. 4; see *ante*, 446.)

SECTION IV.—OVERSEERS' ACCOUNTS.

How kept, and when balanced.] If they continue in office more years than one, they must settle their accounts at the close of *each* year, as directed by the act; otherwise, as the inhabitants of a parish are a fluctuating body, the present inhabitants would be burthened with the expenses of their predecessors. (Rex v. Goodcheap, 6 T. R. 161.) The accounts must be fairly written in a book or books, and specify all sums received, or rated and not received, all payments, all goods, stock, materials, &c. in the hands of the officers or paupers, and all things concerning their office as overseers. (Walrond's Case, 1 Bott. 300.)

What Disbursements allowed.] They are entitled to take credit for all sums properly expended in the discharge of their duty, but not for disbursements to which the rate is by law inapplicable. (Rex v. Seville, 5 Barn. & Ald. 180; Rex v. Bird, 2 Barn. & Ald. 522.) Nor must they include sums given to poor persons, *not registered* in the parish books, unless it be done on sudden and emergent occasions, upon pain of forfeiting £5. (9 Geo. 1. c. 7. s. 2.) And they are to be allowed only for their bare expenses. (Rex v. Glyde, 2 Maul. & Sel. 323.

When Accounts to be delivered.] Besides the intermediate periods, at which the overseers are directed to *produce* their accounts to the guardians at their monthly meetings, and to lay the constable's accounts, delivered to them, before the parishioners for reimbursement quarterly, by 18 Geo. 3. c. 9. s. 4; they are directed by the 43 Eliz. c. 2. s. 2, to make and yield up their accounts *to two justices* within *four* days after the end of their year, and the nomination of their successors, to whom they shall deliver over the balance in hand, and all the stock, goods, &c. of the parish, under a penalty of £20 upon every one, except such as are excused on account of sickness, or other just cause.

The 17 Geo. 2. c. 38. s. 1, without expressly repealing the above act, alters some of its provisions, and directs that the accounts kept in a *book or books* for that purpose, and *verified by oath* before one justice, who shall sign and attest the same, to be delivered *to their successors*, within *fourteen* days after such successors are appointed; and the balance, stock, &c. shall be so delivered over, and the said books shall be carefully kept by the overseers, and open to the inspection of persons assessed, or liable to be assessed, at all seasonable times, upon payment of sixpence, to whom also copies of any part thereof shall be given on demand, on payment after the rate of sixpence for every three hundred words.

And by section 2, upon refusal or neglect, two justices may commit them to the common gaol till they fully comply with the statute. And by section 3, if an overseer removes from the place for which he was appointed, he must deliver up his accounts, and pay his balances to some other overseer before his removal, under like penalties. And where an overseer dies, his executor or administrator must make up the accounts within 40 days, and pay the balance in preference to any other creditor.

Justices auditing Accounts.] Notwithstanding the subsequent acts, the right of examining the disbursements by two justices, and allowing the accounts pursuant to the 43 Eliz., still apparently exists, where the parish chooses to proceed upon it; though, as the recent statutes are much more efficient for these purposes, they will doubtless be generally resorted to. (See Rex v. Whitear, 3 Burr. 1365.) It has, therefore, been held, that though two justices may commit overseers for refusing to *make up and verify* their accounts pursuant to 17 Geo. 2, which requires them to deliver to their successors a just and perfect account, fairly *entered in a book*, of their *receipts and expenditure*, yet the justices cannot refuse to *swear* such an officer upon his delivering an account in gross sums, such as would satisfy the 43 Eliz. (Rex v. Middlesex, 1 Wils. 125.) But the very terms of the 17 Geo. 2, ought to be complied with, and the delivery of a mere summary or balance sheet is not such an account as the statute requires. (Rex v. Worcestershire, 3 Dowl. & Ryl. 299.)

Justices may reduce Items.] The 50 Geo. 3. c. 49, recites the former provisions, and adds, that the account shall be submitted to two or more justices in special sessions, within the said fourteen days, who may examine into, and administer an oath to the overseers of the truth of the accounts, and strike out charges which they deem unfounded, or reduce those which are exorbitant, specifying such reductions, and the cause thereof; and their allowance of the account as directed by the 17 Geo. 2.

Punishable for Neglect herein.] Neglect or refusal herein, or if they do not deliver over to their successors, within *ten days* after the signing and attesting such account, any goods or other things which shall thus appear to be remaining in their hands, two justices may commit them as aforesaid till they comply; or if they neglect to pay over the balance remaining in hand, the same may be levied on the offenders' goods under a warrant by two justices, and if the amount cannot be raised by such distress, they may be committed to the county gaol until payment be made. (50 Geo. 3. c. 49. s. 1.)

Appeal against Reductions.] Overseers *having complied* with these directions, may appeal against an order, making reductions in their accounts, to the next general or quarter sessions, to be holden next after the tenth day from making such order, upon entering into recognizance with two securities in not less than double the amount in dispute, to abide the decision of such appeal. (ss. 2, 3.)

Certiorari, &c.] The 5th section declares that no proceedings, either of justices or of sessions, under this act, shall be removed by certiorari; but the decision upon appeals shall be final.

It has been decided, that this provision does not extend to orders made upon appeals brought by *parishioners* against overseers' accounts, under 17 Geo. 2. (Rex v. Bird, 2 Barn. & Ald. 522.)

By section 6, the act is not to extend to parish officers, who by any local act are exempted from rendering accounts required by 43 Eliz. and 17 Geo. 2, nor to the city of London.

And by the 7th section, no provisions, &c. of 43 Eliz. or 17 Geo. 2, are altered or repealed, except so far as they are *expressly* altered, &c.

Mandamus to pass Accounts.] A mandamus is the only remedy where justices refuse, or make any unreasonable delay in passing overseers' accounts, after they have been laid before them. (Rex v. Townsend, 1 Bott. 305.)

Balances, enforcing payment of.] Two justices may issue their warrant to levy the balance ordered to be paid over, under 50 Geo. 3, in case of default, (supra) upon the application of any *one* of the succeeding overseers, although the others refuse to concur in the application: and the court granted a mandamus to compel the justices to do so. (Rex v. Pascoe, 2 Maul. & Sel. 345.)

And a return to a mandamus, granted for this purpose, stating that the vestry had ordered the former overseers to retain the balance for the fees, &c., incurred in a suit to recover charity money, which they had engaged to pay the attorney, was held insufficient; for the act peremptorily orders the payment over to the new overseers, and the vestry cannot dispense with the statute. (Rex v. JJ. of Somersetshire, 2 Stra. 992.)

Indictable upon Accounts.] The neglect to pay over such balance, (Rex v. King, 2 Stra. 1268,) or refusal to account within the limited time, (Ib. Rex v. Commings, 5 Mod. 179,) or making a fraudulent charge in the account, (Comb. 287,) are respectively indictable, notwithstanding the other remedies given by statute.

Bankrupt Overseer.] And it was held in one case, that where an overseer became bankrupt, and at the end of his year a balance was found against him, he might be committed for not paying it over; on the ground that he had a *right to retain* the money till fourteen days after his office expired, as his bankruptcy did not discharge him from his office, and if the money had been kept by itself, the assignees could not have touched it, as he was a mere trustee for the parish. (Rex v. Egginton, 1 T. R. 369.) But Lord Eldon subsequently held, that the debt owing to the parish might be proved under the commission, before the time for accounting arrived. (Ex parte Exleigh, 6 Ves. 811.) And afterwards, where an overseer, who had so become bankrupt, was committed for not accounting to his successors, although he had accounted for the balance under his commission, it was also held, that the balance was *debitum in præsenti,* although he might be only accountable for it *in futuro,* and discharged him. (Rex v. Tucker, 5 Maul. & Sel. 508.)

Advances, Repayment of] It is a common principle in parish matters, that the *burthens* of the year shall be borne by the parishioners of the year—a maxim so rigidly enforced, till relaxed by statute, that if an overseer made advances, and failed to reimburse himself before he went out of office, he could have no relief from his successors. (Tawney's Case, Lord Raym. 1011, Salk. 531.) But now, if a rate made by overseers is unpaid at the expiration of their year, their successors shall levy such arrears, and reimburse their predecessors all sums expended for the use of the poor, and allowed to be due to them in their accounts, (17 Geo. 2. c. 38. s. 11;) and the 41 Geo. 3. c. 23. s. 9, authorizes them to pay their predecessors, out of *any* rate they may collect, all such sums advanced during the time there was no rate, or whilst it was suspended by appeal; and authorises the general or quarter sessions, upon application made for that purpose, to examine the matter, and order payment to be levied by distress, if necessary. But where an overseer is money out of pocket, and one of his colleagues has a sufficient surplus, the latter may be ordered to reimburse him. (2 N. P. L. 457; see also Banbury Case, Skin. 258.)

Books, &c. compelling Delivery of.] The books of the poor-rates, &c., ought to be accessible to the parishioners, in the custody of the overseers for the time being. They may be summarily compelled to deliver them up to their successors, (ante, 432, 433,) or by mandamus, when necessary; (Rex v. Clapham, 1 Wels. 305: see also 50 Geo. 3. c. 49. s. 1, ante, 433, 434;) as to delivering up goods, chattels, &c. to their successors. A commitment of an overseer for default in this respect should state the particular book, chattel, &c. for the non-delivery of which he is convicted. (Groome v. Forrester, 5 Maul. & Sel. 314.)

Appeal against Accounts.] The succeeding overseers on behalf of the parish may appeal against their predecessor's accounts; or any other person objecting thereto, or aggrieved by any thing done or omitted, &c. in the same manner as in appeals against rates, &c.; but they must specify in the notice not only the objectionable items, but the cause and grounds of the appeal, as required by 41 Geo. 3. c. 23. s. 4. (Rex v. Mayall, 3 Dowl. & Ryl. 383; Rex v. Sheard, 2 Barn. & Cres. 856, 4 Dowl. & Ryl. 480.)

The appeal given by 43 Eliz. and 17 Geo. 2, to parties aggrieved, against overseers' accounts, is expressly reserved to them by 50 Geo. 3. c. 49. s. 3. (Rex v. Dorsetshire, 15 East, 200.) And it has been decided, that where accounts have been duly allowed by two justices, pursuant to 17 Geo. 2, at a petty sessions, a parishioner may appeal against them, although they have not been examined and allowed at a *special* sessions, pursuant to 50 Geo. 3; and the sessions have jurisdiction in such case, and ought to hear the appeal. (Rex v. Colchester, 5 Barn. & Ald. 535.)

Appeal within what Time.] Before the 17 Geo. 2. c. 38, it was held, that an appeal might be made against accounts, years after they had been allowed and confirmed; and once even since that act it has been so held, with regard to such acts as are required to be done by the 43 Eliz. (Rex v. Whitear, 3 Burr. 1365, 2 N. P. L. 462.) But it is now settled that an appeal against overseers' accounts must in every case be made to the next *possible* sessions after allowance, (see Rex v. Dorsetshire, 15 East, 200,) the 17 Geo. 2. c. 38, which directs the appeal to be brought at the next sessions, having virtually repealed the 43 Eliz. c. 2. s. 6. (Rex v. Worcestershire, 5 Maul. & Sel. 457; Rex v. Berkshire, 1 Const. 308.) But the court may adjourn the appeal to the following sessions, if reasonable notice has not been given.

Notice of Appeal.] A notice of appeal against overseers' accounts, merely stating that the party intended to try his appeal against the accounts, on the grounds, and for the reasons thereinafter set forth, and then specifying the items against which he intended to appeal, and the objection he intended to make to each item, was held to be sufficient, although it was not stated, the party intending to appeal was a rated inhabitant of the parish, or a *party aggrieved.* The right of appeal given by 17 Geo. 2. c. 38. s. 4, against overseers' accounts, is not within the principle of the decisions upon the highway act, (55 Geo. 3. c. 68. s. 3, *ante*, 416,) for although the same language, to a certain extent, is found in both, yet the former statute, in addition to giving an appeal to the " party aggrieved," extends the right to a person having any *material objection* to the accounts. (Rex v. JJ. of Somersetshire, 7 Barn. & Cres. 681.)

Prior Allowance by Justices.] The overseers' accounts must be examined and allowed by two justices, before an appeal can be made against them. This is necessary to give the sessions jurisdiction; it should therefore appear on their order that such previous allowance has been made. (Rex v. Bartlett, 1 Bott. 306, 2 Stra. 983.) But it has been held, that the sessions may not only disallow the accounts which have been allowed by two justices, but may order the overseers to pay a certain sum over, which they adjudge to be in their hands. (Rex v. Hedges, 2 Salk. 533.) Though such an order of sessions to repay money *fraudulently* charged, it was said by Eyres, J., cannot be maintained; the sessions have no jurisdiction, but there may be a remedy by indictment. (Moulsworth's Case, Comb. 287.) A magistrate, a rated inhabitant of the parish, cannot vote either on the determination of the appeal, or upon the question of granting a case. (Rex v. Gudridge, 5 Barn. & Cres. 459, 8 Dowl. & Ryl. 217.)

Not to be referred to other Justices.] The accounts cannot be withdrawn from the two justices to whom they were *first* submitted, for the purpose of referring them to others, and if this be done, the allowance or disallowance of such others is void; and though the sessions cannot delegate *their* authority, they may remit such accounts to such two justices before whom they were first laid, as that is merely desiring them to execute their own original authority. (Rex v. Townsend, 1 Bott. 305.)

Balance found by Sessions Enforced.] If the sessions find a balance due from an overseer, but make no order for payment, two justices out of sessions may enforce payment to the succeeding overseers, or a mandamus to compel such justices to do so, may be obtained; for the appeal was to ascertain the amount, upon which the statutes attach, and authorize the justices to compel payment of the balance. (Rex v. Carter, 4 T. R. 246.)

Inspecting Rate.] A rated parishioner is entitled to inspect the books at a reasonable time. Assuming that he has no right to appeal or that the time for appeal is gone by, he may have other good reason for inspecting the books. He has a right to see what has been done. This applies equally to guardians' accounts, although their accounts may not be subject to appeal, as overseers' accounts are, and the court will grant a mandamus, commanding them to allow such inspection. (Rex v. Great Farringdon, 9 Barn. & Cres. 541; see also PARISH BOOKS, *ante*, 134.)

SECTION V.—LIABILITIES AND PROTECTION.

Remedies against Overseers.] The negligence and misconduct for which overseers, &c., are amenable to punishment, need scarcely be more particularly stated than appears incidentally in describing their duties. They *may* be punished in most cases by information or indictment, although penalties are provided by statute for the particular offence, as their disobedience of the statute is a contempt of the law. (Rex v. Commings, 5 Mod. 179.) But the courts do not encourage proceedings *not* according to the statutes. (Rex v. Slaughter, Cald. 246.) The sessions have no power to attach them for disobedience of their order; in such case, the proper mode is by indictment for the misdemeanour. (Rex v. Bartlett, 1 Bott. 342.) If, however, the order be made in a matter over which the justice has no jurisdiction—as to pay a sum of money to a surgeon who had taken care of a pauper, which assistance does not come within the notion of relief to the poor, no indictment lies. (Rex v. Smith, 1 Bott. 343.)

When criminally liable.] Overseers are indictable for not receiving a pauper sent to them by an order of justices. (Rex v Davis, 1 Bott. 378.)

An overseer proceeding through all the stages of an expensive suit, without the concurrence of a vestry, is personally liable. (Rex v. Micklefield, Cald. 507.)

In general, if an overseer absent himself without lawful cause from the monthly meeting enjoined by 43 Eliz. c. 2. s. 2, or is negligent in office, he shall forfeit for every default, 20*s*. to the poor, to be levied by one of his colleagues by warrant of two justices, or in default thereof, any two such justices may commit the offender to the common gaol, there to remain till the said forfeiture shall be paid. But this penalty shall not be inflicted on overseers of extra-parochial places, because they have no church to meet in. (Rex v. Rufford, 8 Mod. 40.)

If an overseer do not provide for the poor, he is indictable, and if he relieve the poor when there is no necessity for it, it is a misdemeanour. (Tawney's case, 16 Vin. Abr. tit. Poor, 415; 1 Bott. 371.)

Mandamus to make a Rate.] Upon a motion for a mandamus to two of the parish officers of Soham, to compel them to *sign* a rate, they having refused to concur with their colleagues in so doing, and the rate being of no avail, if not signed by the majority of the churchwardens and overseers, it was stated, that the funds of the parish were exhausted, that the assessment had been recently made, and was fair and equal, and that if the court did not interfere, the paupers, who were very numerous, would be without the means of subsistence; a large sum having been already borrowed and expended, and no further advance could be obtained, if no effectual rate were made.

The court said, that they could not order the two officers mentioned to *sign the rate*, but the mandamus might issue to the churchwardens and overseers generally to *make a rate*, which would fully answer the purpose. A peremptory mandamus was accordingly granted. (Rex v. Parish Officers of Soham. MSS. H. T. 1830, K. B.; see *ante*, p. 398.)

Actions against Overseers.] An action may be supported against overseers for money lent them to support the poor, or for necessaries supplied under the pressure of *immediate want;* (Simmons v. Wilmot, 3 Esp. Rep. 91;) or for surgical attendance of casual poor, and this upon an *express* or implied promise. (Lamb v. Bunce, 4 Maule & Sel. 275.) In these cases, however, the overseer was aware of, and did not repudiate the supply and attendance; but in the subsequent case of Tomlinson v. Bentall, (5 Barn. & Cres. 738; 8 Dowl. & Ryl. 493,) the court seems to consider it immaterial whether the overseers directed, or knew of, the medical services at the time they were being rendered, as the parish, where an accident happens to a poor person, is *bound* to administer all necessary relief; and if the transaction be *bonâ fide* without any improper attempt to charge the parish, the liability attaches.

Supplying Provisions, &c., for Profit.] By the 55 Geo. 3. c. 137. s. 6, churchwardens, overseers, and other persons concerned in collecting the poor-rates and managing the poor, are prohibited, under a penalty of £100, either in their own or any other name, from furnishing for profit, any goods, provisions, &c., for the use of the workhouse, or the poor of their parish, or being concerned directly or indirectly in any such contract. But upon proof on oath, that no other person competent to furnish such supplies can be found within a convenient distance, two neighbouring justices may, under their hands and seals, authorize such churchwardens, &c., to supply such articles.

Action for the Penalty.] Fairness of price is no answer to such an action; but if an overseer buy provisions, and afterwards, in the event of a scarcity, let the poor have them at the same price, without profit, he will not be within the act. (Pope v. Backhouse, 8 Taunt. 239; 2 Moore, 186.) However a guardian who sold sheep to the master of a workhouse, who provided for the poor by contract, was held liable under this act, (West v. Andrews, 5 Barn. and Ald. 328; 1 Barn. & Cres. 77,) though the act under which he was appointed, (22 Geo. 3. c. 83. s. 42,) imposes a penalty, not exceeding £20, only, for the like offence. But the act extends no further than to prevent the supply to the *workhouse* or poor generally; and therefore, where an overseer, upon an order for relief of a pauper, gave part money and part goods, he was held not liable, (Proctor v. Mainwaring, 3 Barn. & Ald. 145,) though the justices may punish him, if he forces goods upon the pauper.

No Penalty, if not for Profit.] In another case, where the defendant was sued for the penalty for having supplied coals indirectly for the use of the poor, and a verdict was found for the defendant, under the direction of the learned judge, and a rule nisi had been obtained to set the same aside, Abbot, C. J. said, "We are all of opinion that this rule must be discharged." The question in this case arises upon the construction of stat. 55 Geo. 3. c. 137. s. 6, the words are, that "no churchwarden or overseer of the poor, either in his own name, or in the name of any other person or persons, shall provide, furnish, or supply, *for his or their own profit*, any goods, materials, or provisions, for the use of any workhouse or otherwise, for the support or maintenance of the poor in any parish or place for which he shall be appointed such overseer, during the time which he shall retain such appointment, nor shall be concerned directly or indirectly in furnishing or supplying the same, or in any contract or contracts relating thereto, under a penalty of £100." Now, if the overseer himself, in this case, had supplied all the provisions required for the support of the poor, at prime cost, and not with a view to his own profit, it is quite clear that he would not have committed any offence within the words of this part of the act of parliament: that was laid down by Gibbs, C. J. in Pope v. Backhouse, 8 Taunt. 248. Inasmuch, therefore, as an overseer providing, in his own name, the poor of his parish with all the provisions and goods required for their support, would not be liable to any penalty, provided he made no profit, it cannot be supposed that the legislature intended that the same overseer, who is concerned, directly or indirectly, in any contract for supplying any part of the provisions, however small, should be liable to a penalty, although he derived no profit from it. That would involve a manifest contradiction. I think, therefore, that the words, *for his own profit,* must be taken to over-ride the whole clause, and that the legislature intended that no overseer, for his own profit, either in his own name, or in that of any other person, should supply the poor with provisions, nor be concerned directly or indirectly in any contract relating to it. (Skinner v. Buckee, 3 Barn. & Cres. 8.)

Pleadings in an Action for the Penalty.] In penal actions it is essential to state, that the act complained of is against the form of the statute; it was therefore held, that a declaration upon the above statute, to recover the £100 penalty, was bad, for want of an allegation that the act done was "against the form of the statute," and the judgment was arrested. (Wells v. Iggulden, 3 Barn. & Cres. 186.)

As to their duty in producing the books for inspection, (See Parish Books, *ante*, p. 134.)

Protection of Overseers.] The 43 Eliz. c. 2. s. 19, enables an overseer to plead the general issue, to an action brought for any thing done by him under the authority of that act; and in case of nonsuit or verdict in his favour, he shall recover treble damages, together with costs, *i. e. single* costs. (Butterton v. Furber, 1 Brod. & Bing. 517.)

The 7 Jac. 1. c. 5, and 21 Jac. 1. c. 12, enable overseers to plead the general issue, and to give the special matter in evidence, in actions for any thing done touching or concerning *their office,* or by virtue thereof; and the first of these statutes gives them double costs, and the last makes the action local, and that it shall be ground of nonsuit if the plaintiff does not prove the *cause* of action to have originated in the county where the action is brought.

Defects in Rates, Warrants, &c.] The 17 Geo. 2. c. 38. s. 8, provides, that a distress for poor-rates shall not be deemed unlawful (if the sum is really due) on account of any defect in the appointment, rate or warrant; but that the party aggrieved shall recover for *special* damage only in an action on the case,—and not at all if tender of sufficient amends has been made before action brought. (s. 10.)

Limitation of Actions.] They are also within the protection of the 24 Geo. 2. c. 44, when levying poor-rates by distress, which requires a demand of the warrant before an action can be brought, which must also be commenced within six months after the fact committed. (See "Constables," *ante*, 359.)

But the above statute does not extend to the action of replevin; for the party distrained upon, under 43 Eliz. c. 2, may replevy to try the right to levy for the poor's rate, the 19th section of which act, gives a form of avowry. (Fletcher v. Wilkins, 6 East, 283.)

Surplus of Distress.] A formal demand is necessary before an action can be maintained against overseers for the surplus arising from a distress for poor-rates, under the 27 Geo. 2. c. 20. s. 2, and an improper tender does not make such a demand unnecessary. (Simpson v. Routh, 2 Barn. & Cres. 682.)

SECTION VI.—ASSISTANT OVERSEER.

By whom appointed.] The 59 Geo. 3. c. 12, authorizes the inhabitants, assembled for the purpose in vestry, to elect *discreet persons* to be assistant overseers; no other qualification is required, nor is the number limited. Upon being so elected or nominated, two justices are to appoint them by warrant under their hands and seals, with such salary as shall have been fixed by the inhabitants in vestry. They are to execute all the duties of overseers expressed in the warrants, and to continue in office till the appointment is revoked by the inhabitants in vestry, or they resign; and security may be taken by bond, with or without surety, and such penalty as shall be thought fit. The salary shall be paid out of the money raised for the relief of the poor, at such times and in such manner as shall have been agreed upon, between the inhabitants in vestry and the respective persons so to be appointed. (s. 7.)

Stamp on Appointment.] The election, and confirmation thereof by warrant of the justices, of assistant overseer, with salary under the above act, being an appointment in writing to an office or employment, it comes within the stamp act. (55 Geo. 3. c. 184, tit. "Grant.") And where a pauper was so appointed, at a salary of £10 a-year, it was said, "this is an appointment in writing to an office or employment where the yearly salary does not amount to £50 a-year; it is therefore within the very words of the act, and requires a £2 stamp." (Rex v. Inh. of Lew. 8 Barn. & Cres. 655.)

Bound to show the Rate.] An assistant overseer is under the same obligation to allow an inspection of the rates, &c. to parishioners, as overseers. (See *ante*, p. 134, 135.)

Serving as, gives a Settlement.] The appointment is a public office or charge within the meaning of the 3 and 4 W. & M. c. 11; and an assistant overseer executes the office for himsel , and on his own account, and not merely as the deputy of the overseers. And if the warrant fixes a yearly salary to be paid to him, but is silent as to the length of time to which the appointment extends, that is sufficient to constitute it an *annual* office within the above statute, although he may be removed within the year. (Rex v. Inh. of Lew. 8 Barn. & Cres. 655.)

CHAPTER XXII.—INCORPORATED DISTRICTS.

SECTION I.—GUARDIANS AND OTHER OFFICERS.

Origin of Guardians.] The preamble of 22 Geo. 3. c. 83, by which guardians were first established, sets forth, that notwithstanding the many laws and the great sums of money raised for the relief of the poor, their sufferings are nevertheless very grievous; and by the incapacity or misconduct of overseers, the money so raised is frequently misapplied, and sometimes expended in indiscreet litigation. For remedy of these evils, and to introduce a prudent economy into the expenditure of the parish money, this act was passed, the provisions of which are not compulsory, but left to the voluntary adoption of such parishes as choose to avail themselves of its advantages; and its enactments are not to affect any parish, &c., which does not agree to adopt its provisions in the manner prescribed. (s. 44.)

Guardians, &c., how chosen.] Whenever two thirds in number and value of the owners or occupiers, according to their poor-rate, who *actually attend* (by 33 Geo. 3. c. 35. s. 1,) a public meeting, holden pursuant to the direction of the act, shall *there* signify their desire to adopt its provisions, and shall at such meeting nominate to the justices, three persons for guardians, and three others for governors of the poor-house, and fix salaries to be paid to them respectively, and shall procure the consent of two justices to such agreement and salaries, by writing under their hands; they shall thenceforth be entitled to the benefits of the act. (22 Geo. 3. c. 83. s. 3.)

And whenever such two third parts of such persons shall express their desire, that two of the three persons so nominated may be appointed guardians of the poor for such parish, &c., on the ground that one is insufficient, the justices are empowered to appoint *two* accordingly. (33 Geo. 3. c. 35. s. 2.)

And in like manner, where expedient for the like reason, the names of *four* or *more* fit persons may be returned, and the justices may, by writing under their hands, appoint such and so many of such persons to be guardians, as they shall think fit. (41 Geo. 3. c. 9. s. 1.)

Power of Guardians.] Where guardians are appointed, neither churchwardens nor overseers shall intermeddle in the management of the poor, but the guardian shall be invested with all the powers (except in regard to making and collecting rates) *of an overseer.* But the churchwardens and overseers shall continue to make and collect the poor-rate as at present, and shall pay the same to the guardian from time to time, as may be necessary for the expenses of the house and poor; or if two parishes or places are united, they shall pay over the *quotas* respectively to the treasurer of such united district, or shall permit the treasurer to draw a draft upon them, and specify in the receipt and draft, the general purposes for which such money is to be applied; to be allowed to the churchwardens and overseers in their accounts; and the accounts both of them and the guardians shall be examined at every monthly meeting, and examined and passed quarterly by the visitor, after they shall have been verified on oath before a justice. (22 Geo. 3. c. 83. ss. 7, 8.)

Visitor.] The guardians of united parishes shall produce, to two justices, the agreement of union, and the names of three persons, fit in character and fortune for the office of visitor; upon which, the justices shall within three days appoint one to be visitor; if he refuse, then the other; if he refuse, then the third; and if he decline, the guardians shall serve monthly, by rotation, subject to the control of the justices. The visitor if he be not a guardian, may appoint a deputy to act in his absence, and make report to him. The visitor is to superintend every such house, to settle accounts between guardian and treasurer, and all doubts concerning the persons who are to be sent thither, and to enforce the rules and regulations: and the guardian, treasurer, and governor are to obey his directions in all these matters.

The visitor, or deputy, shall be exempt from all parochial offices, and from serving upon juries whilst he continues in office. (Ib. s. 10.)

If two thirds, as aforesaid, in number and value in a single parish, &c., desire to have a visitor, they shall nominate, and the justices appoint, as aforesaid. (Ib. s. 11.)

Treasurer.] The guardians of united parishes shall recommend one of their own body for a treasurer, and the justices shall appoint him, or any other guardian whom they think more fit; which treasurer shall give security for duly accounting, and shall keep accounts, pay bills, and lay his accounts before the guardians at *every* meeting and shall once a year, fourteen days before Michaelmas quarter sessions, make out an account of the expenses, the number of poor persons, their age and sex, how employed, and the amount of their earnings in the year preceding; to be laid before the visitor, and certified under his hand, if he approves of the same, to be then transmitted to the clerk of the peace or town clerk, and by him laid before the sessions: and such treasurer shall be allowed such annual sum, not exceeding £10, as the visitor, if not a guardian, shall think fit; and if there is no such visitor, then as two justices shall appoint. (Ibid, s. 12.)

Two justices, upon the application of two thirds of owners in value, &c., may appoint a treasurer for the-poor house of a single parish, with a like salary. (41 Geo. 3. c. 9. s. 3.)

Governor.] Two justices of the limit may also appoint a governor of each poor-house, upon application by two persons who signed the agreement, removeable for misbehaviour or incapacity by the visitor, with the consent of the major part of the guardians, or if a guardian be visitor, by two justices within the limit. (22 Geo. 3. c. 83. s. 9.) And by the 50 Geo. 3. c. 50. s. 4, the justices in special sessions, upon application of the majority of the overseers, may appoint the *keeper* to be governor, with the same powers and duties as those appointed under the former act, till removed by the sessions. The governor or master of a workhouse shall not inflict corporal punishment upon adult persons under his care, for any offence whatever, nor confine them for longer than twenty-four hours, or till they can be had before a magistrate; (54 Geo. 3. c. 170. s. 7;) nor confine any *sane* person with chains. (56 Geo. 3. c. 129. s. 2.)

Determination of Office.] The offices of guardian, governor, visitor, and treasurer, shall determine in Easter week next after the appointment, at the public meeting held for the purposes of this act; but they may be continued in office by agreement, or others may be recommended to the justices in their stead. (22 Geo. 3. c. 83. s. 14.)

If a vacancy happen in any of the said offices, a meeting shall be called forthwith, and the vacancy filled up in the manner before mentioned. (Ibid, s. 13.)

Money Orders on Overseers, &c.] The guardians present at a monthly meeting, with the approbation of the visitor, who shall sign the same, may make an order on the churchwardens or overseers, or collector of the poor-rates for so much money as shall be necessary for the purposes of this act, and upon neglect to pay the same, the amount may be levied upon the goods and chattels of the said churchwardens, &c. (41 Geo. 3. c. 9. s. 2.)

May hold Lands.] The visitor and guardian shall be a body corporate, and enabled, by that name, to sue and be sued, and to take by purchase or lease any lands not exceeding in any city or town one acre, and in the open country twenty acres, for the site of a house and for lands to be occupied for the purposes of this act, and also all voluntary grants and donations of lands for the use of the poor, (22 Geo. 3. c. 83. s. 21.) And by ss. 22, 23, bodies corporate, trustees, executors, &c. are empowered to sell *to* them, and purchase other lands with the money.

The guardians may also enclose, not exceeding ten acres, from any waste or common near any house, with consent of the lord of the manor, and the major part in value of persons having right of common thereon, for building upon or improving the same for the benefit of such poor-house. (22 Geo. 3. c. 83. s. 27.)

May borrow Money.] The visitor and guardian, where the expenses of erecting the building, &c., or the proportion thereof for their parish, shall amount to 100*l.*, may borrow the same at interest, to be secured upon the poor-rate in sums not exceeding 50*l.* each; and they shall keep down the interest, and if the principal be called for, they may borrow it from some other person, by assignment of the security. (Ib. s, 20.)

The other part of this section, which directs that the assessments shall continue at the *same rate* till such loans are paid off, is repealed by the 43 Geo. 3. c. 110, which enacts that the assessments may be diminished, provided sufficient be raised to pay off *annually* one-twentieth part of the loans, and to keep down all interest, pursuant to 42 Geo. c. 74.

Monthly Meetings.] The guardians shall meet on the first Monday in every month, at the poor-house, at which meeting the treasurer shall produce his accounts, and the money due to him shall be settled and adjusted, in proportion to the sums paid by the respective parishes or places, on a medium of three years next before the date of such agreement in writing. (22 Geo. 3. c. 83. s. 24.) And the churchwarden or overseer who shall have the custody of the poors-rate or account, shall attend on four days' notice, and give an account of what has been the expense at a medium of three years, or in default shall forfeit 5*l.* (Ib. s. 25.)

And if the guardian shall not attend the monthly meeting, or send some *substantial inhabitant* to make payments for him, in case of accident, &c. he shall forfeit not exceeding *5l.* nor less than 40*s.* (Ib. s. 26.)

Inspecting their Accounts.] A rated parishioner has a right to inspect the accounts of the expenditure of the parish, kept by guardians of the poor, appointed under the 22 Geo. 3. c. 83 And the court of King's Bench granted a mandamus to the guardians, &c., commanding them to allow such inspection. (Rex v. Great Farringdon, 9 Barn. & Cres. 541. See *ante*, 437.)

SECTION II.—WORKHOUSES.

Parishes may unite.] When two such third parts of such owners and occupiers within two or more *parishes*, townships, or places, shall think fit with such approbation signified under the hands of two justices, and subscribed at the foot of the agreement, to unite for the purposes of this act, and shall signify their desire at a public meeting in each of such parishes, &c., held as aforesaid, an agreement shall be entered into by the guardians of the poor of each parish for the purpose, the terms whereof shall be entered with the clerk of the peace of the county, city, &c , and a copy left with him within three calendar months from the date of the agreement, and from that time the parishes shall have the benefit of the act, (22 Geo. 3. c. 83. s. 4.)

But no parish, &c., distant more than ten miles from the poor-house, shall unite with the parish, &c., in which such poor-house is established. (Ib. s. 5.)

Public Meetings.] Notice of every public meeting to be held under this act shall be given in the church three successive Sundays, and a copy fixed fifteen days previous to the meeting on the church door, &c.; and none shall vote at such meeting unless he is owner or occupier of lands assessed to the poor after the rate of *5l.* per annum at the least, but when there are not ten persons so qualified, then all who pay poors-rate may vote. (Id. s. 6.)

Poor-houses provided.] The guardians shall provide houses, either by erecting new ones, or renting old ones, and fit them up with the approbation of the visitor, at the expense of the several places respectively, and provide utensils and materials for the employment of the poor. (Id. s. 17.)

Provided, that the same be situate within the parish, &c., or if several be united, then within one of the parishes, &c., so united, and not elsewhere without the consent of three parts in four of such owners, &c. assembled as aforesaid for the purpose. (22 Geo. 3. c. 83. s. 18.)

May sell Poor-houses.] The guardians, with the approbation aforesaid obtained at a public meeting, may sell any house provided for the poor, and, by order of a justice, may remove persons inhabiting the same, or any other house rented, &c. by the parish, &c., if they shall refuse to quit after 14 days' notice. (Ib. s. 43.)

Extended to any workhouse, lands, &c. with consent of justices, notwithstanding any informality in the appointment of guardians, by 1 & 2 Geo. 4. c. 56. s. 1.

And the money arising therefrom, after discharging incumbrances, &c., is to be applied as part of the poor-rates. (Ib. s. 2.)

Houses hired or rented.] The houses to be hired or rented shall be taken for not more than twenty-one years, nor less than three, and be subject only to such parochial and parliamentary taxes as they were at the time of taking thereof. (22 Geo. 3. c. 83. s. 19.)

Parishes not availing themselves of this act are not *compellable* to erect workhouses, but may maintain and employ their poor at their own houses. (Rex v. Wetherell, Cald. 432.)

Rules, &c. in Poor-houses.] There are rules, orders and regulations specified in the act to be observed at every such poor-house, with any *additions* made consistently therewith by the justices at a special sessions, if not repealed at the quarter sessions, and the *governors* shall cause the rules to be printed in plain, legible characters, and fixed up in some conspicuous part of such house; (22 Geo. 3. c. 83. s. 34;) and by the 49 G. 3. c. 124. s. 5, these rules, &c. may be extended, by order of two or more justices in petty sessions, to *any* other *parishes*, &c., as fully as in those incorporated under this act: and by the 50 Geo. 3. c. 50. s. 1, they may in like manner be extended to *any* workhouse or poor-house generally, although there be no *master* or *mistress* to superintend the same.

The 24 Geo. 2. c. 40, enacts, that no spirituous liquors shall be sold or used in any workhouse or house of entertainment for the parish poor.

SECTION III.—MAINTENANCE OF PAUPERS.

Paupers in Poor-houses.] Every person sent to the house shall bring an order for his admission signed by one of the guardians, (22 Geo. 3. c. 83. s. 28.)

But none shall be sent, except such as are become indigent by old age, sickness, or infirmities, and are unable to acquire a maintenance by their labour; and except such orphans as shall be sent thither by order of the guardians, with the approbation of the visitor; and such children as shall necessarily go with their mothers thither for sustenance. (Ib. s. 29.)

Maintenance in Poor Houses.] Poor persons, sent to such houses, shall be maintained at the general expense of the respective parishes or places uniting, including casual poor, (33 Geo. 3. c. 35. s. 3,) according to the terms and proportions before prescribed.

And the treasurer, with the assistance of the governor, shall provide all necessaries for their maintenance, and keep an account thereof. (22 Geo. 3. c. 83. s. 24.)

Clothing of Poor.] "The guardian of the *parish*, &c., shall provide suitable clothing for the persons sent by him to such united poorhouse, which, if he neglect to do, the governor, or one of the guardians of such house, shall complain to a neighbouring justice, who shall summon the guardian so neglecting, and direct him to provide such clothing as shall appear to the justice necessary; and in case of default for ten days after such direction, the justice shall order the governor, or the guardian, making complaint, to provide the same, and demand from the guardian making neglect, the charges thereof, to be levied, with costs, by distress and sale of the goods of such guardian, in default of payment." (Ib. 33.)

Contracts for supplying Poor.] To secure the benefit of an open competition for the contracts for supplying the poor, it is provided, "that notice of the intention to contract shall be given in the local newspapers, or by other public advertisements, at least seven days before the meeting at which such contracts are to be entered into; and of the security which will be required for the performance of such contracts. (55 Geo. 3. c. 137. s. 7.)

Parties who contract for lodging, maintaining, and employing the poor, must be residents within the parish contracting, or within which the poor shall be lodged, &c., in the case of united parishes; and one or more responsible resident householders must also give bond, jointly and severally with the contractor, in the penalty of half the assessment for the year next but one preceding; and the contract must be approved and signed by two justices, or it shall not be valid. (45 Geo. 3. c. 54. s. 1.)

If the contractor cease to *reside* in the parish, the contract shall cease, but the security shall remain as an indemnity against expenses incurred by the non-performance of the contract. (Ib. s. 2.) And by

50 Geo. 3. c. 50. s. 2, contractors are put upon the same footing as *overseers* with respect to the controlling power of justices.

Guardians, &c., not to supply Goods, &c.] The 22 Geo. 3. c. 83. s. 42, prohibits every visitor, guardian, or governor, from furnishing, or being concerned in interest with others in furnishing materials, clothes, goods, or provisions, for the use of any workhouse, poorhouse, or paupers, and from doing any work in the way of his trade for the same, within the parish, &c., for which such officer is appointed, under a penalty not exceeding £20, nor less than £5, on due conviction thereof by a justice of the peace. (See *ante* 440.)

Pauper Children.] "All children of tender years become chargeable where they belong, may be sent to such poorhouse, or be placed by the guardian, with the approbation of the visitor, with some reputable person *in* or *near* the parish, at such weekly allowance as shall be agreed upon, until they shall be of age to go to service, or be bound apprentice. And the visitor shall see that they are properly treated. And when every such child shall attain such age, he shall be placed out at the expense of the parish, &c. Provided, that if the parents, relations, or any other responsible person, shall desire to receive and provide for such poor child, the guardian shall deliver him to such parent, &c. Provided also, that nothing herein shall give any power to separate any child under the age of seven years from his parent, without their consent. (22 Geo. 3. c. 83. s. 30.)

Binding Children Apprentices.] Where a parish has united with others for the support of the poor, according to the provisions of 22 Geo. 3. c. 83, and a guardian has been appointed, the churchwardens and overseers may, nevertheless, bind poor children apprentices; and it is not necessary that the guardian should sign the indentures. The 7th section is calculated to raise a doubt upon the point; for it excludes the interference of the churchwardens and overseers in the care and management of the poor, where guardians are appointed. But in subsequent parts of the statute, various powers are expressly given to guardians of the poor; and by the 30th section, they are authorized to provide for poor children until they arrive at a proper age to be placed out, when they are to be bound out according to the laws then existing. One of those laws was the 43 Eliz. c. 2, directing, that parish apprentices shall be bound out by the churchwardens and overseers of the poor. And it is better that a binding should take place by several churchwardens and overseers, than by a single guardian of the poor. (Rex v. Inhabitants of Lutterworth, 3 Barn. & Cres. 487, 5 Dowl. & Ryl. 343.)

Bastards born in Workhouses.] r Illegitimate children born in such united workhouse shall be settled in the *mother's* parish. (Ib. s. 39.) And a guardian *de facto* is competent to apply to a justice to take the examination of a single woman, pregnant, in order to filiate the bastard, in order to proceed against the putative father. (Rex v. Martyr, 13 East, 55.)

Working Paupers.] "The guardian may agree for the labour of any poor person, (willing to work, but who can get none,) at any employment suited to his capacity, and maintain him until it is procured; and during the time of such work, may receive the money earned, and apply it towards such maintenance. If the money earned exceed the sum so expended, he shall account for the surplus, which shall, within a month, be given to such poor person, if no further expenses be then incurred; but if such person refuse to work, or run away from such employment, the guardian shall complain to a justice, who shall, on conviction, commit the offender to the house of correction, there to be kept to hard labour not exceeding three calendar months, nor less than one." (22 Geo. 3. c. 83. s. 32.)

Farming out Paupers.] "From the time that any parish, &c., shall have adopted the provisions of this act, so much of the 9 Geo. 1. c. 7, as respects the maintaining or letting out the labour of the poor by contract, shall be repealed." (22 Geo. 3. c. 83. s. 1.) "And the visitors and guardians may agree with any person for the diet or clothing of poor persons, sent to the workhouses provided by this act, and for their work and labour, so that no such agreement be for longer than twelve months, and under the control of the visitor, guardian, and governor, and also of the justices where the houses shall be; two of whom, upon proof of abuse, may dissolve such contract." (Ib. s. 2.)

"And if any poor person, maintained in any workhouse, refuse to work at any employment suited to his age, strength, and capacity, or be guilty of drunkenness, or other misbehaviour, he shall, on conviction before any justice, be imprisoned in the common gaol or house of correction, and kept to hard labour for not exceeding twenty-one days." (55 Geo. 3. c. 137. s. 5.)

Paupers embezzling Goods, &c.] "Paupers embezzling, wilfully wasting, or carrying away without permission, any goods or materials belonging to the house, or any person residing there, shall, on conviction, be committed to the house of correction, to be kept to hard labour, not exceeding six calendar months, nor less than two." (22 Geo. 3. c. 83. s. 40.)

The 55 Geo. 3. c. 137. s. 1, provides, "that the overseers shall prosecute paupers who pawn or sell apparel, tools, &c., given them by the parish, or who steal any such tools, apparel, utensils, goods, &c., and the persons who receive or *buy* them; and the property in such goods and chattels shall be laid in the overseers for the time being, without specifying their names." The second section of the act directs, " that the tools, goods, &c., shall be marked, and imposes a penalty of £5, or two months' imprisonment, for defacing such marks, or for buying goods, &c., so marked, or receiving them in pledge, and three months upon paupers absconding with any such goods," &c.

Neglect of Families.] Persons able, but *unwilling*, to work or maintain *themselves and families*, shall be prosecuted by the guardians; and punished as idle and disorderly persons under 17 Geo. 2. (See VAGRANTS, *ante* 380.) " And if any guardian neglect to make complaint thereof against such person, to some neighbouring justice, within ten days after it come to his knowledge, he shall forfeit a sum not exceeding £5, nor less than 20*s.*; half to the informer, and half as other forfeitures are directed to be disposed of by this act." (22 Geo. 3. c. 83. s. 31.)

Casual Poor.] " If any poor person be retarded on his passage through any parish, &c., by reason of any accident, sickness, or bodily infirmity, the guardian living near the place where such distressed object shall be, shall provide him lodging, suitable nourishment, and assistance, and clothing, if necessary; and when he shall be fit to be removed, shall carry him to some *neighbouring justices*, who shall examine him on oath touching his settlement, and make an order for his removal thither, if they think fit. And the parish officer's expenses herein, on being certified by the said justices, or some other neighbouring justices, shall be paid by the guardian of the parish, &c., where such poor person shall be settled, if that can be discovered, and be within the same county; or, in default of payment, the same shall be levied upon the goods of such guardian, so making default after summons, by warrant of a justice; or if such person shall die before he can be so examined, or any poor person shall be found dead in any parish, &c., to which he did not belong, the guardian there shall cause him to be buried; the expenses whereof shall be allowed and certified by a justice, after examining into his settlement, and shall be paid by the guardian of the place where such person shall appear to have been settled, if it be within the same county; but if the settlement cannot be discovered, or shall not be within that county, the same shall be paid by the county *treasurer*, on the production of such certificate." (22 Geo. 3. c. 83. s. 38.) The casual poor, within any parishes united under the above act, shall be relieved by such parishes conjointly, and in the same proportions as they contribute for the other purposes of the act. (33 Geo. 3. c. 35. s. 3.)

Removing, &c. without Order.] Poor children, pregnant women, or persons afflicted with bodily infirmity, are sometimes enticed, or conveyed by parish officers, or others, from one parish, &c. to another, without any legal order of removal, with a view to ease the one parish, &c. and to burthen the other; it is therefore provided, that any guardian or other person, so conveying or enticing, or causing or procuring it to be done, against any parish, &c. which shall adopt the provisions of this act, without an order of removal from two justices, shall forfeit not exceeding £20, nor less than £5. (22 Geo. 3. c. 83. s. 41.)

Notice to Guardians.] Notices, &c. with respect to the management or removal of the poor, shall be given to the guardian, where any shall be appointed; but it shall suffice if given by mistake to the churchwarden or overseer, who shall deliver the same to the guardian, or forfeit 40*s*. for his neglect. (22 Geo. 3. c. 83. s. 7.)

SECTION IV.—JUSTICES' AUTHORITY HEREIN.

Relief ordered by Justices.] On complaint *upon oath* to a justice by or on behalf of any poor person belonging to any parish, &c. that the guardian hath refused such poor person proper relief, the justice, on inquiry into the circumstances *upon oath*, by writing under his hand, may order some weekly or other relief, or direct such guardian to send such person to the poorhouse, if a fit object to be provided for there; which order the guardian must obey within two days after he receives it, or forfeit £5, whereof so much shall be paid to such poor person as the justice shall direct, the remainder to be applied as the other penalties are directed to be disposed of. (22 Geo. 3. c. 83. ss. 35. 37.)

Idle or disorderly Applicants.] But if he appear to be an idle or disorderly person, and has not used proper means to get employment, or that the *husband* or *father* of such person be an idle or disorderly person, who by neglect of, or for want of seeking work, or by spending his money in alehouses or places of bad repute, doth not maintain his wife and children, the justice may commit such husband or father, of such complainant, to the house of correction for any time not exceeding three calendar months, nor less than one. (Ib. s. 35.)

The applicant for relief having first applied to the guardians, should next make application to the visitor, if there be one, and if he refuse, *then* the application to a justice may follow, who is to summon the guardian, and make order as to abode. (Ib. s. 36.) But if it appear that the visitor was absent from home, or is resident more than six miles from the abode of the complainant, the justice may proceed in like manner as in cases where such application has been regularly made to the visitor. (59 Geo. 3. c. 12. s. 27.) But a justice has no power to order pecuniary relief *out of the poorhouse* where the guardian and visitor, being so applied to, has directed the pauper to be received into it. (Rex v. Laughton, 2 Maul. &. Sel. 324.)

Where a Select Vestry.] And by 59 Geo. 3. c. 12. s. 2, it is provided, that when any complaint shall be made to any justice of the peace, of the want of adequate relief, by or on behalf of any poor inhabitant of a parish for which a *select vestry* shall be established by virtue of this act, or in which the relief of the poor shall be under the management of guardians, governors, or directors, appointed by virtue of *special or local acts,* such justice shall not proceed therein, or take cognizance thereof, unless it shall be proved on oath before him, that application for such relief hath been first made to, and refused by, such select vestry, or guardians, governors, or directors; and in such case he may summon the overseers of the poor, or any of them, to appear before any two of his majesty's justices of the peace, to answer the complaint; and, if upon the hearing thereof it should be proved on oath, to the satisfaction of the justices, that the party complaining, or on whose behalf the complaint shall be made, is in need of relief, and that adequate relief hath been refused by such select vestry, guardians, governors, or directors, it shall be lawful for such *justices* to make an order, under their hands and seals, for such relief as *they* in their discretion shall think necessary, reference being had to the character and conduct of the applicant: provided that in every such order the special cause of relief thereby directed shall be expressly stated, and that no such order shall be given for, or extend to any longer time than one month from the date thereof. Provided also, that it shall be lawful for *any one justice* to make an order for relief in case of *urgent* necessity to be specified in such order, so as such order shall remain in force only until the assembling of such select vestry, guardians, governors, or directors, as aforesaid, to which such case shall relate.

Special Sessions.] The justices may hold special sessions for the purposes of this act, on giving proper notices to the several justices, peace officers, and guardians. (22 Geo. 3. c. 83. s. 16.)

Other Justices may act.] And it shall be lawful for justices of any other limit to act, in all cases where there is only one, resident or capacitated, within the limit in which the poorhouse is situated. (Ib. s. 15.)

Recovery and Application of Penalties.] All the penalties inflicted by this act, shall be recoverable before one or more justices of the jurisdiction wherein the offender dwells, by distress, in default of payment after summons, and for want of sufficient distress the offender to be committed to the house of correction, not exceeding six, nor less than one calendar month; which penalties, not otherwise directed, shall be paid to the treasurer towards defraying the monthly expenses of the house. (22 Geo. 3. c. 83. s. 45.)

Appeal] Persons aggrieved by any act done by any justice out of sessions, concerning the execution of this act, may appeal to the next general quarter sessions, giving eight days' notice to the party complained of, and security by recognizance before a justice, with a sufficient surety to pay the costs if the appeal be determined against him; and the justices are to determine such appeals, and award costs for or against appellants, as they shall see cause, which determination shall be *final*, and not removable by *certiorari*; (Ib. s. 46;) and the other acts relating to the poor have a similar clause of appeal.

CHAPTER XXIII.—RELIEF OF THE POOR.

SECTION I. *Poor generally.*
II. *Illegitimate Children.*
III. *Casual Poor.*
IV. *Lunatic Poor.*

SECTION I.—POOR GENERALLY.

Primary Obligation upon Relatives.] The poor laws were never intended to supersede the obligation which the ties of kindred impose upon all mankind to support the helpless or destitute members of their family. Although it is not provided, that before relief shall be demanded of the public, it must *appear* that all who stand in that relation are either incapable or unwilling to discharge this duty, yet the statute which forms the groundwork of the whole system, expressly recognizes the primary right of the indigent to claim support and assistance from their relatives, and affords its sanction to this moral duty.

Enforced by Statutes.] It is enacted by the 43 Eliz. c. 2, that parents, or grandfathers, or grandmothers, may be assessed by justices in their quarter sessions, to the relief of their children or grandchildren; and that children may be assessed to the relief of their parents; the party assessed being of sufficient ability, and the party to be maintained being "poor, old, blind, lame or impotent, or not able to work," or in other words, actually *chargeable;* in the technical language employed on this subject. The sum assessed to be paid under a penalty of 20*s* a month, to be levied by distress; or in default the party to be imprisoned till paid, the amount being in the discretion of the sessions, which, by the above statute, was confined to the quarter sessions, but the power of making such order is now extended to the petty sessions by 59 Geo. 3. c. 12. s. 26.

This mode of relief can only be obtained for persons who, from impotence or infirmity, are unable to work; and by no means requires that those who can, but are unwilling to labour for their subsistence, shall be supported by their relations. (Rex v. Gulley, Fol. 47.) The order must also be made by the justices in sessions of the county in which the person inhabits, for he cannot be so charged in a county into which he comes for a temporary purpose, and is not a resident inhabitant. But he may be ordered to pay the contribution in any other county where the pauper relative is placed. (Rex v. Reeve, 2 Bulst. 344.) The justices cannot send poor persons from their own parish, to their relation who should maintain them, but should make an order of so much a week upon the relation. (Shermanbury v. Bolney, Comb. 379.)

What Relations chargeable.] The act extends to *natural* relations only, and not to such as are acquired by marriage. A father-in-law, therefore, is under no obligation to maintain his wife's child after the mother's death, nor in her lifetime; (Tubb. v. Harrison, 4 T. R. 118;) although the husband acquire an estate with her; (Cooper v. Martin, 4 East, 76;) nor a father his son's wife or widow. (Rex v. Kempson, 1 Bott. 378; 2 Stra. 955;) neither is a son-in-law bound to maintain his wife's mother. (Rex v. Munday, Fort. 303.) But such an order may be made on a grandfather of sufficient ability, though the father be living, if he is unable to support his child. (Rex v. Joyce, 16 Vin. Ab. 423.)

The obligation extends to no other relations than such as are enumerated in the 43 Eliz., and consequently an order cannot be made under this statute, upon a man, to maintain his wife while resident with her, but if he runs away from her he may be punished as a rogue and a sturdy beggar. (Rex v. Davison, 11 Mod. 268.) And if the child to be relieved be a bastard child, this is clearly out of the statute 43 Eliz. (City of Westminster v. Gerrard, 2 Bulst, 346.)

Requisites of Order.] The order must state, that the person upon whom it is made lives within the jurisdiction of the justices who make it; and must adjudge the party charged to be of sufficient ability, and that the pauper is actually chargeable to the parish, and impotent or unable to work. It must direct and *require* the party to relieve the pauper, a mere recommendation being insufficient, and for how long; an indefinite order to pay 2*s.* 6*d.* a week is void; but if it direct him to pay till the court shall order to the contrary, it has been considered sufficiently definite. (Rex v. Tripping, 19 Vin. 424; 1 Bott. 370; 2 Nolan, P. L. 264.)

On whose Application.] The order may be made as well on the application of the indigent person as of the parish officers; and if a sum is directed to be paid weekly, it is due at the beginning of the week. (Rex v. Fearnley, 1 T. R. 316.) It seems the order may be retrospective, as well as for the future relief of the person who is the subject of the application. (Rex v. Joyce, 16 Vin. Ab. 423.) And it may order the party to contribute to the relief of several children in one family. (Rex v. Robinson, 2 Burr. 799.)

Punishment.] Although the statute provides a specific penalty of 20*s.* a month for disobedience to the order, it has been held that the party may be indicted at common law. (Id.)

The remedy, in case an order is illegally made upon a person, is by removing the order into the Court of King's Bench, upon a case, if it can be obtained; or if the defect appears on the face of the order, the court will quash it without being informed of the facts by a case. Where there is neither an apparent defect, nor a case granted upon which to take the judgment of the court above, the only mode of resistance is by disobedience, and proof of the illegality as a defence to an indictment, or by bringing an action for an illegal distress, if the penalty should be levied by distress and sale.

Deserting Family punishable.] And persons *able* to maintain themselves and families, neglecting to do so, whereby they become chargeable, are punishable as rogues and vagabonds. (5 Geo. 4. c. 83. s. 3.)

So husband, father, or mother, absconding from their place of abode, and leaving any wife or children chargeable, the goods or profits of lands, &c., of such party may be seized by order of two justices, and being confirmed by the sessions, they may be disposed of to reimburse the parish for providing for such wife, &c. (5 Geo. 1. c. 8. s. 1.) But the order should show how much of the fugitive's property should be seized, and the *quantum* of relief, and the period of its duration fixed by the sessions, if made prospectively. (Stable v. Dixon, 6 East. 163.) Or if they be navy or army pensioners, the two justices may order payment of their pension to the overseers. (59 Geo. 3. c. 12. s. 31.)

What Parish must relieve.] Paupers whose settlement is unknown must be relieved by the parish in which they become chargeable; and where their settlement is known, they must be forthwith removed to it, unless from sickness, accident, or infirmity, they cannot be removed without danger. (See "Casual Poor," *post.*)

Relief to Poor Debtors.] By the 52 Geo. 3. c. 160, a justice is authorized to order 6*d.* a day to a poor debtor in gaol, not being a county gaol; and if he belong to another parish may make an order of removal, to be suspended till his imprisonment expires, and order the overseers of the debtor's parish to pay the charges of his relief in the mean time. But if the pauper have no settlement, the charges are to be paid out of the county rate.

Merchant Sailors' Families.] If the wives or families of seamen in the merchant's service, become chargeable whilst they are absent on a voyage, the parish shall be reimbursed, by an order, made by two justices, on the owner, ships' steward, or agent of the vessel, to pay such sums as the parish has advanced, out of the wages due; and upon refusal, payment may be enforced as in the case of poor-rates. (59 Geo. 3. c. 12. s. 32.)

SECTION II.—ILLEGITIMATE CHILDREN.

The law has vested very ample powers in magistrates, to compel the parents of illegitimate children to maintain them, so that the parish may be relieved from the burthen, where the parents, or either of them, is of sufficient ability, either wholly or in part, to provide for their subsistence.

Justices' Orders herein.] The 18 Eliz. c. 3, continued and extended by 3 Car. 1, c. 4. s. 15, enacts, that justices within their several limits and precincts, and at their several sessions where any such bastard shall be born, may examine the matter, and make an order for the punishment of the mother and reputed father, as also for the relief of the parish from the charge thereof, wholly or in part, by charging such mother or father with the payment of money weekly, or other sustentation as they shall think meet.

And the father or mother may be committed for non-performance of such order, except he, she, or they, give security to perform it, *or* else personally to appear at the next general sessions, to abide such order as shall then be made by the majority of the justices therein.

Reputed Father to pay Expenses.] The 49 Geo. 3. c. 68, enacts, that all reasonable charges incident to the birth of a bastard child, with the expenses of apprehending the reputed father, and the costs of the order of filiation, not exceeding together £10, shall be borne by such reputed father.

By 13 & 14 Car. 2. c. 12. s. 19, churchwardens and overseers are authorized to seize the goods and chattels, or profits, &c., of lands belonging to a putative father of a bastard child, under an order of justices, to provide for the bringing up of such child.

Father may be apprehended.] By 6 Geo. 2. c. 31, if any single woman shall be delivered of any bastard child, which shall be chargeable, or likely to become so; or shall declare herself to be with child, and that it is likely to be born a bastard, and to become chargeable to the parish, &c., and shall in either case, upon oath before one or more justices, charge any person with having gotten her with child, such justice may, upon the application of an overseer of the parish, or of a substantial householder of an extra-parochial place, issue his warrant to apprehend and bring the person so charged before the same or any other of the justices of the county, who is authorized and required to commit the accused to the common gaol or house of correction of the county, &c., unless he give security to indemnify the parish, &c., or enter into a *recognizance* with sufficient security to appear at the next general quarter sessions, and to abide such order as shall then be made. (See " *Respiting*," &c., *post* 460.)

Committing for not answering.] One justice has not power to compel a woman to be examined under this act, although authority is given to *one justice* to hear the charge, (*i. e.* if the woman shall charge,) and to cause the accused to be apprehended. It is not necessary to infer from that enactment, that one justice has power *to compel* the woman to be examined, for that power was already given to two justices; and although one justice may act if the woman comes voluntarily before him, and charges any person with being the father of her child, that is very different from compelling her to answer interrogatories, and so to make such a charge. Nor does the proviso in the fourth section remove the difficulty, the words of which are, "that it shall not be lawful for any *justice* or justices to send for any woman, before she shall be delivered, or one month afterwards, to answer any question," &c. That is a negative; and if an affirmative was intended to be implied, then, at all events, the justice who makes such a commitment should state on the face of the warrant, that a month had elapsed from the delivery of the woman, before she was sent for in order to be examined. Upon these grounds a woman who had been so committed, upon being brought up by habeas corpus, was discharged. (Ex parte Martin, 6 Barn. & Cres. 80, 9 Dowl. & Ryl. 65.)

Respiting, or discharging Recognizances.] But the 49 Geo. 3. c. 68. s. 6, repeals so much of the above as relates to cases where the woman has *not been delivered;* and by s. 2, requires that the recognizance be entered into within three days, and re-enacts the provisions of the former act in such cases, with this *addition:* that unless one such justice shall have certified under his hand, to the sessions, that it had been proved before him on oath, that the woman *had not* been delivered, or *had been* delivered within *one month,* previous to the day of the sessions; or unless two justices, &c., shall have so certified to the next, or when such woman shall have been delivered as aforesaid, then to the immediately subsequent, general sessions, that an order of filiation *had already been made* on the person so charged, or *was not requisite to be made* on account of the death of the child, or other like sufficient reason; in *each* of which cases *firstly* before mentioned, such sessions may respite the recognizance to the next general sessions, &c., without requiring the personal attendance of the putative father so bound, or his sureties; and in *either* of the *two last-mentioned* cases they may wholly discharge such recognizance, &c.

Neglect to pay Maintenance.] The 3rd section of the same statute enacts, that if any such father or mother, on whom any order of filiation or maintenance has been made, unappealed from, shall neglect to pay the sum ordered to be paid towards the maintenance of the child, any justice of the peace where such father or mother shall happen to be, may, and is *required,* upon complaint by any overseer of the parish liable to the maintenance of such bastard, or of the parish *where such bastard shall then be,* upon proof on oath of such order, and of the money being unpaid, and of a demand and refusal of payment, or that such reputed father or mother hath left his or her usual place of abode, and *avoided* a demand thereof being made by such overseer, to issue his warrant to apprehend and bring before such or any other justice of the same county, &c., such reputed father or mother, to answer such complaint; and if payment be not then made, or some reasonable and sufficient cause for not so doing be not shown, the said justice is required to commit such father or mother to the house of correction or county gaol, to hard labour, for three months; unless the said money shall be paid before the expiration thereof: and so from time to time, as often as any sum shall become due by virtue of such order, after the discharge from any former imprisonment.

Expenses of Filiation, &c.] It is provided by the 4th section, that all such charges, expenses, and costs, shall be in the discretion of the justices or sessions who make the order of filiation, except that the costs of apprehending and securing the reputed father, and making the order of filiation, shall not exceed £10; and that all the powers and provisions of the 18 Eliz. shall be used and respectively observed in the execution of this act.

Bastards of Married Women.] Though formerly doubted, it is now settled that the bastards of married women are within these acts, being *born out of lawful matrimony.* (Rex v. Luffe, 8 East. 204.) And proof whether the husband be alive or not is immaterial, if *non access* be distinctly proved. (Rex v. Bedall, 2 Stra. 1076.) But the rule is, that the issue of a woman married at the time the child was begotten, shall in all cases be *presumed* to be legitimate, until it be distinctly proved that the husband could not, from a natural impossibility, be the father, or had not, or could not have had, access at a time when by the laws of nature he could be the father of the child. (Banbury Peerage, 2 Selw. Ni. Pri. 745.) But marriage, though so recent that the child could not have been begotten in wedlock, is quasi an admission of the husband that the child is his. (1 Roll. Abr. 358; 1 Bla. Com. 456.) But a child born during a divorce *â vinculo matrimonii,* is of course a bastard; if born during a divorce *a mensa et thoro,* it is *presumed* to be a bastard; but if the husband and wife are separated by voluntary deed merely, and not by sentence of the ecclesiastical court, the issue of the wife will be deemed legitimate until non access be proved. (Ib. 1 Salk. 123.)

Complaint, to whom made.] It is immaterial whether the two justices before whom the complaint is made live "in or next unto the limits where the parish church is," &c., so that they have jurisdiction there, these words in the statute being merely directory. (Rex v. Skinn, 1 Bott. 476.) But if the child be born in an extra-parochial place, it seems no order can be made. (Rex v. Baker, 1 Bott. 476.) And not only must the order be *signed* by two justices, but the previous examination must be in the presence of both. (Rex v. Beard, 2 Salk. 478; Billings v. Prinn, 2 Blac. Rep. 1017.)

Complaint, by whom made.] The complaint must be made by the overseers of the poor, or one of them; (Rex v. Fox, 1 Bott. 473;) but if the order state them to be " overseers of a township," it need not add, that the township maintains its own poor. (Rex v. Hartington Upper Quarter, 4 Maul. & Sel. 559.) And if the complaint be by one who is overseer *de facto*, though not *de jure*, or by a guardian of the poor, it is sufficient. (Rex v. Martyr and Fulham, 13 East, 55.)

Reputed Father summoned.] The reputed father must be previously summoned; (Rex v. Cotton, 1 Sess. Cas. 179, 1 Bott. 486;) but it is not neoessary that he should be present at the examination; and if he do not attend, the order may be made in his absence. (Rex v. Upton and Gray, Cald. 308, 1 Bott. 482.) It is said, however, that if the justice has reason to conclude that the putative father will avail himself of the opportunity to abscond, he need not summon him in cases of original complaint. (2 N. P. L. 288.)

Evidence and Order.] The mother may be examined at any time with her own consent, after she discovers herself with child, but she cannot be *compelled* to answer before her delivery, nor sent for and examined against her will until one month after it. But as the 35 Geo. 3. c. 101. s. 6, enacts, " that every unmarried woman with child shall be deemed *actually chargeable*," which extends to married women pregnant under circumstances which would render the child a bastard, (Rex v. Tibbinham, 9 East, 388.) any woman so pregnant may be examined fo the purpose of removal.

The mother may be examined as to all the circumstances of the intercourse, &c., except the *non-access* of her husband, if she be married. (Rex v. Reading, Cas. Temp. Hard. 379.) And the examination of a pregnant woman by a magistrate, in pursuance of the statute 6 Geo. 2. c. 31, has been holden evidence sufficient to warrant the sessions in making an order of bastardy, where the woman died shortly after the delivery, &c., before the making of the order. (Rex v. Ravenstone, 5 T. R. 373; Rex v. Clayton, 3 East, 58.)

Warrant and Appearance.] The warrant for the apprehension of the reputed father continues in force till it is fully executed and obeyed, which may be at any time, however distant, whilst the magistrate who granted it continues in the commission; and therefore where, upon such arrest, the putative father agreed to give a bond with sureties, but one of them not executing, he was taken again under the same warrant, it was held legal. (Dickson v. Brown, Peake's R. 234; Mayhew v. Parker, 8 T. R. 110.) When he is brought before the justice, he must either enter into the security, recognizance, &c., (see *ante* 459 460,) or be committed, the magistrate having no power to enter into the merits of the case.

Order of Filiation.] The first step after the child is born is to obtain an adjudication as to the reputed father; whereupon, if the child be born alive, (Rex v. De Brouquen's, 14 East, 277,) and be chargeable, or likely to become so, (Rex v. Hartington Upper Quarter, 4 Maul. & Sel. 559,) an order of filiation and maintenance is made either by two justices under 18 Eliz., or by the magistrates at sessions. There is no time *limited* after the birth for making such order; (Rex v. Miles, 1 Sess. Cas. 77, 1 Bott. 473;) though, if not made within six weeks after the woman has been delivered, a single magistrate having first summoned the overseers, may discharge the putative father out of custody, where he has been committed before the child was born.

The father should be summoned, (see *ante* 462,) though his presence is not essential, and the examination should be before two justices at the least. If the woman refuse to answer, they *together* (see *ante* 459,) may commit her to prison, (Rex v. West, 6 Mod. 180,) unless *perhaps*, if they are proceeding under 18 Eliz., by which her answers may subject her to punishment. Other evidence is admissible where the mother is dead; or the father's own confession, or the bastard, if competent in other respects, (Rex v. St. Mary, Notts., 13 East, 57, n.) may supply evidence upon which magistrates may act.

Defence of the accused.] If the party charged appears, he may make his defence; but it cannot be made by others in his absence, unless he is incapacitated by illness or otherwise from attending, in which case the justices ought to hear evidence in his defence. (2 N. P. L. 297;) and, upon considering the evidence on both sides, if they are satisfied that the person is justly charged with being the father, they should make the order of filiation accordingly.

Form of the Order.] The order must be made by two or *more* justices. (Hatton's Case, 2 Salk. 477.) It may charge the mother, (Rex v. Taylor, 3 Burr. 1681, 1 Bott. 479,) or putative father, or both, with such weekly sum for the support of the child or children, if more than one are begotten by the same father on the same mother, as the justices shall think meet. (Rex v. Skinn, 1 Bott. 470.)

But the payment should be limited, during so long time as the child shall be chargeable; and an order to pay so much a week, indefinitely, is bad. (Rex v. Mathews, 2 Salk. 475; Newland v. Osman, 1 Bott. 460.)

Requisites of the Order.] But an order for by-gone maintenance is good. (Rex v. Smith, 1 Bott. 667; Ex-parte Addis, 1 Barn. & Cres. 89.) The order must state the child to have been born in the parish; (Rex v. Butcher, 1 Stra. 437; Rex v. Stanley, Cald. 172;) the sex or name of the child must also be stated, (Rex v. England, 1 Stra. 503,) and who begot it; (Rex v. Browne, 2 Stra. 811;) and the order must expressly adjudge him to be the putative father, (Rex v. Pitts, Doug. 661,) and that the adjudication is by two or more justices. (Rex v. Weston, 2 Ld. Raym. 1198.) It must also specify the sum to be paid by the father for the expenses attending the birth, &c. (Rex v. Hartington Upper Quarter, 4 Maul. & Sel. 559.) And the examination of the woman on oath as to her delivery, and the father of the child. (2 N. P. L. 299.) But to render him liable to *any* of these expenses, the child must be born alive. (Rex v. De Broquens, 14 East, 277.)

The county should be stated; but if in the margin, it is sufficient to show that the justices have jurisdiction in the place where the fact arose. (Rex v. Messenger, 1 Bott. 491.) It is not *essential*, though usual and most proper, to state that it is made on complaint of the overseers, &c. (Rex v. Fox, 6 T. R. 148.) The same rule applies to the statement of the putative father having been summoned. (Rex v. Clegg, 1 Stra. 475; Rex v. Clayton, 3 East, 58.)

Appeal against Order by Juotices.] Any person who shall think himself aggrieved by an order of filiation made by two justices, and not originating at the sessions, may appeal to "the next general *quarter* sessions of the peace for the county where such order shall be made. (18 Eliz. c. 3; 49 Geo. 3. c. 58. s. 5; Rex v. Coyston, 1 Sid. 149;) and a notice and recognizance to an *adjourned* sessions will not suffice. (Rex v. JJ. of Lincolnshire, 3 Barn. & Cres. 548, 5 Dowl. & Ryl. 347.)

Notice of Appeal.] The *notice* must be given to the justices who made the order, or to one of them, and also to the churchwardens and overseers of the parish on whose behalf such order shall have been made, or to one of them, ten clear days before the sessions, otherwise the appeal shall not be received or heard. (Rex v. Lincolnshire, *supra.*)

Contents of Notice.] This notice must state the cause and matter of appeal; that is to say, the *objections* to the order which the appellant intends to rely upon at the sessions. (Rex v. JJ. of Oxfordshire, 1 Barn. & Cres. 279, 2 Dowl. & Ryl. 426.) It is not absolutely necessary to be in *writing;* a notice by parol has been holden sufficient. (Rex v. JJ. of Salop, 4 Barn. & Ald. 626; Rex v. JJ. of Surrey, 5 Barn. & Ald. 539.)

Recognizance.] The party must also " enter into a recognizance conditioned to try such appeal, otherwise " no appeal shall be brought, received, or heard." Such is the language of the statute, (49 Geo 3. c. 68. s. 7,) and no alleged practice can prevail against the positive words of the act. (Rex v. JJ. of Lincolnshire, 3 Barn. & Cres. 548, 5 Dowl. & Ryl. 347.)

Time for Appealing passed.] Where an order of bastardy has been made, and the time for appealing has passed, it cannot be enforced by commitment till the party *perform the order*, &c., under 18 Eliz. c. 3; but the magistrate must proceed under 49 Geo. 3. c. 68. s. 3, by commitment for *three months*, or till the money due be paid. (Ex-parte Addis, 1 Barn. & Cres. 87, 2 Dowl. & Ryl. 167.)

Proceedings at the Hearing.] The appellant, (if called upon,) must first prove the service of the notice, and the entering into the recognizance. The respondents then proceed to support their order by sufficient evidence. (Rex v. Knill, 12 East, 50.)

The counsel for the appellant then addresses the court upon the respondents' evidence. But if he call witnesses to controvert it, or to set up a different state of facts, the counsel for the respondents is entitled to a reply. If the objections are formal only, the sessions may amend them under 5 Geo. 2. c. 19. (See 8 T. R. 181.)

Judgment.] After hearing the counsel and the evidence on both sides, the sessions, by a majority of the justices present, merely affirm or quash the order; they cannot adjudge that the appellant is not the putative father. (Rex v. Jenkins, 2 Stra. 1050, 1 Bott. 474.) Though, if the order be substantially good, but directs something additional which is illegal, they may quash such defective part, and affirm the remainder. Their decision is final, and the appellant cannot again be called to answer for the same bastardy, (Rex v. Tenant, 2 Ld. Raym. 1423, 2 Stra. 716,) unless the order be quashed for a defect in form merely.

Costs.] The sessions, upon appeal in cases of bastardy, shall give such " costs to the parties appealing, or appealed against, as they, in their discretion, shall judge proper." (49 Geo. 3. c. 68. s. 5.) And they cannot delegate their authority upon the quantum of costs; therefore, if they award costs to be taxed by the clerk of the peace, it is bad. (Rex v. St. Mary's, Notts., 13 East, 57 n.; Rex v. Skinn, 1 Bott. 470.)

Certiorari.] The defendant, if dissatisfied with the decision of the sessions, may remove the proceedings by certiorari into the King's Bench; and if not in custody for disobedience, he may remove the order of two justices, although there has been no appeal to the ses

H H

sions; (Rex v. Stanley, Cald. 172;) but if in custody, it seems the proper course is by *habeas corpus;* (Rex v. Bowen, 5 T. R. 156;) and in any of these instances he must be in court when the case is heard. (Rex v. Price, 6 T. R. 147; Rex v. Gibson, 1 Bla. Rep. 198.)

Quashing Orders.] The court generally decide upon what appears upon the face of the proceedings; and if there be a substantial defect, as want of jurisdiction, or of an adjudication that the defendant is the putative father, they will quash the whole. (R. v. Tenant, 2 Stra. 716.) And although the justices need not set forth their reasons for the adjudication, yet if they do so, and they appear insufficient, the court will quash the order. (R. v. Browne, 2 Stra. 811.) But where the order is defective in one point, so that the rest may subsist as a good order by itself, they will quash the defective part only, and confirm the rest. (2 N. P. L. 314.)

Security to indemnify the Parish.] Where the reputed father enters into a security, to indemnify the parish against the expenses of supporting the child, the remedy upon his default is by action at law, to be carried on by the overseers for the time being, though the security may have been entered into with any of their predecessors; for the interest in such securities vests in the obligees as overseers, and passes to their successors. (54 Geo. 3. c. 170. s. 8; Addey v. Woolley, 3 B. Moore, 21.)

The security is usually given by bond, but a promissory note to the parish officers is equally legal, (Cole v. Gower, 6 East, 110,) or a sum of money may be deposited. (R. v. Martin, 2 Camp. 268.) The amount is in all cases to be fixed by the overseers, (Dickinson v. Brown, Peake's R. 234,) and it operates as an *indemnity* only; and therefore, in an action on such bond, the obligors cannot be held to bail beyond the amount of damage actually sustained. (Kirk v. Strickland, Doug. 449.)

And if a promissory note be given, the same rule prevails, and a tender of so much as the parish has been damnified is an answer to the action. (Cole v. Gower, *supra;* Townson v. Wilson, 1 Camp. 396.) And in the case of a deposit, the father may recover back the surplus after the child ceases to be chargeable, (Watkins v. Hewlett, 1 B. & B. 1,) for it is contrary to public policy to permit money, or other security to be taken, in such cases, as a *composition* of the entire liability; it can only be received as a *security* to indemnify the parish, (Id. ibid.,) and it is unlawful to take a sum *out and out* for this purpose. (Shutt v. Proctor, 2 Marsh, 224.) The parties receiving the money improperly, cannot discharge themselves by paying it over to their successors; (Townson v. Wilson, *supra;*) and if the obligor of an indemnity bond become bankrupt, the parish cannot prove for the penalty, and receive a sum certain under his commission; but the bankrupt remains liable on the bond for expenses incurred after the bankruptcy. (St. Martin v. Warren, 1 Barn. & Ald. 491.)

Custody of the Child.] It does not seem to be very clearly settled whether the father or the mother has the preferable title to the custody of their illegitimate child. Lord Mansfield said, that neither the father nor the mother has the legal right of guardianship. (R. v. Felton, 1 Bott. 495.) But after an order of bastardy has been made upon him, he may take it from the custody of the *parish* and maintain it himself; or, at least, if he offer to do so, no action can be maintained against him upon his bond of indemnity to the parish. (Ib.; Newland v. Osman, 1 Bott. 460, 2 Saund. 83.) But Mansfield, C. J., held, that within the age of nurture, at least, the mother is entitled to the custody of the child; (Exparte Ann Knee, 1 N. R. 148;) and Lord Kenyon in a similar case said the father has no right to the child; (R. v. Moss Soper, 5 T. R. 278;) and at all events, if he has got possession of it by fraud, the court will interfere to put matters in the same situation as before. (R. v. Mosely, 5 East, 224, n.)

Age of Nurture.] It appears from these decisions, that the courts will support the claim of the mother to the possession of her illegitimate child till it is past the age of nurture. But it seems unsettled in whose custody a child, that has been affiliated, is to remain after that period. (See Strangeways v. Robinson, 4 Taunt. 498.) Wherever it stands in need of support, the parish officers must provide for it, whether it remain in their own, or go with its mother into another parish, (R. v. Hemlington, Cald. 6,) till it acquires a settlement in another parish.

SECTION III.—CASUAL POOR.

Who are casual Poor.] This class of paupers comprehends all such poor persons, who, in consequence of physical accident, sudden calamity, or any other circumstance, require immediate parochial relief, and thus become a burden upon the funds of that parish in which they may happen to be, at the time when the necessity for such relief arises, although their legal settlement be elsewhere.

By whom relieved.] The disbursements made to or for the relief of casual poor, cannot be recovered against the parish to which the pauper belongs, even in the case of continued illness; as the law has cast the burden upon the parish where such pauper becomes chargeable, and raises no implied promise, on behalf of the other parish where he is settled, to repay the sums so expended. (Atkins v. Banwell, 2 East, 505.)

This obligation upon the parish where the pauper becomes chargeable, is so strong, that if a parishioner, not being a parish officer, takes care of one rendered poor and impotent from sudden accident, as by the fracture of a limb, &c., he may recover against the parish officers the sum expended for his care and support, upon an implied promise arising from this their duty. (Per Ld. Eldon, C. J., Simmons v. Wilmot, 3 Esp. Rep. 92.)

Servant becoming casual Poor.] The relation of master and servant does not absolve the parish from the like duty, where the servant becomes suddenly disabled by misfortune; for parishes are under a moral, as well as a legal, obligation to take care of their casual poor. (Newby v. Wiltshire, Cald. 527; see Wennall v. Adney, 3 Bos. & Pul. 247.)

The ordinary class of casual poor, that is, persons who become, by misfortune or otherwise, incapable of obtaining employment, so as to secure the means of subsistence by their own labour, may be relieved and removed to their own parish without delay. But where poor persons by accident, as the fracture of a limb, &c., or by sudden illness, become chargeable, the burden is not to be thus got rid of so speedily. This is an important branch of the poor laws; the principal points of which will be found, as they have been decided, in the following leading cases upon the subject.

The pauper, M. H. was resident with her children in the parish of Inkberrow in Worcestershire, renting a house there, and occasionally receiving relief from that parish. Upon applying as usual for relief, it was refused, and she was desired to go to Feckenham, an adjoining parish in which some of her husband's relations had resided; this she did. F. refused relief, and sent her back to I. Upon her again applying to I. for relief, they refused, and desired her to apply again to F.; and when she expressed an unwillingness to do so, one of the overseers of I. took her to F., without any order of removal, and told her not to return again to I. The officers of F. then relieved her, and at the same time threatened to send her to prison, if she returned to I. She therefore was afraid to return to her house at I., and remained in F. for eight or ten days, when she was removed by an order of two magistrates from F. to Birmingham, which the sessions confirmed. Against this order R. v. St. James, in Bury St. Edmunds, (*infra*,) was cited, to show she was irremovable, as casual poor. Lord Ellenborough, C. J.: That was a very different case. This was the case of a starving vagrant, in whichever of the two parishes she was, who was going backwards and forwards between them, and would have been starved, if she had not received temporary relief from one or the other. She was liable to be removed from either: how then can this oscillation between the two parishes affect the order of removal to her proper parish? Order confirmed. (R. v. Birmingham, 14 East, 251.)

Pauper's Parish not bound to Reimburse.] A poor man settled in Ixworth, was employed by R. H. of the same parish, as a day labourer, on the 23rd Dec. 1807, to drive a load of hay to St. James's, in the town of Bury, and to return with a load of muck. In loading the muck, he fell and broke his leg. On the 24th Dec. two magistrates took his examination, made out an order of removal to his own parish, and the pauper being unable to be removed, they suspended the execution, by an indorsement on the back of the order. The pauper was attended by a surgeon by the order of the parish officers of St. James, and the expense of £16. 13*s*. was incurred for his cure and maintenance. On the 1st April, 1808, the pauper being able to move, the magistrates took off the suspension, and made the order for payment of the £16 13*s*. for the expenses, by indorsing the same on the order of removal, and on the same day the order was executed, and the pauper conveyed to Ixworth.

Ld. Ellenborough, C. J.—No person is removeable from the parish where he is, but by positive statute; the 13 & 14 C. 2. c. 12, after reciting, that poor people endeavour to settle themselves in those parishes where there is the best stock, &c., says that it shall be lawful, in complaint of the parish officers, within forty days after any such person coming so to settle as aforesaid, in any tenement under the yearly value of £10, for any two justices of the peace, of the division where any person likely to be chargeable to the parish shall come to inhabit, by their warrant, to remove him to the place of his last legal place of settlement. The expression of *coming to settle* denotes that the party comes *animo morandi* or *manendi:* it may be for a temporary purpose, but still it must be understood that he comes to settle there. But how can it be said that the pauper went into this parish *animo morandi* at all? Then if he were not removable within the terms of the 13 & 14 C. 2, can we find any enlargement of the power of removal? The 35 Geo. 3. has the words *inhabiting* or *sojourning*, but it would be an extravagant construction of either of those terms to say that it meant to include such a case as this. Then there is no authority for this order, and the sessions have done right to quash it.—Grose, J. agreed, as did Le Blanc, J., and Bayley, J.: and Le Blanc, J. said, that the 35 Geo. 3. c. 101, was meant to provide that persons, who by law were before removable, if likely to become chargeable, should not be removed till actually so; and to make provision for suspending the order of removal when made in case of sickness or infirmity; and that the expenses incurred in the care and maintenance of the persons, between the order to remove and the actual removal of them, should be defrayed by the parish to which they should be found to belong. (Rex v. St. James's, Bury St. Edmunds, 10 East, 25.)

Pauper Irremoveable.] It will have been perceived that the pauper is irremoveable from the parish where the *accident happens*, to the one where he is settled, so long as he remains impotent; and that the former parish cannot recover the expenses of his maintenance, &c. during his illness, against the latter. It seems also that if the accident happen in one parish, and *relief be afforded* in another, without any fraud or device having been practised, to remove the liability from the parish where the accident has taken place, the same rule is applicable. Thus in a case presented to the court upon such facts, and where it appeared that the pauper was carried into an adjoining parish, because there was no house nearer, where the pauper could be received, and assistance obtained, Abbot, C. J. said, this case is not materially distinguishable from Rex v. St. James's, Bury, St. Edmund's; and Rex v. Birmingham, is not at variance with that authority. But if it was necessary to decide between them as conflicting authorities, I should adhere to the opinion of the court in Rex v. St. James's, in Bury, St. Edmund's, for the statute 13 & 14 C. 2. s. 12, only gave a power of removal of those paupers who were *coming to settle.* But it cannot be said this pauper was coming to settle in the parish of L. Nor does the 35 Geo. 3. c. 101, make any difference; for previous to that act, a pauper under these circumstances could not have been removed, and that act only regulated the powers of removal already existing, but did not give any new power to the magistrates for removing paupers who were irremoveable before. (Rex v. St. Lawrence, Ludlow, 5 Barn. & Ald. 660.)

Accident in one Parish, Relief in another.] "It may sometimes happen, that the parish in which the accident happens may not be the proper place to give relief. It may happen that the parish officers, without entering into the question, what are the limits of particular parishes, will do that which *ought* to be done immediately, namely, carry the pauper to the house *nearest* the place where the accident happens, instead of carrying her to a considerable distance. In Lamb v. Bunce, (4 Maul. & Sel. 277,) the impression of the court was, that the parish in which the house was situate, was the proper parish to have given the relief." There is no express decision upon this point, and Mr. Justice Bayley, from whose judgment in Tomlinson v. Bentall,

(5 Barn. & Cres. 746,) the above extract is taken, reserved it in giving his opinion. It can hardly be doubted, however, that whenever this question comes to be decided, that the courts will follow up the manifest impression of these cases, and declare that this expense must be borne by the parish in which the house is situate, where relief is afforded, if such house is the nearest to the spot where the accident has happened, and has been chosen on that account alone, from a laudable anxiety to obtain for the pauper the most prompt and efficient assistance. (See also Rex v. St. Lawrence. Ludlow, *ante* 470.)

Taking Pauper to his, the adjoining Parish.] It is highly prejudicial to the rights of the poor, that when an accident has happened, the question should be agitated, or even pass in the minds of those persons in whose power the sufferer is of necessity placed, whether a burden which must fall somewhere, must be borne by them or can by any contrivance be shifted to others. The various dicta upon this subject seem to establish that a pauper, become so, under such circumstances, *obtains a settlement* pro tempore, in the parish where the accident has left him to be relieved; and that his settlement in his own parish is suspended, till the cause of its interruption is removed. The fact of his own parish being the next adjoining, and near to the spot where the accident happens, forms no exception to the rule. It was held in Tomlinson v. Bentall, already cited, that where a pauper being casually in the parish of A. met with an accident which required immediate medical assistance, and the constable of that parish improperly removed her to her own (which was the next adjoining) parish, and sent for the surgeon of her own parish to attend her, that it was the duty of the parish officers of A. to have taken the pauper to the nearest convenient house in A., and to have provided medical attendance there; and that they could not, by improperly removing her to another parish, relieve themselves from the liability which the law had in the first instance cast upon them: and that they were, therefore, liable to pay the surgeon's bill.

Surgeon attending casual Poor.] The parish officers bound to subsist and take care of the pauper, are also liable for the necessary medical attendance bestowed upon the sufferer. (Gent v. Tomkins, 5 Barn. and Cres. 746.) If they or any of them stand by and see such services performed, and do not object, the law raises a promise to pay for the performance. (Lamb v. Bunce, 4 Maule & Sel. 277.) And although the attendance is not given in their parish, but in the pauper's *own* parish, to which she has been wrongfully removed, yet if they know that the attendance is indispensably necessary, and that the removal was wrongful, it is the same. (Tomlinson v. Bentall, supra.) And the overseers of the pauper's own parish are not liable in such case, although they promise "that if it is right they should pay, they will." (Gent v. Tomkins supra, 1 Dowl. & Ryl. 541.)

Generally speaking, it is doubtful whether parish officers are liable to a surgeon's bill, contracted under any circumstances for the relief of a pauper, where they are *entirely ignorant* that such services have been performed. But a deputy overseer, or even a mere stranger directing a surgeon to attend a pauper, is liable to pay the surgeon's bill. (Watling v. Walters, 1 Car. & P. 132. Atkins v. Banwell, 2 East, 505.)

SECTION IV.—PAUPER AND CRIMINAL LUNATICS.

Statutory Regulations.] The several statutes on this subject were repealed, and their provisions consolidated and amended by the 9 Geo. 4. c. 40. This act relates to England only, and the Royal Hospital of Bethlehem is excepted from its operation by s. 58, but its regulations and directions apply to all asylums erected or established under the repealed acts.

Erecting Lunatic Asylums.] The 2nd section provides, that justices, at the quarter sessions, may direct notice to be given in the local newspapers of their intention to take into consideration, at their next quarter sessions, the expediency of erecting such asylums or houses for the reception of insane persons, or of appointing a committee to treat with the justices of adjacent counties, or the subscribers to any lunatic asylum theretofore established by voluntary contributions, to unite with them for such purpose. Sec. 3, authorizes them at such next general quarter sessions, by a majority not less than seven, to appoint a committee to superintend the erection of such asylum, and to report thereon from time to time; or (by s. 4.) to appoint a committee of not less than five justices to treat with the justices of adjoining counties, or the committee of any lunatic asylum, appointed for the purposes of the act: and by s. 5, the majority of the subscribers to any such lunatic asylum are authorized to appoint a committee of not exceeding five, to treat with such committee of justices; and the agreement entered into between them shall be binding, upon being signed by the majority respectively of the two committees, and approved by the majority of the justices assembled at their next quarter sessions, to whom such agreement shall be reported. The same mode of proceeding must be adopted where the agreement is to be made between counties uniting for the like purposes. (ss. 6, 7.)

And if the asylum be situate in any other county, the justices of the county or counties to which it belongs, may act therein, as far as concerns the regulation of the same, in like manner as if such lunatic asylum were situate within the bounds of their respective counties. (s. 28.)

Committee of Managers.] The 8th section provides, that the justices at their Michaelmas sessions, and the subscribers of any such lunatic asylum, at a general meeting, after notice in September or October of every year, shall elect respectively the members of the committee of visiting justices, or committee of subscribers to act together in the erection and management of such lunatic asylum; and they shall also fill up vacancies in such committees, as they may arise, at a meeting of such justices, or subscribers respectively, upon due notice: the number of justices on such committee to be in the proportion to the share of the expense borne by the county, so that there be not less than seven for any county so united, and the number of the committee of subscribers to any lunatic asylum uniting with any county shall be in the proportion specified in the agreement. But if such vacancies are not filled up, the committee may legally continue to act. (s. 9.) The committee are to meet where and when they please, upon notice by the clerks of the peace; they may appoint a clerk and surveyor for duly exercising the powers of the act, and contract for the purchase of lands and the erection of buildings, &c., such contracts to be entered in a book to be deposited among the records of the county, after the asylum is completed. (s. 10.) And no visitor shall be capable of having any beneficial interest or concern, either in his own name, or the name of any other person, in any such contract. (s. 11.)

Expenses how defrayed.] The justices may make special county rates for the purposes of the act, to be collected in the same manner and from the same places as the ordinary county rate (s. 12.); and may borrow money upon mortgage of the rates so directed to be raised, when it appears that the expense of carrying the act into execution, will exceed one half the amount of the *ordinary* annual assessment for the county rate. (s. 13.) And the rates raised under this act are to be charged with the interest of such loans, and a further sum to be applied in discharge of the securities given for the principal, in the order which they shall be drawn by lot for that purpose. (s. 14.) And the justices at their sessions may direct tenants at *rack-rent* to deduct one half the rate from such rent, which shall go *pro tanto* in discharge of the rent, the same as if it had been actually paid to the landlord. (s. 15.) And the justices may make provision for paying off such loans in a limited time, not exceeding fourteen years. (s. 16.)

Conveyance of Lands for Asylums, &c.] The act has the usual provisions, enabling bodies politic, guardians, &c. to convey lands, &c. to such persons as the visitors shall name in trust for the purposes of such asylums, &c., and for depositing the purchase money in the bank where the owners of such lands cannot be found, or refuse to execute the conveyance; and also for enabling the visitors to accept gifts, or make purchase of lands, &c. to any amount, notwithstanding the statute of mortmain; or they may rent premises for erecting asylums, with liberty to purchase the fee simple, at not more than thirty years' purchase of the rent reserved. (ss. 17 to 27 inclusive.)

The 29th section provides, that the lands, with the buildings thereon for the purposes of this act, shall not be assessed to rates, taxes or levies, at a higher value than at the time of the same being purchased for the use of such asylum; nor shall the buildings erected under this or any former act be assessed to any house or window tax.

Authority and Duties of Visitors.] The major part, not being fewer than three, of the visitors present at a meeting duly summoned, may make regulations for the management and conduct of the asylum, and appoint officers, servants, and assistants, fix their salaries, and dismiss them if they see occasion. They shall fix a weekly rate for maintenance of insane persons not exceeding 14s. per week, to be increased by the justices in quarter sessions, if found necessary. A chaplain shall be appointed for every county asylum; and the visitors may direct repairs, &c., and make orders on the county treasurer for payment of expenses, which he must obey, or subject himself to a penalty of double the sum so ordered to be paid, to be recovered by action; provided that no order, &c. &c. shall be made, unless due notice has been given, and the major part of the visitors at a meeting duly convened, concur, such major part not being fewer than three. (ss. 30 to 33, inclusive.)

The clerk of the committee may convene new meetings of the visitors, at ten days' notice, where they have neglected to adjourn the prior meeting, or in case any emergency arises, requiring them to meet before the day to which they stand adjourned. (s. 34.)

The visitors may sue and be sued in the name of their clerk, whose death or removal shall not abate any such action, but the clerk for the time being shall always be deemed plaintiff or defendant, as the case may be. (s. 35.)

Visitors may deliver any pauper to his relatives or friends, upon an undertaking to the satisfaction of the overseers of the pauper's parish, that he shall be no longer chargeable. (s. 39.)

Visitors' Annual Report.] The visitors shall, within one month previous to the 1st of June in every year, prepare a report of all the patients then confined in their asylum, &c.; and within the twelve months preceding of which a transcript shall be sent by their clerk to his Majesty's secretary of state for the home department, and the clerk shall also send a copy thereof to the clerk of the commissioners under "an act to regulate the care and treatment of insane persons in England," (9 Geo. 4. c. 41.) who shall enter the same in a register kept for the purpose, and the names of all patients mentioned in such report shall be by him entered in one general alphabetical list, with a reference to the asylum from whence such reports shall have been respectively transmitted.

Overseers to make Returns.] The justices of the peace acting in and for any county within England, at their several petty sessions, which shall be held next after the 15th day of August in each year, are hereby required to issue their warrants to the overseers of the poor of the parishes within their respective subdivisions, to return lists of all insane persons chargeable to their respective parishes, specifying the name, sex, and age of each insane person, and whether such insane persons be dangerous or otherwise, and for what length of time they have been disordered in their senses, and where confined, or how otherwise disposed of; and the overseers of the poor as aforesaid, shall, on the receipt of such warrants, forthwith prepare such lists accordingly, and such list shall be verified on oath before any one justice of the peace; and, accompanied with a certificate as to the state and condition of every insane person from a physician, surgeon, or apothecary, shall within fifteen days be transmitted by such overseer to the clerk of the peace for such county, or his deputy, to be by him laid before the justices acting for such county at their next general quarter sessions: and any overseer of the poor, to whom any such warrant shall have been directed and delivered, who shall not return such list so verified on oath, and so accompanied with such certificate as aforesaid, shall for every such offence be subject to a fine not exceeding ten pounds, to be levied by warrant of distress under the hands and seals of two justices; and it shall be lawful for such overseers, and they are hereby required, to defray the necessary expenses of the examination of such insane persons by a physician, surgeon or apothecary, out of the poor rates of the parish, township, or place to which such insane persons respectively belong; or where the legal settlement of such insane person shall not have been ascertained, then out of the poor rates of the parish, township, or place in which such insane person shall reside. (Id. s. 36.)

Penalty on Overseers for neglect.] If any overseer of the poor of any parish or place to which any insane person shall be chargeable, shall, for the space of seven days, wilfully neglect to give information of the state of such person, to some justice of the peace acting within the division of the county, within which the said parish or place is situate, he shall for every such offence forfeit not exceeding 10*l.* nor less than 40*s.*, (half to the informer and half to the treasurer of the county, to be placed to the credit of the county,) to be recovered by distress and sale as aforesaid. (Id. s. 37.)

Lunatic taken before Justices.] Upon its being made known to any justice, that a poor person chargeable to any parish, &c. within the county, is deemed insane, the said justice, by an order under his hand, and seal, may require the overseer of the said parish, &c. to bring the insane person before any two justices of the county, at the time and place appointed by the said order, and the said justices are to call to their assistance a physician, surgeon, or apothecary, at the charge of the said parish, &c., and if, upon examination of the said poor person, or from other proof, the said justices shall be satisfied that such poor person is insane, the said justices shall make inquiry into the place of his last legal settlement; and it shall be lawful for them, if they shall so think fit, by an order under their hands and seals, directed to the said overseer of the poor, to cause the said poor person to be conveyed to and placed in the county lunatic asylum, established under the directions of this or any former act for the county, or district of united counties, for which, or any of which they shall act; and if no such county lunatic asylum shall have been established, then to some public hospital, or some house duly licensed for the reception of insane persons; and it shall be lawful for the said or any other two justices of the peace of the said county, from time to time, as occasion may require, to make order on the overseer of the parish or place wherein such last or legal settlement shall be adjudged to be, for the payment of all reasonable charges of conveying such person to such asylum, &c., and for the payment of such weekly sum to the treasurer of such asylum, &c. as shall be fixed by the visitors of such asylum, &c. or if such poor person shall be conveyed to such licensed house, for the payment of such weekly or monthly sum as shall be agreed, to the keeper thereof, for the maintenance and care of such person; and the said overseer shall not remove such person from the said house without an order made by two justices of the county in which such house shall be situated, unless such person shall have been discharged as cured. Provided always, that the overseer or other person so conveying such insane person to such asylum, &c. shall deliver a certificate from the physician, surgeon, or apothecary so called to the assistance of the justices as aforesaid, certifying his examination and his opinion that the pauper is of unsound mind. (Id. s. 38.)

Parish Medical Practitioners.] Medical practitioners appointed and paid by the overseers, &c. of any parish, &c., shall have liberty eight times a-year, between eight in the morning and six in the evening, to visit pauper patients belonging to such parish, &c. confined in such lunatic asylum, and report thereon to the overseers, &c. (Id. s. 40.)

Where no Settlement found.] If the place of legal settlement of such insane person cannot be ascertained, the said justices may direct such person to be confined in the lunatic asylum for the county, or district of counties within which such person shall have been found; and if no such county asylum shall have been established, then in some public hospital or house duly licensed for the reception of insane persons, and to direct that the reasonable charges for the removal and care of such person shall be paid out of the county rates. (Id. s. 41.)

When Settlement found.] Where the legal settlement of any insane person so confined as aforesaid, has not been ascertained, two justices of the county, at any time, may inquire into the same, and if satisfactory evidence can be obtained as to such settlement, it shall be lawful for such justices to make an order upon the overseers, where such last legal settlement of the insane pauper shall be adjudged to be, for the repayment of the charges, &c., incurred within twelve calendar months previous to the date of such order, for the conveying, care, &c. of such pauper, and to provide for the future expenses necessary for the maintenance, care, &c. of such insane person, in the manner as has been hereinbefore directed. (Id. s. 42.)

And justices of the county in which an asylum is situate, may make such orders upon the overseers of any other county jointly maintaining such asylum. (Id. s. 43.)

Wandering Lunatics.] Upon its being made known to any justice of the peace, that any person wandering about at large within his jurisdiction is deemed to be insane, it shall be lawful for such justice, by an order under his hand and seal, to require the constable, or churchwardens and overseers of the parish, &c., or some of them, to bring the said person before any two justices of the county, at a time and place appointed; and the said justices are hereby required to call to their assistance a physician, surgeon, or apothecary, at the charge of the said parish, &c., and if upon examination the said justices shall be satisfied that such person is so far disordered in his senses, that it is dangerous for such person to be permitted to go abroad, it shall be lawful for such justices to proceed in the same manner as hereinbefore directed, in the case of a person chargeable to any parish within the jurisdiction of the said justices: Provided, if it shall appear upon inquiry, that such person hath an estate more than sufficient to maintain his or her family, the justices shall direct the overseers or churchwardens of any parish or place where any goods, chattels, lands, or tenements of such person shall be, to seize and sell so much of the goods and chattels, or receive so much of the annual rent of the lands and tenements of such persons, as is necessary to pay the charges of removal, maintenance, and care of such insane persons, accounting for the same at the next quarter sessions: Provided always, that nothing herein contained shall extend to prevent any relation or friend from taking such insane person under their own care and protection. (Id. s. 44.)

Justice refusing to make an order for the conveyance of any insane person to any lunatic asylum, &c., on the application of any overseer, shall give his reasons in writing. (Id. s. 45.)

Appeal by Party aggrieved.] Persons aggrieved by any order, or by any refusal of an order, of any justice or justices, may appeal to the next quarter sessions, upon giving the justice or justices against whom such appeal shall be made, ten days' notice thereof, and the determination of the sessions therein shall be final and conclusive, to all intents and purposes whatever. (Id. s. 46.)

Returns made to Quarter Sessions.] Justices shall make a regular return to the next general quarter sessions of the peace of all such cases brought before them; stating in all cases of refusal, the reasons thereof: such returns to be filed among the records of such court of general quarter sessions. (Id. s. 47.)

Sums directed to be paid by overseers under this act are to be levied by distress if they neglect to pay. (Id. s. 48.)

Bastards of Lunatics.] No bastard child which shall be born of any insane person, in any such county lunatic asylum, shall, thereby gain a settlement in the parish in which such county lunatic asylum shall be situated; but the place of the legal settlement of any such child so born, as aforesaid, shall be in the parish where the mother of such child was last legally settled. (Id. s. 49.)

Places not paying County Rate.] Nothing in this act shall extend to render any county lunatic asylum, provided under this act, liable to the reception of insane persons chargeable to, or apprehended in, any city, place, &c., claiming an exemption, and being exempt from the county rate, unless such city, place, &c., shall agree to unite, and shall thereby have contributed to the expense of the same. (Id. s. 50.)

Penalties for suffering Lunatics to go at large.] "No such insane person shall be suffered to quit the said county lunatic asylum, or to be at large, until the major part of the visitors, present at a meeting duly convened, not being less than three, shall order the discharge of such person, under their hands and seals, or until any two visitors shall, by and with the advice and consent of the physician, &c., discharge any lunatic confined therein, whose perfect recovery may be certified by the said physician, &c.; and that if any officer, servant, or assistant in such county lunatic asylum shall, through neglect or connivance, permit such person in any case to escape and be at large, without such order as aforesaid, he or she shall, for every such offence, forfeit a sum not exceeding forty pounds, nor less than forty shillings, to be recovered by distress, &c., to be levied under the warrant of two justices upon the confession of the party, or upon the information of any witness upon oath; one moiety of the penalty to the informer, and the other moiety to the treasurer of the said county lunatic asylum, to be applied to the use of the same." (Id. s. 52.)

Expenses of removal from Asylums.] "On the regular discharge of any pauper, the necessary expenses of removal of such pauper shall be borne by the parish in which such pauper shall be legally settled, upon being allowed by two justices of the county, within which such parish shall be situated, to be paid by the overseers out of the money raised therein for the relief of the poor." (Id. s. 53.)

Lunatic Criminals.] "In all cases where any person shall be kept in custody as an insane person by order of any court, or by his Majesty's order subsequent thereunto, two justices of the peace of the county shall inquire into the place of his settlement, and make order under their hands and seals, upon such parish where they adjudge him or her to be legally settled, to pay such weekly sum, for maintenance in such place of custody, as one of his Majesty's principal secretaries of state shall, by writing under his hand, from time to time direct; and where such place of settlement cannot be ascertained, such order shall be made on the treasurer of the county where such person shall have been apprehended. But if it shall appear that such person is possessed of sufficient property for his or her maintenance, then such justices shall order and direct the same to be applied to such purpose as hereinbefore directed. Provided always, that the churchwardens and overseers of such parish may appeal against such order to the general quarter sessions for the county where such order shall be made, in like manner and under like estrictions and regulations as against any order of removal; giving reasonable notice thereof to the clerk of the peace of such county, who shall be respondent in such appeal." (Id. s. 54.)

Criminals becoming Insane.] "If any person, while imprisoned under any sentence of imprisonment or transportation, shall become insane, and it be so certified by two physicians or surgeons, one of his Majesty's principal secretaries of state may direct, by warrant under his hand, that such person shall be removed to such county lunatic asylum, or other proper receptacle, as the said secretary of state may judge proper; and every such person so removed shall remain until it shall be duly certified to one of his Majesty's principal secretaries of state, by two physicians or surgeons, that such person has become of sound mind. Whereupon the said secretary may issue his warrant to the keeper, &c., directing that such person shall be removed back from thence to the prison, or other place of confinement, from whence he shall have been taken; or if the period of imprisonment or custody of such person shall have expired, that he shall be discharged." (Id. s. 55.)

Inspectors of Lunatic Asylums.] "The principal secretary of state for the home department, if he shall see fit, may employ any medical or other person to inspect the state of any county lunatic asylum, and to report to him the result of such inspection and inquiry; and every such medical or other person so employed, shall be paid such sum of money for his attendance and trouble as to the said principal secretary shall seem an adequate and reasonable allowance; and such expense shall be defrayed in the same manner, and from the same funds, as the other expenses attending the county lunatic asylum so visited." (Id. s. 57.)

Recovery of Penalties.] "All complaints and informations for offences against this act, except in cases where the manner of hearing and determining thereof is hereinbefore otherwise directed, shall be made before one or more justice or justices of the peace for the county or place wherein the offence shall be committed, who are hereby empowered to summon persons complained of, or upon complaint upon oath to issue warrants for the apprehension of any such persons; and upon the appearing or not appearing of such persons, to hear the matter of every such complaint and information, by examination of any witness or witnesses upon oath, and to make such determination thereon as he or they shall think proper, and, upon conviction, may issue a warrant, under hand and seal, for levying the fine, penalty, or forfeiture for such offence by distress, &c.; and it shall be lawful for any such justice or justices to order any person so convicted to be detained and kept in custody until return can be conveniently made to such warrant of distress, unless the said offender shall give sufficient security for his appearance before them on such day as shall be appointed for the return of such distress; such day not being more than seven days from the time of taking any such security. And if it shall appear, by confession of the offender or otherwise, that the offender hath not sufficient goods whereon such penalties, costs, and charges may be levied, such justice shall not be required to issue such warrant of distress, or if, on the return of such warrant, it appear there is no sufficient distress, such justice, &c., may and is hereby required by warrant to commit such offender to the common gaol or house of correction, for any term not exceeding three calendar months, unless such penalty or forfeiture, and all reasonable charges attending the recovery thereof, shall be sooner satisfied; and all such fines, penalties, and forfeitures, when recovered, shall, where the application is not otherwise directed by this act, be paid into the hands of the overseers of the poor of the parish where the offence shall be committed; and the overplus, if any, arising from such distress and sale, after payment of the penalty, and the costs and charges attending the same, shall be returned, upon demand, to the owner of the goods and chattels so distrained." (Id. s. 59.)

Appeal to the Sessions.] "Any person thinking himself aggrieved by any order or judgment, made by any justice or justices of the peace in pursuance of this act may, within four calendar months after, complain to the general or quarter sessions; the person appealing having first given at least fourteen days clear notice in writing of such appeal, and the nature and matter thereof, to the person or persons appealed against, and entering into a recognizance before some justice of the said county, with two sufficient sureties conditioned to try such appeal, and to abide the order and award of the said court thereupon; and if the justices in sessions see cause, they may mitigate any forfeiture, order any money levied to be returned, and may also award such further satisfaction to be made to the party injured, or such costs to either of the parties as they shall judge reasonable and proper; and all such determinations of the said justices shall be final, binding, and conclusive upon all parties to all intents and purposes whatsoever." (Id. s. 60.)

CHAPTER XXV.—PAROCHIAL SETTLEMENTS.

Settlement, Definition of.] A settlement is the right, acquired in any one of the modes pointed out by the poor laws, to become a recipient of the benefit of those laws, in that parish or place which provides for its own poor, where the right has been *last* acquired. It is not forfeitable, and may be communicated from person to person notwithstanding an attainder, which works a forfeiture of most civil rights, (Rex v. St. Mary Cardigan, 6 T. R. 116;) though it ceases and is destroyed for ever in the parish or place where it once existed, upon the acquisition of the same right in any other such parish or place.

Wherever a district of known limits contributes to one common fund raised within it, and which is disbursed within it, for the relief of its own poor, this right may be acquired, whether such district be a parish, a township, or a hamlet, even though the township or hamlet be extra-parochial, for overseers may be appointed to an extra-parochial township or village. (Rex v. Rafford, 1 Stra. 512.)

Who may acquire a Settlement.] It seems to have been doubted at one time whether this right was not limited to natural born subjects; but Lord Ellenborough observed that, " as to there being no obligation for maintaining poor foreigners, before the statutes ascertaining the different methods of acquiring settlements, the law of humanity, which is anterior to all positive laws, obliges us to afford them relief, to save them from starving; and those laws were only passed to fix the obligation more certainly, and point out distinctly in what manner it should be borne." (Rex v. Eastbourne, 4 East, 107.) The result is, that all the natural born subjects of England and Wales,

Scotchmen, Irishmen, and foreigners, may acquire the right by some one or other of the modes hereafter stated.

Settlement how acquired.] A settlement is most commonly acquired by the act of the party, and in one of the following ways, namely, either by hiring and service—by apprenticeship—by renting a tenement—by payment of rates—by estate—or, by office. But neither a feme covert, (Aythorp Rooding v. White Rooding, 2 Bott. 75,) nor an alien enemy, (Rex v. Eastbourne, supra,) as it seems, is competent to gain a settlement in any of these modes, though an attainted felon may. (Rex v. Haddenham, 15 East, 463.)

An infant within the age of nurture, that is, under seven years of age, may acquire a settlement by estate, but by none other of the above modes. (Rex v. Hasfield, 2 Stra. 1131.) And a person residing in a parish under a certificate, can acquire a settlement by three only of the above ways, namely, by serving an office, renting a tenement, or by estate; the two first by 9 & 10. W. 3. c. 11., but as that act declares that no person coming into a parish under a certificate, shall acquire a legal settlement there by any *act whatsoever*, except serving an office or renting a tenement of £10. value, it prevents any settlement being gained by the purchase of an estate, that is bought for a pecuniary consideration; but it does not prevent the acquisition of a settlement by reason of an estate devolving on the pauper by *operation of law*, or acquired by purchase in the *technical* sense of that word. (Rex v. Driffield, 8 Barn. & Cres. 684, overruling Rex v. Deddington, 2 Stra. 193, Burr. S. C. 220.)

Incapacity to gain a Settlement.] A person during a subsisting contract, cannot enter into another inconsistent with the former, so as to gain a settlement thereby. Not being in a condition to contract for the disposal of his time and services, he is not sui juris. For instance, an apprentice cannot make a valid contract of hiring and service, (Rex v. Norton, 9 East, 207,) nor a soldier bind himself to serve, either as a servant, or an apprentice. (Id.)

A person who is residing in a parish under a certificate, cannot acquire a settlement there by apprenticeship, hiring and service, or payment of rates. And a son of a certificated person residing with his father under the certificate, as one of his family, being of the age of nineteen and upwards, bound apprentice, and serving his master out of the certificated parish, but sleeping in it by the master's consent, is affected by the same disability, though if the binding be after he is of full age, he is then sui juris, and may acquire a settlement in the parish to which he had been certificated as a member of his father's family. (Rex v. Manningtree, 6 Maul. & Sel. 214.)

Local Incapacity.] No gate-keeper, toll-keeper, collector, or person renting the tolls of any turnpike road or navigation, residing in any toll-house thereon, or apprentice, or servant of any such collector or person, can gain a settlement thereby in the parish, &c. (54 Geo. 3. c. 170; 3 Geo. 4. c. 126.)

By the former of these statutes it is provided, that persons born in prisons, or houses licensed for the reception of pregnant women, are not to acquire a settlement thereby, nor persons maintained in any charitable institution, nor prisoner for debt in actual custody, by residence under such circumstances respectively.

By 35 Geo. 3. c. 101. s. 4, no act done by any person continuing to reside in any parish, &c. under the suspension of an order for his or her removal, or of a vagrant pass, shall be effectual, either in the whole or in part, for the purpose of giving him or her a settlement in the same. And the 59 Geo. 3. c. 12. s. 11 provides, that workhouses, or buildings hired for the use of the poor, wherever situate, shall be taken to be in the parish hiring them, as far as regards the settlement of persons born or lodged therein. (See also 54 Geo. 3. c. 170. s. 3.)

Derivative Settlement.] Another mode of obtaining a settlement is by derivation., in right of another who has previously acquired it, and without any act of the party entitled to the derivative settlement. In this case such a relation subsists between the two persons, that the settlement of the one, by operation of law, devolves upon the other, who is regarded as dependent upon him.

There are two modes in which a derivative settlement may be acquired—first by marriage, which entitles the wife to the husband's settlement; and, secondly, by parentage, which is the settlement legitimate children acquire in right of one or other of their parents.

Settlement by Birth.] The third and remaining kind of settlement vests in the individual in his own right, but without any act of his own, being acquired by birth. This is the settlement which may be resorted to, in default of any other, if the individual be born in any parish or place, having overseers, in England or Wales, whether legitimate or illegitimate.

Indemnity against Settlement.] A covenant, with the lessor of premises in a parish, to indemnify the parish from all manner of costs, rates and charges whatsoever, for or by reason or means of the covenantor, his executors, administrators or assigns taking an apprentice or servant, who should thereby gain a settlement within or become chargeable to the parish, is valid.

This question was raised upon a demurrer to the pleas which the defendant had pleaded, to an action for the breach of this covenant, and in delivering the judgment of the court, Tindal C. J. said, (inter alia.)

It was contended on the part of the defendant, first, that the plaintiffs had no interest which would authorize them to maintain an action: secondly, that the covenant was void, on the ground that it was unreasonable, that it was in restraint of trade, and that it was against the policy of the poor laws, inasmuch as it took away from the overseers any reasons for economy, and was injurious to the poor themselves. But we do not think any of the objections maintainable; for as to the first, the covenant being an express covenant with the lessor, and not being a covenant running with the land, an action lies for the breach thereof, in the name of the personal representative of the covenantee, who becomes a trustee for the persons, whoever they may be, who are beneficially interested in the performance of the covenant. It is not contended that the covenant is illegal on the ground of the breach of any direct rule of law, or the direct violation of any statute; and we think to hold it to be void, on the ground of its impolicy or inconvenience, we ought to be clearly satisfied that the performance of it would be necessarily attended with injury or inconvenience to the public. But such is not the case. There is nothing in the covenant which will prevent the poor generally from being employed by the defendant; he may employ as a servant or an apprentice the poor of that parish, who may be sufficient for the service of the mill; he may employ in those capacities the poor who have settlements in other parishes, but who have certificates from those parishes; or he may, in the case of servants, hire them for a smaller term than a year, and thereby prevent them altogether from gaining a settlement. There is, therefore, no general restraint of the poor from being employed in the service of the defendant in this parish. And as to any abstract right in a pauper to obtain a settlement in any parish he chooses to select, as he must have a settlement somewhere, the law will not consider a settlement in one parish rather than another as any benefit to the poor. In a case of Hill and others v. Eastaff, which was argued in B. R. in Easter Term 1819, where an action of debt was brought upon a bond, conditioned that the obligors, who were the churchwardens and overseers of one parish, should indemnify the obligees, who were the churchwardens and overseers of another parish, and all the inhabitants of that parish, from all costs, charges, and expenses which might be incurred by the latter parish, by reason of one Stevenson having put himself apprentice to one Moor, in the latter parish, the court gave judgment for the plaintiff; and some of the objections above raised would have applied as well to his case as to the one before us. Upon the whole, we think the judgment in this case should be given for the plaintiffs. (Walsh v. Fussell, 6 Bing. 169.)

SECTION II.—BY HIRING AND SERVICE.

Statutory Provisions.] The division of this subject is suggested by the several enactments relating to settlements of this kind. They are briefly as follows: if any unmarried person, not having child or children, shall be lawfully hired into any parish or town for one year, and shall continue and abide in the same service during the space of one whole year, (8 & 9 W. 3. c. 30. s. 4,) the master not being a certificate man, (12 Anne, st. 1. c. 18. s. 2,) nor the service being to a toll collector, (3 G. 4. c. 126. s. 51,) such service shall be a good settlement therein, (3 & 4. W. & M. c. 11. s. 7,) provided he have resided therein forty days. (13 & 14 Car. 2. c. 12. s. 1.)

Unmarried Person.] It has been held, that the period at which the statute requires the party to be unmarried, is the time the contract is fully and positively completed. Therefore, if he marry during the service, or even between the contract and entering on the service, provided it be not done fraudulently, in order to evade the statute, it will not prevent the settlement. (Anthony v. Cardigan, Fol. 131; Rex. v. Stannington, 3 T. R. 385; Farringdon v. Witty, 2 Salk. 527.) Nor does it make any difference, that both parties think the servant is married at the time of hiring; as where the husband is dead abroad, but the wife entering upon, or in the service, is ignorant of that fact; (Rex v. Hensingham Cald. 206;) nor although the master know the servant is to be married before the service commences. (Rex v. Allendale, 3 T. R. 382.) The servant being married at the time he makes the agreement, is likewise immaterial, if he be single when it becomes absolute and the service commences. (Rex v. Banknewton, Burr. Sess. Ca. 455.)

Without Children.] That is child or children, who, by following their parents' settlement, might become chargeable to the parish in which one may be acquired under the new servitude. Therefore an emancipated child is not within the act, but otherwise, where the emancipation is inchoate. (Anthony v. Cardigan, Fol. 131. 2 Bott, 177; Rex v. New Forest, 5 T. R. 487. 2 Bott. 182.) It will not suffice, that the child has entered into a contract, which will emancipate him if completed; the emancipation must be absolute at the time of the father's contract. (Rex v. Cowhoneyborne, 10 East, 88.)

Lawfully hired.] There must be a contract of hiring, imposing the reciprocal obligations of master and servant. (Gregory Stoke v. Pitminster, 2 Bott, 183.) And, therefore, where A. agreed to teach the pauper to make stockings for two guineas, the pauper paying the master for the use of the frame out of his earnings, this is no hiring. For here the parties merely agree that one shall *teach* the other, without any undertaking by the latter to *serve*. (Rex v. Bilborough, 1 Barn. & Ald. 115.) But the hiring may be either express, or implied from the nature of the service under it, or from other circumstances. (Rex v. Holy Trinity in Wareham, Cald. 141; R. v. Pendleton, 15 East, 449.) Even where there is an *express* hiring for part of the year, and a *continuance* of service for a year or more afterwards, a hiring for a year may then be presumed, in the absence of positive evidence to the contrary. (Rex v. Long; Whatton, 5 T. R. 447.) But if it appear that there was in fact no hiring at all, this of course rebuts the presumption of a hiring. (Rex v. Weyhill. Burr. S. C. 491.) Or if the relation between the parties were that of teacher and scholar merely, this rebuts the presumption of a hiring from a service. (Rex v. St. Mary Kidwelly, 2 Barn. & Cres. 750.; 4 Dowl. & Ryl. 309.) So, if the pauper be the relation of the person he served, who gave him, according to his promise, food, washing, and lodging for his services, that will not amount to an agreement for service, binding upon the parties, and gives no settlement; and the relation of child to the person served, destroys the presumption of a hiring. (Rex v. Sow. 1 Barn. and Ald. 178.) And hence the necessity of proof of an *express* contract in such a case to confer a settlement. The relationship of the parties, however, does not disqualify them from entering into such a contract. (Rex v. Chertsey, 2 T. R. 37.) And it makes no difference whether the child at the time of an actual hiring to his father, were emancipated or not. (Rex v. Chillesford, & Rex v. Winslow, 4 Barn. & Cres. 94.)

Parties must be able to contract.] The person hired must be sui juris, that is, capable of entering into such an engagement; therefore a deserter, (Rex v. Norton, 9 East, 206,) or a soldier, even with the assent of his commanding officer, cannot lawfully hire himself, so as thereby to gain a settlement, even though he be invalided and have leave of absence upon relinquishing his pay; as he is liable to be recalled at a moment's warning, and cannot communicate to his master an absolute right to his service for the year. (Rex v. Beaulieu, 3 Maul. & Sel. 229.) It has certainly been held, that a balloted *militia man*, being hired for a year, with an express exception that he shall be absent on duty for the month, and in lieu thereof serve a month over the year, gains a settlement, without serving that month. (Rex v. Winchcomb, Doug. 391.) And Bayley, J. in a recent case, with reference to this decision, said, "If the master chooses to engage the servant subject to the risk of his being called upon to perform duty as a militia man during the year, it may be considered a conditional hiring; and if during the year the militia be not called out, a settlement may perhaps be gained by serving under it." But as such a person is incapable of making an *unconditional* contract for a whole year, the court decided that, as it did not appear in this latter case that the pauper at the time of hiring informed his master that he was a militia-man, no settlement was gained by serving a year under such a contract. (R. v. Holsworthy, 6 Barn. & Cres. 283.)

Must be a free Agent.] The party serving, as well as the party served, must have been willing to contract, and the contract must be their voluntary act; and therefore a pauper-boy, hired out by the parish officers, into another parish to which he did not object, thinking he had no discretion on the subject, cannot gain a settlement by such service, there being no agreement, but a *submission* merely, by him. (R. v. Rickinghall Inferior, 7 East, 373; R. v. Stowmarket, 9 East, 211.)

But where a poor boy, of the age of fourteen, offered his services to a person in another parish, who agreed to take him into his service upon the overseer of the boy's parish undertaking to supply him with better clothes, for which the master was to pay the parish 1*s.* per week: it was held, that this was a contract of hiring by the boy himself, and his requiring assistance from the parish could not affect his capacity to make such an agreement, under which a settlement might be gained by a year's service. (R. v. Dunton, 15 East, 352.)

Contract by whom and when made.] It is not absolutely necessary that the contract of hiring should be made by the parties themselves; it may be made either by themselves, or by agents for them, (4 Burn's Just. 266,) if it appear that they afterwards adopted the act of the agent; and a son's having served under such a contract made for him by his father, is proof of his adoption of the contract; (R. v. Burbach, 1 Maul. & Sel. 370;) and the acceptance of the services on the terms of a deed, prepared between the parties, and executed by the servant, who was thereby bound to serve, is alike sufficient, although the master did not execute; and the deed ought to be received in evidence to show the terms of the hiring. (R. v. Houghton-le-Spring, 2 Barn. & Ald. 375.) Nor is it necessary that the master should himself have a settlement in the parish; (Chesham v. Missenden, 2 Bott. 178;) or even live in the parish in which the servant performs his service. (R. v. Eldersley, 2 Bott. 274.) If the servant be hired to a college, or other public establishment, and not to any particular individual or individuals, it is sufficient. (R. v. Sandhurst, 7 Barn. & Cres. 557; 1 Man. & Ryl. 95.) If the contract be made on a Sunday, it is not, therefore, invalid, and a service under it will confer a settlement; for the statute 29 Car. 2. c. 7. s. 5, "for the better observation of the Lord's day" only prohibits labour, business, or work done in the course of a man's ordinary calling, and the making of such a contract by master and servant does not come within the meaning of those words. (R. v. Whitnash, 7 Barn. & Cres. 596; 1 Man. & Ryl. 452.)

General Hiring.] Where a person engages to go into the service of a master, without stipulating for the continuance of the service for any particular period, this is a *general* hiring, which the law construes to be a hiring for a year, unless something appear to rebut the presumption. (1 Inst. 42, b.; R. v. Macclesfield, 3 T. R. 76.) But if the agreement be for "as long as the pauper has a mind to stop," (R. v. Christ's Parish, York, 3 Barn. & Cres. 459;) or "for as long time as the pauper please," (Id.) these being hirings at will, the idea of a contract for a year is completely negatived; for it is essential to a contract of hiring, upon which a settlement is to be founded, that there should be nothing in it which *excludes* the notion of the parties having agreed for a year. (Id. 5 Dowl. & Ryl. 314.)

Specific Hiring.] Where the parties agree for a *definite* time, named and settled between them, this is called a specific hiring, and as the statute makes the hiring for a year essential, a specific hiring for a shorter period than a year will not confer a settlement.

There must be one entire contract for a service for one *whole year.* Therefore *successive* hirings following each other in uninterrupted succession, if *severally* less than a year, as from May-day to Lady-day, then from Lady-day to May-day, will not gain a settlement, although they amount to a much longer period of service altogether; (R. v. Lowther, Burr. S. C. 674; Dunsford v. Ridgwick, 2 Salk. 535;) nor will a hiring for fifty-two weeks; (R. v. Astley, 4 Burn's Just. 379; R. v. Bottesford, 4 Barn. & Cress. 84; 6 Dowl. & Ryl. 99;) nor for a certain period, which is considered, by the custom of the country, to be a year. (R. v. Harwood, Doug. 439.)

A hiring from Whitsuntide to Whitsuntide, that is from a moveable feast in one year, to the same moveable feast in the next year, however, will gain a settlement, although it comprise less than three hundred and sixty-five days. (R. v. Newstead, Burr. S. C. 669.) So a hiring from a day after Whitsuntide to Whitsuntide will gain a settlement, because the day of hiring and the feast day should be reckoned inclusive; (R. v. Navestock, Burr. S. C. 719;) or from old Martinmas-day to the Old Martinmas-day following. (R. v. Skiplam, 1 T. R. 490.) But a hiring from *two* days after Whitsuntide to Whitsuntide will not give a settlement. (Coombe v. Westwoodhay, 1 Str. 143; R. v. Standon Massey, 10 East, 576.) Nor will a hiring from the 13th of October in one year to the 11th of October in the next year, which was *leap* year, for such a year comprises three hundred and sixty-six days by the statute, (24 Geo. 2. c. 23;) and a hiring and service in leap year must consist of that number of days, in like manner as ordinary years must comprise three hundred and sixty-five, to give a settlement.

The fact of the hiring being purposely made for less than a year in order to prevent the servant from gaining a settlement, will not make any difference. (R. v. Mursley, 1 T. R. 694; R. v. Haughton, 1 Str. 83.) But if an agreement be merely *colourable* for the purpose of avoiding a settlement, but be in *substance* a hiring for a year, as for instance, a hiring for eleven months, and to give one month over, or a hiring three days after Michaelmas to serve till the Michaelmas following, and it was agreed with the servant, that he should give in three days after the expiration of that time, this would be considered a hiring and service for a year, and a settlement would be gained by it. (R. v. Milwich, Burr. S. C. 433.)

Retrospective Hiring.] A retrospective hiring, that is, hiring for a year, part of which has already expired, will not gain a settlement, notwithstanding the service actually continues *after* such hiring, a whole year. The contract being vicious at the time it was made, no subsequent service can avail to amend it. (R. v. Marton, 4 T. R. 257; R. v. Ilam. Burr, S. C. 304.)

Exceptive Hiring.] Where the parties *stipulate* that upon certain days, or for any other portion of the year to which the contract relates, the servant shall be free from the obligation to serve; this is called an exceptive hiring, and no settlement can be gained under it. (R. v. Macclesfield, Burr. S. C. 458; R. v. Buckland Denham, Id. 696.)

It is essential that the servant should be under the power and coercion of the master for the whole time; (R. v. Kingswinford, 4 T. R. 219;) if, therefore, he *covenant* or *stipulate* in the agreement, to work only a certain number of hours in the day, though the number be in fact a reasonable, or the *usual*, time in the trade, or to have Sundays or holydays at his own disposal, he cannot gain a settlement under such a hiring. (R. v. North Nibley, 5 T. R. 21.) Or, if the pauper have the option reserved of being absent from the service any part of the year, as "two or three days to see his friends," that time is to be considered as excepted out of the contract, and treated as a hiring for a year, *minus* the time the servant is entitled to be absent. (R. v. Leamington Priors, 8 Dowl. & Ryl. 329; R. v. Rushulme, 10 East, 325.)

An *express* stipulation is not necessary, if it is apparent, from the nature of the contract, that the master has not the control over the servant for the whole year. Thus, where a pauper had been hired for three years, at £20 a year, as a looker, the duty of a looker being to superintend the flocks and fences of his employer; when he was hired, his master told him that he should not have full employment for him, but that he would employ him as much as he could. He was not to do any work for his master other than that belonging to the office of looker, without receiving extra wages. During the first year and three quarters he worked for his master only, but was always paid extra for any work not belonging to his office of looker. It was held, that in this case there was not any contract of hiring and service for one *whole* year, and that no settlement was gained under it, as the servant might have employed himself for other masters when the duties of looker did not require his attention. (R. v. Lydd, 2 Barn. & Cres. 754.)

Exception part of the Contract.] But to have this effect, the exception must be part of the contract, and made at the same time; for if, after the hiring is completed, it is agreed that any portion of the year shall be taken away, this will amount either to a dissolution of the contract, or a dispensation of the service, according to the circumstances, but not to an exception. (See R. v. Market Bosworth, 2 Barn. & Cres. 757.) In these cases it is the *contract itself* which must be looked to; if it contain *no* exception, it cannot have one introduced into it afterwards; if it do contain an exception, it is vicious, and cannot be cured of this defect by a subsequent agreement to serve for the period excepted; (R. v. Althorne, 2 Barn. & Cres. 112;) or by substituting an equivalent, as by the servant finding a fit man to do his work for the time; (R. v. Arlington, 1 Maul. & Sel. 622;) or by serving the time out himself after the year has expired; (R. v. Turvey, 2 Barn. & Ald. 520;) or even if the exception is to depend upon a contingency, upon the happening of which the servant is, by the agreement, to be at liberty to serve other persons during its continuance, although in fact the contingency do not happen; in all these cases the contract being essentially defective, no settlement can be gained. (R. v. Edgmond, 3 Barn. & Ald. 107.)

Exceptions implied.] But there is in every contract some *implied* exceptions; as the necessary hours of rest, and for taking meals, &c. And there may be an implied exception from the custom of the country; as that a bleacher, according to the practice of the manufactory in which he was engaged, if he finished his appointed week's, work, calculated at so many pieces a-day, for *six* days, in less time, he had the rest of the week to do as he pleased, and also went where he chose on Sundays, without asking leave; for here was an express hiring for a year, and no express exception in the contract, of any part of the year. (R. v. Horwick, 10 East, 489.) There may be a similar implied exception from the custom of business, as that a clerk is not to serve beyond a certain number of hours. (R. v. All Saints, Worcester, 1 Barn. & Ald. 322.) These implied exceptions do not break in upon the general contracts of hiring for a year.

Conditional Hiring.] The distinction between a conditional and an exceptive hiring, is rather subtle, and at first sight not easily discovered. Mr. Justice Bayley, in delivering the judgment of the court, says, upon this subject: "The proper distinction seems to be this; if the bargain be originally made for an entire year, and terms are introduced applicable to a continuance of the relation of master and servant during the whole year, but there is also a provision, that in a given event it shall be competent to the parties to put an end to or suspend the service for a part of the year, still a settlement is gained, if the service is actually performed for a whole year, and neither party avails himself of the condition. A conditional hiring is, for this purpose, the same as an absolute hiring, unless the condition is acted upon. An exceptive hiring is one by which the relation of master and servant will not subsist for the whole year, unless some further arrangement be entered into; and if, by the bargain, days or hours are excluded from the service, that is an exceptive hiring." (R. v. Byker, 2 Barn. & Cres. 120; 3 Dowl. & Ryl. 375.)

It would seem, however, that a conditional hiring, as above defined, becomes an exceptive hiring, if the proviso be added in the contract, that in case the service should be suspended, the servant shall be at liberty to contract with or serve *another master* during such suspension. (See R. v. Edgmond, *ante*, 491.)

Instances of conditional Hiring.] Where in the contract for a year, a stipulation is included for determining the service by a month's or fortnight's notice, or, what is equivalent to a notice, payment of the wages for the same period; (R. v. Birdbroke, 4 T. R. 245;) or where the master stipulates that he may dismiss the servant for misconduct without any notice at all. (R. v. Sandhurst, 7 Barn. & Cres. 557; 1 Man. & Ryl. 95.) Or if the servant goes on liking a month, to have £5 a year wages, the contract is such as will give a settlement; though, if at the end of the month the master tell him he must leave a fortnight before the end of the year, and he does so, this will defeat the settlement, although he receive the whole year's wages. (R. v. Coggeshall, 6 Maul. & Sel. 264.) A hiring at so much per week, a month's wages, or a month's warning, is a hiring for a year. (R. v. Pershore, Worcestershire, 8 Barn. & Cres. 679.)

A hiring coupled with a condition, whereby, from subsequent circumstances, the service and wages may be suspended for a short period, as to repair machinery, &c., if there be not, in fact, any suspension of the service, will gain a settlement. (R. v. Byker, *supra.*) So where the master doubts whether the servant is strong enough, but bids him try the service, and he continues therein. (R. v. Northwold, 2 Dowl. & Ryl. 790.) A hiring for a year to work for the master's benefit, though at the same time to learn a trade, not being an apprenticeship, will gain a settlement. (R. v. Coltishall, 5 T. R. 193; R. v. Shinfield, 14 East, 541.) But a contract merely on the part of the master to *teach* the servant a trade during the year, will not, for it is no hiring at all. (R. v. Bilborough, 1 Barn. & Ald. 115; R. v. St. Mary, Kidwally, 2 Barn. & Cres. 750; 4 Dowl. & Ryl. 309.) And a stipulation for a deduction from wages for illness, will not prevent a settlement. (R. v. Martham, 1 East, 239; 2 Bott. 228.) Where there was an express hiring "to do the offices of a servant," a stipulation that the servant might have what she could earn by her own labour besides, was holden not to defeat the settlement. (R. v. Chertsey, 2 T. R. 37; 2 Bott. 204.)

Implied Hiring.] It is not necessary that an express hiring for a year should be proved; if it can be inferred as a fact, from other independent circumstances which properly lead to such a conclusion, or that the parties intended the pauper to serve for a year, it will be sufficient. Thus a general indefinite hiring, is a hiring for a year, unless something appears that may raise a presumption to the contrary; (R. v. Worfield, 5 T. R. 506; R. v. Seaton & Beer, Cald. 440; 2 Bott. 202; R. v. Market Bosworth, 2 Barn. & Cres. 757; 4 Dowl. & Ryl. 306;) so telling a man to go into the place of another who was a yearly servant, implies a hiring for a year; (R. v. Berwick, St. John's, Burr. S. C. 502; 2 Bott, 197;) so hiring for eleven months "and then on an end," will gain a settlement; (R. v. Macclesfield, 3 T. R. 76; 2 Bott. 206;) so a hiring for a year, and then a continuance in the same service without any new agreement, implies a *new* hiring for a year. (R. v. Croscombe, 2 Stra. 1240; 2 Bott. 278.) But this presumption, like all others, may be rebutted by circumstances appearing in the contract itself, or otherwise. (See R. v. Stokesly, 6 T. R. 757, 2 Bott. 190.) Thus a hiring "for as long a time as the pauper pleased," is a hiring *at will*, which excludes the presumption of a yearly hiring. (R. v. Christ's Parish, York, 3 Barn. & Cres. 459; 5 Dowl. & Ryl. 314.)

The same Service.] The words of the act are, "and shall continue and abide in the *same* service for one whole year." (See *ante*, p. 486.) "The same service" does not mean a service entirely under the same hiring; for if there be a hiring for a year, and a continued service for a year, though not under the same hiring, it will be sufficient. (R. v. Overnorton, 15 East, 347.) Thus a hiring for half a year, or even for a week, and then a hiring for a year, and a service, part under the one, and part under the other, will gain a settlement, (R. v. South Moulton, 1 Ld. Raym. 426,) even although there be less than forty days' service under the yearly hiring, provided it be in the *same* parish. (R. v. Adson, 5 T. R. 98.)

So if there be several consecutive hirings, and then a hiring for a year in the same service, they may be coupled in like manner; (R. v. Bagworth, Cald. 179;) and this whether the yearly hiring followed or preceded the others; (R. v. Grendon Underwood, Cald. 369; R. v. Fillongley, 1 Barn. & Ald. 319;) or whether the services under these different hirings be on similar wages or not; (R. v. Underbarrow and Bradley Field, Doug. 309, Cald. 65;) or although the service under any, except the *yearly* hiring, were under an invalid contract, or without contract at all, for a service without a contract may be coupled with a service under one. (R. v. Dawlish, 1 Barn. & Ald. 280.) But if after a yearly hiring and service, a hiring take place for a *shorter* period, and the parties remove into *another parish*, and the service is there completed, no settlement is gained in this latter parish, as there is *no service* in that parish under a yearly hiring. (R. v. Apethorpe, 2 Barn. & Cres. 892; 4 Dowl. & Ryl. 487.)

But services in successive years without a new agreement, will connect only when the servant at the commencement of the succeeding year is unmarried; (R. v. St. Giles's, Cald. 54;) and the service for the last forty days, to give a settlement in the parish where it is performed, must be under a hiring, made when the pauper was unmarried. (R. v. Great Chilton, 5 T. R. 672.)

The Service must be unbroken.] The several services must be continued and uninterrupted, even by the interval of a day; but the interval of the fraction of a day, even although during that time the pauper actually quit the service and take away his clothes, is not material. (R. v. Fifehead, Magdalen, Burr. S. C. 116.) Thus if B. be hired from Michaelmas to Michaelmas, and A., the master, dispense with his service till the Wednesday after Michaelmas day, and on that day B. goes to A. who, wishing B. to serve in a different capacity to that in which he was hired, and B. refusing, it is agreed between them that B. is at liberty to hire himself elsewhere, and goes away; but on the same day meeting A. again, B. agrees to serve in the manner A had desired; here was a renunciation and agreement to dissolve the contract, with the resumption of it for a different kind of service; but as all these circumstances took place within one day, they are overlooked by the law, which does not regard the fraction of a day. (R. v. Grendon, Underwood, Cald. 359.)

Serving Executor or Assignee of Master.] If the servant live part of the year with the master who hired him, and the remainder with his executor, (R. v. Ladock, Burr. S. C. 179,) or widow, (R. v. Hardborn with Newton, 12 East, 51,) or with a person to whom the master assigned his farm, upon which the service was to be performed, no words dissolving the contract with the servant having passed between them, (R. v. Ivinghoe, 1 Stra. 90,) it is sufficient.

Service for a Year.] The person hired mus tabide, either actually or constructively, in the same service for the space of a year.

A person is constructively in the same service, who is absent any part of the year for a reasonable or justifiable cause. Thus, if the servant during any part of the year be prevented serving by illness, yet the time of his illness shall be reckoned in the year; (R. v. Islip, 1 Stra. 423; 2 Bott. 300, 322;) no matter whether it happen at the beginning, middle, or end, if it be after the *service* has actually commenced. (R. v. Wintersett, Cald. 298; 2 Bott. 263, 310.) But where the pauper, being ill about a fortnight before the end of his year, *left his master's* service, and the master paid him the whole year's wages, this was held a dissolution of the contract, and no settlement was gained. (R. v. Sudbrooke, 4 East, 356.) Though whether the master deduct from the wages on account of the servant's illness or not, is immaterial. (R. v. Maddington, Burr. S. C. 675.)

So if the servant be imprisoned by order of a magistrate, upon the complaint of the master, the time of his imprisonment is reckoned in the year, even although it occur at the end of the year. (R. v. Hallow, 2 Barn. & Cres. 739; 4 Dowl. & Ryl. 299.)

Sometimes the year of hiring, as from Whitsuntide to Whitsuntide, may comprise more, sometimes less, than three hundred and sixty-five days; if less, a service from Whitsuntide to Whitsuntide is sufficient; (R. v. Newstead, Burr. S. C. 669;) if more, a service of three hundred and sixty-five days is sufficient. (R. v. Ulverstone, 7 T. R. 564, sed vide *ante*, p. 490.) In this respect more liberality of construction is observed with regard to the *service*, than with regard to the *hiring*. (R. v. Ackley, 3 T. R. 250.) And where the pauper entered the service the day before New Year's day, having hired himself "at £8 and his washing," and quitted two days after Christmas, receiving his full wages, that being the usual time that servants in that part of the country go into and quit their places, the court thought this not a yearly hiring; but as the sessions had found it to be a hiring and service for a year, they held themselves bound by it. (R. v. Tyrley, 4 Barn. & Ald. 624.)

Yearly Hiring implied by Wages.] If the reservation of weekly wages be the only circumstance from which the duration of the contract can be collected, the presumption is, that it is to continue for a week only; but a stipulation for a month's wages, or a month's warning, shows clearly that the contract was for a longer period; and no precise time being fixed, it was a contract for an indefinite period, or, in other words, a general hiring for a year. (R. v. Pershore, Worcestershire, 8 Barn. & Cres. 680.)

An *express* hiring for a year, though at weekly wages, will gain a settlement; (R. v. Newton Toney, 2 T. R. 453;) but an *indefinite* hiring at weekly wages is but a weekly hiring, unless there be something in the agreement which shows the intention of the parties to have been otherwise. (R. v. Lambeth, 4 Maul. & Sel. 315.) As where the relation of master and servant cannot be put an end to by either party without a month's notice, then the hiring must be understood to be a hiring for a year; (R. v. Hampreston, 5 T. R. 205; R. v. Great Yarmouth, 5 Maul. & Sel. 114;) but any number of years' service at weekly wages, and a week's notice, will not gain a settlement. (R. v. Hanbury, 2 East, 423.)

Nor does it seem to make any difference, where instead of being hired at yearly, monthly, or weekly wages, the servant is to work by the piece; at least where the hiring is expressly for a-year; (R. v. King's Norton, 2 Stra. 1139; R. v. Birmingham, Doug. 333;) but a hiring to serve as a brickmaker from Michaelmas to Michaelmas, and to make a certain quantity of bricks at a stipulated price, it was held conferred no settlement, as it was a contract to serve till the completion of the job, and not for a year's service. (R. v. Woodhurst, 1 Barn. & Ald. 325; see 1 Bla. Rep. 443.)

Dispensation in the Service.] If the servant absent himself from the master's service during the year, this absence is either dispensed with by the master, or is justifiable upon the part of the servant, or amounts to a dissolution of the contract altogether; in the two first cases the time of absence is reckoned, in the latter not, but the time of service is reckoned up to the time of dissolution only.

If the servant absent himself with the leave of the master, (R. v. Potter, Heigham, 2 Bott. 316; R. v. Beccles, 2 Stra. 1207; R. v. Goolaston, Id. 1232,) and his master receive him again into his service within the year, this is a dispensation merely; (R. v. Islip, 1 Stra. 423;) even though the servant ran away, was brought back by a warrant, and consented to a deduction from his wages for the time he was absent. (R. v. East Shefford, 4 T. R. 804; R. v. Barton upon Irwell, 2 Maul. & Sel. 329.)

Dissolution of the Contract.] If before the end of the year a master discharge his servant, this, if *consented* to by the servant, is a *dissolution* of the contract of hiring, (R. v. Mildenhall, 12 East, 482; R. v. Bray, 3 Maul. & Sel. 20,) whether the full year's wages be paid or not. (R. v. Maidstone, 12 East, 550; R. v. Seagrave, Cald. 247; R. v. Castlechurch, 2 Stra. 1022.) But if the master discharge the servant by his own will, who is at the time willing to stay the whole year, and merely *submits* to leave the service at the master's request, or is turned away by the wrongful act of the master, this is but a dispensation, and not a dissolution of the contract. (R. v. St. Philip, Birmingham, 2 T. R. 624.) And whether the whole or only part of the wages be paid, is immaterial in such circumstances. (R. v. Hardhorn with Newton, 12 East, 51.) So if a master, leaving his house or the country, or becoming bankrupt, dismiss his servant on that account only, it amounts to no more than a dispensation. (R. v. St. Bartholomew, Cornhill, Cald. 48; R. v. St. Mary, Lambeth, 8 T. R. 236.) Nor will the wrongful act of the servant, *of itself*, put an end to the contract; it only gives the party aggrieved a right to do so; it puts him in a condition to elect whether he will dissolve the contract or not; and if the master chooses to act upon the right which the misconduct of the servant gives him, then the contract is legally dissolved between them, just as much as if the free consent of both parties had been given for the purpose. (R. v. Barton, Irwell, 2 Maul. & Sel. 329; Spain v. Arnott, 2 Stark. Rep. 256.) Upon the whole, whether it be a dispensation or a dissolution is more a conclusion of fact from the circumstances of the case, than matter of law; the only rule that can be depended on is this:—That when the parties stand in such a situation, that neither the master can compel the servant to come back into his service, nor the servant can compel the master to take him back, and neither of them have the legal means of compelling redress against the other, there is a dissolution of the contract. (R. v. King's Pyon, 4 East, 354.)

Dissolved by Absence.] A servant may in some few cases justifiably absent himself from his master's service without his consent.

As, for instance, near the end of his year he may absent himself, even against the master's will, to attend at a statute or fair to hire himself for the ensuing year, or for any other reasonable cause which the master ought to have allowed; and his so doing does not prevent his gaining a settlement, though his master refuse to take him back. (R. v. Polesworth, 2 Barn. & Ald. 483.)

But if the absence be wrongful, and the master do not, although he has the opportunity, take the servant back, the law will conclude that the master left the servant to the consequences of his own act; (R. v. Westmean, 2 Bott. 320;) or if he has no such opportunity, as where the servant is detained in custody to the end of his year, the contract is at an end in either case, from the misconduct of the servant. (R. v. North Cray, 2 Bott. 322.)

Dissolution by a Justice.] The acts of Parliament which give the magistrates jurisdiction in these cases, (see 20 Geo. 2. c. 19; 4 Geo. 4. c. 34) confine their power herein to cases where a complaint has been made against the servant: and where, in the exercise of their discretion, they put an end to the contract, their order must be under hand and seal.

The dissolution of the contract, effected by an order of removal, is of the like nature; which, however wrongfully, separates him from the master, if unappealed against. (R. v. Kenilworth, 2 T. R. 598.) And though he may return in a few days to, and continue in, his master's service, the effect is the same, the contract having been determined by the submission to the order of removal; but if there be a new hiring after his return, he may, it seems, gain a settlement under that; (see R. v. Fillongley, 2 T. R. 709;) for although heretofore the return of the pauper after removal, was an offence against the law, yet since the 35 Geo. 3. c. 101, this may admit of considerable doubt, as that act renders a person irremoveable, unless actually chargeable, and he may after his removal return with the means of subsistence; it is difficult therefore to say that so returning he commits an offence. (See R. v. Barham, 8 Barn. & Cres. 104.)

But in the case of an imprisonment under the 20 Geo. 2. c. 19. s. 2, upon the complaint of *the master*, the servant is still to be considered as virtually in the master's service; for the act gives the magistrate authority to put an end to the contract; and if upon hearing the complaint that be not done, the contract still subsists. Consequently, if the imprisonment be for the last month of the year for which the servant is hired, he in this case gains a settlement. (R. v. Hallow, 2 Barn. & Cres. 739; 4 Dowl. & Ryl. 299.)

Whether the contract has been *dissolved* or not, or there has been a *dispensation* of part of the service, or the agreement for putting an end to the service, is *fraudulent* to defeat a settlement, is for the sessions to determine, and they ought always to find the fact in such cases. (R. v. Bottesford, 4 Barn. & Cres. 84; 6 Dowl. & Ryl. 99.)

And in all such cases of fraud, whether by the master, (Eastland v. Westhorsley, 1 Stra. 526,) or by the servant, (R. v. Frome Selwood, 2 Bott. 312,) or by the contrivance of both, (R. v. Sulgrave, 2 T. R. 376,) it is a dispensation merely, and not a dissolution.

Forty Days' Residence.] In order to complete the settlement, there must be a residence at a place of rest, that is, the place where the *servant* takes his ordinary and sufficient sleep, without regard to the master's place of abode, (R. v. Mildenhall, 3 Barn. & Ald. 374), of forty days; either consecutively or at different times within the year. (R. v. Denham, 1 Maul. & Sel. 221.) The parish in which he last completes a forty days' residence, is that in which he is settled; (R v. Hedsor, Cald. 51; R. v. Great Bookham, Cald. 290; R. v. Croscombe, 2 Stra. 1240;) whether it be in the parish in which he serves or not, provided the residence be with a view to the service, which condition is satisfied by the servant being there working for himself, with his master's permission; for he is still constructively in his master's service. (R. v. Nympsfield, Cald. 107.) But if he be sent to another parish on account of his becoming lunatic, his settlement remains in the former parish. (R. v. Sutton, 5 T. R. 657.) If, however, his services require him, or he have leave without fraud to reside some days in one parish, and some days in another during the last forty days, the parish in which he sleeps the night of the *last* day, is his place of settlement, provided he have slept the remaining thirty-nine days, to make up the requisite number at some period during the year, in the same parish; (R. v. Ivestone, Cald. 288; R. v. Findon, 4 Barn. & Cres. 91; 6 Dowl. Ryl. 116;) and this whether the master ever resided in the parish or not. (Id. ib. St. Peter's in Oxford v. Chipping, Wycombe, 1 Stra. 528.) But the service, or some part of it, while he is living in that parish, must be under a yearly hiring. (R. v. Apethorpe, 2 Barn. & Cres. 895.)

But the servant cannot gain a settlement in any parish in which his master or himself are, during any part of the forty days, residing under a certificate. (R. v. Egremont, 14 East, 253.)

SECTION III.—BY APPRENTICESHIP.

General Requisites.] The statute upon which settlements by apprenticeship are founded, is the 3 W. & M. c. 11.; which by s. 8. enacts that "if any person shall be bound an apprentice by indenture, and inhabit in any town or parish, such binding and inhabitation shall be adjudged a good settlement." It is sufficient, therefore, if he is *bound* and inhabit as an apprentice, even though he be married at the time he enters into the contract, (Titchfield v. Milford, Burr. S. C. 511,) provided the master whom he serves is not a toll-collector, (*ante* 484,) and that the parish is not protected by a certificate from some other parish. But forty days' residence is equally necessary in this as in the former kind of settlement. (See *ante* 499.)

Distinction between Binding and Hiring.] An imperfect contract of apprenticeship is not available for the purpose of gaining a settlement; it is, therefore, important to notice the distinction between these contracts, especially as contracts of hiring are sometimes unnecessarily executed with the formalities which are essential to an apprenticeship. If the contract has for its object the instruction of the party who is *to learn*, it is an actual or intended contract of apprenticeship, but if the principal object be a *service* to be performed to the master, it is no more than a hiring and service, although mention is made therein of the master teaching, and the servant learning, any particular art or trade. (Rex v. Bilborough, 1 Barn. & Ald. 115; Rex v. Burbach, 1 Maul. & Sel. 370; Rex v. Mountsorrell, 2 Id. 460.)

No technical expressions are essential to a binding, provided the parties show by the words they do use in the instrument, an evident intention to create the relation of master and *apprentice*. (Rex v. Laindon, 8 T. R. 379; Rex. v. Rainham, 1 East, 531.) Though an agreement be, in all its terms, and in the intention of the parties, for an apprenticeship, if no valid *indentures* are executed, no settlement is gained by the service as an apprentice; nor as a hired servant, because the party was engaged to serve *as* an apprentice, not as a hired servant. (Rex v. Margram, 5 T. R. 153; Rex v. Kingsweare, Burr. S. C. 839; Rex. v. All Saints, Hereford, Burr. S. C. 656.) And though the instrument be signed and sealed by the father and master, by which the latter agrees to teach his art and mystery, &c., but is not signed by the boy, it is equally nugatory. (Rex v. Cromford, 8 East, 25.) So where a premium is given, and the master undertakes to teach a trade, but no indentures are executed in order to save the stamp duty, it is held to be a contract of apprenticeship, but void, and no service under it can give a settlement, either as an apprentice or hired servant. (Rex v. Highnam, Cald. 491.)

Defective Apprenticeship.] It is clearly established by the authorities, that if an apprenticeship, only, was contemplated by the parties, and there was an imperfect contract of apprenticeship, the service will give no settlement. Thus, where the father of a pauper was about to put him out to service, when it was suggested to him by A., a carpenter, that it would be better for him to learn his, (A.'s) trade, instead of going to service; and A. afterwards hired the pauper to learn his trade, and to do any other work as well as that of a carpenter; and the pauper went to A. and served him for five years, living during that time with his parents, who provided him with victuals and part of his clothing, the remainder being provided by A., and the pauper did any work that his master ordered him to do; and at the end of that time he agreed to work for his master as a journeyman at weekly wages; it was held, that this was a defective contract of apprenticeship, and not a contract of hiring, and that no settlement was gained thereby. (Rex v. Combe, 8 Barn. & Cres. 82; Rex v. St. Margaret's, King's Lynn, 6 Barn. & Cres. 97, 9 Dowl. & Ryl. 160.)

Hiring to learn a Trade.] But where none of the above circumstances, tending to establish that an apprenticeship was intended, occur, and the party is to *serve*, and his object in entering into the contract is to learn a trade, but he is also to do the service of a servant, or any work his master sets him about, and no premium is given, that is decisive to show that he must be considered as a hired servant, and the instruction in the trade as part of his wages. (Rex v. Coltishall, 5 T. R. 193; Rex v. Martham, 1 East, 239.) And the cases seem to proceed upon the principle, "that all contracts of service for the purpose of *instruction*, which are not in form contracts of apprenticeship, are to be taken as contracts of *hiring*, unless it appear that an *apprenticeship was intended;* and that under such a contract a settlement may be gained." (See Rex v. Laindon, 8 T. R. 379; Rex v. Little Bolton, Cald. 367; Rex v. Shinfield, 14 East, 541.)

The Binding essential.] This must be by *indentures*, that is by *deed*, duly stamped and executed with the usual formalities; but *indenting* is dispensed with, by 31 G. 2. c. 11, and is, therefore, not necessary. (Rex v. Ditchingham, 4 T. R. 769.) In the case of *voluntary* bindings, that is where the apprentice binds himself, both master and *apprentice* should be parties to, and execute the deed. (Rex v. Cromford, 8 East 25; Rex v. Ripon, 9 East, 295.) But trustees of a charity, authorized to advance a sum of money upon the binding out of poor boys, need not in such case be parties also. (Rex v. Quainton, 2 Maul. & Sel. 338.) The age of the person binding himself is immaterial, so as he be not under the age of seven years.

Binding to whom.] The master's condition in life is immaterial if there is no fraud; thus, a female may be bound to a day labourer, to learn the art of a housewife. (Rex v. St. Margaret's, Lincoln, 1 Bott. 613.) And though the master has no right under the statute to take an apprentice, (2 Bott. 370.,) or be himself a minor, (Rex v. St. Petrox, Dartmouth, 4 T. R. 196.,) or the apprentice be not more than seven years old, (Rex v. Saltren Cald. 444., but see as to parish apprentices, *post* 508,) or put out by the parish officers to a master in another parish or county, (Rex v. St. Nicholas, Notts. 2 T. R. 726,) the binding is good: nor is it material whether the master be of any, or what trade. (Rex v. St. Margaret's, Lincoln, Burr. S. C. 728.) So, though the parent's consent do not appear; because an infant may make a contract for his own benefit. (Newberry v. St. Mary's, Fol. 154.) And the rule is the same where an infant is bound from the workhouse, by the privity of the parish officers who made the agreement, and paid the premium, but did not execute it as a *parish binding*. (Rex v. Arundel, 5 Maul. & Sel. 257.)

But a binding to a *certificate man* confers no settlement, (12 Anne, st. 1. c. 18. s. 2.,) in the place where the certificate is in force, and the act extends to a binding and service with the *widow* of the certificated person. (Rex v. Hampton, 5 T. R. 266.) It also extends to a *service* with a certificated person, where the apprentice has been previously *bound* to one *not* certificated; (Ramsey v. St. Michael's, Southampton, Burr. S. C. 640;) and likewise to the case where the *service* is by agreement or assignment, under another person, if the *binding* is to a certificate man. (Rex v. Hinckley, 4 T. R. 371.)

Term for which bound.] The 5 Eliz. c. 4. directs, that the binding shall be for seven years, and the 43 Eliz. c. 2. enacts, that *male* apprentices shall be bound till they are 24 years of age, (altered by 18 Geo. 3. c. 47. to 21 years,) and *female* till they are 21, or the time of their marriage; but it is held, that these statutes are merely directory, and that indentures not made in conformity thereto are not void, but voidable only, at the option of the parties. Thus a binding for 4 years, (Grey v. Cookson, 16 East, 27.) or till the apprentice is 23, or 21, (Rex v. Chalbury, 1 Bott. 610,) or till the female is 21, omitting the alternative of her marriage, will confer a settlement. (Rex v. St. Petrox, Burr. S. C. 248.) And it is said, that an indenture is good under the act, although it covenants for no certain time. (Rex v. Woolstanton, 1 Const. 606.)

Execution of Indentures.] A father has no power to bind his son apprentice without his assent, which assent must be signified by his execution of the indenture; nor is his adoption of the contract by serving under it, equivalent to execution. In the case of a parish apprentice, a special power is given by statute (43 Eliz.) to parish officers, and there an apprentice may be bound without his assent till he come of age. (Rex v. Amesby, 3 Barn. & Ald. 584.) He may bind himself for seven years, to serve one master for the first four years, and his own father or any other master the last three, to learn two different trades, and this by one indenture, with one stamp only. (Rex v. Louth, 8 Barn. and Cres. 247.) Execution by the apprentice is essential, (except in parish bindings) whether the apprentice be an infant or an adult; but neither the master to whom he is bound, nor the father, or other friend taking such part in the contract, need add his execution. (Rex v. St. Peter's-on-the-Hill, 2 Bott. 367; Rex v. Ribchester, 2 Maul. & Sel. 139. See Execution of Parish Indenture, *post* 508.)

Indenture properly stamped.] The indenture must be properly stamped, according to the premium or *consideration* given, and the particular kind of stamp; and if the sum so paid, or contracted for, be not truly inserted in words at length, the indenture is void, and no settlement is gained. (Rex v. Edgeworth, 3 T. R. 353; Rex v. Chipping Norton, 5 Barn. & Ald. 412, 1 Bott. 545.) If an indenture bind an apprentice to two masters in different trades, to serve part of seven years with the one, and the rest of the term with the other, one stamp suffices. (Rex v. Louth, 8 Barn. & Cres. 247.) And if his friends covenant to maintain and provide him with clothes, this is not such a benefit as is liable to the duty imposed by 8 Anne, c. 9. s. 45; (Rex. v. Leighton, 4 T. R. 732;) nor if the master stipulate for 4*d*. out of every shilling of his earnings. (Rex v. Wantage, 1 East, 691.) And if he is to allow his master two shillings a-week, and to have wages and provide for himself during the term, the indenture does not require the additional stamp charged by 44 Geo. 3. c. 98. sched. A. (Rex v. Bradford, 1 Maul. & Sel. 151.)

Stamp Duties.] It is not very probable that the question as to the requisite amount of the stamp, before the 10th day of October, 1804, will hereafter arise. On that day all former duties upon indentures were repealed, and a new duty was imposed according to the following schedule. (44 Geo. 3. c. 98, sched. A.)

	£.	*s.*	*d.*
Upon every indenture of apprenticeship, where the sum or value given, paid, contracted, or agreed for, did not exceed £10, a duty of	0	15	0
Exceeding £10, and not exceeding £20	1	10	0

	£.		£.	£.	s.	d.
Exceeding	20,	and not exceeding	50	2	10	0
	50		100	5	0	0
	100		300	12	0	0
	300			20	0	0

The above duties continued until the 10th day of October 1808, on which day a new scale of duties came into operation. (48 Geo. 3. c. 149. sched. part 1.)

			£.	s.	d.
Upon apprenticeship, where the premium did not amount to £30.			0	15	0
Where it amounted to	£30, and was under	£50	1	10	0
	50	100	2	10	0
	100	200	5	0	0
	200	300	10	0	0
	300	400	15	0	0
	400	500	20	0	0
	500	600	25	0	0
	600	800	30	0	0
	800	1000	40	0	0
	1000		50	0	0

In the event of there being no premium to the master, then if the indenture did not contain more than 1080 words, there was a duty of 15 shillings.

And if it contained more than that quantity of words, there was a duty of £1 10*s*.

And where there were duplicates, or two parts of such indenture, each part was charged with the duty imposed by this act, in all cases where the duty did not exceed thirty shillings. And where it exceeded that sum, only one part was charged with the *ad valorem* duty, and the other part was charged with a duty of £1 10*s*.

These latter duties were in force till the 31st of August 1815, when the 55 Geo. 3. c. 184 fixed the duties which at the present day are to be paid upon indentures of apprenticeship: as under

			£.	s.	d.
If the premium does not amount to £30			1	0	0
If it amount to	30, but not to	50	2	0	0
	50	100	3	0	0
	100	200	6	0	0
	200	300	12	0	0

			£.	s.	d.
If it amount to	£300, but not to	£400	20	0	0
	400	500	25	0	0
	500	600	30	0	0
	600	800	40	0	0
	800	1000	50	0	0
	1000		60	0	0
And where there is no premium, if the indenture do not contain more than 1080 words, a duty of			1	0	0
Or if it contain more than 1080 words			1	15	0

Duty on Assignments.] An assignment of an apprentice to another master, if by indorsement on the indenture, or other written agreement, must also be stamped as under:

	£.	s.	d.
From 1783 to 1804, with an agreement stamp	0	6	0
—— 1804 to 1808	0	15	0
—— 10th Oct. 1808 to 31st Aug. 1815	0	15	0
But if the indenture contained more than 1080 words	1	10	0

And if a new consideration or premium were given, the same rate of duty as for the original consideration. From 1815 the duty on assignments is charged upon the same plan, where there is a new premium, &c.; or if no premium, then the same duty as on an original binding without premium. The same rules apply to any subsequent assignment.

Serving another during the Term.] How far he may gain a settlement by any other means, whilst the indenture remains in force, is fully stated by Lord Kenyon, who says, "It is clear, that in general an apprentice is not capable of contracting the relation of servant to any other master until the end of the term for which he was bound. But it is equally clear, that if the master and apprentice put an end to the apprenticeship by mutual consent, it is the same as if the indentures had never been executed, and the latter may gain a settlement by hiring and service with any other master, before the expiration of the time which he was bound to serve as an apprentice. Then there is a third case: that where the apprentice leaves his master and enters into the service of another, if the indentures still subsist, he is not *sui juris;* but is incapable of gaining a settlement by serving another master, unless he serve with the *consent* of his former master, and in such case he gains a settlement, not as an hired servant, but as an apprentice." (Rex v. Chipping Warden, 8 T. R. 108.) Service to another with the master's consent, being a service to the master.

Parish Apprentices—Stamp.] Indentures and all other instruments for placing out poor children apprentices, by, or at the sole charge of any parish, &c. or public charity, since 10th Oct. 1804, (and before that period a duty of 1*s.* only, or if the premium exceeded 10*l.* a duty of 11*s.*) or pursuant to the 32 Geo. 3, passed for the further regulation of parish apprentices, are exempt from all stamp duties, by the present act. (55 Geo. 3. c. 184.) The prior stamp act, (44 Geo. 3. c. 98,) contains the like exemptions; and where an apprentice was placed out with the consent of trustees of certain funds bequeathed for such purposes, and the recited premium was paid by *them,* but they did *not execute,* the case was held to be within the exemption. (Rex v. Quainton, 2 Maul. & Sel. 338.) But where the indenture recited that the premium was paid out of a charitable fund *belonging to the parish,* and the master proved that it was paid by the parish officers, who *said* at the time, it came out of such fund, but there was no proof, *in fact,* that it came out of such fund, it was held that this declaration was not sufficient evidence that it came from such fund, and the indenture being without stamp no settlement was gained. (Rex v. Skeffington, 3 Barn. & Ald. 382.) And Bayley, J. in this last case, observed, that an indenture of apprenticeship is no evidence of the facts recited in it; if it were, the inconvenience would occur, that in order to defraud the revenue, a party might always recite that the premium was paid out of a public charity, whether the fact were so or not. But Holroyd, J. is reported to have said, "If the recital in the indenture of apprenticeship, and the declaration of the parish officers, had been the only evidence of the fact of payment of the premium, I should have been of opinion, that there was sufficient evidence also, that it was paid out of a public charity. But on looking at this case, it is clear to me, that the fact was proved substantially by the master." (Rex v. Skeffington, 3 Barn. & Ald. 386.)

Binding Parish Apprentices.] "The churchwardens and overseers, or the greater part of them, by the assent of two justices, one of whom must be of the quorum, may bind any such children, whose parents they shall adjudge not able to maintain them, to be apprentices where they shall see convenient till such man child shall come to the age of 21 years, (so altered by 18 Geo. 3. c. 47,) and such woman child to the age of 21, or marriage; the same to be as effectual to all purposes as if such child were of full age, and by indenture of covenant, bound him or herself. (43 Eliz. c. 2. s. 5.)

Although it is required, that one of the justices must be of the quorum, it is not necessary on any occasion to state that he is so. (See 26 Geo. 2. c. 27.) But if it is *proved* that the fact is otherwise, it vitiates the indenture, and a binding for a term different to that pointed out by the act, or for an unlimited period, does not make the indenture void, but voidable only. (Rex v. Chalbury, 1 Bott. 610; Rex. v. Woolstanton, Id.)

Parties to Parish Indentures.] The parish officers *must* be parties to a parish indenture; but to obviate some objections which had arisen, (see Rex v. All Saints, Derby, 13 East, 143,) it was enacted by 51 Geo. 3. c. 80, " that all indentures for the binding of parish apprentices which have been heretofore executed and signed by two persons only, acting or purporting to act in the capacity of churchwardens as well as overseers of the poor, and also all such indentures as shall have been so signed, shall be considered as good, valid, and effectual, as if the same had been executed and signed by distinct persons as churchwardens, and distinct persons as overseers." Under this act the signing by two parish officers, one being both churchwarden and overseer, was held valid; (Rex v. St. Margaret's, Leicester, 2 Barn. and Ald. 200;) and under the 13 & 14 Car. 2. c. 12, an indenture executed by the overseers of a township which has *no churchwardens*, has been held valid. (Rex v. Nantwich, 16 East, 228.)

And still further, to prevent objections of this kind from being set up, it is provided by 54 Geo. 3. c. 107. s. 1, that all indentures for the binding of poor apprentices, heretofore or hereafter signed and executed by a person or persons, who at the time of his or their signing and executing *acted as* churchwarden or churchwardens, chapelwarden or chapelwardens of the *township*, *hamlet*, or *chapelry*, binding such poor apprentice, shall be as valid and effectual as if the same had been signed by a person or persons actually sworn into such office: provided such person or persons shall have been sworn into the office of churchwarden of the *parish*, wherein the township, &c., is contained, or into the office of churchwarden of such township, &c. (See Rex v. Crowland, 8 Barn. & Cres. 711.)

And the 2nd section of the act renders indentures signed and executed by overseers and churchwardens of such townships, &c. as valid and effectual, as if signed and executed by the officers of the *parish* in which the township, &c. is situate. And by 1 & 2 Geo. 4. c. 32, parish indentures and certificates signed before 28th May 1821, by one church or chapelwarden, *purporting* to *act* in that capacity for any parish, township, &c. in *England*, for which two had been formerly appointed, shall be valid and effectual as if executed by one or more *legally* appointed.

Execution of Parish Indenture.] Where the apprenticeship is voluntary, the execution by the apprentice is essential, (*ante* 502); but the law has given parish officers the power of putting out pauper children as apprentices, and, therefore, it is not necessary that the pauper should be an executing party to the deed. If the master and parish officers sign the indenture, though the apprentice omits to do so, the instrument will be valid; (St. Nicholas, Notts. 2 T. R. 726;) for his consent shall be *implied* if he lives under the binding, even where he was originally carried to the master by the parent without his consent. (Rex v. Woolstanton, 1 Const, 606.)

The churchwardens and overseers of a united parish, for which a guardian has been appointed under 22 Geo. 3. c. 83, are still competent to bind parish apprentices as before, and it is not necessary in this case that they should sign the indentures. (Rex v. Lutterworth, 3 Barn. and Cres. 487; 5 Dowl. & Ryl. 343.)

Assent of two Justices.] The 43 Eliz. further requires the assent of two justices, given in each other's presence, to the binding, though it need not be executed either by the master, (Rex v. Fleet, 2 Bott. 371,) or by the apprentice. (Rex v. St. Nicholas, Notts, 2 T. R. 726. 2 Bott. 373.) But if one justice sign alone, and is present when the other signs, that will suffice. (Rex v. Winwick, 8 T. R. 454.) The assent seems to be properly signified by the signing, and the master, having executed the counterpart, is not at liberty to give evidence that at the time of the execution it was signed by one justice only. (Rex v. Saltren, Cald. 444.) The justices may describe themselves in signing as "justices of the county aforesaid," the name of the county appearing in the body of the indenture. (Rex v. Hinckley, 1 Barn. & Ald. 273.)

But neither the assent of justices, nor the execution by parish officers, is necessary where the minor (though a pauper at the time,) is *not* put out by the parish; although the officers interfere and pay the premium, but the infant with the parents' consent binds himself. (Rex v. Arundel, 5 Maul. & Sel. 257; Rex v. St. Mary's, Reading, 1 Bott. 609.)

Regulations in Parish Bindings.] The last statute, (56 Geo. 3. c. 139,) passed on this subject, and which governs all bindings after 1st Oct. 1816, contains some new and important regulations to be observed in the binding of parish apprentices. The 7th section forbids the binding of any child under nine years of age, as a parish apprentice; and the act expressly provides by s. 5, that no settlement shall be gained unless the *order* be made, and the indenture be signed, as is directed by the statute; and by s. 9, any assignment of the apprentice's services must be made with the consent of two justices, as directed by 32 Geo. 3. c. 57, or the settlement will be defeated.

Inquiry as to Master, Distance, &c.] Sect. 1 provides, that the child before being bound shall be taken before two justices, who shall inquire into the propriety of binding the child to the person proposed, his character and circumstances, and may examine the parents of the child, and consider whether it is fit that the child shall be placed out at a greater or less distance from the parish, the means of communication therewith, &c.; and if they are satisfied on all these points, they shall make *an order*, declaring, that such person is a fit person to whom such child may be properly bound an apprentice; which order shall be delivered to the overseers, as their warrant for binding such child, and which order shall *be referred to in the indenture*, by the date thereof, and the names of the justices: after which the justices are to sign their allowance of such indenture before it is executed by any of the parties thereto. But the binding is not to be more than forty miles from the parish to which the child belongs, unless it be in the same county: except the parish be more than forty miles from London, in which case the special circumstances must be stated in the order.

If the justices, on inquiring into the fitness of the person to become the master of the pauper, are imposed upon, that will not destroy the settlement. Thus, where the grandfather and mother of a pauper having colluded together, and fraudulently imposed the grandfather upon the justices and parish officers as a proper master for the pauper, it was held, that as there had been no fraud on the part of the parish officers, a settlement was gained. (R. v. Great Sheepy, 8 Barn. & Cres. 74.)

It has been held, that the part of the act which requires that the order of justices shall be referred to in the indenture by the date thereof, is *compulsory*, and that an indenture in which the date of the order is omitted is void, and no settlement is gained by serving under it. (R. v. Bawbergh, 2 Barn. & Cres. 222; 3 Dowl. & Ryl. 338.)

Binding into another County.] Sect. 2 provides, that where the apprentice is to be bound into another county, the indenture shall be allowed by two justices of that county, as well as the two justices of the county from which he is sent; but *previous* notice must be given to the overseers of the place where it is intended he shall serve; and such notice shall be proved before any such justice of the county into which the apprentice is bound, shall sign such indenture, unless one of such overseers shall attend such justice, and admit the notice. It also provides, that no indenture shall be allowed by any justice of the peace for the county into which such child shall be bound, who shall be engaged in the same business, &c. in which the person to whom such child shall be bound, is engaged.

Where a pauper settled in the parish of N. C. in the county of Nottingham, was, pursuant to an order of two justices of the county, bound apprentice to A. B. of another parish, in a borough situate in the same county, but having justices who had exclusive jurisdiction therein, the indenture was allowed by the two county justices; but *no notice was given to the overseers* of the parish in the borough, of the intention to bind such apprentice, nor did any of them attend before the county justices who allowed the indenture, and admit such notice. It was held by three judges, Abbott, C. J. dissentiente, that under this act the indenture was void for want of such notice, and that no settlement was gained by serving under it. (R. v. Newark-upon-Trent, 3 Barn. & Cres. 59.)

Thus a two-fold allowance will be requisite wheresoever the master's parish and the parish of the apprentice happen to be under the general jurisdiction of *different* justices; and the second allowance must be by the justices of the local district, within which the master's parish is situate, whether it be in the *same* or a *different* county; but if the two parishes happen to be in the *same* county, and the parish of the apprentice is in a local district, and that of the master in the county at large, the second allowance must be by the justices of the county. (Per Abbott, C. J. ib. 83.)

It is necessary that the magistrates of the two counties should be different persons, and it will not satisfy the statute if the indenture is allowed by two justices having jurisdiction in both counties; that is, the indenture in such case must be allowed by four justices, two of them being of the county in which the binding parish is situate, and the other two, of the county in which the parish wherein the apprentice is intended to serve, is situate. (R. v. Shipton, 8 Barn. & Cres. 772.)

Sect. 3, the allowance by two justices of the county shall be valid and effectual, although the service is to be in a corporate town, having justices of its own.

Sect. 4, directs that cities, &c. which are counties of themselves, shall, as to distances to which apprentices may be bound, be considered as part of the county in which they are locally situated.

Binding at Parish Expense, &c.] By Sect. 11, after the 1st of October, 1816, (when the act is appointed to commence) no indenture, by reason of which any expense *whatever* shall at any time be incurred by the public parochial funds, shall be valid, unless approved by two justices, under their hands and seals, according to the 43 Eliz. and of this act.

This enactment does not relate merely to a premium advanced by the parish officers; therefore, where, before the execution of an indenture, the master said the intended apprentice should have better clothes, upon which the apprentice applied to the parish officers, who agreed to give him £2. on the execution of the indenture for the purpose of buying clothes, which they did accordingly; it was held, that this was an expense incurred by reason of an indenture of apprenticeship, within the meaning of the above section, and that, consequently, the assent of two justices was required. (R. v. Matteshall, 8 Barn. & Cres. 733.)

The parish officers were not parties to the indenture in the above or in the following case, though as an expense was incurred by the parish in both instances, they were within the act. The point determined in the following case was, that under this act the approval of the justices must be under hands *and seals*, and that an indenture approved under their *hands only* was void, and not voidable, and that no settlement was gained under it. (R. v. Stoke Damerel, 7 Barn. & Cres. 563; 1 Man. & Ryl. 458.)

Apprentices to Sea Service.] Any boy of the age of ten years or upwards, who is chargeable to any parish, or whose parents are so, or who begs for alms, may be bound by two justices, or by chief officers of any corporation, or by the churchwardens and overseers of parishes, or overseers of townships, with the consent of such justices or chief officers, to any British subject who is master or owner of any vessel belonging to some port of England, or Wales, or to Berwick-upon-Tweed. (2 & 3 Anne, c. 6.)

The binding may be till the boy attain the age of twenty-one: his age must be inserted in the indenture, and the indenture is to be registered by the collector at the port to which the master belongs, and the counterpart sent to the parish officers. The parish is to pay down to the master fifty shillings for the boy's outfit, and he is not to be liable to be impressed till he is eighteen years of age.

Apprentices to Chimne-ysweepers.] Churchwardens and overseers, with the consent of two justices, or of the parents, may bind or put out any boy of the age of eight years, who is in like manner chargeable, or a beggar, as above, to be an apprentice to any chimney-sweeper, until such boy attain the age of sixteen; the age to be inserted in the indenture. (28 Geo. 3. c. 48.)

All indentures and bargains, made after the passing of this act, for taking any boys under eight years old, as apprentices or servants, employed as climbing-boys or chimney-sweepers, shall be void, and the person so keeping or employing such boy, shall forfeit, not exceeding £10. nor less than £5. (Id. s. 4.)

In a late case it was argued that this statute only applied to *parish* indentures, and that the indenture of a boy five years of age, made between the father, the boy, and the master, was *voidable* only; and that by a service under it, a settlement was gained. But the Court thought the act applied to all apprenticeships to chimney-sweepers, whether voluntary, or by the parish, and that consequently no settlement was gained. (R. v. Hipswell, 8 Barn. & Cres. 466.)

Assignment of Parish Apprentice.] A parish apprentice might before the 1st of October, 1816, (as a common apprentice might at all times, and still may,) be transferred to a new master, by what is called a particular consent of the former master, or in any more formal manner. But since the 56 Geo. 3. c. 139, a parish apprentice can only be assigned by the consent of two justices. This assignment is to be made in the manner prescribed by 32 Geo. 3. c. 57, which is directed to be by indorsement of the new master's acceptance of the apprentice, upon the indenture, or by other writing, by which he becomes bound by all the covenants; the former master making the assignment by the same instrument, with the consent of two justices, testified under their hands. The 32 Geo. 3. c. 57, did not affect the question of settlement, which might still be gained, though the act was not complied with, (R. v. Barleston, 5 Barn. & Ald. 780,) its only object being to make the new master liable to the covenants of the indenture, where a limited premium had been given; but the 56 Geo. 3. c. 139, which applies to *all* parish apprentices, whether a premium be given or not, also provides that no settlement shall be gained unless the assignment is sanctioned under the hands of two justices: and the *putting away* a parish apprentice to any other, or discharging him from the service without such consent, is unlawful; for which a penalty not exceeding £10. is imposed by s. 10 of the act.

Thus, where the master of a parish apprentice, not having work sufficient for him, proposed to him to go to a farm occupied by the master's sister, and the pauper assented to the proposal, and agreed with the sister to work there for a twelvemonth for meat and drink, and he worked for her four years and four months, during the third and fourth years of which period he received wages; it was held first, that no settlement was gained by the service with the sister, the service not being under the indentures; and secondly, that there had been a *putting away* of the apprentice, without the consent of the justices within the meaning of the 56 Geo. 3. c. 139. s. 9, and that the pauper did not, by his service with the sister, gain any settlement by hiring and service. (R. v. Shipton, 8 Barn. & Cres. 88.)

Hands and Seals of Justices.] As already observed, the statute just cited requires certain forms to be observed, in the execution, and allowance of indentures of apprenticeship, in which parishes are concerned. The following case explains the circumstances under which magistrates, in such bindings, must sign and *seal*, as distinguished from those in which their signing is sufficient.

The pauper, Jane Bishop, in 1818 was bound an apprentice by the parish officers of Tedburn, St. Mary, to one Henry Belworthy: the indenture by which she was so bound was made in pursuance of a previous order of two justices, to which reference was made by its date, and was duly executed by the said parish officers and the master. An allowance thereof was written at the foot, which was signed by two justices, but was not under seal. On occasion of this binding, an expense of seventeen shillings was incurred by the parochial funds of the parish of Tedburn, St. Mary; namely, seven shillings as the costs of préparing the indenture, and ten shillings which were given to the master of the pauper.

The Court, after hearing the argument upon the case, held that where an apprentice is bound by indenture, to which the parish officers *are parties*, an allowance by the justices, under the 56 Geo. 3. c. 139, will be sufficient, if it be under the *hands* (without the seals) of the justices. But where, upon the binding, a part of the premium, or *any expense* in respect of the indenture, comes out of the parish funds, and the parish officers are *not parties* to the indenture, the allowance in conformity with the above act must be under the *seals* as well as the hands of the justices.

The judgment of the Court was delivered by Mr. Justice Bayley, who, after stating the facts, said,—" We have considered the case, and we have consulted with my Lord Tenterden, who concurs in opinion with us. We think the ten first sections of the act apply to cases where the parish officers are parties to the indenture, and that the 11th section is applicable only to cases in which they do not join in the indenture. This has been intimated, but not expressly decided, in former cases. The preamble to the 11th section shows this by the use of the word " clandestinely." (The learned judge read the preamble.) And to remedy the mischief there described, it provided, that there should be an allowance by justices, and that their allowance should be under their hands and seals. The former ten sections, which were evidently confined to parish bindings, provided for an allowance merely under the hands of the justices. Therefore, the only case to which that section is applicable, is where the parish officers, by not joining in the indenture, may be considered as binding the apprentice clandestinely." (R. v. St. Paul, Exeter, M. T. 1829. MSS.)

Assignment and new Indenture.] The principle of a service under another by assignment or permission, is, that it is constructively a service under the original master; it must, therefore, be in the same trade, with the express consent of the master, he having at the time power to control the apprentice; and it must be under the indentures, so that he is in effect still serving as an apprentice under the original contract. (R. v. Whitchurch, 1 Barn. & Cres. 574; R. v. Shipton, 8 Barn. & Cres. 88.) Thus, where the pauper, or parish apprentice, bound till he should be twenty-one, served about eight years, when it was agreed that he should go to C., who was of the same trade, to serve him the remainder of the term, and C. agreed to pay his master 1*s*. 6*d*. per week during that period, and the pauper accordingly went to C. and continued serving him with his master's express consent, and after he had been there three weeks, the original indenture was given up by his master to C., and a *new indenture* of apprenticeship was made between the pauper, his father-in-law, his master, and C., without reference to the original indenture, and for a longer period than the original term, and containing some provisions differing from those in the original indenture: it was held, that the pauper did not gain a settlement by serving C. as upon a constructive service, under the first indenture, with his master's consent, although C. continued to pay his master the 1*s*. 6*d*. per week under the agreement. (R. v. Ecclesfield, 6 Maul. & Sel. 173; R. v. Christowe, 11 East, 95.)

Assignment on Death of Master.] The 32 G. 3. c. 57, provides, that in case of the death of the master, two justices may, upon application being made within three months afterwards by the widow, son, daughter, brother, sister, executor, or administrator, by indorsement on the indenture or counterpart, order the apprentice to serve the remainder of his term with any one of such persons making the application; such person having lived with, and been part of, the family at the time of the death of the master, as they shall think fit: the person at the same time declaring his acceptance of such order by signing his name thereto, upon which the relation of master and apprentice is to subsist, the same as if the original binding had been to such person. But if no such application be made within three calendar months from the death, or being made, the justices should not think fit to transfer the service as aforesaid, the indenture shall be at an end, the same as if the term thereof had fully expired. But this regulation is only to extend to parish apprentices living in the family of their masters at the time of the death. (s. 5.)

Upon this latter provision it has been held, that where a parish apprentice served the son of the mistress to whom he was originally bound, she having given up her farm to her son, and continued with *him* till *her* death, he could not gain a settlement in another parish by serving another person, with the son's consent given after the mother's decease. For the act recites, that the service is at an end upon the mistress's death; and service by which a settlement is to be acquired, according to section 5, means a service with a subsequent master or mistress, who becomes so by the provisions of the act; it is the service under the *authorized* substitution that the act applies to. (R. v. Sheepshead, 15 East, 59.)

Inhabitancy by Apprentice.] There must be an inhabiting for forty days under the indenture. The inhabitancy is where the apprentice *lodges*, and the settlement is gained there, though the service be in another parish. (St. John v. St. James, Bishop's Kenny, 1 Stra. 594.) And the settlement is gained where the apprentice lodges *the last forty days* of the apprenticeship, even although he do no service during that time; (R. v. Charles, Burr, S. C. 707;) unless he lodge merely on account of illness, (R. v. Barmby-in-the-Marsh, 7 East, 381,) for the lodging must be for the purposes of the apprenticeship. But if he perform services generally, for, and at the command of his master, in the parish where he sleeps on account of illness, though he do not actually work at his trade, he gains a settlement there. (R. v. Stratford-upon-Avon, 11 East, 176.)

Where an apprentice to a barge-master, who had slept thirty-five nights in the master's parish during his service, went with his master on a voyage to London, where the master absconded, and never returned during the period of the indentures; but the apprentice returned in the barge to the master's parish, and remained on board two days, when, in consequence of illness, he was, by direction of his master's wife, conveyed to the poor-house, she being unable to accommodate him in her own house, but was maintained there entirely at her expense, in the expectation of her husband's return, during three weeks, while he continued there; it was held, that his residence in the poor-house, at the expense of the master's wife, was virtually a residence in the master's house, under a continuance of the contract, and that the apprentice acquired a settlement in the master's parish. (R. v. Foulness, 6 Maul. & Sel. 351.)

Sleeping Saturday and Sunday Nights.] If the apprentice be allowed to sleep at his father's, in another parish, on Saturdays and

Sundays, he gains no settlement there in consequence. (R. v. Ilkestone, 4 Barn. & Cres. 64, 6 Dowl. & Ryl. 64.) But where the apprentice worked with his master during the week in one parish, and returned with him from their work to his master's house in another parish on Saturday evenings, where he slept on Saturday and Sunday evenings, he gained a settlement by inhabitancy under the indenture in the latter parish. The case of R. v. Ilkestone is very distinguishable from the present. There the apprentice was allowed by his master, as a matter of indulgence to go to his *father's* every Saturday, and to sleep there every Saturday and Sunday, and it was expressly found there that the apprentice during those periods of absence did no work for his master. Here the apprentice passes the Saturday and Sunday nights at his *master's* house, and on the Monday again accompanies him to his work, having been in the interval under the eye and control of his master, and, for aught that appears, performing all his biddings. (R. v. Warden, 2 Man. & Ryl. 27.)

Where the master and apprentice were both in the local militia at B. during the last forty days, the apprentice was holden to have gained his settlement in B. (R. v. Chelmsford, 3 Barn. & Ald. 411.)

Residence on board Ship.] Apprentices to seafaring men, lodging on board ship, gain their settlement in that parish in which the ship lay during the last entire forty days they slept on board. (St. Mary Colechurch v. Radcliffe, 1 Stra. 60.) It may be doubtful whether this rule holds, if the ship go into the port for a mere *casual* purpose, as to repair a leak, or the like; (R. v. Barton Bradstock, Burr. S. C. 537;) but if the ship go there for the purposes of trade, or the like, a residence there will confer a settlement in the parish to which such port belongs.

Residence and Service must concur.] But where the apprentice is absent from the master, the service must be actually or *constructively* going on, to enable an apprentice to gain a settlement during that time; (R. v. Brotton, 4 Barn. & Ald. 84;) but, it suffices if he is serving another person with his master's consent. (R. v. Iddesleigh, 4 Dowl. & Ryl. 332.) But where an apprentice, not being wanted, went back to school, it was holden that his residence at school did not gain a settlement, for the service did not continue while he was at school, and the apprenticeship was suspended for the time. (R. v. St. Mary Bredin, Canterbury, 2 Barn. & Ald. 382.) So a mere *casual* residence will not gain a settlement, as where an apprentice, who had been hired out by his master to a person in another parish, where he slept, and the service to such other person being determined, returned and slept one night in his master's parish, without any intention of returning into his master's service, and without his master's knowledge, and in fact never did return to his master's service; (R. v. Smarden, 13 East, 452;) or where an apprentice left his master's parish and service, and went and slept in a parish where he was allowed occasionally to sleep before, (R. v. Ribchester, 2 Maul. & Sel. 135,) it was holden in these cases, that the apprentice gained no settlement in the parish he slept in last.

And if the apprentice serve another, under a *general licence* from his master to serve whom he chooses, (R. v. Holy Trinity, 3 T. R. 605,) there being no express assent of the master to the particular service, (R. v. Whitchurch, 1 Barn. & Cres. 574; 2 Dowl. & Ryl. 845,) or serves another with the *knowledge* of the master, but without his actual *consent*, (R. v. Ideford, Burr. S. C. 821; see a note on this case, Cald. 129,) no settlement is gained. An apprentice bound to one who lives in one parish, with intent to serve another who lives in another parish, and he serves the latter accordingly, gains a settlement in the parish of the latter; (Holy Trinity v. Shoreditch, 1 Stra. 10;) and the rule is the same if the indenture be assigned. (St. Olave's v. All-Hallows, 1 Sess. Cas. 215; R. v. Barnsley, 1 Maul. & Sel. 377.)

Consecutive Days' Residence.] It will be seen by the previous cases, that forty days' residence *consecutively*, is not necessary. (See also, R. v. Cirencester, 1 Stra. 579.) If the apprentice live with his master forty days at A. and forty days at B., and then one day at A., he is settled in A. (R. v. Brighthelmstone, 5 T. R. 188.) And although the forty days' residence must be within a year to give a settlement by hiring and service, (see R. v. Denham, 1 Maul. & Sel. 221,) the rule does not apply to cases of apprenticeship.

Discharging from Indentures.] The Court of King's Bench has no authority to discharge an apprentice from his indentures. (Exparte Gill, 7 East, 376.) But the indentures may be discharged,—1st, by application of either party to two justices, or to the quarter sessions;—2nd, by death of the master;—3rd, the apprentice attaining his majority;—4th, by consent.

Discharge by Justices.] The power given to two justices over indentures, is created by 20 Geo. 2. c. 19; and before the 1st Oct. 1816, extended only to *parish* apprentices, and to any other apprentice, upon whose binding no larger premium was paid than £5, (altered now by 4 Geo. 4. c. 29, to £25.) The 3rd section enacts, that in such cases, upon complaint by the apprentice, of any misusage, cruelty, or ill-treatment by his master, &c., they may summon such master; and, upon proof upon oath of the complaint to their satisfaction, may discharge the indentures by warrant or certificate under their hands and seals, without fees.

Sect. 4, gives the like power, in case of complaint by the master, &c., concerning any miscarriage or ill-behaviour by the apprentice, to punish the latter by commitment to the house of correction and hard labour, not exceeding one calendar month, or by discharging him in manner and form aforesaid.

It has been determined upon this section, that although the complaint must be verified upon *oath*, it need not be the oath of the master, &c., who may know nothing of the facts themselves. (Finley v. Jowle, 12 East, 248.) It has likewise been held, that this act is not repealed by 6 Geo. 3. c. 28. s. 21, which empowers justices, when an apprentice absents himself at any time thereafter, when he shall be found, if within seven years after the expiration of his term, to order him to serve his said master for so long as he shall have absconded, unless he makes satisfaction for the loss sustained thereby; the remedy by this statute being cumulative. (Gray v. Cookson, 16 East, 13.)

An appeal is given, except against any order of commitment, to the next general quarter sessions; but no certiorari is allowed. By the 33 Geo. 3. c. 55, justices may fine masters for ill using their apprentices, whether bound by the parish or otherwise, where the premium does not exceed £10, extended by 4 Geo. 4. c. 29, to £25. And by 32 Geo. 3. c. 57. s. 8, two justices may discharge any *parish* apprentice with whom not more than £5 premium has been given, upon the master becoming insolvent or unable to maintain his apprentice.

Discharge by Sessions.] The 5 Eliz. c. 4. s. 35, gives a more extensive power to the sessions in like cases, though it directs that the first application may be to one justice, or mayor, or other head officer of the place, who is to endeavour to compound the matter between the parties; but if he fail therein, he is to take bond for the appearance of the master at the next sessions, which means, sessions having jurisdiction where the *master lives*, although the apprentice is bound elsewhere (R. v. Collingburne, 1 Stra. 663.) The power of discharge is confined in counties to four justices at the least, assembled at a general sessions; and if the order be made at a private sessions, it may be set aside. (Anon. Skin. 98.)

The sessions possess jurisdiction, although no application has been made to one justice, &c. (R. v. Johnson, 1 Salk. 68; R. v. Easman, 2 Stra. 1014.) And the sessions may proceed in the master's absence, if he has been duly summoned. The discharge may be upon the complaint of either party, but the sessions must set forth some cause in their order. (Id. Ditton's case, 2 Salk. 490.)

Form of the Order.] If an order merely states that the master "misused his apprentice," or "used him unkindly," or "refused in court to take him again," &c., it does not show a sufficient ground for his discharge; neither is it enough that he has married without his master's consent; and there is no power to discharge for sickness, (R. v. Hales Owen, 1 Stra. 99,) though idiotcy is a sufficient ground for such discharge. (Anon. Skin. 114. Burn's Justice, "Apprentice.")

Money given with the apprentice may be ordered to be returned upon such discharge. (R. v. Johnson, 1 Salk. 68; 2 Salk. 491; see Bac. Ab. C. "Master and Servant.")

The order of sessions must be under the hands and seals of four justices, and enrolled as the act directs, or the superior court will set it aside. (R. v. Hales Owen, 1 Stra. 99.)

Discharge by Death, &c.] The relation of master and apprentice is determinable by the death of either, though the latter may continue the relation with the master's representatives, at the option of the parties, and his executors are liable upon his covenants if they have assets. (R. v. Peck, Salk. 66.) But the 32 Geo. 3. c. 57. s. 2, provides, that the covenant for the maintenance of *parish* apprentices with whom no more than £5 shall be given, shall continue in force no longer than three months after the death of the master, &c., during which time the apprentice shall continue to serve the executors as their apprentice: but if within that period the indentures are not assigned, &c., (see *ante*, p. 513,) they are at an end.

Discharging voidable Indenture.] An indenture which is voidable for some defect, is dissoluble in any of the ways in which a valid indenture may be determined, that is, by cancelling, delivering up, or by judicial sentence. It may also be avoided by some act of either of the parties, declaratory of his election, to avail himself of the defect. Thus, persons bound for a time extending beyond their minority, may upon attaining the age of twenty-one, put an end to the indentures, unless bound to serve beyond it under the authority of an act of parliament. (Exparte Davis, 5 T. R. 715.) But in all these cases of avoiding indentures on account of some defect therein, the apprentice must regularly declare his intention, during the service, to do so; and an apprentice who is brought before a magistrate for running away from his master's service, cannot then allege his right to avoid the indentures, in justification of his absconding, for he cannot make use of his offence in order to avoid the punishment that attends it. (R. v. Evered, Cald. 26; Gray v. Cookson, 16 East, 28.)

A minor is competent to elect to dissolve a voidable indenture.

Discharge by Consent.] If the apprentice bound by a valid indenture is an infant, his master cannot discharge the indentures by his consent *alone;* (R. v. Austrey, Burr. S. C. 441; R. v. Hindringham, 6 T. R. 558;) but it may be done with his father's consent, or any person in *loco parentis.* (R. v. St. Mary Kallendar, Burr. S. C. 274.)

In the case of parish apprentices under age, the parish officers, as well as the other parties, must concur; (R. v. Langham, Cald. 126; R. v. Heddington, Burr. S. C. 766;) but the master and *parish apprentice* of *full age,* may cancel the indentures by agreement. (R. v. Harberton, 1 T. R. 139.)

Manner of discharging.] The discharge of indentures should be by actual cancellation, as by drawing a pen through them, or tearing the names and seals off; (R. v. Spaunton, Burr. S. C. 801;) or by exchange, or mutually delivering them up, either with or without an indorsement. (R. v. Mountsorrell, 3 Maul. & Sel. 497.)

But the discharge has been held complete, in several instances, where the indentures *have remained* undefaced with the master. Thus where he receives money of the apprentice of *full age* to vacate them, the relation is dissolved; (R. v. Devonshire, Cald. 32;) so where a *parish* apprentice, bound till he should be twenty-four, ran away a month before he was twenty-one, and the father, at his instance, some months afterwards bought out the remainder of his time, and took a receipt for it, but left the indentures in the master's hands, it was held that they were put an end to. (R. v. Harberton, 1 T. R. 139.) But unless they are actually cancelled, or the master agrees unconditionally to give them up for a good and valid *consideration,* they still subsist; (R. v. Skeffington, 3 Barn. & Ald. 382;) and in a recent case, where the master verbally agreed upon being paid £3 to set his apprentice at liberty, and to give him up his indenture, it was held that the indenture was not thereby discharged so as to fix the settlement of the apprentice in the parish where he slept last, before the making of such agreement. (R. v. Warden, 2 Man. & Ryl. 24.)

If the agreement is conditional, the indentures remain in force till the condition is performed, although the apprentice is treated in the interim as one *sui juris,* uncontrolled by the indentures. (R. v. Chipping Warden, 8 T. R. 108; R. v. Shebbear, 1 East, 73.) And a mere agreement, without sufficient consideration, does not put an end to the indentures. (R. v. Bow, 4 Maul. & Sel. 383.)

SECTION IV. BY RENTING A TENEMENT.

Period of the Renting.] In order to discover whether a person has acquired a settlement by renting a tenement, it is necessary in the first place, to ascertain the *date* of such renting, as there are three several periods in which the conditions necessary to obtain a settlement by this means, differ from each other.

The subject therefore divides itself into three parts: first, a renting before the 59 Geo. 3. c. 50, that is, before the 2nd July 1819; secondly, a renting under that statute, or within that date and the 22nd of June 1825, which is the date of the 6 Geo. 4. c. 57; and, thirdly, rentings at any time since the passing of this latter statute, which regulates the mode of acquiring this species of settlement to the present time.

Renting, &c. anterior to 2nd July 1819.] The 13 & 14 Car. 2. c. 12. s. 1, made it lawful for justices to remove, within forty days, all such persons as came to settle upon tenements of less *yearly value* than £10, provided they were likely to be chargeable to the parish.

Thus a person, by remaining forty days in a parish, as an occupier of a tenement of the yearly value of £10, gained a settlement; and if he afterwards removed to another parish, and was found likely to become chargeable before he had resided forty days there also, he might be removed to the former parish, which was his last place of settlement.

Who might gain such Settlement.] With the exceptions stated, (*ante*, p. 483,) any person might acquire a settlement in this way: thus, a soldier who is not *sui juris* to make a contract of service, (R. v. Brighthelmstone, 1 Barn. & Ald. 270,) and a foreigner who is incompetent to hold a dwelling-house, or shop, by lease, might gain a settlement by occupying a tenement of the proper yearly value. (R. v. Eastbourne, 4 East, 103.)

A certificate man, who is disabled in many ways, may, by taking a *lease* of a tenement of the annual value of £10, gain a settlement. (9 & 10 W. 3. c. 11.) And although the terms of this act are more precise than those of 13 & 14 Car. 2. c. 12, yet the two are to be considered together, being in *pari materia*, and no distinction is to be made either as to the nature of the tenement, or of the taking thereof. (R. v. Croft, 3 Barn. & Ald. 178.)

But by the general turnpike act, (3 Geo. 4. c. 126. s. 51,) no toll-collector, or renter of tolls, or apprentice, or servant of such collector or renter, shall, by residing in the toll-house, gain a settlement.

Before the passing of this act it was held, that a person might gain a settlement in the parish where he resided, and rented a tenement of above £10 per annum, although his residence was in a turnpike house, as the toll-collector's servant; as the 13 Geo. 3. c. 84. s. 56, did not extend the provision to servants and apprentices of toll-gate keepers; (R. v. Denbigh, 5 East, 333;) and the collector of bridge tolls was also held to be exempt from the prohibition. (R. v. Bubwith, 1 Maul. & Sel. 514.)

So prisoners in the King's Bench Prison, or within the rules thereof, (23 Geo. 3. c. 23. s. 1,) or in any other prison; or being confined or detained as prisoners within any district, (54 Geo. 3. c. 170. s. 4,) shall not gain a settlement by renting a tenement.

And where A. took a tenement, and, after having occupied it a week, was carried to prison, but his family remained therein more than forty days, it was held that no settlement was gained. (R. v. St. George the Martyr, Southwark, 7 T. R. 466.)

Persons residing within the forest of Alice Holt, cannot thereby gain a settlement. (52 Geo. 3. c. 72. s. 8.)

Nature of the Tenement before 1819.] For the purposes of obtaining a settlement under the 13 & 14 Car. 2, a liberal construction has been given to the word tenement. Lord Kenyon upon this subject says, " Any thing is a tenement which is a *profit out of land;* (R. v. Tolpuddle, 4 T. R. 675;) and an incorporeal tenement would confer a settlement, (R. v. Chipping Norton, 5 East, 242,) or uses, offices, dignities which concern lands, &c., because all these savour of realty.

Thus renting a rabbit-warren, although the party have no right except that of entering to kill the rabbits, (R. v. Piddletrenthide, 3 T. R. 772,) or the renting of a fishery, (R. v. Old Arlesford, 1 T. R. 358,) or the taking of sand or gravel from a river, (R. v. All Saints, Derby, 5 Maul. & Sel. 90,) or rushes or flags from a pond, (R. v. All Saints, Cambridge, 1 Barn. & Cres. 23; 2 Dowl. and Ryl. 47,) or a cattle gate, (R. v. Whixley, 1 T. R. 137,) or right of common in gross, (R. v. Dersingham, 7 T. R. 671,) or the tolls of a market, (R. v. Chipping Norton, 5 East, 239; R. v. North Duffield, 3 Maul. & Sel. 247,) or a water-mill, (Evelyn v. Rentcomb, 2 Salk. 536,) or a windmill, (R. v. Butley,) or hay-grass and aftermath, (R. v. Stoke, 2 T. R. 451; R. v. Brampton, 4 T. R. 348,) or a dairy, (R. v. Hollington, 3 East, 113; Rex v. Darley Abbey, 14 East, 280,) provided the land on which the cows were fed were of the annual value of £10, (R. v. Minworth, 2 East, 198,) or the agistment of cows, (R. v. Sutton, St. Edmunds, 1 Barn. & Cres. 536; R. v.

Cherry, Willingham, 1 Barn. & Cres. 626; 3 Dowl. & Ryl. 13.) But in these cases, unless it was stipulated that the cows, &c., should be *pasture fed*, that is, upon growing produce, it would confer no settlement; (R. v. Bardwell, 2 Barn. & Cres. 163; 3 Dowl. & Ryl. 369;) for if fed in any other way, as upon green tares bought in the market, the pauper would not thereby obtain an *interest* in land by the mouths of his cattle. Thus, a contract "to have twenty-one ewes going," means, in the absence of proof to the contrary to have the ewes fed in the ordinary way, either upon hay, &c., or growing produce, as the other flock was fed; and in order to confer a settlement, it must be part of the bargain itself, that the cattle shall be pasture fed, and therefore no settlement was gained in this case. (R. v. Thornham, 6 Barn. & Cres. 733.)

What Holding insufficient before 1819.] But the occupation of premises by a servant, for the due performance of his service, and not in the character of tenant, (R. v. Kelstern, 5 Maul. & Sel. 136; R. v. Shipdham, 3 Dowl & Ryl. 384,) though a deduction from the wages were made for it, (R. v. Cheshunt, 1 Barn. and Ald. 473; Rex v. Benneworth. 2 Barn. & Cres. 775; 4 Dowl. & Ryl. 355,) or a licence for a year, to use a part of the machinery of a mill, (R. v. Dodderhill, 8 T. R. 449;) even though the party had also the use and liberty of grazing for his horses, and of a stable and cart-house, without paying any thing for them, (R. v. Hammersmith, 8 T. R. 450, *n.*) or the renting of a *standing place* in a mill, for the party's own machinery, to be fixed and worked by the steam machinery of the mill, (R. v. Miller, 2 East, 189,) would not confer a settlement.

What Interest in Tenement.] Before the passing of the 59 Geo. 3. c. 50, a settlement might be gained by the possession of a tenement of the yearly value of £10, although the occupant had neither a freehold, copyhold, or leasehold interest therein, and whatever might be its nature, so that it came within the ordinary and legal definition of a tenement. It was generally considered, that the possession *must* be obtained by *renting* or holding in the ordinary character of tenant; (4 Maul. & Sel 212;) but this opinion is not *strictly* accurate, as lawful possession of such a tenement, when absolute and independent, with *some* interest therein sufficiently permanent to denote a *coming to settle*, according to the words of the 13 & 14 Car. 2. c. 12, upon which this species of settlement was founded, conferred a settlement, although the occupier or tenant was exempt from paying rent, or might pay in services. (Rex v. Cherry, Willingham, 1 Barn. & Cres. 626.) So that a voluntary donation, where the occupier had not an interest of sufficient permanency to entitle him to acquire a settlement by *estate*, was sufficient. (See Rex v. Lakenheath, 1 Barn. & Cres. 534, 2 N. P. L. 4.)

If the party held several distinct tenements, each of less value, but amounting in the whole to £10 a year, (North Nibley v. Wotton-under-Edge,) and one part in one parish, and another in another, a settlement would thus be gained where he resided. (Rex v. Fillongley, 1 T. R. 458; Rex v. Culmstock, 6 T. R. 730.) But an occupation as tenant, could not be coupled with an occupation as landlord or freeholder for this purpose, (Rex v. St. John's, Glastonbury, 1 Barn. & Ald. 481.) although renting a tenement of £10 a-year, and letting a part of it to an under-tenant, would have gained a settlement. (Rex v. Llandverras, Burr. & S. C. 571; 1 Bla. Rep. 603.) So, on the other hand also, if two or more held tenements as joint tenants, partners, &c., if the moiety of one of such joint tenants were of the yearly value of £10, he might gain a settlement there. (Little Tew v. Duns Tew, 2 Bott. 118; R. v. Newnham, Burr. S. C. 756.) But if the joint occupation of two or more do not yield to each a rateable proportion of £10 annual value, the tenement confers a settlement upon none of them. (Marden v. Barham, Burr. S. C. 311.) But if one rent be £5 in severalty, and £10 as joint tenant with another, it would confer a settlement; (Rex v. Tissington, Burr. S. C. 499;) or if a person came into a parish as a servant, and during his servitude rented a tenement, without residing thereon, of £10 value, he gained a settlement. (R. v. Kenardington, 6 Barn. & Cres. 70; 9 Dowl. & Ryl. 72.)

Value of Tenement before 1819.] The tenement must have been of the yearly *value* of £10, that is, the value if let by the year, (R. v. Hellingley, 10 East, 44,) whatever might be the amount of the rent *agreed* to be given for it, (South Sydenham v. Lamerton, 1 Stra. 57;) although part of the occupation were given to the individual out of private charity, for the rent is merely evidence of the yearly value, (R. v. Fillongley, 1 T. R. 458; R. v. Fritwell, 7 T. R 197.) and it must have been of this value at the time the person came to settle upon it, (R. v. Hellingley, 10 East, 44,) independently of any merely collateral and distinct matter; and in the case of a lease for years, the estimate must be made at the time the tenant entered upon the tenement, not sooner or later. (R. v. Cramore, 2 Maul. & Sel. 132.) But in the case of a lease from year to year, every year is considered as a new lease; and if the tenement be of the yearly value of £10, being one year of the tenant's occupation, he thereby gains a settlement. (R. v. Bilsdale, Kirkham, Burr. S. C. 833.) However, if the value be increased by merely collateral and distinct matter, that will not suffice;—as the erection of a *post* windmill upon the tenement, removeable at the tenant's pleasure; (R. v. Londonthorpe, 6 T. R. 377.) although the holding a windmill attached to the *ground* will give a settlement, (*ib.*,) and *erections attached* to a mine may be considered as part of the tenement, so rabbits in a warren. (R. v. Minworth, 2 East, 201.) It was also held immaterial, that the landlord agreed to pay taxes, &c. (R. v. St. Paul's, Deptford, 13 East, 320.) But a weekly value amounting to £10 in the year would not have been sufficient, if the value by the year, at a yearly letting, would not have amounted to £10. (R. v. Hellingly, 10 East, 41.)

The rule that the tenement shall be of the prescribed value at the time the tenant comes to settle upon it, has received this modification, "that the tenement must be of the value of £10, at the time of entry, or to be made of that value at the expense of the landlord," for "the tenement is of that value within the meaning of the statute, (13 & 14 Car. 2, c. 12,) although the improvement was not made until after the time of entry;" and consequently a settlement would be gained in such case. (R. v. Poulton-with-Fearnhead, 6 Maul. & Sel. 256.) And this rule extends not only to ploughing, digging, and manuring, (R. v. Ringwood, 1 Maul. & Sel. 381,) but even to the case where the tenement has been cropped by the landlord, and was thereby rendered worth £10. a-year, but without which it would have been of much less annual value. (R. v. Purley, 16 East, 261.)

Where Surety for the Rent is taken.] The person who actually occupied as *tenant*, is the person who gains a settlement, (R. v. Berkswell, 1 Barn. & Cres. 542; 3 Dowl. & Ryl. 9.,) although a surety be demanded and taken by the landlord for the rent. (R. v. Butler, Burr. S. C. 107; (R. v. Hooe, 4 East, 362.) And where the house was taken by A. without the knowledge of B., but the latter with his family removed into, and occupied, it for more than two years, A. paying the rent and taxes, and being assessed in the parish books, and A. directed B. to quit without notice, which he did; but it was proved, on the other hand, that the landlord said he had let to B., and A. had guaranteed payment, and A. stated that he considered B. responsible to him for the rent, it was held, that B. gained a settlement as tenant. (R. v. Chediston, 4 Barn. & Cres. 230. 6 Dowl. & Ryl. 269.)

A soldier, whilst at barracks, took a house for himself and family, and resided forty days; it was holden, that he thereby gained a settlement; (R. v. Brighthelmstone, 1 Barn. & Ald. 270.) but where taken by a soldier's wife in his absence, and he afterwards deserted and concealed himself in this house for forty days, he did not thereby gain a settlement. (R. v. Ashton-under-Lyne, 4 Maul. & Sel. 357.)

Term for which taken.] A taking for less than a year, provided the yearly value of the tenement were £10, and there were forty days' occupation, would have been sufficient to confer a settlement. (R. v. Shenstone, Burr. S. C. 474.) Thus, the taking of a room by the week, or if no time were mentioned, would suffice. (R. v. Whitechapel; R. v. Brampton, 4 T. R. 348.) And a soldier who took a house for himself and family while his regiment lay in barracks, was held to have gained a settlement. (R. v. Brighthelmstone, 1 Barn. & Ald. 270.)

Although it was at one time said, that two distinct tenements in two parishes, making together £10 per annum, would give no settlement, yet it was afterwards expressly decided, that two distinct tenements, one being in one parish, and the other being in another, constituted a sufficient tenement within the act. (R. v. Sandwich, Burr. S. C. 46.)

Residence.] There must be a residence of forty days in the parish, &c., in which the tenement or part of it is situate. (R. v. Knighton, 2 T. R. 48; Rex v. South Lynn, 5 T. R. 664.) But where a person had a residence in two several parishes at the same time, and he resided in one of them for forty days, at intervals, and *slept* there the last night when both tenancies expired, the settlement was gained there, though his family resided on the tenement in the other parish all the time. (R. v. St. Mary's, Lambeth, 8 T. R. 240.) But *passing* the last night there, though he was occupied in packing up his goods, and did not sleep, was held sufficient to determine the settlement. (R. v. Ringwood, 1 Maul. & Sel. 381.) If the tenant remove, or be removed even forcibly from his tenement, before the forty days, he gains no settlement. (R. v. Llanbedergoch, 7 T. R. 105.) A residence of forty days is indispensably necessary for that purpose. (*ib.*)

But a residence as a widow, and a residence as the wife of her late husband, cannot be coupled so as to form a forty days' residence in all. (R. v. South Lynn, 5 T. R. 664.)

It was at one time thought that the residence must be an actual residence upon some part of the tenement. (See R. v. Bardwell, 2 Barn. & Cres. 162—164.) But it has since been decided, that a residence in any part of the parish was sufficient. (R. v. Kenardington, 6 Barn. & Cres. 70.)

Settlements between July 1819, *and June* 1825.] The 59 G. 3. c. 50, was passed on the 2nd July 1819, and was repealed on the

22nd June 1825. All settlements, therefore, acquired in this interval, by renting a tenement, must be governed by this statute. It is as follows:—

" Whereas, many disputes and controversies have arisen respecting the settling of the poor people in parishes in England, by the renting of tenements, be it enacted, That from and after the passing of this act, no person shall acquire a settlement in any parish or township maintaining its own poor, in England, by, or by reason of, his or her dwelling for forty days in any tenement rented by such person, unless such tenement shall consist of a *house or building* within such parish or township, or of both, *bona fide* hired by such person at, and for the sum of ten pounds a-year at the least for the term of *one whole year*; nor unless such house or building shall be held, and such land occupied, and the *rent* for the same actually *paid* for the term of one *whole year* at the least, by the person hiring the same; nor unless the whole of such land shall be situate within the *same parish* or township as the house wherein the *person* hiring such land *shall dwell* and inhabit; any thing in any act or acts, or any construction of, or implication from, any act or acts, or any usage or custom to the contrary, in any wise, notwithstanding."

It will be perceived, by the parts marked in italics, which indicate the several conditions precedent to the gaining of a settlement by renting a tenement, that the law was very materially altered by the statute.

Operation of 59 *Geo.* 3. *c.* 50.] If the pauper has not resided for forty days *before* the passing of this act, it operates upon the case just the same as if there had been *no* previous residence. (R. v. St. Mary-le-bone, 4 Barn. & Ald. 681.) Thus, though the pauper took a tenement on the 21st May, under a written agreement, and paid rent from that time, yet, as he did not actually take possession till the 4th June, between which and the passing of the act only twenty-eight days elapsed, he gained no settlement under the old law, and consequently, as the case fell within this statute, a year's occupation became necessary. (R. v. Brighton, 1 Dowl. & Ryl. 313.)

Renting £10 *a-year,* 59 *Geo.* 3. *c.* 50.] The rent must have been at least £10 a-year; therefore, where a pauper held a house at the annual rent of £8, from Lady-day, to Michaelmas 1821, and a different house from Michaelmas 1821, to Lady-day 1822, at the annual rent of £9, and during the whole of that period was the tenant of a piece of garden ground, at the rent of £2 2*s.*, but had agreed with a third person to share the expense and profits arising from cultivating the garden, and the person paid half the rent to the pauper, but the latter paid the whole to the landlord, it was held, that no settlement was gained by the operation of this act, as the pauper *occupied* to the amount of £9 1*s*. only during part of the year. (R. v. Tonbridge, 6 Barn. & Cres. 88; 9 Dowl. & Ryl. 128.)

But a *holding* of a *house* or *building* is sufficient, and therefore, where the pauper occupied together a house and garden, and paid rent during the year, though taken at different times, and of different persons, the house at six guineas, and the garden at £3. 15s. per annum and he underlet one room at thirty shillings a-year, by which *he* actually *occupied* less, though he *held* more than to the amount of £10, yet this was considered sufficient to give a settlement under this act. (R. v. North Collingham, 1 Barn. & Cres. 578; 2 Dowl. & Ryl. 743.) But if the pauper occupy a piece of potatoe land, and have the keep of two cows in addition to his house, by the *kindness of his master*, this will not now suffice, though the annual value be sufficient. (R. v. Benneworth, 2 Barn. & Cres. 775; 4 Dowl. & Ryl. 354.)

Hired and occupied, 59 *Geo*. 3. *c*. 50.) In analogy to the case of a hiring and service for a year, the hiring of a tenement under this act was good, notwithstanding it was accompanied with stipulations which rendered it defeasible. (See R. v. Herstmonceaux, 7 Barn. & Cres. 551; 1 Man. & Ryl. 426.) And *prima facie*, a general hiring must be presumed to be a yearly hiring, and that presumption is the stronger where the subject matter of the hiring is land. (R. v. Wainfleet, 8 Barn. & Cres. 229.)

But the taking must have been *bona fide* by the party, and a fraudulent intent vitiated the contract, in which respect the *value* of the tenement would still be material, because an agreement to pay £10 a year for that which was not worth near so much, would be cogent evidence in some instances of a fraudulent intent. However, a person by whom a tenement is hired and occupied, and the rent paid for a year, gains a settlement, under the 59 Geo. 3. c. 50, although a third person be surety to the landlord for payment of the rent, for that does not make the surety the party hiring the tenement; especially as the occupier, did not, for any thing which appeared, know that the person who had been employed in the commencement as his agent, had become his surety. (R. v. Kegworth, 2 Man. & Ryl. 28.)

And the holding must be for a year; therefore, where a house was hired by A. for a year, at the rent and of the annual value of £12, and he died three days before the year's occupation was completed, but his corpse continued in the house till after the expiration of the year, and his widow continued to reside there, and paid the last quarter's rent, he having paid the previous three quarters, it was held that his widow and children did not gain any settlement. (R. v. Crayford, 6 Barn. & Cres. 68; 9 Dowl. & Ryl. 80.)

Houses held, Lands occupied, 59 *Geo.* 3. *c.* 50.] If the tenement consisted of a house or building, it was to be *held* for a year; but if land, it must have been occupied for a whole year, by the particular words of the statute; consequently the party might underlet part of the house or building, in such manner as such house or building could still be charged as his, in an indictment for burglary. (R. v. Great Bolton, 8 Barn. & Cres. 71; R. v. North Collingham, 1 Barn. & Cres. 578.)

But if the tenement consisted of land, there must have been a sole occupation by the person taking it. (R. v. Tonbridge, 6 Barn. & Cres. 88.) But where a tenant of land from year to year underlets the *whole* to another party, at so much per week, whose tenancy was to commence at the ensuing Lady-day, but no time was specified for which the land was to be taken, this was considered a good contract of yearly hiring of the land by the under-tenant, the tenant having received no notice to quit, as the tenant by such an agreement was taken to have conveyed her interest to the under-tenant. (R. v. Wainfleet, 8 Barn. & Cres. 229.)

Rent paid for a Year, 59 *Geo.* 3. *c.* 50.] The statute did not require that the holding or occupation should be for the *same* year as the hiring, but only that such holding or occupation should be for the term of one whole year; and therefore, where the pauper hired a house three weeks *after* May-day, for a year from such preceding May-day, at £15 a-year, and at the expiration of that time hired it again for another year, at the same rent, and occupied from the time of the first till six months after the second hiring, and paid the rent for the whole period, he gained a settlement. (R. v. Stow, 4 Barn. & Cres. 87.)

It was held, that where a person hired and occupied a £10 tenement for more than a year, and the rent was paid after his death, out of the proceeds of the sale of his effects, no settlement was gained under this act, as it was not *paid by him;* nor under the 6 Geo. 4. c. 57, although the year expired, and the payment was made after that statute passed; because there was no payment of one whole year's rent, *at the time of his death,* the subsequent payment out of his assets being insufficient to supply the requisites of that statute. (R. v. Carshalton, 6 Barn. & Cres. 93; 9 Dowl. & Ryl. 132.)

Payment, Tenant become a Pauper.] There are two cases, in each of which, before the payment of the rent, the tenant became chargeable to the parish, and in one it, was held, that a settlement was gained, in the other, that it was not. The only difference in the facts seems to have been, that in the one case the tenant became chargeable *before* he had completed a year's holding of the tenement which he had hired; and though he was removed by an order of justices to another parish, yet he returned to his tenement the same day, continued his holding, and at the end of his year paid his year's rent, namely £12. In this case the court held, that the statute had been complied with, and that a settlement was gained. (R. v. Barham, 8 Barn. & Cres. 99.) In the other case, after the tenant had completed his year's tenancy, he applied for parochial relief, and was removed to another parish, after which he paid the year's rent by the sale of the furniture left by him in the tenement, which he had so hired and occupied for a year. It was held in this case, that as the rent was *due and unpaid* at the time of his removal by the order of justices, no settlement was gained. (R. v. Ampthill, 2 Barn. & Cres. 847.) At the time of his removal, he had clearly not complied with all the requisites of the act, although by his contract he ought to have done so, as he had held the tenement for a year, and the subsequent payment of the rent could not cure this defect; but in the former case, the pauper had committed no breach of his contract at the time of his removal, and he afterwards went on to complete it in all its parts.

Residence, 59 *Geo.* 3. c. 50.] A settlement might be gained under this statute, by a residence of forty days in a parish, provided the party comply with the other conditions mentioned in the act; and therefore, where a pauper hired land for a year at the sum of £10, paid the rent, and occupied for the whole year, but resided only forty days in the parish, though not upon the land, it was held that he gained a settlement. (R. v. Wainfleet, 8 Barn. & Cres. 227.)

Settlements under 6 *Geo.* 4. c. 57.] The date of this statute, which repeals the former one, is 22nd June 1825, and no settlement by renting a tenement can be acquired since that period, except upon the condition stated in this act, which is as follows:

" No person shall acquire a settlement, in any parish or township maintaining its own poor, by or by reason of settling upon, renting, or paying parochial rates for any tenement, not being his or her own property, unless such tenement shall consist of a separate and distinct dwelling-house or building, or of land, or of both, *bona fide* rented by such person, in such parish or township, at and for the sum of ten pounds a-year at the least, for the term of one whole year; nor unless such house, or building, or land, shall be occupied under such yearly hiring, and *the rent* for the same to the amount of ten pounds, *actually paid for the term of one whole year* at the least; provided always, that it shall not be necessary to prove the actual *value* of such tenement; any thing in any act or acts, or any construction of or implication from any act or acts, or any usage or custom to the contrary notwithstanding."

With respect to the tenement—term of hiring—and amount of rent, the same construction is to be put upon this statute, as upon the one which it repealed.

Holding under the two Statutes.] A holding before the 22nd June, when the 6 Geo. 4. c. 57, was passed, and the holding subsequent to that period may be connected, provided the occupation before the 22nd June be such as will satisfy the requisites of the 6 Geo. 4. c. 57; and therefore, if a party, before this act began to operate, was in possession of a yearly tenement, and held it under such circumstances as that statute says shall be requisite in order to gain a settlement, a settlement will be conferred. There are no words in the act which import that the taking shall be subsequent to the time when the statute came into operation. (R. v. Ditcheat, 9 Barn. & Cres. 183.)

Renting One whole Year under 6 *Geo.* 4.] The taking of a tenement at twenty guineas a-year, the rent to be paid weekly, but either party to be at liberty to give three months notice from any quarter-day, is a yearly hiring within this act. (R. v. Herstmonceux, 7 Barn. & Cres. 551; 1 Man. & Ryl. 426.)

Payment of Rent under 6 *Geo.* 4.] The former act required that the house should be *held*, and the land *occupied*, and the rent paid, by the *person hiring the same.* The language of this statute is different; it is wholly silent as to the occupation or payment of rent by the person hiring, and it has been decided in Rex v. Kibworth Harcourt, (7 Barn. & Cres. 790; 1 Man. & Ryl. 691,) that, according to the true construction of the statute, the payment need not be made by the party hiring. The words, "by the person hiring the same," are to be considered, therefore, as struck out of this statute, and the law so far altered, that it is now sufficient if it be paid either by the person hiring, or by any other person. (R. v. Ditcheat, 9 Barn. & Cres. 181.) Still, if the tenant were to die before the rent were actually paid, he could not be considered as having acquired a settlement, by the rent being afterwards paid out of his effects. (R. v. Carshalton, 6 Barn. & Cres. 93.)

Under this statute, the *whole* year's rent must be actually paid, whatever be its amount, and the payment for a portion of a year, though the sum so paid exceed £10, will not suffice. (R. v. Ramsgate, 6 Barn. & Cres. 712; R. v. Ashley Hay, 8 Barn. & Cres. 27.)

Occupancy under 6 *Geo.* 4.] Some difficulty has arisen upon the construction of the word "occupied" in this act. Mr. J. Bayley inclined to think, that occupation by any other person than the person hiring, by assigning or underletting, is not an occupation under the yearly hiring within the meaning of the statute. But Littledale, J. and Parke, J. held, that the occupation of part by the person hiring the tenement, though the other part was for nearly the whole period underlet to another person, was sufficient; though it might be otherwise, if the person hiring underlet the whole house, and occupied no part of it, per Littledale, J. And the other of these learned judges observed, that the statute "does not require the payment of rent or *occupation* by the person hiring the same, but occupation *under* the yearly hiring; and these words may be satisfied by the continuance of the term and occupation by a *sub-tenant* or assignee, during the continuance of the term. But it is not necessary to decide in this case, whether occupation by an *assignee* would be sufficient or not." (R. v. Ditcheat, supra.)

This construction of the act has been further confirmed in a subsequent case, the facts of which were nearly the same. It will suffice to give the judgment of Lord Tenterden, who said: "The question was upon the act generally called the Tenement Act, 6 Geo. 4. c. 57. Upon consideration, we think, that all that was required by that act has been done by the pauper in this case, so as to entitle him to a settlement, by renting the tenement in question. The words of the act are, 'No persons shall acquire a settlement by renting, &c., unless such tenement shall consist of a separate and distinct dwelling house, or building, or land, or of both, *bonâ fide* rented by such person, in such parish or township, at and for the sum of £10 a-year at the least, for the term of one whole year, nor unless such house or building, or land, shall be occupied under such yearly hiring, and the rent for the same to the amount of £10 be actually paid for the term of one whole year at the least.' Now the hiring in this case was for a year, the rent was paid for a year, and the rent exceeded the sum required. But it was objected, that as the pauper had not *occupied* the *whole* of the premises hired, the clause in question was not satisfied, the words being shall be occupied under *such yearly hiring,*' and it was said, that as another person had occupied part, there could not be a year's occupation by the pauper, under the yearly *hiring* by the pauper; but this renders it necessary for us to look at the statute, 59 Geo. 3. c. 50, which the statute 6 Geo. 4. repealed. That statute provided, in terms, which for the present may be considered as substantially the same as those of the 6th Geo. 4, except that it also contained the words, '*by the person hiring the same,*' after the words which provided for the occupation and payment of rent. Now those words are omitted in the present act. We must understand the legislature to have had under their consideration the terms of the very act which they were repealing, and so understanding, we must consider, that they left out the words for some particular purpose. Then, were the premises held by the pauper? It is not denied they were; that being the case, all which is required by the terms of the statute has been complied with, the pauper has gained the settlement in dispute. We think it much the safer course to go by the *words* of the statute, than to enter into an inquiry as to the supposed intention of those who framed it. If we entered into such an inquiry, we might often be mistaken, but by adhering to the very words, we take, in our opinion, the safer course. The consequence is, that the order of sessions must be quashed." (R. v. Great Bentley, H. T. 1830. MSS.)

Residence under 6 *Geo.* 4.] Although the act does not in express terms require a residence of forty days, that has always been essential to complete a settlement by renting, and is so still.

SECTION V.—BY PAYMENT OF RATES.

Origin of this Settlement.] The 3 W. & M. c. 11. s. 6. enacted, that if any person, who comes to inhabit in any town, or parish, is *charged* with and *pays* his share towards the public taxes, or levies of the said town or parish, he shall be deemed to have a legal settlement there, though no notice in writing has been given to the parish.

By force of the above enactment, any one, except a certificated person, (9 & 10 W. 3. c. 11,) by residing forty days in the parish after such payment, might in this manner gain a settlement, whatever were the value of the tenement, up to June 22nd, 1795. From that day, when the 35 Geo. 3. c. 101. was passed, to the 22nd June, 1825, the condition was added, that the tenement must be of the yearly value of £10. (See s. 4.) And upon this last mentioned day, by the 6 Geo. 4. c. 57, the acquiring a settlement by payment of rates, is virtually abolished; for, in order to acquire a settlement by paying rates, all the conditions must be observed and fulfilled, which suffice to give a settlement by *renting* a tenement; the party, therefore, need not go further, and prove that he has paid rates, when his settlement is already established by proof of all the preliminary conditions, and which are in themselves sufficient to entitle him to a settlement by renting a tenement.

General Rules.] The party must be *rated*—he must be rated *before* payment—he must make payment—the rating may be in any manner, which notifies to the parish that he is rated—if the rate itself be void, his right is not thereby prejudiced—the rate need not be strictly, though it must be in the nature of, a parochial assessment—and he must have resided forty days in the parish after the time when he paid it.

The expression in the 3 W. & M. c. 11. s. 6, " the public taxes or levies of the parish," appears to embrace all rates whatsoever, without regard to the subject matter, in respect of which the rates are imposed, and, therefore, the gaining a settlement is not confined to cases in which the party is rated in respect of a tenement. Nor do the subsequent statutes make any such restriction, and, therefore, a settlement may be still claimed by virtue of a rate upon personal property, (see 2 Peck, 251,) subject of course to the other conditions, as actual payment, residence, &c.

Rating necessary.] Though the rate be in form or in the manner of making it void, yet if the party be rated and pay the rate, he gains a settlement. (R. v. St. Bees, 9 East, 203; St. Giles, Cripplegate, and St. Mary, Newington, 19 Vin. Ab. 386.) But his name must be inserted in the rate *before* he pays it, for he gains no settlement by its being inserted afterwards. (R. v. Edgbaston, 6 T. R. 540; R. v. St. Olaves, Burr. S. C. 787.) Though he need not be expressly *named,* if he be otherwise described, so as to show that the parish *knows* he is an inhabitant: (R. v. Painswick, Burr. S. C. 465:) thus, " Thomas Clifford, *or* tenant," was held a sufficient rating of a succeeding tenant. (R. v. Walsall, Cald. 37.) But where the landlord's and tenant's name are in the rate, if it be stated in the rate itself, that the landlord is the person rated, the tenant cannot be considered the person assessed, although he pay the rate. (R. v. St. John's, Southwark, Cald. 62.)

But as the poor-rate is an occupier's tax, the tenant was held to be rated, although it appeared that the landlord's name was *also* in the rate, without declaring which of them was assessed; and it was proved that the landlord had been formerly rated, and that the tenant, after paying four years, had his name taken off the rate at his own request, on account of his poverty, and no one paid afterwards. (R. v. Endon, Cald. 374.) The land-tax being also a tenant's tax, falls within the same rule; (R. v. St. Lawrence, Winchester, id. 379;) but where, in addition, the *receipt* given to the tenant stated, that the sum was assessed upon the landlord, it was held, that the tenant did not acquire a settlement. (R. v. Bury St. Edmund's, *ib.* 385.) But rating the farm or *house* is insufficient where the landlord pays the rate, and the tenant pays him again, if it is *expressly proved* that the parish (the overseer,) does not know who is the occupier. (R. v. Langammarch, 2 T. R. 628.)

Payment of Rates, &c.] It is necessary that the person rated should *pay* the tax; but if it be wrongfully imposed for premises occupied by another, it will suffice, for rating and paying are facts of recognization of his inhabiting in the parish. (R. v. Stapleton, Burr. S. C. 649.) So if the rate be afterwards repaid him by agreement with the landlord. (R. v. Bramley, ib. 75.) So a custom-house officer rated to and paying the land-tax, although the amount is given him beforehand, or allowed him afterwards by the collector of the customs. (R. v. Axmouth, 8 East, 383.) And it is enough if the money be paid through the intervention of an agent or other person for him. (R. v. Bridgewater, 3 T. R. 550.)

It is sufficient, likewise, if the money be paid *bona fide* by the pauper, although it may have been received by the overseer through a mistake, and is afterwards returned to him. (R. v. Corhampton, Cald. 108; Doug. 621.) But where an exciseman was rated to the land-tax for his salary, but never paid the rate, it being paid by the collector, and not deducted out of the pauper's salary, no settlement was gained. (R. v. Weobly, 2 East, 68.)

What kind of Rates, &c.] The settlement may be gained, not only by payment of taxes and rates strictly parochial, but also of such other public tax which is charged and payable within a parochial limit, (R. v. Blood, Comb. 410,) such as the church-rate, (R. v. St. Bees, 9 East, 203,) the land-tax, and other king's taxes. (Anon, Comb. 282.) But he must pay in quality of a *parishioner*, therefore payment towards a county bridge gives no settlement. (Cases of Sett. 1.) Payment for less time than a year is sufficient. (R. v. Bramley, Burr. S. C. 75.)

It is expressly provided by statute, that payment of the following taxes shall confer no settlement. The scavengers' rate for the repairs of the highway, by 9 Geo. 1. c. 7, s. 6; duties on houses worth £5 yearly rent and upwards, by 18 Geo. 3. c. 26; duties on houses and windows, by 21 Geo. 2. c. 10, s. 13; or any of the assessed taxes, by 43 Geo. 3. c. 161, s. 59. And a party does not gain any settlement by reason of his having been assessed to, and paid the watch-rate in the city of London. (R. v. Christ Church, 8 Barn. & Cres. 660.)

Forty Days' Residence.] It is equally necessary that the person should reside in the parish; for if he inhabit in one, and is rated in another, he gains no settlement in either, under the statute of 3 W.

& M. It is also necessary that he be an inhabitant for forty days; (R. v. St. Michael, 6 T. R. 536;) and the forty days' residence must in all cases be *after* the rating and payment. (R. v. Ringstead, 7 Barn. & Cres. 607; 1 Man. & Ryl. 448.)

Requisites under 59 Geo. 3. c. 50.] It has already been observed, that before 1795, the value of the tenement was immaterial; and that after that period, until June 22nd, 1819, it was required that the tenement should be of the annual value of £10; and as the tenement itself, in most cases, would give a settlement independently of the rating, but few instances would occur of settlements gained by being rated within that period. But when the 59 Geo. 3. c. 50, limited the nature of the tenement, by *renting* of which a settlement could be gained, the other kinds of tenement, which were stripped of this privilege of conferring a settlement, might serve as the medium of a settlement by payment of rates in respect thereof, if such tenements were of the yearly value of £10. (R. v. St. Pancras, 2 Barn. & Cres. 125; 3 Dowl. & Ryl. 343.) It was not necessary that the tenement should have been assessed at £10 annual value; it was sufficient, if it could be proved, that it was actually of that value. (R. v. St. Dunstan's, Kent, 4 Barn. & Cres. 686; 7 Dowl. & Ryl. 178.) And in estimating the value, whatever forms part of the freehold must be included as fixtures, even though they are such as a tenant might remove, if they are put in by the landlord, and form part of the demise. (R. v. St. Dunstan's, Kent, supra.)

SECTION VI.—BY ESTATE

Foundation of this Settlement.] The principle upon which these settlements are founded, viz. that the party shall not be removed from his own, but is entitled to the care of his property, goes beyond estates in land, and seems to extend this right to all interest in things *immoveable,* situate within a town or parish, which, as a party cannot take with him to the place of his settlement, he must be allowed to remain where they are, for the purpose of superintending them. (2 N. P. L. 69.)

The 9 Geo. 1. c. 7, introduced a modification of the general right of settlement by estate, which before existed, and since the passing of which act no settlement can be gained by an estate, of which the party has become the owner by purchase for a less sum than £30.

Since the passing of this statute, a person may be irremoveable on account of residing on his own estate, and yet not gain a settlement by such residence, however long it continues; or, in other words, living upon an estate irremoveable for forty days, and gaining a settlement, have not been convertible terms in all cases. (See R. v. Brington, 7 Barn. & Cres. 550.)

By what Estate gained.] With the exception of estates purchased for less than £30, any estate in lands, whether freehold or copyhold, and whether it be held in fee simple, fee tail, for life, term of years, or from year to year, even though the party in possession is not the original lessee, will suffice to confer a settlement, with a residence of forty days in the parish. (R. v. Stone, 6 T. R. 295.)

If a man have an estate by descent, &c. whatever be the value, (2 Bott. 457,) or in any other manner than by *buying* it, and reside on it, or *in* the same parish, for forty days, either together or in the whole, though he part with it immediately afterwards, he thereby gains a settlement. (Ryslip v. Harrow, 2 Salk. 524; R. v. Houghton le Spring, 1 East, 247; R. v. Dorstone, 1 East, 296.)

Must be a present Estate.] It has been thought that a reversionary interest in an estate was sufficient for this purpose, and the case of R. v. Houghton le Spring has been cited in support of this doctrine; there, however, the party was seised in fee, though he had let his freehold, and the question was not, whether an estate in reversion would suffice, but whether it was necessary that the party should *occupy* the estate, and it was held that he need not. And it has since been said, that it is a clear principle of settlement law, that a party cannot gain a settlement by estate unless he has a freehold in *possession*. He must have an estate, of which he may be disseised. (R. v. Ringstead, 9 Barn. & Cres. 221.)

But the estate may be either a legal or an equitable estate, and the party may gain a settlement, whether he be alone interested in the estate, or one of several joint-tenants, parceners, or tenants in common. (R. v. Brington, 7 Barn. & Cres. 550; R. v. Dorstone, 1 East. 290.)

Although the title be disputable, yet it may be sufficient. (R. v. Calow, 3 Maul. & Sel. 22; Ashbrittle v. Wiley, 1 Stra. 608.) Thus an *undisturbed* possession, no matter how acquired, for twenty years, will gain a settlement, (*ib.*) even though a portion of the time, the possession is in his mortgagee; (R. v. Bitton, Burr. S. C. 631;) for the strict rules to be observed in the trial of an ejectment, ought not to be applied to settlement cases, and the court will not permit the title to an estate to be determined upon an order of removal. (R. v. Buttes-ton, 6 T. R. 554.)

By an equitable Estate.] With regard to an equitable interest giving a settlement, the test by which cases of this description are to be decided is, whether the estate on which the party resides is substantially his property, and not merely such a claim as might possibly induce a court of equity to interfere in some way or other. (R. v. Horndon-on-the-Hill, 4 Maul. & Sel. 565.)

If a party is *sole* next of kin to a person deceased, that is, if he has exclusive right to take out administration, he has an immediate equitable interest in any term of years of which the deceased was possessed, and may gain a settlement thereby before taking out administration. (R. v. Horsely, 8 East, 405.) But where A. at his death left a widow, a son, and a daughter, and the widow and daughter, with her husband, were living in the house at A.'s death, no one of these could say that the property was his or her's at that time. There was neither exclusive right nor exclusive possession, and in order to make it the property of one or the other, it was necessary to obtain letters of administration; and as none had been obtained in this case, though there was an occupancy for a series of years, no settlement was gained. (R. v. Canford Magna, 6 Maul. & Sel. 355.)

If A. assign to trustees, to raise a certain sum by the rents and profits, and by sale or mortgage, and after payment of that sum, in trust to reassign the premises, the estate substantially remains in A., and suffices to give him a settlement. (R. v. Edington, 1 East, 288.) So if an estate be devised to trustees to sell and pay the money over to A., and A. lives upon the estate till it is sold; (R. v. Natland, Burr. S. C. 793;) or if the devise be of a house to a party, with a provision in the will that A. should have free power and liberty to dwell in it for life, A. may thereby gain a settlement. (R. v. Woburn, Burr. S. C. 785.)

What Interest insufficient.] If a lord of a manor grant a licence to a party to build on the waste, and he does so, and occupies the house, this confers no settlement, for the licence gives no *legal* title; and though a court of equity might probably interfere, a court of law cannot say with certainty that it would. (R. v. Hayworthingham, 1 Barn. & Cres. 634.) So, if a son build a house on his own land, and agree *by parol* with his father, who lent part of the purchase-money of the land on this condition, that he should occupy it for his life, this amounts to no more than a licence to occupy; and no estate, either legal or equitable, was conveyed to the father, nor any such interest probably as a court of equity would decree to be conveyed. (R. v. Standon, 2 Maul. & Sel. 461.) So, if J. C. agree by parol to purchase an estate, and, upon paying part of the money, is let into, and continues in possession for six months, and then, failing to pay the rest, the contract is abandoned, he can gain no settlement thereby, for a court of equity would not acknowledge his claim to the estate, without paying, or offering to pay, the residue of the purchase-money. (R. v. Long Bennington, 6 Maul. & Sel. 403;) and even where, in addition to the like state of facts, it appeared that the party, after a year's possession, sold the estate, and gave up possession to his vendee, and afterwards paid the remainder of the purchase-money owing to his own vendor; it was held, no settlement was gained. (R. v. Llantillio Grossenny, 5 Barn. & Cres. 461, 8 Dowl. & Ryl. 320.)

The principle deducible from these cases is, that the relation of trustee and cestui que trust, at least, must be created, to give a settlement by purchase; and even when the agreement for the sale and purchase of an estate has been made in writing, as required by the statute against frauds, and part of the purchase-money was paid, and the vendee let into possession, and a distant day (seven months afterwards) named for the payment of the residue, the court held, as that payment was not made, and no conveyance was executed, the contract being ultimately abandoned, the party gained no settlement. (R. v. Geddington, 2 Barn. & Cres. 129; 3 Dowl. & Ryl. 403.) This decision seems to carry the principle further than any of the preceding cases, and raises the distinction between an equitable *estate* and a mere equitable right, and shows, that in cases of *constructive* trusts, a settlement is not gained by the cestui que trust. There are cases in equity, according to which, the interest enjoyed by the party in Rex v. Geddington, would be considered a substantial estate, which he might have sold, or incumbered, and would have descended to his heir; (see "Observations on the case of R. v. Geddington, by A. Amos, Esq.;" also Green v. Smith, 1 Atk. 572; Seton v. Slade, 7 Ves. 274;) but the court thought an uniformity and consistency in the decisions would be best preserved by the judgment then pronounced, and that it was desirable the sessions should have cases settled for their guidance upon plain grounds, rather than that they should be called upon to entertain and decide difficult questions of equitable law. It was also observed, that this was a case of an estate or interest *purchased*, and the statute (9 Geo. 1. c. 7. s. 5,) requires that the consideration shall be *paid*.

So a devise to trustees to receive the rents and profits for the benefit of A., (an uncertificated bankrupt,) his wife and children, all or any of them, during his life, as they should think proper, does not give A. such an interest as will enable him to acquire a settlement; for he takes neither a legal nor an equitable interest in the estate, and is only one of several persons to whom the trustees might, in their discretion, have given the rents. If he had taken an equitable interest, the intention of the testatrix would have been defeated, because, being an uncertificated bankrupt, it would have passed to his assignees. (R. v. Darlington, 5 Maul. & Sel. 493.)

The rules applicable to persons having a *sole* interest in an equitable estate, are equally applicable to persons having a *joint* interest only. (See R. v. Brington, 7 Barn. & Cres. 546.)

Right of Franchise insufficient.] A mere right of franchise falling short of an interest in land, is not sufficient to give a settlement by estate; as, for instance, the right of freemen of a borough to turn cattle on the waste, which is only a *personal* privilege; (R. v. Warkworth, 1 Maul. & Sel. 473;) or a specific legacy out of land, or schoolmaster's salary, payable, among other things, out of the profits of lands held by trustees; (R. v. Melborne, Burr. S. C. 244;) a widow's dower before assignment; (R. v. Northweald Basset, 2 Barn. & Cres. 724;) the right which a mortgagor has from his equity of redemption; (R. v. Catherington, 3 T. R. 771,) or the next of kin to an account from the administrator for the rents and profits of leasehold lands; (R. v. Barkswell, 1 Barn. & Cres. 542;) or the right which a party, conveying land to trustees to be sold, has to the residue after payment of incumbrances and debts; (R. v. St. Michael's, Bath, Doug. 630;) in all these cases no sufficient interest in land exists in the party to confer a settlement.

Who may gain this Settlement.] A settlement by this means may be gained by infants, (R. v. Hasfield, 2 Stra. 1131,) or by executors, (*ib.*) even before the will be proved, because probate is unnecessary to vest a term in an executor; (R. v. Stove, 6 T. R. 295;) but generally administrators have no vested interest till the letters of administration are obtained, and therefore they cannot gain a settlement till after that has been done. However, a *sole next of kin*, who is thereby entitled to *exclusive* administration, may gain a settlement before administration, as he cannot be considered as an intruder in the parish having nothing of *his own*, within the scope of the poor laws. (R. v. Horsley, 8 East, 405.) So the husband of an administratrix may gain a settlement in right of his wife. (Mursley v. Grandborough, 1 Stra. 97.) A widow having right of dower, may gain a settlement for herself during her quarantine after her first husband's death, but she cannot communicate a settlement to a second husband, and her children by him, until dower has been actually *assigned*. (R. v. North Weald Basset, 2 Barn. & Cres. 724; 4 Dowl. & Ryl. 276; R. v. Painswick, Burr. S. C. 783.) So trustees in whom estates are vested; (R. v. Offchurch, 3 T. R. 114,) even for the purpose of sale, (R. v. Natland, Burr. S. C. 793;) the husband of a parcener; (R. v. Dorstone, 1 East, 296;) so an heir claiming right to the possession, and residing on the estate without right, being in fact a reversioner merely, upon a term of 1000 years, if there be no fraud; (R. v. Staplegrove, 2 Barn. & Ald. 527;) or a guardian in socage; (R. v. Oakley, 10 East, 494;) in all these cases a settlement is gained, but there cannot be a guardian in socage of an equitable estate, even for this purpose. (R. v. Poddington, 1 Barn. & Ald. 560.) A devise of a house to W with liberty for T. to reside in it during his life, and residence accordingly; (R. v. Woburn, Burr, S. C. 785;) a schoolmaster, appointed by trustees under a will, residing in the school-house, &c., (R. v. Oversby le Moor, 15 East, 356;) and a mortgagor in possession, respectively gains a settlement. (R. v. Catherington, 3 T. R. 771.) So where a cottage was conveyed by a pauper to a trustee for sale or mortgage to raise £10, to be paid to the parish, and afterwards to the assignees, and it did not appear that the money was ever raised, but the party always continued in possession, this was held a good settlement by estate; (R. v. Edington, 1 East, 288;) and it is not clear that an alien during the time he is in possession of an estate has not such an interest as will entitle him to a settlement; for, till office found, the interest in lands may vest in him; (Com. Dig. Alien, c. 2;) and as executor or administrator, he has such an interest in a term of years as renders him irremoveable, (Id. c. 7.)

Restrictions by 9 Geo. 1. c. 7.] The fifth section of this act provides, that no person shall gain a settlement by a "purchase of any estate or interest," whereof the *consideration* does not amount to £30 *bonâ fide* paid, for any longer time than he *inhabits* the same; *after* which he may be removed.

Nor do his children thereby gain a settlement; (R. v. Salford, Burr. S. C. 516, Bla. Rep. 433;) and even though he mortgage it, and reside upon it as mortgagor, it will not confer a settlement. (R. v. Tarrant Launceston, 3 East, 226.) But land (under £30) bought by a woman before marriage, will confer a settlement on her after taken husband, and thus derivatively on her, (R. v. Ilmington, Burr. S. C. 566, 1 Bla. Rep. 598,) for he is not a purchaser of the estate within the meaning of the act.

The Consideration under 9 Geo. 1.] The statute means *pecuniary* consideration, and therefore, a conveyance in consideration of natural love and affection, (R. v. Marwood, Burr. S. C. 386; R. v. Ingleton, Burr. S. C. 560,) or of that and money, (R. v. Upton, 3 T. R. 251,) is not within the statute, and a settlement may be gained by an estate so conveyed, although of less value than £30. But a grant of land by a lord of a manor at a quit rent of 2*s.* 6*d.* is a purchase within this act, and being under £30, confers no settlement. (R. v. Hornchurch, 2 Barn. & Ald. 189; R. v. Martley, 5 East, 40.) So a mere licence to build on the waste, rendering an annual quit rent, and building and residing thereon, confers no settlement, being a licence only, and not a *grant* of any interest in land; (R. v. Horndon-on-the-Hill, 4 Maul. & Sel. 562;) nor will a subsequent purchaser thereof for £30, without a conveyance, although no adverse claim is made. (R. v. Hagworthingham, 1 Barn. & Cres. 635; 3 Dowl. & Ryl. 16,) thereby obtain a settlement.

But if the price amount to £30, although part of it be paid by the parish officers, if without fraud, it is no objection. (St. Paul's Warden v. Kepton, Fol. 238.) So a purchase for £39, and £30 of it borrowed on mortgage of the premises, gains a settlement; (R. v. Tedford, Burr. S. C. 57;) but a purchase for £60, the property being *already* mortgaged for £50, and £10 only being paid, the mortgage to remain, (R. v. Chailey, 6 T. R. 755; R. v. Olney, 1 Maul. & Sel. 387,) is a purchase for £10 only, and not sufficient: but if the mortgage be satisfied, though another be immediately granted of the same amount, it is otherwise. (*Id. ib.*) So money laid out in a purchase *under* £30 will not give a settlement; (R. v. Dunchurch, Burr. S. C. 553;) but where £28 was stated in the deed as the consideration, but £30 was *actually* paid, it was holden to be sufficient. (R. v. Scammonden, 3 T. R. 474.) A settlement, however, is in no case gained until the purchase is actually completed. (R. v. Geddington, 2 Barn. & Cres. 129; R. v. Woolpit, 4 Dowl. & Ryl. 456.)

A mortgagee is a purchaser within the meaning of this act; (R. v. Stockland, 2 Stra. 1162;) and a purchase by a felon unpardoned has been holden sufficient. (R. v. Haddenham, 15 East, 463.)

Sum paid is the Test.] Though payment of a fine, or money borrowed upon mortgage, is part of the purchase-money, yet the only touchstone in these cases is, was £30 *bonâ fide* paid; and consequently, subsequent improvements of an estate, for which a smaller sum was originally given, will not give such purchaser a settlement, though the value thereof may be greatly increased. (Dunchurch v. South Kilworth, 1 Bla. Rep. 596.)

It will appear by the above authorities, that the word *purchase* is not to be taken in its largest sense, but is confined to cases where a pecuniary consideration is paid. It has been held, that, in the consideration for a copyhold estate, the fine to the lord, and the fee to the steward, are to be taken into the account; but the expenses of a surrender, paid to the purchaser's own attorney, cannot be computed as part of the purchase-money. (R. v. Cottingham, 7 Barn. & Cres. 603; 1 Man. & Ryl. 469.)

These instances show that the amount of the *purchase-money paid by the purchaser* is the criterion by which the question of settlement is determined, and not the *value* of the estate, which is quite immaterial; for if the estate devolve upon the party by act of law, as by executorship or marriage, &c., though it is of much less value than £30, it will suffice. (R. v. Ynyscynhanarn, 7 Barn. Cres. 233.)

A certificate man may gain a settlement in this way. (Barclear v. Eastwoodhay, 1 Stra. 163; R. v. Deddington, 2 Stra. 1193.)

Residence.] In order to acquire a settlement by estate, the party must *reside* forty days in the parish in which his estate lies, and while his interest continues. An order, therefore, removing a person to an estate which had descended to him, but where he had not resided, was quashed. (Wookey v. Hinton Blewet, 1 Stra. 476.) But the days need not be consecutive, and it makes no difference whether he reside on his own estate, in an alehouse, or any where else in the parish, so that the estate continues vested in him. (R. v. St. Neott's, Burr. S. C. 132; R. v. Dorstone, 1 East, 296; R. v. Horsley, 8 East, 410.) In short, the inhabitancy required depends upon the same principles which govern in other kinds of settlements, and may perhaps be safely considered as regulated by such determinations as have taken place respecting them. (2 N. P. L. 117.) No one can be removed from the parish in which his estate lies; but if he quits voluntarily, and becomes chargeable, he cannot be removed *thither*, unless he has before resided forty days.

This rule respecting residence admits of this qualification, that there must be a complete title; and where the title is incomplete without possession, as in the case of a sole next of kin, it seems that a residence on the estate itself is necessary, and that no settlement is gained by a residence in the same parish. As, where the party is kept out of possession by a wrong-doer, or suffers it to continue in a mortgagor, the party fails to gain a settlement, not because he does not *reside* upon the estate, but because he has not completed and perfected his title to the estate. (See R. v. Catherington, 3 T. R. 771; R. v. Darlington, 5 Maul. & Sel. 493; R. v. Canford Magna, 6 Maul. & Sel. 358.)

SECTION VII.—BY SERVING OFFICE.

Origin of this Settlement.] "If any person who shall come to inhabit in any town or parish, shall for *himself*, and on his *own account*, execute any public annual office or charge in the said town or parish during one whole year," he thereby gains a settlement. (3 & 4 W. & M. c. 11. s. 6.)

Mere Employment insufficient.] An *office* must be derived either immediately or mediately from the crown, or be constituted by statute. Whatever employment, therefore, is not derived from the one source or the other, is not an office for the purposes of gaining a settlement. (R. v. Mersham, 7 East, 171.) Thus the master of a workhouse has not such an office; his is merely an *employment* arising out of a contract; (Id.) nor has the master of a charity school such an office, his appointment being of a private nature, not derived from any public source; (R. v. Melborne, Burr. S. C. 247,) and as the statute is intended to apply to inferior offices, and not to those of any dignity, a curate of a parish has not such an annual office in his curacy as will give him a settlement. (Helsington v. Over, Burr. S. C. 746; R. v. Wantage, 2 East, 65.)

What Offices give a Settlement.] The statute was evidently intended to be confined to inferior annual officers. The office of parish clerk is within the act; (Gatton v. Milwich, 2 Salk. 536;) so is that of churchwarden; (St. Maurice v. St. Mary, Kallender, 2 Bott. 158;) and wardens of a borough, (St. Mary v. St. Laurence Reading, 10 Mod. 13.) The office of sexton is also within the act, (R. v. Liverpool, 3 T. R. 118,) and tithingman, (Burlescomb v. Sandford Peverell, 1 Stra. 544.) A borsholder and hogringer are also respectively *officers* within the statute. (Wingham v. Sellinge, 2 Stra. 1199; R. v. Holy Cross, Westgate, 4 Barn. & Ald. 619.) So, holding the situation of collector of the land tax, (R. v. Hammond, 2 Bott. 156,) and bailiff and ale-taster of a borough, (R. v. Bow, 8 T. R. 445,) confers settlements when duly executed. So a constable, though he serve by deputy, gains a settlement; (R. v. Hope Mansell, Cald. 252;) but a deputy constable does not; (R. v. Winterbourne, 1 Bla. Rep. 452.) And although, as already stated, a master of a workhouse at an annual salary, appointed by the parish, does not thereby gain a settlement, yet where the sessions stated *in the case*, that the party was legally appointed governor of the workhouse at an annual salary, and that the said *office is a public annual office*, that was held decisive in favour of the settlement. (R. v. Ilminster, 1 East, 83.)

An assistant overseer, elected and appointed under the 59 Geo 3. c. 12, at an annual salary of £10, will gain a settlement by serving such office for a year. But the appointment in writing, under the hands and seals of the justices, requires a £2 stamp, and the settlement is defeated if that be wanting. (R. v. Lew, 8 Barn. & Cres. 655.)

Limits of the Office.] The office, as it will be perceived by the instances of such as give a settlement, must have some especial relation to the parish in which the settlement is gained, for the notoriety in the parish is the ground upon which the statute gives the settlement, to the person exercising any public office. But it need not extend over the *whole* parish, nor be confined within its limits. However, the office must in some measure, at least, be executed in that part of the parish where the officer lives. (R. v. Liverpool, 3 T. R. 118.) Thus a party, by serving the office of clerk to a chapel situated in an extra-parochial vill, may gain a settlement in the adjoining parish, if he reside there, and if part of the duties of his office of clerk be exercisable within that part of the parish where he resides. (R. v. Amlwch, 4 Barn. & Cres. 757; 6 Dowl. & Ryl. 626.)

Serving the Office.] The mere appointment, though legally made, and an execution of its duties for a short time, will not suffice; although the service be put an end to by other persons. Thus, if A. be appointed to an office, and during the year is irregularly removed by two magistrates, and another person is appointed, and he, submitting to the discharge, does not in fact afterwards execute the office, he gains no settlement. (R. v. Westgate, 4 Barn. & Ald. 619.) Though, if he serve by deputy, he gains a settlement, and the deputy does not. (R. v. Hope, Mansell, 2 Bott. 166.)

The office must extend, but need not be limited in duration to a year; but in all cases the person must have *served* one whole year consecutively. (R. v. Fittleworth, Burr. S. C. 238; R. v. Yalding, 3 Dowl. & Ryl. 352; R. v. Bow, 8 T. R. 445.) He may be removed before he has served one whole year, if he become chargeable; or if removed for any other cause, in such case he gains no settlement. (Id.) And, if after serving an office for half a year he is removed, and sometime afterwards he executes the same office another half year, this is not sufficient to give him a settlement. (R. v. Cold, Ashton, Burr. S. C. 44.)

Residence.] The 13 & 14 Car. 2. c. 12, which enacts, that no person can gain a settlement in any parish by coming to inhabit there, unless he reside in the parish forty days, extends of course to this species of settlement.

A certificate man may gain a settlement in this way. (9 & 10 W. 3. c. 11.)

SECTION VIII.—DERIVATIVE SETTLEMENTS.

Acquired by Marriage or Parentage.] Derivative settlements are of two kinds; first, that which a wife derives from her husband; and secondly, the settlement which children derive from their parents, that is, from the father whilst he is living, being the head of the family; and after his death, as the mother becomes the head of the family, whilst she continues a widow, she communicates any settlement which she may acquire, in her own right, to the children. But when she marries again, she is no longer capable of acquiring a settlement in her own right, being herself a subordinate member of the family, of which her second husband is the head, and cannot, therefore, during the second coverture, communicate any settlement to the children of the first marriage.

Among the subordinate members of a family, which includes the wife and all the legitimate children not emancipated, is to be reckoned a posthumous child.

Wife's Settlement.] If a woman marry a man who hath a known settlement, she, instanter and *ipso facto*, by the marriage, acquires the husband's settlement; and the same as to any new settlement he may obtain until his death; and this although the marriage has been brought about by the fraud of parish officers; (R. v. Birmingham, 8 Barn. & Cres. 29,) and whether she have ever lived with him in his place of settlement or not. (St. Giles, Reading, v. Eversley, Blackwater, 1 Stra. 580, 2 Ld. Raym. 1332.) And she cannot gain a new settlement by any act of her own during his lifetime, even by residence on her own estate, after he has deserted her and his children. (Berkhamstead v. St. Mary, Northchurch, 2 Bott. 33, 1 N. P. L. 291.) After his death, she retains his last settlement until she acquire a new one. (St. George's v. St. Catharine's, 4 Burr. 289.) But if he is in the progress of acquiring a settlement, as by renting a tenement for a year, and he dies a few days only before it is completed, the widow cannot, by continuing to reside, and paying the year's rent, perfect the settlement for herself and children. (R. v. Crayford, 6 Barn. & Cres. 68; 9 Dowl. & Ryl. 80.)

Where Husband has no Settlement.] But if she marry a foreigner, who has no settlement, or a person whose settlement is not known, she still retains her maiden settlement, and may be removed there after her husband's death, or if he leave her, and it is not known whether he is living or dead. (R. v. Ryton Cald. 39.)

Alteration by 59 Geo. 3. c. 12.] Before this statute was passed, it was held, that even where the husband and wife were living together, but he had no settlement, and was unable to support her, she might be removed to her maiden settlement with *his consent*. (R. v. Eltham, 5 East, 113.) But it has been since held, that by the 33rd section of the above act, this power is taken away in such cases, and that the justices cannot now remove the wife and family of a Scotchman to her maiden settlement, thereby effecting a temporary divorce, although the husband consent; but that he and his family must be sent by a pass to Scotland. (R. v. Leeds, 4 Barn. & Ald. 498.)

Before that statute passed, it was clearly established by a series of authorities, (see R. v. Harberton, 13 East, 311,) that where a woman who had a settlement, married, and was deserted by her husband, who had no settlement, the maiden settlement of the wife was revived, and she might be removed thither. This statute, however, in the thirty-third section, reciting that poor persons born in Scotland and in Ireland, and in the Isles of Man, Jersey and Guernsey, frequently become chargeable to parishes in England, and cannot be removed unless they have committed some act of vagrancy, authorizes and requires two magistrates, upon complaint of the parish officers, that any person born in Scotland or Ireland, &c. has become chargeable to such parish by himself or his family, to cause such person to be brought before them, and to examine him touching the place of his birth, or last legal settlement; and if it shall be found that such person was born in Scotland or Ireland, &c., and has not gained any settlement in England, then the justices are empowered, *by a pass* under their hands and seals, to cause such person *and his wife*, &c. to be removed to the place of his birth in the manner therein mentioned.

The object of the legislature was to relieve parishes from the necessity of maintaining as casual poor, persons born in Scotland or Ireland, &c. But the statute does not authorize the removal of the *wife alone* to the place of her husband's birth. The law, therefore, remains as it was before, in those cases where a Scotch or Irish husband has *deserted* his wife. In R. v. Leeds, cited above, it was only decided, that where the husband (who was born in Scotland,) and his wife were *living together*, the wife must be sent along with him to Scotland. No mischief will result from this decision; for during the absence of the husband, the family will be maintained by the parish, which is bound to maintain them; and upon his return, that parish may pass him and his family to Scotland or Ireland, &c., whichever is the place of his birth. (Rex v. Cottingham, 7 Barn. & Cres. 615; 1 Man. & Ryl. 439.)

It follows, therefore, notwithstanding this statute, that if the husband, being such foreigner, dies, or quits his family, and after his death, or while he is absent, they become chargeable, the removal must be to the wife's maiden settlement. (Id.; Rex v. Heaton Norris, 7 Barn. & Cres. 619.)

Expenses of Removals to Jersey, &c.] The provisions for removing vagrant and poor persons born in the Isles of Jersey and Guernsey, and chargeable to parishes in England, by passes which cast a burden upon the respective parishes, through which they passed, under the 17 G. 2. c. 5. the 59 G. 3. c. 12, and the 5 G. 4. c. 83, have been repealed, and instead thereof, it is enacted, that it shall be lawful for two justices of the peace, and they are hereby required, upon the complaint of the churchwardens and overseers of the poor of any parish, that any person born in either of the Isles of Jersey or Guernsey hath become chargeable to such parish, by himself or herself, or his or her family, to cause such person to be brought before them, and to examine such person, and any other witness or witnesses, on oath, touching the place of the birth or last legal settlement of every such person, and to inquire whether he or she, or any of his or her children, hath or have gained any settlement in that part of the United Kingdom called England; and if it shall be found by such justices, that the person so brought before them was born in either of the isles of Jersey or Guernsey, and hath not gained any settlement in England, and that he or she hath actually become chargeable to the complaining parish, by himself or herself, or his or her family, then such justices shall, and they are hereby empowered, by an order of removal under their hands and seals, to cause such poor person, his wife, and such of his or her children so chargeable, as shall not have gained a settlement in England, to be removed, *by and at the charge and expense of the complaining parish, to the place of his or her birth.* (11 Geo. 4. c. 5.)

Proof of Settlement by Marriage.] Though the pauper is a married woman, it will suffice to prove her maiden settlement; the other side must prove the husband's settlement, and whether he is dead or living, to get rid of it. (Rex v. Hedsor, Cald. 371; Rex v. Harberton, 13 East, 311.)

Whichever party means to rely upon a settlement by marriage, must be prepared to prove the marriage, and the husband's settlement.

For the purposes of a settlement, the marriage may be proved by an examined copy of the register, and the identity of the parties; and the witnesses who sign the register are not *essential* for this purpose. The proof may also be by any persons present at the ceremony, even the husband and wife, who are also competent to *disprove* the fact. (Standen v. Standen, Peake Rep. 32; Rex v. Edmonton, Cald. 435.) But neither husband nor wife is admissible to prove the fact of marriage, where it directly tends to criminate the other in the offence of bigamy, &c. (Rex. v. Cliviger, 2 T. R. 263; 1 Phil. Ev. 79.) The fact of marriage may also be presumed from long cohabitation as man and wife. (Leader v. Barry, 1 Esp. R. 353.)

Foreign Marriages.] Marriage in Scotland, even between English subjects who go there for the purpose, (Bull, N. P. 113,) being merely a civil contract, is proved either by express evidence of the contract, or by evidence of the admission of it by both parties, or presumptively, by cohabitation and being reputed man and wife. (See Dalrymple v. Dalrymple, 2 Haggard's Reports; 54 Ilderton v. Ilderton, 2 H. Blac. 145.)

A marriage in a foreign country, if good by the laws of the country in which it takes place, is valid here; (Lacon v. Higgins, 3 Stark, Rep. 178; Dowl. & Ryl. N. P. Rep. 38;) and upon proof of a marriage *de facto,* the court will presume it to have been legal, unless the contrary be shown. (Rex. v. Brampton, 10 East, 282.)

But the strongest of all proofs is the admission of the parish itself, against which it is sought to establish the marriage, by having granted a certificate in which it acknowledges the parties to be man and wife. (Rex v. Ullisthorpe, 8 T. R. 465.)

Void Marriages.] The party interested to controvert the marriage, must prove either that it was solemnized in a manner which renders it void by the marriage act, or that one of the parties was already married to a person living at the time; which may be proved by oral testimony. (See Rex v. Twyning, 2 Barn. & Ald. 386.) No settlement can be gained by marriage with an idiot or insane person, unless celebrated during a lucid interval. (15 Geo. 2. c. 30; 1 Bla. Com. 439.) But a marriage of a female pauper, brought about by the fraud of parish officers, will not prevent her from acquiring a settlement by the marriage in the husband's parish. (Rex v. Birmingham, 8 Barn. & Cres. 29.) And a marriage by licence of a minor, without his father's consent, is valid; the marriage act (4 Geo. 4. c. 76, s. 15) being directory only. (Id. See *ante Marriage.*)

Settlement by Parentage.] The father's *last* settlement is the settlement of his legitimate children who have not been emancipated, or gained a settlement for themselves, whether it was his settlement at the time of their *birth* or not. (Coxwell v. Shillingford, Fost. 313, Fol. 269.) And therefore, proof of the settlement of a father is *primâ facie* evidence of the settlement of his child; (Rex v. Stone, 6 T. R. 56;) and this rule prevails, although before the birth of the child the father die; (Reg. v. Clifton, 19 Vin. Abr. 382;) or if he be attaint, the settlement which he had *previously* acquired is communicated to his children born *after* his attainder; (Rex v. St. Mary Cardigan, 6 T. R. 116;) and if he acquire a fresh settlement after his attainder, as it seems he may do, if during the performance of the necessary conditions to obtain a settlement, his civil disability on account of his attainder is not objected against him by a competent authority, such settlement is communicated to his children. (Rex v. Haddenham, 15 East, 463.)

If the father's settlement be unknown, or he have none, the settlement of the wife, acquired previous to her existing marriage, shall be that of the children, until emancipated. (Westerham v. Chidingstone, Fol. 252; Berkhampstead v. St. Mary, North Church, 2 Bott. 33; 1 Nolan, P. L. 308.) But since the 59 Geo. 3. c. 12, (see *ante* 547,) if the father be an Irishman or Scotchman, &c., and has gained no settlement, and any unemancipated child of his becomes chargeable, though he is not so himself, such child may be removed, not to the mother's settlement, but to the place where such child was born. Thus, where an unmarried daughter of an Irishman, being pregnant, became chargeable, it was held, that this did not make her father and the rest of the family removeable by a pass, under the above act, to Ireland, but that she might be removed to the place of her birth, in England. (Rex v. Whitehaven, 5 Barn. & Ald. 720.)

If a husband die, and the widow marry again, the children of the first husband do not thereby acquire the settlement of the second husband, but retain that which their mother *last* had, before the second marriage. (Wangford v. Brandon, Carth. 449; 2 Salk. 482.)

But the mother becomes the head of the family, on the death of her husband; and therefore a settlement acquired by her in her own right, during widowhood, as by estate, renting a tenement, &c., is communicated to her unemancipated children, although past the age of nurture. (St. George v. St. Catharine's, 2 Ld. Raym. 1474; Rex v. Long Wittenham, 2 Bott. 38; Rex v. Paulsperry, 1 Barnard. 11.)

Age of Nurture.] Children under *seven* years of age shall not be removed from their parents, but go with them for nurture; and the parish where the children are legally settled shall relieve them in the parish where the *parent* is settled. (Wangford v. Brandon, Carth. 449; 2 Salk. 482.)

Emancipation of Children.] The right of children to take the parents' settlement is at an end by their obtaining a settlement in their own right; or assuming a relation which wholly and permanently excludes the parental control. (Rex v. Wilmington, 5 Barn. & Ald. 525.)

Emancipation may be effected in various ways; one of which is, by the party gaining a settlement, in his or her own right, by any of the modes before pointed out. And if a person under age thus acquire a settlement, and afterwards, during minority, return to and continue to reside in the father's family, such child does not follow the parent's settlement subsequently gained, but retains his own *acquired* settlement. (Rex v. Bleasby, 3 Barn. & Ald. 377.)

Emancipation by Marriage.] A party marrying contracts a relation incompatible with parental control. If a son, he becomes the head, and if a daughter, she becomes a subordinate member, of a *new family;* and the emancipation is complete, although the son or daughter continue to live with the parents. (Rex v. Everton, 1 East, 526.)

By living away from Parents.] A child may be emancipated by living separately from, and independently of, the parents, *after twenty-one years* of age, whether the separation commence before or after full age; provided the means of support are not derived from, but are obtained independently of the parents. (Rex v. Roach, 6 T. R. 247.) And where the pauper, while he was under age, quitted his parents, and went to sea, serving sometimes in a king's ship, at other times in trading vessels, and remained in such service, and so separated from his father's family when he attained the age of twenty-one years, it was held, that he was then emancipated, and that his settlement did not afterwards shift with that of his father. (Rex v. Lawford, 8 Barn. & Cres. 271.)

By enlisting as a Soldier, &c.] A son becomes emancipated by enlisting as a soldier or marine, if he continue in the service till he is of full age; but if he be a minor at the time of his enlistment, and, quitting the service, return to his father's family during his minority, and continue a member thereof, thus returning to the father's control, he is not emancipated; because, during the minority of a child there can be no emancipation, unless he marries, and so becomes the head of a family, or contracts some other relation, so as wholly and *permanently* to exclude the parental control. (Rex v. Rotherfield Greys, 1 Barn. & Cres. 345; 2 Dowl. & Ryl. 628.)

But if the son enlist only into the militia, he places himself under the government or control of others, for only that part of the year for which the militia is called out; and the parental control not being thereby entirely excluded, he is not emancipated. (Rex v. Woburn, 8 T. R. 479.)

Emancipation not perfected.] The circumstances essential to emancipation will further appear, by considering the instances in which it has been held that the emancipation was incomplete.

Thus, if a son who was bound apprentice to a master, by serving whom he could gain no settlement—as to a *certificated* person, (Rex v. Hardwicke, 11 East, 578;) or who was bound by a void indenture, (Rex v. Edgeworth, 3 T. R. 353,) or who has served under a hiring and service in an extra-parochial place, (Rex v. Collingbourn Ducis, 4 T. R. 199,) returns, during his minority, to reside with his parent, he is thereby re-incorporated with the family, and is not emancipated. So, as has already been seen, if he enlist for a soldier, and, being discharged, resume his home with his father, before he is of age. (*Supra.*)

And it is not sufficient, to be of age, and have an independent business of his own; for if he remains under the parent's roof, he thereby makes his election to remain a member of his father's family, and is not emancipated; (Rex v. Sowerby, 2 East, 276;) or if he be living separate from his parents, but either of the other requisites be wanting—that is, full age, or support from a source independent of his parent—the result is the same. (Rex v. Witton *cum* Twambrookes, 3 T. R. 355.) And where a child had lived with and been maintained from the age of four years, by her grandfather, till his death, who by his will directed the grandmother to educate and maintain the child out of a fund given to the grandmother for life, and after her decease to the granddaughter, and this maintenance continued until she was twenty-one, it was held, that this did not amount to an emancipation; as, in the eventual failure of the funds, or if the grandmother had refused or neglected to maintain the child, the father might have been obliged to provide for her; and he again might claim to have had the control and custody of her at any time. (Rex v. Uckfield, 5 Maul. & Sel. 214.)

Emancipation, when completed.] In the case of emancipation by gaining a settlement, it is accomplished when the settlement is *completed.* (Rex v. New Forest, 5 T. R. 478.) When it results from a marriage, it commences immediately upon the marriage, though she never lived in the place. (Rex v. Pincehorton, 4 Burn. 333.)

In the case of a minor enlisting for a soldier, if he remain in the army till he is twenty-one, his emancipation relates back to the time of his enlistment. But there is a distinction between the case of the soldier, and the minor contracting to serve another person, as the captain of a merchant ship, or for any other employment not under the state: for by the law of England the parental authority continues until the son attains the age of twenty-one; and any contract of service made by the son subjects him to another authority, not paramount, but subordinate to that of the parent. The policy of the law, however, requires that a minor shall be at liberty to contract an engagement to serve the state; and when entered into, it becomes inconsistent with the duty which he owes to the public, that the parental authority should continue. He thereby becomes severed from his father's family, and is subject to the paramount control of the state. The case of a soldier, therefore, is an exception to the general rule. (Rex v. Lytchet Matraverse, 7 Barn. & Cres. 226.) But if a son, at the age of eighteen, live apart from his parents, and independently of them, and continue to do so till he is twenty-one, he is then emancipated; but his emancipation does not relate back to his age of eighteen; for till he is of age, his domicile, in law, is supposed to be with his parents; and the parental control, though not exercised, is not absolutely at an end till the son, in addition to these other circumstances, has attained to his full age. (Rex v. Uckfield, 5 Maul. & Sel. 214.)

It remains to be observed, that a father who is a widower becomes competent to acquire a fresh settlement, by hiring and service, after all his children are emancipated. (Rex v. Cowhoneybourne, 10 East, 88.)

SECTION IX.—BY BIRTH.

Foundation of this Settlement.] Before the passing of the 13 and 14 Car. 2. c. 12, there were several statutes, by which the right of the poor to resort for relief to the place of their birth was recognized. So early as the time of Richard 2, there is an act to this effect, and the reigns of Henry the 7th, Edward the 6th, and James the 1st, are distinguished by similar enactments.

But the 13 and 14 Car. 2. c. 12, more particularly fixed this species of settlement, by directing justices to remove such poor persons as are pointed out in the act, to the parish where they were last legally settled, either as natives, servants, householders, &c.

Who may acquire this Settlement.] Legitimate children whose parents have no settlement, or whose parental settlement is unknown, acquire a settlement in the parish or place where they are born. And it is a general rule, that illegitimate children born within any particular parish, &c., without fraud or contrivance, are so settled; to which there are, however, some exceptions introduced by particular statutes, for the protection of parishes against the accumulation of this burthen, by charitable or other public institutions, in which children of this class may be born, being situated within such parishes or places.

Another exception was made by the statute for encouraging Friendly Societies. In the case of a woman, who, at the time of the birth of her bastard child, was a member of a Friendly Society, and was residing in any parish not her own, under the authority of the act; in such case it was provided, that the child should have the same settlement as the mother had at the time the child was born. (See 33 Geo. 3. c. 54; Rex v. Idle, 2 Barn. & Ald. 149.) But this statute was repealed by the act for consolidating the laws relating to Friendly Societies, which does not contain a re-enactment of the like provision. (See 10 Geo. 4. c. 56.)

Legitimate Children.] The place of birth, or first known place of abode, (Comb. 364. 372,) is *primâ facie* the place of settlement of legitimate children. (R. v. Heaton & Norris, 6 T. R. 653.) But this is the case only until the parish find the father's, or in default thereof, the mother's place of settlement, if either of the parents had acquired a settlement. As to the children of a father born in Ireland, Scotland, &c., and having acquired no settlement in England, (see *ante* 547.)

Illegitimate Children.] It is a general rule, that the place of birth is the place of settlement of a bastard child. (Whitechapel v. Stepney, Carth. 433; 2 Bott. 12.) But if it be born in an extra-parochial place, it has no settlement by birth, and being a bastard, it can derive none from its parent; it is therefore entitled to remain with its mother as long as the purposes of nurture require, and it will afterwards be entitled to relief as casual poor. (R. v. St. Nicholas, Leicester, 2 Barn. & Cres. 389; 4 Dowl. & Ryl. 462.)

But if a woman be delivered of a bastard, in another parish than that in which she is settled, by *collusion* or *fraud*, (Masters v. Child, 3 Salk. 66; Tewkesbury v. Twining, Buls. 349;) or if after an *order* of removal of the mother to her legal settlement, and *before* actual removal, the bastard be born, (R. v. Ickleford, 2 Bott. 4;) or be born whilst the mother is being removed, (Jane Grey's case, 2 Bott. 4;) or whilst the mother is in a state of vagrancy, (17 G. 2. c. 5, s. 25;) or in the house of correction, (Suckley v. Whitborn, 2 Bulst. 358.; see 54 G. 3. c. 170, s. 2;) or in prison, (Elsing v. Hereford, 1 Sess. Cas. 94; see 54 Geo. 3 c. 170, s. 2;) or in the house of industry of an incorporated district, (20 Geo. 3. c. 36;) or in the Lying-in Hospital, (13 Geo. 3. c. 82, s. 5;)—in all these cases the settlement of the bastard shall be that of its mother at the time of the birth; and by the 13 Geo. 3. c. 29, no child received into the Foundling Hospital shall thereby gain a settlement in the parish in which the hospital is situated.

If a woman is removed from a parish in which she has no settlement, to another parish in which she has also no settlement, and the order of removal is afterwards quashed; and whilst she is in the parish to which she has been thus removed, her bastard child is born, it does not thereby acquire a settlement in that parish, but in the parish from which the mother was removed. (R. v. Great Salkeld, 6 Maul. & Sel. 408.) And the same rule applies with respect to districts, as to parishes. Thus, where a parish was divided into two districts, (A. & M.) each separately maintaining its own poor, and removing from one to the other, and a woman who was settled in M. was removed from a third parish to A. by an order of removal directed to A, which order was quashed upon appeal; and pending the appeal, the woman was delivered in A. of a bastard child, and afterwards the woman and her child having been received back by the removing parish, were removed by order to M.; it was held, that the child's settlement was not in M., but in the removing parish. (R. v. St. Andrew's, Holborn, 6 Maul. & Sel. 411; R. v. Martlesham, M. T. 1829, MSS. 9 Barn. & Cres.)

Where the Mother is certificated.] A bastard born whilst the mother resides in another parish under a certificate, is settled where *born*; (New Windsor v. White, Waltham, 1 Stra. 186; Lydlinch v. Hilton, 2 Stra. 1168;) unless the certificate undertake to provide for the woman and her child, she being then pregnant. (R. v. Wyke, Burr. S. C. 264.) But it must appear on the certificate that it refers to an illegitimate child, as the parish will not be bound to do so where the undertaking is, in general terms, to provide "for the woman and her child," as that will be intended to signify her legitimate offspring. (*Ib.* R. v. Mathon, 7 T. R. 362.)

A bastard, however, cannot be removed from its mother whilst a nurse child, that is, until seven years of age, although it is settled in the place where it is born. (Cripplegate v. St. Saviour's, Fol. 265; Skiffreth v. Walford, 2 Bott. 4;) but the parish in which it was born must maintain it, though it may be resident with its mother elsewhere. (R. v. Hemlingham, Doug 9, n. (2.)

CHAPTER XXVI.—REMOVAL OF PAUPERS.

SECTION I.—ORDERS OF REMOVAL.

Authorized by Statute.] The authority of magistrates to remove paupers, exists only as it is derived from the express provisions of acts of parliament. The principal statute giving this power is the 13 & 14 Car. 2, by which poor persons might be removed within forty days after their coming to settle in any parish, by an order of two justices, upon complaint made by the churchwardens or overseers, that such poor persons were *likely to become* chargeable. But the power of removal in anticipation of chargeability, was in the late reign taken away, and now no poor person can be removed by an order of justices till such person has become *actually chargeable* to the parish or place where such poor person shall be inhabiting. (35 Geo. 3. c. 101. s. 1.)

But an unmarried woman with child shall be deemed to be actually chargeable. (Id. s. 6.) And if she be married and pregnant with a child, which when born will be a bastard, the husband having been for a long time, and being still abroad, she is alike within the act with an unmarried woman. (R. v. Tebbenham, 9 East, 388.)

But though the act says that such a person shall be " deemed and taken to be actually chargeable," yet that must be understood to be *secundum subjectam materiam;* or as the act itself expresses it, " chargeable within the true intent and meaning of this act," the interpretation of which is thus given by Lord Ellenborough: " Was it not the meaning of the act to prevent the removal of persons until *actually* chargeable, who were before removable, if likely to become so; but not to make persons removeable who were not proper objects of removal before that act? Could it be meant that a person in this situation should be torn away from her parents, whatever her condition in life may be, and however far removed from probability of being a charge upon the parish? The substance of a person so situated repels the idea of her being chargeable; and the act did not mean to make any one removeable who was not so antecedently to the passing of the act." It was therefore held, that a single woman, serving a master under a contract of hiring and service, cannot, though pregnant of a child which will be born a bastard, be removed from her service, against her consent and *his*. (R. v. Alveley, 3 East, 563.)

To what Place removeable.] The removal must be to the place of the pauper's last legal settlement. But if that place has, since the pauper acquired a settlement there, ceased to have overseers and to maintain its own poor, as where the houses within it were taken down, and there were no residents remaining capable of being appointed overseers, no removal to it can take place; and the pauper must remain to be subsisted as casual poor in the place where he became chargeable; and the justices have no power to remove him to any prior settlement, for the last acquired settlement extinguished all the former; and in a new case, the court form their judgment upon the very words of the act. (R. v. Saighton-on-the-Hill, 2 Barn. & Ald. 162.)

In like manner, where a district previously extra-parochial, was by act of parliament made a township, and it was provided, that from thenceforth it should maintain its own poor, &c., and have the same privileges and immunities, and be subject to the same regulations as other townships within the county; it was held, that this provision was prospective only, and that a bastard born within the district previously to passing the act, was not settled there. (R. v. Oakmere, 5 Barn. & Ald. 775.)

Where two justices made an order of removal to the parish of

Tamworth, adjudging the pauper's settlement to be at Sirescote in the said parish of Tamworth, and ordering the overseers of the said parish of Tamworth to receive and provide for the pauper, it was held a good order, as it appeared that there never had been any overseers for the hamlet of Sirescote, which consisted of one house only, which was not assessed to the poor of Tamworth, though it always had been to the church. (R. v. Tamworth, Cald. 28.) And where an order of removal was made to a parish, when it ought to have been made to one of several townships into which the parish was divided, and which townships removed poor from one to the other reciprocally, the court held, that the removal unappealed against was conclusive upon the parish. (Spitalfields v. Bromley, 2 Bott. 890; R. v. Kirkby Stephen, 3 Burr. S. C. 664.)

But in the case of R. v. Swalcliffe, Cald. 248, it was determined, that the removal of a pauper to Ascott, a large populous village, part of the parish of Whichford, but maintaining its poor, *in common with Whichford*, and not separately, was a mere nullity, and not conclusive, although unappealed against.

Refusal to receive the Person removed.] The 13 & 14 Car. 2. s. 3, makes it an indictable offence in churchwardens and overseers refusing to receive and provide work for persons removed to their parish. And the 3 W. & M. c. 11, provides, that if any person be removed by virtue of that act from one county, riding, town, &c. to another, under a warrant of two justices, the churchwardens or overseers are required to receive such person under a penalty of £5.

The punishment provided by this latter statute does not necessarily supersede the other. In a case where it was moved in arrest of judgment, upon an indictment for this offence, on the ground that the more recent statute had provided a pecuniary penalty, it was said by Denison, J.: If one statute gave one punishment, and another statute gave another punishment, the prosecutor has his election; and Foster, J. observed, that in all cases where a justice has power given him to make an order, and direct it to an inferior ministerial officer, and he disobeys it, if there be no particular remedy prescribed, it is indictable, and the judgment was given against the defendant. (R. v. Davis, Say 163; 4 Burn's Justice, 829.)

The Complaint, by whom, &c.] The complaint may be laid before a single justice, and need not be upon oath. (R. v. Westwood, 1 Stra. 73.) But if the order of removal do not set forth any complaint made, it is bad, for this is the foundation of the justice's jurisdiction. (R. v. Harely, Andr. 361.) And if it state that it is made upon complaint only, and not of the churchwardens or overseers, this omission is equally fatal, for no one can disturb a man coming to settle in a parish but those to whom the law has given authority to do it, viz. the churchwardens and overseers; and if they do not complain, it may be that the parish is willing to keep him. (Western Rivers v. St. Peter's, 2 Salk. 492.)

But if the order be directed to the officers of the two parishes, and state, " Whereas complaint has been made by you," &c., without saying which is the complaining party, this is sufficient, for it must be intended to be made by the party aggrieved; for it is upon complaint of the right parish if both complain. (Spalding v. St. John Baptist. Fol. 267. 2 Nolan, P. L. 218.)

The complaint, as set out in the order of removal, should state, that the pauper has become actually chargeable, since 35 Geo. 3. c. 101, or it should set out facts from whence that conclusion necessarily follows. If it merely recite that the person was reduced to great poverty, and had been relieved by the churchwardens and overseers, that is not sufficient, as it does not appear to have been at the parish expense. (Great Bedwin v. Welcot, 2 Stra. 1158.) But where the complaint stated that the pauper was with child, which was likely to be born a bastard, and there was an *adjudication* that she was actually chargeable, this was held sufficient, although the complaint did not state that the pauper was actually chargeable. (R. v. Inskip-with-Sowerby, 5 Maul. & Sel. 299.)

Justices, their Style on the Order.] The complaint may be made to one justice, though two are necessary to adjudge and remove, and they ought to hear, determine, and sign together, though an order altered by one magistrate in the presence of the other, after sealing a ndbefore delivery, was held good. (R. v. Llanwinis, 4 T. R. 473.) And if the merely ministerial act of signing be performed, separately where they have previously agreed, upon a joint investigation, the order is at most voidable, and not void. (See R. v. Stotfold, 4 T. R. 596; R. v. Hamstall, Ridware, 2 Bott. 503.)

But an order of removal made by two justices, one of whom at the time was churchwarden of the removing parish, is bad. Because as churchwarden he must be considered as one of the complainants seeking the removal, and then the person who was complainant heard and adjudicated upon the complaint, which cannot be in point of law. (R. v. Great Yarmouth, 6 Barn. & Cres. 646.)

The order of removal should state the justices to be justices *of the peace*, and not merely justices of the county; (4 Burn's Justice, 799;) and it was held a fatal objection to an order, that it said, " unto us, two of his Majesty's justices of the peace *in* the said county, instead of *for* the county," for by that it merely appeared, that they lived in the county. (R. v. Owlton, 2 Sess. Ca. 76; 2 Salk. 474.) But it is not essential that it should appear that they are justices of the division. (Anon. 2 Salk. 473.)

Where the order, being addressed to parish officers in two different counties, described the justices as justices, &c., in and for the *said county*, so that it was not expressed in terms, on the face of the order, for which county they were acting, this was held a fatal defect. (Rex v. Moor Critchell, 2 East, 66.) But the authority of this decision was afterwards much questioned, in a case where, after describing the parishes and counties respectively, as above, the order went on, "Rutland to wit," and then styled the justices as justices, &c. in and for the said county; and it was held, that it sufficiently appeared that they were justices for the county of Rutland. (Rex v. St. Mary's, Leicester, 1 Barn. & Ald. 327.) And if the language employed leaves no doubt upon the point, when reasonably construed, it is sufficient.

By the 26 Geo. 2. c. 27, it is enacted, that no order shall be set aside for not setting forth that one of the justices is of the quorum.

Description of the Paupers.] The name of the pauper must be inserted in the order, or if it is unknown, it must be so stated; and this rule applies where a whole family is removed, and an order to remove a man and *his family*, or, and his *then children*, is bad, being too general, and may include persons not removeable. (Johnson's Case, 2 Salk. 485, Beaston v. Scisson, 1 Stra. 114.) Nor can two families be removed by one order; for it may be illegal as to one, and then a difficulty would arise in settling costs, upon an appeal. (Chewton v. Compton Martin, 1 Stra. 471.)

The established rule is, that in every order where the children are directed to be removed to their father's settlement, the ages of the children must be set out, (to show that they are of such tender years as not to have gained a settlement for themselves,) or there must be an express adjudication of their having gained no other settlement. (Rex v. Bowling, Burr. S. C. 177.) Seven years is an age that the court will presume a child could gain a settlement at, in his own right. (Rex v. Trinity in Chester, 2 Bott. 867.)

There must also be an adjudication that the pauper has become chargeable to the parish from whence he is removed, and that the parish, &c. to which he is removed is the place where he was last legally settled. (2 Nol. P. L. 224, 226.)

Stating the Examination.] The examination ought to be taken before two justices. If the order state, " It appears, upon examination before us, *or one of us*," it is bad, because both are to make the judgment of removal. (Ware v. Stanstead, 2 Salk. 488.)

But now, by 49 Geo. 3. c. 124, s. 4, if the pauper be, from age or other infirmity, unable to be brought up to be examined as to his settlement, one magistrate may take his examination, and report it to another, who together, upon such report, may adjudge the settlement. And the order thus made need not state the special circumstances of taking the examination, as the statute does not require any alteration to be made in the form of the order. (Rex v. South Lynn, All Saints, 4 Maul. & Sel. 354.)

Although it is directed by statute that the examination shall be upon oath, yet if the order profess to be made " upon *due* examination," without saying, upon oath, it shall be intended to have been upon oath; or if it be stated that it was " upon his affirmation," &c., it will suffice, without adding, that he was a Quaker. (Munger Hunger v. Warden, 2 Nolan. P. L. 222.)

It is usual, though not essential, that the pauper himself should be examined before the order of removal is made; for he may produce a certificate, give security, or show other cause against the removal. (Rex v. Wykes, Andr. 238.) It is obvious, however, that this cannot be always done, as in the case of infants of tender years, extreme infirmity, or dangerous sickness. Holt, C. J. says, on this subject, " If it can be, it is fit it should be so, but not absolutely necessary." (Comb. 478.) And this seems to afford a safe rule in such matters. (See Rex v. Everdon, 9 East, 105.)

By 59 Geo. 3. c. 12, s. 28, any justice of the peace may take, in writing, the examination, on oath, of any person having a wife or child who shall be a prisoner in any gaol or house of correction, or in the custody of the keeper of any such gaol or house of correction, or who shall be in the custody of any constable or other peace officer, by virtue of any warrant of commitment, touching the place of his or her last legal settlement; and such examination shall be signed by such justice, and shall be admitted in evidence as to such settlement before any justices, for the purpose of any order of removal, so long only as the person so examined shall continue a prisoner.

The Adjudication.] The adjudication must be certain and positive; as, " We do adjudge," which is the most unexceptionable form; or, " It appears to us," &c., which has been held sufficient. (2. Nol. P. L. 224.)

Thus, where the order stated, " We, on examination, do believe the same to be true," this was held insufficient. (Stallingborough v. Hartray, 1 Ses. Cas. 131.) So, where it adjudged the pauper to be settled in A., "according to their knowledge;" for this is uncertain. (2 Nol. P. L. 224.)

As the complaint, since 35 Geo. 3. c. 101, must state, so must the order adjudge, that the party is actually chargeable to the parish complaining, (Ufculm v. Clysthydon, Burr. S. C. 138,) and that he is legally settled in the parish to which the order directs he shall be conveyed, unless it be a removal back to a parish giving a certificate; in which case the justices need not adjudge it to be his settlement. (Malden v. Fletwick, 2 Salk. 530.) Thus, "We order him to be removed to A., as the place of his last legal settlement" is bad, as there is no adjudication. (Rex v. Westwood, 1 Stra. 73.) "That the pauper was legally settled in B., *according to their knowledge;*" or, "That C. is the place of his legal settlement, as we are credibly informed," are alike defective. (Trowbridge v. Weston, 2 Salk. 473.)

If the order merely state, that it appears, on the oath of A., that her husband was last legally settled at H., it is bad; for the oath of the woman is not tantamount to an adjudication by the justices. (Rex v. Hackney, 2 Salk. 478.) And if they do adjudge that the husband was last legally settled at H., the pauper being his widow, they must further state, that she has not gained any other settlement since his death. (Egburn v. Hartley Wintly, 1 Sess Ca. 45.)

In like manner, if children *above* the age of seven are removed, it is not sufficient to adjudge, that the place to which their removal is made was the legal settlement of the father; for they may have acquired a settlement in their own right. (Rex v. Middleham, Fol. 271.) But if children under the age of seven are removed without their parents, and the order adjudges the parish to be their last legal settlement, by name, it need not adjudge it to be the settlement of their father. (Rex v. Bucklebury, 1 T. R. 164.)

It was objected, that the order which adjudged that the paupers *were* last legally settled in M. was imperfect for want of an adjudication of a *present* settlement; but Lord Ellenborough said, that it referred to the time of the complaint made, and the court could not intend an intermediate settlement, betwen the hearing of the complaint and the making the order of removal. (Rex v. Binegar, 7 East, 380.)

Where the words were, "the last legal place," omitting "of settlement" in the adjudication, the omission was held fatal. (Rex v. Warnhill, 2 Sess. Ca. 91; 2 Nol. P. L. 229.)

Direction of the Order.] The order should be directed to the officers of *both* parishes, and should require those of the complaining parish to remove the pauper, and those of the parish in which the settlement is adjudged to be, to receive and provide for him. If, therefore, it do not state which is to convey, and which to receive, it is bad. (Binfield v. Banstead, 11 Mod. 268.)

A mistake in the name of a parish does not vitiate the order, if that used be sufficiently descriptive to a common intendment, especially if the parish, by appealing, or otherwise recognizing the order, acknowledge the sufficiency of the name. (Rex v. Topsham, 7 East, 466; 2 Nol. P. L. 231.)

And it seems no objection to the direction of an order, that it is to the churchwardens and overseers of the *parish, township,* or *division* of U. (Rex v. Ulverstone, 7 T. R. 565.) Or to the churchwardens and overseers of the township of H. (Rex v. Holbeck, in Leeds, Burr. S. C. 198.

But a removal to "a parish or *hamlet*" has been held bad for uncertainty, the court saying, that a vill and a parish they would intend co-extensive, but a hamlet was nothing else but part of a parish. (Rex v. Grimston, 1 Barnard. 11.)

Form of a subsequent Order.] An order of removal is, in effect, a judgment. If it be unappealed from, or be affirmed upon appeal, it concludes the parish to which the removal is made, as against all the world. (Rex v. Corsham, 11 East, 388.) But if quashed, it only concludes the litigating parishes. (Rex v. Bradenham, Burr. S. C. 397.) So long, therefore, as these judgments are in force, the justices cannot make a fresh order repugnant to them.

It follows, that if an order be made upon a parish which appears to be exempt, by a prior judgment, the order must state that a settlement has been acquired there subsequently to such judgment or adjudication. (Rex v. Leigh, Cald. 59.) But if an order be quashed for a defect in form, it concludes nothing between the contending parishes; and the pauper may be again removed, without setting forth a fresh settlement subsequent to the making of the first order. (Rex v. St. Andrews, Holborn, 6 T. R. 613.)

Suspending Orders of Removal.] The power of suspending orders of removal is given by the 35 Geo. 3. c. 101; the 2nd section of which enacts, "And whereas poor persons are often removed or passed to the place of their settlement during the time of their sickness, to the great danger of their lives; for remedy, therefore, be it further enacted, That in case any poor person shall, from henceforth, be brought before any justice or justices of the peace, for the purpose of being removed from the place where he or she is inhabiting or sojourning, by virtue of any order of removal, or of being passed by virtue of any vagrant pass, and it shall appear to the said justice or justices that such poor person is unable to travel, by reason of sickness or other infirmity, or that it would be dangerous for him or her so to do, the justice or justices making such order of removal, or granting such vagrant pass, are hereby required and authorized to suspend the execution of the same, until they are satisfied that it may safely be executed, without danger to any person who is the subject thereof; which suspension of, and subsequent permission to execute the same, shall be respectively indorsed on the said order of removal, or vagrant pass, and signed by such justice or justices,"—or any others. (By 49 Geo. 3. c. 124.)

The obvious danger and inconvenience of a *literal* observance of the words, " if any poor person shall be *brought* before any justice," has led the courts to give them a reasonable and practicable construction; and it has been decided, that the meaning of the act is, " not that where any person was brought personally, but where his *case* was brought *judicially* before the magistrates, for the purpose of his removal, that they should have power to suspend the execution of the order of removal, if it appeared to them, that is, by due examination of the facts, that, from sickness or infirmity of the party, the removal could not then be safely made." (Rex v. Everdon, 9 East, 101. See 49 Geo. 3, c. 124, *ante* 561.)

The 49 Geo. 3. c. 124, s. 1, enacts, that in all cases where an order of removal has been suspended, under the former act, any other justices within the same jurisdiction as those who made the order, may afterwards direct the execution of it, and the charges to be paid, &c., as fully and effectually as those who made the order.

The 3d section of this latter act also provides, " And in order to avoid any pretence for forcibly separating husband and wife, or other persons nearly connected with, or related to each other, and who are living together as one family, at the time of any order of removal made, or vagrant pass granted, during the dangerous sickness or other infirmity of any one or more of such family, on whose account the execution of such order of removal, or vagrant pass, is suspended; be it further enacted and declared, that where any order of removal,or vagrant pass, shall be suspended, by virtue of this or of the said recited act, on account of the dangerous sickness, or other infirmity, of any person or persons thereby directed to be removed or passed, the execution of such order of removal, or vagrant pass, shall also be suspended for the same period, with respect to every other person named therein, who was actually of the same household or family of such sick or infirm person or persons, at the time of such order of removal made, or vagrant pass granted."

A suspended order of removal must be served within a reasonable time. Therefore, where an order of removal was made, and suspended on the same day, on account of the age and infirmity of the pauper, and she survived three years, but no notice of the order of removal was served upon the parish to which she was ordered to be removed, till after her death, it was held, that the service not being within a reasonable time, the order of removal was a nullity. It is just that the parish sought to be charged should have an opportunity of investigating, within a reasonable time, whether they are liable to the burden so sought to be thrown upon them. (R. v. Lampeter, 3 Barn. & Cres. 454; 5 Dowl. & Ryl. 310.)

Expenses during Suspension.] The act 35 Geo. 3. also provides, that the charges incurred on behalf of the pauper, during the suspension, are to be paid by the officers of the parish to which the removal is ordered; which may be levied, with costs: though, if they exceed £20, an appeal to the quarter sessions is given.

The power given to the magistrates, of ordering these intermediate costs, is confined to two cases:—viz. the removal, and the death of the pauper. When, therefore, such an order was made, but the pauper had never been removed, he having, during the suspension, inherited two freehold houses, such order was held to be a nullity. (R. v. Chagford, 4 Barn. & Ald. 235.) And the proper course is to take off the suspension, by another order of the justices. But where, upon the death of the father, during a suspended order of removal of himself and family, his widow and the children were removed, without any such order removing the suspension of the original order, and the justices made a third order, stating the death of the husband and amount of the charges, directing the same to be paid by the parish removed to, the court held, that as these several orders were good upon the face of them, they could not be quashed, on account of no order having been made to take off the suspension. (R. v. Englefield, 13 East, 317.)

Pauper returning, punishable.] The statute of Charles, so often cited, also provides, that if paupers refuse to go, or do not remain in the parish where they ought to be settled, but return to that from which they have been removed, any justice of the city, county, town, &c., where the offence is committed, may send such person to the house of correction, to be punished as a vagabond, or to the workhouse, to be employed in hard labour. The vagrant act, 17 Geo. 2. c. 5, which also applied to this subject, is now repealed. (See 3 Geo. 4. c. 40; 5 Geo. 4. c. 83, and *ante* "Vagrants.")

It seems clearly settled, however, that a commitment for returning can only be made when the person returns in a state of vagrancy; (see R. v. Fillongley, 2 T. R. 709;) though returning without a certificate, is *prima facie* evidence of his being an idle and disorderly person, and then it is for the defendant to show that he has a lawful excuse for returning. And Best, J. is reported to have declared, "I must say that the parish officer acted most inproperly in taking up a man as a vagrant who was at work in the harvest-field. But when he was before the magistrate, and alleged no fact to show that he was not, as he appeared to be, in a state of vagrancy, the magistrate could do nothing but convict him. Had he stated to the magistrate that he returned for the purpose of working, it would have been a question for the court, whether the magistrate should not have used the language of this court in the case of R. v. Fillongley." (Mann v. Davers, 3 Barn. & Ald. 103.)

SECTION II.—APPEAL AND SUBSEQUENT PROCEEDINGS.

The manner of commencing and conducting all appeals is nearly similar; the *general rules* and principles of law, therefore, as stated under the head of "Appeal against a Rate," and incidentally in treating of the other subjects throughout the volume, will be applicable to appeals against orders of removal.

Who may appeal.] The several statutes authorizing the removal, give a right of appeal to the parish to which the removal is made. (See 13 & 14 Car. 2. c. 12; 3 W. & M. c. 11.) The words of these acts of parliament are, "all persons who think themselves *aggrieved*," &c. may appeal, and the pauper himself, therefore, may appeal against his removal. (R. v. Hartfield, Carth. 222.)

The 35 G. 3. c. 101. s. 2, enables justices to suspend orders of removal on account of the sickness of the pauper, and to give the costs of such suspension, with an appeal against such costs, *if they* amount to £20. Upon which it has been held, that the appeal may still be made against the order of removal, which was suspended, and the subsequent order for costs, notwithstanding the death of the pauper *before* removal, and the costs are *under* £20, as such costs are by consequence a grievance on the parish, if the pauper were not settled there, and the appeal against the order for costs is not against the *quantum*, but against the liability of the parish to pay any costs at all in this case. (R. v. St. Mary-le-bone, 13 East, 51; R. v. Bradford, 9 East, 97.)

Where an order of removal is appealed against, and is quashed *generally* by the sessions, the appellant, on the trial of another appeal, may show by evidence the distinct ground on which the former order was quashed. (R. v. Wheelock, 5 Barn. & Cres. 511.)

To Sessions of what Place.] The appeal must be to the sessions, for the county, division, or riding, from which the removal was made, and not to the sessions of a corporate town, &c. (R. v. Wendover, 2 Salk. 490; R. v. East Donyland, Burr. S. C. 592.)

Where by charter the magistrates of a borough, which was a *county of itself*, held only *general* sessions twice a-year, and not quarter sessions, it was decided, that an appeal against an order of removal might be made to such next general sessions. (R. v. Carmarthen, 4 Barn. & Ald. 291.)

What Sessions as to Time.] The appeal must be to the "*next* general or quarter sessions," that is, to the next practicable sessions *after* the removal, for it is thereby the parties are aggrieved; (R. v. JJ. of Essex, 1 Barn. & Ald. 210; R. v. JJ. of West Riding, York, 4 Maul. & Sel. 327;) or after due service of a copy of the order, and at the same time showing the original, where the execution of the order is suspended, by reason of the pauper's sickness, &c.; (R. v. Alnwick, 5 Barn. & Ald. 184;) or after the demand of charges, &c. where the order is suspended, and the pauper dies before removal. (R. v. St. Mary-le-bone, Middlesex, 13 East, 51.)

Thus where a sessions commence before the cause of complaint accrues, and is continued by adjournment afterwards, the appeal should be entered, not at the adjournment, but at the following sessions. (R. v. Hendercleave, 19 Vin. Abr. 336; 2 Bott. 714.) But an appeal may be lodged at an *adjournment* of the next sessions, (Ib. R. v. JJ. Sussex, 7 T. R. 107,) though if no sessions are held pursuant to such adjournment, the original sessions are completed, and then the opportunity is gone. (R. v. West Torrington, Burr. S. C. 293.)

And where the sessions commenced the next day after the removal, and sat *de die in diem* for fourteen days, and was then continued by two several adjournments, with an interval of one week in the first instance, and nearly a month in the second; so that there was abundant time to enter the appeal, and it was the practice to do so in such cases in that county; yet the court held, that the party was not bound to take this step till the next quarter sessions. (R. v. JJ. Surrey, 1 Maul. & Sel. 479.)

Notice of Appeal.] "Reasonable" notice of appeal (usually a week's notice) must be given to the respondent parish, and if it appear to the justices at sessions that reasonable notice has not been given, they shall adjourn the appeal to the next quarter sessions, and then finally determine the same. (9 Geo. 1. c. 7. s. 8; R. v. JJ. of Wiltshire, 10 East, 404.) But service of the order of *respite* is tantamount to a notice that the party intends to *try* the appeal at the following sessions. (R. v. Lambeth, 3 Dowl. & Ryl. 340; R. v. Bucks, 6 Dowl. & Ryl. 142.)

But the sessions are bound to receive the appeal, even although no notice has been given. (R. v. Staffordshire, 7 East, 549.) Hence the practice of moving the court of quarter sessions to enter and respite an appeal. And a mandamus may be obtained to compel them to try, or to receive the appeal, and adjourn the consideration of it, according to the circumstances of the case. (Ib. R. v. JJ. Gloucestershire, Doug. 191.) An appellant may countermand his notice at any time before the sessions.

Length of Notice.] The sessions have the power in most cases of determining what is "reasonable" notice. No general rule can be laid down upon the subject, and the usage and practice of the particular sessions governs, unless there be some peculiarity in the case which would lead to a denial of justice, if the rule were strictly enforced. In the county of Surrey, the practice requires service of notice eight clear days previous to the first day of the sessions in appeals against rates, and six clear days against an order of removal, and the rule is the same in many other places.

It seems that it is unnecessary to enter and respite an appeal at the next sessions, where the order of removal is served so late as to render it impossible *to try* the appeal at those sessions. (R. v. Kent, 8 Barn. & Cres. 639.) And the court held, that if due notice be given under such circumstances of the intention to prosecute the appeal at the second sessions, the court of quarter sessions are bound to hear and determine it. (R. v. Devon, 8 Barn. & Cres. 640.)

Where an appeal was dismissed on the ground that the appellant had given one day's notice less than was required by the rules of the justices, the Court of King's Bench thinking it reasonable that the appeal should be heard, granted a mandamus to enter continuances and hear the appeal. For, although the justices have a discretionary power to make rules for the governance of the practice of the sessions, yet, for the purposes of justice, the Court of King's Bench will interfere to control that discretion. (R. v. Lancaster, 7 Barn. & Cres. 691.)

Form of Notice.] The notice of appeal should be addressed to the churchwardens and overseers of the parish from which the removal is made, and must be signed by the parish officers of the appellant parish, or, as is most usual, by their attorney; and if it be signed by, or on behalf of, a majority, it is sufficient. (R. v. Beeston, 3 T. R. 592.) It is safe, and usual likewise, to date it, though not absolutely necessary, and all that seems requisite besides is, that it describe the orders complained against with sufficient certainty. And, though it is the practice, and obviously most prudent to give the notice in writing, yet it does not appear to be *essential* that it should be so. (R. v. JJ. Surrey, 5 Barn. & Ald. 539.)

Adjourning Appeals.] Although the words of the statutes before referred to, seem to require that appeals shall not be adjourned beyond the *next* sessions after that at which they are lodged, yet a further postponement may be obtained by consent of parties, and assigning a sufficient reason, as the absence of a material witness, &c. to induce the court to allow it. And the justices may adjourn them at their own discretion, as for further consideration; (R. v. Langley, 1 Ld. Raym. 481; R. v. Bucks, 3 East, 342;) or, on account of their being equally divided in opinion; (Bodmin v. Warligen, 2 Bott. 733;) or to submit a question in the case to a judge of assize. (Ib. R. v. Hedingham, Burr. S. C. 112.) But *quære* whether the sessions ought to adjourn, instead of quashing an order, when they are equally divided; and, where they adopted the latter course, thinking that it lay on the respondent parish to make out their case to the satisfaction of a majority of the justices, the Court of King's Bench refused to interfere. (R. v. Monmouthshire, 4 Barn. & Cres. 844; 7 Dowl. & Ryl. 334.)

An adjournment of a sessions, is not to be to a time beyond that fixed for holding the next original sessions; (R. v. Grince, 2 Bott. 723;) but the justices may respite an appeal to an adjourned sessions, and then determine it. (R. v. Stansfield, Burr. S. C. 205.) If there are not justices enough to *hold* a sessions, there are not enough to adjourn it legally, and, therefore, acts done *after such* adjournment are void. (R. v. Westrington, 2 Bott. 725.) And, consequently, if it do not appear upon the caption of the order of sessions, that it has been regularly respited, by continuance or adjournment, the Court of King's Bench will quash such order as void. (R. v. Polsted, 2 Stra. 1263.)

But where the lapse arises from the act, or inadvertence of the court, or its officers, the Court of King's Bench will, it seems, upon proper application, grant a mandamus to re-enter and hear the appeal. (R. v. Carnarvon, 4 Barn. & Ald. 86.)

Proceedings at the Hearing.] Appeals are heard in the order in which they were entered. The first step is, for the appellants to prove their notice, unless it is admitted; they next produce the original order of removal, if it has been served upon them, and the pauper, if he has been delivered to them. These preliminary steps being over, the respondents' counsel states his case, and calls his witnesses to prove that the pauper was last settled in the appellants' parish. If he is aware that the counsel for the appellants intends to rely upon the cross examination of the pauper, without calling witnesses himself, where the respondents are obliged to put the pauper into the box, he of course anticipates, and attempts to confute the case so to be set up. When his evidence is closed, the appellants' counsel is heard in the same manner, but if he call witnesses, the counsel for the respondents may reply.

If there are two counsel on a side, which is usual where there are several witnesses, the junior counsel addresses the court *after* the delivery of the evidence on their part *respectively*.

Defects in Form.] It has already been observed, that the legislature have provided that all defects of *form* shall be amended by the justices without costs, and after such amendment *they shall proceed* to examine the truth and merits of the case. (5 Geo. 2. c. 19. s. 1.) But it may be a question, whether the defect be one of form merely, or of substance. It has been held, that the omission, in the order, of a *complaint* by the churchwardens and overseers, and of an *adjudication* of the pauper's settlement, cannot be amended, as they are matters of substance. (R. v. Great Bedwin, 2 Stra. 1158.) It was never designed that they should insert new facts, but only amend the informal way of setting out the facts which were stated. (Id.) And the want of jurisdiction in the justices making the order, is matter of substance, and such order is a nullity, though unappealed against. (R. v. Chilverscoton, 8 T. R. 178.) Lord Kenyon is reported to have said, that by the construction which had been put upon the act, it had become a dead letter. (R. v. Moor Critchell, 2 East, 66.)

An order of removal was directed to the *churchwardens* and overseers of the *parish* of L. In fact, L. was a vill, and there were no churchwardens in it; it was held, that the word "churchwardens" might be rejected as surplusage, and that the sessions might, under the statute, insert the words, "or vill." Because, although there were no churchwardens, the persons for whom the order of removal was intended, received it, and appealed; and the other objection amounted to no more than a plea of misnomer; that was a mere matter of form. (R. v. Amlwch, 4 Barn. & Cres. 757; 6 Dowl. & Ryl. 626.)

Judgment upon Appeal.] The justices by whom the order is made, and also those who are rated, or rateable, in either of the contending parishes, or whose interests may be affected by the judgment, have no right to vote upon the determination of the appeal. (R. v. Yarpole, 4 T. R. 71.)

If the magistrates are equally divided, no judgment can be given; but whether they must in such case adjourn the appeal from sessions to sessions till a majority shall be of one opinion, seems doubtful. At all events, if they quash the appeal on the ground that the respondent, like a plaintiff in an action, ought to make out his case, or suffer defeat, the Court of King's Bench will not interfere. (R. v. Monmouthshire, 4 Barn. & Cres. 844. *ante* 569.)

If the majority results from miscounting, it must be rectified during the sessions, for the Court of King's Bench will not grant a mandamus to re-hear the case. Except in matters of a criminal nature, the court cannot look dehors the record. It cannot sit as upon a scrutiny before an election committee. (R. v. Leicestershire, 1 Maul. & Sel. 442.)

Though the justices cannot refer the appeal to others to decide, yet this may be done by the cqnsent of the parties, or even, it seems, of their attornies, who also attend the reference. (R. v. JJ. Northampton, Cald. 30.)

The sessions cannot make an original order, but must either quash or affirm; (R. v. Bond, 2 Show. 503;) and they cannot affirm one *without* appeal. (R. v. Leverington, Burr. S. C. 279.) They are not bound to state the reasons of their judgment; (South Cadbury, v. Braddon, 2 Salk. 607;) and they may alter their judgment at any time during the *same* sessions; (St. Andrew's, Holborn v. St. Clement Danes, 2 Salk. 494;) but not at any subsequent sessions, unless the appeal be regularly continued to it. (Ib. R. v. Cuckfield, 2 Salk. 477.)

It is a general rule, that one session cannot quash the order of a former sessions. (Ib. 2 Bott. 711.) That can only be done by the Court of King's Bench for some objections appearing on the *face* of it, upon a review of all the facts and circumstances stated in the *case*.

Pauper, how disposed of.] If the sessions affirm the order, the pauper of course remains in the parish to which he was removed; but if they quash it, he may be sent back to the respondent parish by order of two justices of the county in which the appellant parish is situate. (Honiton v. South Beverton, Comb. 401.)

Special Case.] The sessions are not *bound* to state a special case, but may exercise their discretion in granting one upon the application of the unsuccessful party. (R. v. Oulton, 2 Bott. 738.) And where they have no doubt in their own minds, they ought to refuse, in order to avoid unnecessary expenses. (R. v. Darley Abbey, 14 East, 285.) But if the justices will not state the facts specially, though requested to do so, when the matter is doubtful, this is very blameable conduct in them, and it is to be wished that it might be avoided; per Lord Hardwicke. (R. v. Preston-upon-the-Hill, 2 Burr. S. C. 77.) It is commonly settled and signed by the junior counsel on each side, and if they cannot agree upon the facts, and mode of stating them, the chairman, with the concurrence of a majority of the justices, may state and sign a case himself. Care should be taken to have all the material facts clearly ascertained, and if there be any fraud, in the conduct of any of the parties, affecting the settlement, that should be specially found and stated as a fact. (R. v. Tedford, Burr. S. C. 57; R. v. Llanbedergoch, 7 T. R. 105.)

A bill of exceptions doth not lie to the quarter sessions; for this matter of the settlement of the poor, which ought to be rendered cheap and speedy, might by such means be rendered dilatory, expensive, and burdensome. (R. v. Preston-upon-the-Hill, *supra.*)

Costs of the Proceedings.] When the appeal is determined, the justices may order such costs and charges as to *them* shall seem just and reasonable, to be paid by the overseers, or other person, against whom the appeal is determined; so where notice of appeal is given, and the appeal is not further prosecuted, costs may be awarded to the party to whom such notice was given. (8 & 9 W. 3. c. 30. s. 3; and see R. v. JJ. of the county of Nottingham, 1 Sess. Cas. 422; 2 Bott. 776.) It is usual, however, for the sessions to allow 40*s*. costs, unless the case has been attended with circumstances of vexation or fraud.

Maintenance of Paupers.] If the appeal be determined in favour of the appellant, that the pauper was unduly removed, the justices shall, at the same quarter sessions, order to the appellant such sum as appears to have been reasonably expended, in maintaining the pauper from the time of the removal to the determination of the appeal. (9 Geo. 1. c. 7. s. 9.)

It is *imperative* upon the sessions to allow the costs of *maintenance* to the appellant, where the appeal is decided for him; (St. Mary's Nottingham v. Kerklington, 2 Sess. Cas. 67;) and they cannot direct that such costs shall abide the event of another appeal. (R. v. Chart. Burr. S. C. 194.) A mandamus lies if the justices refuse to hear evidence, where the costs are in their discretion, or do not allow them where the statute is imperative. (R. v. JJ. Nottingham, *supra.*)

But the Court of King's Bench, upon a case being brought up

from sessions for their decision, have no power to award the expenses of maintaining the pauper, in the interval between the judgment of the sessions and the time when their own judgment is pronounced. Nor will they remit the original order of removal to the sessions, to enable the justices, by quashing the order, to give the appellant parish those expenses under the 9 Geo. 1. c. 7. s. 9. (See R. v. Moor Critchell, 2 East, 222.)

Certiorari.] Although the sessions do not grant a special case, the appellant parish may, nevertheless, at the discretion of the Court of King's Bench, bring both the order of justices and the order of sessions under the review of that court, for defects appearing upon the face of them. For this purpose, the same course must be taken in suing out the *certiorari*, as where it is to bring up a special case. The first step is to give a six days' notice of the motion to any two of the justices (if so many) who made the order; (13 Geo. 2. c. 18. s. 5;) then the motion paper (indorsed, the King against the Appellant parish " to move for a *certiorari*,") signed by counsel, should be delivered to a clerk in court, and he will sue out the *certiorari* on behalf of the appellant. All this must be done within six calendar months after the first day of the sessions which confirmed the order, or after the original order made, if it be intended to impugn that. (13 Geo. 2. c. 18. s. 5; R. v. JJ. Sussex, 1 Maul. & Sel. 631.)

The writ is to be delivered to the clerk of the peace, and it will be returned accordingly, together with the order, special case, &c., and it is then set down in the crown paper for argument.

The application for the *certiorari* must be founded upon an affidavit of the *date* and substance of the proceedings to be removed; and if there are any other circumstances where the application is out of the ordinary course, they should be inserted. (R. v. Glamorganshire, 5 T. R. 279.) And in this latter case, the court usually grants a rule *nisi* only, which must be served upon the magistrates, who have been previously served with six days' notice of the application.

Recognizance to prosecute, &c.] Before the *certiorari* is allowed, the party must enter into a recognizance, with two sufficient sureties, before a justice of the place or a judge of the King's Bench, in £50, to prosecute the same at his own costs and charges, without wilful delay, and to pay the costs of the opposite party, within a month, if the order, &c., be confirmed. (5 G. 2. c. 19. s. 2; R. v. Boughey, 4 T. R. 281.) But if the necessity for a *certiorari* arises from a mistake of the clerk of the peace in recording the judgment, the court will, it seems, regulate the question of costs according to the justice of the case, upon motion to that effect. (R. v. Ashton Underhill, Cald. 416.)

If the party *in whose favour* an order has been made, wishes to remove it into the King's Bench, with a view to enforce the execution of it; or, it being defective, for the purpose of having it quashed, to give the justices an opportunity of making a valid one, the removal may be *after* six months, and *without* any recognizance for costs, &c. (2 Nol. P. L. 590.)

Returning the Certiorari.] "All *certioraries,* though directed to divers jutsices, may be returned by one, and so is the usual practice." (Comb. 25.) The practice in Surrey is to make the return in the name of the justice who is chairman of the sessions, and to sign, but not seal it; but it must be stated that he is a justice, &c.; (R. v. Newton, Burr. S. C. 159;) and the return must be on parchment, or it will be quashed as no return. (R. v. Stow Barden, Cas. Temp. Hard. 173.)

The remedy for a false return is by action on the case, or criminal information, or attachment for contempt where the party refuses to make a return. (4 Hawk P. C. 162; see R. v. Battams, 1 East, 298.)

The general practice is as follows:—the attorney for the applicant receives the writ from the crown office as soon as the rule of court or judge's *fiat* has been obtained. He then carries it, along with the recognizance to prosecute, to the clerk of the peace, who, when a case has been granted, draws up at length, on parchment, a record of the order of sessions from the entries in the sessions-books. It commences with the caption, and terminates with the case, generally omitting, in the caption, the names of the justices who made the orders appealed against. But in Surrey, and some other sessions, the clerk of the peace indorses on the writ, "The answer of A. B., one of the justices within named." "The execution of this writ appears in certain orders to the same writ annexed." Opposite to this is a seal affixed, supposed to be the justice's in whose name the return is made; and the orders directed to be removed, with the recognizance to prosecute, are then annexed to the writ.

But whatever form is followed in this respect, the orders are *annexed* to the *certiorari,* and the clerk of the peace sends the return, usually by the agent of the applicant, who must deliver it to the proper officer at the crown-office. (2 Nol. P. L. 596-7.)

Judgment in Banc.] When the case is called on, it is first argued by the counsel for the appellant, then by the counsel for the respondent, and lastly, by the appellant's senior counsel, in reply. After which, the court deliver their judgment, and quash or affirm the order of sessions accordingly. And they will quash an order in part, and affirm it as to the remainder, where it appears necessary from the facts, in order to meet the justice of the case. (R. v. St. Mary, Lambeth, 6 T. R. 615.)

But if the case be insufficiently stated, the Court of King's Bench may send it back to be re-stated, and the sessions may thereupon hear fresh evidence, or re-state the case upon the former evidence, as may be necessary. (R. v. Bray, Burr. S. C. 682.)

Costs after Certiorari.] Though the judgment of the court be in favour of the party removing the order, he is not entitled to costs; and he must pay them to the other side, as taxed by the master of the Crown-office, if the decision is against him, within ten days after demand made, or he is liable to an attachment. But if he succeeds in quashing the orders, in *part* only, *upon the merits,* he is not liable to costs. (R. v. Madley, 2 Stra. 1198.) Nor is he so liable if the certiorari is superseded, *quia improvide emanavit,* for the improvidence is the act of the court. (R. v. Wakefield, Say's Law of Costs, 306, 2 Nol. P. L. 622.) If a case is sent back to be re-stated, and upon the return thereof, the removing party abandon the further prosecution forthwith, before counsel are instructed, he is not to pay costs. (R. v. Edgeworth, 4 T. R. 418.)

The party's recognizance is discharged, if he succeeds, as a matter of course, but if the decision is against him, he cannot apply for the discharge till he has paid the costs. (R. v. Bray, Burr. S. C. 687.)

SECTION III.—EVIDENCE IN SETTLEMENT CASES.

It will be collected, from the statement already given of the facts upon which the different kinds of settlement depend, in what manner each particular case is to be supported: a brief analysis, therefore, of the rules of evidence and of the necessary proofs applicable to the subject, will complete this digest of the poor laws.

Who may be Witnesses.] The pauper whose settlement is in dispute, is supposed to stand so far indifferent between the parties, that he may be called by either, and examined with much the same latitude on behalf of the one parish as the other. And by the 54 Geo. 3. c. 170. s. 9, (see *ante* 14.) persons rated, or liable to be rated, or holding or executing any office in the parish, are made competent witnesses in these matters, so that all objections to the competency of any witness on the score of interest are wholly removed.

Soldier's Examination.] The general rule which excludes an ex-parte statement, when there is no opportunity of cross-examination, is relaxed in the case of a soldier; to perpetuate whose testimony respecting his settlement, power is given by the annual mutiny acts, under particular circumstances, to any justice of the peace for the district within which the soldier is quartered, to take the examination of any non-commissioned officer or soldier, having at the time a wife or child, and to make it evidence as to their settlement, whenever afterwards it may come into dispute.

But as all persons having a special authority under acts of parliament, must show it upon the face of the order, or other document which they are thus empowered to execute or effect, it should be proved aliunde, or be stated in the examination itself, that the examinant was a soldier, and was quartered within the jurisdiction of the magistrate. (R. v. All Saints, Southampton, 7 Barn. & Cres. 735; 1 Man. & Ryl. 663.) Either this examination, or an *attested* copy (and no other can be admitted, (R .v. Warley, 6 T. R. 534 ;) given by the magistrate to the soldier, and by him delivered to his commanding officer, may be produced in evidence as to the settlement of the soldier, although he be dead, or absent from the kingdom, at the time when the appeal is tried. (R. v. Warminster, 3 Barn. & Ald. 321.)

Some proof should also be given, that the person whose settlement is the subject of inquiry, was the person whose examination is produced. And the original examination, if produced, must be proved to be in the hand-writing, or to have been signed by the justice.

But if the attested copy be produced, that must be proved to have come out of the custody of the commanding, officer to whom the mutiny act directs it to be delivered; and it should be further authenticated by proof of the hand-writing of the magistrate; (R. v. Bilton, 1 East, 13 ;) and of the attesting witness also, if he cannot himself be produced ; though this would probably not be considered indispensable.

Prisoner's Examination.] A similar rule in the case of a prisoner is established by the 59 Geo. 3. c. 12. s. 28, (see *ante* 561 ;) but with two limitations, that the examination is only to be so admitted for the purpose of any order of removal, and that it is evidence so long only as the person continues a prisoner.

Admissions by the Parish.] The common rule of evidence, that if a party, upon whom an obligation or duty is sought to be enforced, has antecedently acknowledged his liability, to the particular claim, applies to parishes in settlement cases, with this limitation, that the acknowledgment must be by the act, or conduct of the parish, and not merely verbally by any of its officers. These admissions are either by relief, by certificate, or by non-resistance to an order of removal;

and if such an order be appealed against, and is affirmed, it is equally conclusive.

Relief, Evidence of Settlement.] Relief given to a pauper while she is residing *out* of the parish, is *prima facie* evidence of a settlement in the relieving parish. Thus, where the overseer of Edwinstowe happening to be at a public-house, at Mansfield, on a market-day, seven miles distant, and there being applied to, relieved the pauper, and promised further relief if applied to at Edwinstowe, and the pauper applied accordingly a fortnight afterwards, when he and his colleague refused to give her relief, telling her she must throw herself upon the parish of Mansfield, the court held, that this was sufficient evidence to warrant a finding by the sessions, that the pauper was settled in the relieving parish. (R. v. Edwinstowe, 8 Barn. & Cres. 671; R. v. Stanley, *cum* Wrenthorpe, 15 East, 350.)

This, however, is only *evidence*, which may be rebutted by satisfactory proof, that the pauper at the time he was relieved, while residing out of the parish, was actually settled elsewhere. (R. v. Maidstone, 12 East, 553.)

But the bare fact of giving relief to a pauper, while resident *in the parish*, is not evidence of a settlement in that parish, for it may be bestowed upon him as casual poor, in which case they would be bound to maintain him till they could find out his settlement. (R. v. Chatham, 8 East, 498.) And giving him money to enable him to return to a particular place, after having relieved him for three weeks, does not carry the acknowledgment of settlement in the relieving parish any further. (R. v. Trowbridge, 7 Barn. & Cres. 252; 1 Man. & Ryl. 7.)

The fact of such relief may be proved by the pauper himself, or any other person who saw the payment, or by the *admission* of the overseer, or of any rated inhabitant of the relieving parish; and it is the province of the court before whom the evidence is given, to judge of and determine its value. (R. v. Hardwicke, 11 East, 578; R. v. Whitley Lower, 1 Maul. & Sel. 636.) In such cases it is prudent to give the parish notice to produce their books, or any book which contains an entry relating to the question.

Certificate, Evidence of Settlement.] A certificate being an acknowledgment in writing, made by a parish, in a certain prescribed form, that the persons included therein have a settlement in that parish, it is *conclusive* between the *certificated* and the certifying parishes, as to the settlement of such persons at the *time* it was *granted.* (R. v. Buckingham, Cald. 64; 2 Nol. P. L. 141.) But in a question between *either* of these parishes and a third parish,

(R. v. Lubbenham, 4 T. R. 251; R. v. Clifton, 2 East, 168,) or between a third and fourth parish, though it is evidence, it is not conclusive. (R. v. St. Margaret, Leicester, 8 East, 332.) Certificated persons, therefore, may be removed to other besides the certificating parish, upon becoming actually chargeable, and it appearing that their settlement is elsewhere. (R. v. St. Martin-at-Oak, 16 East, 303.)

Whenever a certificated man leaves the certificated parish without an intention to return—not indeed for a temporary purpose only, but where the residence there is permanently at an end—the certificate is determined. (R. v. Newington, 1 T. R. 354; R. v. St. Michael's, Coventry, 5 T. R. 526.) And if he gain a settlement in the certificated parish, as he may do by serving an annual office, or by renting a tenement, or by estate, the certificate is discharged. (R. v. Ufton, 3 T. R. 251; R. v. Findern, Cald. 426.)

Certificate, how proved.] Certificates thirty years old, produced out of the proper custody, require no extrinsic proof to make them evidence.

The 8 and 9 W. 3. c. 30, requires that the certificate shall be allowed by two justices of the county, city, &c.; and the 3 Geo. 2. c. 29, s. 8, directs, that the witnesses who attest the execution of certificates by the churchwardens or overseers, shall make oath before the justices who are to allow the same, that they saw the churchwardens sign and seal, and that the names of such witnesses to the attestation are of their own proper hand-writing. And the justices are also to certify that such oath was made before them. It is therefore necessary, in cases where the certificate is less than thirty years old, to prove the signatures to the allowance, and to the certifying of the oath.

The same proof must be given in the case of a lost certificate; the loss or destruction thereof being first established, in order to let in secondary evidence of its contents.

Where the parish is in two counties, an allowance of the certificate by the justices of one county is sufficient. (R. v. Austrey, 6 Maul. & Sel. 319.)

It seems to be quite clear, that the certifying parish may take advantage of any defect or informality, not the effect of fraud, in the certificate granted by its own officers; (R. v. Catesby, 2 Barn. & Cres. 814; 4 Dowl. & Ryl. 434;) because, the power being given to the parish officers to bind the parish by their act, that power must be strictly pursued. (R. v. Clifton, 2 East, 174.)

The certificate should be under the hands and seals, of the major part of the *aggregate* body of churchwardens and overseers. (See R. v. Whitchurch, 7 Barn. & Cres. 573; 1 Man. & Ryl. 480.) And if the certificates are signed by two persons only, who acted, or purported to act, in the capacity of churchwardens, as well as of overseers, they are as valid as if signed by distinct persons, as churchwardens and distinct persons as overseers. So, if the certificate be given in behalf of a township, &c., and is signed by the churchwardens, &c. of the parish in which the township is situated, it will suffice, provided they have been sworn in for the parish or township. (See 51 Geo. 3. c. 80; 54 Geo. 3. c. 107, *ante* 507.) But it seems doubtful whether the officers must be strictly officers *de jure*, or whether they have sufficient authority to execute certificates, if they are so *de facto* only, that is, before they are sworn in; but the court will, in the case of an old certificate, presume that they have been sworn. (See R. v. Whitchurch, *supra.*)

In some parishes or townships, a practice had crept in of electing one churchwarden or chapelwarden only; and as the execution of a certificate by such one was clearly bad, where no legally established custom to elect but one such officer existed, the 1 and 2 Geo. 4. c. 32. was passed, declaring, that all certificates which had been executed in this manner *before* the 28th May, 1821, should be as valid and effectual as if executed by officers legally appointed. But the act does not cure any defect of this kind in certificates granted since the date of the act.

It has been decided, that the magistrates who allow the certificate, may also be the attesting witnesses of its execution by the parish officers; but it must appear on the certificate that they act in both capacities. (Horncastle v. Boston, 1 Stra. 94.)

Order of Removal, Evidence.] If an order of removal be executed, and the parish acquiesce in it, without appeal or resistance, this is an admission of the pauper's settlement at the date of the order; and, being an adjudication that the settlement is in that parish, it has the same force as a judgment *in rem*, and is conclusive to all the world. (R. v. Kenilworth, 2 T. R. 598; R. v. Corsham, 11 East, 388.)

Where Order has been resisted by Appeal.] The order is equally conclusive if, being appealed against, it is confirmed. (Harrow v. Ryslop, 2 Salk. 524.) If it is quashed upon the *merits*, that is conclusive evidence in favour of the parish upon whom the burden is sought to be cast, as against the *removing* parish. (R. v. Bentley, 2 Bott. 919.) But a third parish may be able to give better evidence; and its right to do so is not affected by the prior failure, where it was not a party;

and, therefore, the quashing of the order can have no effect upon the question with a third parish. (R. v. Cirencester, Burr. S. C. 17.)

If the order be quashed for defect in form, and not upon the merits, it is no evidence as to the settlement. (R. v. St. Andrew, Holborn, 6 T. R. 613.) And in that case, the appellant parish should take care to have a special entry made by the clerk of the peace, to facilitate the proof at any future time that it was quashed for want of form merely; though this may be shown by other evidence, where no such entry has been made. (R. v. Wheelock, 5 Barn. & Cres. 511.)

Order of Removal, how proved.] If the original order is in existence, it should be produced; for which purpose a subpœna *duces tecum*, or notice to produce it, according as it is in the custody of a witness, or the opposite party, should be given. If it is not produced upon such notice, then proof of its having been in their possession, and of the service of the notice, must be given, in order to let in secondary evidence of its contents; and if lost or destroyed, the same course must be taken, for the like purpose, as in the case of lost certificates. (See *ante* 578.)

The authentication of the order should be by proof of the handwriting of the magistrates, and some general evidence that they were magistrates: though it seems doubtful whether this will not be presumed, in common with all the other requisites directed to be observed by the statutes, until the contrary is made to appear. But if the order is in the custody of the opposite party, who decline to produce it, upon due notice, no proof of authentication is required.

If the order of removal be to a place which has no overseers, it is no removal at all, but an absolute nullity, and may be so treated by all the world. (R. v. Swalcliffe; Cald. 248.) And if the order be made, but the removal is never carried into execution, it may be impeached at any time for any defects therein, or in the jurisdiction of the magistrates; because the parish, not being aggrieved. could not appeal. If it be bad upon the face of it, the order is also a nullity, and may be so treated, even by the parish to which the removal has been made, and has acted under it for years. (R. v. Chilverscoton, 8 T. R. 178.)

Order, void or voidable.] It has already been observed, that an order of removal bad on the face of it, is void at all times, and under all circumstances; but that if the validity of an order can only be impeached by extrinsic evidence, and it is not so impeached and invalidated at the time when it is executed upon the parish removed to, it is not, at any time afterwards, *voidable* by any such extrinsic evidence. (See R. v. Stotfold, 4 T. R. 596.) Such objections, therefore, are only available against the order when it is the subject of appeal, and not when it is produced as *evidence* of a settlement, unless, indeed, the party has had no previous opportunity of contesting its validity.

It has been already stated what are the requisites of a valid order; and upon an appeal against it, the parties may be put to the proof that all those requisites have been complied with. (See *ante* 558, *et seq.*)

If it be produced as *evidence*, the parish which is in a situation to raise any such objections, may prove them accordingly; and if the defect made out be, that the *adjudication* includes a greater number of persons than the *complaint*, (R. v. Newington, 2 Bott. 760,) or that the persons removed are not properly described, as, a man *and his family*, (Johnson's Case, 2 Salk. 485,) or any other defect, vitiating the order in part only, that part may be quashed, and the rest remain good. But if the defect vitiates the whole order, it cannot then be admitted in evidence.

If the order produced be a valid one, it is still competent to the opposite party to show, that it was abandoned by the parish which obtained it; in which case it is no longer evidence. This abandonment is usually signified by the parish taking back the pauper, without putting the other parish to the trouble of an appeal. (R. v. Llanrhydd, Burr. S. C. 658; R. v. Diddleburgh, 12 East, 359.)

Settlement by Hiring and Service: Proofs.] A hiring may be either express or implied; and if express, it may be either by oral or written contract.

An oral contract may be proved by either master or servant, or any other person present at the time it was made.

If the contract was in writing, the document must be produced, or proof given that it is lost or destroyed. If it is thirty years old, it is, by the common rule of evidence, admissible, without proof of hand-writing, upon its genuineness being exonerated from suspicion by the custody out of which it comes.

If it is less than thirty years old, it must be proved by the attesting witness, if there be one; unless he is incompetent to give evidence, from blindness, insanity, infamy of character, or interest, acquired since the execution of the instrument, or if it be proved, that upon diligent inquiry he cannot be found; in either of which cases, proof of *his* hand-writing is sufficient to authenticate the instrument. (1 Phil. on Evid. 454.) If there be no attesting witness, any person acquainted therewith may prove the hand-writing of the executing parties, or their adoption of it, signified in some other mode: as, by assent expressed at the time, or by other written document, which is produced and proved in like manner. No such written agreement requires a stamp, unless it be a deed.

When the instrument is in the possession of the opposite party, notice to produce it should be given, and the serving or giving of such notice; for it is not essential, (though much best,) that the notice be in writing. Secondary evidence may then be given, by copy, or otherwise, of its contents, without any proof of its execution, if the party neglect or refuse to produce the original.

If the instrument has been destroyed, proof of that fact should be given; if lost, the person or persons who, from having an interest in the instrument, would probably have the custody of it, should be called, or their representatives, if dead, or some one having the care and custody of such person's papers, &c., to prove a search and non-discovery in the place or places where it was considered most likely the instrument should be found.

Where a search for a document was made among the papers in the custody of an executrix of a person who had acted as executor of another person, the latter having had possession of the document in his lifetime, it was held that this was sufficient for the purpose of considering the person who had so acted to have been in law the executor, although the probate was not produced. (R. v. Witherly, Oct. 30, 1829, K. B. MSS.)

But the *execution* by the parties of a lost or destroyed instrument must be first proved, before secondary evidence can be given of its contents.

Effect of the Evidence of Hiring.] Whether the contract, when proved, amounts to such a hiring as will suffice to give a settlement, must be determined by ascertaining whether it contains the requisites for that purpose. (See *ante* 489, *et seq.*) And although upon questions of *fact*, as questions of this kind of settlement generally are, the court of King's Bench is very reluctant to interfere with or review the decisions of the quarter sessions, yet, where the facts stated in the case do not warrant the conclusion at which the sessions have arrived, the court will vacate their determination. A few instances will illustrate this rule.

The mother of a boy asked J. S. whether he wanted a boy. He said, "Yes." She then asked what wages he would give; to which he replied, "Let him stop what time he will, I will give him satisfaction in money or clothes." The sessions found, that this was no *general hiring;* and the court said, that there were premises to warrant the conclusion; and their decision, therefore, ought not to be disturbed. (R. v. Rosliston, 8 Barn. & Cres. 668.)

The pauper, when a lad, went along with his father to an innkeeper, and asked if he wanted a lad; who said he expected one in a fortnight, but the lad might stay till then. He was to fill the situation of boots and tap boy. He was to have his board and lodging in the house, and the vails which he might obtain in his employment. The other lad, when he came, was not engaged by the innkeeper, and the pauper remained in the service for three years and a quarter, without any thing further passing; at the end of which time, the pauper hearing that the place of ostler was vacant at another inn, went and engaged it, without consulting his master, and removed into it the following day, his master telling him, that if he had a mind to go, he believed he must. The sessions found this to be an implied yearly hiring; and the court, on the like grounds, refused to disturb their decision. (R. v. St. Martin, Leicester, 8 Barn. & Cres. 674.)

The pauper was hired for a fortnight by a straw bonnet maker; and after that period she went into her mistress's house, being told that she might sleep there, and that when she wanted clothes her mistress would find them for her. She went home to see her mother on several occasions, with the leave of her mistress, and was told two or three times, during her stay with her mistress, that she might provide herself with a place elsewhere when she could. She stayed, altogether, fifteen months in the service, did the household work, and after having done that, went to the straw bonnet work. The sessions found, that this was a hiring and service for a year; and the court, considering there were some premises to warrant the finding, confirmed it, although in both these cases it was intimated, that an opposite finding might have been more in accordance with their own impressions, derived from the evidence. (R. v. St. Andrew the Great, Cambridge, 8 Barn. & Cres. 664.)

But where, upon a contract for weekly wages, with a month's warning, or month's wages, and nothing further was said as to the duration of the service, the sessions found, that this amounted to no more than a *weekly* hiring; the court said, the sessions had no premises to warrant their conclusion that this was not a yearly hiring. The reservation of a month's warning or a month's wages clearly showed that the service was intended to continue longer than a week; it then became a hiring unlimited in duration: in which case the law implies a hiring for a year. The order of sessions, therefore, was quashed. (R. v. St. Andrew, Pershore, 8 Barn. & Cres. 679.)

But service under a yearly hiring, by which the servant was to serve from six in the morning to seven in the evening, and might make as much *overwork* as he chose, was held insufficient to confer a settlement. Because the servant, according to this contract, was not under the control and coercion of the master during the *whole time*. Mr. Justice Bayley, in giving judgment, said, " The case is very different from that of R. v. Byker (see *ante*, 492). There the agreement gave the term merely as the measure of the wages, and the pauper was bound to work; he had no right to be absent. Here the pauper could not have been compelled to do any overwork; the coercion and control of the master were clearly limited to thirteen hours a-day; beyond that time the master had no right to compel work, nor was the pauper under a duty to perform any." (R. v. Atherstone, Oct. 30, 1829, K. B. MSS.)

Settlement by Apprenticeship: Proofs.] To establish a settlement by apprenticeship, the indenture must, if possible, be produced and proved; and a residence by the apprentice for forty days, in some parish or place under the indenture, that is, under the authority and control which is given by it over the apprentice, must be proved. In short, proof of a forty days residence must be given in every species of settlement.

The same rules apply as to the mode of proof of deeds of apprenticeship when produced, or when lost or destroyed, as govern in cases of written contracts not under seal. (See *ante* 582.) It must not be forgotten, however, that a deed can only be executed in one of two ways; namely, by signing, sealing, and delivery by the party, in the ordinary way, or by some one on his behalf, who is constituted, by deed, his attorney, for that purpose, who must sign, execute, and deliver, in the name of his principal, and not in his own name. (See Berkeley v. Hardy, 5 Barn. & Cres. 355; 8 Dowl. & Ryl. 102.)

Secondary evidence of a deed is also admissible under the same circumstances which render secondary evidence of a written contract not under seal admissible. (See *ante* 582.) Although, if it be *proved* that the indenture was not stamped, no evidence can be given of its contents, in any way; but in the absence of proof to the contrary, it will be presumed to have been properly stamped.

The best secondary evidence in this case is a counterpart, or other copy, if there be one, which must, of course, be proved to be correct; but if no such copy exists, then oral testimony may be received. The following instance will illustrate the rule as to the reception of oral testimony in these cases:—It was proved by a pauper that he had been bound apprentice twenty-three years ago, by the overseers of the parish, to A. B., for seven years; that the indenture was signed and sealed; and that he served the seven years, and that A. B. had the indenture; that when the apprenticeship expired, the pauper asked A. B. for the indenture, who said the overseers had it. Upon these facts it was held, that the declarations of A. B., who might have been called as a witness, were not admissible in evidence; and that parol evidence of the contents of the indenture was not admissible, the indenture not having been sufficiently accounted for. (R. v. Denio, 7 Barn. & Cres. 620; R. v. Castleton, 6 T. R. 236.)

If the apprentice bound himself, it is material to show his execution of the deed. If he was bound by the parish, before the 56 Geo. 3. c. 139, the execution by the majority of the churchwardens and overseers must be proved, and likewise the signature of the two magistrates who allowed the indenture; and that they were magistrates, should be made out by some witness who knew them to be acting in that capacity at the time. If the binding be since that statute, and to a master residing in a parish out of the county in which the pauper lives, there must then be, in addition to the above evidence, proof of the allowance of two magistrates having jurisdiction over the parish or place into which the apprentice is bound. (*Ante* 509.) As to bindings to the sea-service, or to chimney-sweepers, (see *ante* 511.) The other points of evidence respecting the want or insufficiency of the stamp—the jurisdiction on the justices—the proper parties to the indentures—the forty days' residence—assignment of the apprentice, &c., will be found under the head of "Settlement by Apprenticeship." (*Ante* 499.)

Defective Apprenticeship: Proofs.] The evidence by which it may be concluded that the parties intended to enter into a contract of apprenticeship, but have failed to observe all the legal forms, has already been explained, and the consequent inability to gain a settlement thereby, either as an apprentice or a hired servant, (*ante* 500, *et seq.*) Where the question is, whether a contract is a contract of this kind, or a contract of hiring and service, the point to ascertain appears to be, what was the principal and what the subordinate object of the parties, and whether the service was not treated by them as the means of effecting the purpose of apprenticeship.

Upon such a question, the presence or the absence of certain facts found only in a contract of apprenticeship, or only in a contract of hiring and service, is not decisive of the question, though such presence or absence is a circumstance to be considered, as bearing upon the question.

Accordingly, a contract being entered into, by which a person engaged to serve as an "articled servant," at certain wages, but the father was a party to the agreement, and engaged to provide the intended servant with board, lodging, and necessaries, and the master engaged to teach and instruct the servant in his own business, and it was also provided that the servant should be considered as an out *apprentice*, and there were other provisions of the same inconsistent character; the court held, that no one of those circumstances was to be taken as of itself decisive of the question whether this was a contract of apprenticeship, or one of hiring and service; but the sessions having, on the whole, found it to be a defective contract of apprenticeship, the court confirmed their order. (R. v. Tipton, Nov. 2, 1829, K. B. MSS.)

Settlement by renting a Tenement: Proofs.] The subject of settlements by renting a tenement, being divided into three parts, (see *ante* 521,) it is proper to state what evidence will suffice, before the 59 Geo. 3. c. 30, (2d July, 1819;) secondly, what will be required under that statute, (to 22d June, 1825;) and lastly, the evidence necessary to be adduced since the passing of the 6 Geo. 4. c. 57.

Renting, &c., before 1819: *Proofs.*] A settlement might be gained before this period, by renting any of the several species of tenement already enumerated. (See *ante* 522.) But it must be remembered, that in the case of buildings, if they are not inserted, or fixed into the land in some way, they are not tenements for this purpose. As, for instance, if a windmill merely rest upon brick pillars, without being attached or fastened to them, the *windmill* is no tenement, but a mere chattel. (R. v. Londonthorpe, 6 T. R. 377.) The evidence on this subject is obvious. But the party must be a *renter* of a tenement, either as a lessee, sub-lessee, or tenant from year to year. An assignee, or purchaser of a tenement, does not rent a tenement in this sense, though he may probably gain a settlement by estate, in right of such an interest.

A tenancy may be proved by evidence of an express contract between the parties, with proof of occupation; or by proof of occupation and payment of rent; or by establishing the fact of occupation, and by showing some other person to have been landlord or owner of the tenement at the time; or lastly, where the person is dead whose tenancy is sought to be established, by proof of his having been the occupier, and of declarations made by him whilst in possession, showing on what terms he held.

An express contract, if in writing, must be proved in the same manner as other written instruments. (See *ante* 581.) If the agreement was by parol, either of the parties, or any one present when it was made, may give evidence of it; and any one cognizant of the fact may prove the occupation.

Where the case rests upon occupation and payment of rent, the same mode of proof, that is, either by one of the parties, or some other person who has a personal and express knowledge on the subject, may be adopted; or if the landlord or his agent who received the rent be dead, any receipt given for the rent may be substituted, on proof of the hand-writing of the deceased.

A *primâ facie* case may be made out in this way, sufficient to give a settlement, unless it be opposed by proof, on the other side, of circumstances which either destroy such case, or render additional evidence essential to establish it. It may be shown, for instance, that the occupation was not as tenant, but as bailiff or servant of the owner, or against his consent, or as a privilege attached to, or allowed in respect of an office, or a personal hiring, which is the principal thing. (R. v. Seacroft, 2 Maul. & Sel. 472.) It may also be made to appear, that the person, whose settlement is in dispute, came into the occupation under one who was the original taker, in which case the question arises, whether he was assignee of a term, or a subtenant; as, in the former case, his occupancy will give him no settlement, and the party therefore who sets up the settlement must prove by the ordinary evidence of a tenancy, that he occupied in the latter character.

Abstractedly considered, there is no stronger ground to presume that the party occupied as sublessee, than as assignee of the term, held by the prior occupier. But, if A., the tenant, quit the premises, and upon his quitting B. take possession, and no other fact appears, such as payment of rent by B. to A., it may be presumed that B. came in as assignee of A. (Doe d. Morris v. Williams, 6 Barn. & Cres. 41; 9 Dowl. & Ryl. 30; Doe d. Batten v. Murless, 6 Maul. & Sel. 110.) However, it may be proved that he occupied as under lessee, so as to entitle him to a settlement, either by evidence of the agreement for such an occupancy, whether in writing or by word of mouth, or by proof that the first tenant again occupied, subsequent to the occupation by the second tenant, and *before* the expiration of the original term; for then it may be presumed that the original term was *not* assigned to such second tenant, but that a subtenancy was created; or, by proof of payment of rent by the second tenant to the first, for then the relation of landlord and tenant is established between them.

Proof of yearly Value.] It is the value of the tenement at the time of coming to settle, that is material, though in case of a tenancy from year to year, the beginning of each succeeding year is the period at which the value is to be estimated. It must also be recollected, that a joint-tenancy, or tenancy in common, is sufficient, if the value of each tenant's share is sufficient, and that, if a person who rents a tenement of the proper value let off part of it, he does not thereby lose his settlement.

The yearly value of a tenement is the sum which it is worth to let by the year, and the rent actually received is usually the best evidence of value in such cases. This may be proved either by the landlord or the tenant, and even where there is a *written* agreement, payment of rent, as rent, is evidence of tenancy, and may be proved without producing the written instrument, nor need it be produced to prove the yearly value. (R. v. Hull, 7 Barn. & Cres. 611; 1 Man. & Ryl. 444.) But proof of the rent actually paid does not estop the other side from proving the real annual value by the opinion of competent persons, who have made their estimate upon a survey of the premises; a species of evidence which may be resorted to by either party, and the only proof where payment of rent cannot be proved.

If a renting by the *week*, or month, be shown, which, in the aggregate for the year, amounts to a sufficient value, this is not so decisive as an *annual* renting, and may be more readily impugned by proof of the actual yearly value being less than such aggregate amount.

The forty days' residence in the parish in which the tenement, or some part of it is situated, must be proved as in other cases.

What Tenement, since 1819.] Since the passing of the 59 Geo. 3. c. 50, it is necessary that the tenement, in respect of which the settlement is claimed, should lie in one parish, and that it consist of a distinct and separate dwelling-house or building, or of land, or of a house or building and land. Evidence to this effect may be given by any one acquainted with the parish and the tenement; or, if the bounds of the parish be in dispute, those bounds may be proved by perambulations, in which the two adjoining parishes were parties, or, which were made under an act of parliament. Or, the boundaries may be proved by evidence of reputation, that is, by the declarations of old persons deceased, or other owners and occupiers, who had, at the time such declarations were made, no particular interest in favour of the one parish or the other. So, also, proof of the exercise of parochial rights over the place in dispute, as the taking of tithes, payment of parish rates, &c. is evidence for this purpose.

By an act for making the river Cam navigable, authority was given to the commissioners to let the tolls, toll-houses, &c. They accordingly granted a lease of the house, tolls, &c. at £56 a-year. The toll-house was licensed as a public house, and the lessee underlet the whole demised to him to one Unwin, who stipulated to purchase all the ale and beer sold on the premises of the lessee, who was a brewer. Under this agreement, Unwin occupied for more than a year, and paid the year's rent, and had been charged by the parish of St. Andrew, in which the house was situated, to the rates, "for public-house, four pounds;" and it was found by the sessions, that the house was worth, as a public-house, twenty-five pounds a-year; but if not rated or used as a public-house, then the value was estimated at four pounds a-year; and the sessions quashed an order removing Unwin to the said parish, holding that no settlement was gained by the above hiring and occupation. The case was considered as coming within the 54th Geo. 3, c. 170, s. 5, which provides, that no person renting the tolls, &c., of any turnpike road or navigation, and residing in the toll-house, shall thereby gain a settlement. The Court of King's Bench held that the sessions were right, saying, it was better to adhere to the words of the act in such cases; and observed, that the house, land, and tolls were let at one *entire rent*, and that they could not inquire into the value of one part, as distinct from the other, in order to bring the case within the 59th Geo. 3, c. 50, or the 6th Geo. 4, c. 57.

It seems from the above case, that where a tenement, which may happen by itself to be of more than the value of ten pounds a-year, is let together with some other matter, at an entire rent of more than ten pounds a-year, a residence on the tenement will not confer a settlement under either of the above statutes. Mr. Justice Bayley having expressed it as his opinion, that the subject matter of the letting could not be apportioned, in order to fix a value of ten pounds a-year upon the tenement. (R. v. St. Andrew the Less, Cambridge, E. T. 1830, MSS.)

The locality, and the nature of the tenement being established, it must be next proved, that the party hired the tenement for a year at the rent of £10 at the least. For this purpose, the agreement, if in writing, should be produced, and proved in the ordinary way. Or, if by word of mouth, the usual testimony in such cases is sufficient. (See *ante* 581.)

It has already been stated, that the fact of *tenancy*, and of yearly *value*, may be proved by oral testimony, even where there is a written agreement, which the party fails to produce. (*Ante* 588.) But the *terms* of the tenancy must be proved by the written instrument, where one exists between the parties.

Thus, where a *primâ facie* case of tenancy was proved, and the respondents attempted, in answer, to show by parol testimony, that the pauper was not the sole tenant, and that the premises were let to him jointly with two others; but the witness, on cross examination, having stated that the letting was by a *written instrument*, the court held, that such letting could only be proved by the production of that instrument. (R. v. Rawden, 8 Barn. & Cres. 708.)

It seems to follow, that as under the 59 Geo. 3. c. 50, it is material that the party should *rent* at £10 a year at the least, and the demise must be by the year, in all cases upon tenancies since that statute, the written agreement cannot be dispensed with, if there be one capable of being produced; it being the best evidence of the *terms* of such renting.

Where no direct means of proving an agreement between lessor and lessee, or landlord and tenant, exist, circumstantial evidence of a *bonâ fide* hiring, according to the conditions of the statute, may be adduced. Thus, proof that A. was the landlord of the premises, that B. occupied them for a year, and paid a year's rent amounting to £10, justify the inference that they were *hired* agreeably to the terms of the statute.

If the tenement consist of different parcels, hired of different persons, and at different times, the same proof must be gone through with respect to each hiring, to complete the evidence of the settlement.

Proof that the party held or occupied for a whole year, (see *ante* 529,) may be given by any one cognizant of the fact.

Payment of a whole year's rent, whatever the amount, (*ante* 531,) may be proved by the landlord or tenant, or if the agent of the person for whom it was received be dead, a receipt given by him is good evidence for this purpose.

As the law considers a tender of payment, duly made, as equivalent to payment, for certain purposes, it is probable that a legal tender of the rent upon the premises before sunset, or the last hour of the day when it became due, and proof also that the party was always ready afterwards to pay it, would be held equivalent to actual payment for the purpose of gaining a settlement. (See R. v. Ampthill, 2 Barn. & Cres. 854.) But, of course, the tender must be made with all the exactness required in other cases, that is, it must be the proper sum, the money must be produced, and the payment must be offered unconditionally.

The proof of forty days' residence in the parish, must, of course, be added.

Proofs under 6 Geo. 4. c. 57.] With regard to the evidence necessary to establish a settlement acquired under this statute, that is to say, since the 22nd of June, 1825, it is requisite to prove the nature of the tenement, and that it is within the parish, in the same manner as under the former act; (*ante* 588;) the hiring in this case, it is presumed, must be *one* hiring, and that several hirings, as in the former case, will not suffice, the words of this statute being, "such yearly hiring." An occupation under such yearly hiring must, of course, be proved, and the payment of the year's rent, with a residence also of forty days in the parish.

Settlement by payment of Rates: Proofs.] Settlements by payment of rates were virtually abolished by 6 Geo. 4. c. 57; before that period, down to June 22nd, 1795, they were governed by 35 Geo. 3. c. 101. s. 4, having, anterior to the passing of which statute, rested upon the law as it stood upon the 3 W. & M. c. 11. s. 6.

In all cases, whatever the period in which the settlement by payment of rates is to be established, there must be proof that the person was either actually or constructively rated in respect of his tenement; that he paid such rate, and that he resided in the parish forty days after payment.

The rate itself is the best evidence of the rating, but if it be in the custody of the opposite party, who refuse to produce it upon due notice, or if proof be given of its destruction or loss, then secondary evidence is admissible of its contents. In this latter case, some evidence must be given for the purpose of authenticating it; if, however, it be proved to be in the possession of the opposite party, and they having had notice, refuse to produce it, no further proof is necessary to entitle the party to give secondary evidence of its contents.

In all other cases it must be duly authenticated, the best proof of which authentication is afforded by evidence of the hand-writing of the justices who allow it.

As by 17 Geo. 2. c. 3. s. 2, the churchwardens, &c. are to give to the inhabitants of the parish, copies of the rate on demand; such copy, proved to have been so given, seems to be good secondary evidence of the rate without being proved to be an examined copy; but any other copy must be proved to have been compared with the original rate.

If no copy is produced, and it is not shown that one exists within the knowledge of the party proving the rate, oral evidence may be given of its contents.

If the rate refer to the person by name, his identity as the person so referred to, may be proved by any one who knows the fact. If he is not named in the rate, it must be shown by distinct evidence, that he was the person contemplated by the parish officers in rating the tenement of which he was possessed; and that the fact of his occupation at that time was known to the parish officers.

Thus, for instance, if the assessment be upon "J. S. *or the tenant*, of Black Acre." Here it is necessary to prove that J. S. was the landlord, and that A., whose settlement is in question, was the tenant.

Or, if the rate had been upon J. S. a former occupier, who was dead, it must be shown, that the parish knew of the death at the time they made the rate, and that A. was at that time in the occupation of the premises.

As to what in law may be considered a payment, and the time when such payment should be made, (*ante* 590.)

To establish a settlement by rating between the 22nd of June, 1795, and the 22nd of June, 1825, in addition to all the above proofs, it must be shown that the tenement, in respect of which the party is rated, was of the yearly value of £10 at the time the rate was made.

Settlement by Estate: Proofs.] As the law has provided that a purchase of an estate for less than £30, shall not suffice to give a settlement, it seems necessary in all cases to prove that the title of the owner is not liable to this objection, before it can be held sufficient to give him a settlement.

The nature of the evidence necessary for this purpose will depend upon the nature of the estate, and upon the mode by which the party acquired it.

Thus, proof of possession by an ancestor, and succession by an heir, which may be given by any one who knows the facts, discloses enough of the title to make out a *primâ facie* case, that the latter did not purchase for a money consideration. And, his relationship as heir may be proved by persons belonging to the family, speaking from their own knowledge, or from what they have heard from deceased members of the family, respecting the relationship of its different members, aided by parish registers, &c. (See 3 Stark. Ev. tit. Pedigree.)

In the case of a widow found in possession of an estate, which was her husband's, proof of possession on the part of the husband, before, and at the time of the marriage, proof of the marriage itself, of his death, and of her subsequent possession, will *primâ facie* establish her an estate as confers a settlement.

If the party hold the estate as tenant, by the curtsey or otherwise, in right of his wife; the marriage, and either possession by the wife before marriage, or the title by which it came to her after marriage, must be proved.

Where the party holds, as executor, administrator, guardian in socage, or as tenant by elegit, his title must be shown, according to the character in which he holds.

To prove him executor, the probate must be produced, which requires no authentication, or a copy thereof, proved to be an *examined* copy, may be given in evidence, or the Probate Act Book of the Ecclesiastical Court, or an examined copy of the entry in that book is admissible. If the probate has been lost, it is the practice of the Ecclesiastical Courts to grant what is called an exemplification of the probate from their records, which exemplification, in such cases, or an examined copy of it, may be given in evidence. (2 Phill. Ev. 342-3.)

If the party was administrator, the same course of evidence with regard to the letters of administration may be taken. (Davis v. Williams, 13 East, 232.) But instead of an exemplification, it is usual to give a certificate that administration was granted, which is equally effectual where the letters of administration are lost.

In order to establish the title of guardian in socage, it will be necessary to prove the seisin of the ancestor, the death of that ancestor, the heirship of the ward, the fact of his being under the age of fourteen at the time of the guardian's entry upon the land, (which fact may be proved by any witness acquainted with the family of the ward,) and the relationship of the guardian to the ward, as nearest in degree among those relations to whom the inheritance cannot descend.

If the estate was held under an elegit, it is requisite to prove the judgment recovered; the elegit taken out upon it; the inquisition made by a jury, and the sheriff's return, by which the land is assigned to the creditor. (See 2 Phill. Ev. 252.)

If the party possessed the estate, or was reversioner, or remainder-man, or had some equitable interest under a devise, marriage settlement, conveyance in consideration of natural love and affection, mortgage, deed of trust, or some written agreement, the ordinary mode of proving title in any such case must be observed.

The devise, if of a copyhold interest, does not require a signature or attestation, as a devise of lands in fee simple. It is sufficient in this case to prove a will by the testator, of the same force only as that required for passing personal property. (Doe d. Cook v. Danvers, 7 East, 299; 2 Phill. Ev. 248.)

If the devise be of a lease for a term of years, the interest is a chattel interest, and therefore the probate, and not the original will, is the proper medium for proving it. (2 Phill. Ev. 247.) This proof, coupled with proof of possession under the will, would probably be deemed sufficient to show that the party had such an estate as would give him a settlement, without further evidence, as it would make out that the party occupied by a title not derived from a money-purchase.

If the claim is under surrenders and admittances to a copyhold estate, either the original entries on the court rolls of the manor, or stamped copies of those court rolls must be produced. (Doe v. Hall, 16 East, 208.)

It seems that land held as appurtenant to an office will not give a settlement by estate. The case was as follows:—By an award made by the authority of the lord of the manor and certain commoners, an allotment of a portion of the lands inclosed was awarded to "the shepherd for the time being." It was also provided by the award, that the shepherd was to keep the fences in repair. The shepherd had been for many years appointed by the commoners, and was liable to be discharged, like any other yearly servant. It was held, that a person who had in fact filled the situation of shepherd, and enjoyed the allotment for several years, did not thereby gain a settlement by estate. His situation being yearly, from which he was liable to be discharged, and he taking to the allotment, not by virtue of the award, (to which he was a stranger,) but by virtue of his situation as shepherd, the court considered his occupation of the allotment to be a part of the consideration or wages for his service, and that he had no title, either legal or equitable, to the land, but merely the right to occupy so long as he was in the place of shepherd. (R. v. South Newton, E. T. 1830, MSS.)

Nor will residence upon an estate at will, under the value of ten pounds a-year, give a settlement, unless there has been an adverse possession for twenty years: and a person who has only such an estate is removeable, though he may have resided more than forty days upon the estate. (R. v. Chew Magna, E. T. 1830, MSS.)

To the various proofs by means of documentary evidence, must, in each case, be added some proof of the identity of the party.

The instances in which a title, apparently good, may be most frequently impeached by matter of fact, are cases of estates purchased for a money consideration. In the instrument of conveyance, the sum *stated* may be large enough, while, in point of *fact*, it may have been less than is required by the statute. In every such case the party opposing the settlement may show, that the full sum of £30 was not paid, or that it was not paid by the purchaser, but by some person who did not pay it on the purchaser's behalf.

A residence for forty days in the parish which contains some part of the estate must be proved, as in the other kinds of settlement.

Settlement by Office: Proofs.] To establish a settlement by serving an office, an appointment to such an office as will confer a settlement must be proved; the execution of the office for a whole year must also be shown, and a residence for forty days in the parish, or in a part of it where some of the duties of the office are performed, must likewise be made out in evidence.

The appointment may be proved by the books or rolls of a manor or parish, or by the oral testimony of witnesses who were present, if no formal record, warrant, or written entry, were made at the time. It must be remembered, that the appointment of an assistant overseer requires a stamp. (R. v. Lew. 8 Barn. & Cres. 655.)

In the absence of direct proof of the appointment, it may be inferred from the proof given of the exercise of the office by the party, subject to its being impeached by the opposite side. That he exercised the office for a whole year, may be proved by himself or others, or by evidence that another person, who discharged the duties, acted as his deputy.

If a legal appointment is established by direct evidence, it will not be required to give very strict and precise proof of the execution of the office, nor will it be necessary in any case to make out that the party served the whole year, otherwise than by general evidence of his having discharged the duties of his appointment at different times within that period.

The office of town crier and bellman is an annual office, within the 3 W. & M. c. 11, s. 6, by which a settlement may be gained. And if the town comprises several parishes, the settlement will be gained in that parish in which such officer has last resided forty days, while serving the office. It was before undecided (see 2 N. P. L. 629) whether a year's *residence* and a year's *service* in the same parish were not essential in such case. But the court said, that as the notice in writing of a coming to settle required to be delivered, according to the 3d section of the above act, and from the delivery of which the forty days are to be calculated, is dispensed with in the case of an annual office, by the 6th section, a residence of forty days, without notice, by analogy to the cases of settlement by hiring and service, renting a tenement, &c., is sufficient. So that neither a year's residence, nor a year's service, in the parish where the settlement is claimed, is essential according to the words of the act. (R. v. St. Nicholas, Hereford, E. T. 1830, MSS.)

Derivative Settlements: Proofs.] To establish a derivative settlement, whether it be claimed on behalf of a wife or child, it is necessary that satisfactory evidence of the marriage, which is the foundation of this settlement, should be given. In some instances this question is put beyond dispute by the acknowledgment by certificate, &c., of the parish, sought to be charged.

Settlement by Marriage: Proofs.] Where no such acknowledgment exists, the most usual course to prove the marriage is, by a person who was present; and either husband or wife is a competent witness for this purpose, and the production of the parish register, with proof of the identity of the parties; if, however none, of the persons who were present on the occasion can be found, the other evidence will be sufficient. (See *infra.*)

Although by the policy of the law, husband and wife shall not be permitted to be witnesses for, or to criminate each other, yet where, upon a question of settlement, a marriage between A. and C. was set up, but the opposite party proceeded to prove that A. had been previously married to B., and B. was called, who gave evidence of the fact, the court held, that she was properly received as a witness, as her evidence could not be used to criminate him; and it also appeared that he had not been called as a witness, so that she was not produced to contradict him; though the court thought, under the circumstances of the case, that was not material. (R. v. All Saints, Worcester, 6 Maul. & Sel. 194.)

If the marriage took place in a *chapel* before the 23rd August, 1808, (see 48 Geo. 3. c. 127) it is necessary to prove that the chapel was *consecrated;* or if the chapel were not consecrated, or the marriage took place subsequently to the above date, then it must be proved that the chapel was one in which marriages might legally be solemnized, which proof may be afforded by the production of old registers of marriages solemnized in the chapel, and by living testimony that it is customary to celebrate marriages there. (2 Stark. Ev. 933.) And under the present marriage act, if the marriage take place in a chapel where banns could not lawfully be published, it cannot be invalidated on that account, if the parties were not cognizant of that circumstance. (See *ante,* 117.)

The declarations of persons deceased, as of either of the immediate parties, their relations, servants or intimate friends, as to the fact of marriage, are also evidence, so that such declarations, whether oral or written, were made before any dispute had arisen as to the fact, upon its being proved that the connexion of such persons with the family to which the tradition relates, was of a nature to give them peculiar means of knowledge on the subject. (1 Phill. Ev. 227.)

Another mode of establishing a marriage is by evidence of reputation. Proof, therefore, by any of the above means that the parties cohabited together, and were received by relations and friends as man and wife, will suffice in the absence of more direct evidence.

A marriage may also be proved by a sentence in the spiritual court affirming the marriage, which is conclusive for all purposes, unless it can be impeached on the ground of fraud or collusion. (1 Stark. Ev. 141.) The sentence itself is to be proved by the book which contains the official entry of the proceedings, or an examined copy of such entry.

It is competent, on the other hand, to show, that a marriage has been annulled by the spiritual court, or that it was not performed in a manner to render it valid; or that no marriage in fact took place, in cases where the proof in its support rests upon hearsay evidence, or reputation; and the same species of evidence is admissible to destroy a marriage by reputation, as is produced to establish it, the court having then to determine upon the balance of testimony.

It may be proper to remark, that a marriage is presumed to have been celebrated with the formalities necessary to its validity, till the contrary be shown; and that it is not necessary to prove that the minister was in orders, or to prove any of the proceedings preliminary to the actual solemnization of the marriage. (See 2 Stark. Ev. 932.) And, although in cases of marriages by banns, the law requires that the true names of the parties should be given in the publication of the banns, yet if they were known by the names used, for some time, (in one instance sixteen weeks,) though it be a false name, which has been assumed to prevent a discovery in some other matter not at all connected or relating to the marriage, (as where the party is a deserter, for instance,) the marriage cannot be invalidated on that ground. It is also good, if the names by which they have been long known are used, though there might be some intention of a fraud in other respects. But if a totally false name be assumed for the purpose of the marriage, then it cannot be considered that such name is a true designation, and the fraud would vitiate the marriage. But partial variations, where no fraud was intended, and the parties have lived together a long time, would not be considered as rendering the marriage void. (2 Stark. Ev. 935; 3 Maul. & Sel. 266.) See further on this subject, tit. "Marriage." (*Ante* 111, *et seq.*)

Settlement by Parentage: Proofs.] To prove that B. the person for whom a settlement by parentage is claimed, is really the legitimate child of A., in addition to the marriage of the parent, which has been already discussed, the birth of the child within lawful wedlock must be shown, which may be either by direct proof of the birth, and time of birth, as by means of the mother, or any one else personally acquainted with the fact, or by the declarations, oral or written, of deceased relations who may be acquainted with the circumstances, (3 Stark. Ev. 1101—1116,) or through the medium of the register, accompanied with proof of identity.

Or it may be shown that the child was reputed to be the legitimate child of its parents, and was so treated by the family.

In whatever way the legitimacy of the child may be attempted to be proved, it is still open to the opposite party to show that the child in question was not in law and fact a child of the marriage. (Goodright v. Moss, 2 Cowp. 591.)

Even if the marriage be unimpeachable, and the child was born after the marriage, and the husband was even living in the same house with the wife at the period when, according to the ordinary course of nature, he might be the father of the child, yet evidence may still be adduced to show that the husband was not the father of the child. (See "Illegitimate children," *ante* 461.)

Settlement by Birth: Proofs.] Although in questions of pedigree hearsay evidence of birth is admissible, yet in a case of settlement the point to ascertain is, whether the person was born in a *particular place,* and upon this question hearsay evidence cannot be received. (R. v. Erith, 8 East, 539.)

It is obviously the best mode of fixing the locality of the birth, to call some person who was present, or who knew and saw the mother in the parish, just before and immediately after that event, and who also saw the offspring, and can give evidence upon the question of identity. Or these several facts may be proved respectively by different witnesses, according to their knowledge. It is clear that the party himself can have no recollection upon which to presume that he was born in a particular place. (See R. v. Trowbridge, 7 Barn. & Cres. 252.)

The register of baptism is, *per se,* no evidence that the child mentioned in it was born in the parish. If the age of the child, when it was baptized, could be ascertained, the register might in some cases be evidence of the place of birth. If the child was then very young, the register would be presumptive evidence that it was born in that parish where it was baptized; but if the child were not then young, the circumstance of its having been baptized in a particular parish would afford no presumption that it was born there. (R. v. North Petherton, 5 Barn. & Cres. 510; 8 Dowl. & Ryl. 325.)

Though a parish register is not conclusive evidence of the place of birth of the person baptized, it is admissible in evidence, to be considered with other facts, upon the question as to the place of birth.

The declaration of a deceased mother, as to the time of birth, is admissible in evidence, upon a question as to the place of birth of the child, though the father be living. (R. v. Birmingham; R. v. Aston, Oct. 29, 1829, K. B. MSS.)

CHAPTER XXVII.

LIGHTING AND WATCHING PARISHES.

An act has passed in the present session of parliament, upon this subject, with a view to supersede the necessity of incurring the expense of private bills, by parishes desirous of availing themselves of a regularly digested system for this purpose, under the sanction of the legislature.

The act is intituled, "An Act to make Provision for the Lighting and Watching of Parishes in England and Wales." (11 Geo. 4. c. 27.)

The following abstract is in the language of the act itself, the repetitions and multiplied expressions being omitted, in order to reduce the whole into a smaller compass. The provisions relating to nuisances arising from the manufacture or use of gas, are the same as those usually found in local acts on the like subject. The first section is as follows:—

Whereas it is desirable to make provision for the lighting and watching of the several parishes in England and Wales; be it therefore enacted, that this act shall apply to and may be adopted by all or any, or either of the parishes in England and Wales. (s. 1.)

Meeting to adopt the Act.] That upon the application of three or more rated inhabitants, the churchwardens shall, within ten days after, appoint and notify a time and place for a public meeting in vestry of the inhabitants of the parish, for determining whether the provisions of the act shall be adopted in the said parish; provided that the meeting shall not be less than ten, nor more than twenty-one days, from the delivery of the said application; and that the notification of the time and place of meeting shall be forthwith affixed on the principal outer door of every parish church or chapel situate within such parish, and also by publication in the church or chapel, on the Sunday previous to the day appointed for such meeting, during or immediately after divine service. (s. 2.)

Plurality of Votes.] That at any such meeting, every inhabitant present, who shall by the last poor's rate have been assessed in respect of any annual rent, profit, or value, not amounting to fifty pounds, shall have one vote only; if assessed upon fifty pounds or upwards, (whether in one, or more than one sum or charge,) shall have one vote for every twenty-five pounds of annual rent, profit, and value, upon which he shall have been assessed in such last rate, so that no inhabitant shall give more than six votes; and where two or more inhabitants present are jointly rated, each shall vote according to the proportion borne by him of the joint charge; and when one only of the persons jointly rated attends, he shall vote according to the whole joint charge; provided, that when any person become an inhabitant, or become liable to be rated, since the making the last poor's rate, he shall be entitled to vote in respect of the property for which he shall have become liable to be rated, and shall consent to be rated, as if he had been actually rated for the same: provided also, that no person who shall have refused or neglected to pay any poor's rate due, and which shall have been demanded of him, shall vote or be present at any such public meeting in vestry, until he shall have paid the same. (s. 3.)

Chairman elected: his duty.] The inhabitants present shall elect a chairman at such meetings, who shall determine any controversy as to the qualification, right, or eligibility of any person claiming to vote, or as to the qualification or eligibility of any candidate. (s. 4.)

The chairman shall read, or cause to be read, the requisition for the meeting, and shall require the persons assembled to determine, by majority of votes, whether this act shall be adopted. The majority of the rated inhabitants present may adjourn such meeting from time to time. (s. 5.)

Act to operate from adoption.] That if at such meeting it shall be determined by a majority of three-fourths of votes, ascertained as aforesaid, to adopt the provisions of this act, the same shall from thenceforth come into operation in such parish; and it shall forthwith be determined, that not more than eleven, nor less than three inspectors, shall be elected to carry such purposes into effect. The inspectors shall be elected in manner hereinafter mentioned. (s. 6.)

Maximum of Rate.] The inhabitants adopting the act shall, at the first meeting, or some adjournment thereof, fix the highest amount of rate which the inspectors shall have power to call for in any one year, for the purposes of this act. (s. 7.)

Rejecting the Act.] If the meeting determine against adopting the act, the inhabitants shall not meet again in less than one year from such meeting. (s. 8.)

Electing Inspectors.] The inspectors shall be elected in manner following:—Each candidate, being a resident within the parish, and assessed to the poor in respect of a tenement, &c. of the annual value of fifteen pounds or more, shall be eligible, and shall be proposed and seconded at the meeting by persons duly qualified to vote; and if there are more candidates than the number of inspectors authorized to be elected, and a poll be demanded by any ten persons qualified to vote, the chairman shall proceed with such poll, and in a book or books prepared by the churchwardens, shall enter or cause to be entered, the name of all such candidates, and the name of every duly qualified voter, with his description and abode, and for whom he votes; and if all the votes cannot be conveniently registered by four o'clock, the chairman shall at that hour adjourn such poll to the day next succeeding, unless such day shall be a Sunday, Christmas day, or Good Friday, and in that case, to the day following, and then proceed with the same. But the poll shall finally close at four o'clock on such second day, or sooner, provided all persons duly qualified and desirous to vote shall have voted, and after the lapse of one hour, without any person offering to vote; and as soon after the close of the poll as may be possible, the result shall be declared at the place of election, and certified by the chairman to the overseers of the poor; and the said churchwardens shall be reimbursed all reasonable expenses incurred in providing clerks, books, and otherwise, in the performance of the duties hereby required of them, by the candidates at the said election for the said office. (s. 9.)

Inspectors: duration of Office.] The inspectors so elected shall go out of office on the 29th day of September, in the third year from the said first election; and in their place other inspectors, elected as hereinafter provided, shall come into and remain in office for three years, who at the expiration of such three years shall in like manner go out of office, and be succeeded by other inspectors, who shall remain in office for a like term of three years, and so on for ever;

provided that any of such outgoing inspectors may be re-elected. (s. 10.)

Elections when to be made.] The triennial meetings for electing inspectors are to be held on the second Monday in September. And such meetings are to be regulated and governed in all respects by the provisions herein contained, as applicable to the first meeting. (s. 11.)

In case of any vacancy happening in any manner whatever, so that the number of inspectors shall be reduced to less than three, notice shall be immediately given by the acting inspectors to the churchwardens, who shall forthwith call a meeting of the inhabitants, as aforesaid, for the purpose of filling up such vacancy. (s. 12.)

Meetings of Inspectors.] The inspectors shall meet on the first Monday in every month, at noon, at some convenient place previously publicly notified; and at such monthly meeting any inhabitant rated to the poor may there prefer any complaint concerning any thing done in pursuance of or under pretence of this act. (s. 13.)

The inspectors shall meet as often as at any previous meeting shall be determined upon; and any one inspector, when three only have been appointed, and in all other cases any two, by writing under his or their hands, may summon, at forty-eight hours' notice, the inspectors, for any special purpose, and for such time as shall be therein named; and that at such meetings not less than one third of the whole number, except when only three shall have been appointed, and then not less than two inspectors shall constitute a quorum for transacting business. (s. 14.)

Officers appointed by Inspectors.] The inspectors for the time being shall appoint, during pleasure, such treasurer and other officers as they shall think necessary, and hire a sufficient office or room for holding their meetings and transacting their business; and they also shall appoint suitable salaries and allowances for such treasurer and other officers, and pay the same, and the rent of the office, &c., out of the monies received by them under the authority of this act. But no person shall at the same time hold two offices under the said inspectors. (s. 15.)

Treasurer to give Security.] The inspectors, or any two or more of them, shall take security from the treasurer, for the due execution of his office, to the full amount of the sum likely to be in his hands at any one time; and if he neglect or refuse, for three weeks next after his appointment, to give or offer satisfactory security, his appointment shall be void, and the inspectors shall, within three weeks then next, assemble and appoint some other fit person to the office of treasurer in his stead, and shall so assemble and appoint, from time to time, until security shall be given to their satisfaction, as aforesaid. (s. 16.)

Officers' Accounts.] Every such treasurer and other officer shall, under his hand, and in such time and manner as the inspectors shall direct, deliver to them, or such person as they shall appoint, true accounts in writing of all matters and things committed to his charge by virtue of this act, and of all monies by such officer received by virtue of this act, and of his disbursements, together with proper vouchers for such payments; and every such officer shall pay all such monies as remain due from him, to the treasurer, or to such person as the inspectors shall appoint; and in case of refusal or neglect herein, or to deliver to the inspectors, or to such person as they shall appoint, within three days after being required, in writing, under the hands and seals of any two or more inspectors, left at the usual abode of such officer, all books, papers, and writings in his custody or power, relating to the execution of this act, or to give satisfaction to the inspectors, or such other person, respecting the same; then and in every such case, upon complaint to any justice of the peace, such justice shall issue a summons under his hand and seal for such officer to appear before two justices; and upon his appearing, or, having been so summoned, not appearing, without some sufficient excuse, the said justices may hear and determine the matter in a summary way; and if upon confession, or by credible testimony upon oath, it shall appear that any monies remain due from such officer, such justices shall, upon non-payment thereof, cause such money to be levied by distress; and if no goods of such officer shall be found sufficient to satisfy the said money, and the charges of distraining and selling the same, or if it shall appear to such justices that such officer had refused or wilfully neglected to render such account, or to produce the vouchers relating thereto, or that any books, papers, or writings, as aforesaid, remained in the custody or power of such officer, and he refused or wilfully neglected to deliver or give satisfaction respecting the same, then such justices shall commit such offender to the common gaol or house of correction for the county or place where such offender shall be or reside, there to remain until he shall have given a perfect account, or paid such monies, or compounded for such money, and shall have paid such composition, (which composition the said inspectors are hereby empowered to make,) and until he shall have delivered up such books, papers, and writings, or given satisfaction in respect thereof, as aforesaid; but no such offender shall be imprisoned for want of sufficient distress, for any longer than three calendar months. (s. 17.)

Sureties not exonerated.] No such prosecution or commitment, shall acquit or discharge any surety or security given to the inspectors for the due execution of his or their office. (s. 18.)

Officers not to accept Fees, &c.] If any treasurer, officer or servant in anywise employed by the inspectors, shall take, or accept any fee or reward, other than such salaries, allowances, and rewards as are appointed under the authority of this act, on any account whatsoever relative to putting this act into execution, or shall in anywise be concerned or interested in any bargain or contract made or to be made by the inspectors, every such offender shall be incapable of ever being employed under this act, and shall also forfeit the sum of fifty pounds to any person who shall sue for the same. (s. 19.)

Inspectors to sue, and be sued.] The inspectors may sue and be sued in the name of any one of the inspectors for the time being; and no action or suit brought, by or against the inspectors, by virtue of this act, shall abate or be discontinued, by the death of such inspector, but such inspector shall be deemed plaintiff or defendant in any such action or suit (as the case may be): provided, that in all cases in which the inspector shall be the plaintiff or defendant, in which in effect the said inspectors shall be suing or sued in the name of such one inspector as aforesaid, he (although appearing as the plaintiff or defendant on the record) shall nevertheless (if not otherwise interested or objectionable) be a competent witness either for or against the inspectors; and affidavits of debt or service in the prosecution or defence of any such action or proceeding, may be made by such one inspector, notwithstanding he is nominal plaintiff or defendant: provided also, that any such inspector in whose name any action or suit shall be so prosecuted, or defended, shall be reimbursed all costs and expenses which he shall be put to or become chargeable with by reason of his being made plaintiff or defendant therein, unless such action or suit shall arise in consequence of his own wilful default, or have been commenced or be defended without the order of the said inspectors. (s. 20.)

Proceedings to be entered in a Book.] All acts, orders, and proceedings of the inspectors at their meetings shall be entered in a book, and be signed by two of the inspectors then present; and such books may be read as evidence of such acts, orders, and proceedings, upon any proceeding, civil or criminal, and in any court or courts of law or equity whatsoever. (s. 21.)

Books for Accounts.] The inspectors shall direct a book or books to be kept, in which shall be entered true accounts of all money received, paid, and expended for the purposes of this act, and of the several articles and things for which such sums of money shall have been paid; and such book or books shall at all reasonable times be open to the inspection of the inspectors and of every rated inhabitant, without fee or reward, who may take copies or extracts without paying for the same; and in case the inspectors do not permit the persons aforesaid to inspect the same, or take copies or extracts as aforesaid, such inspector shall forfeit not exceeding £5 for each default, to be levied and applied in manner hereinafter provided. (s. 22.)

Annual Accounts.] In the month of September in every year, a true account shall be made in writing of all monies received and paid during the preceding year, ending upon the thirty-first day of August in every year; and a copy or duplicate of such account, verified on oath before any two justices of the peace by the said inspectors, or any two of them, shall be deposited with the said inspectors, and shall be open to the inspection of all parties interested. (s. 23.)

Order to levy Rates.] The inspectors, or any two or more of them, may from time to time issue an order under their hands to the overseers of the poor, requiring the said overseers to levy the amount mentioned in the said order: such order to specify the rate in the pound at which the sum mentioned therein shall be computed. (s. 24.)

Rates proportioned and enforced.] The overseers shall, for the purpose of collecting and levying such rate, proceed in the same manner, and have the same powers, remedies, and privileges, as for levying money for the relief of the poor, provided that the owners or occupiers of land shall be assessed in the proportion of one-fourth of the rate so authorized to be demanded by the inspectors, and the owners or occupiers of houses, buildings, and other property rateable to the relief of the poor, shall be assessed in the proportion of the remaining three-fourths of the said rate: provided also, that the sum so to be levied shall not exceed in the whole in any one year the rate of so much in the pound on the fair annual value of all property rateable to the poor, as shall have been determined on at the meeting assembled in manner hereinbefore directed, such fair annual value to be according to the last valuation acted upon in assessing the poor's rate for the said parish. (s. 25.)

Overseers to pay Amount required.] The overseers to whom such order shall be issued, shall pay the amount mentioned therein to the treasurer appointed under this act, within forty days from the delivery thereof, to one of the overseers, and shall keep the accounts of the said rate levied for the purposes of this act, separate and distinct from the accounts of the poor rates; and on payment to the treasurer, the overseers shall deliver to him a note, signed by them, specifying the amount so paid, which note shall be kept by the treasurer as a voucher for his receipt of that particular amount; and the receipt of the said treasurer, specifying the amount paid to him by the overseers, shall be a sufficient discharge to the overseers for such amount, and shall be allowed as such in passing their accounts with their respective parishes. (s. 26.)

Where any persons other than the overseers shall, by virtue of any office or appointment, make and collect the rate for the relief of the poor in any parish to which the provisions of this act shall be extended, such persons, by whatever title called, shall be deemed to be overseers of the poor within the meaning of this act. (s. 27.)

Overseers may be distrained.] In case the amount directed by such order shall not be paid to the treasurer within the time specified, any justice, upon complaint to him by the treasurer, shall issue a summons under his hand and seal for such overseers to appear before two justices, who may, in case the said money is not paid, issue their warrant for levying the amount by distress; and in case the goods of all the overseers shall not be sufficient to pay the same, the arrears thereof shall be added to the amount of the next levy, which shall be directed to be made in such parish for the purposes of this act. (s. 28.)

Watchmen, &c. to be appointed.] The inspectors shall appoint and employ such number of able-bodied watch-house keepers, serjeants of the night, watchmen, patrols, street-keepers, and other persons, as they shall think proper, by day and by night, and provide them with such clothing, arms, ammunition, and weapons, and shall assign to them such beat and duties, and appoint such hours for them to be on duty, and also such wages, rewards, and gratuities, and also make such rules, orders, and regulations relative to them and their duties, as to the inspectors shall seem meet; and also may give them, as well as any other persons not specially employed by them, such rewards for apprehending felons and others, offenders within the limits of this act, as to them shall seem proper; and may defray the expenses of prosecuting any such felons and offenders, for the protection of the inhabitants of any parish adopting the provisions of this act, or in defending any of the said persons or other officers of the said inspectors in the execution of their duty, as they shall think proper; and the said and all other expenses incurred by the inspectors for the protection and guard of the inhabitants, shall be paid by the inspectors out of the monies received in pursuance of this act. (s. 29.)

Duties of Watchmen, Patrols, &c.] The watchmen, serjeants of the night, &c. appointed under this act, shall, when on duty, use their utmost endeavours to prevent mischief by fire, robberies, burglaries, misdemeanors, and other outrages, disorders, and breaches of the peace, and to apprehend all felons, rogues, vagabonds, and disturbers of the public peace, or persons wandering, secreting, or misbehaving themselves, or whom they shall have reasonable cause to suspect of any evil designs, and to secure and keep in safe custody every such person, in order that he or she may be conveyed, as soon as conveniently may be, before a justice of the peace, to be dealt with according to law; and it shall be lawful for the said watchmen, serjeants of the night, &c. to require any persons to assist them in taking such felons, and disorderly or suspected persons as aforesaid; and any person who shall assault or resist, or encourage the assaulting or resisting, any of the said watchmen, &c. in the execution of their duty, shall for every such offence forfeit and pay any sum not exceeding forty shillings. (s. 30.)

To be sworn as Constables.] The watchmen, serjeants of the night, and patrols, shall be sworn in as constables before any justice, and act as such under this act, with the like powers, privileges and immunities, and shall be subject to the like penalties and forfeitures, as constables are invested with, or shall or may have and enjoy, or are or shall be subject or liable to by law. (s. 31.)

Fire Engines to be provided.] The inspectors shall provide and keep up fire engines, with pipes and other utensils proper for the same, and a proper place or places for the keeping of the same, and shall place such engines under the care of proper persons, and make them a reasonable allowance for their trouble; and the expenses herein shall be paid out of the money received as aforesaid. (s. 32.)

The inspectors are hereby empowered to cause lamp-irons, or posts, to be put upon or against the walls or palisadoes of any houses, tenements, buildings, or inclosures, (doing as little damage as may be practicable thereto,) or in such other manner as they shall think proper, and also to cause such lamps to be provided as they shall think necessary for lighting the streets and places, with gas, oil, or otherwise, and also to cause such watch-houses or watchboxes to be provided, as they shall think necessary. (s. 33.)

Gas Pipes on private Premises.] Nothing herein contained shall empower the inspectors, bodies politic, or persons contracting with the inspectors for lighting with gas such streets, &c. to lay any pipe, cocks, or branches from any mains or pipes, against, into, or through any dwelling-house, public or private buildings, or to continue the same, without the consent in writing of the owner or occupier, nor to enable any persons so contracting for lighting such streets, &c. to enter into or upon any private lands or grounds, without the consent in writing of the owner or occupier first had and obtained. (s. 34.)

In case the soil or pavement be broken up, with the consent of the owner, and after the same shall have been so laid and placed, he shall be desirous of having the same removed, he may at his own charge, alter and vary the position of such pipe or pipes, main or mains, and re-lay the same, so that no damage be done thereby to the said persons, contracting with the inspectors, so that such contractors be not thereby obstructed in lighting any public or private lamp, unless such damage or obstruction be unavoidable. (s. 35.)

Stopping escape of Gas.] Whenever any gas shall be found to escape from any such pipes, the persons whosoever, supplying the gas, shall, at their own expense, immediately after receiving notice by parol or in writing, at their office or usual place of business, from any person whomsoever, cause the most speedy measures to be taken to prevent such gas from escaping; and in case they shall not, within twenty-four hours after such notice, satisfactorily remove the cause of complaint, they shall for every such offence forfeit any sum not exceeding five pounds, for each and every day, after the expiration of twenty-four hours from the time of giving such notice, during which the gas shall be suffered so to escape, which penalty shall be recoverable in a summary way, on the oath or affirmation of one or more credible witness, before any two justices, with all reasonable charges, by distress and sale, in like manner as herein directed touching other penalties. (s. 36.)

Washings, &c. from Gas Works.] The party supplying any gas for lighting the streets, &c. within any parish adopting this act, may lay iron pipes as they shall think expedient, under the streets, &c. for the purpose of carrying off the washings or other waste liquids which arise in their works, doing thereby as little damage as may be, and immediately repairing, at their own expense, all such damage; provided that no such washings, &c. shall be conveyed into any river, brook, canal, or running stream, and that no such pipe shall be laid where the same may in any manner prejudice or affect any of the present or future public or private wells, sewers, or drains, or without the consent of the inspectors. (s. 37.)

Conveying Washings, &c. into River, &c.] If any such persons, supplying such gas, shall at any time empty, or cause or suffer to be emptied, or conveyed, or to flow, any such washings, &c. into any river, brook, or running stream, reservoir, canal, aqueduct, waterway, feeder, pond, or spring-head or well, or into any drain, sewer, or ditch communicating with any of them, or do or cause to be done any annoyance or thing to the water therein, whereby such water shall or may be spoiled, or corrupted, such persons so offending shall forfeit for every such offence the sum of two hundred pounds; and such penalty may be recovered, with full costs, in any of his majesty's courts of law, by regular or summary action of debt or on the case, or by bill, plaint, or information, wherein no essoign, protection, privilege, wager of law, nor more than one imparlance shall be allowed; and the whole penalty shall be paid to the person or persons who shall inform or sue for the same; provided that such penalty shall not be recoverable unless sued for within six calendar months from the time when such annoyance or thing shall have ceased and determined: provided also, that in addition to the said penalty, whether it shall have been sued for or not, upon notice in writing given by any person whomsoever, to the persons supplying such gas, or to any person in their employ, of the commission of any such nuisance and offence as aforesaid, if they shall not, within twenty-fours after such notice, prevent all such washings, waste liquids, &c. from being conveyed, or from flowing in manner aforesaid, and every such other annoyance, damage, or thing, from being done as aforesaid, then such persons so offending shall forfeit and pay the sum of twenty pounds for each and every day such washings, &c. shall be so emptied, conveyed, or suffered to flow in manner aforesaid, or such other annoyance, damage, act or thing shall be so done as aforesaid; and such last-mentioned penalty may be recovered in like manner as any other penalty is by this act directed to be recovered, and shall be paid to the informer, or to the person or persons who, in the judgment of the justices before whom the conviction shall take place, shall have sustained any annoyance, injury, or damage by any such act so done or committed. (s. 38.)

Gas Pipes distant from Water Pipes.] The pipes or other conduits used for the conveyance of gas in any parish adopting the provisions of this act, shall be laid at the greatest practical distance, and, whenever the width of the carriage-way will allow thereof, at the distance of four feet at least from the nearest part of any water pipe under any of the said streets, &c. excepting where it shall be unavoidably necessary to lay the gas-pipes across any of the said water-pipes, in which cases the said gas-pipes shall be laid above the water-pipes at the greatest practical distance therefrom, and shall form therewith a right angle, and shall be at least nine feet in length, so that no joint of the said gas-pipes shall be nearer to the said water-pipes than four feet at least; and in laying down the gas-pipes the said persons supplying gas shall in no case join two or more gas-pipes together previous to their being laid in the trench, but shall lay each pipe as near as may be in its place in the trench, and shall in such trench properly form the jointing with the other pipes with proper materials, and shall also keep all and every such pipes, and all pipes communicating therewith, and all the screws, joints, inlets, apertures, or openings therein respectively, air-tight, and in every respect prevent the gas from escaping therefrom, upon pain of forfeiting for every offence the sum of five pounds. (s. 39.)

Gas contaminating Water.] Whenever the water of any company shall be contaminated by the gas used for lighting any street, premises, &c. within any parish adopting this act, the persons supplying such gas shall forfeit and pay the sum of twenty pounds, to be sued for, and shall be applied to the benefit of the said company supplying such water; and the persons supplying such gas shall, within twenty-four hours after notice in writing, signed by the treasurer or other officer of such water company, or by any person using such water, to be left at the usual place of business of the said persons, cause the most proper measures to be taken to prevent gas from escaping from their mains, works, or pipes, or contaminating or affecting the water of such company; and in case of neglect for twenty-four hours after such notice effectually to stop the gas from so escaping, and satisfactorily to remove the cause of every such complaint, that then the said persons, as aforesaid, shall on such and every complaint forfeit and pay to such water company, over and above the before-mentioned penalty of twenty pounds, the sum of ten pounds for each and every day during which the water of the said before-mentioned company shall be and remain contaminated or affected by such gas; and in default of payment, such penalty or penalties may be recovered by information exhibited on the oath of one credible witness, by and in the name of the treasurer or other officer for the time being of the said water company, or by and in the name of any one or more of the directors of the said company, at the option of the parties prosecuting such information against the said offending party, before any two justices, with costs, to be assessed by such justices, and to be levied by distress and sale of the goods and chattels of the offending party, together with the charges of such distress and sale, by warrant of such justice. (s. 40.)

Contamination, how ascertained.] If it become a question upon such complaint as aforesaid, whether the said water be contaminated or affected by such gas, it shall be lawful for the proprietors of any waterworks to dig to and examine the mains, pipes, conduits, and other gas apparatus, to ascertain the fact; and if it shall appear that the said water has been contaminated by any escape of gas as aforesaid, the costs and expenses of the said examination, and of the repair of the pavement so disturbed, shall be borne by the said persons supplying such gas as aforesaid, the amount to be ascertained and determined, if necessary, by such justices as aforesaid, and to be recovered in like manner as any penalty under this act: provided that if it appear that such contamination has not so arisen from any such escape of gas, then the said proprietors of such waterworks shall pay the expenses as aforesaid, and shall make good any loss or damage occasioned to the said mains, pipes, &c.; the amount to be ascertained by such justices as aforesaid. (s. 41.)

Gas nuisances indictable, &c.] Any person may proceed by indictment or otherwise, notwithstanding this act, against any of the officers or servants of any persons whomsoever, making, furnishing, or supplying any gas used within any parish adopting this act, in respect of any works or other means employed in making, using, or furnishing the said gas as aforesaid, as a public or private nuisance, or may bring any action for the same, against such proprietors, or any of their workmen, for any injury sustained by such works, or the use of the said gas, or method of lighting therewith, or from any other cause whatsoever. (s. 42.)

Destroying Lamps, Posts, &c.] If any person wilfully break, throw down, or damage any watch-house, watch-box, lamp, lamp-post, pale, rail, chain, or other furniture thereof, or wilfully extinguish the light of any such lamp, any person who shall see the offence committed, may apprehend, and any other person or persons may assist in apprehending the offender, and deliver him to any constable, who is with all reasonable dispatch to convey him before any justice, who shall examine upon oath any witness touching such offence; and if the party accused be convicted, he shall forfeit not exceeding forty shillings for every lamp or lamp-post so broken, thrown down, or damaged, and shall also make full satisfaction for the damage done thereby, and not exceeding five pounds for any other such offence as aforesaid, and shall also make full satisfaction for the damage which shall have been done thereby; one moiety of such forfeiture to be paid to the party apprehending such offender, and the other moiety shall be applied for the purposes of this act; and if such offender do not pay the said forfeiture and satisfaction, such justice is hereby required to commit him to the house of correction, to hard labour, if such justice shall so order, for not exceeding three calendar months, unless such forfeiture and satisfaction shall be sooner paid. (s. 43.)

Accidental damage to Lamps, &c.] If any person shall carelessly or accidentally break any of the said lamps, &c. or do any other such damage as aforesaid, and shall not, upon demand, make satisfaction to the inspectors for the same, any justice of the peace, upon complaint upon oath, may summon the party, and upon hearing the parties, or on the non-appearance of the party complained of, may award such sum of money as such justice shall think reasonable; and upon neglect or refusal forthwith to pay such money, the same, and all expenses attending the recovery thereof, may be levied as any penalty in other cases. (s. 44.)

Contracts for lighting, &c.] The inspectors may enter into any contract or contracts with any person or company for lighting the streets, &c. or any part thereof, with oil, gas, or any other material, or in any other manner whatsoever, or for furnishing lamps, lamp-posts, watch-boxes, chains, rails, and other things necessary for the purposes aforesaid, or any materials for the same; which contracts shall specify the works to be done, the prices to be paid, the time when the works shall be completed, and the penalties to be suffered in cases of non-performance thereof, and shall be signed by two or more inspectors, aud also by the persons contracting to perform such works respectively; which contracts, or copies thereof, shall be entered in a book kept for that purpose; but no contract above twenty pounds shall be entered into unless fourteen days' previous notice be given in one or more newspapers published in the county wherein the parish shall be situate, in order that any persons willing to undertake the same may make proposals, to be presented to the inspectors at a time and place in such notice to be mentioned: provided, that if the inspectors shall be of opinion that it will not be advantageous to contract with the persons offering the lowest price, they may contract with such other persons as they shall think proper. (s. 45.)

Remedy for breach of Contract.] In case such contract shall not be duly performed, or completed at the time specified in such contract, the inspectors may bring an action against any such contractor for any penalty contained in his contract; and on proof of his signing the said contract, or non-performance thereof at the time therein mentioned, the inspectors shall be entitled to recover the full penalty, to be applied for the purposes of this act: provided that the inspectors (if they think fit) may compound with any contractor for any penalty for such sum of money as the inspectors shall think proper, not being less than the damage sustained by the breach of such contract, and all expenses occasioned thereby; and the inspectors may cancel or make void any contract by mutual consent, if they shall think proper. (s. 46.)

Ground for Watch-house.] The inspectors may treat with the owners and occupiers of any buildings and grounds, for the purpose of erecting a watch-house thereon, for such sum or yearly rent, or for such time, as to them shall appear reasonable, and in such place or places as they may think proper. (s. 47.)

Lamps, &c. vested in Inspectors.] The property of and in all the lamps, posts, watch-houses, watch-boxes, chains, pales, and rails in or belonging to the said streets and places, and of and in all the iron, timber, stone, bricks, and other materials and furniture and things of, in, and belonging thereto, (except when the same shall be otherwise regulated by contract with the said inspectors,) shall be vested in the inspectors, and may be sold and disposed of from time to time as they shall think proper; and the inspectors may bring any action in manner as herein-before is provided, or prefer, or direct the preferring, of any bill of indictment, against any person who shall steal, take, or carry away, (as the case may be,) all or any part of such lamp-irons, watch-boxes, iron, timber, stone, or other materials and things as aforesaid; and in such actions or indictment it shall be sufficient to lay the property generally in the inspectors, without specifying the name of any of the inspectors. (s. 48.)

Parishes may unite.] It shall be lawful for the inspectors appointed in one parish, to unite with the inspectors of any adjoining parish or parishes, for the better carrying into effect the purposes of this act. (s. 49.)

Forms to be used.] Justices before whom any persons shall be convicted or prosecuted for any offence against this act, shall, and may cause the information and conviction respectively to be drawn in the form following, or in other words to the same effect; (that is to say,) (s. 50.)

Form of Information.] *County of* ——— *to wit.*—" Be it remembered, that on the day of A. B. of informeth me [*or* us] of his majesty's justices of the peace for the said of that of in the of [*here describe the offence, with the time and place, and follow the act as near as may be,*] contrary to the provisions of an act made in the eleventh year of the reign of king *George* the Fourth, intituled [*insert the title of this act,*] which hath imposed a forfeiture of for the said offence. Taken the day of before me "

Form of Conviction.] *County of* ——— *to wit.*—" Be it remembered, that on the day of in the year of the reign of and in the year of our Lord A. B. is convicted before us of his majesty's justices of the peace for the said for [*here specify the offence, and when and where committed,*] contrary to the form of the statute made in the eleventh year of the reign of king *George* the Fourth, intituled; [*here set forth the title of this act;*] and we do hereby declare and adjudge that the said hath forfeited for the said offence the sum of [*or* shall be committed to for the space of *as the case may be.*] Given under our hands and seals the day and year first above written."

Recovery of Penalties, &c.] All fines, penalties, and forfeitures, imposed by this act, or by virtue of any rule or order made in pursuance hereof, (the manner of levying and recovering whereof is not herein before particularly directed,) may be recovered in a summary way by order and adjudication of any two justices, on complaint to them exhibited, and afterwards be levied, as well as the costs, (if any,) by distress and sale, by warrant under the hands and seals of such justices, who are hereby required to summon and examine any witness, upon oath or affirmation, of and concerning such offences, matters, and things, and to determine the same; and the overplus, (if any,) of the money so raised, shall be rendered to the owner of the said goods; all which penalties, not herein directed to be otherwise applied, shall be paid to the inspectors or their treasurer, to be applied for such purposes of this act as the inspectors shall direct, except where the forfeiture shall be incurred by the inspectors, and then the same shall be paid to the informer; and the said justices may order offenders so convicted to be detained in custody until return can be made to such warrants of distress, unless the said offenders give security, to the satisfaction of such justices, to appear before the said justices on such day or days as shall be appointed for the return of such warrants, not being more than seven days from the taking such security, and which security they may take by way of recognizance or otherwise; but if upon such return it shall appear that no sufficient distress can be had, and the penalty be not forthwith paid, or in case it appears to the satisfaction of any such justices, that the offenders have not sufficient goods whereupon such penalties and expenses can be levied, such justices shall not be required to issue such warrant of distress; and thereupon they shall, by warrant under their hands and seals, commit such offenders to the common gaol or house of correction of the county or place in which the parish is situate, there to be kept, with or without hard labour, for not exceeding six calendar months, or until such offenders shall have paid such penalties, and all costs and charges attending such proceedings, to be ascertained by such justices, or shall otherwise be discharged by due course of law. (s. 51.)

Inspectors not personally liable.] Nothing herein shall be construed to render the inspectors personally, or any of their goods, (other than such as may be vested in them in pursuance of this act,) liable to the payment of any sum of money by way of compensation or satisfaction, in the cases in which such compensation or satisfaction is herein-before directed to be made by the inspectors. (s. 52.)

Inhabitants Witnesses.] No inhabitant of any parish adopting this act shall be deemed an incompetent witness in any action, suit, or information, complaint, appeal, prosecution, or proceedings, to be had, made, prosecuted, or carried on under the authority of this act. (s. 53.)

Appeal to the Sessions.] If any person shall find himself aggrieved by any order or appointment of the inspectors, or any order or conviction of one or more justice or justices of the peace, such person may appeal to any general or quarter sessions for the county, city, riding, borough, town, shire, division, liberty, or place in which the parish is situate, within four calendar months next after the cause of complaint shall have arisen; or if such sessions shall be held before the expiration of one calendar month, then such appeal shall be made to the secondly succeeding sessions, either of which court of sessions is hereby empowered to hear and finally determine the matter of the said appeal, and to make such order therein as to them shall seem meet; which order shall be conclusive upon all parties: provided that the person so appealing shall give at least fourteen days' notice, in writing, of his appeal, and of the matter or cause thereof, to the inspectors, or other the respondent or respondents; and within five days after such notice, shall enter into a recognizance before some justice, with sufficient securities, to try such appeal at the then next general sessions or quarter sessions of the peace, which shall first happen, and to abide the order of, and pay such costs as shall be awarded by such sessions, or any adjournment thereof; and such justices, upon determining such appeal, may, according to their discretion, award such costs to the party appealing, or appealed against, as they shall think proper; and their determination concerning the premises shall be conclusive and binding on all parties, to all intents and purposes whatsoever. (s. 54.)

Tender of Amends.] No plaintiff or plaintiffs shall recover in any action for any trespass, or other proceedings made or committed in execution of this act, if tender of sufficient amends be made by or on behalf of the party who has committed such trespass or wrongful proceedings, before such action brought; and in case no tender shall have been made, the defendant or defendants in any such action may, by leave of the court, at any time before issue joined, pay into court such sum of money as he or they shall think fit; whereupon such proceedings shall be had, as in other actions where the defendant is allowed to pay money into court. (s. 55.)

Limitation of Actions.] No action or suit shall be commenced for any thing done in pursuance of or under colour of this act, until twenty-one days' notice has been given thereof in writing to the inspectors, nor after sufficient satisfaction or tender thereof has been made, nor after six calendar months next after the fact committed; and every such action shall be brought and tried where the cause of action shall have arisen; and the defendant or defendants may plead the general issue, and give this act and every special matter in evidence; and if the matter or thing appear to have been done under this act, or that such action was brought before twenty-one days' notice thereof was given, as aforesaid, or if not commenced within the time limited, or be laid in any other county or place than as aforesaid, then the jury shall find a verdict for the defendant; and if a verdict shall be found for any such defendant, or if the plaintiff become nonsuit, or suffer a discontinuance, or if upon any demurrer judgment be given for the defendant, then such defendant or defendants shall have double costs, recoverable, as in any other case, by law. (s. 56.)

Defects of Form.] No proceedings had and taken in pursuance of this act shall be quashed or vacated for want of form, or be removed by *certiorari*, or any other process whatsoever, into any of his majesty's courts of record at Westminster or elsewhere. (s. 57.)

Act how limited.] Nothing herein shall interfere with the powers of 10 G. 4. c. 44, intituled, "An Act for improving the Police in and near the Metropolis," or extend to any parishes or places within the city of London or the bills of mortality, or to any parish or place already wholly or in part regulated by the provisions of any act of parliament for any of the purposes herein-before provided for, or to interfere with the powers which any corporate body may have with respect to watching and lighting. (s. 58.)

Nothing herein shall prejudice the rights of the commissioners of sewers, nor affect the rights and privileges of the universities of Oxford or Cambridge. (ss. 60, 61.)

Inspecting Gas Works.] It shall be lawful for any surveyor, or other person or persons acting under the authority of commissioners of sewers, at any time or times in the day time, to enter into any manufactory, gasometer, receiver, or other building belonging to any gas company, or the said inspectors, in order to examine if there be any escape of gas, or any washings, or other things whatsoever produced in the prosecution of the said gas works, into any public sewer or drain ; and if such surveyor, &c., shall be refused admittance for such purpose, or, on being admitted, shall be obstructed in making such examination as aforesaid, the said gas company, or the said inspectors so offending, shall forfeit, for every such offence, the sum of twenty pounds. (s. 59.)

Construction of the Act.] The powers given to watch and light any parish shall be understood to be given to any wapentake, division, city, borough, liberty, township, market town, franchise, hamlet, tithing, precinct, and chapelry ; and that the powers given to a churchwarden shall be understood to be given to any chapelwarden, overseer, or other person usually calling any meeting on parochial business ; and that the words " justice of the peace" shall be understood to mean justices of the peace for the county, city, borough, town, division, riding, shire, liberty, or place in which the parish which may adopt the provisions of this act shall be situate ; and the words " rated inhabitant," to include all persons assessed to and paying rates for the relief of the poor. (s. 62.)

This act shall be deemed to be a public act, and shall be judicially taken notice of as such, without being specially pleaded. (s. 63.)

ADDENDA.

THE following cases have been decided since those parts of the work to which they belong have been printed.

Parish Lands.] By the following decision it is established, that the statutes on this subject are not limited to lands held merely for the benefit of the poor.

Lord Tenterden, in delivering the judgment of the court, observed :—

" There were demises in the name of the parish officers, and the tenements were certainly held for parish purposes. The lessors of the plaintiff contended that the premises were vested in the parish officers by the 54 G. 3. c. 12. The other side contended that the statute was inapplicable, for two reasons ; 1st. Because the persons in whom the legal estate was vested were *trustees* only ; 2dly. That they were held for the benefit of the *church*, and not of the poor. As to the first of these objections, we are of opinion that there is nothing in the act of parliament to limit the right of persons under that act to those who fill the situation of parish officers, and it would be highly inconvenient to give the act so limited a construction. It is often difficult for persons who claim under an ancient trust, (where the trustees are numerous,) to show who was the survivor of those trustees ; and even if they should succeed in ascertaining that fact, it will not be less difficult to show who is the heir-at-law of that survivor. Upon the second point, whether this act extends to tenements which are applicable for the benefit of the church, or is confined to those which are applicable merely for the benefit of the poor, it is undoubtedly correct, as was insisted on in the argument, that the primary object of the act was directed to tenements of the latter description; and it may be assumed that this was the primary object. But s. 17 goes in its terms much further. (Here his lordship read the section.) It uses the words, 'and also all others.' To these there is no limitation. We think, therefore, that the safest course will be to give full effect to that generality of expression, as nothing appears to show that that which is held for the benefit of the church does not, under these circumstances, require the assistance of this act, as well as that which is held for the benefit of the poor. In both cases the difficulty is the same; and we see no reason to doubt that the operation of the act was intended to be co-extensive with the mischief. The *postea*, therefore, is to be delivered to the plaintiff." (Doe d. Jackson, v. Hiley, E. T. K. B. 1830, MSS.)

Highways.] Where a road has been made under a turnpike act, which act is afterwards repealed, the parish is not bound to repair the road. The court considered the point too clear for argument, and observed, that a road made under such authority might be called an act of parliament road, which ceases as such road when the act expires. If the road had been used long previous to the act of parliament, it did not follow that it was dedicated to the public, so as to cast the burthen of repairing it upon the parish; (see R. v. St. Benedict, *ante*, 164;) though it might be doubtful whether a road originally made under an act of parliament was not thereby dedicated to the public; notwithstanding the act was afterwards repealed, and the public were not bound to keep the road in repair afterwards. (R. v. Mellor, T. T. K. B. 1830, MSS.)

Bridge Tolls rateable.] The Hammersmith suspension bridge is at one end in the county of Middlesex, and the other in the county of Surrey. It was erected by a company, and the surplus receipts are divided among the shareholders. The gate at which the tolls are received is on the Middlesex side, and the company paid to the poor rates on that side; but upon being assessed on the other side, where no tolls were taken, they appealed, and the sessions granted a case. It was contended, that as the tolls of a sluice or lock upon a navigable river had been held to be rateable only in the parish where such sluice, &c., was situated, and the tolls received, (see *ante*, 411, 414,) the same rule must be followed in this case. The court, however, was of opinion, that as the company were beneficial occupiers upon both sides of the river, it was immaterial at what part of the bridge the tolls were taken; and they were clearly liable to be assessed to the parish in the county of Surrey, as well as in the county of Middlesex. (R. v. Barnes, T. T. 1830, K. B. MSS.)

Relief—Evidence of Settlement.] The rule of law, that the fact of giving relief to a pauper while resident *in the parish,* is no evidence of a settlement in that parish, (see *ante,* 577,) has been strongly confirmed in a recent case. The pauper with his family had resided for some considerable time in the parish, during which he had received relief from the parish, and the overseers had also put one of his children out as an apprentice, within the same period. His prior settlement in another parish was afterwards discovered, and an order of removal made, against which there was an appeal, which the sessions allowed; the magistrates being of opinion that under all these circumstances, the pauper's settlement was in the respondent parish. Upon the case being argued in the King's Bench, it was contended, in support of the order of sessions, that the whole was a question of *fact* for the decision of the sessions, who were to judge whether the relief given under the circumstances, was such as to warrant the conclusion that the respondent parish, by relieving the pauper for such a length of time, and exercising the right to place one of his children out as an apprentice, *admitted* that he belonged to them, and that they, having found, upon a consideration of all the facts, that the pauper was settled in the relieving parish, it was not competent now to reverse their decision, although the *prior* settlement in the appellant parish was fully established by the evidence.

The court, however, were of opinion that the order of sessions could not be sustained upon either of these grounds. The question was not one of fact, to be determined by the balance of legal evidence, but depended upon the law applicable to the case, which the sessions had mistaken. They had in fact acted upon that which was *not* evidence on one side, *against* the evidence on the other, and had afterwards sent the case for the opinion of this court, which has jurisdiction, and is bound to correct their error in this respect. The King v. Chatham (*ante,* 577) has established rightly that relief given to the pauper whilst in the parish, is no evidence of settlement, and the circumstance of one of the pauper's children being put out apprentice by the parish, does not alter the case. It is not provided by any of the acts of parliament on this subject, that overseers by being parties to the binding out of pauper children, thereby give them a settlement in their parish; it is, in fact, a mode of relief to casual poor which they may adopt without bringing any such liability upon their parish. (Rex v. Coleorton, T. T. 1830, K. B. MSS.)

Written Agreement—Evidence.] The necessity of producing the written agreement, (see *ante,* 590,) if there be one, in support of a settlement by renting a tenement, since the passing of the 59

Geo. 3. c. 50, and 6 Geo. 4. c. 57, has been fully confirmed since that page was printed. Mr. J. Bayley observed, that before these statutes passed, it was sufficient if the *value* of the tenement was £10 a year, no matter what were the terms; but under the above acts, the *terms* of the tenancy were material, and the settled rule of evidence, that the best evidence must be produced, cannot be dispensed with. It followed, therefore, that as the party had the written agreement, but would not produce it, the oral testimony ought not to have been received by the sessions, and their order must therefore be quashed. There was another point in the case,—whether payment of part of the rent in money, and leaving fixtures upon the premises more than equivalent to the residue, amounted to payment of the whole year's rent, as required by the statutes, and the court intimated that it did not. (Rex v. Merthyrtidvil, T. T. 1830, K. B. MSS.)

Appeal, Overseer against Overseer.] The overseers of the poor are not so united and identified in their office and duties, as to preclude one from appealing under the 17 Geo. 2. c. 38. s. 4, against the accounts of the other. Upon a motion for a mandamus to the justices of Gloucestershire to hear an appeal against an overseer's accounts, it appeared that upon an appeal against the accounts, after the case had been shortly gone into, it was objected, on behalf of the overseer, that the appellant was his co-overseer, appointed with him contemporaneously, and answerable alike to the parish for the faithful discharge of the duties of the office, and that, therefore, the appellant being joint overseer with the respondent, he was in effect appealing against *his own* accounts, which was manifestly absurd, and not sanctioned by any thing to be found in the above, or any other, statute on the subject; the sessions yielded to this objection, and dismissed the appeal with costs. Upon these facts the court of King's Bench granted a rule *nisi* for a mandamus: upon showing cause, it was contended, first, that the sessions had heard and determined the case, as they had examined a witness, quashed the appeal, and given costs to the respondent; and although they might have come to a wrong conclusion, yet as they had decided the question, the mandamus ought not to be granted. But the court said, that it was clear the justices had dismissed the appeal, not upon the merits, but because they thought they had no jurisdiction, which was a question of law; and if they were mistaken in that, the mandamus ought to go.

It was then contended, upon the same grounds as had been taken at the sessions, that one overseer could not appeal against the accounts of the other; that although they were several individuals, their duties were not several, both having the same authority, and the same liabilities in the management of the poor. The court, however, were of opinion that the rule for the mandamus ought to be made absolute, and observed, that in this case it appeared each overseer kept a separate account; and it was clear that each overseer may act by himself, and make separate disbursements, against which the other would have a right to appeal. It might happen, that one overseer might have grounds for appealing against the accounts of his colleague, which would be unknown to other persons. Besides, his being an overseer does not take away his right as a parishioner to appeal against the accounts of the other. The words of the act fully bear out this interpretation; and it is obviously for the benefit and protection of parishes that it should be so acted upon whenever a proper occasion presents itself. (Rex v. Justices of Gloucestershire, T. T. K. B. 1830, MSS.)

Overseers for Extra-parochial District.] The district of Borough Fen is extra-parochial. It contains a considerable population; and it had been for some time the practice for the inhabitants to support the poor requiring relief, who were resident among them, by rates, &c. Overseers had been in several instances appointed, who discharged the ordinary duties of that office. But the liability of the inhabitants within the district to pay rates for this purpose being at length disputed, the magistrates appointed overseers, and a motion was now made in full court for a *certiorari* to bring up such appointment, for the purpose of moving that it be *confirmed*, and thus obtaining the decision of the court, whether, under all the circumstances, overseers could be legally appointed for the district.

In support of the application it was stated, that both parties were anxious for, and ready to abide by, the judgment of the court; and a note in 4 Burn's Justice, 26, was relied upon, which says, "The law has likewise permitted a confirmation of the appointment by the court of King's Bench, on motion to that effect, when it is brought up by *certiorari*;" and R. v. Standard Hill, 4 Maul. and Sel. 382, was also referred to.

The court, however, said they were not aware of any instance in which such an application had been granted with a view to *confirm* the appointment, though there were many cases in which an appointment of overseers had been moved into this court for the purpose of quashing it, as was done in R. v. Standard Hill, to which reference had been made; the rule was therefore refused. (R. v. J. J. of the Liberty of Peterborough, T. T. K. B. 1830, MSS.)

INDEX.

THE END.